The Psychic Stream

THE
PSYCHIC STREAM

OR

The Source and Growth of the Christian Faith

BY

ARTHUR FINDLAY

Honorary Vice-President of the Spiritualists' National Union.
A Founder, and past Chairman of The International Institute for Psychical Research.
Founder and Vice-President of the Glasgow Society for Psychical Research.
Past President of the London Spiritualist Alliance.
Vice-President of the Leicester Society for Psychical Research.
Membro d'Onore dell' Universitaria Accademica Spiritualistica Italiana.
Honorary Member of the Edinburgh Psychic College.
Founder of the Quest Club.

"The discovery of what is true and the practice of what is good are the two most important objects in life."—Voltaire.

THE HEADQUARTERS PUBLISHING CO. LTD.
5 ALEXANDRIA ROAD, WEST EALING
LONDON W13 0NP.

First Impression, September, 1939
This Impression 1992

THE SPIRITUALISTS' NATIONAL UNION was left the copyright to all of Arthur Findlay's books, with the request to keep the titles in print. The SNU is the largest Spiritualist Church organisation in the UK. The SNU also owns the Arthur Findlay College at Stansted Hall.

The SNU is based at Redwòods, Stansted Hall, Stansted Mountfitchet, Essex, CM24 8UD.

All of the Arthur Findlay books are now published by one of the foremost publishers in the psychic sphere:-
THE HEADQUARTERS PUBLISHING COMPANY LIMITED. Booksellers, publishers of books and two Spiritualist monthly magazines "TWO WORLDS" and "HERE AND THERE."
5 Alexandria Road, West Ealing, London, W13 0NP.

ISBN 0 947823 31 X

CONTENTS

FOREWORD.

THE PSYCHIC STREAM has been the cause of every religion. By this I mean that the interaction which has taken place between earth and heaven, and which is today known under the name of psychic phenomena, has brought every religion into being since the time of primitive man. The Psychic Stream has, moreover, germinated and fertilised all theology and all mythology, in fact, all aspects of religious belief. Revelation, through those termed mediums, is the essence of all religion, as I hope to make clear in the following pages.

Every god worshipped by mankind was once a man on earth who returned to earth after death to be seen, and at times heard. Others who thus visited the earth after death received the names of angels and spirits, and round these beings mankind has draped his religious beliefs. Women, for the same reason, have been deified, and also because they were the mothers of the men who became gods.

The source of the psychic stream is in man himself, and the more he realised from observation and experience that he was other than a creature of the flesh, the stronger was its course. Thus was germinated that which came to be known as religion. He saw apparitions of those called dead, and he observed supernormal occurrences which he could only explain by believing that beings, with intelligences like his own, were behind them.

He saw, moreover, growth and movement without physical contact, such as the apparent daily journey of the sun across the heavens. To explain what he could not understand, he adopted the simple course of attributing everything mysterious to immaterial beings, whom he termed gods or spirits.

At an early date in human history he became conscious of the fact that these immaterial forces which surrounded him were governed by intelligences of varying degrees. In time, he divided them into two categories, one of which he termed nature spirits and the other spirits of the dead. Thus he learned to make the distinction between the effect of natural law and individual thought. The first man who realised the difference between nature spirits and the spirits of the dead discovered the source of the psychic stream. He made the greatest of all discoveries, and one which has had a more profound effect on human thought than any other.

Since that date the stream has never ceased to flow, as contact has continued between the physical and the etheric orders of existence till the present day. At times it flowed strongly and swiftly, at others sluggishly and slowly, but the movement has never ceased. Never before in history has the volume been so great as in our own times, and everything points to this increasing until someday it will carry on its flood the religious beliefs of the human race.

The purpose of this book is to trace this stream from early times to the present day. It is to be found under many names, according to those given to the etheric beings the people worshipped. During its onward course it has produced many and wonderful ideas ; it has so fertilised the imagination of man that what ultimately came to be believed was very often far different from the parent stream which gave rise to the belief. Still, there was always a connecting link, a chain of cause and effect, between the final idea and the psychic event which was the first cause of the idea's conception.

In the pages which follow, the influence of the psychic stream will be traced from the most primitive form of religious thought, through the various forms of religious belief it created, till it brought the Christian Faith into being in the fourth century of our era. As Christianity was the outcome of beliefs which had come down from earliest times, our survey must commence from those early days so as to enable us to trace, step by step, the evolution of ideas which finally ended in the Christian religion as we know it.

My study of this subject is not of recent date ; in fact, I can claim to have given it almost life-long consideration. My age as I write this is fifty-five years. I began to study comparative religion and mythology when I was seventeen years old. That was thirty-eight years ago, and, from that date to this, my interest in the subject has never flagged, much of my spare time being spent in collecting information and thinking out the deeper problems of life.

In the early days of my study I was considerably hampered by my parents' belief that all such subjects were sinful, and that any knowledge which in any way conflicted with the Bible could only lead me to perdition. Consequently, for a number of years, every book I bought on the subject was burned by them until an entire library was thus destroyed. It was only after I had a home of my own that I could set about the collection of this class of literature, and, since that date, I have gathered together many of the leading books on this and kindred subjects.

Until I was about thirty-five years of age I adopted the Rationalist outlook on religion, believing that every form of faith was the outcome of man's ignorance of nature, and his fear of the unknown. From that time onwards, however, my outlook changed because I happened to experience psychic phenomena in the presence of a medium more than usually endowed with mediumistic gifts. For five years I had this experience in his presence but, as this will all be found recorded in my book *On the Edge of the Etheric*, there is no necessity to go over the story once again.

That was twenty years ago, and from that date to this mythology and religion became to me entirely new subjects. I had discovered the key to unlock the door which stood between me and the truth. What had hitherto been mysterious to me, gradually became as clear as daylight. I had discovered the origin of all religious belief and the reason why man was a religious being. With this increased knowledge I returned to my study of mythology and comparative religion, and then it was only a step forward to apply my discovery to unravelling the tangled skein which we call the Christian Faith.

Christianity has its roots straggling back into the past, and cannot be understood until these are discovered and traced, one by one, to their junction in the stem. These roots are the mythologies of the ancients which, when once understood, open the door to an understanding of the Christian religion.

This book is the outcome of over thirty-five years of thought, study and patient research and, though it has taken me two years to write, it is the result of these many years of consideration and investigation. Step by step I have trodden the path of reason, and each step I took will be found recorded in the pages which follow. Piece by piece I shall put together the Christian jigsaw puzzle, until what appears a hopeless mass of confusion becomes natural and easy to understand.

The reason why it has been so difficult to piece everything correctly together until now is because the picture we have had before us was incomplete. The missing part was the cause of all the mystery. This missing piece has now been found, and the purpose of this book is to place it in its proper place. To write this book has required the combined knowledge of psychic phenomena, comparative religion and mythology, and, because of this new method of approach, this book is revolutionary in its conclusions. When everyone is able to accept its contents, an entire change will take place in our religious outlook, just as great a change as took place in consequence of the discoveries made, and the conclusions arrived at, by Darwin in biology and by Copernicus in astronomy.

Armed with this greater knowledge, we can now approach the history of man from an enlarged angle and, in consequence, appreciate his thoughts, aspirations and outlook better than ever before. Likewise we shall understand the reason for the present-day religious beliefs and the way in which they are likely to develop in the years to come.

Nothing of any value is destroyed by this inquiry,

though much that is of no value is swept away. Our highest aspirations will be strengthened and increased by traversing the road of man's mental evolution, as recorded in the pages of this book. Faith will be turned into knowledge, and fear and doubt into courage and certainty. The firm basis on which our aspirations rest will be realised when the solid structure of natural law is uncovered and appreciated. The fear of death will be removed and our reason for existence understood in a way never before realised.

Nothing is so true as the fact that the kingdom of heaven is within us and that our destiny is our own making. That which makes us what we are, our personality and everything about us of a non-material nature, survives the death of the physical body. They pertain unto the mind which constitutes the individual. It is our mind which is our self. It remembers the past, controls the present, and contemplates the future. Our character, our virtues and our vices, in fact, all that makes us what we are, are centred in the mind, this immaterial, but very real, substance which is temporarily inhabiting an instrument of flesh.

The mind must always have an instrument with which to express itself, and, that being so, nature has provided it with one which does not decay. This is the etheric body, the structure round which gather the cells comprising our physical body. At death this etheric body, which is a duplicate of the physical body, passes over into another order of existence, but it still remains governed by the same mind that controlled it on earth. So it becomes evident that as we are here, so shall we be hereafter. What constitutes ourself never dies, as it is indestructible.

The fact that man is an etheric being, in the likeness of his present bodily form, accounts for the fact that apparitions have been seen down the ages in the form of men and women. Not only have apparitions been seen but clairvoyants, on many occasions, have seen the etheric body parting from the physical body at death, and starting on its new life in the other order of existence which surrounds and interpenetrates this earth of ours. The universality of the belief in apparitions, and its age-long acceptance, should help to convince the doubters that this duplicate body exists, and that it passes with the mind into that other order of existence at the change called death. Unless this is accepted the past actions of mankind are a mystery, for which there is no known explanation.

We can understand all the follies, the cruelties and the absurdities of our ancestors in their beliefs and actions. They were but children in their mental development. Religion, however, was as essential to them as meat and drink, it satisfied a natural craving which was as real as hunger and thirst. It fed the immaterial or mental quantity in the trinity called man. If that part had not existed there would have been no craving for the sustenance supplied by all those ideas about the gods and the after life. So when we read on and discover the many curious and stupid beliefs of our ancestors, let us always remember that this was all that they could mentally digest. They received the comfort they needed from this simple diet, and it made life possible for them.

This book has been written in the spare time of a busy life, often after a busy day devoted to everyday affairs. My only reason for undertaking this rather laborious task was to help my fellow men and women towards a clearer understanding of much that is dark and mysterious. My wish has always been to increase general knowledge on religious questions, and so satisfy the increasing present-day craving for more light on the deeper problems of life.

It is quite impossible to expect this to be done by theologians who have their own outlook on religion, the one into which they have been trained from youth upwards. One does not expect a capitalist to write in favour of communism, and so one cannot expect a theologian to undermine in any way the form of belief by which he lives. For that reason the public will never be told the truth by the theologians and the priests, who confine their thoughts to the beliefs set down by the organisation of which they are members. They do not relish the people thinking for themselves and forming their own religious ideas. They live on past tradition and obtain their livelihood from its propagation. Only one who has no vested interest in the old theological outlook, and who is quite independent of popular criticism, can express an unprejudiced opinion on orthodox religious beliefs in the light of modern knowledge.

I am no mystic and am eminently practical. Any success I have attained in everyday affairs I attribute to a capacity for taking pains and being thorough with whatever I take in hand. I mention this because I have been unable to give individual references to all the numerous facts mentioned throughout this book. To do so would have increased its size to double its present dimensions and I was anxious to confine its contents to one volume. The critical reader can be assured, however, that behind every statement made there is good authority, and that I have taken the same scrupulous care with this book, as I did with my previous books, in order to ensure that my facts are accurate. As far as possible I have quoted from standard books when I thought that certain statements required additional authority.

Finally I wish to thank my friend, Dr. Albert Neale, for so kindly compiling the index to this work. He would have liked, if time and space had permitted, to have produced an index similar to the very comprehensive one he compiled for my trilogy, which task occupied him nine months. I am deeply grateful to him for his labour of love which will enable every important item referred to in the pages of this book to be discovered without any difficulty.

ARTHUR FINDLAY.

Stansted Hall,
Essex, July 1939.

CHAPTER I.

INTRODUCTION.

THE greatest study of mankind is man himself. History is a record of his achievements, his follies and his mistakes. History is a record of his thoughts put into action. To each one of us life is made up of the individual mind creating mental images, to which we give the name of ideas. Thinking consists of these images and, as we image, so we think, so are our thoughts or ideas. Apart from our mind, which creates these ideas, we could experience nothing, as all our senses concentrate in our mind. As we think, so we act. Consequently, every action is preceded by a mental image.

Our ideas can be grouped under various names, such as political, social, economic and religious. This book is devoted to man's religious ideas which, till the age of science, satisfied him as an explanation for his existence, his destiny and his relationship with those natural forces which were beyond his control. Humanity has for ever asked the two greatest of all questions, Whence? and Whither? We long for light on innumerable problems, about which we can obtain no satisfactory answer. Especially do we wish to know about our destiny after death, which desire is the foundation of all religious thought. We feel instinctively that though we are in a material environment, we are not of this environment. We cry aloud, and many only hear an echo in reply.

Is our conscious existence confined to the short span between the cradle and the grave ? Are we aware of our surroundings only for this limited time which we call life, and is consciousness no more than a light which, lit at birth, is extinguished at death ? Is life just an enigma never to be solved, or is there an explanation which by seeking we can find ? To think, to wonder about the reason why we are here on earth, and what is our destiny, is as natural as to eat and sleep, which we do to satisfy a natural craving. We ponder over the reason for our existence because it is a natural problem, and this exploration into the mysteries of life gives us satisfaction, it makes life more tolerable and in consequence gives increased happiness.

The thoughts which are formed daily in our minds, concern not only our happiness and comfort on earth, but also our destiny ; a well-balanced individual gives reasonable thought to the future as well as to the present. In this connection a proper mental balance is required, as in no other walk of life is instability more noticeable. Neither the monastery nor complete immersion in earthly affairs can appeal to the well-balanced mind. The wise and thoughtful realise that when on earth their primary duty consists of attending to the affairs of earth, but that this does not prevent them from giving rational thought to the hereafter.

As we have developed mentally on earth, so shall we be after the change which we call death. One's mind is oneself and is indestructible. Just as a child

in the nursery prepares himself for a fuller life, when
the nursery days are over, so it is wise for us on earth
to develop our character and grow in wisdom while,
at the same time, we enjoy our present surroundings
and make the most of them. Mankind has spent much
time in the past observing religious ceremonials and
conforming to religious observances. Man's pleasures
and his delights have been spoiled by religious taboos,
and in many ways he has inconvenienced himself in
order to obtain religious comfort.

Only the superficial live for the day, those of deeper
thought realise that our earthly experiences are temporal, and that the mysteries of existence require
rational explanation. The most profound thought
that enters the mind of man is that he survives death.
It conjures up endless speculations which only knowledge can answer. Ignorance makes it all a mystery,
and desire intensifies the wish for enlightenment.
Those who have such thoughts, therefore, cast them
forward from time to time and ponder as to whether
this valley of life, through which we are travelling, is
bordered by heights too lofty to scale or whether we
can, by greater knowledge, perceive the vista beyond.

These thoughts receive sustenance and guidance
from the aspirations and mistakes of those who have
lived before us. The study of past religious and
philosophical ideas is an aid to knowledge and wisdom,
as thereby we discover that man down the ages has
had the same longings and aspirations as we have
ourselves. Moreover, by commencing our study of
religious thought from primitive times, and following
it through step by step, we can arrive at a correct
understanding of the causes which brought the

Christian Faith into being. Surely no study is of greater importance, because it furnishes us not only with the religious ideas of humanity throughout the ages, but it also explains the source and growth of the Christian Faith, which form of belief has had such a powerful influence on a third of the human race, since it became an organised religion in the fourth century of our era.

At some far distant date, when our primitive ancestors had developed mentally to the stage when they were being guided by reason as well as by instinct, the seed of the Christian Faith took root, and from that date to the fourth Christian century is one succession of cause and effect, which produced the beliefs we now associate with Christianity. Christian beliefs have a long line of ancestors stretching right back in one unbroken sequence to the first rational thought of the first primitive man. The Christian Bible emphasises this in allegory. The Christian Faith is a system of thought which only slowly, over thousands of years, came into being. From a simple beginning it grew and developed, because mankind, throughout his pilgrimage on earth, has required such a crutch to aid him in finding, to his own satisfaction, the reason for his existence on earth, and what was likely to happen to him after death.

Man is a mental being. The mind constitutes the man. This mind is housed in two bodies, one of which we call the etheric body and the other the physical body. The etheric body interpenetrates the physical body ; what we call death is the separation of the etheric from the physical, when the etheric carries with it the mind into another environment. As man is an etheric being his body of flesh has been a constant worry to him. There has been incessant warfare between his carnal desires and his etheric aspirations. The desire of the flesh has always pulled in one direction, while his aspirations have pointed in another. His mind has never been quite at home during its association with the physical body. It has always been pulled in two directions : towards the earth in the one case and towards heaven in the other, towards satisfying the desires of the physical body and the desires of the etheric body.

On this unstable foundation is based what we term our earth life, made up of mental ideas concerning earth and heaven. A realisation of this explains much that is difficult to understand. It explains how religion, which stands for our etheric aspirations, has been for ever tarnished by the weakness and greed of the flesh. Man's greatest handicap is that part of him which we call the physical body, with its craving for carnal satisfaction. Here on earth we need food, clothing and shelter. Life is a warfare against our fellows and against nature, as each one strives for himself and those whom he protects and cherishes. All these carnal desires come from our having a physical body ; the trouble ceases in the etheric world, as there we need not strive to live. The etheric body does not require to be sustained as does our physical body, and our desires are met by thought and not by direct action.

Because many have realised this weakness of the flesh, they have confined themselves to mental contemplation and tried to keep from satisfying bodily desires. This they have done for the purpose of keeping the mind undefiled by its association with the earth through the body. Religious history tells of multitudes who have sacrificed earthly desires·for the sake of mental peace ; but we have still to learn how to live naturally on earth with the carnal desires under rational control.

This will come by mental development, but the constant warfare between the flesh and the spirit is obviously intended to develop our characters and strengthen our minds for our environment after death, as there the mind plays a much larger part than it does on earth. There thought creates our surroundings even more than it does on earth, and, as our thoughts are, so shall be our environment and our happiness. We can make a heaven or hell of life on earth, but, in the etheric world, this capacity which we possess is increased beyond our powers of understanding.

The realisation of his relationship to a higher order of existence, and his own flesh weakness, has been the cause of man's constant endeavour to reach at-one-ment with those he called the gods. Consequently, religious history consists of a record of the numerous attempts man has made to please and appease the gods. Because of this he has given as much time and thought to his religious speculations as he has to his well-being on earth. Man is an etheric being temporarily housed in a body of flesh, and if we keep this in mind, we shall understand much more clearly what the following pages have to unfold. To ignore this great factor is to miss one of the most striking facts in history. To dismiss religion as just due to illusion, in any contemplation of the past, is to ignore a great reality which has had as much effect on man's welfare, comfort and happiness as have his political and social aspirations.

Past history emphatically pronounces that man is a religious being. Present-day knowledge equally emphatically declares that he is so, because he is a mental creature, that mind is the man and that his physical body is but the mind's temporary habitation. Our modern psychic knowledge proves to us that this mind survives the decay of the physical body, and that the real body is the duplicate etheric body which is the permanent habitation of the mind. Mind, we now know, survives death and uses this etheric vehicle, composed of higher and finer vibrations than those which make up our physical body and the earth from which it comes.

By knowledge we have learned to separate man into three categories—mind, etheric body and physical body. He is a trinity, a three-in-one, and, just as he is a trinity, so is the universe, which is composed of vibrations similar to those which make up the human being. The universe is composed of vibrations which constitute mind, etheric matter and physical matter. What we on earth appreciate in our physical body is the physical universe which is vibrating in harmony with our organs of sense. Thus we can only see, hear, touch and smell that which is within the range of physical vibrations.

Psychic phenomena, however, have proved to us that beyond the physical lies the etheric, and that there is not only a physical world, but also an etheric world, a world which is vibrating in harmony with our etheric bodies. This etheric world interpenetrates and surrounds the physical world and is in many respects like the earth. The reason we do not sense it is because our physical, and not our etheric, sense organs function on earth. Everything, however, in connection with our body is in duplicate and, when we discard our physical body at death, our mind will be housed in our etheric body capable of seeing, hearing and feeling etheric matter. At death we enter an order of vibrations in harmony with the etheric body, and consequently everything etheric will be real to us, while everything physical will cease to be real. We shall have made the change over from the physical to the etheric, which will then become our home. This new abode will be as real and as solid to us as is this earth, and there dwell the multitudes who have passed through this nursery called the earth to take up their permanent abode in the etheric world, which we call heaven.

If we keep clearly in our minds the fact that man is a trinity, of three orders of substance, and that the universe is the same, we shall have made our first step towards discovering the origin and history of everything we place under the name of religion. Owing to the fact that some individuals are so made that they can sense the etheric order, man discovered that he was an etheric being. Only because such individuals down the ages have been able to see and hear the inhabitants of the other world, has the revelation from heaven to earth come to mankind. In consequence of what they saw and heard, our ancestors turned those etheric beings, who once lived on earth, into gods, angels, demons, devils, all of whom figure prominently in every religion. From his speculations on their doings and their attitude towards him, have come all religious doctrines, dogmas, creeds and the legends to be found in mythology.

Religion is based on the interaction between the two worlds, which is appreciated by those sensitive people called mediums. Because of them man has become aware that surrounding him is another order of life, and another order of beings. In his ignorance he believed that these beings were the cause of all the phenomena of nature, and that on their whims and caprices his welfare on earth, and his destiny hereafter, depended. Because he failed to appreciate his true relationship towards them he produced those beliefs which make up the various world religions. From what was true and real, he erected a mass of speculation which in many cases has hidden the truth from view.

Early man, in a hazy way, began to realise that here on earth he was but a temporary sojourner and, as we proceed, it will be discovered how this idea developed and branched out in various directions. These branches formed different religious beliefs, all of which grew from the parent stem, which was the belief that man was an etheric being and survived the change called death. When he came to recognise that death was not the end but the beginning of a new career, not a wall but a door, a liberation from the confines of matter to an expanse of life which we in the physical body can only dimly surmise, greater and greater vistas opened out before him and these we find expressed in the religions of the past.

These facts explain history and give the historian a reason for the range of ideas which have done so much to make history. Physical science has never attempted to explain the cause of religious ideas because it confines its attention to physical vibrations. Psychic science, which has been neglected up till within recent years, is now explaining the cause of the religious idea in man, and in time this new science must come to have an equal standing with all the other sciences. It is only now, because its findings are definitely established, that it is possible to write this book and make clear past religious beliefs which have been mysterious and difficult to understand. This book lays the foundation for a correct and proper understanding of religion, theology and mythology, and it is the first serious attempt to utilise our present-day psychic knowledge for the purpose of explaining the Christian Faith and all the other past religions.

To separate and single out one religion and attribute it alone to supernatural causes is contrary to the facts of history. What caused one caused all. Of one thing, however, we can now be sure, they were not the result of man's imagination any more than they were the result of supernatural causes. We know nothing of the supernatural because anything beyond nature must relate to something outside the universe. The universe is natural and is governed by natural law. Its range of vibrations, so far as our knowledge goes, extends from mind vibrations, which are of the highest frequency, to long electric waves which are of the lowest frequency. We know nothing outside of this range of vibrations, but we do know that what takes place within the range is natural and subject to natural laws.

The etheric world is natural and conforms to natural laws. Consequently, nowhere throughout this book is reference made to the supernatural, and in every case where the word supernatural has heretofore been used, the word supernormal is employed. Though nothing supernatural is known to science, yet much that is supernormal occurs today, and has occurred down the ages. Religion has developed from the supernormal, not from anything miraculous. Miracles never happen, but psychic phenomena have often been turned into miraculous stories. All religions have evolved out of something which was natural but not normal, from something which happened to one or more people, who were not normal, but who experienced quite natural phenomena which do not come the way of the ordinary normal individual.

We, therefore, live in a world of phenomena, both normal and supernormal, and now that mediums are allowed to live, and are not burned as witches, supernormal phenomena are increasing and may someday be considered quite normal, especially so as mediumship is an hereditary gift. The wholesale destruction, during the Christian era, of witches and wizards, as they were called, had the effect of so curtailing psychic phenomena that they were nearly obliterated from the experience of those living in Christian countries. Then followed the age of Materialism from which we are now only slowly emerging.

One cannot understand the first principles of religion and mythology without taking into account psychic phenomena, which occur today just as they occurred in the years gone by. This I know, because I have experienced the phenomena, and so also have many others whose judgment I much respect. These supernormal experiences are as much facts as other natural experiences, and the reason why so few people

understand or accept them, is because they occur in
the presence of only a small number of people, who are
endowed by nature with a higher sensitiveness than
pertains to the ordinary individual.

Those who have not made contact with these
peculiar people, known as mediums, cannot understand
their constitution and how advanced they are in their
range of sight and hearing compared with the average
individual. Anyone who has not seen a medium in
deep trance cannot understand what takes place while
this occurs. Anyone who has not heard the direct
voice, in the presence of a medium, cannot realise how
it brings all who hear it into close and intimate touch
with the etheric being who uses the ectoplasm drawn
from the medium to materialise, temporarily, his voice
organs for the purpose of making himself heard on
earth. Lastly, the full form of a materialised etheric
being, which can be seen, touched and heard, makes
us appreciate the numerous references in the Old
Testament, and mythology, to the gods who came to
visit the earth.

As one who has experienced the entire range of
psychic phenomena, and has studied deeply the
religions and mythologies of the past, it will be my
pleasure in the following pages to explain and clarify,
in the light of present-day psychic knowledge, the
numerous mysteries which surround them. Only
someone armed with this knowledge can make clear
and easily understood what is dark, and has always
been regarded as a divine mystery. Those in the past
who have studied mythology and religion have
entirely neglected this fundamental branch of knowledge. The orthodox have, in ignorance, considered

all psychic phenomena to be the work of a devil, and the rationalists and materialists have ignored it because they never grasped its reality. In consequence, they attributed it to faulty observance. For these reasons religion and mythology have never been correctly understood ; they have always been approached by those ignorant of psychic science.

As our study proceeds we shall realise that the Christian Faith is no break in the religious pattern which stretches back into antiquity. Christianity continued quite naturally the weaving of the same religious thought which preceded it. The death of Jesus, and his appearance after death, only caused the old beliefs to become known under a new name. His appearance after death caused his intrusion into age-old beliefs under the new name of Christ, which his followers bestowed upon him. The old stream of religious thought flowed on as before under the new name, just as the Rhine does when it enters Holland under the name of the Waal.

Christian beliefs evolved out of age-old ideas which were held in much reverence nineteen hundred years ago in the lands surrounding the Mediterranean. These old beliefs were the children of previous beliefs, which in turn were the offspring of earlier beliefs, and so we go back, step by step, to those of our first ancestors who ceased to accept their surroundings just as they found them.

To find the source of the Christian Faith, we must therefore travel up the stream of religious thought to the point where the first drop trickled from the mind of man. We must follow this drop, observe it being added to first of all by other drops, then by tiny streams

and larger streams, and finally by rivers, all of which
went to swell the main stream of religious thought
prevalent in the world when the Christian Faith was
born.

As we follow this stream down the ages we find
that it is for ever dividing into smaller streams, which
break away from the parent and flow on in the same
direction, but at varying distances. Today, standing
as we do, looking down on the delta of this mighty
stream of thought, we can pick up each of these offshoots and trace it back to the parent, and thence to
its source. So, to vary the metaphor, we might say
that every link of the chain stretching between then
and now is complete and unbroken. Religious history
is made up of these links, and the historian, when
writing the story of the past, must give each one
consideration before he can arrive at a true explanation
to account for the source and growth of the Christian
Faith.

The history of the human race is that of the development of mind. If we grasp this development aright,
then the evolution of the race can be understood and
appreciated. Before we can understand the history of
the rise and development of Christianity, it is imperative that we have the knowledge of the world
religions which preceded it, right back to the religious
ideas of early man.

It is in the nature of man, when ignorant of his
surroundings, to worship. Thus we find that worship
has left one of the most indelible marks on the sands
of time. Cromlechs and ruined temples abound everywhere, in fact without these ancient monuments our
knowledge of primitive man would be much more

meagre than it is. These relics of his fear, these ruins of his ignorance, tell us unmistakably that early man was a religious being, one who feared the gods and therefore did all in his power to placate them. To him life was an unending mystery, a continuous war against the caprices of the unseen and the unknown.

Out of the past we discover the beliefs of early man, which were the foundation on which were erected the religious beliefs of the present day. Each belief gave rise to another, and though it is no longer believed that Isis wanders along the bank of the sacred Nile searching for her dead Osiris, yet the descendant of this idea is part of the religious beliefs of today. Though the belief no longer exists that Prometheus died a victim chained to a rock, in order to save sinful humanity from the wrath of Zeus, yet its descendant is with us today. Though the idea that, by eating the actual body, and drinking the actual blood of the slain god-man, at-one-ment with the gods could be attained, does not prevail today in civilised countries, yet its descendant is still part of our religious worship. Names change and ideas are put into different words, but the beliefs and aspirations of our primitive ancestors are much the same today in the Christian religion as they were thousands of years ago.

To find an explanation for these beliefs, to trace the thread of thought through the primitive religions, and then through the Pagan religions, till they came to be consolidated under the name of Christianity, is the task I have set myself. As I take the reader on step by step, I trust that no chapter will be omitted, as otherwise a link in the chain of thought will be missing.

In the space at my disposal I have gathered together

all the important threads of present-day religious knowledge. Unless, however, these threads are kept apart,
they become a tangled skein, as indeed they are to the
great majority. Only knowledge can unravel what past
ignorance has so tangled up, but when this confused
mass is untangled, what has been mysterious will
become clear, and what has caused controversy, confusion and discord will appear as one harmonious
whole.

This study will give the reader a clear, rational and
logical history of the source and growth of the
Christian religion. New ground will be opened up,
and what has hidden the truth from view will be
cleared away. By the time the book ends, I hope that
I shall have led the reader along the right path of
thought, to a height from which he will be able to
look back, and obtain a clearer and truer perspective
of everything essential that has taken place from a
religious point of view in the past. Shorn of all its
theological accretions, Christianity will then become
intelligible and find its place in a world governed by
natural law.

For good or ill, the Christian religion has had a
profound influence on the history of a large section of
the human race. Surely a correct and proper understanding of the origin and development of this mighty
idea is one of primary importance. Besides the
exaltation, the comfort and the misery it has caused
to untold millions, the organisation which protected
it has been the factor behind the government of the
most important and influential of the world's states for
fifteen centuries. This organisation determined policy,
it placed kings, princes and governors in powerful

positions, but, if they rebelled against its authority, withdrew from them the support it had so freely given. This being so, no more worthy subject can be dealt with by the historian, especially as the discoveries of psychic science, over the past hundred years, have added greatly to our capacity to understand what was mysterious to our ancestors, and which, in consequence, they misunderstood and misinterpreted.

A new approach is therefore needed, more today than ever before as, with the breakdown of Protestant authority, the people are now left in the wilderness. The supernatural approach, with the march of science, is being rapidly discarded, and many are turning to a materialistic outlook on life, unaware that another is open to them. This other is rational and logical and, moreover, it accepts all the scientific findings of the present day. It explains the reason for all religious beliefs of the past, while, at the same time, it gives us a reason for our highest aspirations and the knowledge that there is nothing to fear. This new approach makes clear to us that we are on a road which leads through death to a happier, fuller and better life than the one we can experience on earth.

The birth, in a Jewish atmosphere, of what ultimately became known as Christianity, its discarding of this influence, and its rise to power out of the ashes of Paganism is a story of absorbing interest. If treated honestly, if none of the facts surrounding its origin and growth are neglected, if all our present-day knowledge is focused on our quest, which is to reach truth and truth only, one of the most important events, if not the most important event in world history, will become understood as never before.

We must begin at the beginning and take one step at a time. To do so we must know something about the ancestry of the Christian religion, and this brings us to the next chapter, which is devoted to a review of the religious beliefs of primitive man.

CHAPTER II.

CHRISTIANITY—ITS ANCESTORS.

The difference between an animal and a savage is that the one entirely accepts his environment and the other does not. The animal is afraid of the forces of nature and seeks shelter from danger. The savage, likewise afraid, not only seeks shelter but does something more, something an animal does not do. He seeks a reason for what he experiences and attempts to placate these unknown forces by prayers and gifts.

We have no written records of what primitive man believed, but it is reasonable to think that his ideas more or less corresponded with those of the most backward of present-day savage tribes. This is confirmed from an examination of the scattered remains which have been found in the oldest graves, all of which point to the fact that his outlook on nature was of the most simple description. His ideas can best be compared with those of a very young child who believes anything and everything, no matter how absurd.

Our principal sources of information are the Vedic literature of India, the religious literature of China, the sacred book of the followers of Zoroaster known as the Vesta, the Homeric poems, the religious and mythological traditions preserved in the literature of

Rome and Germany, the Egyptian Book of the Dead, the Chaldean tablets, the Christian Bible and comparative philology, or the comparing of words in different languages.

The first indications we have of intelligent thought comes from the effort evidently made by early man to reach a compromise with nature. Our first ancestor who reasoned tried either to appease or cajole the forces with which he was surrounded. From his store of food he offered some to the thunder or the storm, and tried to harness them by other cunning devices. These two primitive ideas developed into magic and then into worship, both of which play such important parts in the religious history of the human race.

The thunder rolls, and the storm destroys man's handiwork. They are his enemies, which, though unseen, he pictures as like himself and as having passions and desires akin to his own. An animal has not this reasoning power. An animal accepts, but man, however undeveloped, has this faculty of reasoning. The first animal to reason became a man. The first man to reason put the words science and religion in the vocabulary of the human race.

The forces of nature were far beyond his comprehension, and he could only think that they were caused by beings who were like himself, but larger and stronger. Behind the phenomena of nature he imagined beings who roared more loudly than he could or who blew more strongly than he could. This sufficed to explain the reason for thunder and wind, and gradually the idea developed in his mind that these unseen forces were none other than supermen to whom he gave the name of gods. The cause of each phenomenon he attributed to an individual god and mistook the echo for their voices.

Experiencing as he did the destructive forces of lightning, rain and wind, he implored these unseen gods to spare his home and children. When perishing of cold he prayed for heat, and welcomed the rising sun as his friend and protector. Little wonder that the imagination of man evolved extraordinary and wonderful ideas about the powers of nature. As his mind developed these ideas increased, so much so that to the gods was attributed everything he was unable to explain or understand. From these speculations developed the earliest and crudest form of religious thought which we today call

MAGIC.

The gods, these invisible beings, were conceived slowly in the mind of primitive man, and, as this occurred, there came the natural desire to treat them all as friends. This was discovered to be impossible as all would not be friendly, though there were exceptions. The sun came to be looked upon as a friend, whereas thunder and lightning were enemies. Thus all the forces of nature were classified as either good or bad gods.

Those gods who caused growth and movement were in time grouped under the heading of nature gods and to these man worshipped and prayed for his daily needs. Besides these gods, however, there were others with whom he was on much more intimate terms. They showed themselves to mankind from time to time, sometimes as shadowy beings and sometimes as materialised beings. They spoke and could understand when they were replied to. They came and went in a most mysterious way. Moreover, they could take control of certain individuals, speak through their mouths, and carry on at times conversations of great length. These beings man also termed gods, and, from earliest times, certain individuals have been on close and intimate terms with these immaterial beings.

It was discovered that the gods appeared, and made their presence felt, in the neighbourhood of those individuals, who were but passive instruments and could in no way command their presence. Only when the gods, or spirits, controlled them could these earth instruments respond, and this the spirits did just when they pleased. The gods, so to speak, were in control, but their earth instruments had the power to receive or refuse them as they could not be controlled against their wish.

The consequence of this was that these earthly instruments revered those who controlled them. They prayed to them, told them their troubles and implored their help and sympathy. As language developed a name was given to those people who were sensitive to the visitations of the gods. Many names have been applied to them and today they are known as mediums, because they act as the medium between the gods and mankind. One or more gods would attach themselves to one particular medium and become efficient in controlling their instrument. Names were given to such gods and today they are known as controls. In the old days, as in our own times, a medium occasionally attracted a control who was a very powerful character. He, through his instrument, assumed direction over the tribe. He became the tribal god and nothing would be done without first consulting him and obtaining his sanction and direction.

According to the number of mediums so there were gods, because one or more of these discarnate beings attached himself to each medium. So the gods of the past were as numerous as the mediums. When the mediums were plentiful the gods were plentiful, and when they were scarce the gods were scarce. The gods, of course, were plentiful enough, but to mankind they could only be appreciated when they discovered a human instrument who could respond to their attentions. Man only knew the gods through their human instruments, the mediums. These gods were none other than human beings who had lived on earth and died, to continue functioning in another world of finer vibrations. As they had taken with them their earth memories their interest in earth affairs was still great, and they were always pleased to have a chance of getting into contact with their past environment through these sensitive individuals we today call mediums.

The Old Testament tells us of one of these gods who was a very powerful character and showed all the virtues and vices of the human being. His aim was to direct the activities of one of the tribes of those days, the people of which came to be known as the Hebrews. He told this tribe, when communicating through his medium Moses, that he was a jealous god and that they were to have no other gods but him. From time to time this god was seen and we are told that he had a face, hands, arms, that he could smell, that he winked, laughed, and could make others laugh. He could be angry and pleased and in every way he showed himself to be a very human character. This god, however, is only one of many who have come down to us in the mythologies of the past, all of whom showed human qualities, which is just what we find today with those etheric beings who come back to earth and communicate with us through our present-day mediums.

In those old days, just as now, the mediums could only act as instruments if "moved by the spirit", but there were others in the tribe who tried to imitate what took place in their presence. This also happened in the Hebrew tribe, because we read in Exodus and Deuteronomy that the Hebrew god, through his instrument Moses, gave stern injunctions against these imitators of his medium. These were known as sorcerers and severe laws were made against them. Unfortunately the translators of these two books from the Hebrew called these sorcerers by the names of witches and wizards, and the laws which were originally intended for the purpose of preventing charlatans imitating the genuine medium were used throughout the Christian era against the medium.

Primitive man, by his constant fight for life against the beasts and the elements, developed qualities of cunning and resource, which very qualities some applied to imitating the mediums. They pretended to be mediums and, by sleight of hand and deception, they duplicated what took place in the medium's presence. They assumed trance and imitated the utterances of the gods. By deception they imitated the direct voice and caused the movement of objects without visible physical contact. Thus, though not mediums themselves, they pretended to be and, as they could do this when and where they desired, the natural medium, who could not do so, was very often left out in the cold.

The genuine phenomenon comes spontaneously without any effort on the part of the medium, but now we come to the time when fraudulent phenomena were produced so as to give the people the impression that it came from one of the gods. This, then, is the origin of magic and the beginning of that profession of deception and cunning. The one who deceived the people was called the magician and, as he had much more skill and cunning than the medium, and could make the people think that he could bring the gods to earth at his pleasure, he became all-powerful in the tribe.

How much early man understood about the nature of psychic phenomena is difficult to say. That he experienced them there is not the least doubt. Ancient literature is full of these experiences and the speculations which developed from them. Some may have realised that the gods had once been people on earth, but others seem to have looked upon them as a different order of beings and something quite apart from humanity. Amongst the inaccessible mountains lived the gods and they were a race of beings quite apart from the rest of creation. The mountain-tops became holy and sacred and whoever tried to approach them was courting death. When the thunder roared it was the voice of the Lord and the lightning was his sword.

Knowing, as we do, that fraudulent phenomena occur today we can be sure that they also occurred in the time of early man. Consequently, we are not surprised to find that traces still remain in some of the temples of Greece, Egypt and Italy of the appliances used to deceive the people. By this time the magician had developed into the priest, but he has always remained wedded to his original profession, that of the magician. He has always loved mystery and deception. "Great is the mystery of the Godhead !", "Great is the mystery of salvation !", and suchlike exclamations, have always come from priestly lips. The priests have always loved mystery more than understanding, ignorance than knowledge, and this outlook they instilled into the minds of the people who found their pleasure and comfort in being deceived by the priest-magicians.

So when one visits the ruins of ancient shrines, over which the priest-magician presided, we find the traces of their craft, such as appliances, behind the view of the people, for the purpose of levitating the images of the gods, so as to make them think that the god was being raised without human contact. Often steam was used for this purpose and steam-pipes under the images have been discovered. A visitor today to one of these temples can easily imagine the effect on the people, fresh and childlike, who simply accepted everything they experienced. The effect was doubtless increased by the dim light and the silence which would prevail. By mechanical contrivances the priests were able to manipulate under these conditions all sorts of delusions. Mysterious voices would be heard singing, whispering and sighing all round, lights would gleam from above and below, while figures appeared and disappeared. All the arts would be taxed to the very utmost to make these performances as mysterious as possible, and yet attractive to the people.

In Egypt the visitor is shown a recess in a temple where in the old days the priest sat. This communicated with the mouth of a crocodile of stone through which the priest spoke. When the people desired to know the will of the gods they knelt before the beast and took its instructions. They told it their troubles and gave it their worship.

In *The Illustrated London News* of 15th January, 1938, a photograph was reproduced of an altar found in Syria, believed to date from 2300 B.C., which showed the mouth of a speaking-tube which enabled a priest in a recess behind to make oracular utterances. Another altar was discovered which contained a gold finger-ring which the devotee had slipped down the speaking-tube in order to attract the attention of the god. It never reached its destination as it had stuck half-way, and the poor deluded creature returned home without her ring and also, doubtless, without the comfort of having had a conversation with the Lord. At Corinth, a recent discovery, behind an old altar, has disclosed the trap-door through which the priest entered to enable him to speak as a god to the worshippers at the altar.

Such priestly contrivances have been in use from earliest times up to the present day. The people, however, where education exists, cannot now be deceived by such crude methods, though in the more backward countries such methods are still in vogue. In some Roman Catholic churches, behind an image of the virgin sits a priest with a cord attached to one of her legs. According to the number of times she kicks her leg is the devotee answered, if beforehand a coin has been slipped into the money-box alongside. Today the priests deceive the people in other ways, one of the most conspicuous being their claim to turn a wafer of bread into the body of Jesus and the wine into his blood.

The medium was the cause of the first magician, out of which developed the priest-magician. So priest-craft owes its origin to the medium. Rather than disappoint those expecting something unusual to happen how tempting it was for the clever and cunning individual in the tribe to pose as a medium, and produce his own mysteries without any interference from the gods. The simpler the audience the easier it was to produce the delusion, and in the old days those more cunning and unscrupulous than the rest were able to reap a rich harvest, gleaned from the work of the simple. Magic became a lucrative profession and the magician became the chief of the tribe, he was the wonder-worker who claimed to make the gods do his bidding. So successful was he that he became nothing less than a god himself to his credulous tribesmen. It only required a beginning and its development came naturally.

When the magician found that he could deceive the people on most, if not all, occasions, deception became a skilled profession and his miracles went far beyond those of the genuine medium. He seated himself within a magic circle which was sacred, and within which no one could enter. As the people also looked upon him with awe and reverence all this mystery made discovery less likely. A strong character, with a magnetic personality, acquired a power in the tribe to which no other could aspire. His ambition did not, however, end there. If he could deceive his fellow-men could he not likewise deceive the gods ? As he could make his own people do his will, why not also the gods ?

So his work and power increased. He became the intermediary between the gods and man, and this deprived the genuine medium of the place intended by nature. The magician was the first priest, the first to take on this ecclesiastical office, the first to tell the gods what they were to do, and the first to claim to act as their chosen representative on earth. This being so, the priest-magician was no friend of the genuine medium. Fraud and honesty cannot live together and this feeling of antagonism has come down to us from these ancient days. Even in our own time the medium has no more bitter enemies than the priest and the magician. The priests have never wished competition from nature, as, if nature succeeded in revealing the other world to everyone through mediumship, the priest would find his occupation gone.

We find a very interesting story in the Old Testament which is evidently intended to convey the impression that, when given a fair chance, the "man of god" can do better than the magician. So we are told of a contest between Moses and the magicians of Pharaoh. Moses surpassed the magicians to such an extent that Pharaoh was amazed. This contest evidently greatly pleased the spirit control of Moses, who told him, "Have I not made thee as a god to Pharaoh ?" Whether Moses ever came to be looked upon as a god to Pharaoh or not matters little. The interest to us lies in the fact that in those old days we find the belief that so-called miracles could be performed by divine aid which could not be imitated by the magicians.

Though Moses may have succeeded in making himself appear as a god to Pharaoh, the history of magic relates that the magician had always a much larger following than the medium, because he could produce his wonders at will. He lost no chance of depreciating the medium in the eyes of the people, who, in their simplicity, accepted his claims. These claims were to the effect that if the right incantations were correctly said, the correct spells laid, and the appropriate rites performed, then the sun would rise, the rain would fall, the crops would grow, diseases would be healed and all desires met. Only certain words and deeds, which the magician alone knew, could make the gods respond. He, and he only, could control nature; through him, and him only, could the gods be approached, and every method was used to suppress and destroy all who exhibited genuine psychic power—all who were really used by the gods to manifest their presence on earth.

There is, however, still another supernormal achievement which the genuine medium can do today and which, for this reason, it is quite likely could be done by certain mediums in the days of long ago. Some people have such a delicate sense of touch that they can, by handling an article, tell its history. This gift is called Psychometry and anyone having this power, while holding an article in his hand, can tell what has happened in the surroundings of this article, just as if the article had experienced it and was communicating its experience to the psychometrist. It would seem as if so-called dead or lifeless matter contained some kind of mind which became indented with what happened in its surroundings, just as a gramophone record can be indented and give back the impressions it has received.

Whatever is the ultimate explanation of psychometry, the fact remains that certain sensitive people can psychometrise articles, and, as this seems to have occurred down the ages, it is doubtless the explanation of the belief held by the ancients that articles had souls which could convey an influence for good or ill. Amulets and talismans were treasured because they were looked upon as charms and as having protective powers. Some things were lucky to possess and others unlucky. Some articles brought health, wealth and happiness, others disaster. A certain article would be treasured as a fetish because it either gave out a good or an evil influence.

Other things were treasured because they belonged to the dead, it being believed that the dead were still interested in them and would come back to those who possessed them. The people had totems which have come down to us today as crests. Each tribe had its own totem or clan mark. Some had bears, others hawks, lions, deer or fishes. A man would dream that he had been a buffalo, for instance, and he took a buffalo as his totem. Articles had magical effects if certain passes were made over them, or spells were pronounced on them, and the magician made the most of the belief, generally held from the time of primitive man in all lands, that certain things could affect humanity as each possessed a soul which could exert an influence for good or evil.

Amongst a superstitious and ignorant people, such as our primitive ancestors, the magician had plenty of material with which to deceive them. This art of deceiving became so much a part of the life of the magician that he accepted it as a matter of course, deceiving himself into the belief that his deception was real and that he had the powers he claimed to have. He was the genius of the tribe and nothing could stop his progress to the top. On him devolved its welfare and to him was left its entire management. The magicians became the religious and temporal rulers of the people, and still are in some places.

The life of the priest-magician was not always easy. In exchange for the power he obtained he had to satisfy the people. If he did not he was either murdered or deported. Consequently the most sagacious, the most cunning, arrived at the top and became both the chief priest and the king. Once there, with all his enemies under his feet, he was comparatively safe. He then turned from deceiving the people to ruling them. Kings thus came into being, but the link which binds them to the priesthood has never been broken. Even to this day a king is first ordained as priest and then crowned as king.

Primitive man was conservative in both his religion and politics and rigidly bound by the tradition of his ancestors. In this mental state progress was exceptionally slow. He was a slave to invisible masters and what his ancestors did was always his pattern. Till the rise of the priest-king, with his superior talents, a dead level of thought prevailed, custom and tradition holding the mind in their deadly grip.

The next development was the deification of the

priest-king. , He was the representative on earth of the principal tribal god and thus he could do no wrong. Those god-kings either led their people to victory or defeat, on the path of progress or reaction, to greater or less happiness and contentment. At least they made an effort one way or another and the people followed them. When the kings were great, courageous and wise, empires rose, only to fall when they were stupid and timid. The great civilisations of China, Babylon, Persia, Egypt, India, Peru and Mexico were built up by men who were looked on as gods, they having attained the position of chief priests. Either by themselves, or through some ancestor, they had attained the rank of kings by being first magicians, through cleverly impressing on the people that they could control the forces of nature.

What are termed miracles, or nature being diverted from its course by the magic of some superman, were accepted as a matter of course in these early days. It was the regular profession of the magician, his stock in trade. The magician could, it was believed, make crops to grow, bring rain or sunshine, victory or defeat, health or sickness, in fact, he claimed to do exactly what his followers desired. No wish within reason could not be granted. He would heal the sick, make hands and legs to wither, and kill enemies by making their images and piercing them with pins. He could even make barren women fruitful, in fact he was omnipotent.

He had charms, spells and sacred words which he doled out, and when nature did not respond his excuse was that the charms and words had not been used aright. His astuteness had only to be sufficient to overcome the doubts of his dupes. He mingled his magic with his prayers and had always the excuse that the gods were angry, or busy, and that, when things settled down again up above, all would be well.

As the representative of the gods he healed the people's diseases, which he told them were sent by the gods as a punishment for their neglect of the use of his powers. Thus the role of the priest-magician included that of the medicine-man. As disease came from the gods, only he could cure the sufferer. So he had his quack cures, some of which have come down to us in the Old Testament, which book the Archbishop of Canterbury, at every Coronation, hands to the King with the words, "These are the Oracles of God". The Archbishop then proceeds to turn him into a god-man by pouring holy oil over his head and pronouncing the prescribed words.

According to these Oracles, all the diseases from which man suffers come from God, who told his priest-magician-medicine-men how his inflictions on humanity could be cured. So we read that the leprosy of Uzziah was sent by God, just as were the plagues of Egypt and the boils of Job, which latter had developed because of a wager between God and the Devil. Here we find that the Hebrew medicine-men claim that their tribal god prescribed the cure for leprosy, the prescription being given in the 14th chapter of Leviticus as follows :

And the priest shall take one of the he-lambs and offer him for a guilt offering, and the log of oil, and wave them for a wave offering before the Lord :

And he shall kill the he-lamb in the place where they killed the sin offering and the burnt offering, in the place of the sanctuary : for as the sin offering is the priest's so is the guilt offering ; it is most holy.

And the priest shall take of the blood of the guilt offering, and the priest shall put it upon the tip of the right ear of him that is to be cleansed, and upon the thumb of his right hand, and upon the great toe of his right foot.

And the priest shall take the log of oil, and pour it into the palm of his own left hand.

And the priest shall dip his right finger in the oil that is in his left hand, and shall sprinkle of the oil with his finger seven times before the Lord.

And of the rest of the oil that is in his hand shall the priest put upon the tip of the right ear of him that is to be cleansed, and upon the thumb of his right hand, and upon the great toe of his right foot, upon the blood of the guilt offering.

And the rest of the oil that is in the priest's hand he shall put upon the head of him that is to be cleansed ; and the priest shall make atonement for him before the Lord.

And the priest shall offer the sin offering, and make atonement for him that is to be cleansed because of his uncleanness ; and after he shall kill the burnt offering. And the priest shall offer the burnt offering and the meal offering upon the altar ; and the priest shall make atonement for him and he shall be clean.

One has only to read what are termed the Laws of Moses, and the other books of the Old Testament, to find how magic and priestcraft worked together, and how the priest-magicians have managed to bluff their way through, and delude the people at the same time. This still occurs in our own times, as will be discovered by anyone who reads the prayers about health and sickness in the Church of England Prayer Book. On the other hand, the magician was our first scientist, the medicine-man was our first doctor and from them have developed all that we know today. The beginning was certainly crude and their

knowledge was meagre, but time and mental development have worked wondrous changes.

So we find in ancient literature that the priest-
magician is accepted by the people as the mouthpiece
of the gods or their instructor. In Egypt the magicians
declared that they would scatter the bones of Osiris
and reveal his secret legend if this god worked against
them. The Indian trinity of gods, Brahma, Vishnu
and Siva were subjected to the same threats from
the priest-magicians who, by means of spells, claimed
the power of making these gods submit to their
desires.

When the arrogance of the magicians reached this
height a split occurred between those who adopted
this dictatorial attitude and those who advocated
supplication to, and worship of, the gods. Thus the
supplicants broke away from the others and reserved
their magic to control the people. The gods were
approached by prayer and sacrifice, and the people
were stimulated in their worship by magical rites.
As there was a stone age, so there was an age of
magic. As the stone age was world-wide, so was the
magic age, to which we can trace the rites and ceremonies of the Christian Faith.

This adoption of supplication in place of magic
was the beginning of religion, which word comes
from the Latin words *re-* again, and *ligare*, to bind ;
the idea being that through religion we return to the
original state of union with the gods from which man
fell through disobedience to their wishes. This idea
of original sin evolved only after it became evident
that the claims of the magician were baseless. In
time, the recognition of the folly of accepting the

promises of the magician dawned on the human mind, which found by experience that the crops grew, and the sun rose and set, no matter what the magician said or did. Our ancestors found that the sprinkling of water on the ground, or the making of imitation clouds, did not make the rain to fall and prevent droughts. They began to realise that to stop drinking water and only eat dry food did not stop floods. Nature, whatever they did, pursued her course and was quite indifferent to their behaviour.

When this fact became embedded in the mind of man, when he perceived that magical incantations and ceremonies did not really affect the course of nature, that the verdure of Spring appeared without the necessity of his painting himself, or clothing himself in green, that the crops grew, the rain fell, the thunder rolled and the seasons came and went, no matter what he did, he turned from magic to worship. By slow evolution, through experience, primitive man came to realise that he was powerless before the forces of nature, and that something greater than himself was behind all phenomena. He came to realise human weakness and human ignorance.

The rudiments of science and religion were thus implanted in his mind by experience. He began to reason from effect to cause. He began to think of the causes behind the things he experienced, and he ceased to imagine that he had found the bottom to the fathomless sea of nature. He came to realise that he was born to sorrow and toil. By mental development he turned himself out of the Garden of Eden by eating the fruit of the Tree of Knowledge.

When he had digested this he turned from magic to religion. Instead of relying on the magician he began to pray to the gods.

He gave up ordering the universe by magical rites and became a suppliant and worshipper. He cut himself adrift from past ideas and thus reached peace by accepting the fact that there were powers in nature greater than his own. He found that happiness followed the accepting of the inevitable, and through making the best terms possible with those he imagined were his superiors in the skies.

Religion developed as man humbled himself sufficiently to admit that the handiwork of nature far exceeded his puny understanding, and that other causes must be found for all that he experienced. The change was slow and only step by step did his mental progress develop. One by one he yielded up each phenomenon of nature to the gods. What he thought he could control became a mystery which could be solved only by imagining some power greater than his own. Slowly he gave over the control of nature to the gods and busied himself by devising means to keep on good terms with powers mightier than himself.

From standing erect and instructing the course of nature by his magic and cunning, man adopted the prostrate and supplicant attitude before its mysterious and unseen powers. Instead of making magic circles he built temples. Instead of incantations he said prayers. Instead of performing magic to make the sun rise, he prayed to it as a god to come and perform its daily round. Instead of incantations to bring about the different seasons, he observed festivals of prayer, imploring the gods to remember his needs and pardon his frailties.

Thus religion and religious ceremonies came into being though, in the transition process, magic and religion were combined. Only as development proceeded did he discard the former. This combination of magic and religion is especially noticeable in the religions of Egypt and India where the priests also acted as magicians. The present-day aborigines of Australia are an example of primitive man who resorted to magic and the worship of his ancestors. The magician, to these natives of Australia, is the priest who rules them and they rely on charms and sorcery as did early man. Their gods are the spirits of their ancestors with whom they try to make contact through magic and prayers. These aborigines are now fast dying out and are the last link we have with primitive man. They are present-day examples of the outlook of early man, and their study has been a great aid to anthropologists in forming conclusions as to the religious ideas of prehistoric man, who groped and stumbled towards some explanation of the mystery of existence.

Much can be learned of the magical arts of the past in the Old Testament. In Ezekiel (xxi, 21) one finds an interesting passage relating to three modes of magical divination. The Babylonian and Assyrian clay tablets have also revealed many of the magical formulas of antiquity and these are set out clearly in *Magie chez les Chaldéens* and *Divination chez les Chaldéens* by Lenormant. Researches in Egypt have also been very fruitful in the same direction, as will be realised by a study of Sayce's *Records of the Past.*

Doubtless the sun was the first natural object on which primitive man expressed his incipient religious emotions. Because it moved, and gave heat, a god must be within it so as to guide and direct its daily life. What he imagined it was who can say, but at least he felt happier when it was shining than when it was not, and he would observe that its rays had a beneficial effect on growth. From these feelings of satisfaction and gratitude developed

SUN WORSHIP,

which, along with magical rites, gave comfort to humanity for thousands of years.

Here we arrive at the stage where our primitive ancestors began to develop a sense of reverence, and a sense of awe and gratitude. Here we find the acorn of religious feeling which was to grow into a mighty oak and profoundly affect existence on earth. Here we find the germ of the realisation of the divine in nature and of a power outside ourselves.

In the early days of sun worship there were no priests, no altars and no sacrifices. All these came later when man discovered that he had a spirit, which he thought the sun-god relished. Man, being a cannibal, believed that the sun-god was one also. The first sun worshippers were grateful for its benign rays, and in simple terms expressed themselves as such, together with the hope that the sun-god would not hide his face behind the clouds, and that when he left them at night he would return in the morning.

In our search for the religious beliefs of primitive man the data which carries us furthest back is that obtained from names expressive of the divine, which have been preserved in the most ancient languages. Languages carry us much further back than do the ruins of temples and shrines. Long before the erection of the oldest places of worship language shows us that man conceived the gods as powers outside himself, which he worshipped, either from fear or gratitude. Language is the only real guide we have to the beliefs of primitive man, though it by no means carries us back to the earliest beliefs of the human race.

By the study of languages we can, however, go back a long way. The Egyptian word *nutar* and the names of the Egyptian gods, found in their inscriptions, prove that at a date long before they wrote history they conceived the gods as responsible for natural phenomena. The Chinese language likewise, by its word *T'ien*, proves that this race conceived the gods as overruling powers thousands of years before the Christian era. All members of the Semitic family of languages have the word *El* or some modification of it. In Sanskrit we find *Deva*, in Latin *Deus*, and in the Teutonic group of languages the word is *God*, or some slightly modified form of the word. The Slavic group has the word *Bog* or some modification thereof.

Doubtless there were divine names much older than these, as, from the reconstruction of prehistoric languages, we find words expressing ideas of the divine. The reconstruction of languages takes us far back in the history of the race, but there is every reason to believe that further back than this can take us, names were used in speech which referred to the gods as the cause of everything experienced by early man.

Research has shown us by fossil remains the great antiquity of man, and, from these relics, as far as we can go back, we discover that he was awed and comforted by thoughts of beings beyond the material. Between this far-off date and the date of even the oldest language, there stretches an unmeasurable expanse of time so that the first religion of man must remain a conjecture. Considering the age of man, history is but a streak of light amid surrounding darkness.

From the places of worship still existing, such as Stonehenge, the large, well-preserved Druid's temple discovered in 1937 near Glasgow, and others of a similar kind, we know that early man gave much of his thought to the influence of the sun on his condition. As the sun gave heat, and caused growth, it became at an early date the principal god of the ancients. Traces of sun worship are to be found in all parts of the world, and constitute the first evidence we have of organised religion. All the phenomena by then had been deified, but all took secondary place to the sun, which became the God of Gods and Lord of Lords. To early man the sun was the vital force 'which intimately affected life from birth to death, "The Shining One" it was called by the Hindus, and "He by whom all men live" by the Mexicans. The fact that its presumed daily journey across the heavens could be seen by all, that its heat could be felt by all, that its power to produce growth was noticed by all, caused the worship of its greatness to be translated into numerous ceremonies. To recount them all is impossible, but a few examples will suffice.

The sun was the cause of rain, and so innumerable ceremonies were performed when rain was wanted, or the reverse. An eclipse was a bad omen. The sun was angry and human lives and the fruits of the field were offered to it, with prayers for forgiveness. Fire-tipped arrows were shot into the air in the hope that they would help to bring back its beneficial heat. On such occasions, incantations, ceremonies and prayers were numerous.

To prevent such a recurrence innumerable methods were resorted to. In ancient Egypt, for instance, the king, who was the sun's representative on earth, walked in great solemnity round the walls of the temple as an aid to the sun in its daily journey and to prevent another eclipse. Festivals were held at the autumnal equinox when the sun's power was felt to be waning, the one in Egypt being called "The Nativity of the sun's walking-stick", the idea being that it was tired and needed some support. Again, elsewhere, bleeding hearts of men and animals were offered up for the same reason.

Offerings were made before sunrise and prayers were repeated that it would make its appearance. In the evening, after sunset, thank-offerings and prayers were offered for its appearance. Regular sacrifices were made of human victims and animals to feed the sun with their life, and altars were soaked in blood everywhere by this holocaust. Countless legends were told of the prowess of the sun, and each race had a sun-god to whom cities, temples, groves and altars were dedicated. Traces of sun worship still remain in the orientation of churches, of graves and of priests when repeating the creeds.

The ancient Greeks believed that the sun was the chariot of their god, and chariots and horses were sacrificed to this vain idea. From the Esquimaux in the north to the Australian bushmen in the south the sun was looked upon as the God of Gods, and received from them their sacrifices, their prayers, their incantations and their offerings. Each time of the year the ceremony was different, to accord with the diversified power given out by this luminous orb.

The development of sun worship into a regular and sustained form of belief can best be understood by a study of the religious beliefs of the Egyptians, that great nation which dwelt on either bank of the sacred Nile. These beliefs centred round the sun and can be traced back to a date before 3300 B.C., when the historical age began. Each district worshipped its own gods, who were the prototypes of the sun, and had attributed to them the stories told of the sun in its apparent daily and annual journey in the heavens.

The Egyptians regarded the sun as the creator of the universe and the source of all life. The centre of the Sun-god cult was Heliopolis, a short distance from the modern city of Cairo, and from this centre its influence spread throughout the whole of Egypt, so much so that every local god came to be identified with the sun.

The sun was worshipped as a god under the name of Rā, and it was believed that Rā sailed across the sky, the sun being his boat. At dawn he was a new-born child, at midday a man in his prime, who became older as the day wore on, ending finally at sunset as an old man. To him hymns were composed and sung, in which we find poems of gratitude because it was believed that he lifted the waters of the Nile, which fertilised the land, and thus gave the people their sustenance. Monuments, walls of temples, and coffins in Egypt bear witness to the wonderful powers of the sun, and quite three-quarters of these relate to the religious beliefs of the people.

Rā, like Jehovah, waxed wrath at the sins of the people and decided to destroy every living creature; this he carried out in the same cruel way as did Jehovah. What really happened was some natural disaster from which few escaped. This story spread as far as India and the countries surrounding the Mediterranean. The people believed that this whole-sale destruction was a punishment by the gods for their sins, which fact the priests kept constantly before them so as to prevent them from neglecting sacrifice and worship. The same story is recorded on Babylonian tablets and in Greek literature.

The reason for Rā's cruelty can be better understood when we realise that he, like all the other gods of the past and present, was imagined as having the characteristics of man. When the people were cruel the gods were cruel. When the people were kind the gods were kind. The Egyptians were cruel, because we find on the reliefs carved on the walls of the temples, scenes depicting Pharaoh sacrificing prisoners of war in the most brutal manner in the presence of the god, of whom he was considered the earthly embodiment.

The god of the Egyptian pantheon who played the most spectacular part during the period of Egypt's greatest conquests was Amen. To this god was given the nation's thanks and worship for leading his people to victory. No other god, whose worship did not conform to the rites and ceremonies surrounding sun worship, had any hope of success amongst the people to whom the sun was an ever daily presence. So, as with the gods who preceded and followed, Amen was identified with Rā the sungod and became Rā-Amen. After prayers and proclamations the people always exclaimed "Amen" and this custom of exclaiming "Amen", like many others connected with these old religions, has come down to us in the Christian religion. In 1938 a temple was discovered at Karnak, near Luxor, and on the lintel of one of its doors is engraved the following : "Erected by Senusrat I to the glory of his faith in Rā-Amen, in good white stone from Tura."

The pastoral staff of present-day bishops, and the scull-cap of present-day priests, are found on these reliefs to be part of the vestments of the Pharaohs, back into early times. Besides these, each Pharaoh, as the sun-god's incarnation on earth, carried a sceptre on which were three symbols. The one which has survived, doubtless because of its importance, and also because of the influence Egyptian beliefs had on early Christianity, is the cross in the form of a T on which was a circle, thus ♀. This symbol is known to Egyptian students as the *ānkh*, which means life.

Each sun-god was also represented with a disc behind his head, to depict the sun. This, likewise, has come down to us in the halo which is so often placed behind the head of Jesus, because the Christian

Church adorned its god, when Jesus became the Christ, with this solar emblem, and much else that was attributed to Osiris, the much-beloved sun-god of Egypt, who followed Rā-Amen in the affection of the Egyptian people.

Some of the Egyptian temples were of vast size ; Karnak, for instance, occupied over sixty-one acres. They were magnificent buildings, and even today excite the wonder and admiration of visitors. In the inmost precincts of the sanctuary was the Holy of Holies, where rested what corresponded to the Hebrew Ark of the Covenant. This, and everything to do with each temple, and the worship therein, was in charge of the priests, over whom ruled the chief priest.

On the sun-god was showered the best of all that the land produced, which, after being offered to him in all solemnity, was retained by the priests for their own use. Here we find the origin of our present-day tithes. Another resemblance of the Egyptian worship with that of Christianity is that the Egyptian priesthood owned nearly one-seventh of the cultivated land of Egypt, and had allotted to it a multitude of slaves and vast herds of cattle. In the middle ages the Christian Church owned about half of Europe, and is even today the wealthiest organisation in the world. It was also the largest owner of slaves, Pope Gregory the Great having no less than a thousand. How man has impoverished himself in his attempt to be on friendly terms with the gods through their representatives the priests !

As we proceed we shall discover the source of all that we today call Christian, as the Christians copied much from the Egyptians, either direct, or through the Jews, who previously had framed their rites, ceremonies and beliefs on those practised by their Egyptian neighbours. We must, however, proceed step by step, just as the beliefs, rituals and ceremonies grew up and developed. From Egypt came the ritual performed by present-day Christian priests before the altar in Roman Catholic, Greek and High Anglican churches. Incense, carried in censers, filled the air with its fragrance to convey to the gods, by means of the fumes, the spirits released from the food which had been offered to them. Incense is in use today in many churches, but few of the worshippers know the reason for this practice.

So the sun rose and set, crops grew and died. Winter came with unfailing regularity, to be followed by Spring, Summer and Autumn, and our ancestors likewise came and went with the same unfailing regularity. In Spring they prayed for Summer, so that the earth might yield its increase, and when Autumn came they thanked the sun for all it had given to them. So came our various festivals which have all a close connection with the position of the earth to the sun throughout the year.

We still use expressions which have come down from the early days. The sun by the ancients was the first to die. So we speak of life's day being over, of it having set, and of the dead going west. The sun was supposed to be the first to have found the way to the realms of the dead. It was known as "The Lord of the departed", and, when man discovered his spirit, it was termed "The Lord of the risen dead". It was supposed to symbolise life on earth, which passes through the various phases of the sun ; birth, strength and the weakness of old age, only to rise in the after life refreshed and young again.

Sun worship, and the rites connected with it, would require volumes to describe, because it was world-wide and lasted for thousands of years. Besides the sun, the moon was worshipped to a lesser degree. By some it was considered to be the sun's wife, by others his son. Ceremonies were performed to the moon, and prayers and sacrifices were offered to this ruler of the night. An eclipse of the moon called for an intensification of worship and sacrifice. Each month special ceremonies were performed to this god of the darkness which to some was the god of evil. This latter belief brought about the idea that it caused mental unrest. Hence our word lunacy, from the Latin luna, the moon. Others looked on it as the god of fecundity because its waxing and waning coincided with the process of life-giving in women.

Besides these two heavenly bodies, the planets were worshipped and received adoration. The sky was worshipped as the dwelling-place of the gods, and, when praying, the people looked upwards. Besides the sky, and the heavenly bodies receiving the worship of our ancestors, trees, the fruits of the fields, animals and fire received worship in different ways. To early man the effect of life, growth and movement was seen and experienced, and to all a god was made the cause who had to be thanked or placated.

Fire, when it was discovered, was symbolised, deified and likened to life, because it lived for a time, only to die. As man advanced in knowledge he learned how to keep in being a continuous flame, and this was sanctified, and rendered holy, because it symbolised life everlasting. Round this symbol, rites and ceremonies grew up which are found in so many ancient faiths. Temples were built to protect it, and its protectors were vestal virgins of spotless lives.

Early man doubtless discovered fire by rubbing two sticks together. This crossing of two sticks, which produced fire, may have been the reason why the cross has been a sacred symbol to so many nations who professed different faiths, and who looked on it as a symbol of life everlasting. Fire was considered a purifier, and the smoke it caused was looked on as the avenue by which the spirit of the sacrificed victim travelled to the gods. Like the human being, alive one minute and dead the next, so smoke is seen one minute and disappears the next. Smoke, like the word breath, was used as a symbol of life, and the spirit was supposed to rise to heaven as did smoke. The poets described the spirit as a bird, giving it wings, and we still find angels depicted with these birdlike attributes.

To early man the world must have been a very mysterious place in which to live. True, he would accept his conditions very much as the rest of us do, but to one of a more thoughtful nature, in these early days, there was so much that could not be understood. He saw movement everywhere, growth and decay, life and death. The heavens were to him a panorama of moving lights. One wonders who was the first man with sufficient intelligence to come to the conclusion that nothing moves of itself, that there must be a force behind all motion. Whoever reached this conclusion, and someone must have been the first to do it, was the first scientist. He reached one of the most important decisions arrived at by the human race, that there can be no movement without a cause, which is one of the fundamental axioms of science.

In these early days science and religion were one and the same, and represented the effort made to find a cause behind movement and life. Prehistoric man adopted the idea of a god, which meant to him very much the same as it does to many today. It expressed his solution of the puzzle, and satisfied his conviction that there was a cause behind every effect, the infinite behind the finite. It stood for the unknown quantity which he could not grasp but which he realised was within all movement and life. The idea stood him in good stead and has satisfied trillions for thousands of years. Till the scientific age the idea was considered a sufficient answer, and satisfied his religious longings.

Some authorities think that all religion is due to illusion and fear, that there is a material explanation for everything that happens, that every effect can be understood, that every cause can be explained, that the universe is but one vast machine, each cog fitting into its place, all moving with precision, without friction, without direction, and that man himself is just one of the cogs in this great revolving wheel.

To those who think thus the human body is an active, thinking mechanism, moved by chemical action within. To such, the universe, and all it contains, is matter combined with force which have been from all eternity, and will be to all eternity. To them, all religious beliefs and emotions, all the beliefs, from the days of primitive man up to the present time, and all the demonstrations of psychic phenomena, are mere delusions, and mean only one thing, that humanity has been mistaken in believing that the human being is other than flesh and bones, and that there exists anything beyond matter and force which alone constitute the universe.

Those who adopt this line of thought concentrate on the effect and misjudge the cause. They concentrate on the mass of humbug, folly, cruelty and ignorance which makes up the religious history of the human race. They forget that all this accumulation of error would never have been had there not been a cause, that delusion cannot be the cause of its origin, and that something more fundamental than delusion must be assigned to so great an effort, however much the effort has trespassed beyond the bounds of reason and reality.

There is a cause for every effect, and the greater the effect the greater the cause. Illusion can surely not be assigned to the effect, as represented by religious history, which tells us of mankind sacrificing his time and wealth in building temples, in handing over to others a tenth of what he has won from the earth by the sweat of his brow, so that they might instruct him as to his destiny, and how he could secure happiness and contentment after death. Illusion cannot be the cause of the taboos he has scrupulously kept, thinking that they were pleasing to the gods, and that by observing them he would be happier hereafter.

Illusion would not have made him offer up his most precious possessions to the gods had he not instinctively felt that there was something about him related to the gods. Man may be a fool, but not quite such an abject fool as the materialists represent him to be. His ignorance of the facts of nature was profound, but he knew one thing, and that was his own inmost feelings, which were due to one cause only, that he possessed a spirit. His ideas of the causes behind the phenomena of nature were as simple as those of a child, but at least he knew the limitations of his knowledge and put gods into the void his mind could not fathom. He had sufficient sense to know that he must put some cause behind each effect he experienced.

Surely the evolution of the human mind, its growth from ignorance to knowledge, explains its past mistakes and follies. These were due to the fundamental reality that man valued his spirit more than anything else ; to him it was the greatest reality and he would suffer misery and privation of all kinds to secure its future happiness. His ignorance of his future abode, his fear of punishment there for his mistakes here, his ignorance of the universe in which he lived, his belief that in sacrifice he returned life to the gods, and his slow moral development, produced the folly, the cruelty, the intrigue and all those phases of religion which disgust us in this more enlightened age.

Some have emerged from this ignorance to knowledge and yet, in spite of our greater intelligence, the Infinite and man's spirit still remain the greatest problem. We still pursue our quest to reach an understanding of the mysteries which surround us. Because of this earth being the starting-place of a journey, as "here we have no continuing city, but seek one to come", the Infinite means much to our inquiring minds. Like the ancients we feel that we are related to it and that somewhere, some time, this relationship will become closer. We cry aloud for light, more light, but to many the answer to the cry is but an echo. Like Sisyphus, in Greek mythology, some are for ever trying to roll a huge stone to the top of a hill, only to find that it slips back, and they see no possible end to their quest.

So long as the human mind is limited by the limitations of the human body it cannot do otherwise than think in terms of boundaries, of limits and of time. So long as to it, finite and changing matter is reality, it cannot imagine a universe which has been from eternity, will endure to all eternity, and that cause and effect go round a circle which has no beginning and no end. So long as the human mind is incapable of reaching out to grasp reality apart from physical matter the universe can be none other than a problem, which it will be for ever trying to solve.

So long as mind remains beyond human conception, beyond the reach of touch and sight, so long as there are no boundaries to the mind and one horizon leads to another, one peak to a higher one, so long as there are no frontiers, so long as the finite cannot plumb the Infinite and the part embrace the whole, humanity must fill the gaping void by believing that some power exists which is beyond its comprehension.

To some it is a personal being, called God, somewhat larger and stronger than themselves. To others it is a giant with human attributes but all of enormous proportions. To a smaller number it is an indefinite being without parts or substance. To the philosopher God is Mind, which produces the cause and appreciates the effect. To others God represents something behind or within the material universe, which keeps it in motion, and is the cause of life and growth, the omnipotent and omnipresent life-force of the universe which links up cause and effect, and of which every thinking, moving thing is a part.

Whether we say that God is behind or within nature, or Mind is, matters little. Until, however, we accept the fact that this life-giving and controlling force exists, the universe is an enigma incapable of being understood. Mind, or God, is the universe which has been from all eternity and will be to all eternity. All material things are but an expression of this immaterial something, sustaining life, producing growth, causing thought and ordering the universe.

Primitive man, living close to nature, though ignorant of science, as we understand it today, accepted like a child what seemed obvious : that the sun circled round the earth, which movement he could only explain by believing that behind it was an invisible superman. Though our physicists today express it all in different language, and have other words for the gods, to the ordinary individual God fills the infinite gap his reason cannot fathom.

All past history emphasises that man has been unable to abstain from acknowledging the existence of some unseen power, or cause, or thought, which produced the panorama we call nature, and also some energy within himself, apart from the material universe. In spite of all the discoveries of science, God, or Mind, or whatever other name we care to use, still remains as the unknown factor in the mechanism of the universe. The blank in our understanding exists and each one fills it as best he can.

Whatever has been beyond our grasp has always

been related to the Divine or Infinite. The Infinite, from the time man began to think, has grown from being an invisible man, a little larger and a little stronger than he was, to something more and more inscrutable as our knowledge advances. All the sacred and philosophical writings of the past, the characters on stone, the temples and burying-grounds which are now in ruins, are the relics of man's attempt to fathom the Infinite, that magnetic power which has raised him from the beast to what he is today. To what further heights it will raise him who can say ?

One after another the old ideas were abandoned, and something new accepted, as his mind pressed onwards in its search for an explanation of the Divine in nature. Ever was he striving to reach beyond the finite into the infinite. First he tried magic and then worship. When he discovered that the sun was not a god then he worshipped the god who produced the sun, which he termed the Father of Mankind. This again the thoughtful had to abandon because they could not explain who produced this Father, and so he has gone on in his philosophical reasonings down the ages. Finally, Xenophon, Plato and Aristotle gave up all attempt to apply names and concepts to the Divine, as they realised that it was something beyond human understanding.

We are still confronted with the same problem and no progress will be made in solving the Infinite till we place ourselves mentally outside the physical body, and the physical universe, and accept the fact that each one of us is Mind and Mind only, that what we term the Infinite is likewise Mind and only Mind, and that Matter is but the expression of Mind. When the individual mind can grasp this mighty truth it will realise that the Infinite is only the Infinite to Mind encased in a body having limitations, and that only when it is freed of such limitations will it become possible to begin to comprehend the Infinite.

It is impossible to understand the Infinite through the eyes of finite matter, physical or etheric. The finite cannot possibly comprehend the Infinite but, if we accept the Infinite as Mind, of which we each are part, we come to realise that the problem is not the enigma it seems to be. Thinking of it in terms of physical or etheric matter, with boundaries and duration, will always retain the mystery, but by thinking of it as Mind, without duration and without boundaries, we are on a higher plane of thought, which makes the problem comprehensible. Mind has no limitations, either in time or space. These limitations only refer to matter, and, if we can think of the universe as Mind, and that matter is but an expression of Mind, we are not looking at the problem upside-down as we do when we consider the Infinite through the spectacles of matter. When the human mind can reach up to this angle of thought, religion will develop into philosophy and worship into contemplation.

The universe is undoubtedly held together by cause and effect. If it were not so there would be chaos. Because there is order instead of chaos man has conceived one or more minds behind the phenomena of nature. This has been the cause of his belief in the existence of many gods, or of one supreme god, and of his conception of a god as a thinking being like himself.

All the thinkers before the scientific age found it

necessary to explain phenomena by attributing them to one or more invisible non-material agents. Because things move of themselves, argued Plato, there must be some invisible cause to produce the movement. For the same reason he argued that man must be possessed of a mind, which is the cause of thought and movement. It must be something quite apart from the inert body. This mind Plato relates to the cause which orders the universe. Reasoning thus he concludes that everything which moves must have a mind and be related to the cause. Thus he argues that the sun, the planets, all the phenomena of nature in motion, are each possessed of a mind and are related to the Divine. A god is behind each, and all things that move, he asserts, are Divine.

The Greeks were roused to the worship of the gods by art, the Egyptians by the personification of animals and the river Nile. Others have been roused by fire, trees, thunder, lightning, the sun, the moon and the sky. The Divine has always been personified in something material, as only through the material could it be imagined by man. Images have from early times aided mankind in his conception of the gods, they were the material symbols of things mental, and still remain as such in many churches and temples.

All these aids to worship were later developments. We must not proceed too fast as, during the ages of magic and sun worship, or perhaps before them, who can say, man was making his most important discovery, a discovery which entirely altered his outlook on life.

From trying to control nature he had become a suppliant. If he had stopped there we would have found that, round this impulse, caused by gratitude, and the desire for more from nature's storehouse, religion would never have developed. Something much more vital, much more personal, was necessary if his development were to proceed. Without this, religion, as we understand it, would never have been. So the time came, no one can say when or where, as the development came about very slowly in the process of evolution, that man made his greatest discovery.

MAN DISCOVERS HIS SPIRIT

What the spirit is he probably knew as little as do the vast majority of his descendants of the present day. The word spirit occurs in all religions but is never defined. In more modern terminology let us say that early man came to realise, more or less indefinitely, that he was not just a material creation, but that he was, in fact, very different from what he appeared to be. To outward eyes he appeared as a body of flesh, but this he discovered was an illusion as he found that he had certain psychic attributes which functioned apart from the physical body. To account for these he employed the word spirit which embraced them all, everything, that is to say, which is apart from the body of flesh and blood.

Before we proceed further let us first of all understand exactly what is meant by the words spirit and mind, and also the word soul. These words are constantly being confused, owing to the fact that the Greek word *psyche* has always been translated soul and the Latin word *spiritus* has been translated spirit. Psyche and spiritus mean the same and they correspond

to the Sanskrit word *prâna.* These three words
originally meant breath, which it was thought constituted what we now call the Etheric Being. The
mind is something far different from the spirit or the
soul, as it is the intangible, unseen, image-making
substance within our brain which controls the physical
body on earth through the duplicate etheric body.
After death it controls the etheric body through the
etheric brain, which is a duplicate of the physical brain.

As it is the custom to talk about *a* spirit I shall use
this word when referring to an etheric being, that is
an individual without a physical body, one with an
etheric body controlled by mind. If I ever refer to
the spirit it will mean the etheric body only. I shall
not use the word soul as this is so often used in error
for the mind, and to use two words, soul and spirit,
for the etheric body is confusing. The mind, the
directing quantity, the spirit or etheric body, and the
physical body make up the man on earth. At death he
becomes an etheric being or spirit, a being guided by
mind, which latter consists of that image-making
substance which produces thought and directs our
movements. Man *is* a mind, not *has* a mind, because
he can live and function after death apart from the
material body. This proves that the physical body is
only a covering to house the mind during the time it is
in contact with physical matter. Both the physical
and etheric bodies are but habitations to enable the
personality to function.

The ancients could only express the immaterial
part of man by words such as breath, blood or heart,
just as they described the gods behind natural phenomena by the words storm, fire, wind and sky. They

noticed that when death occurred the breath left the body, so some thought that the breath was the spirit and mind, but, as the heart stopped beating, some thought that they were the heart. Others thought that the mind was concentrated in the liver or other internal organs. In a Babylonian tablet we find the expression "His liver rejoiced", but the Greek word psyche, meaning breath, was certainly the most natural description for that part of us which is not material, because the breath is the least seen and felt substance connected with the body.

We know that the breath exists during life and ceases at death, but it is likewise true that blood flows when life is present and ceases to do so at death, which was the reason why some believed that the blood contained the spirit. Blood poured from a wound during lifetime but not at death. We are familiar with the quotations in the New Testament relating to the blood sacrifice of Jesus, who became the Christ. Here we are told that "Without the shedding of blood there is no remission of sin", and that "The blood of Jesus Christ cleanseth us from all sin". Blood, meaning life, occurs in all old literature and what has been believed about the saving qualities of the life of Jesus was likewise believed of all the Saviour gods of the past. Kritias, a Greek philosopher, stated that the mind was seated in the blood, and the Arabs when referring to the death of anyone used the expression that "his mind flowed away".

Blood was poured on the altar of the gods because it was thought to be life, that it had come from the gods and was thus returned to them. Christians talk about "the precious blood of Jesus", and the legend of the soldier piercing his side, when he was on the cross, is symbolic of a sacrifice, when the knife was placed into the side of the victim for the purpose of releasing the blood. From the belief that the blood contained the spirit and life, which the gods could eat, arose sacrifice, with all its cruelty, but it is well to remember that sacrifices were offered up in all reverence, and in the firm belief that they were pleasing to the gods. It was not for the purpose of inflicting suffering on the victim that a sacrifice was made.

The Jews believed, as did other nations, that blood contained the spirit and belonged to their god. Consequently we read of the stringent regulations about bleeding an animal before eating it. Our ancestors believed that drinking the blood endowed them with the life and strength of the one whose blood they drank. This became one of the rites of the Pagan eucharist which was copied by the Christian Church. To drink the blood of the slain god imparted to the one who drank it the immortality that the god had achieved.

The same applies to the heart. It was seen that the heart ceased to beat at death and so the word heart was also used as meaning the life and spirit of the individual. It was eaten for the same purpose as the blood was drunk. It was offered to the gods for the same reason, just as were the other organs of the body, such as the liver, the kidneys and the bowels, each of which, at one time or another, was believed to be the seat of life. In the English translation of the Bible we read such expressions as "Refresh my bowels in the Lord", "Create in me a clean heart, O God", and "In meekness of heart, fearing God",

The breath vanishes at death and so man's mind was described as a breath which vanishes at death. It was also believed that the spirit came out of the body at death through the mouth, which, more or less, corresponds with what clairvoyants tell us today, that at death they can see an immaterial substance coming out of the top of the head and gradually forming into a complete body.

In many languages we find that the expression "to expire" or "to breathe out" means to die, and so the word breath became generally adopted as referring to the mind. It is because of this that the word psychic has come down to us from the Greek. When alive man breathed, when dead he ceased to breathe. Everything was there but the breath. Everything changed when the breath stopped, the body did not move, the heart did not beat, and finally all ended in dust. The only explanation which could be given for this was that all thought, life and movement had departed with the breath.

We are told in Genesis that "God breathed into his nostrils the breath of life". The correct translation is that "the gods breathed into his nostrils the breath of life". Elohim, which has been translated God or The Lord, is a plural word meaning the gods. It occurs two thousand times in the Old Testament and in each case should have been translated in the plural. So what the gods gave they could also take away, and it was believed that life at death returned to the gods.

How was it man discovered that he had a mind, that he was something different from what he appeared to be, that the body was not the man but the mind within, which did the thinking, caused the movement and survived the death of the body ? It must have dawned on him slowly. It must have taken ages for him to be able to evolve the words body and mind, and this could only have come about by a process of deduction. We can look at a locomotive without steam and one with steam. They have both very much the same appearance but they are very different in performance. When we find that a locomotive will not move we say that it has no steam. It is a process of deduction drawn from our experience of what a locomotive is capable of doing with and without steam.

Early man adopted the same process. When a body moved it was said that it had life and when it was inert it was said to be without life. The steam in a locomotive is unseen, just as life is unseen, but when the locomotive moves we know that the steam is there, just as we know that when a body moves it has life. So early man inferred that this unseen something, which animated the body and left it at death, was something very real.

Moreover, he personally experienced sleep and dreams, and some experienced swoons, trance, clairvoyance and clairaudience, but much the most conclusive proof he received, that the mind and spirit existed apart from the physical body, came from his seeing apparitions and ghosts, when in a normal state, and visions when in a state of ecstasy. Primitive religion combines all these factors which are today grouped under the name of psychic phenomena.

Not only did early man come to believe that he himself had an undying mind, which he considered was a god within him, but he also believed that behind each phenomenon of nature there was likewise a mind or god. All nature was thus endowed. This development of his religious beliefs is now known as

ANIMISM,

which explained all growth on the hypothesis of spirit agency. Its beliefs are amongst the earliest to be discovered in the religious history of man and they are still prevalent amongst savage races. Animism may rightly be described as a distinctive philosophy of primitive culture and is the outcome of early man's contemplation of life, growth and decay. To him all life was animated by mind ; he sees life everywhere, in animals, trees and plants. Hence we have the name from the Latin word *animus*, meaning the mind.

The mystery of growth defied early man, and, just as he had to put a god behind the thunder, a god behind the storm, so he had to explain growth in the same way. He developed his philosophy round the belief that a god was in every living thing, both animal and vegetable. Certain animals were considered sacred and so were trees. Amongst the Celts the oak was sacred everywhere in Europe. Not even the bark of a tree could be cut because the sap was supposed to be its blood, and it was believed that when trees were cut they suffered and bled. Severe punishments were inflicted on anyone who damaged a tree in any way.

The Greeks associated the oak with Zeus, and when Zeus was taken over by the Romans and called Jupiter, they continued the belief that this god of the sky, rain and thunder, called Zeus by the Greeks, and Jupiter by the Romans, was the god of the Oak. The

Teutonic god of thunder, Thor, was also identified with Jupiter and Zeus, and to him also the oak was dedicated. The Slav thunder god, Perun, was also identified with the oak. When rain was wanted the oak was prayed to, and the mistletoe, to the Druids, was the most sacred part of the tree. The groves of oak trees were the scenes of their services and ritual, and oak leaves always formed part of their rites.

The present-day dance round the Maypole or Maytree is a survival of tree worship, when the people sat round a tree, worshipped it, and then danced round it. This ancient form of worship was held in the Spring, when it was believed that the spirit came to take up his abode in the tree for the Summer. The May Queen, a young girl, was the symbol of life entering vegetation. She was usually clad in green leaves and, after the festival, was often carried in procession.

Evil spirits were kept away from sacred trees by imitation birds being placed on the tops of the trees because it was thought that, as they swayed in the wind, the spirits would be afraid to come near. The weather-cocks on church steeples are a survival of this super-stition, and, at one time, no church was ever built without the effigy of a cock being placed on the top of the steeple so as to keep away evil spirits.

If we imagine ourselves in Europe in those early days, we can easily realise how much the growth and death of trees would influence our imagination and religious emotions. Europe was then covered by dense forests in which were to be found scattered clearings, where lived our ancestors. One forest, for instance, stretched eastward an unknown distance from the Rhine, and its density and silence so impressed the Emperor Julian that he tells us he knew nothing like it in his Empire. England was likewise covered by immense forests, and the wild bull and boar were hunted, up till the twelfth century, in the woods of Hampstead.

Vegetation was not always treated with awe and respect, because some thought that certain trees contained evil spirits, and much shouting and noise took place to drive them away. Again, some tribes believed that the spirits of the dead animated certain trees, which trees received reverence and protection. Human spirits were supposed to prefer certain trees to others, and we find that these trees were offered food and such things as it was thought the spirit of the departed would like. Elsewhere it was believed that tree-spirits came and went, that sometimes they were there and sometimes they were not, which brought about a new form of belief—that these spirits came to give the trees life and then returned to the sky. This idea brings us back again to the belief that the gods, who controlled nature, lived in the heavens.

The tree-spirits could make the crops grow, the cattle to multiply, give rain and sunshine and make women fruitful. Various devices were resorted to by women who wished children. Those gods who inhabited the trees were looked upon with the same reverence, the same respect, and received the same worship from our primitive ancestors as did the sun, the moon and the planets. Whatever moved incited in their minds the sense of worship, and vegetation received its full share.

Primitive man also believed that each animal had

a spirit body and that the bodies of some could be taken possession of by the gods, as was a medium's body by the controlling spirit. An animal's spirit is a duplicate of its physical body and it was believed that this duplicate body passed into another world at death. For this reason they were sacrificed, to return their spirits to the gods as food. All kinds of animals down the ages have been considered sacred, such as bulls, cows, crocodiles and so on. It would be difficult to find some animal that was not at one time or another considered sacred and consequently worshipped.

Closely allied to this was the belief that the spirits of men and women after death found their way into animals and replaced those of the animals. This belief followed many tortuous ways, but it has been one which has prevailed down the ages and is still in being in India and elsewhere.

All disease was accounted for by the explanation that the sufferer was possessed by one or more demons, and this was especially so in convulsions, delirium or insanity. Good or evil gods were the cause of all the good or ill that affected humanity. Every brook and well, every rock and glade was peopled by nature spirits who have come down to us as fairies.

From this primitive belief, that all nature was alive with gods of different kinds, a system of thought developed which became so comprehensive as to hold all nature in a web of vital action, so multiform that it encompassed almost every order of phenomena. It was so coherent as to create a perfect plexus of ideas that mutually support and interpret one another, and so persistent that its most extravagant developments have survived for ages. Development was slow and gradual, but its philosophy took firm root and cast its branches far afield, so much so that the more advanced religions, which developed later, adopted almost entirely its expressions and ideas. It held its place not only in ancient philosophy and theology but up till recent times.

Customs prevail today which are the result of this primitive belief. As recently as 1781 a soldier's horse was sacrificed at Treves when its owner died, to enable him to ride into the other world. This idea still persists by the leading of horses of kings and soldiers in their funeral processions to their graves. It is also the relic of the custom when wives and slaves were slain to do service to their master in the other world. Besides these, horses and cattle were slaughtered in order to transfer their spirits to his new abode, as it was thought that he would there have need of them. Clothes, ornaments and other necessary articles, which the deceased might need, were burned so that he might have the use of their etheric counterparts in his new abode. In Ireland pieces of money are still put in the hand of the corpse, and in some countries of Europe the custom still prevails of setting out offerings of food for the spirit of the departed.

The very general belief in reincarnation can likewise be traced to the fact that some individuals, when in trance, are controlled by personalities claiming to be those of people who once lived on earth. When thus controlled such people behave and speak as did those purporting to control them. This control, by the departed, of another human body is perhaps the origin of the numerous conceptions of reincarnation.

It was also believed that each individual had

previously lived on earth, and that as his deeds were so was his reward when he returned to earth. The human being was either ascending or descending. If he lived aright he ultimately quitted matter for good and all, but if he did not do so he would go down through the animals and finally perish. This belief in reward and punishment developed until ultimately it was believed that the sky was reserved for the good and some place under the surface of the earth was reserved for the wicked. This was termed the underworld. Certain gods were allotted to the underworld and others to the sky. Above, the departed enjoyed life much as they did on earth, but below was a dark and rocky region where there was constant misery.

In the former the good gods reigned, and the hierarchy of earth was believed to exist in heaven, presided over by divine beings of great power, under whom came archangels, angels and various grades of heavenly beings. Likewise hell was presided over by the chief god of evil who, like the good gods, had under him different grades of beings. These beliefs in divine potentates, archangels, angels and demons have persisted throughout all religious history and, except for changes in ceremonials, ritual, dogmas and doctrines, the beliefs of primitive man are still the basic religious beliefs of humanity.

War, it was believed, reigned in the heavens between the gods of the underworld and the gods of the skies for the ultimate possession of humanity. Finally it became a settled belief amongst the most cultured in Greece and Rome that there was a supreme God of good and a supreme God of evil. The good God was surrounded by good angels and the bad God by bad angels, which belief was taken over by Christianity, along with the Pagan belief that the God of evil was intent on gathering to himself as many lost spirits as possible, much to the annoyance of the God of good, who was for ever trying to thwart the plans of the God of evil.

Animism can be considered the main principle of the philosophy of religion throughout the various grades of civilisation, and its beliefs make themselves apparent just as theological and theosophical speculations developed. What was originally simple became complicated, and primitive beliefs were evolved into doctrines and dogmas, supported by ritual and ceremony. These primitive beliefs were the origin of religion, philosophy and science. In the earliest literature they abound. They constituted the science of early man and formed the basis of his religion. They are the ancestors of present-day religious creeds, doctrines and dogmas. The two worlds have continually interacted throughout the history of man, and what he is today is largely due to this fact.

Besides the beliefs of early man that all nature was animated, it must be remembered that his own spirit took first place in his thoughts. Doubtless he was anxious to discover the cause of life and movement, the reason why the planets moved and why vegetation grew and died. All this was interesting as a branch of knowledge, but man's own spirit was his first concern. What happened to him at death was the great question to which he always wanted a definite answer. Though none came, yet he obtained many indications as to his destiny.

We have seen that at some time man discovered

his spirit and that various reasons were the cause of this discovery. We have also noticed that he had visions, dreams, saw ghosts and apparitions. This seeing of apparitions was one of the most convincing proofs he had that he survived death, as some could actually see that the dead lived. This was only experienced by the few, and the many had to take on trust what was told them. The proof was therefore confined to the few and the many could only believe that these clairvoyant experiences were either real or imaginary.

Primitive man accepted them as true, it being only in our more critical days that doubts have been cast on their reality. In the age we are considering they were generally accepted, and, out of this belief, that the departed really lived and could be seen, grew the saviour-god religions. Consequently this important development makes it a subject which deserves some further consideration. The next few pages will therefore be devoted to a consideration of

APPARITIONS.

Occasionally, as happens today, early man saw the form and likeness of his friends, though their physical bodies were dead. I maintain that apparitions are also occasionally seen in our own times and this remark is not made hastily. There is now sufficient evidence to leave the matter in no doubt.

Two very evidential cases of apparitions being seen have come to my knowledge during the period of writing this book. The first I shall mention refers to an apparition being seen in my own neighbourhood, the facts of which are as follows : A few miles from my home, near the old market town of Great Dunmow, there lived a woman who shot herself one evening, Monday, 5th December, 1938, after having shot her husband. They were alone in the house at the time, and the discovery was not made until 7.45 on the following morning when the servant, who came by the day, arrived at the house, to find the woman in the garden with part of her head shot away. She immediately informed the police, who were on the scene by 8.30, with a doctor, who certified that they both must have been dead since the previous evening. The radio had not even been turned off.

There is therefore no doubt that these two people were dead at 8.30 in the morning. A husband and wife, both friends of mine, who do not wish their name mentioned, gave me the following information : They were motoring to London on the morning the discovery was made, and they passed the house where the tragedy occurred, about 9.20. As they came in sight of the house they saw the woman who had shot herself walking along the road towards them dressed, but without a hat. She was seen first of all by the man, who was driving the car, who said to his wife beside him, "Oh, there is Mrs. ——. She gives me the creeps." His wife replied, "Oh, so it is," as she also saw her, and, as they passed within six feet of her, they smiled in recognition, and she acknowledged this with a bow and a smile.

They thought nothing more about the affair, and, after spending the day in London, they bought an evening paper on their way home, in which they read the story of the tragedy. This was the first they had heard about it, and my friend went to the police on his return home and told them that the woman could not have been dead at the time stated as he and his wife had seen her at 9.20 that morning. The police, however, assured him that they were in the house by 8.30, and that the doctor had certified that the woman they saw had been dead since the previous evening. Such is the story which was told to me by my friends, who agree about all the facts. They have not the slightest doubt that the woman they saw was Mrs. ——, who had killed her husband, and then herself, the previous evening. There was nothing about her dress which occasioned my friends any surprise, and when I asked if she looked happy or sad, I was told, "She looked just as she always did." All these details as to time of death came out at the inquest and are to be found in the local newspaper.

This is an interesting case because, when my friends saw the apparition, they were unaware that the woman was dead, and only discovered, some twelve hours later, that the woman they had seen that morning walking along the road had died the previous evening. Because they remembered when they left home they knew the time they saw her, and the police and the doctor were able to certify that the woman was dead when they arrived at the house an hour earlier. Both my friends saw the apparition and are quite definite that it was Mrs. ——, the dead woman. Thus we have two witnesses who saw the apparition at the same time, which greatly strengthens the evidence.

The other interesting case occurred in Scotland. Friends of mine rented for the summer a large old country house in Dumfriesshire. It had the reputation of being haunted but, as they were quite uninterested in such subjects, this did not worry them. One evening their daughter, who told me this story, went out of the drawing-room to interview the cook, whom she thought she saw at the end of a passage. She spoke to her but received no reply. Then she realised that the person she was looking at was a woman who had no resemblance to the cook. She went towards her, but the figure vanished. She returned in an agitated state to the drawing-room and told her parents, whose only remark was that she must have been dreaming.

Not long afterwards she saw the same figure and went straight forward with her arm outstretched, determined to touch her, but she vanished from view. She was not the only one, however, to see this visitor from another world, because some days later the apparition was seen in an upstairs passage by three young women guests, who were so overcome that they collapsed on the spot. I know personally all the people connected with this experience and what I have related is what was told by those who experienced it.

Such stories are not uncommon and most people are aware of one or more of a like nature. So as to put the matter on a scientific basis The Society for Psychical Research, of London, sent out a questionnaire, for the purpose of discovering what proportion of those who replied had ever experienced the seeing of an apparition. The result, which was published in 1894, revealed the fact that, from the thirty-two thousand replies received, a sufficient number had met with this experience to establish apparitions as scientifically demonstrated. Twelve per cent. of the women and nine per cent. of the men, who replied, declared that under good conditions they had seen one or more apparitions on one or more occasions. Others have made the same inquiry, The American Society for Psychical Research, for instance, having obtained a similar result from its questionnaire. Various scientific men, who have done likewise, have had similar results.

Hallucination cannot be given as an explanation, as medical science knows nothing of hallucination amongst ordinary sane and healthy individuals, such as these were. Apparitions, as seen today, have been seen since the time of early man, and probably also before his time, as there is good reason to believe that animals can often see apparitions when they are invisible to human beings.

Anyone who doubts the fact that those we call dead can, and do, return to earth to be seen and heard, should read W. H. Salter's recently published book, *Ghosts and Apparitions.* Coldly analytical, he examines the claims made by those who declare that they have had such experiences. Apparitions are seen and are heard, is the author's verdict, and no one is more competent than he to give this decision, because, as Honorary Secretary of The Society for Psychical Research, he has had exceptional opportunities to enable him to arrive at the truth.

We, today, look upon apparitions as the spirits of individuals who have lived on earth, whereas early man related them to the supernatural, to something beyond nature. These apparitions he termed gods, but a distinction must be drawn between them and nature gods. Mythology is a mixture of both. The ancients, as we have seen, looked upon the heavens as the dwelling-place of life. The sun, moon and planets were alive because they moved, and where they lived also dwelt the gods. All things that moved on earth and in the heavens were believed to have etheric counterparts, or, as the ancients believed, to have a god within them.

Early man even went to the length of believing that everything had a phantom duplicate, because in dreams he saw his clothes, weapons and the things with which he was in daily contact. He saw also that everything had a shadow, a duplicate body as he thought. So he called this extra body a shade because it was a shadow of the material body. When he saw this fall on some upright object he had before him a duplicate of himself, and, when he saw an apparition, it was very natural to call it also a shade. It was something immaterial, yet real, because it could be seen. Someone, we can imagine, had an idea, on one occasion, to copy his shadow and ran a charred ember, or some paint-like stuff, round it, and found that he had before him a likeness of himself. Thus, it may be, the art of drawing was discovered.

The heavens to the ancients were a stage and the earth was the auditorium. The sky was the dwelling-place of the gods, and, as some clairvoyants saw those who died ascend there, it was likewise the dwelling-place of those who had lived on earth. First of all they were looked upon as demi-gods because they dwelt with the gods. Those, however, who had been out-standing men and women on earth were elevated to rank with the gods of nature and were given the attributes which had been allotted to the sun-god, the thunder god and the gods behind all the other natural phenomena.

Because of their visits to earth it was believed that the gods were still interested in the people and the affairs of this earth, so much so that our ancestors called themselves the children of the gods, a little lower than the demi-gods or angels, to whom they told their troubles and thus obtained their comfort. The Egyptians have left on record their belief that during the age when the world was young the gods reigned on earth and had close intercourse with man, just as we read in the early chapters of Genesis.

For this feeling of close relationship with the dead acknowledgment must be made to those sensitive people who were able to feel the departed beside them, hear them speak and also see them. The records of history show that nature has always endowed some with a greater range of sight and hearing than ordinary mortals. This we today term clairvoyance and clairaudience. One has only to read through the pages of ancient literature to find how frequently reference is made to what these supernormal people are believed to have experienced. Both the Old and the New Testaments contain numerous incidents of clairvoyance and clairaudience, as does also Greek and Roman literature. Apparitions are also mentioned on many occasions in writings both secular and religious.

It is no exaggeration to say that these have played a very large part in the formation of man's religious ideas, and have had a great effect on the religious development of the race. This is admitted by scholars who have studied the origin and growth of religious beliefs. From north to south, from east to west, wherever the inquirer goes to trace religious origins, he is met with the primitive belief that man has a duplicate body, which parts from the physical body at death, and is occasionally seen and recognised.

It is likewise no exaggeration to say that if primitive man, and those of later civilisations, had not held strongly to this belief the entire religious history of mankind would have been different from what it is, in fact, there might have been no religious beliefs whatever to record. It would be equally logical to go even further and say that the fact that man survives death accounts for religion. If he did not religion would never have originated. Religion exists because of the fact that man survives death and instinctively knows it.

Apparitions and psychic phenomena, pointing as they do to the reality of another order of existence (which each one of us will one day experience) together with the inner conviction of survival, so firmly held by the great majority right back to the days of primitive man, can be given definitely as the cause of all religious beliefs from the most primitive to those of the most developed civilisation.

This opinion is expressed by the leading anthropologists and mythologists. They admit the cause, but set it down to delusion and hallucination. If these men had had the experience of psychic phenomena which those who have studied the subject have had they would not have resorted to such a foolish explanation. They have suffered from the prejudice of the civilisation in which they lived. From childhood upwards they had been taught that all psychic phenomena, such as ghosts, apparitions, visions, clairaudience and clairvoyance were a delusion, fitted only for a world of children. The most they probably knew

of psychic science was what they had been told in the
nursery about ghosts and spooks. They were unacquainted with the discoveries of the last fifty years,
and because of this they were unable to form a correct
opinion.

These men of science were under a considerable
handicap when they started to try and solve the origin
of the world's religious beliefs. When they got down
to facts they had to admit that there was only one
cause for these, and that was the belief held by primitive man, in every country in the world, that he saw
apparitions and experienced things which were quite
apart from the material world. The facts were there
and a reason had to be given. What other could be
given than the one which had become embedded in
their minds, namely delusion and hallucination ?

The scientific age, which started in the sixteenth
century, was confronted with the only explanation so
far put forward to account for natural phenomena,
that each phenomenon was produced by a god. Gradually bit by bit the science of early man, which had been
built up during the ages, and which had become
accepted by all, was pulled to pieces and discarded.
Instead of a god behind each phenomenon was found
a regular sequence of cause and effect which, when all
were put together, gave us an entirely new picture of
the universe, a cosmos moving and developing
according to law.

The gods were thus abolished and they gradually
faded from men's minds. The nineteenth century was
the period when this outlook reached its height.
During this same century inquiring minds worked
back to discover the cause of everything that we now

experience, including religious beliefs, and found that they also were all based on belief in the gods. As the gods had been abolished from the universe the conclusion likewise followed that such religious beliefs were based on the same delusion as all the other beliefs of the pre-scientific age, when the gods were made responsible for everything.

It was therefore so natural, in fact it was inevitable, that those responsible for the discovery of the beliefs of early man should adopt the only explanation of which they could think, namely illusion and delusion, to account for their discoveries. But we never stand still, as each century has its own discoveries and its own contribution to make to the world's book of knowledge. The one which the twentieth century is giving to the world is the knowledge gained by the discoveries of psychic science.

Those who have studied this science, and made themselves acquainted with all it stands for, can now take up and continue the investigations of the anthropologists and mythologists of the nineteenth century. They have laid their science on a firm and sure basis. The results of their research are unquestioned and our greater knowledge makes them understandable. The facts are there; all that I dispute is the reason they gave for what they discovered. In the pre-scientific age our ancestors claimed too much of the gods, but this was due entirely to their ignorance. They had not the mental capacity to reason things out and attribute, logically and rationally, the correct cause behind each phenomenon of nature. This could only come about as mind developed, but because our ancestors claimed too much is no reason why everything that they claimed should be swept aside and attributed to their deluded minds.

It was because primitive man accepted naturally what psychic science is discovering today that he believed the gods to be the cause of everything he experienced. That was his mistake, but we now know that he made no mistake in believing in apparitions, visions, clairaudience, clairvoyance and all the phenomena which come from mediumship. We know this because such happenings are experienced today. All the supernormal phenomena which occur today have been observed from the time of primitive man by every race and in every land.

Everything now dovetails in, each bit fits the other. We find no records in the past of any psychic phenomena with which we are unacquainted today, and we find recorded everything that happens today. We now know the cause of religious beliefs, rites and ceremonies and the origin of mythology. The basis of them all is the same throughout the world, as all have sprung from the same root. The trunk of the religious tree is the same, and the branches differ only because of the different grades of civilisation and intelligence prevailing in different parts of the world.

The belief in the reality of apparitions is to be found in all ancient literature and has been preserved in writing on stone. Mythology, without this belief, would be meaningless and never would have been. The gods of all nations, and all languages, were once human beings on earth and, owing to being seen after death, they came to be regarded as gods in heaven, round whom the legends and tales were wrapped. Their humanity has been distorted, and in many cases obliterated, so as to increase their godlike attributes in the heavens, but this does not in any way detract from the fact that they were once men and women on earth like the rest of humanity. Because of this we have the belief in personal gods, or one personal god, in the likeness of a man, but each step in the deification of those who were once men on earth will be better understood as we proceed.

Hesiod, Homer, Herodotus, Plutarch, Æschylus and Sophocles in Greece, Pliny in Rome, the Babylonian tablets, the Egyptian Book of the Dead, the Indian Vedas and Bhagavad Ghita, the literature of China, the Hebrew Scriptures, the Koran and the New Testament tell us of the activities on earth, and in the heavens, of these discarnate beings. During the Christian era, however, they were not considered welcome visitors, and their human instruments were, in consequence, destroyed so as to prevent them making their presence felt on earth.

Numerous standard books have been published within the past fifty years by men and women of integrity, known for their care and caution, which record and classify cases of the appearance of the dead after death. Those who claim to have seen these apparitions have been interrogated and carefully examined to ascertain that what they reported was accurate, and to make sure that hallucination was not the cause. As these supernormal experiences happen today there is no reason why they should not have happened in the days gone by. We need not accept the elaboration surrounding these ancient stories, because this was the outcome of the imagination run wild, but because of their number, and their unanimity in recording the appearance and activities of the dead, we can at least accept the fact that those supernormal experiences, which happen today, also occurred to our ancestors.

Out of apparitions being seen grew mythology, which draped those of the departed, who were in any way out of the ordinary on earth, with stories which had been evolved to recount the wonderful power of the sun, the moon, thunder and storm. Natural phenomena were symbolised to clothe the departed with experiences in the skies which were as absurd as they were untrue. All the phenomena of nature were also marshalled to symbolise the belief that life survived death. Seeds and grain were taken as examples that man died only to rise again. The sun died at night to rise in the morning. Rivers shrunk in size to swell again, and vegetation died to live again.

These natural events were turned into stories, and the corn and other grain were deified just as were the other phenomena of nature. So we find, in the pantheon of ancient gods, that those who had once been men were worshipped and given the attributes allotted to the sun, rivers, and vegetation. Fantastic stories were told of their deeds, all of which had either a close connection with the movement of the sun, the increase or decrease of rivers, the growth and death of vegetation, or other natural phenomena. The stories and legends are not what is important but the belief which we find behind them, and it was because of this that these tales so appealed to our ancestors. Apparitions brought about ancestor worship, which in turn produced mythology. "Here we find the first germ of all religion," says Herbert Spencer when writing on the age-old, world-wide belief in the return of the dead with the form and the characteristics they had on earth.

Besides seeing apparitions, when in a normal state, some had the faculty of seeing and hearing what was denied to those with normal sight and hearing. Some people have this gift in our own times. Their description of the dead and their utterances convinced their friends that they either gave messages from the dead, or that the dead spoke through them. On occasions the dead person communicated by means of his own voice in the presence of these supernormal people. Expressions such as "possessed by a spirit", or "possessed by an evil spirit", or "by a good spirit", or "by the spirit of a god", occur in many parts of the world, and in languages quite unrelated to each other.

The age-long opposition of the priest-magician has never been able completely to prevent these sensitive people from exercising their psychic powers, and convincing those with whom they came in contact that death is not the end of life. When they were not persecuted and destroyed the belief in survival was very real to the people. When the priest-magician was powerful enough to prevent their powers being exercised the belief in survival was weak, and religion consisted only of dogmas, rites and ceremonies, with the priest as the intermediary between the gods and man.

When a sensitive person is in a condition of trance his mind seems to leave his body and, with his etheric body, travels considerable distances. On its return to its physical body it can at times remember what it has experienced. Thus we have records in ancient literature of these experiences which sometimes relate to what has been seen and heard on earth, or to what has been experienced in the realm of the dead, who were discovered to be alive and pursuing occupations in another order of existence much as they did when on earth.

Indian and Greek literature contains stories of the travels of the spirits of different individuals. One Greek record tells us of a medium named Hermotimus whose spirit made distant visits and, on its return to its earth body, remembered what was seen and heard. The secrets thus revealed created enemies who took the opportunity, when the medium was in trance, and his mind on its travels, to seize his body and burn it.

Ancient and modern literature abounds in the records of the experiences of these abnormal people, all of which could not be the result of hallucination or delusion. The number of recorded cases rules out such a theory. As they were accepted as true and real by the most primitive races up to the most cultured, such as the Greeks and Romans, we are not surprised to find that they were responsible for the formation of their religious beliefs. Whatever may be thought of such matters by some in this materialistic age, the fact remains that when religious beliefs, as we know them today, were being formed, such supernormal experiences as trance, clairvoyance, materialisation and clairaudience were accepted as due to the gods, or spirits, by all races and all peoples up to the fourth century of the Christian era.

The Bible is a psychic story-book from start to finish and many opportunities will occur, as we proceed, to demonstrate this fact. The story, for instance, of the voice heard by Samuel, which he took to be the voice of Eli, and other similar Biblical stories, have their counterparts in the religious history of all nations down the ages.

There is, however, further proof that our ancestors experienced the return of the departed, because they not only saw them, but worshipped them. This brings us now to the consideration of

ANCESTOR WORSHIP.

The worship of the spirits of the dead forms all that can be called religion at one period in the evolution of religious ideas. It is not difficult to imagine how this developed. The wife was stricken by grief at the death of her husband and so were the children. They experienced his return, either through the medium of the tribe or as the result of their own psychic senses. They perhaps saw him or heard his voice. This would not happen in many cases, but often enough to make people believe that the dead returned, and could occasionally be seen and heard.

What occurs today happened in primitive times, the only difference being that we consider the departed to be human like ourselves, whereas our ancestors looked on them as gods. When one comes to think it out they were not far wrong in this assumption, because a being who can withstand death, and has the power of thought and movement, superior to man on earth, is the nearest we can experience to anything beyond the material universe. Here was something beyond matter. Here at least they found something they could worship which was beyond the physical.

Here, indeed, was an immaterial being to whom the name god applied. If the husband, or the father, now functioned in this god-like body, then a god could not be imagined as being other than in the likeness of man, or the dead as other than gods.

So the spirits of the departed became the gods of our ancestors. The departed father was known as the Father God, the mother as the Mother God, and the longer time elapsed after their deaths the more exalted did they become in the opinion of their descendants. But it did not end here. The tribal chief became likewise a god after death, and it was believed that he continued to rule the spirits of the dead men and women of the tribe. When the tribe became a nation and the king died, he likewise became a god and ruled the spirits of his people in the other world.

The deification of great men did not happen only after death. A great king, a famous soldier, an outstanding magician, or one who was a great medium, endowed with gifts of healing, of clairvoyance and clairaudience, who could foretell the future, and in whose presence the entire range of psychic phenomena would occur, were all looked upon in the light of god-men. Such were considered sacred, and became part of the ecclesiastical organisation, because it was thought that the gods influenced and guided them as their chosen servants.

When Mythology was in the making those spirits who controlled the mediums received much honour and worship, and, from what takes place today, it is not difficult to realise how in those old days many gods were believed to come to earth and visit the children of men. Even in our own times those spirits who control mediums are spoken of in terms of great respect, and even of adoration, and one can easily appreciate how, in the days gone by, imagination would weave round them very interesting stories. Herbert Spencer accounted for Zeus by suggesting that he was once an Aryan medicine man, or chief, named Sky, which is what the name means, and that after his death some believed that they saw him as an apparition. As he had been known on earth by the name of Sky all natural phenomena associated with the sky were attributed to him. Consequently he became the god of the sky, and was looked upon at times as a sun-god, a thunder god and so on.

This idea can be even further developed. One who had once lived on earth returned to control a medium, giving his name as Sky. He became a much-revered spirit control about whom many stories were told. Round his name a cult was formed and he was worshipped as a god. In time his earth medium died, but the god Sky would not be forgotten, as the stories surrounding him would be passed on from generation to generation. In time it would be forgotten that he was a spirit control, and so he came to be looked upon as a god quite apart from humanity, the powerful Zeus who reigned over the other gods and goddesses on Mount Olympus.

If the people of today had the mentality of the people of those days we would find the controls of our leading mediums deified in the same way. Red Cloud, the famous control of Estelle Roberts, would by now be worshipped by his many admirers on earth, and round his name stories relating to natural phenomena would be told. Likewise we would find the other well-known controls who call themselves White Hawk, Silver Birch, White Feather, and so on, deified and worshipped as gods in heaven. About them it would not take very long to work up a mythology such as has come down to us from Greece concerning their gods, who in many cases were none other than the spirit controls of their mediums. These controls continue to use names for themselves similar to the ones they adopted in the old days, and this consistency is certainly interesting and evidently indicates that they have a long tradition on the other side which they wish to maintain.

Those who came to be called Zeus, Jehovah, Apollo, and all the other gods and goddesses of mythology were once men and women on earth who returned after death and, as spirits, made themselves beloved and admired. Their admirers on earth could only think of them living and behaving as earth people would do, and so we find these tales concerning them which both shock and amuse all students of mythology. Love affairs take a prominent place, and the gods and goddesses marry and produce children. Not satisfied with the goddesses as wives the gods also come to earth and produce earth children. Thus we find stories of men, who came to be considered great, being born of virgin mothers, in consequence of each being overshadowed by a god from heaven.

Men and women also came to be looked upon as gods and goddesses if they had been outstanding people on earth and were seen after death. We shall discover in the next chapter how some, who had been reformers, and were taken by the priests to die on the sacrificial altar, returned after death, and in consequence came to be looked upon as gods because it was believed that their reappearance was a sign that death had been conquered. These came to be regarded as saviour gods and received the titles of Mediator and Redeemer. In this way the belief in saviour gods developed, and they became heavenly beings with attributes different from those who had become gods in consequence of controlling mediums on earth.

This, then, is how mythology came into being, but before we give this subject further consideration there are some interesting beliefs surrounding ancestor worship which it would be well to recount. Some races believed only in this form of worship, whereas others combined it with the worship of the gods of nature. The Zulus of today are a typical race of ancestor worshippers, but they recognise a supreme spirit who is greater than their ancestors and exercises his authority over nature. So far as the Aryan race is concerned, nations as widely separated as Greeks and Indians differentiated from early times between the gods of nature and those they looked upon as their ancestors. Ancestor worship and nature worship thus existed together and have continued right on down the ages to the present day.

The return of the spirits of the departed was either appreciated or dreaded in accordance with the way the people looked upon death and the gods. Some tribes thought that they could cause disease and death to the other members of the family, whereas others believed that their return was a good omen and that good luck would follow a reappearance.

Many ceremonies were instituted either to encourage or discourage the return of the dead. Some believed that when they returned it meant that they were happy, whereas others thought it was a sign that they were unhappy or angry.

At an early date what we now call séances were held, which meant that a number of people would gather in the presence of a medium and observe the phenomena which took place when he became controlled by his controlling spirit. This evidently was the origin of what is in our time known as the Eucharist. Under the influence of the priests, what originated as a séance developed into a ceremony with rites and beliefs which came to surround the saviour gods. To begin with, however, it was a simple Spiritualist séance, and what came to be known later as the Real Presence was none other than the return to earth of those who had died. From this natural event developed the Greek Mysteries, the Agape, or Love Feast, the Pagan Eucharist and the Christian Eucharist or Holy Communion, comprising doctrines and dogmas relating to sacrifice. In the first four Christian centuries Christians continued to hold séances in connection with their religious services, but gradually, as the priests obtained control, these were superseded by the Eucharist, and the people were taught to believe that at this ceremony their Lord and Saviour was always present.

Historians, in their search for man's primitive religious ideas, always find the psychic stream running through them all, watering and fertilising new ideas and beliefs. Fiske, the historian, tells us that "among all races of men, as far as can now be determined, ancestor worship was the earliest form of worship—prevailing in Africa, Asia, China, Japan, among the Aryans of Europe and the American Indian tribes". Allen, in his *History of Civilisation*, writes that "rude tribes the world over are found to have ideas of a human soul, a spirit world, and generally a belief in immortality. Savages consider the next life to be simply a continuation of this ; they also recognise an other self which has mysterious powers. Death is the abandoning of the body by this mysterious other self, which is conceived of as still existing in the near neighbourhood. The loves and hates of this world are transferred to the spirit world".

Professor Max Müller thought that ancestor worship was not the only source of religion, but that it had exercised an important influence on the development of all religious thought. Out of it grew the festivals of All Souls and All Saints. Ancestor worship is not peculiar to the inferior races, because at one time it dominated the whole of the social, civil and political life of the human race. It comes second in time of origin to the worship of the powers of nature. Nature religion came first and then religion surrounding man's spirit. How long nature religion lasted before man discovered his spirit, no one knows, but this we do know, that both nature worship and ancestor worship continued together for many thousands of years.

After the discovery of the etheric body and that the dead could return after death, some tribes and nations slowly grew out of nature worship and developed religions based solely on the surviving spirit. They never, however, quite broke away from the influence of nature worship as they endowed their gods with the powers of nature and symbolised their lives in heaven with these attributes. All past religions have traces of nature worship, even those which accept the idea of one God only. Such was the power of the forces of nature to raise the religious emotions of mankind !

Those religions which have emphasised most strongly the belief in one God have had the haziest ideas as to the fate of the spirit. The Jews are an outstanding example. No nation believed more intensely in one god, and one god only, than did the Jews after the captivity, and no nation had a fainter belief than they had about the spirit and the after life. Some believed in Sheol, which was a kind of Hades where the dead wandered about with no memory and no purpose. One searches the pages of the Old Testament for expressions of belief in survival and only here and there does one find a vague reference to the after life. In many passages one gains the impression that the writer did not believe in the surviving spirit.

This is quite understandable when it is thought out. The more majestic one's god is, the more distant he is from the everyday life of the people ; the more he is approached in abnegation and fear the more distant is the other world from the minds of the people. To the Jew, God was an unapproachable being, and the more unapproachable a nation makes its God the less it believes in survival after death. Christianity took over the god of the Jews and their hazy belief in the hereafter, as will be discovered by a study of the Thirty-Nine Articles of the Church of England,

"Rest in Peace" is the usual Christian slogan on tombstones.

The Greeks, on the other hand, imagined the future far differently, as will be discovered from what their tombstones tell us. This subject will receive our consideration in Chapter IV. They were on the most intimate terms with their gods, who visited them on earth and knew all about their troubles and pleasures. Consequently, the Greeks represented Heaven as being like Arcadia, one of the most beautiful parts of Greece, noted for its peacefulness and the happiness of its inhabitants. They considered death to be only a transition to something higher and better, and one has only to read Plato's account of the conversation Socrates had with his followers, prior to his death, to realise how intensely real the other world was to this great seer. The Greeks termed the dead "the blest", and we find in some writings the belief that the departed awaited the friends they had left on earth, and welcomed them on their arrival.

Another reflection which arises from this same subject is that we find amongst those who burned the bodies of their dead a much more vivid belief in the survival of the spirit than with those who buried the dead bodies. To the former there was no question of sleeping in Sheol, or wandering aimlessly about the underworld awaiting the final judgement. The Greeks, Romans and Hindus burned the dead bodies and we see the result in their mythology. On the other hand, the Hebrews and Egyptians buried their dead bodies to await the last day when the spirit would return to the body and take up its abode again on earth. This was the foundation of Christian belief, which was adopted by the Christian Church in the fourth century, though it was not the belief of Paul and many early Christians.

Just as the ancients gave much thought to the conditions of their friends in the other world, so they likewise, out of love and affection, gave considerable attention to the graves of the dead bodies. The Greeks purified themselves after entering a house where a dead body lay by touching water in a vessel placed at the door, which is the origin of holy water. Outbursts of sorrow and emotion were popular at Greek funerals, but later it came to be believed that violent grief caused sorrow to the departed. When this idea gained root the outward show of sorrow ceased.

Before the common burying-ground was started by the tribe the dead were buried under the family hearth, which became the family altar. The altar originally was the stone over the grave, and where a great man was buried was often erected a temple. Every one of the temples of antiquity was built round the grave of some great man.

At funerals, hymns were sung and passages were read from sacred literature. On the return from a funeral in Greece the people purified themselves by sprinkling their bodies with holy water. Then they adorned themselves with wreaths and had a meal in honour of the dead. During the period of mourning offerings were made to the departed; in fact, we find that most nations remembered the dead at various times during the year. In Athens, All Souls' Day was celebrated in the Spring.

The belief was general that if the graves of the departed were not carefully tended they would be unhappy and come back to visit them. Some thought that they would come back and do their relations injury. Valuables were often thrown into the graves and this custom still persists in parts of Europe, when something treasured by the departed is left in the grave.

It was quite a common custom, immediately after death, to throw a handful of earth on to the dead body to let the spirit realise that its body would receive a proper burial, which custom is still continued at most Christian funerals. As civilisation increased the people gave great care to the graves, and often brought food and presents which they thought would be useful to the departed. The proper funeral rites had to be performed ; if not, the spirit could not join his friends in the other world. Some tribes believed that if the correct funeral rites were not performed the dead would reappear, but that if they were he would join his friends happy and contented. A Babylonian tablet tells us that those whose bodies are properly buried are happy after death, but when this is not so they wander about like beggars.

Euripides (480–406 B.C.), the Greek poet and dramatist, calls graves "the sacred temples of the dead". They were usually placed round the temples, and became places of solemn meetings of friends and relations, who used these graveyards as places of prayer. The great national festivals of Greece, out of which developed the national games, were each instituted in honour of one who had been a hero or a benefactor. After some great victory a festival would be instituted in honour of the hero who had fought and conquered. It was believed that the spirits of departed generals came back and again fought for their country. After a victory the Greeks would reserve the first portion of wine for the dead hero in whose honour the festival had been arranged. Hero worship in Greece became an important part of the life of the country, and Pliny tells us that all heroes were exalted to rank with the gods.

In the thoughts of the Greeks and the Romans the departed were believed to rank very close to the level of the gods. Cicero writes that the ancestors of the Roman people wished the dead to be considered as gods, and that when an apparition is seen it is a god returned to earth. This conveys to us the atmosphere of religious thought apparent in the years just before the opening of the Christian era, and the chapters which follow, dealing with the conception, birth, and childhood of the Christian religion, will not be understood unless I am successful in making this pre-Christian mental atmosphere clearly understood. It is most important that it should be realised that Christianity did not grow out of a mental environment such as we know today, but out of one when all things that moved were believed to be endowed with life from the gods. Everything which was not understood was termed a miracle and believed to be the act of a god. In those days heaven and earth were much more closely related than they are in the minds of people today.

The nations surrounding the Mediterranean, just before the opening of the Christian era, were giving much thought and consideration to the relationship of the two worlds. They were trying, to the best of their ability, to solve the mystery of death and explain the reason for existence. Instinctively they felt that, in the presence of death, they were witnessing something which transcended the limits of their understanding, and that it brought them within the region of the gods. Whether death was sudden or violent, or life ebbed slowly away, the feeling it aroused in their minds made them think seriously as to its meaning. What we feel today was equally felt by the Greeks, the Egyptians, the Babylonians and the Romans.

Round their speculations they built up religious ideas which dominated their beliefs and customs. They seriously contemplated the god within the body and its relationship to the gods without. A profound philosophy comprising beliefs both mystical and theosophical evolved in consequence. The soil was there awaiting any acorn which would produce a new religious system. The people were growing beyond the old mythology, and they were ready for something new which would combine their philosophical and mystical reasoning with the religion of their forefathers. They had no difficulty in explaining the universe, since their science consisted in attributing everything to the gods, but there was a hunger and thirst after righteousness, and a longing for a greater at-one-ment with the Infinite.

Then, as now, the idea of extinction was inconceivable to the human mind. No one has ever had the capacity to imagine himself out of existence. One can talk about it, but cannot imagine it. That one who yesterday was like ourselves should today be lying inert required explanation, and this the philosophers of Greece and Rome were continually pondering over. It was one of the first things about which early man began to think and it is a problem which makes all thoughtful people pause and consider. "Man, know thyself" was one of the first problems he set himself to solve. It is a subject intimately related to each individual and not something apart, like the forces of nature, which became more and more neglected as objects of worship as man came to appreciate the reality of his spirit and mind. Death first made man conscious of life, and round it have grown the beliefs, customs, rites and ceremonies of all the world religions.

When man was more individualistic than he is now, with not so much government either by Church or State, his religious philosophy and science were settled by attributing everything to the gods. After duly appeasing them he obtained his comfort from his knowledge that he would follow his ancestors into the world beyond. His religious comfort followed much on the same lines as that obtained by Spiritualists today. They obtain satisfaction and comfort from the communications which they believe they have with the departed, thus assuring themselves of their own survival and of the survival of those they love. They do not worship the spirits but, apart from this, there is a very close link between Spiritualism of today and ancestor worship of the past. One has grown out of the other, and it may be fairly claimed that Spiritualism is the oldest religion in the world.

Gods have come and gone, but the belief which

Spiritualists hold today—that the individual lives on, in another order of existence surrounding this world, in a body a duplicate of his physical body, and that he can return to earth and communicate his thoughts to the people on earth—has outlasted sixteen hundred years of Christian persecution. Spiritualism and ancestor worship have preserved the belief that the departed are not far from us, that they take an interest in us, and that we shall join them some day.

Ancestor worship still persists in many parts of the world and is as strongly entrenched in China and Japan as it was four thousand years ago. There they believe that God is imminent in nature and diffuses himself in his creation. He is present in the flux which causes evolution. He is present in the trees and in all nature. He is present in each one of us. God is everywhere and suffers with every creature, just as his happiness is increased with human happiness.

In China and Japan the dead are never forgotten. There are feasts in their honour, and it is believed that the spirits of the departed watch over and help those living on earth. They are prayed to and the people tell them all their sorrows and all their joys. Ancestor worship, which goes back into the dim past, is thus still with us today and comforts a third of the human race. In China it has enjoyed the highest respect for more than four thousand years, but the ancestors worshipped have always been confined to relations or members of the tribe.

Love and affection have been as deeply rooted in the past as they are today. At each cradle we ask whence ? and at each grave we ask whither ?

These questions are as old as man, and an immense amount of thought and energy has been expended in answering them.   Besides this, speculation has been rife as to what the other world was like, where it was and how its inhabitants lived.   All tribes and nations have given their answers, but the ones that concern us in dealing with the Christian religion relate to the religious ideas of the inhabitants of Greece, Persia, India, Babylonia, Palestine and Egypt prior to the Christian era, and go under the name of

MYTHOLOGY.

From these six countries came the Christian beliefs, as will be discovered by reading their sacred literature.   The Roman beliefs were similar to those of Greece as they borrowed the Greek gods and gave them Roman names.

We have now traced man's early religious beliefs from Magic to Sun worship, from Sun worship to Animism and from Animism to Ancestor worship. The next step is from Ancestor worship to Mythology. As ancestor worship developed and translated those of this earth into gods in the sky wonderful stories were spun about their doings.   They were credited with everything from the creation of the universe in general to this earth in particular.   They were on the best of terms with humanity at times, whereas at other times they were angry and were the cause of all the disasters on earth.

What stories the name Mythology conjures up in our minds !   What thoughts relating to the inmost being of man and his relationship to the powers which guide the universe. On the other hand, what senseless nonsense is mixed up with what is profound and beautiful. All nations have their mythology, but that of India, Palestine, Greece, Babylon, Egypt and Mexico is the best preserved. Mythology, like everything else on earth, is the result of a slow evolution, and what has come down to us is doubtless the product of earlier stories, which were in turn the product of still earlier legends.

Much thought over the last hundred years has been given by students to the origin and meaning of these legendary stories of the gods and their dealings with mankind. Who were the gods and why were they created? What is the reason for the drapings which have come to surround them? Were they only mental creations or was there something real behind it all? Was Hesiod, the father of Greek mythology, right in believing that the gods once lived with man on earth and then migrated to heaven?

These questions have been answered by scholars who have studied the subject, and their answer has an important bearing on a proper understanding of much which follows in this book. All the gods were once men, the goddesses were women and the myths relate symbolically to history or natural phenomena. Their symbolic meaning can be imagined, as for instance that when it thundered the gods were angry, and that storm and lightning indicated a war in the heavens between the gods. Rain falling on the earth, turning into mist, and ascending to heaven, gave the idea that the rain-god had married the earth, which marriage produced the mist-god.

Evemerus (4th century B.C.), the Greek mythographer, was the first to put forward the opinion that mythology is history in disguise, or natural phenomena symbolised, and that all the gods and goddesses were once men and women whose real lives have been decorated and distorted through their being associated with the gods of nature. He became famous and was considered an atheist because of the sacred history he published, in which this view was set out. Cicero expressed the same opinion in these words : "Is not almost all Heaven filled with human beings ? Those very gods themselves had their origin here below and ascended from hence into Heaven". This opinion was shared by Augustine. Sahagun, our greatest authority on the Mexican religious myths, came to the same conclusion, and Herbert Spencer, who made a deep study of ancient religious beliefs, was also of the same opinion.

From what I shall bring forward, to show how psychic phenomena are the basis of all religion, this opinion is now proved to be the only one possible to hold. It is important that at this stage this should be emphasised, as otherwise what follows will not be understood. Since the opening of this century a number of books have appeared, written by men of eminence, for the purpose of proving that the gods originated in the imagination of their worshippers, first in heaven and then on earth, with especial reference to Jesus. Christ the god came before Jesus the man. Their arguments, though supported by much learning, are worthless because they omit entirely the psychic factor so essential in understanding how men and women became elevated to the rank of gods.

These scholars are limited in their outlook on life. They believe that psychic phenomena are nothing more than hallucination, or are due to fraud, and that nothing supernormal has ever happened. Their view is that no apparition was ever seen by anybody at any time, that clairaudience is the result of a distorted mind, that no voices have ever been heard except those spoken by physical beings, and that all trance utterances can be explained as due to a wandering imagination. As to the direct voice, due to an etheric being materialising his vocal organs, throat, mouth and lungs, or a full-sized materialisation, such things are too absurd even to discuss.

Such people will never be able to understand the origin of religion in general, or the Christian religion in particular, as they are entirely lacking in the knowledge of what really was their cause. Only one who has experienced such supernormal phenomena as I have just mentioned can see the cause behind the effect. I, myself, have experienced every variation of psychic phenomena under the severest test conditions against fraud, and only very slowly did I allow myself to be convinced of their reality. Only then did the origin and development of religious legends become clear to me, only then did I come to understand why the ancients believed in gods and saviours, and only then was I able to penetrate the maze in which everyone gropes when trying to use their reason in connection with religion.

Since this happened, as I said in the foreword, I have spent twenty years studying the origin and growth of religion from the time of primitive man, and only now do I feel capable of writing about the Christian Faith. This presentation of its origin and history would have been impossible if I had not had the experiences recorded in my book *On the Edge of the Etheric* and also many others which are not referred to therein. Those who have not the knowledge thus acquired are quite unable to write about the origin and history of any religion, because they are unacquainted with the alphabet in which every religion is written, namely psychic phenomena.

To expect those who deny the reality of psychic occurrences to explain immaterial happenings is absurd. It cannot be done any more than oil can mix with water. It is not religious emotion that is needed, or faith, or respect for tradition. All these can be ruled out and one's reason given full play. What is needed in those honest attempts to solve an age-long problem is increased knowledge, and because few have it is not their fault, but their misfortune. They have not had the opportunity to undergo what I and others have experienced, and, until they have these experiences, their labour in the religious field is in vain, and can lead to no correct conclusions.

We are entering a new era of thought. The materialism which developed as a reaction to the age of superstition, and in consequence of the discoveries of science, cannot, in these days of greater knowledge, be justified. Our early ancestors just accepted what they experienced. They did not put supernormal phenomena down to illusion. They explained it as divine action, as something supernatural. Today we explain such phenomena as something beyond the normal, not as expressions of a god or gods, but as those of individuals like ourselves, who, though dead, still function in a world of finer matter, which is just as much part of our world as is the earth.

When these discarnate personalities are in the presence of one we term a medium, who has a superfluity of ectoplasm, or one with clairvoyant sight or clairaudient hearing, they can make their presence known to us on earth. With our greater knowledge we can accept their return without worshipping them, or turning them into supernatural beings, which was the mistake our ancestors made, and, in consequence, produced all the religions of mankind.

There is no doubt that the apparitions of the dead have been worshipped since early times. Likewise there is little doubt that unnatural stories were told about these beings, concerning their lives on earth, and imagination supplied the details about their lives in heaven. As time passed these were further adorned by what their worshippers thought such heavenly beings would have done and said when on earth, and so their earth lives became as unreal as their imaginary doings in the heavens.

Such additions and adornments in no way diminished the primary truth that these gods and goddesses once lived as men and women on earth, and that they were deified and worshipped for the reasons already given. Here truth ends and fancy begins, because no sooner were they deified than imagination began to run riot. Round the names of those who had been men and women, like the rest of us, were entwined myth and legend for which originally there was a meaning, but which, as time passed, was forgotten.

Max Müller attempted to arrive at a rational understanding of the meaning behind the myths and legends of the gods, and reached the opinion that originally they were nature stories woven round the lives of men who had become gods through it being thought that they appeared again after death. He arrived at this conclusion by tracing words back to a common source. He discovered the connection between the root words in the Aryan languages and proved that the group of languages under this heading, Celtic, Germanic, Sanskrit, Latin and Greek, could all be traced back to one family of speech. Thus Zeus and Athene may have no intelligible meaning in Greek, but their counterpart in Sanskrit reveals the original significance of the names, just as the word Christ can only be understood by a knowledge of Greek.

In his *Lecture on Languages* Müller remarks that "To understand the origin and meaning of the names of the Greek gods, and to enter into the original intention of the fables told of each, we must take into account the collateral evidence supplied by Latin, German, Sanskrit and Zend philology". A name may be intelligible in Sanskrit which has no sense in Greek. Thus Athene is a divine name without meaning in Greek, but, as Müller points out, it means "the dawn" in Sanskrit. So the stories told of Athene originally referred to the dawn of day, and, when this is remembered, the legends and myths surrounding this Greek goddess can be understood. Zeus can be traced in Sanskrit to refer to the sky, and, so Müller remarks, "there was nothing that could be told of the sky that was not in some form or other ascribed to Zeus".

Adopting this reasoning he argues that much which is stupid, cruel and unreasonable can become understood as originally referring to nature worship. These legends can thus be proved to have a natural meaning as descriptions of the sky, sunrise or sunset, water, fire, dawn, darkness and twilight which were woven round the life of a god-man to whom was given a name to correspond to the phenomena.

Each phenomenon, it is interesting to observe, was thus considered to be either a male god, female goddess or sexless, and this dividing up of objects into these three classes was the origin of genders in languages. Fortunately the English language considers that all things except humans and animals are neuter, and distinction is only made between those who are male and female. In the other European languages, besides some other world languages, each thing is either male or female or neuter. To the English-speaking race this seems absurd and quite unnecessarily involved, as not only is it necessary to know the gender of the noun but to remember that this gender governs the entire sentence, the frame of which differs accordingly. The fact that primitive man imagined that different phenomena and things were animated by spirits of different sexes, or of no sex at all, is the reason for this complication in languages which fortunately our English speech has been able to overcome.

Though much that is crude and cruel has come down to us in mythology, and though the evolution of languages may account for the change in the meaning of words, let us always remember that legends are the survival of savagery, when man's mind was so childlike, and so akin to the beasts, that nothing was too absurd and nothing too revolting to weave round the doings of their gods. We have an example of this in the Old Testament, in which senseless, obscene and revolting stories have come down to us from an early age when men pictured their gods in the likeness of themselves. Thus we have a foolish, cruel, savage and obscene Jehovah, who came to be considered more civilised as time went on.

What intelligent Christians feel today towards these old Biblical legends was likewise felt in Egypt, Greece and elsewhere when the peoples' intelligence rose to a higher level. The better educated, in those days, were disgusted and shocked because similar cruel, revolting and silly stories about their gods were attached to a higher and purer faith. The human mind, however, was very much the same then as it is now, and the priests were so wedded to tradition that the old and the new remained intertwined in much the same way as they are in the Christian Faith. Beliefs had come down from generation to generation and, because of their age they were to the majority considered sacred and true. To find a place to break off, and cast aside the old from the new, was impossible then just as it is today. To give up the Bible is to give up Christianity. To cast aside Jehovah, and the beliefs of a savage tribe, makes the events recorded in the New Testament illogical, as the scheme of salvation runs through the Bible from beginning to end. Therefore the old must be retained if the new is to be believed.

There is, however, another aspect which should not be overlooked. In the past the Old Testament was looked upon as the inspired work of Jehovah and as literally true. This idea prevented its being compared with the mythology with which it was contemporary. In our more enlightened days we now realise that its stories and legends are similar to those of the countries surrounding Palestine, and that Hebrew mythology was on no higher a level than any other produced at the same time.

To make a correct comparison we should keep in mind that when the Hebrew scriptures were originally written the word "gods" took the place of "God" and that it was at a much later date, when monotheism developed amongst the Jews, that the singular word, instead of the plural one, was adopted. Further, the word translated "The Lord" should in most cases have been translated "A spirit" or "The Spirit". It is the monotheism of the later Hebrews which so distinguishes their sacred literature from that of other nations, but, now that it is admitted by Hebrew scholars that the difference is due to errors in translation, the legends of the Hebrews and those of Greece, Babylon, India and Egypt are found to be on the same level, and produced by the same cause.

Just as Mythology teems with gods coming to earth, and walking and talking with men, so we find similar stories in the books of Genesis, Exodus, Daniel and Ezekiel. In the books of Exodus, Deuteronomy, Ezekiel and Samuel reference is made to the Direct Voice, and in the books of Genesis, Ezekiel and

Daniel accounts are given of mediums in trance. The story of Adam and Eve, and their seeing and conversing with the gods, has its parallel in the mythology of many lands. The intercourse of Abraham with the gods, his walking, talking and bargaining with them, makes us think of the god Mercury, the messenger of Zeus, who came to convey the instructions of Zeus to his people on earth. Just as Mercury was called "the Messenger of Zeus" so we read in Genesis "The messenger of the Lord called to Abraham out of heaven".

The stories of Joseph and Jacob and their dreams find many parallels in mythology. In those old days most people were guided by dreams, and Jacob's remark after his dream, "Surely the Lord is in this place", was quite in keeping with the prevailing opinion of the time.

Moses is represented to us as medium, priest and magician. Mixed with his magic, one finds stories which may have had a psychic origin. His finding water may have come about because he had the power of a water diviner, as some have in our own times. His intercourse with Jehovah on Mount Sinai makes us think of the stories about Zeus on Mount Olympus, and the story of the burning bush reminds us of one relating to Apollo. The tale of Moses and Aaron outwitting Pharaoh's magicians takes us back to the magic age and reminds us of similar incidents in mythology.

The story of Balaam, who we are told was a medium, and his talking ass which was stopped by a spirit, is on the same level as the talking snakes, crocodiles and other animals in mythology. It was not the animals who talked, and the original story of Balaam quite likely indicated that the voice came from the spirit who was standing beside him. The gods in those days were believed to use many vehicles to convey their instructions to mankind, and the more unusual the instrument the more the child-like minds of those days relished the story.

The gods also sent their messages by direct writing. We are told in the *Book of Daniel* that a hand wrote on a wall, which writing only Daniel, "in whom is the spirit of the holy gods" (Daniel v, 11), could interpret. In other cases similar writings took place in the sky. We would today call Daniel a medium as in those days it was believed that he had the spirit of the holy gods in him, which belief grew into the Christian god known as the Holy Spirit, about whom I shall have much to say in later chapters.

We find also accounts in the Old Testament of men disappearing and going up to heaven in clouds of fire, and of the gods appearing in a similar way. Elijah, we are told, reached heaven by means of a whirlwind, after being parted from Elisha by "a chariot of fire and horses of fire", which is similar to a story about Zeus and various other mythological beings. Xisuthrus, the Babylonian Noah, his wife, daughter and ship's captain were translated to heaven in their physical bodies just like Enoch.

One could go on relating these stories and legends which, as they have come down to us, are absurd and stupid. I do not, however, wish to dwell on this aspect as it is quite unimportant. What is important is the idea behind all these old stories which comforted the ancients of all lands. Their comfort came from the belief that those they called the gods, or the spirits of men and women, were frequently making visits to earth, to be seen as apparitions or in other ways, just as is happening in our own day.

These legends in the mythology of the Hebrews, as in those of other nations, have a psychic background however much it may have been distorted by later fancy. On the other hand, in other cases, some stories have come down to us without so much exaggeration. For instance the story of the prophet Shemaiah, called the "Man of God", and the clairaudient messages he gave to King Rehoboam; the clairaudient message heard by Samuel; and the voices heard by the medium Deborah, the Hebrew Joan of Arc, who led the Israelites to victory guided by a voice, are straight records of something which we know can happen. The story of Gideon is that of a clairaudient, clairvoyant and materialising medium who was instructed by a spirit, whom he saw, heard and spoke to, to overthrow the altar of Baal.

In places in the Old Testament we are told that the Angel of the Lord appeared, and that the Angel of the Lord said this and that. One appeared to the wife of Manoah, who was told clairaudiently that she would have a son, who became known as Samson. When Samson grew up he evidently developed psychic gifts, as we are told that "the spirit of the Lord began to move him" and he is reported as having done many wonderful things.

Here is the case of a wonder worker with psychic power, and the story which has been woven round his name is similar to some of the stories which have come down to us about Hercules. His mother being told that she would have a son, reminds me of a woman at a séance, at which I was present, being given the same news. She was quite unaware of her condition, but what she was told by the spirit, who communicated the information to her, proved to be correct.

Again we read of the "inner shrine" of the Hebrew Temple, the "Holy of Holies", which was in thick darkness, the dwelling-place of the Lord, and of the luminous cloud which filled the temple "for the glory of the Lord filled the house of the Lord". This happens today when clouds of ecto-plasm roll out of the cabinet, in which sits the medium in darkness, and out of which the spirits materialise. In the Old Testament the expression occurs from time to time that "The Lord appeared", which was just another way of expressing the same phenomenon, as the word Lord in the original is Spirit.

The materialisation séance King Saul had with the "Woman of Endor" does not astonish those who have witnessed a materialisation in our own times. This medium has always been called a witch, the word used when the Bible was translated into English, but the same word in Aramaic was used by Jesus when addressing his mother as "woman". Such were the liberties which were taken by the Christians when translating the Bible into English, because of their hatred of mediums. She has received much scorn and contempt, but anyone who reads the story will find that she was a woman of sweet dis-position, generous, kind and worthy of praise for what she did to help the King.

Greece was the least priest-ridden of all the countries surrounding Palestine during the six hundred years prior to the opening of the Christian era, and there mediums were held in honour and respect. Their mediumship was taken advantage of by the highest and the lowest in the land, and repeated reference is made to this in Greek literature. Mediums officiated in the temples and we read that at the Apollo Temple at Larissa the medium, after partaking of the Eucharist, became entranced when a god took control and spoke through her mouth.

Herodotus (5th century B.C.) states that these gods had human forms and looked like men and women. Freed of the incubus of priestcraft the Greeks consulted the oracles, through whom their dead spoke, and, from what they discovered, they spun their marvellous legends and tales which delighted the people, and have interested those who came after them. Greece became great and produced men who expressed thoughts which have resounded down the centuries. Rome adopted the same policy of free speech, and freedom of thought, and priestcraft never blighted the nation's intellect. In Rome, as in Greece, great men spoke and wrote great thoughts, many of which are immortal.

Elsewhere it was far otherwise, and in Judaea, hedged in by the Laws of Moses, mediumship was suppressed and every medium murdered. It was a dangerous place for a reformer with psychic powers to appear, and there is a very close connection between the text in Exodus "Thou shalt not suffer a witch to live" with the origin of the Christian Faith, as we shall see as we go on.

Another matter which must not be overlooked is the belief of the ancients in signs and wonders. This also has a close connection with the origin of the Christian Faith. As it will be referred to from time to time, I would like to take this opportunity of making some reference to the belief of the people in those days that God, or the gods, sent messages to earth by means of signs and through the working of wonders.

This belief in signs and wonders, which has travelled down the ages to the present day, is one of outstanding importance when we come to consider the reason why men were turned into Saviour gods. The belief was everywhere prevalent that divine messages came to the people on earth by means of odd or unusual occurrences. There were many different signs sent from heaven to man on earth, such as dreams, earthquakes, eclipses, trees dying or reviving, fleece being soaked in dew, water being bitter to drink, and so on.

Miracles and wonders, no matter how they were performed, were also taken to have certain meanings. If some sick person went into a sacred river and recovered, a miracle had been performed. Seeing an apparition or a ghost was a sign from the gods that they desired to impart something very important to the people on earth. Apparitions were taken to be messengers who had come to convey good tidings, or warnings, or who had come as a sign that something had been done which should not have been done, or that something had not been done which should have been done. In those superstitious days all things unusual, or supernormal, immediately carried the people away into thinking that they were messages from the gods to humanity on earth.

Out of happenings, such as the foregoing, and countless others experienced by people of all lands, races, tongues and religions, grew mythology. In those far-off days the gods were not only very real, but life without them would have been impossible. Homer aptly remarks that "All folk yearn after the gods" and what was applicable to cultured Greece is equally applicable to the savage. A prayer which has come down to us: "O Cagn! O Cagn! are we not your children, do you not see our hunger? Give us food!" is what the Australian bushman has long prayed, just as a Christian prays "Give us this day our daily bread".

Frail humanity has received untold comfort, and its life has been made possible, because it felt that it could talk to the gods and tell them all its troubles. Prayer, we now know, does not alter the course of nature, but it makes life possible and easier to those who feel that they can face the battles and storms of life with greater fortitude, after they have laid bare their sorrows and troubles to the particular saint or god they believe is specially interested in them.

This adoration and supplication to the gods has assumed weird and strange forms, and the gods have been, and still are in some lands, worshipped with cruel, obscene and irrational rites. They have been worshipped, and still are amongst savages today, in the form of beasts, birds and fishes. The Egyptians explained this absurdity by declaring that the gods had concealed themselves from their foes by assuming the shapes of animals, but here again the explanation probably is that these gods originally represented some phenomena of nature such as thunder, fire or storm, and were imaged by the people as like unto some beast. The god of thunder became symbolised as a lion because this beast roared, and this accounts for the images, worshipped by the ancients, which have come down to us of gods in animal form.

The gods, we must remember, were very real to our ancestors and were accepted by everyone as a matter of course. The early Christians believed in the gods of the Greeks, but gradually the opinion gathered weight that, though they were such, they were demons and comprised the bodyguard of Satan. This belief, that the gods of Greece were demons, but yet very real, prevailed right up to the seventeenth century of the Christian era, when a book was published to prove that the Bible contained the pure revelation from God, and the myths of Greece were only a distorted form of revelation. The revelation which had been made to the Christians had come from God but the revelation which had been made to the Greeks had come from the Devil and his angels. It was not, however, until last century that students attempted to obtain a true perspective of these ancient stories and legends. Before then the Egyptian and Chaldean languages were closed books and little was known of Sanskrit.

Sir Henry Rawlinson was responsible for deciphering the old Chaldean language, which was forgotten. In 1835 he took from the Behistun Rock, near Babylon, a copy of what turned out to be a decree of King Darius, written in Babylonian, Scythian and Persian. He made paper casts of this inscription, and it was

E*

possible, owing to the fact that the Persian was known, to translate the Babylonian and the Scythian. In consequence of this discovery the numerous Babylonian tablets, since found, have been translated, and much of what is found in the Old Testament can now be traced to Babylon. The stories of Adam and Eve, the Flood, and other events, were all current in Babylonia long before a book of our Bible was written. They were copied there by the Jews when in captivity. The story of Moses being hidden in the bulrushes was perhaps taken from Babylon, as we have discovered a similar story relating to Sargon, an early king of Babylon, the river in his case being the Euphrates.

Just as we have learned much of Babylonian history from the discovery of how to read their cuneiform writing, so have we discovered much of Egyptian history through learning how to read the Egyptian hieroglyphics. This came about through the discovery, at the mouth of the Nile near Rosetta, of what is called the Rosetta stone, when Napoleon invaded Egypt in 1798. It contains a decree in honour of Ptolemy and is written in Hieroglyphic, Demotic and Greek. As the Greek was known, Champollion, the French Egyptologist, discovered how to read the hieroglyphics. These discoveries also throw much light on the political and religious history of the Jews.

Our being able to read these languages, and obtain the meaning of their writers, has enabled scholars to realise the thoughts and feelings of these great people who left such a mark on the religious history of the world. The study of the evolution of religious institutions, from the lowest savagery to civilisation, has also helped to throw much light on mythology, though the knowledge which is given to us today by the discoveries of psychic science does more than anything to enable us to understand the origin and development of all mythological legends.

To believe, as was believed by their worshippers, that the gods originated first in heaven and then came to earth to walk and talk with its inhabitants, is wrong, just as another school of thought is equally wrong in attributing their creation to human imagination. The gods of mythology, I again emphasise, were originally men and women like ourselves. They have not flown from the skies as the result of our increased knowledge. Quite the reverse. Our greater knowledge has discovered the identity of those our ancestors called gods, and what was a mystery is one no longer. What was attributed to the supernatural can now be related to the natural.

So much for this aspect, but there is another which should be briefly mentioned. How is it that some tribes believed that men and women were directly related to certain beasts? Why did a man consider that his grandfather was a lion or a buffalo or something else? They had not anticipated Darwin, as this belief was far different from the idea that man had slowly evolved from some primitive life, stage by stage. The relationship with animals was far closer, within a generation or so. How is this to be made intelligible?

Herbert Spencer explains how this may have come about. Early man applied to himself names taken from nature. The chief might call himself

Lion, someone else Elephant, others would take the names of Bear, Wolf or Eagle. In time their descendants forgot that the name was a mere name, and were misled into the opinion that their ancestors were really these animals and that they were the descendants therefrom. This idea, once current, would naturally stimulate and diffuse the belief that human descendants from animals were possible and that the animals are closely akin to men.

Thus is explained the origin of the legends found in mythology which are in many cases similar throughout the world. Precisely similar irrational stories, as we find in Greek literature, and as were current amongst the Chaldeans and Egyptians, exist amongst the Australian aborigines, South Sea Islanders, Esquimaux, Bushmen of Africa, among the Solomon Islanders, and the natives of South America.

Ancestor worship could only have come into being by the dead revealing themselves from the other world. So this explanation by Spencer can be developed further. The dead, bearing the names of beasts or natural phenomena, returned to earth, just as they return today. They would announce themselves then as they announce themselves now by giving their names. Those who returned were looked on as gods, as beings superior to humanity. These gods would consequently be known by the names by which they were called on earth, and stories would be told about the one bearing the name of Shining Sun, that he fought the darkness and conquered it, to be again slain by night and sent to the underworld. In time the individual, who had actually existed on earth and had returned, giving the name of Shining Sun, would be forgotten, but the stories that had been told about him would be remembered and related to him as a god in heaven.

So have come down to us the irrational elements in the myths of primitive man. If traced to their source they become understandable when we consider that the mind of primitive man was as simple and pliable as that of a child of tender age. Thus we find an explanation of all these stories, which were just as plentiful in Mexico as they were in Greece, as to how the world was created, what caused it, how man and woman, the beasts and vegetation appeared on earth, how evil came into the world and how it fought with good, how the good gods were continually at battle with the bad gods, and how both sides came to earth and mixed with human beings.

The gods of India, in the imagination of believers, behaved just as people behave on earth. They had their love experiences and their hatreds, their wars and their banquetings. Running parallel with this, is also to be found ethical teaching of a high order. Many Vedic hymns reach in their religious fervour to heights as great as those touched by the Hebrew psalmist. The hunger and thirst after righteousness stands out in sharp distinction from that which is unrighteous, and the contrast is just as noticeable in the Indian religious literature as it is in the Bible. The Vedic deities, so imposing when regarded as vast natural forces, become benign and kind when appealed to as forgivers of sins.

The legends about the god Indra, one of the gods of India, are survivals of a time when natural phenomena were regarded, not as we regard them today, as impersonal forces, but as savage persons, and, just as elsewhere throughout the world of primitive man, these personified phenomena became the centres of legends and myths. As nature has its kinder side, when the days are calm and the skies are blue, so there has come down to us the legends of Indra, of the gods Vishnu, Agni, Soma and others, who are therein depicted as kind, loving and generous.

The idea of Heaven for the sinless and Hell for the sinner developed along with the growth in the belief in sin. The gates of Hell, it was thought, were guarded either by devils with flaming swords or by fierce beasts, and once this place was reached there was no escape. The Egyptians drew particularly lurid pictures of this region, which to them was a lake of fire. To all, Hell was the region of the other world inhabited by the demons, or bad gods, and Heaven was the region occupied by the good gods. In these matters, just as in all others connected with their religious beliefs, the imagination of our ancestors went wild.

Just as children revel over fairy stories, and everything that is impossible and absurd, so in the age of mythology man did likewise. His innate belief in another world, and another order of being, caused him to spin stories by the hundred about their doings. Taking as his basis what took place on earth amongst human beings he imagined that the gods lived as he did. They had human frailties and compassions, though they were somewhat stronger, more powerful and swifter in their movements.

Our early ancestors, like ourselves, were curious about their surroundings and wanted to know the why and the wherefore of everything, as we do today. They were easily satisfied, just as children are, with any explanation so long as it was an explanation. Their philosophy was derived from a scanty stock of acquired ideas and these ideas and conceptions now seem to us ludicrous and absurd. As early man turned all phenomena and nature into gods and goddesses, he easily found an explanation for everything. Religion and science came into being by man's curiosity and yearning for an answer to the eternal questions Whence and Whither, Why and How. What was the origin of the world of men and of beasts ? How came the stars ? Why do the sun and moon move, the one to rule by day and the other by night ? Why is this tree green and this flower red ? Why am I here and how long will I remain a conscious being ? From these yearnings and wonderings came mythology, which was both science and religion to our ancestors.

The earth was supposed by certain tribes to have grown out of some original matter or vapour, and the myths dealing with the origin of man partake of conceptions sometimes resembling evolution and sometimes creation. This problem received so many explanations that only a few can briefly be mentioned. To some, man was made from clay, the gods fashioning him as a potter fashions a vessel. Others believed that he evolved out of the lower animals, and yet again some believed that he came from trees and plants.

The Babylonians tell us that their god Murduk, the god of Light, created mankind, the beasts of the field and all living things, vegetation, man and woman.

Before this happened everything was water. Out of this was created primitive matter. Then came light, the sun, the moon, the planets and the other stars, which were followed by a fight between the god of light and the god of darkness, similar to the story of the fight between the Egyptian god of darkness named Set and the sun-god Horus.

The Greeks believed that in the beginning the world was a shapeless mass, or chaos, out of which came the spirit of love, the god Eros, then the earth, then darkness and then night. The union of the two latter produced the sky and day, all of which were given divine names. The earth then produced the firmament which was deified as Uranus. Eros made all things on earth to come together in pairs. Uranus, and the god of earth called Gaea, representing heaven and earth, then peopled the earth with titans and giants. Then came man and woman. Love thus brought order out of chaos, it brought the opposite elements together and so prepared the world for mankind.

The Hebrew account of the creation is similar to the Babylonian, as we would expect, because the book of Genesis, and the other books attributed to Moses, were not written till after the captivity in Babylon. The various versions of the creation are now believed by some authorities on comparative religion to be fairly accurate accounts of a ritual observed in each country, where they originated, for the purpose of stimulating creation. Appropriate ceremonies were performed annually to prevent the world running down.

Each ceremony was an extensive system of rites performed for the purpose of regenerating creation, and what has always been looked upon as a legend may now be more correctly considered as a form of service, such as the one performed in remembrance of the dying and risen god, to which reference will be made in the following chapter. Quite possibly it was also performed as a drama, to teach and interest the people in the order of creation, each day allotted to the work of the gods being an act in the play.

The mystery of death was another great problem to our ancestors. Death to them was something supernatural, which had come about through sin, or because some early ancestor had offended the gods. The New Zealander believed that it was because the first man had not been properly baptised, the Australian that it was because a woman disobeyed the commands of one of the gods and went near to a tree from which she was told to keep away. Another race believed that man became mortal because he had bathed in a river to which the gods had forbidden entrance. The Greeks, in the days of Hesiod, considered that all diseases that brought death to men came as the result of a box, containing all the diseases and troubles of mankind, being opened against the wish of Zeus.

The belief that man, through trying to acquire knowledge, had brought on himself the displeasure of the gods, was doubtless of priestly origin, as history tells us that all knowledge, apart from belief in the gods, was always opposed by the priests. Each story, found in every country where there was an established order of priesthood, and amongst the organised pre-Christian religions surrounding Palestine, contained the belief that man had sinned at an earlier date in an attempt to attain the knowledge which only belonged to the gods.

This belief was the outcome of man's mental development. He had come to realise the difference between right and wrong, which knowledge the priests declared should belong only to the gods. This evolution of the idea of right and wrong has a long history and goes back into the mists of the past. If we are to understand how the saviour-god religions came into being we must go back to the beginning and trace out the development of the belief in

SIN AND SACRIFICE.

Sacrifice was a gift to the gods, a gift of the spirit of the victim. Whether the sacrifice was an animal or a human being the idea behind it was always the same. It was a return for something received or hoped for. We have now reached the point in history when religious ideas commence to develop in different directions, the human family pursuing their devotions in three different ways.

These three forms of belief have continued for thousands of years and formed the trunk and roots of the tree which comprised man's religious ideas. As time went on, one or other of these determined the beliefs of the religions which developed out of them into organised systems of worship. The tree sent out three branches and to one or other of these every present-day polytheistic religion in the world is closely related. Ancestor worship is represented by the beliefs of the Chinese and Japanese. Animism is represented by Buddhism, which grew out of it, and lastly we have Christianity and Hinduism as the religions which are based on sacrifice.

As Christianity developed out of the belief in sacrifice we shall leave aside the other religions which grew out of animism and ancestor worship, and confine ourselves to the beliefs surrounding sacrifice. The basis of sacrifice is reciprocity. If one asks for something one likes to give something in return. If someone does us a kindness we like to give a gift in exchange. If we are afraid of someone we try to win his friendship, and sometimes the method pursued is the presentation of a gift. Our ancestors had this quality of reciprocity fully developed but, besides this, they had the feeling that the more they gave to the gods the more they received. Just as they bargained with each other so they thought that they could bargain with the gods. The more they gave to the gods the more they expected in return. The more they gave of the produce of the fields, or of their livestock, or in the way of human victims, the better crops they expected to have in return, just as they expected that their animals would be healthy and fruitful. They dealt with the gods on a business basis.

Our ancestors believed that the gods had feelings like themselves and that all things with life had spirits, which were released at death. So the idea arose at an early date that by killing animals, and human beings, or burning corn and fruit, they gave their spirits to the gods. When man was a cannibal he thought that the gods were likewise cannibals and relished the spirits just as he relished the flesh. The spirits were the gifts that man gave to the gods in the expectation that they would treat him kindly, and order the course of nature so that he could live as comfortably as possible with all the food he required. Only when man ceased being a cannibal did he cease sacrificing human beings, as he naturally imagined that the gods had also given up this type of food.

The mental darkness in which our ancestors groped kept them from realising the folly and wickedness of sacrifice. Regularly they took their nearest and dearest, killed them, and offered them to the gods. Prescott, in his *History of the Conquest of Mexico*, says, "It is safe to conclude that thousands were yearly offered up on the bloody altars of the Mexican divinities". Wholesale butchery took place when multitudes were slaughtered, and the annual total throughout the world, for countless thousands of years, of those who became victims to the priests on the altars of sacrifice, is incalculable. After a victorious battle it was the custom to kill all the prisoners and offer them to the gods as a thank-offering. These wholesale offerings were considered special occasions, but amongst the tribes and nations, who adopted sacrifice, either a human being or an animal was offered each day to the gods, the number being greatly increased on the weekly or monthly festivals. In other words, they were presented with these regular gifts by the tribe so as to retain their friendship.

It was not the flesh that the gods were believed to desire, but the spirit, the part of man which is akin to the gods. All that the gods could receive and appreciate was the spirit freed from the flesh. Only through death could the spirits of humans, animals and vegetation be set free. The material body meant nothing to the gods, but they greatly relished the spirit. As man ate the flesh of humans and animals, and the material part of vegetation, he imagined that the gods needed the spirit in each for their sustenance, as it was on this that they fed. As primitive man gave slaves, captives and animals as presents to his friends, so he presented their spirits as a thank-offering to the gods. The sacrifice of an animal, however, produced more succulent spirit-food than came from vegetation and so we read that the Lord preferred the sacrifice of Abel, the shepherd, to that of Cain, the gardener.

Thus we see that the reason for sacrifice was the belief that the gods ate the spirits of the victims. As our ancestors ate human bodies, and the bodies of animals, it was quite natural for them to think that the gods ate the etheric duplicates. The idea behind the earliest form of sacrifice was simply a payment or present to the gods for their favour and protection. As time went on, and our ancestors thought more of their future after death, the fear arose as to what happened to the individual when he entered the presence of the gods. If the gods ate the spirits of the victims sacrificed, why should they not also eat the spirits of everyone at death?

The conclusion primitive man reached was that unless he continued to sacrifice, so as to meet the voracious appetites of the gods, they would be so hungry that the people in general would stand a poor chance of escape when they reached their presence. So slaves, sheep and oxen, and the fruits of the field, were regularly offered in large quantities to satisfy the appetites of the gods. Every new temple was consecrated and rendered sacred by the body of a sacrificed victim being built into its walls, and a reflection of this ancient rite still survives in our day through the custom of depositing coins, and other objects, within the foundation stone.

Mankind, in consequence of his ignorance, has always feared death and meeting the gods. When we think it over from his point of view it was quite a reasonable fear and not unnatural. The saviour-god religions were the outcome of this fear of being devoured by cannibal gods. Like everything else, in the beginning the ideas surrounding these religions were simple, engendered by the belief that the victim, who was seen and recognised, after death, had not been eaten, but allowed to return as a sign that each individual after death would not become a meal for the gods.

This germ, once planted, grew and developed as the result of man coming to realise more and more the difference between good and evil. The knowledge of good and evil, however, brought with it a fresh terror, namely, that of punishment, or separation, from the good gods. So his fate after death seemed not to be much improved by his belief in the saving power of the Mediator and Redeemer. Instead of being eaten, his fate was evidently to pass into a region of misery and live with the gods of evil.

The next, and last step, was that the saviour-god had taken his punishment and had been a sacrificed victim for the sins of believers. The place of punishment, however, remained and it was reserved for those who did not believe in the Saviour's atoning deed, the idea being that those who could not accept this belief were not fitted to live with the good gods. As we proceed we shall discover how the belief in sin, wickedness, salvation and punishment developed under the influence of evolving mind.

Holding intensely to the belief that the gods expected something in exchange for their compassion, and believing that the victims at death passed into the presence of the gods, it is evident that religious sacrifice was not the result of blood lust, or for the purpose of inflicting suffering on the victim. We know that in the later phases of sacrifice the victims in some cases were elevated to the rank of god-men before they were sacrificed. In Mexico and elsewhere this was a common custom and there they were fêted and given license, sometimes for as long as a year, to pursue their carnal desires without hindrance. The chiefs willingly offered their sons for this honoured position. Nothing in the minds of the people could rank higher than this form of sacrifice, and their comfort came from the feeling that they had given to the gods the best that they could conceive.

This offering up of sacrifice required time and preparation and where the sacrifice occurred was considered a holy place, which had to be protected and kept in order. So from amongst the men of the tribe were chosen those of a more mystical type of mind who were given charge of the temple, or grove, wherein the sacrifice took place. They were made responsible for keeping the gods in good humour, and so it is not difficult to realise how important this profession became in an age when men believed that the gods could affect their happiness here and hereafter. Being human, like other people, as their power increased the priests claimed to be above and beyond the laws and customs which bound the tribe together.

They set themselves up as a separate class, consider-ing themselves to be holy men and superior to the rest of mankind.

With a natural desire for power, it was to be expected that they would make the people do their wishes by impressing on them that what they said was the will of the gods. Being human, with a desire to live well and comfortably, they managed at an early date to arrange that the gods were well provided with food and sustenance. This was duly offered up to the gods and then consumed by the priests. The gods were supposed to enjoy the spirit but the nutritive value of the food was in no way spoiled. In *The National Geographic Magazine* of March, 1939, is a photograph of fruit being offered to the gods by the natives of Java, with the remark, "Gifts for the gods who enjoy the essence", which proves that this idea prevails even in our own times.

In the Old Testament there are thirty-nine separate references to the "sweet savour", or savoury dish, which the priests sent to Jehovah. These palatable dishes he relished so much that we are told that he decided not to curse the earth any more, or act as universal slaughterer again, because Noah's enormous meal consisting of the spirits of every clean beast and every clean fowl smelled so appetising (Gen. viii, 21). Jehovah was very particular as to how his food was to be cooked and the way it was to be served up to him. He was most fastidious about the seasoning, pickling and the sauces (Lev. ii, 1). Every-thing in connection with his meal was sacred and holy. The priest was a holy man, and everything he touched was holy, such as the table off which the Lord dined, the oil and gravy used in the cooking process, and the knife the priest used to cut off the joints exactly as the Lord directed. (Lev., chaps. i–iv.) Priests have always surrounded themselves with this atmosphere of holiness to increase the mystery of their calling.

From the earliest records we have of those countries which have handed down to us their literature we find that the least the priests obtained to offer to the gods was a tenth of the produce of the land, and from this custom came our system of collecting this amount annually for the purpose of maintaining the priesthood. The Christian Church took over this system when it modelled its priesthood on the Jewish ecclesiastical structure in the fourth century, and this has prevailed throughout Christendom to the present day. It was a very clever and cunning arrangement, but so very natural. The priests told the people that their offerings satisfied the gods, which meant that the priests were satisfied. The people had to do with less but, in exchange for this, they had the satisfaction of believing that they had received the favour of the gods.

This payment to the gods for favours received, which was used to support the priests, and is still in vogue today, means that all land in any country, such as our own, which is burdened with tithes, has to pass over a tenth of its produce, in the form of money, to support the ecclesiastical organisation which still acts as the agency between the gods and man. The tenth of the produce of the land, which it receives by way of a first charge, is used to support a priest in every parish of the country and also their superiors, Archbishops, Bishops, Deans and others,

The gifts which our ancestors offered to the gods were made in many different ways. If a god were believed to inhabit a sacred stone or a sacred tree, these were daubed over with oil, blood, milk or wine. Cereal gifts were presented either by being laid on the ground beside the stone or the tree so that they might die, or by being burned so that the spirit within could be released at once. In other cases the food was laid on a sacred spot; the priests sat round it and consumed it after offering the spirit to the gods.

Other methods were adopted to feed the gods, but in general the idea prevailed that the spirits within the gifts could best be transferred to the gods when etherealised by fire. The gods in the heavens thus received their gifts by means of burnt offerings, and the gods of the underworld by their being buried or thrown into the sea. The natives of Java today feed the devils by reserving for them all the refuse of their food. This idea that the gods fed on the spirits of men, animals and plants is the reason for sacrifice. Each sacrifice was a meal offered to one or more of the gods.

Sometimes the sacrificial meal was given over entirely to the gods and at other times they and the worshippers partook of it together. The latter method of paying the gods for favours received, or hoped for, was known as a feast, to which the gods were invited, or expected to be present without invitation. This idea developed still further, so that in Greek and Roman days it was not thought fitting to rise from a meal without offering first a portion of it to the particular god the family worshipped. The food was taken from the table, burned on the hearth, and a prayer of thanks was tendered for the bounties received. This ceremony might take place before the meal began, or both before and after the meal, and to this we can trace the custom of grace before and after food.

When the gods were supposed to be present certain ceremonies were performed, just as is done today at ceremonial banquets when some important person is the guest of honour. There was music and intoning. Garlands were placed on the spot where it was thought that the god would sit. Incense was freely used as it was believed that the gods relished its odour. Wine, which we are told in the *Book of Judges* "Cheereth God and man", was seldom lacking at these festivities, if they took place in wine-growing countries. The portion for the gods was transferred to heaven by being placed in a bowl and, by heat, turned into steam. If the gods, who were present, were not satisfied with what had been given to them they showed it in different ways which were only understood by the priest-magician.

Out of these feasts developed the mystic rites and ceremonies, still with us today, which became so pronounced in the Mystery Cults held in such high esteem in Greek and Roman times. The ritual surrounding these feasts, together with that surrounding the sacrifice, developed into these mystical rites and customs about which we shall have more to learn later on. Their special feature was that the victim, who represented the Saviour-god, was not simply slain and burned, and his remains cast away, but that his worshippers partook of the body and blood so that they themselves would be strengthened with the immortal spirit within the sacred flesh and blood. These rites, in their early days, were orgies of blood in which the communicant, who attended for the first time, was drenched so as to bring about the complete union with the god worshipped.

Thus the communicant was introduced into the cult by being baptised in the blood of the lamb, or the bull, or whatever animal was used for the purpose. This idea was continued by the Christian Church and so we read in the *Epistle to the Hebrews* : "Since then the children are sharers in flesh and blood, he also himself in like manner partook of the same that through death he might bring to naught him that had the power of death, that is, the devil". Here the writer associates Jesus with the victim whose body and blood was partaken of at these mystical ceremonies, and we shall find as we go on how much they influenced the beliefs of the early Church.

From the 7th century B.C. onwards, when political convulsions were beginning to shake men's faith in the atoning sacrifice of the saviour-gods, believed in by their forefathers, these Mystery Cults carried on the beliefs and strengthened their faith. The worshippers at these ceremonies, by re-enacting the death and sacrifice of their saviour, felt that by so doing they participated in his saving power, just as much as those who in the days gone by partook of the actual sacrifice, and strengthened themselves by consuming part of the victim's body and blood. What they felt, Christians have likewise felt and so they continued the rites and beliefs of the Mystery Cults, relating them to Jesus instead of to one or other of the older saviour-gods.

Prayer always accompanied sacrifice. The act of prayer goes back to the time when man talked to the gods as if they were beside him. He wanted something, so he asked for it. He told them aloud his difficulties, believing that they heard him. Then came the time when he prayed silently in the belief that his thoughts were registered in heaven. He did not realise, as has now been discovered by those who have investigated psychic phenomena, that every thought is a mental image. Thoughts are things because they are mental images. When we say that we have an idea it means that an image, made up of mind stuff, exists for the time being in our brain. That image, by a mental process, enables us to say the word horse if the image formed is of a horse. When we hear the word horse the mind becomes the image of a horse. Thinking is image making and as we image so we think. As we relate one image to another so are our thoughts. If we do this rationally, we think rationally, if not, we think irrationally.

This I have proved in the séance room when in conversation with friends on the other side. They told me that they could read my thoughts and tell me about what I was thinking. They described to me the process of thinking, and, after numerous tests, I had to admit that their explanation was the only one possible. Whatever I thought about was told to me by the direct voice and a mistake was never made.

With this knowledge is it possible to find an explanation for the origin of prayer ? If etheric beings can read one's thoughts today, as I know they can, they could do so in the days of old, and primitive man may have discovered that his secret thoughts could be revealed. The Psalmist tells us that "The Lord knoweth the thoughts of man" (Psalm xciv, 11), so perhaps he had an experience similar to my own. Prayer is something one is taught as a child. If no child were taught to pray it is unlikely that he would do so when he grew up. It is, therefore, an acquired and not a natural habit, and it seems to me that man acquired it in the days when he and the gods were on very close terms, as they evidently were at one time in the world's history when psychic gifts seem to have abounded.

From some such beginning the idea may have developed that the gods could read our thoughts. It was a great relief to many to be thus able to unburden their troubles. The feeling that there was always some living, thinking being who, though unseen, was willing to hear and answer prayer has been a source of untold comfort down the ages, and is so today. By means of prayer the people on this earth try to keep up a regular service of communication with the gods in heaven.

The evolution of the idea of prayer can only be stated in a general way. From speaking his wants aloud to the gods, whom primitive man believed inhabited the trees, the wind, the thunder, the sun, the moon and the planets, he in time developed the process of thinking his wishes to himself and not expressing them aloud. This may have come about by his knowledge of telepathy, which in those days may have been more developed than it is today. We know that primitive people in our own days adopt this method of communication amongst themselves, and there is no reason why our early ancestors should not have done the same. Habit and custom hold us today in many ways and people do things without knowing why. For ages children have been taught to pray, and when they grow up they continue to do so because they find that it is a simple way of easing their minds of daily worries. It is possible that early man prayed without speaking because he knew by experience that thoughts can carry from one human mind to another. So he argued that if this were so on earth his thoughts could be picked up just as easily by the gods.

At a time in history when gods or spirits were believed to be in daily contact with humanity the reason for silent prayer can be understood. In later times the belief was held that everyone had a guardian angel, or particular saint, to whom was allotted the charge of one or more people on earth. Through them it was thought prayers were answered as they acted as messengers, which is the meaning of the word angel, between the gods and mankind, but how those who do not believe in such things as telepathy, guardian angels or saints, justify their belief that prayer is heard and answered is hard to say.

Prayer unburdens the mind and its simple exercise causes relief. Probably those who pray give little logical thought as to how it is answered so long as they feel relieved by its exercise. After a prayer how usual is the remark made by the one in trouble : "Well, I cannot do more and I must now leave it in God's hands, but I feel so relieved." This feeling of relief is doubtless the cause behind this frequent religious exercise, and Psychology in our day is just adopting methods which man has practised for ages. Psychologists find that the best way to relieve the mind is to get the one in trouble to express the worry, and the way to aggravate a mental worry is to suppress it. When the trouble is deep-seated it is now found that through hypnotism it can be located and, by means of questioning, expressed. When the hypnotic state passes, that which was upsetting the harmony of the mind is often found to have vanished.

Along with prayer our ancestors made vows. A favour was asked and something was promised in exchange. If a god or the gods would only meet the supplicant's wish then he would give them something in exchange. To begin with it was in the form of a sacrifice and, in consequence of such vows, many wives, children, slaves and cattle have perished, but, as the idea in the efficacy of sacrifice declined, it was believed that the gods wanted some penance or personal abnegation in exchange for the favours asked. So vows were made that the first-born son would be dedicated to the priesthood. A vow would be taken that if some danger passed, or if some great desire were realised, the supplicant would fast, or give a gift to the temple, or go on a pilgrimage, or endure poverty.

In effect he said to the gods, if you give me something I shall do something that you would like me to do. A vow was just a contract entered into with the gods that if they did something the supplicant would in his turn do something for them. Instead of vows many now do penance at the instigation of the priest. They do not make a bargain with God but perform the penance because of some sin, in the hope that God will accept the present misery endured and in consequence not mete out punishment in the hereafter.

The false idea that the gods were for ever standing over man like a schoolmaster could only have taken root in childish minds. Not till the time of the Greek philosophers do we find these simple beliefs scoffed at, and, in their place, the view advanced that the Creator of the heavens and earth had other things to think of than man's petty troubles. Why, they asked, should the Creator wish to eat a spirit he had created ? The people, said they, were imagining the Creator as a cannibal, which was just what they had done for thousands of years, and the first voice raised in protest came from Greece six hundred years before the Christian era, to be endorsed by the later Hebrew prophets. This belief in the necessity of sacrifice is one of the most deplorable aspects which we come across in the study of religion, and so it is with some relief that we now turn to a brighter page in the history of man's climb from mental darkness into the light of knowledge.

After man discovered his spirit he gradually developed a sense of right and wrong towards his neighbour and the gods. As his mind developed so did his moral sense. Instead of thinking only of himself he began to think of others. He found by experience that when every individual thought only of himself, and pursued his own wishes and desires, without thought of others, chaos reigned, and that fighting, quarrelling and snarling was the order of the day.

Just as he preferred the peace and harmony of a Summer day, when the sun-god was reigning, to stormy, thundery weather, when the gods of thunder, storm and rain were in power, so he came to see that for his own peace of mind, for his own greater happiness, it was wiser not to be so selfish, and much wiser to think of himself less and of others more. He found that when he ceased beating his wife he received, in exchange for giving up this pleasure, her love and sympathy, and the same with his children. Though he lost the satisfaction of clubbing his enemy he gained in exchange a greater tranquillity of mind, because he was not so fearful of being clubbed by someone who considered him an enemy. Though he lost the satisfaction of letting loose his unbridled rage he did not suffer from the rage of others. He also found that it was wiser not to interfere with his neighbour's property and so he obtained greater security for his own. In other words, by slow mental evolution, he found that his happiness increased as he concentrated less and less on himself. He thus exchanged a turbulent life for one of greater peace and security.

This explains how morality developed. It had nothing whatever to do with religion, as it came about by expediency. Every individual is by nature selfish, and if happiness could have come about better by fighting, quarrelling, cruelty and persecution, this would have become the order of the day. The race would consequently have become obliterated and the strongest man would have been the last to survive. Because man is a selfish individual, he thinks of himself first, but, as he grew in intelligence, he realised that to think of others and their feelings was the height of wisdom, and that the more he thought of others the happier he was.

This policy is called unselfishness, but it is really due to intelligent selfishness. It is due to his own wish for happiness and the happiness of those he loves, whom he wishes, because of this love, to be happy like himself. He thinks of the happiness of others because he found that by making others happy he increased his own happiness. Love is the greatest force in the world, comprising as it does this thought for the feelings of others. It means that one's mind is telepathically in touch with the minds of others, and that to upset another mind reacts on the mind responsible, which is in turn upset. In other words, as our minds become more developed and refined, as they become less encased in the physical, they reach out and blend with the minds of others. Anything done or said which creates disharmony in one mind reacts on those with which it comes in contact, thus upsetting the mental harmony of all.

Morals and ethics have developed just as the human mind has become more refined. They have no more to do with religion than has marriage. Marriage is a social contract, and the moral law is a social law which has grown up and developed through the experience of thousands of years. Right and wrong, having nothing to do with religion, are in quite a different category from sin, which is a contravention of the religious code and not of the social code. The sinner is the one who does not conform to the orthodox or prevailing religious opinions of his time. So we have the sin of unbelief, the sin of blasphemy, the sin of disobedience to the divine will as expressed by the priest, the sin of not keeping the religious taboos, the sin of communicating with the departed, and the sin against the Holy Ghost, which has never been defined, but which we shall discover before our study ends.

Throughout religious history it has been a sin

to do other than respect the priests who were the representatives of the gods on earth. Anyone who ridiculed them, or doubted the claims they made, was one of the worst sinners, because he was undermining the standing of this class in the minds of the people. We remember the terrible punishment inflicted on forty-two little children when they called out to Elisha, "Go up, thou bald head". Humour was evidently not one of the strong points of this representative of Jehovah on earth, as he cursed them and then two bears came along and devoured them all. This story served as a warning to both big and little children that the priests had to be respected, and that if they were not the gods would be angry.

One who denied the existence of the gods was a sinner. One who did not perform the sacrifices to the gods was likewise a sinner. One who scoffed at the waste involved in sacrifice, or in the religious beliefs of the time, was a sinner. In other words, anyone who in any way did anything, or said anything, which could affect the social status of the priests, or endanger the regular supply of offerings to the gods, which were reserved for the priests, was a sinner.

I am aware that the word sin is often used when the word evil or wrong-doing should be used. We talk of the seven deadly sins, namely pride, covetousness, lust, anger, gluttony, envy and sloth, just as we talk of the sin of breaking any of the Ten Commandments. It is foolish to be proud, but not sinful. One can covet something, but so long as one does not steal it no wrong is done. Lust and anger are not sins, but they often lead to wrong-doing. Gluttony is no sin, but it is unwise if one wishes to keep healthy. To envy your neighbour often acts as a spur to harder work. Certainly it is not a sin any more than are slothfulness or indolence.

Only two of the Ten Commandments refer to sin. It is sinful to take the name of the Lord thy God in vain, just as it is sinful not to keep holy the Sabbath day. Anyone who works on Saturday, which is the Sabbath, or causes anyone to work, is a sinner if he is a Christian or a Jew, but not if he is a Hindu. But if a Christian, Jew, or Hindu steals he violates the moral law and becomes a wrong-doer, transgressor or evil-doer. This makes clear my point. The moral law is world-wide but the religious law relates only to the religion professed. To sin is to break the religious law but to commit a crime is to contravene the moral law. As to honouring one's father and mother, it depends on whether they deserve it or not. If they do not deserve to be honoured, it is neither sinful nor wrong not to honour them. Is it possible for a child to honour a father who is a drunkard and a criminal and a mother who is vindictive and spiteful? To commit murder is a crime. To commit adultery is the breaking of a contract and comes under wrong-doing. Theft is a crime just as is perjury or bearing false witness. And the last commandment is covetousness, which we have already considered.

These ten commandments are interesting as shewing a stage in the development of the race, but it is strange that they should still be repeated in most churches, on each Sunday of the year, as if they contained the entire moral code. If the Hebrews had been more developed they would have attributed the following to Jehovah, "Thou shalt not be cruel to animals", "Thou shalt not hunt them or cause them painful deaths", "Thou shalt not be cruel to children and make them suffer", "Thou shalt not permit poverty amidst plenty. Those who have must give something to those who have not", "Thou shalt not go to war against thy neighbour", "Thou shalt not permit mediums to be burnt, as it is through them man's destiny is revealed", "Thou shalt permit free speech and free thought, as only through them is progress possible", "Thou shalt acquire knowledge which is vital for thy health, comfort and happiness".

All these things, and many others, were omitted because the people had not risen enough in intelligence and wisdom to incorporate them in their rules of life. They had only reached the position of realising that murder, theft and perjury were crimes against the community. They were no further on than the savage of today whose moral and social code also recognises these as crimes. So long as savages do not murder, steal or bear false witness against their neighbours, as long as they keep the taboos of the tribe, and believe in the tribe's priest-magician they are good citizens, just as were those who kept Jehovah's Ten Commandments amongst the tribe of savages led by Moses out of Egypt.

A man might be an exemplary husband and father, fair and straight in his dealings with all men, generous and kind, have lived a pure and unspotted life and yet, if he rejected the religious beliefs of his time and was clever enough to realise the mistakes of the priests, or scoffed at the powers attributed to the gods, he would be one of the blackest of sinners. On the other hand, belief in what the priests told the people were the wishes of the gods ensured happiness hereafter.

To believe that the gods were just human beings like ourselves made the order of the priesthood unnecessary. One who made such a suggestion was a sinner. Heaven and Hell have always been the special preserves of the priests and, from early times to the present day, they have opposed to the utmost of their power any attempt to solve the mystery of death by experimental methods or rational thinking. To find, as some have now discovered, that the other world is a natural one, that its order of existence resembles this one, that its inhabitants are men and women like ourselves and that to enter it requires no special passport, is, in the eyes of the priests and the orthodox, nothing less than giving up religion.

When the discovery of the few becomes accepted by the many it will certainly change the religious outlook, and make the profession of priesthood unnecessary, but it will never abolish the religious instinct in man. This comes from his mind, related to the divine, which is sustained by the psychic stream, and it can function apart from churches, temples or priests. Just as a child grows up and can discard the use of a nurse, so the human race is gradually growing in intelligence and throwing off the priests, who are becoming unnecessary to the community.

When mankind becomes intelligent enough to realise that sin, in its correct meaning, has no more existence than has a nightmare he will be able to order his own life without ecclesiastical help. Sin and Hell, both priestly inventions, without substance or reality, are the basis of all organised religion. On the wealth the priests of the Church of England and the Church of Scotland received from the faithful and the fearful, who mortgaged their lands and gave large endowments to the Church in the days gone by, on the labours of their deceased brethren who held the Holy Office and expounded volubly on Sin and Hell, the present occupiers now live quite independent of the small collections contributed by their meagre congregations.

Sin, Hell and Priestcraft are a trinity which has thrived on ignorance. When knowledge takes the place of ignorance the ecclesiastical organisation will become a skeleton without public support, and kept in being only by its accumulated wealth. Not till religion is purged of priestcraft will it occupy the place it should in the minds of an intelligent community. The teacher will then replace the priest, and churches will become places of instruction instead of worship.

Unfortunately every saviour-god religion, as it developed, adopted the view that there was a heaven and a hell. Hell came to be looked upon as the destination of those who did not accept the Saviour, and Heaven as the future abode of those who did. Little did these ancient people realise that as one sows so one reaps and that punishment comes from mental remorse, just as happiness comes from mental content-ment. We make our own heaven or hell both in this world and the next. That, however, was beyond the grasp of the people, whose thoughts we are now con-sidering, and in consequence they imagined the misery of the sinner, just as they thought of the happiness of the good.

The sinner's misery hereafter reached its height

when they pictured the damned in a never-dying fire forever suffering the torture of burning. Their ideas about Heaven were just as extravagant as their ideas about Hell. Those living in towns imagined that it was a place with streets paved with gold, others who enjoyed music, as one continual praising of the gods, while to those living in the country it was a happy hunting-ground where they could hunt and kill to their hearts' content.

Just as they let their imagination run wild about the condition of the departed, so did they likewise when thinking of the journey the dead made before they reached their new abode. The Egyptians believed that they went first of all to the underworld and that their journey there was one of many perils and difficulties. There they remained until rescued by Osiris, whom they termed their Saviour, Mediator and Redeemer, who took them to his kingdom. On the Day of Judgment they expected to return and live with him on earth in their old physical bodies, which they in consequence tried to preserve. This, we shall discover, was also the belief of the early Christians about the Old Testament worthies who were rescued from Hades by the Christ.

Plato speaks for the Greeks in the following passage :

Now we must believe the legislator when he tells us that the spirit is in all respects superior to the body and that even in life what makes each one of us to be what we are is only the mind, and that the body follows us about in the likeness of each of us, and therefore when we are dead the bodies of the dead are rightly said to be our shades or images ; for the true and immortal being of each one of us, which is called the spirit, goes on its way to other gods, that before them it may give an account, an inspiring hope to the good but very terrible to the bad, as the law of our fathers tells us.

Besides paying priests to show the people the way to the other world, our ancestors also paid them to pray for the spirits of the departed, and this method of raising money is still in vogue in our own times. The Christian religion is in no way peculiar in its methods of raising funds for the upkeep of the organisation. The Buddhist religion, which is not one of gods or saviours, but of the spirit ultimately reaching Karma through successive reincarnations, teaches the faithful that the more liberal they are to the priests the sooner will Karma be reached. To this end much money has been given by the faithful for the erection of pagodas and the upkeep of the priests.

Just as our ancestors were morally, so were the gods, because the gods were made in the image of man. As man improved, so did the gods. Thus a religious morality developed alongside a social morality, which latter is known as ethics, or the science of living happily with one's neighbour, whereas religious morality relates to what the priests declare must be done so as to live happily with the gods. Not to observe the social code is a crime, not to observe the religious code is a sin, and just as our ancestors advanced in intelligence so has the moral and social code developed.

The religious code, unlike the social code, never remains constant. What was once considered a sin is one no longer. In the early days it was a sin not to feed the gods with sacrifices, but in our time this neglect would not be considered a sin. Sin has changed its meaning and is sometimes used in error for wrong-doing. With the development of the moral sense we find words like transgression, evil-doing, wickedness, and such like, coming into use, and, as this happens, so the gods use similar words. As man develops so do the gods, because they are none other than man himself in a changed environment. As his moral sense developed so the idea behind sacrifice developed, till he felt that his load of guilt could only be released by a god taking the punishment he himself deserved.

Morally this is a wicked doctrine, and has been the cause of untold crime and wrong-doing, because each believer felt that all that was necessary was to unload his transgressions on to the saviour-god, and not to worry further about his transgressions. Thus there was no restraint on wrong-doing and the saviour-god religions in no way helped man to develop morally. They were just a stage in his development, and now that some have evolved ethically to realise that no one can carry another's guilt, that as each one sows so must he reap, that wrong-doing can only be alleviated by regret and restitution to the one wronged, the idea of a whipping-boy to carry one's evil deeds is coming to be regarded as morally wrong. This idea has led many up the wrong path in the days gone by, and still does those who believe this doctrine.

Just as wrong-thinking does not differentiate between sin and wrong-doing, so it causes people to say that it is not Christian to do this, or it is not Christian to do that. It is only Christian to believe the creeds of the Church and it is un-Christian not to believe them. Christianity only applies to the beliefs surrounding Christ and his saving power. The rites, sacraments and ceremonies of the Church are for the purpose of preserving this belief in the minds of believers. Christianity has nothing to do with peace or war, or ethics, or marriage, or anything apart from its creeds. The Church has always accepted men and women of all shades of character as communicants, if they accepted its creeds, because it does not stand for anything apart from its creeds.

It is well to keep this in mind in our time when the Church is being blamed for doing or not doing something it was not founded to do. It is now, and always has been, composed of men and women of saintly and noble character on the one hand, and, on the other, of the most disreputable blackguards, because they all professed belief in its creeds and doctrines. Its history comprises deeds done by its priests and members deserving of all praise, just as it includes those which all Christians now look back upon with horror and shame. Because its priests and members had, and still have, human failings, the history of the Christian religion is what it is, but it is well to remember that it is incorrect to apply the name Christian to anything apart from the beliefs for which the name stands.

Numerous attempts were made in the days of old to explain how evil came into the world. The people wanted to know how it originated, and how the trouble started. So as to satisfy their longings the priests in every land told them stories of how this came about. One story was that the principal god of evil turned himself into a serpent and tempted a woman by holding out the promise that if she ate the fruit of a certain tree she would learn as much as the gods knew.

Because of man's thirst for knowledge she accepted the offer. As this was against the wishes of the gods she and her husband were turned out of Paradise, which was imagined to have been a land where no one needed to work, where there was no sickness, no death, no sin and wickedness and everything went on happily, in such a contrast to the world as it really is. But a promise by the gods was attached to this story of man's loss. A Saviour would come to earth to save his people, suffer for them, and then set up a kingdom on earth for all who acknowledged him. Then Paradise would be regained. This story, with different names for those concerned, has been believed for thousands of years from Greece to India.

The Greek goddess Persephone, the daughter of the much revered goddess Demeter, the Universal Mother, like Eve, allowed herself to be tempted by the magic flower which stretched its sunny petals towards her. She plucked it, and, after sensing its intoxicating perfume, her senses were so dulled that Pluto, the Greek god of the dead, carried her off. Demeter searched for her and she was finally rescued by Triptolemus, who returned her to her mother. This in drama was enacted each autumn at Eleusis by women actresses only, and the Greeks regarded it as symbolic of the fall of man from grace and his return to at-one-ment with the gods.

The Greeks had also another legend embodying the same idea. In it the one who had sinned was Epimetheus, whose wife Pandora possessed a box which the god Zeus had commanded was not to be opened. Quite enough to make anyone want to open it! The thirst for knowledge on the part of

Epimetheus caused him to open the box and out jumped all the troubles which have since afflicted mankind. For this inquisitiveness on the part of Epimetheus, Zeus cursed mankind with death. He, however, gave the world another chance just as did Jehovah, and Rā, his prototype in Egypt, but the people started building a tower for the purpose of examining the heavenly bodies, and this was too much for Zeus, as it was for the other gods. So the story goes on to relate how Zeus decreed that all mankind was to be destroyed. Then came the flood from which only a few survived. Prometheus, taking pity on humanity, decided to come to earth to suffer in its place. This he did, chained to a Scythian crag. By his death mankind was freed from the curse of death.

This curse of death, the priests declared, the gods had inflicted on man because of his attempt to attain knowledge which was the perquisite of the gods. Knowledge was the one thing that the priests did not wish the people to have. The mystery of life and death must be retained, or their work as the representatives of the gods on earth, as the intermediaries between the gods and man, would cease.

"As in Adam all die, so in Christ shall all be made alive," wrote Paul, while to the Greeks it was, as in Epimetheus all die so in Prometheus shall all be made alive. As Prometheus was the saviour-god of the Greeks so Osiris was the saviour-god of the Egyptians, Mithra of the Persians and Romans, Krishna of the Indians, Bel of the Chaldeans, and Quexalcote of the Mexicans. All this shows that, for a period going back more than two thousand years prior to the

Christian era, the belief was held in different parts of the world that sin had become an affliction through man attempting to obtain knowledge. This sin was the cause of death, which curse could only be removed by the death of a god-man victim, who, by this sacrifice, restored to man his birthright which he lost through his sin of disobedience.

Thus by the development of this line of thought the priests tightened their grip on the people. Before priestcraft developed, entrance into the other world was accepted more or less as the destiny of the human spirit. Savages today accept this as a matter of course, as a natural event. When, however, the saviour-god religions developed into organised systems the power of the priests greatly increased. Death, to those who did not accept their system of belief, meant everlasting suffering in Hell. Belief in their system, on the other hand, meant eternal life through the death of the saviour-god.

Thus a Church organisation came into being, with sacraments, rites and ceremonies. There was the Church of Dionysus in Greece, the Church of Bel in Babylonia, the Church of Osiris in Egypt, the Church of Krishna in India, the Church of Quexalcote in Mexico, and the Church of Mithra in Persia and Rome. Here we have the foundation of the beliefs on which was built up the Church of Christ when the time came for it to rise out of the ashes of the Church of Dionysus, the Church of Bel, the Church of Osiris and the Church of Mithra. How this all came about we shall see as we proceed.

Other nations had different types of saviour-gods about whom stories were told. The Polynesians, for instance, believed that man lost his right to immortality because Manui, the saviour-god, could not pass through the body of night, which was represented as a woman asleep. She awoke, thus preventing the passage, and because of this all men were doomed to die. One might read into this that Manui could not incarnate on earth, as did the other saviour-gods, but the story, however it originated, is just another of the numerous sun-myths wound round a saviour-god, it being a legend relating to the sun at sunset. Manui, however, tried again and on this occasion night was conquered and so he rose the next morning.

Stories such as these are world-wide, but there is another aspect of sin which must not be overlooked. There were many things man felt it was a sin to do, or not to do, to which I have not yet referred. This brings us to the subject of taboos, which figure so largely in religious history. The religious code included numerous taboos, many of which are of great antiquity, and originated in the magic age when the magician's spell included formulas that such things would happen, or not happen, if certain things were done or not done. Out of this developed religious taboos. To name them all is quite impossible because their name is legion. Some things were pleasing to the gods, such as offering up sacrifice and conforming to the religious etiquette of the tribe. Other things were displeasing and had to be avoided.

These taboos, both positive and negative, included the preparation and eating of food, how animals were to be killed and prepared, what work could be done on certain days and what work was to be avoided. It was thought that iron was obnoxious to the gods, and that they could not approach anyone who had it about him. Iron was therefore tabooed, and is even to this day in Java, no iron ploughs ever being used. To do so means bad harvests. On the other hand, when the spirits were troublesome iron was used to drive them away. This reminds us of the belief held in this country by all, up to a hundred years ago, that spirits would never cross running water. Women had taboos about the dressing of their hair, just as they had about wearing ornaments and rings. Certain names were taboo, some were sacred and others profane. Some words were taboo and reserved only for the priests, and so on.

Taboos existed at one time or another, in some place or other, over nearly everything in life. Some things were sinful or not sinful to do, just as the priests or king, representing the gods, decreed. The reason is obvious. Those in authority worked on the fear of the people to make them do their pleasure. It was the easiest way to command obedience and the simplest way to keep the people in order. To promulgate laws amongst people little better than children was useless. They had to be frightened by fear of punishment, here and hereafter, and the bringing of the gods into the regulation of everyday life served the purpose.

As time went on the difference between sin and wrong-doing widened, and so we find, with the advance of civilisation, that laws were enacted and enforced without the aid of the gods. This came about as man's moral sense developed and he began to consider what his attitude should be towards his neighbour. The priests, however, continued their taboos, as by them they found that they could hold the people. What a burdensome affair life was in the age of taboos! How progress was checked to please the gods! What pleasures have been lost out of fear of the gods! Fear made life miserable, unhappy and uncomfortable, for no other reason than the belief that the pleasure or anger of a god or the gods followed man's actions on earth.

Gradually, as intelligence developed, so did the social code. The moral law slowly evolved and kings started regulating society by making laws, by laying down what could and what could not be done. Theft, we find, was one of the earliest crimes, as was murder, so decrees were ordered by the king or chief inflicting punishment by death on all thieves or murderers. Thus the social code grew up by the addition of one crime after another, as will be found in Egypt from the 17th century B.C. onwards. With the rise of the Egyptian Empire, from this date, we discover increasing evidence of ethical evolution and the importance attached to the moral law, to justice, goodness and truth.

The following, taken from Egyptian monuments, make clear how high a value they attached to righteousness :

Established is the man whose standard is righteousness, who walketh according to its way. (2700 B.C.)

More acceptable is the virtue of the upright man than the ox of him that doeth iniquity. (2300 B.C.)

Righteousness is for eternity. It descendeth with him that doeth it into the grave . . . his name is not effaced on earth, but he is remembered because of right. (2300 B.C.)

A man's virtue is his monument, but forgotten is the man of evil repute. (2200 B.C.)

The people of his time shall rejoice, the son of man shall make his name forever and ever. . . . . Righteousness shall return to its place, unrighteousness shall be cast out. . . . (2200 B.C.)

The moral code of Hammurabi, who founded the Babylonian dynasty, and made Babylon the capital about 1550 B.C., is the oldest known code of laws. They cover the entire field of social life and are remarkable for their justice, considering the times. The Sabatu, or Seventh day, was prescribed as the day of rest from work, and many of our present-day laws can be traced back to this great monarch. The Jews, when captive in Babylon, copied some of them, and, on their return home, attributed them to Moses.

Solon, the famous Greek legislator in the 6th century B.C., regulated every department of life. His laws were humane, enlightened and just. They prescribed, for instance, attendance of youths at school till eighteen years of age, in strange contrast to the closing of all schools everywhere when the Christian Church obtained control of affairs. Philosophy and learning which, as the result of Greek influence, were making men free, intelligent and kinder, were thus abolished, and Christendom in consequence entered a night of darkness from which we are only now emerging. It is well to keep this in mind as it illustrates clearly the point we have just considered that social and religious morality are entirely different. So much is this the case that they have often worked against each other in world history, the priests invariably being found in opposition to legislative reform and social advancement.

How the fear of the gods has retarded social and mental development, and yet, when the gods are rightly understood, as they are today by those who have made a study of psychic science, how different is our outlook. Instead of fear we have courage. Instead of thinking that knowledge is sinful we find that the greater our moral and mental development is on earth the happier we shall be hereafter, that to seek after knowledge is the height of wisdom, and that to pursue the path of ignorance is the depth of folly. "Ignorance is the curse of God, knowledge is the wing wherewith we fly to Heaven", was Shakespeare's way of putting it.

Sin and ignorance are twin brothers because both reign together wherever man's mind is small and cramped. Knowledge develops the mind, and, just as this happens, sin and ignorance wither away. Knowledge destroys sin, but it is wisdom that destroys wrong-doing. It is well to mark the contrast because it is all-important. There is no such thing as sin apart from religion dominated by priests. Ignorance is mental darkness. Selfishness is the basis of every evil, and with knowledge and wisdom come happiness, comfort and content.

Sin and sacrifice run through the history of all the sacrificial religions, from early times up to the present day, the only difference being the form of the sacrifice offered up. In most primitive times it was a human being, often the son of the chief of the tribe, as the gods had to be given the very best food that the earth produced. In time, animals took the place of human beings, and the gods seem to have been satisfied because things went on just as usual. In truth the gods thought and did just as man desired, since the instructions they gave to those on earth originated in the minds of the priests.

It was a roundabout method, but this way of putting first things last and last things first occurs in connection with the history of all the saviour-gods, and the object of this book is to put first things first and last things last. When that is done the source and growth of Christianity will be understood and appreciated, whereas when we look at it as a fully developed and completed system we find that emphasis is laid on the points which should be avoided and vice-versa. What came first has been put last, and what came last has been put first, with the result that a story has been produced which no thinking person can understand, and only those who do not think deeply or honestly can profess to believe.

In Genesis we are told that "The Lord smelled the sweet savour" of Noah's sacrifice, but in the original this read "The gods smelled the sweet savour". As the Hebrews developed morally so did their gods, and thus we find as we go on that a higher and deeper outlook on life slowly evolved, till we come to the days of the Psalmist when he chants :

> Thou desirest not sacrifice.
> Thou delightest not in burnt offerings.
> The sacrifices of God are a broken spirit.
> A broken and a contrite heart, O God, thou wilt not despise.

The prophet Micah, after asking if God requires the sacrifices of thousands of rams, or the first-born child, answers that what is required is "to do justly and to love mercy and to walk humbly with thy God". These moralisings were certainly a decided step forward, but the people did not respond. Sacrifice therefore continued, though the thoughtful in China, India, Palestine, Greece and Egypt, in the five hundred years before the birth of Jesus, continued to dwell on righteousness as more pleasing to the gods than sacrifice. This was the theme of all philosophic writings in those days, but the priests and the people could not get away from this age-long method of placating the gods, and so sacrifice continued till it merged into the saviour-god religions.

The history of sin and sacrifice is long and gory. Commencing with animal and human sacrifice the idea developed till it was believed that sin, like disease, could be transferred to an animal or some individual, who, with the accumulated sins of the tribe on him, was driven out into the wilds.

Dogs, goats and various animals were used for the purpose of carrying the sins of the community. The priests laid the people's sins on them and then drove them out to die. On the Jewish day of atonement the Chief Priest laid both his hands on the head of a goat. During this ceremony he confessed all the sins of the Israelites, and then the poor goat was chased away, no one daring to touch it. The same ceremony was performed by other tribes, a man often taking the place of the goat, the victim being purchased from his master by those who felt heavily the load of sin. After the sins of the community had been thus easily disposed of he was driven out to starve, no one being his friend.

Such is the story of sacrifice, and a gruesome story it is indeed. The grief it caused can best be realised when that pathetic Biblical story is read of the offering up by Jephthah of his daughter as a sacrifice to Jehovah. The grief of Abraham when he was told by Jehovah that he must offer up, as a sacrifice, his only son Isaac can easily be imagined. We find that the Babylonians had a story similar to this, but, when we remember that Abraham is said to have come from these parts, it is not unlikely that the story in Genesis originated in Babylon and refers to the same event. These pathetic stories reveal to us the grief and suffering of mankind in his attempt to please the gods. What a holocaust it has been !

What misery has been endured through ignorance of the meaning of life and death. Mind encased in matter has never felt the earth to be its real home, it has forever been pulled by some irresistible force into other realms of thought apart from the material. As a sojourner in a strange land longs for the land of his birth, so religious history tells us man has longed for an existence other than the material. The history of religion is the history of his speculations on the meaning of life, death, and the hereafter. His ignorance has led him into innumerable follies and sufferings, though, on the other hand, from these speculations he has obtained untold comfort, without which life would have been impossible.

CHAPTER III.

CHRISTIANITY—ITS RELATIONS.

STEP by step part of the human family has advanced to a higher level of thought and, in its upward climb, it has left the less intelligent behind, to remain wedded to the customs, beliefs and mode of life from which it has emerged. In greater or less degree man has advanced in proportion as he has developed his reasoning powers, and made use of the faculties with which nature has endowed him. The more he has inquired and doubted and wondered, the more he has learned. As his mind became stored with new ideas, with facts and experiences, so it developed. As it evolved so his ideas changed. What seemed perfectly natural in one state of mental development was looked back upon by succeeding generations as crude, cruel and stupid.

So wherever there is mental development there is progress, and wherever there is progress the generation which follows always thinks differently from the one which has preceded it. Evolution is apparent in customs, morals, ideas, science and religion, whenever we look back upon the history of a progressive community. Nothing can escape change when confronted with developing mind.

When mind is so undeveloped as to be forever dominated by fear, progress is impossible. Only as fear lessens is progress possible, and this comes about as man relies more and more on himself and less and less on the gods. When under the constant fear of offending the gods, stagnation was general. The first man to think for himself, and ignore the prevailing opinion as to what the gods would think, was the first to lead the race on the path of progress.

The first man to suggest a better method than one hitherto adopted was probably murdered. The road of progress has been strewn with the bodies of its martyrs. The first to suggest that the gods would be quite satisfied with the spirits of animals, instead of those of human beings, was probably seized by the priests to become the next sacrificial victim. Gradually, however, the number of human victims lessened and probably nothing helped more to bring human sacrifice to an end than the development of the belief in the saving powers of the saviour-gods. This advance brings us to the consideration of

THE SAVIOUR-GOD RELIGIONS.

When and where this form of religious worship started we do not know. All that we do know is that it has left its record on the pages of history and tradition over the past four thousand years.

In the previous chapter we commenced our inquiry into religious beliefs far back in the misty past, where we discovered primitive man groping his way out of the animal stage into that of the human. Here we found a creature who was beginning to think and reason. His observation of natural phenomena made him believe that behind each phenomenon there was an invisible being like himself who was both larger and stronger. He observed effects and argued that there must be a cause. He observed nature doing things which he could do in a small way, and decided that natural phenomena were caused by invisible men who were larger and stronger than he was.

From small beginnings it gradually came to be believed that there was an invisible superman behind each phenomenon of nature. Thus man built up in his imagination a group of invisible beings whom he believed to inhabit the sky and to whom he gave the name of gods. There was the thunder-god, the wind-god, the rain-god and so on. The method was simple, but primitive man had a simple mind. He observed an effect and his imagination supplied the cause. Everything not understood was explained by the name of god, and this method continued till the sixteenth century of the Christian era, when, what is today called the scientific method was introduced for the observation and explanation of natural phenomena.

After primitive man had found a cause to explain each experience he next turned to examine himself as a problem requiring explanation. Many things about himself puzzled him. He realized that he was different from the beast and that, though he was not so strong as some animals, he could circumvent their strength by intelligent thought. He noticed that he was conscious for a certain length of time and then lost consciousness of his surroundings, when he would dream and picture what he had experienced when awake. He also began to appreciate the duration of life and how some of his friends died, or were killed, and how their bodies reverted to the earth.

At times he saw as apparitions those who had died, and how one of the tribe became entranced and assumed the characteristics of the one who had died. Some of his friends would hear voices clairaudiently and experience the movement of objects without physical contact. Gradually the feeling developed that invisible beings, in the likeness of himself, were living in his own surroundings and could occasionally be seen and heard. When he reached this stage he imagined that he had finally solved the problem of natural causation. Consequently he looked upon these beings as responsible for the ordering of nature and his own creation. To them he expressed his wants and told them his troubles, which supplication of the gods by mankind came to be known as prayer and worship.

From what occurred in the presence of the medium of the tribe man came to realise that certain individuals had the power to attract the gods who, in the presence of these mediums, delivered their messages. Here we find the beginning of public worship. Thus the gods and man were brought together, and the medium was regarded as the instrument used by them when communicating with earth. He was treated with such veneration and respect that he came to be considered a god-man.

This position, was, however, challenged by the magician who, by cunning, duplicated what took place in the presence of the medium, and, as the magician could do this at will, the people came to look upon him as the instrument of the gods, often neglecting the natural medium, who could only function when the gods willed. The magicians claimed that they only had access to the presence of the gods, and that they only could receive their instructions. By deception and cunning they misled the people into thinking that they could order the course of nature and, when they found that this was accepted, their next claim was that they could make the gods do their bidding. The magician thus set himself up as a being superior to nature, and the instructor of the gods. This was the beginning of the priest-magician, out of whom developed the priest.

When man came to realise that he was endowed with a spirit and mind, which was the cause of his movement and his thoughts, he associated this immaterial part of him with the gods, and so thought that in some way or another he was related to this higher order of life. In those days man was a cannibal, making his meals off human flesh, and he believed that the gods were cannibals like himself. When he wanted his crops to grow and the sun to shine, he asked the gods to grant his wishes. With each prayer he sent them a present, consisting of the spirit of an animal, or a man, which he released by killing the creature.

This desire to send offerings to the gods, in the form of spirit-food, was the reason for sacrifice, out of which grew religious rites and ceremonies. Incidentally it was through sacrifice that soap was discovered, by the fat of the victim mixing with the wood ashes left by the fire, thus producing a hard substance which it was discovered removed dirt. So from this barbarous custom man discovered how to clean himself, which makes us realise the aptness of the saying that cleanliness is next to godliness.

For thousands of years magic and sacrifice went on side by side, until the time arrived when man came to realise that he could not control the forces of nature and that these must be left to the gods to manage. So he decided to keep them well supplied with spirit-food and get on with his everyday work. To enable him to do so undisturbed he appointed, from amongst the tribe, a certain number whose duty it was to keep the gods fed and on good terms with the people on earth. This was the beginning of priestcraft, as now understood, which has been associated with every religion since man gave up ordering nature by magic, and became a supplicant.

As man developed mentally he realised that there were such things as right and wrong. He found by experience that certain things were right to do and others were wrong to do. Those things he believed affected him adversely he considered to be wrong, and those things that made life happier and easier were right to do. It was right to feed the gods because, by so doing, the crops grew better and life generally was more tolerable. It was right to try and please the gods because nothing could happen without them and his life was in their hands. It was wrong to ignore the gods and try to live without recognising their power. Consequently it was wrong not to pray to them and ask for what was wanted. In this way developed a religious morality which had for its object the pleasing of the gods, and thus making the best of man's lot on earth.

Mental development proceeded, and, along with religious morality, there developed a social morality, that which was right and wrong to do so far as one's neighbour was concerned. As man developed morally so did the gods. Consequently he came to think that righteousness was more pleasing to them than un-righteousness. He imagined the gods to be like himself, and when he thought an action was wrong he believed that the gods would think likewise. Thus mankind was guided in all his doings by his belief that the gods were ever-present beings, who either approved or disapproved of what he did.

Mental development brought about a sense of unworthiness, a growing feeling of the weakness of the flesh. As his mind developed so likewise did his belief that he was not quite at home on earth, and that he was destined for another order of existence. He came to believe that after death he would dwell with the gods in the heavens if he lived in accordance with their wishes on earth. If not, they would not allow him to reach their presence where only happiness could be attained. The more unrighteous he felt the more he sacrificed and, by rites and ceremonies, tried to please them. As his mental development continued, this feeling of separation from the gods, owing to the wickedness of the flesh, increased, until the problem of how at-one-ment could be attained became his constant thought.

The priests set about speculating as to the meaning of it all. A reason must be found to satisfy the human mind. Death, the greatest of all mysteries, must be solved, and yet it was something quite beyond human intelligence to explain. Man had the feeling that he existed after death and yet how this came about was something that he could not grasp. He felt that at death he left his earth surroundings and went alone, as a wanderer, into some unknown land where dwelt the gods. Some of these, he had already decided, were wicked, while others were good. As he felt his increasing burden of wickedness so he imagined that after death, if the gods did not eat him, he would be placed by the good gods in the underworld, which was the region inhabited by the bad gods, where he would be unhappy. As he preferred happiness to unhappiness he naturally wished to be allowed to live in the company of the good gods, where happiness could be attained.

However, it was all a mystery, and out of ignorance the idea developed that death was a curse, placed on mankind by the good gods for his wickedness, and that no amount of sacrifice could ever put things right. He came to look upon himself as a fallen being, and to feel that because of this there would be continued enmity between him and the gods. This idea was encouraged by the priests who naturally wished him to believe that he was a sinner, because the more he did so the more they were employed in making intercession for him. The more he was weighed down by his sins, and the fear of death, the greater was their power over him. As the intermediaries between heaven and earth, his fate was in their hands.

A time came, however, when one less servile and more intelligent than the rest preached another doctrine, one of hope and not of fear. The gods, he said, were not angry with humanity and death was not a curse but a blessing. He preached a gospel of courage and trust in the justice of the gods. Quite possibly he was a medium in close contact with the etheric world, one who had discovered from the gods that death was not a curse but the entry into a better and fuller life. He revealed to mankind a new outlook on his destiny and taught that righteousness, and not sacrifice, was pleasing to the gods. They were not cannibals, he told his followers, and did not desire their sacrifices. Sacrifice must stop as the gods did not eat the spirits of the dead. Instead of sacrifice they wanted repentance for wrong done, and an attempt to live justly and love mercy. This gave the gods their pleasure and brought them and mankind together.

Deeds more than words appealed to the people in those days, and, by means of his psychic gifts, this reformer impressed them with the conviction that he was revealing to mankind the divine message. Such a man naturally alarmed the priests, who realised that, if this new outlook were accepted, their sacrifices would cease, their power over the people would go, and their profession would come to an end. So they arrested this upstart and condemned him to death. They thus shewed the people the error of the new gospel by taking this man, who claimed to be a messenger of the gods, and offering him up as a sacrifice, and as a peace-offering, for all the wrong he had done.

Such an event may have happened from time to time before there was any outstanding effect. To begin with, the priests would crush the rebellion, and though the reformer might be forgotten, his teaching was remembered. The seed was thus sown for a later reformer to gather the grain, but, with a powerful priesthood, the reaping seemed to be beyond human effort. A time, however, came when an event happened which changed the entire outlook, so much so that the people refused to be satisfied any longer with priestly denunciations.

An occasion came when a reformer, who was probably a medium, was seized by the priests and offered to the gods on the sacrificial altar. Again it was thought that his life-work had ended in failure. But no. To some of his followers he appeared after his death, and this they took to be a sign from heaven that he was the one chosen by the gods to break the fear of death, and to end human sacrifice, because the gods had given up eating the spirits of the dead.

Consequently he was termed the Saviour. He was regarded as the Chief Priest who had gone before to make intercession on behalf of the human race. His reappearance opened a new chapter in the history of man's relations with the gods and round this event grew up all manner of doctrines and dogmas. A vast theology accumulated over the centuries, composed of mystical speculations relating to sin, sacrifice and atonement. Stories were told of how the promise of a Saviour had been made to the first man and how the gods had now fulfilled their promise.

A new era had in consequence opened in man's religious history, and those who accepted the saviour-god idea were comforted by the thought that their Saviour had gone before, and was making intercession for them in the presence of the gods. Here, as heretofore, we find the psychic stream to be the cause of this new religious development, which embraced all the countries from India westwards until, as Christianity, it covered all Europe, America and Australasia.

The gratitude of the tribe or nation towards the victim was unbounded. The people, remembering his supernormal powers, spun marvellous tales which, as time went on, had no relation whatever to the actual events. The psychic happenings which had occurred in his presence were turned into miracles, and all the things he had said and done were considered to be the utterances and actions of a god. He came to be looked upon as a god-man who had lived a sinless life on earth, and had gone about doing good. It was impossible for such a being to be born in a natural way, so he was given a god for his father and a virgin for his mother. Imagination ran wild as to his status in heaven and he was ranked as equal with the chief of all the gods. Around his name grew up a cult which developed into a religion, and though his first worshippers believed that his death had abolished sacrifice and the priesthood, both remained. The sacrifice of victims continued as a eucharist (thanksgiving), and this was surrounded by rites and ceremonies which made the priesthood necessary.

In the previous chapter it was noticed how what is called in our day the Holy Communion probably originated in a séance. Perhaps the first one to be called Saviour returned to earth, not only as an apparition but as a communicating spirit in the presence of a medium. Perhaps he materialised and spoke with his own voice. The Saviour thus revealed to his assembled worshippers his real presence on earth. This came to be known as the Real Presence, who is believed to be present at every celebration of the Eucharist.

Because etheric beings can only reveal themselves in the presence of developed mediums, who are often scarce, this original holy communion with the departed Saviour could not be preserved indefinitely in this way. Gradually this holy séance came to be surrounded with the beliefs and customs relating to sacrifice, and these are now preserved in the rites and ceremonies of the Christian Eucharist. The priests thus elaborated a séance and took the place of the medium.

In spite of the saving power of the Saviour, the sacrifice of victims continued, just as it did amongst the early Christians. While maintaining the ancient ceremony of sacrifice the priests developed this Eucharist service which had for its object the bringing of the people into closer mental contact with their risen Saviour. They took the dead body of a sacrificed animal, or human victim, and cut it up into small pieces which they handed round to the assembled people to eat. The blood they passed round for them to drink. They told the communicants that, by the priests repeating certain words over the body and blood, they had transubstantiated them into the Saviour's body and blood, which were believed to have saving properties.

Thus began the belief in transubstantiation. This the people accepted, as many Christians do to this day, and found their comfort in the belief that by eating the flesh, and drinking the blood of the Saviour, they fortified themselves with his saving power. The story has come down to us of how the body of Dionysus, the Greek saviour-god, was broken for his worshippers and handed round to them to eat so that they could thus absorb his immortality. The only change we find today, from those far-off days, is that bread and wine are now changed into the body and blood of the Saviour, and the body and blood of a sacrificed victim are not now consumed.

The change over from eating a victim's flesh and drinking his blood was gradual. In time, however, this substitute was found in the form of bread and wine. Instead of a victim being placed on the altar and sacrificed, an image in bread, in the likeness of the Saviour, took its place. Into this dummy at each Communion celebration the priest stuck a knife to represent the killing process. He then said some magical words over the corpse of bread and declared that, by this solemn and holy rite, he had turned the bread into the actual body of the victim.

If the king or chief were present the priest would cut out a piece from the part of the body where the heart lies and, after again pronouncing certain magical words over it, hand it to him to eat. When the king or chief had finished eating, the rest of the body was cut up into small pieces so that each of the worshippers received a portion to eat. This they did in the firm belief that they were eating the actual body of the victim, and that by so doing they ensured the salvation of their spirits. Wine, by the same magical process, was turned into blood, and so we discover how it was that bread and wine took the place of flesh and blood.

During these services of remembrance and thanksgiving the priest took the occasion to tell the people the stories about the growth and decay of vegetation, the rising and the setting of the sun, and the rise and fall of rivers. Their sermons were based on natural phenomena, and had for their purpose the impressing of the people with the belief that what happens in nature happens to all mankind, that after death comes life, that from decay there always follows resurrection. Paul made use of the same symbolic language by telling the Corinthians that that which is sown is not quickened except it die. Such simple parables appealed to those simple people in these far-off days. They lived under the dome of heaven unprotected, as we now are, against the elements. They lived much closer to nature and had little to distract them from its daily lessons. Nature stories, and the stories of the deeds of the gods in heaven, interested them, giving them comfort in life and hope at death.

Besides listening to sermons, and partaking of the Eucharist, our ancestors, who worshipped the saviour-gods, found much delight in music and singing. Hymns were composed to the saviour-god and sung with as much heartiness as they are sung today by Christians to their Saviour. Music had the effect of stimulating the emotions of the assembled congregation. In those days of almost complete illiteracy, music and the drama had a deep emotional effect on the people, who were raised to a height of ecstasy which only occasionally occurs in our time. Often during a dramatic performance, or much hymn singing, they lost all self-control and indulged in every form of excess. Music has contributed much, down the ages, towards religious fervour, and hymn singing, which became an important part of the service, had the same effect on the emotions in those days as it has on some people in our own times.

Some pages further on we shall go through the entire performance of what took place at a Passion Drama in Babylon. Now we can realise what these ancient saviour-god worshippers experienced at this display when his atoning work of mercy was re-enacted. If he were a sun-god the drama took place at

the times we call Christmas and Easter, when the sun
enters the winter solstice and spring equinox, and also
at other periods during the year according to its position
in the heavens. If the gods symbolised vegetation,
the festival was held when the crops were coming
to life in the spring, or at reaping time, and at the
times of ploughing and sowing.

The old method of sacrificing for the purpose of
feeding the gods was one stage in mental development
and, though this continued, even amongst the worshippers of the saviour-gods, yet this belief in their
saving powers is an indication that man had attained a
degree of intelligence which enabled him to realise
that what one sows one must reap. His sense of
justice had developed to the point that he demanded
an eye for an eye and a tooth for a tooth. Consequently his gods did likewise. Because of this
sense of justice, which developing mind produced,
the saviour-god idea, commencing from the theories
surrounding an apparition, evolved, based on the
belief that the gods would not be just if they did
not require a victim for man's shortcomings.

Justice, our ancestors believed, demanded a
victim, and righteousness demanded that this victim
must be a holy man, so as to satisfy the demand of the
gods that one righteous man must suffer for the
nation. This belief is associated with all the saviour-
god religions. Justice and righteousness prescribed
this path and to follow another meant union with the
gods of evil. Out of this belief in justice developed
repentance. The wrong-doer had to acknowledge
his sins and transgressions, and accept the Saviour's
sacrifice as one for him personally. Salvation thus

became a personal matter between the saviour-god and each individual. Through the Eucharist service he entered into direct communion with his Saviour, and reached mental harmony through this at-one-ment, or atonement, which belief followed from the original idea of the Real Presence. Thus he felt that he was brought into tune with the Infinite.

By baptism he became a fellow member of a community, holding similar views, whose members, by this rite, were purified and fitted to enter their Saviour's presence at the Eucharist and also at death. Thus we find that the partaking of the Eucharist gave the same satisfaction to the people as their ancestors had received from sacrifice. Moreover, it eased their minds with regard to their unrighteousness, which had become so apparent as the result of their increased mental development. Now they dwelt on the suffering of the Saviour on their behalf, and on his life in heaven where he acted as their mediator and judge. Naturally he was raised in their minds to the highest status amongst the gods, and received all the praise and gratitude his sin-stained worshippers could bestow upon him. His name was to them above every other name, he was the Lord of Lords and God of Gods.

The fifty-third chapter of Isaiah gives an account of the sufferings of a saviour-god, "For the transgression of my people was he stricken". We are told that he carried the peoples' sorrows, was wounded for their transgressions, bruised for their iniquities and that with his stripes they were healed. He was oppressed, was led as a lamb to the slaughter and on him the Lord had laid the iniquity of the people. His spirit, we are told, was made an offering for sin, he bore the sin of many and made intercession for the transgressors.

Here we find clearly expressed how it was that he suffered because we are told that his spirit was made an offering for sin. So, like all the others, he was a sacrificed victim and his spirit was sent to the gods to eat. They, however, did not accept this spirit-food and it was believed that they allowed the victim to return and show himself to mankind as a sign that they wished to eat no more human spirits. That was how our ancestors interpreted the meaning of the reappearance of those they turned into saviour-gods. It was likewise believed about Jesus that he was a priestly victim offered as food to Jehovah, as we are told that "Christ hath given himself for us as an offering and a sacrifice to God for a sweet smelling savour" (Eph. v, 2).

As human sacrifice slowly came to an end in consequence of man's moral development, so the priests gradually turned from being murderers to being butchers only. They, however, could not get away from the idea that it was necessary to feed the gods with the spirits of animals, and in consequence sacrifice amongst so-called civilised people continued till the fifth century of our era.

To begin with, the recognised victim who returned was just a sign that the gods had ceased eating the spirits of the people of earth, but, as the idea developed, the argument ran thus :

(1) A reformer is seized by the priests.

(2) He is sacrificed so that the gods can eat his spirit.

(3) He is seen after death in his etheric body.

(4) This is taken to mean that the gods have permitted him to return to let mankind know that they wish no more human spirit-food.

(5) This means that humanity will now be allowed to survive death and not perish.

(6) This brings human sacrifice to an end, and animals only are sacrificed from now onwards as thank-offerings.

As man ceased to be a cannibal, and likewise the gods, he continued his moral development and became more and more conscious of the weakness of the flesh. As the gods were not handicapped by the flesh he came to look upon them as beings morally superior to himself. He felt that he was not fitted for their presence after death, and so developed the feeling that there was an estrangement between him and the gods. This developed naturally, just in proportion to his moral development, until the time came when he believed that the gods were angry with him, and would punish him hereafter for his wickedness on earth by sending him away from them to the underworld. He realised his own wickedness, and that in justice he deserved punishment. Out of this moral background the saviour-god idea made further progress, and so we find that in time there was added to the previous six stages five others, namely :

(7) The priests resent the activities of a reformer who tells the people that the gods are not now angry with them, and will not send them to the underworld after death. Probably this reformer is also a medium whose supernormal deeds and utterances are also influencing the people from sacrificing to the gods.

The priests kill him and he is seen after death. This is taken to mean that his teaching was true and that he has come back to prove that the curse of death is now broken. He dies a martyr, but, because the priests were his murderers, he is regarded as a sacrifice.

(8) Gradually the belief develops that the gods have accepted him as a sacrifice for the sins of humanity, and consequently he is regarded as

(9) The Saviour, because, by taking the punishment due to mankind, he has opened heaven to those who believed in his atoning deed. He is also regarded as the Mediator because he has brought the gods and man together as friends. He is the friend of mankind because he has influenced the gods to allow the people of earth to live in their presence after death.

(10) As his death is looked upon as the price the gods demanded before they could overlook human weakness, he is also considered the Redeemer because he has redeemed all his worshippers at the price of his suffering. Lastly he is regarded as

(11) The Judge, because a judgement is necessary to separate the good from the bad. The unbelievers in this doctrine of salvation are wicked and must receive punishment because the Saviour died only for believers. The believers are good and have been saved. Before, however, this separation of believers from unbelievers took place the dead after death went to the underworld, or Hades, to await the judgement. On the Day of Judgement the good would be separated from the bad, the wicked sent to Hell and the good to Heaven.

The strained situation which was believed to exist between the gods and mankind had now come

to an end. It was now believed that the price had
been paid for the sin committed by the first man
who had angered the gods by his attempt to equal
them in knowledge and wisdom. All the requirements of justice had now been satisfied and all past
sins and wickedness had now been atoned for. Heaven
was now open to all believers as the curse of death
placed on the first man and his descendants was now
removed. Man's sins and wickedness were now
pardoned and death had lost its sting, because the
divine victim, who had been offered up on the altar,
or had been put to death by the priests by some
other means, had opened the door of heaven to all
who accepted his sacrifice on their behalf.

Imagination developed ideas as to the life after
death. The general belief prevailed that the dead
did not reach heaven until they were judged by the
Saviour. The judgement was believed to come
about at the end of the world. Opinions differed as to
what this really meant as some held that the world
would be destroyed by fire and others that the Saviour
would come and reign on earth surrounded by his
worshippers. Consequently it was believed that the
dead went first of all to the underworld, which
must not be confused with Hell.

The Greeks termed this place Hades, the Egyptians the Underworld, and the Hebrews Sheol. These
terms all meant the same place, where the dead existed
till the arrival of the Saviour-Judge who would
separate believers from unbelievers. The believers
then went with him to Heaven while the unbelievers
were consigned to Hell, a lake of fire under the earth,
volcanoes being its chimneys. The Egyptians, how-

ever, thought that believers returned to their earth bodies to live in Paradise on earth, and the Hebrews believed that this would be their destiny when the Messiah fulfilled his mission on earth.

Because of this widespread belief in Hades which prevailed in Egypt, Babylonia, Persia, India, Greece and Palestine for, in some cases, as far back as two thousand years before the opening of the Christian era, we find records of a number of saviour-gods descending to Hades, after they have suffered as victims on earth, there to judge the people who have been awaiting this event. The idea always seemed to prevail that the Saviour, after his resurrection, would shortly return as judge, that his death ended the old era of sin and wickedness, and ushered in the era of righteousness. When Jesus, as the Christ, was credited with this descent to Hades in early Christian literature, we find that the first he released was Adam, who had been awaiting the successful completion of the Saviour's work of redemption. This story was produced because it was thought that the one on whom the curse of death had first been placed was the first to be released when the curse was withdrawn.

The one who had performed this great atoning work could be none other than a divine being, and so the priestly victim came to be looked upon as a god-man on earth and a god in heaven. His saving powers were enlarged and dwelt upon to an increasing extent, with the result that all the terms of affection and adoration which it was possible to conceive were showered upon him. On these ideas a great speculative theology in course of time developed, right up to the opening of the Christian era.

Such then was the position the saviour-god idea had reached when Jesus reappeared after death, and further on we shall see how all the beliefs this theology produced came to be wrapped round him till he likewise was turned into a saviour-god, receiving all the terms of affection which the Pagans bestowed upon their saviour-gods. Because Jesus was a priestly victim he was termed The First Fruits, The Sin Offering and The Anointed One. Because it was believed that by his death mankind was saved he was called the Saviour, because of his intercession he was called the Mediator, and, because of his having paid the price Jehovah demanded, he had redeemed mankind and was termed The Redeemer. At this stage of our study, we are, however, not dealing particularly with Jesus, but with the relations of Christianity, and with what was believed by the Pagans before the time of Jesus, as well as during the period Christian beliefs and doctrines were being manufactured in the first three centuries of our era.

All this can be discovered from the records of ancient religious beliefs, if one has the psychic key to unlock the door to this mysterious room wherein lies the secret. All these ideas run through the New Testament and are clearly expressed in *The Epistle to the Hebrews*, wherein the writer tries to prove to the Jews that the priesthood and sacrifice have come to an end by Jesus having been adopted by Jehovah as the final sacrifice.

It will thus be seen how everything hinged on the victim being seen again as a spirit after death, and how impregnable is this fact, because, if this had not happened, not one single doctrine, dogma, ceremony or rite would have followed. Because the victims, who became saviour-gods, were actually seen in their etheric bodies, all else followed logically. We can follow the way the minds of the ancients worked. We can realise how, with their beliefs about sacrifice and the gods, everything they evolved about the saviour-gods was logical. The mistake they made was in not realising that the gods were those who had once lived on earth, that they did not eat the spirits of the dead, and that they neither ordered the course of nature nor were the judges and punishers of mankind for his shortcomings.

The Spiritualists of today understand correctly who these beings are who return to earth and, through mediums, communicate with mankind. They call them spirits, not gods, but our ancestors were just as ignorant about their relationship to the gods, and who they were, as they were of the earth's relationship to the sun. If, however, we put ourselves in their place, and think as they did, the evolution of the saviour-god idea is quite logical, and the natural outcome of a reformer, who became a priestly victim, returning after death and being seen in his etheric body.

God is a spirit, says the Scottish Shorter Catechism. We cannot define the Infinite, but, so far as the gods are concerned, we can say that a god is a spirit and that man is a spirit clothed in flesh. When he is released at death from his earth body he becomes a god or a spirit, whichever word one cares to use, but if we say that he becomes an etheric being, or an Etherian, we then realise better the distinction. He ceases to be a human being and becomes an etheric being ; he ceases to be a man and becomes an etherian, and the same with a woman. Unfortunately the English language has no personal pronoun to include man and woman, and when using the comprehensive word "man" or the personal pronoun "he" this must also be taken to apply to woman.

The chapter in Isaiah to which reference has just been made has been inserted between two others to which it bears no relation, and is probably the ritual recited at the Eucharist service to the Saviour-god Bel. Bel was known to the Hebrews as Baal, and we know that under this name he was worshipped in Palestine by the Hebrews and surrounding tribes. In the reign of Ahab the Hebrews had rejected Jehovah in favour of Baal, much to the annoyance of Elijah, who helped to rehabilitate Jehovah by his sacrifice catching on fire, whereas the priests of Baal were not so fortunate.

This story is interesting, not because of this magical performance on the part of Elijah, which is on the same level as the ones Moses performed before Pharaoh, but because it brings us into contact with Bel, the famous saviour-god of the Babylonians, who was to them what Christ was, and still is, to all Christian believers. We shall hear more about this saviour-god a few pages further on, but this chapter in Isaiah, dealing with his suffering and meekness, is of especial interest as it gives us such a graphic and moving account of the suffering saviour.

It was part of the beliefs of the saviour-god cults, in the centuries just before the Christian era, that the saviour they worshipped would some day return to earth and gather his elect from the unbelievers on earth. This idea undoubtedly sprang from the sun worship of earlier days, which was so intertwined with all the saviour-god religions. The sun rose to set again. The sun set to rise again. The saviour-god died to rise again, he left the earth to return at some future date. Psychic happenings were material-ised and turned into parables. The people were like children and could not think in an abstract way. Things etheric had to be connected with things material. It was the only possible method then, as it was the only one in the time of Jesus, and is still today amongst the mentally undeveloped.

The belief in the return of Christ, which has prevailed throughout the Christian era, is just the descendant of this old belief that the saviour-god would return to earth. At the time of the birth of the Christian Faith this belief in a saviour-god's return to earth was much in evidence, all the races round the Eastern Mediterranean anticipating this great event. This idea had a great influence in forming the beliefs of the Christian Faith. Forty years before the birth of Jesus, Virgil wrote of the coming Christ for whom the people were longing. Then would follow the golden age on earth when war, poverty and hardship would disappear and the whole world would be ruled by equity, love and justice.

This return of the Saviour was associated with astronomical calculations made by the Babylonians and Egyptians in relation to the sun. For thousands of years the ancients pursued their astronomical studies, during which they elaborated their various systems of solar worship. They mapped out an imaginary zone in the heavens, within which lay the paths of the sun, moon and principal planets. It was divided into twelve signs, marked by twelve constellations called the Zodiac, and there was a ceremony or feast to celebrate the entrance of the sun into each sign. The ancients regarded the various heavenly bodies as visible expressions of divine intelligence, and the twelve constellations were considered to be the sun's bodyguard, this number being given to the saviour god-man as the number of his disciples. Theology, with all its rites and mysteries, is like a tripod, its three supports being the gods, vegetation and the heavenly bodies, which sustain every religious rite, ceremony, doctrine and dogma.

The word Christ means the anointed one, the one anointed with oil before he was laid on the altar of sacrifice, so that the flames would better consume the body. Thus the saviour-god worshippers looked upon their saviour as the Christ, which word has come down to us from the Greek word Christos, meaning the anointed. A similar word was also used for these saviours, meaning good, excellent, beneficent and gracious. The word the Greeks used for these expressions was Chrestos and we find these two words Christos and Chrestos in use prior to the Christian era.

Of all the countries surrounding the Mediterranean in those days the Jews alone were without a saviour-god, and their comfort came from their anticipation of his coming to earth and reigning over them as a god-man. This idea was not peculiar to the Jews as, at least fifteen hundred years before the Hebrews thought of a Messiah, the Egyptians were writing of the coming just ruler who would lead the people on the road of righteousness. He came to them as Osiris, about whom there will be much to say before this chapter ends. The Jews evidently borrowed the belief from Egypt, and called this anticipated righteous leader by the name of Messiah, which conveyed to them the same idea as Christos did to the Greeks. He was the expected anointed Jewish king, who was to subdue all their enemies, whereas the Christ of the Greeks, and the neighbouring nations, was the anointed victim who had suffered on the altar as a sacrifice for their sins.

What a strange history the Jews have handed down to us ! Up to the opening of the Christian era they were the only people without a saviour-god, and yet, when the opportunity came for them to adopt this form of belief, they rejected the one who was a victim of their priests and returned after death. They had the opportunity of believing like their neighbours, and yet they preferred to be a peculiar people. They could not get away from Jehovah and so they continued to anticipate the coming Messiah king, rather than accept the Messiah saviour.

What a grip Jehovah has had over the minds of the Israelites, and yet not one of the promises they believed that he had delivered to them has been fulfilled. Always expecting and never receiving, always hoping and forever disappointed, this strange race has lived as a minority for thousands of years amongst those who have believed in the saving power of the saviour-gods. They have never compromised and never lost their belief in Jehovah, and yet, if they had but accepted Jesus as the Messiah, what a difference it would have made to the happiness of millions of the Jewish race.

Who the first Christ was we do not know. Who the first reformer was who exposed the false claims of the priests we do not know. History does not tell us the name of the one we can call the first Christ, the first priestly victim who returned after death as an apparition to become the first Saviour and Mediator. What we do know, however, is that history records quite a number of these saviours, and our knowledge of those who became national celebrities is now fairly extensive, though somewhat scattered. Over the last thirty-five years I have gathered together all the information I have been able to discover and I now present this in a compact and readable form. This research has entailed much study, patience and careful investigation, as I have always rejected anything doubtful. What follows has been assembled over these years from only standard works, the findings of leading authorities, and the ancient records to be found in the British Museum.

One of the earliest records we have of a saviour-god relates to Thulis, who was born in Egypt about 1700 B.C. He is believed to have lived a life of grace and truth. When twenty years old he was taken as a victim and sacrificed on a cross. His body was then buried in a rock tomb which was discovered last century in a well-preserved condition. He was seen in his etheric body after death by some of his followers, and this was taken to mean that he had conquered death and secured safety hereafter for mankind from the appetites of the gods. In consequence it was imagined that he had been a god-man on earth, and

he was considered to be the Saviour and Judge of
the dead. This was believed to have happened these
many hundreds of years ago, but, if we delve into the
history of the neighbouring country, we find much
the same story about the Saviour-god Crite, who was
worshipped by the Chaldeans.

The date of the birth of Crite is believed to be
about 1200 B.C. He was offered up to the gods as a
sacrificial victim and his death came about by crucifixion, during which event the earth was shaken by a
great earthquake. He reappeared after death and
consequently was worshipped as the Redeemer.
He was called The ever blessed Son of God, The
Saviour of the race and The atoning offering to an
angry God. After his death he received the usual
posthumous honour of being raised to the position of a
god-man, while his status in heaven was made equal
to that of the principal gods.

The natives of Travancore worship Wittoba as
their saviour-god. He is represented with nail
holes in his hands and in the soles of his feet. His
followers believe that he was born about 552 B.C.
and crucified as a sacrificial victim, just as the followers
of the saviour-god Iao believed that he was their
saviour. Iao is believed to have been born about
622 B.C. and crucified on a tree in Nepal. Alcestis,
the wife of the King of Pheræ in Thessaly, is one of
the few cases we have of a woman who was believed
to have suffered for the sins of her people. She is
believed to have been born about 600 B.C. and to
have suffered death by crucifixion, when she entered
heaven to become one of a trinity of gods.

The followers of Quirinus believed that he was

born in Italy about 506 B.C. His mother was looked upon as a virgin and it was claimed that he was of royal descent. The reigning king attempted to kill him. He was taken as a sacrificial victim and we are told that "He was put to death by wicked hands". When this took place the whole earth was enveloped in darkness. These beliefs came about in consequence of his being seen after death.

The foregoing saviour-gods were not national celebrities like the others we shall soon be considering. Their saving power did not extend far enough to embrace great nations. Consequently not much is known about them, and, if there ever were any records of their lives, they have been lost. They are referred to only because we discover, from the scanty information which has been found concerning them, that there was a widespread belief in salvation through the death of one who came to be looked upon as a Saviour, because he had died the death of a sacrificial victim, and had reappeared after death to prove that death had been conquered.

We now come to those national Saviours about whom much more is known. The story about each will be found in the pages which follow. They became either vegetation-gods or sun-gods, or they had attributed to them the qualities of both types of nature-gods. Some were partly associated with vegetation and some partly with the sun. When the saying "I am the bread of life" was attributed to a saviour-god we know that behind it were the beliefs associated with the growth and death of vegetation. When another was called "The Light of the World" he was associated in the minds of his worshippers with the beliefs surrounding the sun. The saviour-gods were therefore either sun-gods, or vegetation-gods, or a mixture of both, and this will become apparent when we learn what was attributed to each.

In the days when the saviour-god religions came into being, and right up to last century, the people could not read or write and many received their religious comfort from witnessing a reproduction of the death and resurrection of their Saviour. In the previous Chapter reference was made to the fact that the Creation story, as we have it in Genesis, was taken from a Babylonian drama, which was produced for the people in order that they might dwell on the handiwork of the gods. In this drama of the creation the priests informed the people, in seven dramatic acts, as to how the earth was created. So likewise the people were kept informed of the atoning work of their Redeemer by means of a dramatic production.

Legends quickly grew up about each individual saviour-god after the people came to believe in him as their Mediator. His uniqueness on earth was emphasised, and all he did was quite contrary to the ordinary course of nature. He, in fact, held nature in the hollow of his hand and could divert her laws at will. That was one side of his life which interested the people, but what was much more vital was his atoning death. Consequently the priests reproduced this in the form of a drama which the people witnessed to their comfort and religious satisfaction. It was a great moving spectacle for which much preparation was made beforehand. Little change has taken place in these dramatic performances down the centuries from what we can today witness at Oberammergau in Bavaria.

It is important to remember that the cause of the legends and the drama was the belief that the Saviour had come to earth and been offered up as a victim for the sins of humanity. Because of this belief all that we are told of each, from the time of virgin birth to ascension into heaven, is a story of what the people believed because of this atoning deed. These legends are the finished story and the result of the mystical speculations of believers. They are a biography written backwards.

To understand these legends aright we must not accept the final records but go back to the cause and work onwards throughout the building process. By so doing we discover how a man became, in the eyes of the people, a god who came to earth for their salvation. Because of this the stories of his life and death were elaborated and elaborated, and all that remains for us is the finished production, a story about a god who came to earth, lived here as a god-man, and is now in heaven acting as the mediator and judge of the dead.

The drama performed was believed to be an actual representation of the Saviour's trial before he became the sacrificial victim. This was for the purpose of testing his fitness to carry the sins of the people. Then came the death scene and finally his resurrection and ascension to heaven. A few pages further on will be found the programme of the drama performed to commemorate the death and resurrection of the saviour-god Bel. This is one of the greatest religious discoveries of the age, as we are now in possession of a genuine record, relating to the worship of a saviour-god, which is the same today as on the day it was first produced.

We have been aware that these dramas were performed in memory of each saviour-god, and from the scattered facts which have come down to us we were in a position to realize that the drama consisted of different acts showing the arrest, trial, death and resurrection of the victim. Now, however, we are in possession of the complete programme and one, moreover, which has not been tampered with, as have so many writings of the past. What was actually believed and witnessed by the people some four thousand years ago in Babylon, has come down to us intact, without a single alteration, because it was printed in the cuneiform writing on soft brick tablets, which were then placed in the sun to harden. When this took place the writing was indelible, and could not be altered. It was from this, and similar dramatic performances, that the gospel writers made up their story of the great Christian drama relating to Jesus, as we shall discover as we proceed.

Our interest at the moment, however, lies with those saviour-gods who were worshipped before the Christian era and we shall commence our study with

THE STORY OF THE SAVIOUR-GOD BEL.

This much beloved god was worshipped for many centuries by the Babylonians. He took the same rank in the Babylonian trinity of gods as does Christ in the Christian trinity. The Babylonian triad consisted of Ea, Bel and Anu, the father god being Ea and Anu was the name for what Christians call the Holy Spirit. As Babylonia bordered Palestine the influence of the worship of Bel spread among the Hebrews, and there was constant friction between the priests of Jehovah and the priests of Bel. Consequently, in the references to Bel (Baal) in the books of Judges and Kings of the Old Testament, we are apt to obtain a wrong idea of the beliefs surrounding this deity.

Christians are taught that the priests of Bel were constantly trying to take the people away from the worship of the one and only God, namely Jehovah, but, if they had been brought up on Babylonian instead of Hebrew literature, they would have found that in the eyes of the Babylonians the priests of Jehovah were for ever trying to make the people depart from the faith surrounding the saviour-god Bel. In first Samuel (xxii, 17–19) we find that King Saul turned over to worship Baal and slew the priests of Jehovah.

Babylonian civilisation, for thousands of years before the Christian era, dominated the lands and tribes on either side of the great rivers Euphrates and Tigris. What the Nile was to the Egyptians, these two rivers were to the Babylonians. Their capital was Babylon, which means "the gate of the gods", and was known to the Greeks as Babel. It was here, according to the ancient Babylonian legend, that the tower was built which so offended the gods that they made it impossible for the people to understand each other. Recent discoveries show that the Babylonians were advanced astronomers, and excavations reveal the site where it is thought the tower was erected. It was probably built for astronomical purposes to serve the same object as our observatory at Greenwich.

Evidently this attempt to gain further scientific knowledge was as much opposed by the priests of Bel as was Galileo's effort in the same direction. The priests of Christ made Galileo recant and cease his astronomical observations, just as the priests of Bel forced the Babylonian scientists to cease their explorations into the heavens. How extraordinary is the human mind ! So conservative and yet so daring. History reveals that there have been these two types down the ages, those who never wished for progress and those who were always anxious for further knowledge. In this instance the priests won in Bablyon just as they won in Rome, and the tower was destroyed. Some time earlier, in consequence of what is now believed to have been a great tidal wave, the Euphrates burst its banks and caused a great disaster. This the priests attributed to the sinfulness of humanity, and from this event grew the story of the Flood which covered the earth and drowned all the people except a chosen few.

One of the greatest discoveries relating to the Babylonian race is that of the Gilgamish epic, believed to be at least four thousand years old. It was found at Nineveh. The hero, Gilgamish, was King of South Babylonia, and the poem deals with his adventures and those of his friend Enkidu. Though some tablets are lost, and there are gaps in the narrative, yet what we have of it is one of the most extraordinary documents in existence. Professor Jensen, one of the foremost Assyriologists in Germany, considered that this poem is the parent of innumerable tales, legends and myths which were taken up by all the surrounding countries and incorporated in their mythology.

His first volume dealing with it exceeded a

thousand pages. The tablets include the famous legend
of the Deluge and from them we discover the source
of many legends with which we are familiar in Greek
and Hebrew literature. It is a long tale of the adventures of these two heroes and of how Gilgamish set
out to find the elixir of life. It contains accounts of
dreams, visions, prayers and psychic occurrences
and tells how, after Enkidu died, Gilgamish, with
the help of one named Nergal, a medium, saw, spoke
to and embraced his dead friend. Thus he found the
elixir of life which was not never-ending life on earth,
but life after death in the etheric world. This must
be one of the oldest psychic stories in the world, and
from it the Greeks probably copied their legend of
the expedition of the Argonauts in their search for the
Golden Fleece.

The City of Babylon, at the height of its fame,
was encircled by a wall three hundred and thirty-five
feet high and eighty-five feet wide. Herodotus tells
us that this great wall was fifty-six miles long and
enclosed an area of about two hundred square miles.
Within this space were beautiful gardens, parks,
fields, and orchards studded with houses, three and
four storeys high. There were two Universities and
several great libraries. Unfortunately, in 690 B.C.
Sennacherib, King of Assyria, plundered the city
and, in the words of Herodotus, "pulled down, dug
up and burned with fire the town and part of the
palaces, root and branch, destroyed the fortress and
the double wall, the temples of the gods, the towers of
brick and threw the rubbish into the river". Babylon,
though a mass of ruins, greatly astonished the Greeks,
when, after the defeat of Darius by Alexander the

Great, they reached the ruined city. In our own times they also astonish the visitor.

The principal sanctuary, erected to Bel, stood in the centre of the city. It was an imposing temple, built of brick, which rose like a pyramid above all the other buildings in the city. Its base was in the form of a square, two hundred yards each side, and from this rose a series of eight towers, one built within the other. A winding road led to the summit on which stood a golden image of Bel forty feet high. In the topmost tower there was a spacious shrine, devoid of images, where the worshippers met to sing praises to their god.

Such then was Babylon, where reigned great kings who were looked up to as god-men by the people over whom they ruled. Here was the centre of the worship of Bel, and his temple in Babylon was regarded with the same sacred devotion as is St. Peter's in Rome. At the time we now call Christmas, when the sun enters the winter solstice, a great feast was held in remembrance of his birthday and at Easter another festival was celebrated in remembrance of his resurrection. The name of Bel, at the height of his worship, could raise the emotions of his people to as great a height as the name Christ the emotions of his worshippers. He was the Christ of the Babylonians and was as much revered by them as was ever Jesus the Christ by his followers.

The beliefs surrounding Bel were similar to those which came, at a later date, to surround Jesus. This we know because there has been discovered, engraved on baked clay, the programme of the drama of the arrest, trial, death and resurrection of Bel which was in use at the time when Bel was worshipped in Babylon. Consequently it was in existence when the gospels were being compiled and we shall find, when we come to consider the compilation of the gospels, how it was used as the basis for the Christian drama.

This clay tablet is accepted by Babylonian scholars as the programme used by the priests at the drama depicting the death scenes of the life of Bel. Its discovery was made by Professor Zimmern and·this is of comparatively recent date. When I called to discuss it with the Curator of the Babylonian Section of the British Museum, I found that the translation, which I shall give, is accepted as "a list of parallel instances found both in the story of the Bel and of the Christ. Zimmern deduced the incidents of the story of Bel from ritual texts which seem to describe a primitive kind of religious play".

The foregoing was written out for me by the Curator, when I was in his private room, and I have this beside me now as I write. The tablet is believed to have been produced about two thousand years before the Christian era, and it was evidently used by the priest who acted as the announcer at the drama. He would have the tablet before him and before each scene would announce what was about to take place. This tablet is probably just a copy of others relating to the same subject, as in Babylonian libraries copies were kept of all their literature. They had a large selection of religious books, including books of Psalms, which were looked upon as inspired. When a book was wanted the number of the tablet was given to the librarian, who handed it out.

The Babylonian Bible contained their mythology relating to the doings of the gods in heaven and on earth, who were associated with the sun, the moon and planets. From their religious literature we find that the early Babylonians were believers in Animism. They believed that behind all phenomena were good or bad spirits, but gradually these were reduced in number to a hierarchy of good and evil beings in Heaven and Hell, the former being presided over by a trinity of gods who personified the sun, moon and air respectively. Bel was pre-eminent amongst the gods and was associated with the sun. Their descriptions of Heaven and Hell so resemble those of the book of *The Revelation of John* that we can only believe that the writer of the Revelation was acquainted with them, and also with the similar ideas held by the Egyptians and the Greeks.

What follows is the translation of the tablet giving the programme of the Passion Drama enacted in memory of the sacrifice of the Saviour-god Bel, the Christ of Babylonia.

(1) Bel is taken prisoner.

(2) Bel is tried in the Hall of Justice.

(3) Bel is smitten.

(4) Bel is led away to the Mount.

(5) With Bel are taken two malefactors, one of whom is released.

(6) After Bel has gone to the Mount the City breaks out into tumult.

(7) Bel's clothes are carried away.

(8) Bel goes down into the Mount and disappears from life.

(9) A weeping woman seeks him at the gate of burial.

(10) Bel is brought back to life.

Let us now go through the performance, and, with the help of the fragment preserved for us in the fifty-third chapter of Isaiah, realise what the Babylonian worshippers of four thousand years ago experienced. We can imagine them sitting in a great amphitheatre, such a one as was so common in those days. The stage was before them and its roof was the dome of heaven. Thousands of people could thus be accommodated, and, from the programme, it is evident that it was situated on the side of a small hill. It was in all probability built at the foot of one of the slopes of this hill, which curved inwards. On the top of the hill may have been a sacred grove.

The people assemble and the actors take up their places behind the stage. We can imagine that the service begins by the singing of one or more of their numerous psalms, of which many of the *Psalms of David* are more or less copies. Here are the first lines of some which have been discovered :

(1) May God my creator take my hands.

(2) Guide thou the breath of my mouth, Guide thou my hands O Lord of Light.

(3) In heaven who is high? Thou alone, Thou art high! In earth who is high? Thou alone art high!

(4) As for thee thy word in heaven is declared, the gods bow their faces to the ground.

(5) As for thee thy word on earth is declared, the spirits of earth kiss the ground.

(6) Lord my transgressions are many, great are my sins.

(7) The Lord in the anger of his heart set himself against me.

(8) God in the strength of his heart set himself against me.

(9) O Land of the silver sky where the gods know no evil.

After the singing of one or more of these hymns a priest pours forth the following prayer :

Merciful and Gracious Father who holds the life of the entire land in his hand.

Lord, thy divinity is like the distant heaven, a broad sea full of fruitfulness,

Who createth the land, foundeth the temples, nameth their names.

Father, who begetteth gods and men, causeth dwellings to be set up, and initiateth offerings,

Who summoneth the kingship, handeth over the sceptre and fixeth the destiny to distant days.

Mighty prince whose spacious heart no god seeth through.

Lord who fixeth the decision of heaven and earth, whose command no one altereth,

Who holdest fire and water, who guideth the living creatures.

What god is thy peer ? In heaven, who is exalted ? Thou alone are exalted !

On earth who is exalted ? Thou alone are exalted !

When thy word resoundeth in heaven, the gods of the lower world kiss the ground.

When thy word riseth aloft like the wind it maketh to flourish meadow and springs.

When thy word sinketh down to earth, the green herbage is brought forth.

Thy word maketh fat, stall and herd, it spreadeth out the living creatures.

Thy word bringeth forth truth and righteousness, so that men speak the truth.

Thy word is the distant sky, the covered earth which
no one seeth through.
Thy word who can comprehend it? Who can equal it?
Look upon thy house! Look upon thy city! Look
upon Babylon!*

After this prayer was ended a priest rose and
read out :

"Scene I—Bel is taken prisoner."

The actors come on the stage and the one representing Bel is arrested. One can imagine the various
forms which this could take. He may have been
denounced by a traitor or by one who led the soldiers
in and pointed out the victim. After the arrest the
prisoner, surrounded by the soldiers, is taken off the
stage and the announcer then rises and calls out :

"Scene II—Bel is tried in the Hall of Justice."

Here we have the scene of a trial. There is a
judge and witnesses to testify for and against the
victim, who is found innocent but sentenced to death.
This is for the purpose of testing his worthiness to
suffer for the sins of the people. His innocence
was essential, just as it was essential that he should be
sentenced to death, which explains why it was that
Jesus, though found innocent, received the sentence
of death. After the prisoner is sentenced the next
scene is announced :

"Scene III—Bel is smitten."

Here we have enacted what was the usual practice
in those days, the jeering and baiting of a prisoner
after the sentence of death. When this ends the
priest rises and says something like this :

---

*The foregoing prayer is taken from a Babylonian tablet which is about four
thousand years old.

He hath no form or comeliness ; and when we see him there
is no beauty that we should desire in him.   He was despised,
and rejected of men ; a man of sorrows, and acquainted with
grief ; and as one from whom men hide their face, he was
despised, and we esteemed him not.

Such is the fragment which has been preserved
for us in Isaiah, though we can imagine that the
occasion·would be taken to enlarge on the suffering
which the god endured.   After which would be
announced :

"Scene IV—Bel is led away to the Mount."

The actor representing the victim is now led
away under guard to the top of the hill where was
situated the sacred grove and probably an altar.
To make the event more realistic, and to impress on
the people the good and evil in humanity, the scene
which follows is included in the performance.   The
priest now announces :

"Scene V—With Bel are taken two malefactors,
one of whom is released."

Two malefactors come on to the stage and are
likewise tried.   One of them is found guilty and the
other innocent.   Here we have the symbolism of good
and evil which we find so well expressed in the case
of the saviour-god Hesus, who is believed to have
been slain by the Druids in Gaul about 834 B.C.
He is represented as crucified with a lamb on one side
of him and an elephant on the other, which has a
similar symbolic meaning as has the legend of the
two malefactors who suffered on either side of Jesus.
One repented, to go to Heaven after death, and the
other's destination was presumably Hell.   The one
signified salvation by faith and the other the fate of

all unbelievers. In the case Hesus, the lamb on one side of him represents the good and faithful, and the elephant, the largest animal known, the magnitude of the sins and wickedness of humanity. In the drama which we are considering one malefactor is released as innocent and the other is slain.

The programme does not contain a scene of the god's death. This may be because it took place on a hill where he was hung on one of the trees in the sacred grove, or crucified, or slain on an altar, and so could not be enacted on the stage. By now the theatre is empty and everyone has climbed to the top of the hill to witness the death scene. As the actor, taking the place of Bel, and the one representing the malefactor, are not actually killed, it may be that the death the saviour-god actually suffered was not enacted. This is unlikely and it is more probable that the tablet which has been found referred only to the performance in the amphitheatre, which accounts for the death scene not being included thereon. They were heavy to carry and would not be brought away from the theatre. After the scene, when the two malefactors appeared, and one was sent after Bel to be sacrificed, the people would know that for the time being the performance in the theatre was over. For that reason, and because the death scene was not taking place in the theatre, it is not engraved on the tablet.

After the death scene the people return to the amphitheatre and the priest announces :

"Scene VI—After Bel has gone to the Mount the city breaks into tumult."

This scene is evidently for the purpose of depicting the religious frenzy which later generations believed took place when the saviour-god Bel suffered as a victim. We know that at these sacrifices the people often lost all control of themselves, cutting themselves with knives and otherwise throwing off all self-restraint. Here then in this dramatic representation is enacted what the priests believed happened at the death of Bel, and we can imagine an excited mob appearing on the stage shouting, yelling and screeching. After this is over the priest announces the next scene :

"Scene VII—Bel's clothes are carried away."

By now Bel has returned from the Mount and, as a dead corpse, he lies on the stage. The undressing process begins. His clothes are taken away from him and he is prepared for the burial which constitutes the next scene. The priest now rises and announces :

"Scene VIII—Bel goes down into the Mount and disappears from life."

The stage is near the side of the hill and so it is not difficult to visualise a tomb cut into it, into which the body of Bel is placed. During the burial service the priest officiating would say words somewhat like these :

Surely he hath borne our griefs, and carried our sorrows : yet we did esteem him stricken, smitten of God, and afflicted. But he was wounded for our transgressions, he was bruised for our iniquities : the chastisement of our peace was upon him ; and with his stripes we are healed.

All we like sheep have gone astray ; we have turned every one to his own way ; and the Lord hath laid on him the iniquity of us all. He was oppressed, yet he humbled himself and opened not his mouth.

As a lamb that is led to the slaughter, and as a sheep

that before her shearers is dumb ; yea, he opened not his mouth.

By oppression and judgement he was taken away ; and as for this generation, who considered that he was cut off out of the land of the living ? for the transgression of my people was he stricken and they made his grave with the wicked . . . although he hath done no violence, neither was any deceit in his mouth.

Yet it pleased the Lord to bruise him ; he hath put him to grief : when thou shalt make his soul an offering for sin. . . .

Because he poured his soul out unto death and was numbered with the transgressors : yet he bare the sin of many and made intercession for the transgressors.

The burial service being over, the next scene is announced :

"Scene IX—A weeping woman seeks him at the gate of burial."

The legend had probably come down that after the death of the saviour-god a woman visited his grave. Perhaps she was his wife, mother, sister or lover. It is a natural touch to the drama, but why it was thrown in we can only imagine. It may have been just to keep the people's attention during the time the final act was being prepared behind the stage, but I think that it has a greater significance than this.

The beliefs surrounding Bel included the belief that he was seen after death in his etheric body. Quite possibly he was seen first of all by a woman, as women are today, and always have been, more clairvoyant than men. The wording of the programme is such that it conveys the idea that the woman went to the tomb in the expectation of seeing him, quite forgetting that he was not there and that his spirit left his body at the place of sacrifice. However, like other mortals, she could think only of him being in the tomb. Now he could only be seen as a spirit and not as a physical being. Quite probably this act represented the woman seeing him as a spirit and displaying either terror or joy. Then comes the final scene depicting what all this display has been leading up to. The priest rises and announces :

"Scene X—Bel is brought back to life."

We can imagine the enthusiasm and excitement this announcement would cause. The people rise and there is thunderous noise and shouting. Then comes a hush and they reseat themselves, awaiting in eager expectancy the dénouement of this great drama. During the silence the stone which has been pushed up against the tomb is seen to move, and slowly it is pushed aside. Out of it comes Bel in his burial clothes. As he emerges from the tomb the audience rises and shouts in its frenzy till all are hoarse. The great drama has reached its climax. Their god has reappeared to prove to them that death has been conquered, and that he has secured for all life in the hereafter. As the actor could not reappear as a spirit, as did Bel after his sacrifice, the reappearance had to be a physical one, just as the Christian drama depicts Jesus having left the tomb as a human being.

So ends this moving spectacle, which must have been performed thousands of times to assure the people that death had been conquered, and that it now held no terror for believers. This great religious service has never been forgotten. It was copied by the Greeks and is still performed in memory of Christ. It has been preserved for us throughout the Christian era in the four gospels. Up till now it has been accepted as a prophecy of what would happen to Jesus, but now we know that when Christianity was in the making those who were responsible for its furtherance adopted this passion drama relating to Bel, and the other gods about whom we shall soon be reading. The Christian dramatist made such changes in the details as were required, so that the people should believe that it was an historical event which happened in Jerusalem, and that the actors were those who were believed to have been the disciples of Jesus.

This Babylonian drama was given to the people the wrong way round and all who copied it made the same mistake. The event which was the origin of the ideas which produced the drama is given last. This should have been given first if the true story had been told. What really happened was this. Bel, a mortal man, when on earth, was killed as a sacrificial victim. After his death he reappeared in his etheric body, and this was taken to mean that he had been sent to earth by the gods to show mankind that he had conquered death. From this event the ideas which were built up on it were evolved, in the following order, and if this is carefully remembered, all the beliefs, doctrines and dogmas, which have come to surround the saviour-god religions, become quite comprehensible.

The people four thousand years ago reasoned thus, just as they did after the reappearance of Jesus :

(1) Bel has been seen after death.
(2) Bel has therefore conquered death.
(3) Bel must have been a god-man on earth.
(4) Bel must have been the son of a god.
(5) Bel must have been the son of a woman who was in contact with a god.
(6) Bel must now be equal to the other gods in heaven.

(7) Because Bel has conquered death he is our Saviour.

(8) Bel, having conquered death, has broken the power of the gods of evil.

(9) Therefore the gods of good are satisfied and will not punish us for our transgressions by devouring us at death or by sending us to the underworld.

(10) Therefore our transgressions are pardoned and Bel is our Mediator and Redeemer.

(11) Bel will come back again some day and, as a King-god-man, rule the earth, when Paradise, which was lost through man's transgression, will be regained.

What, of course, interested the people was the fact that their sins had been forgiven and life with the good gods secured. So the legend grew up about Bel being "the only begotten son of God" who came to suffer for the sins of humanity, that he was born of a virgin, led the life of a god-man, performed miracles, was arrested as a victim, suffered as such, reappeared after death and ascended to heaven, from whence he will come some day to gather together his elect on earth. That is how the story was told and how his death and resurrection were presented in this great drama, but it is always well to remember how the story originated, as unless this is done the Christian religion will never be understood.

Bel, which means The Lord, was given all the adoration his faithful followers could bestow upon him, being known as The Mighty Lord, The Lord of the Covenant, The Lord most High, and The Lord of Heaven. These titles were given to all the saviour-gods, and no one received more terms of affection than did Osiris, the beliefs about whom we are now about to consider.

Such, then, is the story I have to tell about this

greatly beloved Babylonian god Bel, who brought to
the Babylonians, and surrounding races, the same
comfort as Christ brought to his worshippers. Another
saviour-god about whom an equally interesting story
can be told is the saviour-god of Egypt. So I shall
now follow on with

THE STORY OF THE SAVIOUR-GOD
OSIRIS,

which will tell what the Egyptians believed about him,
and the religious comfort and consolation he brought
to this great nation. The Babylonian cuneiform tablets
have made it possible for us to reconstruct the beliefs
about Bel, and the Egyptian hieroglyphics have enabled
us to learn what was believed about Osiris. Besides
these we have what we might call the Gospel of
Plutarch, the Greek historian, who, in the first century
of the Christian era, recorded the legends then current
regarding this god, both in heaven and on earth, and
the beliefs with which his worshippers surrounded
him.

According to Plutarch, whose story in many
respects has been confirmed by modern discoveries,
Osiris, hundreds of years before the Christian era, was
King of Egypt, a human being born in a natural way.
But it was so far back, perhaps about four thousand
years ago, that he has become a semi-mythical character,
somewhat resembling our own King Arthur. When
he came to the throne the Egyptians were savages, but
he enforced laws and civilised the people. He, moreover, taught them how to cultivate wheat and barley,
which changed them from being cannibals to being

vegetarians. He encouraged the planting of fruit trees and made wine out of grapes. After civilising the Egyptians, and thus starting them on the road to prosperity, he handed over the government of Egypt to his wife Isis, and went off as a missionary to teach other lands the blessings of civilisation and the value of agriculture. Besides teaching the people how to make wine out of the juice of grapes, he was the first to teach them how to brew beer from barley.

The tradition which has come down about Osiris marks him out as a wise and beneficent man and one of the first great agriculturists. From now onwards the Egyptians turned slowly from being only meat-eaters to being vegetable-eaters. Instead of living as cannibals, of going out as hunters, they stayed at home and tended their fields and crops. Instead of leading a nomadic life, chasing after game, they settled down and built homes.

Here we come to the beginning of civilisation in Egypt, and to Osiris the Egyptians gave their thanks for all the benefits his wisdom had showered on the land. This is all quite reasonable and possible, but in these old stories it is difficult to know what to believe as they are so surrounded with myths and legends.

This is certainly so with Osiris, as no one received more adoration, praise and glorification than he did from those who lived after him. Stories were told about his being the son of a god and how his brother Set plotted against him and ultimately put him to death. Set made a box, the exact size of Osiris, and when Osiris and Set, together with some other companions, were dining, Set promised to give the box to the one it exactly fitted. One by one they lay down in it and when Osiris did so it fitted him exactly. Before, however, he could rise, Set, with the help of the others, nailed down the lid and soldered it round with molten lead. Osiris, in the box, was thrown into the river Nile, and, after many days, the box was cast up at Byblus on the coast of Syria. From then onwards his wife Isis, in great distress, searched the banks of the Nile for her dead Osiris until ultimately she received word that the box was at Byblus. So off she went in a boat to bring home his body and the box.

On her return she went to see her son Horus, and during this visit Set found the box, which he opened, cut the body of Osiris in pieces and threw his remains about. When Isis returned she set about finding these remains and buried each piece in a different part of Egypt. This is the explanation of why Osiris has so many graves in Egypt.

If the foregoing were all it would be a very interesting old story about the origin of agriculture in Egypt, the brewing of beer and the making of wine. It would also be interesting in that it showed how in those days, as in ours, one strong wise mind could lead the people upwards to a higher level of life and thought. It also teaches us that in those far-off days, thousands of years ago, hatred could make man sink to any depth, and love could raise a woman to almost any height.

The story of Osiris, however, does not end here as he reappeared after death, and this event started his fellow-countrymen off on the path of imaginative story-making because his appearance was taken to be a sign from Heaven that death had been conquered. Osiris, they thought, must in consequence have been a god-man, and Set came to be looked upon as personifying the god of evil who tricked the god of good to his death. Set was therefore compared with darkness and Osiris with light.

As there is an apparent constant fight between light and darkness in the physical world so there is a constant fight between good and evil in the moral world. Horus, the son of Osiris, set out to revenge his father and became identified with the sun. He was deified and looked upon as the sun-god Horus, because he fought the god of darkness. Such is the legend round which grew dogmas, doctrines, rites and cere-monials just as they were entwined round the legend of Jesus.

Horus was given many terms of affection and adoration. He was called The Good Shepherd, The Morning Star, The Lamb of God, The Only Beloved Son, Our Lord, The Mediator and Redeemer, The Cross, and The Intercessor with the Father for the Sins of the World. Other terms which were bestowed upon him were The Way, The Truth and The Life, The Path of Life, The Door of Life, The Only Begotten Son of God, The Prince of Peace, The Sun of Righteous-ness with Healing in His Wings. To him was sung the hymn "Sun of my Soul, thou Saviour dear", and others which might have been taken from the Christian hymn book.

Horus was born at Christmas. When he died he descended into Hades and rose again at Easter, when "he ascended to the Father" and became one with the Father. He, like his father Osiris, was believed to have suffered for the sins of mankind and to be at perpetual war against Set, the God of Evil. He is pictured as a child in the arms of his mother Isis, who, after his birth, takes him on a journey to escape from Heru, who massacred all the infants in his attempt to kill him. He is heard of again at the age of twelve and we are told that he was lost and his mother searched for him. At his baptism the Holy Spirit, as a dove, descended on him. Horus is represented as offering up thanks before a meal, which was the usual custom in those days. Set, on the other hand, was looked upon as the god of evil and he is still known to us under the name of Satan.

Osiris died and reappeared after death. So he was deified as a corn and wine god and his wife Isis was deified, because from her came life and growth. Thus we come to this Egyptian trinity of gods, Osiris, Isis, and Horus, which had such an influence on early Christianity. In Egypt the cross was a symbol of life for thousands of years, and in an ancient sculpture on the wall of a temple at Luxor the annunciation to the Egyptian virgin mother is depicted, the Egyptian Holy Spirit being shown as holding a cross before the face of the virgin mother. In consequence of this she is depicted in the next scene as having given birth to a god-child and being surrounded by figures in adoration.

Imagine Egypt, with its clear atmosphere, the sun day after day giving evidence of its power, its all-enveloping glory, and the mighty Nile swelling and overflowing its banks in summer, then receding, to repeat this same fertilising process when summer returns the following year. This has gone on as long as man has lived on earth. What a profound impression it made on the religious feelings of those dwellers on its banks. Since the Nile brought salvation to Egypt, it was deified, like the sun, in Egyptian mythology, and became the basis of their religious beliefs. As the Nile was responsible for the corn and the wine it was associated with Osiris, just as Horus was associated with the sun.

The annual decrease and increase in the power of the sun, and the yearly rise and fall of the Nile, made the Egyptians, dependent on them both for their food and sustenance, realise that life and death came by their waxing and waning. Osiris and Horus were considered the divine saviours of the race and, like the Nile and the sun, both died to rise again so that by their resurrection man might live after death. The people required something material to enable them to comprehend the immaterial, and so the Nile was symbolic of the psychic stream.

Osiris was termed the father and Horus the son, because of their close relationship to the life of Egypt. It was argued by the Egyptians that as vegetation died and came to life again, as the sun died to rise again, so man did likewise. What was obvious in nature Osiris had proved, by his resurrection, occurred to man himself. Vegetation died and returned to life by the help of the sun and the Nile. So man died to return to life by the help of Horus, the prototype of the sun, and of Osiris the prototype of the Nile. Mother Earth was likewise deified as Isis, the creator of vegetation. Thus we have Isis, representing the earth, and her husband Osiris representing the Nile, the life-giving stream. This pair produced the sun. Osiris, and Isis his wife, whom he fructified annually, and Horus their son, comprised the Egyptian Trinity of gods, the three essentials to growth.

Round this trinity circled the religious beliefs of the Egyptians for the two thousand years prior to the Christian era, and for the first four hundred years after this era commenced. Round these three gods was woven a story of their deeds for the salvation of mankind, and what I am now about to relate with regard to Osiris is taken from papyri, from coffins, from inscriptions, ritual texts and scenes on the walls of temples in Egypt which go back two thousand years before the commencement of the Christian era. From these well-preserved relics we can read and appreciate the religious faith of the Egyptian people, who gave as much thought to the after-life as to this one. They found their comfort in the belief that Osiris had risen from the dead, broken the curse of death, and awaited each spirit at death to pilot it through the dangers and difficulties which beset the newcomer to the other world.

Osiris became the Christ and Saviour-god of the Egyptians and stood to them in the same relationship as Christ has stood to Christians. Just as the Christian story should be read backwards so should the story of Osiris. Because the Christian story is read the wrong way round it has been misrepresented and misunderstood. It should start with the appearance of Jesus after death and tell how, because of his reappearance, and his victory over death, he was elevated to the highest position in Heaven amongst the gods, just as he was raised after death to the highest position among men, that of a god-man. It should then tell how, because of the high status he reached in Heaven, the people came to believe that he was born of a virgin, was the son of a god, and that all the miraculous stories of his life on earth, and the drama of his death, were then added. Instead of starting off with his birth, the gospels should have commenced with his reappearance and explained how all the beliefs grew up because of this.

This may seem repetition, but it is the very kernel of this book, and only by repetition can I break a false idea which has lived four thousand years and been the cause of all the misunderstanding which has accompanied the saviour-god religions, including the Christian religion. The orthodox presentation of the lives and deaths of all the saviour-gods is as false as the idea that the sun travels round the earth each day. Both errors have come about as the result of regarding the subject at the wrong angle. Copernicus put forward the truth about the relationship of the earth to the sun, but, because it was at variance with what seemed obvious, it took several hundred years before it became accepted that the earth travelled round the sun.

How long will it take Christians to realise that the story of the birth, life, death and resurrection of Jesus has been falsely presented by the Christian gospel writers because they told the finished story and not how the story was compiled ? The Christian Church has, throughout its reign, been giving as false a presentation of the facts as the people had, in the days before Copernicus, of the relationship of the sun to the earth. The truth will come slowly but the priests will fight every inch of the ground in defence of their age-old beliefs.

Because the gospel writers made this mistake I shall not now make a similar one when I relate the beliefs which came to surround Osiris. I shall first of all start with the reappearance of Osiris and then consider the myths and legends which followed in consequence of this event. Osiris was believed to have been a slain victim and to have appeared after death. Because of this all that I have now to tell was added to make him into a god-man on earth and a god in heaven. When on earth he was looked upon as a saviour from famine and after death as the saviour from the wrath of the gods. He was elevated by the people to the position of Lord of the Underworld because it was believed that the dead went there to be judged. He was given the position of Judge of the Dead and, from the representations of the Judgement of Osiris, which appear on the walls of temples, he was believed always to judge justly and with righteousness.

The reappearance of Osiris brought all this about, and so he became a god to the people, because he had proved himself, by his survival of death, to be equal to the gods. Consequently, his life on earth was draped with fancy. He had to be tried to test his fitness for the role he now had to play, but before this trial, which the people believed preceded his death, he had a triumphal procession to the temple. Then followed a supper with his friends when he was betrayed during the eating of bread. From the supper Osiris went to Seman, where he poured out his soul in agony because of the load of guilt he was carrying. Seman may be the source of Gethsemane, about which nothing is known in the time of Jesus. Arrayed as a king Osiris was then taken to the Judgement Hall and found innocent. Like Pilate, the judges were vacillating. He was depicted as the silent one and wore a seamless robe.

Osiris was then slain and his body broken. In a

temple on the island of Philae, he is represented as
crucified. Then followed the mortal struggle between
Osiris and the deadly serpent Apophis. This symbolised death, from which Osiris emerged the conqueror. When the victory was won he exclaimed,
"I have bruised the serpent I have passed". After
death, Osiris went to the underworld to help those
living in darkness. He became the god of the underworld and the judge of the dead.

The body of Osiris was put in a tomb swathed in
linen bandages, which were thrown aside when life
returned. As Osiris rose from the tomb two protecting
angels held a cross before his face. A similar story is
told about the risen Christ in the non-canonical *Gospel
of Peter*. The cross, to the Egyptians, was the symbol
of immortality, and every believer considered that after
death he would be transported from the underworld
by Osiris, who had conquered death. On the other
hand, the destiny of unbelievers was a sea of flame
which they entered through two fiery gates.

While Osiris was in the tomb two women, who
were sisters, mourned at the grave. When the tomb
was opened his body could not be found, but two
angels were seen to be guarding the tomb. While the
body was lost the people fasted and mourned, and when
it was found they rejoiced, saying, "We have found
him, rejoice !"

Then Osiris was seen as a spirit. Because of this
all the foregoing was added. Before his reappearance
he was an ordinary human being, after it he became in
the minds of the people a god in heaven who had
deigned to come to earth, to be born of a virgin, to live
the life of a god-man on earth, where he performed

miracles, exorcised evil spirits, cured the halt and the lame, raised the dead, made the blind to see and the deaf to hear.

Thus we have the paradoxical belief, which runs through this religion, as it runs through the Christian religion, that a god came to earth, lived on earth as a god-man, conquered death, returned to heaven and resumed his place among the other gods. Immortality was a perquisite of the gods and a god conquering death was no assurance to man that he had become the heir of immortality because of this sacrifice. One, cannot, however, expect logic and reason from theology produced by men who had minds like children and were absolutely devoid of logic and reason.

What became an absurd form of belief was in its original form quite simple. Someone died and was seen again, which was proof that man survived death. In this simple form religion became ancestor-worship without the need of an ecclesiastical organisation. From this no saviour-god, and the accompanying beliefs, could ever have been evolved. Then came sacrifice and priestcraft, and from it developed the beliefs surrounding the saviour-gods. A victim was seen after death and this fact, combined with the beliefs surrounding sin and sacrifice, brought into being a complicated religious system symbolising the sun and vegetation. The beliefs surrounding this, and the psychic gifts of the victim, formed the basis of all the legends and myths which grew up over the centuries, and which came to be believed as facts, as actual happenings, as true and historical.

This psychic stream, flowing between the two worlds, germinated the acorn, from which has grown a huge oak of beliefs, ideas and speculations. Here is the acorn which has produced theology and mythology. Such is the acorn which has caused mankind to erect temples, churches and pagodas. It has prompted him to forego his comforts in order to support priests so that they might interpret their own inventions, speculations, and all the paraphernalia which surrounds ecclesiasticism.

Doubtless all this had to be, as man-made theology and mysticism are quite irrational, and only when materialised in the form of parables, symbols and legends could they be understood by the people. The priests were required to translate their own speculations into stories which all could understand, just as they were needed to perform the rites they invented as the only method of making contact with the gods. Otherwise priestcraft would never have come into being, as humanity always gets the government and religious system for which it is fitted. It always has been so and ever will be.

Osiris, like all the other saviour-gods, was seen after death, and, according to the records which have come down to us, when the one who saw him went up to touch him, he said, "Touch me not". On another occasion, however, he remarked, "Give me your arm, I am made as you are". Here we are back again to the dramatic presentation, the mixture of the true and the false, due to the latter account being taken from what was seen at the drama, and not from what actually occurred. At the drama the actor, taking the· place of Osiris, and wishing to impress the audience that he was really alive again, says to someone, "Give me your arm, I am made as you are". The same drama was performed of the death and resurrection of Osiris as was performed of the death and resurrection of Bel. We have not found its programme, but Herodotus, the Greek historian, who lived in the 5th century B.C., tells us that he was present at a passion drama held in memory of Osiris.

A ritual sacrament was observed to commemorate the death of Osiris, the partakers of which believed that by eating his body and drinking his blood, which the priests miraculously produced, they shared the god's immortality. At Egyptian funeral services the priests committed the departed to the keeping of Osiris, who, the people were told, could raise their spirits to life eternal. Because of this he was worshipped as the Father God, the Lord of Eternity, and the Judge and Saviour of Mankind. It was believed that he termed himself The Resurrection and the Life, and The Bread of Life.

In the devotional literature of this religion we read, "Osiris is the Saviour and Leader of Souls, leading souls to the light and receiving them again. He raises the dead, he shows forth the longed-for light of the Sun to those who see, whose holy tombs contain multitudes of sacred books. We never can escape him, he will save us. After death we shall still be the care of his providence".

The Egyptian temples, from the descriptions given, must have been in many respects like our present-day Roman and Greek churches. Instead of the Virgin Mary was the image of Isis with the child Horus in her arms, and before it knelt worshippers in the light of numerous candles. Isis was termed The Queen of Heaven, as is the Virgin Mary.

Osiris was looked upon as the God of Truth, The God of Righteousness, The God of Justice and The Judge of all the Earth. He is represented as a scourge-bearing god and elsewhere as the Shepherd of the Flock. He was the most beloved of all the gods of Egypt, and was known as the Good Being.

Believers in Osiris were born again and saved from their sins. He was the giver of immortality, the risen and glorified Lord who had returned to his kingdom. He was known as The Lord of Eternity. He was represented as a king with a sceptre and hailed as Lord of All. He was called The First Lord of the Harvest and had twelve reapers as his bodyguard. His reappearance after death drew all men unto him. He was the Lord and Saviour, the Justifier and the Redeemer, the Substitute, the one who had suffered vicariously for the sins of mankind. He was the Water of Life and the Vine. He gave his body to be broken, and died so that his followers might live.

For this reason Osiris is placed in the category of a vegetation-god. Some of the terms which surrounded him are symbolic of vegetation. They are also symbolic of the Nile, when he is called the Water of Life, which he gave freely to those that thirsted. Some of the thoughts which revolved round the worship of Osiris likewise circled round other vegetation-gods, and one is particularly reminded of the Greek goddess Demeter, in whose keeping were all the seeds of vegetation. In her they fructified. Her daughter Persephone represented the new life which came annually from the mother, and so these two goddesses were always worshipped together. They were called "The two in one" and styled "The great deities",

because they typified the development of growth from
the seed which is planted and dies, only to rise again.

At Abydos in Egypt there still stands the beautiful
temple of Seti I, the second king of the Nineteenth
Dynasty, which he erected in honour of Osiris. It is
a most impressive monument, containing halls, chapels,
and seven main sanctuaries. The coloured reliefs
decorating the walls are amongst the finest achievements of Egyptian sculpture, the delicacy of execution
and splendid composition delighting all lovers of art.
Behind this temple lies one of the most extraordinary
buildings in the world called "The Osireion", consisting of a large subterranean hall which is reached
by a passage leading down from the ground-level.

This underground building, carved out of sand-
stone with huge granite piers supporting the roof,
contains a representation of the creation in the form
of an island surrounded by water. The island consists
of a hill on which it was thought the creator stood,
and every morning at sunrise came to touch the land
with his golden beams. This hill became the symbol
of resurrection, the rising sun emerging out of a realm
of darkness symbolising the victory of life over death.

Beyond this hall is a large chamber, shaped in the
form of a sarcophagus, the roof of which is inscribed
with religious texts. This is known as the "false tomb",
and is looked upon as the burying-place of Osiris,
though it was known that his body was buried elsewhere. What was the motive behind this idea ? For
answer we must go back to the passion drama of the
arrest, trial, death, burial and resurrection of Osiris,
one scene of which doubtless showed the body,
representing Osiris, being put into the tomb, which

was then closed. The next act was the opening of the tomb, which was seen to be empty, and then followed the third act when Osiris appeared alive after death.

So that the people could realise that Osiris had conquered the grave it was necessary for the tomb to be empty. It was the only way to impress them with the fact that the Lord had risen. It was impossible for the audiences to see, lying in the tomb, the dead body of Osiris and his spirit-body standing beside it. So the only way this event could be dramatised was by showing the tomb as empty. This symbolism conveyed to the people the idea of resurrection from the dead, and it was perpetuated, when this temple was erected, by the empty rock tomb in which it was assumed that the body of Osiris had been laid. It was there no longer because he had conquered the grave.

We can now understand the mystery of the empty tomb related in the gospel narratives. The writers made use of the Egyptian symbolism, taken from their passion play, and told the story, just as it happened on the stage, of the corpse being put into a rock tomb and not being there when the disciples visited the grave. As an actual record of facts the story is absurd, since Jesus rose from the dead as a spirit and left his material body behind him at the place where he died. This will be made clear in Chapter VIII. Now that we know that the gospel record of the empty tomb was probably taken from the Egyptian passion drama all our difficulties disappear and what appears to be absurd and impossible becomes understandable.

In the Egyptian religion we also find a story resembling the transfiguration recorded in the gospels, and one similar to the story of Jesus at the well, talking to a woman with five husbands. The Egyptian Pool of Peace, in which the infirm were healed, when an angel descended, reminds us of the Pool of Siloam. From Egypt came the stories of the miracle of the loaves and fishes, of the devils entering the swine, and their god bringing back the dead to life. On one occasion Osiris addressed a mummy with the words, "Come forth". He wept over Rem-Rem and had his feet washed by a woman called Meri. When the Egyptians prayed they did so in the name of Osiris, and, if they had known the words of our hymn "Rock of Ages", they could have sung it with the same fervour, and received from it the same comfort, as Christians do today. How true are the words in Matthew (ii, 15), "Out of Egypt did I call my son".

Such were the beliefs of the Egyptian people about Osiris, who stood so highly in their affections that his worship continued till the fourth century of the Christian era, and made such an appeal to the people of all classes that the Emperor Hadrian (A.D. 76–138), tells us that when he visited Alexandria he found the Christians there worshipping both Christ and Osiris, and, from what he could discover, the beliefs surrounding both these gods were so closely related as to be almost identical.

Before concluding this account of the beliefs relating to this much-beloved god a few observations are necessary. That Osiris died a violent death may be inferred, though how he died we do not know. The story Plutarch tells us is just a legend as to how he met his death, and is doubtless symbolic of what actually occurred. The story of Set killing Osiris by nailing him in a box, at least conveys to us the impression that he was killed by violence, and that he was a victim. Symbolised it means that the god of evil tried to box the god of good, and send him forever out of Egypt by way of the Nile.

The actual life history of Osiris meant as little to the Egyptians as did the life of Jesus on earth to Paul and the early Christians. What the story conveyed to the Egyptians was that Osiris died a violent death at the hands of the god of evil, just as it was believed that the devil was behind those who crucified Jesus. It was a fight between God and Satan for the possession of humanity. If Jesus and Osiris had not conquered the grave by reappearing after their sacrificial deaths the devil would have been the victor, and life for mankind after death with the good gods unattainable. Because they emerged the conquerors so the God of Righteousness, who had planned it all for the salvation of humanity, was victorious. Such was the mystical meaning behind the whole story.

Set was looked upon as the prototype of the god of evil, and may have been in real life the priest who slew Osiris as a sacrificial victim. As time passed he came to be looked upon in much the same light as were Pilate and Caiaphas, the High Priest, in the case of Jesus, who, we are told, was slain "by wicked hands". In the minds of Christians these two men were, and still are, regarded as the servants of the Devil because of the part they took in crucifying the Lord of Glory.

The reappearance of Osiris put a new complexion on a sacrificial event, which was an everyday occurrence, and so we have the elaborate story which grew out of it. We have, however, to go back to this event to find the psychic link which connected the etheric with the material. Of course Osiris may not have been a victim in that he was an actual sacrifice, but there must have been, in some form or another, a psychic seed to cause this elaborate story about which we have just been reading. Such a story, it is impossible to believe, could have evolved from some purely material event. Like produces like in this world, and though kings and heroes became deified for no other reason than the fact that they were kings and heroes, yet they were never worshipped as were the saviour-gods. They were never looked upon as conquerors of the grave and referred to as Saviours, Mediators and Redeemers.

It is well to note carefully this difference which emphasises the power of the etheric over the material in the mind of man. All the Egyptian, Babylonian and Indian kings were considered divine, in the sense that their people believed that they represented a god or the gods. At the most they were looked upon as god-men. Alexander the Great brought this idea with him from the East, and the Roman Emperors found it a great help in governing the mixed and ignorant races over whom they ruled. The deification of monarchs, however, lasted only during their lifetime. At death even a Caesar turned to clay, we are told. They received divine honours on earth but their divinity was soon forgotten after death. With the saviour-gods it was just the reverse, they were mostly unknown till after death, when they then received the love and adoration of their worshippers, which continued for many hundreds of years.

Julius Caesar, the most deified of all the Roman Emperors, never reached a higher status than that of

a god-man on earth, and at death his deification died
with him. It never followed him to the other world.
These deified Emperors and Kings were just reflections
of the gods the people worshipped. They were given
the attributes of the gods because the people could not
think of anything higher with which to endow them.
If the gods had not existed in the minds of the people
the deification of kings would never have taken place.

Now notice the difference between what the
people considered real and those they honoured by
associating with the real. No monarch, as such, became a god in their mythology. No monarch, as such,
was worshipped as the founder of a religion. No
monarch, as such, was the centre and head corner-
stone of a Church, or an organised priesthood, or had
countless churches and temples built in his name for
his worship. No monarch, as such, had the Eucharist
celebrated in his memory. No monarch, as such, was
worshipped in Heaven as Lord and Saviour, and held
his worshippers' affection for, in some cases, thousands
of years after his death. No monarch, as such, had
attributed to him what was attributed to the saviour-
gods. Nothing relating to the spirit of man and the
etheric world was ever attributed to these monarchs ;
nothing to rouse the emotions, to raise men's thoughts
to ideas beyond the material.

The Kings and Emperors received the adoration
and worship of their subjects only during their lifetime,
because they were Kings and Emperors. The saviour-
gods never sought fame or glory and never received it
during their time on earth. They came, as a rule, from
the ranks of the people, and yet, after their deaths, they
received in love and adoration far beyond what

monarchs ever received from their subjects. While the spurious received divine worship during their lifetime, when the others were unknown and humble members of society, death changed the scene and reversed the position. Those who claimed to be god-men, and were considered as such during their earth lives, were soon forgotten as divine beings, while those who never thought of such an idea were, after their deaths, looked upon by their worshippers as god-men on earth and gods in heaven.

But that is only half the story. After their deaths these humble individuals were raised in the minds of their worshippers to a position in heaven which required all the imagination and exaggeration the human mind was able to achieve. They received gratitude such as no human being ever gave to each other. They received adoration, love and affection such as has never been expressed by man for man, by man for woman, or woman for man. Down the ages their memories have been cherished, and expensive organisations have been maintained for this purpose, along with extensive rites and ceremonies. A code of beliefs, doctrines and dogmas developed round their names which were held to be above all other names, at which every knee must bow.

Is this the result of some material delusion? If so, it happened not once but often, and produced numerous identical saviour-gods. A delusion could not always produce the same effect. We can only imagine the cause from the effect, which we know, and there is only one possible cause to explain it all. We have not a choice of causes but only one, so the answer is neither difficult nor uncertain. The one who

was deified after death reappeared in some form or
other to prove that he had conquered death. This was
taken to be a sign, or a message from heaven, that he
had broken the curse of death.

No other explanation is possible. If the old
records did not tell us that this happened we would
have had to imagine that some such thing had occurred,
that some link between heaven and earth had been
forged, to lift the people's minds from earth to heaven,
to the contemplation there of one who had lived and
died as an ordinary mortal on earth, but who had been
caught up by the psychic stream to become a god in
heaven.

Another inference we gather, by arguing from
effect to cause, is that the one who died was in some
way or another a victim. He must have died as a
sacrifice or as a martyr. If he had died an ordinary
death and reappeared it would have meant nothing in
particular. If every apparition seen had been turned
into a saviour-god, and worshipped as such, their
names by now would have been legion. Those who
became saviour-gods were associated with sacrifice, or
martyrdom, in the minds of the people, and with
having suffered in some way to satisfy the gods.

This inference rests on a solid basis of circumstantial evidence, and these two facts, the reappearance,
and the one who reappeared being a victim, can be
taken as established, because it is rational and in
accordance with our psychic knowledge. This opinion
is arrived at by a process of deduction, through
arguing from effect to cause. Every saviour-god we
can thus assume died as a victim, in some form or
another, and was seen again after death. On this basis

the various religious structures which have been raised can be understood and explained. Without it the origin of the saviour-god religions could never be fathomed, and would forever remain in the limbo of mystery as one of the wonders of the world for which there is no known reason.

Therefore, we can come to the conclusion that the material world could never have been the cause of these non-material legends and myths. If there had been no psychic link our ancestors could never have imagined the etheric or such an array of immaterial ideas. Before the material and the immaterial could be joined, as they were by these beliefs and stories about the saviour-gods, a connecting link was essential, and there is only one link possible, namely an apparition or a materialisation.

On the reappearance of Osiris all else was added in the course of years, just as it was added to the lives of all the others who came to be looked upon as Saviours, those who caught the imagination of the people through their reappearance after death. So it came to be believed that Osiris, the good one, had fought and conquered Set, the evil one, and thus saved his people from the curse of death. Then Osiris came to be looked upon as the god of the good, and the mediator for all the dead, who would appear before him in the underworld after death. Here he would judge them, and, if they were accounted righteous, take them with him to heaven above. Consequently the dead were provided in their coffins with a chart to enable them to find their way about till they came into contact with Osiris.

Most copies of the Book of the Dead, which

contains the Egyptian sacred literature, included an elaborate picture of the dead being judged before Osiris. In the Judgement Hall, called The Hall of the Two Truths, sits Osiris on a throne within a shrine. A great balance stands in the centre of the hall; on one pan of the balance rests a feather, which symbolises truth, and on the other the heart of the one being judged, the heart being regarded as the seat of consciousness. Here the dead man's life is gone over, and his every thought and action weighed in the balance. Osiris sits, presiding over it all, and we read the following pleadings by the one being tried: "Behold I am in thy presence O Lord of the West; There is no iniquity in my belly; I have not told a lie knowingly; There is no wickedness in me. Grant that I may be like the favoured ones who are in thy following". Osiris then rises and, if he is satisfied that all is well, he takes the suppliant by the hand, saying: "Well done, my good and faithful one, enter thou into my kingdom".

If Osiris had not appeared again after death evil would have been victorious and there would have been no judgement. He, however, did appear, and the curse of death was broken. This fight between life and death comes in all the saviour-god religions. Life after death being desired more than anything else, it was represented as being the gift of the good gods. Annihilation, which was not desired, would have followed in consequence of the good gods being overcome in their attempt to save man from the clutches of the gods of death. Death and evil are represented as the curse of the wicked gods, just as life and goodness are the gift of the good gods.

When reading these old stories of apparitions and materialisations one is struck with the reality of it all, as the ancients tell them just as they appeared to them, which is just as they appear to us today. Apparitions and materialisations are due to two different causes. An apparition is that which is seen by clairvoyant sight. The clairvoyant catches the vibrations of the etheric body, but a materialisation is something quite different. It is caused by the etheric body clothing itself in ectoplasm drawn from a medium, who has a superfluity of this semi-material substance which is part of everyone. One can see an apparition but cannot feel it. One's hand goes through it. On the other hand, a materialised etheric being can be touched and treated just like a human being.

Again, when an apparition is seen it does not appear to come out of the ground, but rather as a being within our own atmosphere, so to speak. It may appear suddenly or gradually, or, again, seem to be treading the surface of the earth. A clairvoyant, when a death takes place, can see the etheric friends of the one just dead floating with a downward sweep to take the one who has died back with them to the etheric world, to a surface in space above the surface of the earth.

In the case of a materialisation just the opposite impression is obtained. The materialised being builds up from the floor, covering itself with ectoplasm from the medium, but using the earth as a basis. Thus it appears to rise out of the floor, should this take place in a house, or the earth should this take place outside. Though in reality the being has come down, just as did the apparition, yet the apparition is seen in its natural state. The materialised being, on the other hand, is seen in an artificial state, because those on earth cannot see it come and go, but only when it is clothed in ectoplasm. This process of clothing itself in its own likeness, by using part of the medium's bodily sub-stance, produces an entirely different effect from an apparition in its coming and going, as, when it dis-appears, the being appears to sink into the floor, leaving the ectoplasm behind it on the floor, to be re-absorbed into the medium's body. Two classes of religious beliefs have thus developed, as we shall discover.

So an apparition can be seen to come down and to ascend, while a materialisation is seen to rise out of the earth. This knowledge of psychic science is essential if one is to differentiate between a materialisation and an apparition in these old stories. From the way they are told we can note the difference. When the ancients tell us that a spirit or god came out of a hole in the ground and went back into the earth we know that they refer to a materialisation. When we are told that a god or spirit came down and ascended we realise that the story refers to an apparition.

Those who became gods, as the result of their appearances after death, were considered either gods of heaven or of the underworld, according to the manner of their appearance after death. If one appeared as an apparition he was considered a god from heaven. If he appeared as a materialisation he was looked upon as a god of the underworld because he appeared out of the earth, below the surface of which the Egyptians believed that the dead went to be judged. If Osiris found them righteous they passed to heaven, if the reverse they suffered in hell and were finally annihilated. Just as we know why certain gods became associated with the sun, and others with vegetation, so we know also why some were considered gods of the underworld and others gods of heaven.

Osiris was considered to be a god whose care was the underworld because, on this reasoning, he reappeared after death as a materialisation. Because of this fact the Egyptians evolved different eschatological beliefs from those of the Greeks, whose gods were seen as apparitions and not as materialisations. This also explains why amongst some tribes and nations it was believed that the dead lived under the surface of the earth which it was expected would some day give up its dead. The Egyptians embalmed the dead because they believed that their spirits would again take possession of their physical bodies on the great Resurrection Day at the end of the world.

The Greeks and others believed that at death the spirit entered the etheric world immediately, thus holding quite contrary views to the Egyptians as to the state of the dead and the last judgement. To the Greeks death was the door to the etheric world, whereas the Egyptians believed that there was an interval of time, during which occurred the judgement and then the return of the spirit on the last day to its earthly body. These two opposite beliefs, one taken from Greece and the other from Egypt by the early Christians, were the cause of the contradictory eschatological beliefs expressed by Paul, who was influenced by Greek thought, and those of the Church fathers, who followed Egyptian beliefs. In the burial service of the Anglican Church these two contrary opinions are expressed, which produce the effect of leaving the mourner in complete bewilderment as to what exactly has happened to the departed spirit.

A reappearance after death was looked upon differently in those old days from what it is in our day. We understand the meaning of psychic things better now than then, though they occurred then just as they occur now. They were certainly used then as the basis for religious belief, and out of them beliefs grew in a way they do not do today. If we were as ignorant today about physical and psychic science as were our ancestors we would still be producing religions and saviour-gods, and building up legends and myths around natural and supernormal occurrences. As it is we now analyse each effect to find the cause and so separate the phenomena of nature into the respective compartments to which they belong.

Thus, while not attributing the ordering of nature to the spirits of the departed, as did our ancestors, yet we find that a compartment must be allotted to them if we are properly to understand the past history of mankind and the destiny of the human race. Just as humanity has its place on earth so has it its function in the etheric world surrounding this earth. The spirits no more order the phenomena of nature there than do human beings here, and, when this is accepted and understood, we can retain the age-old belief in the gods without making the mistakes of our ancestors who, by believing too much, have produced in our day such a reaction that many believe too little.

One might say that religion, as it has come down to us, is the product of our ancestors' faculty for imagination, but to expect intelligent people to believe as true these ancient legends and myths is not only absurd but impossible. They are only respected by those who do not think deeply, and who imagine that the more thickly a story is embedded in the dust of tradition the more sacred it becomes. What our ancestors wove round their psychic experiences need not be accepted by us today.

One similarity, however, is evident which is that now, as then, they have the effect of raising our thoughts to ideas above the material, and impressing on us that we are all etheric beings, with a destiny after death in another order of existence. This knowledge is the foundation of Religion, and, though its meaning has been much abused, by the follies and ignorance of the past, yet it will remain with us even when these follies have been swept away.

The psychic stream between the two worlds is the cause of all religious belief, from the time of primitive man up to the present day, and if we are to make anything of the legends which grew up around the men who reappeared after death, and became accepted as saviour-gods, this immaterial link must receive first place. It is the basis of all mythology. Without it mythology cannot be understood, and till it receives its right place Christian and Pagan mythology will continue to be regarded upside down, the wrong way round. The same revolution in thought is as necessary today towards mythology as it was in the day of Copernicus towards astronomy.

One last observation before proceeding to the consideration of the next saviour-god, about whom I wish to give some details. Some of the wonders attributed to the saviour-gods, when on earth, may have been taken from the doings of the magicians or mediums of the time and exaggerated. Doubtless both the medium, when he was allowed to function, and the magician, when he was successful in mystifying the people without being discovered, were considered in the light of god-men or god-women. The pheno- mena, supernormal or magical, that they were able to produce were consequently attributed to the saviour- god when his life was being recast after his deification. It is also possible that during their earth lives the saviour-gods were either magicians or mediums, or perhaps both, and that, when they proved that they rose superior even to death, this was also a cause contributing to their deification.

It is impossible, in the stories which have come down to us, to pick out something and say that this is a definite instance of psychic phenomena, because a magician can duplicate so much. Again, an apparently absurd story may have had either a psychic or magical background. One thing, however, a magician could not do then and cannot do now by magic, and that is to cause someone who is dead to reappear after death, either as a materialisation or as an apparition. This is something which is definitely related to the psychic realm.

As to the mighty works the saviour-gods were reported as doing on earth, the information we have about them is insufficient to enable us to judge how they were performed. They may have been the result of mediumship, or magic, or of the imagination of those who recorded their lives. Doubtless these legends are a composition of all three, and came into being for no other purpose than to magnify and glorify the gods who had done so much for mankind. They, in many instances, are based on previous stories, which, in the first instance, related to the doings of the sun, the planets and the growth and death of vegetation.

These observations are necessary in view of the information I have still to give in this chapter. We have gone back to be with the Babylonians at their remembrance service to their Saviour-god Bel. Then our minds turned to their neighbours, the Egyptians, when we discovered similar beliefs surrounding their much-beloved Osiris. Let us now cross the Mediterranean to Greece, the land of culture, art and literature. Here we find an old story which is well worth recording and remembering.

THE STORY OF THE SAVIOUR-GOD PROMETHEUS.

This is an old Greek legend and will be found in the writings of Hesiod, who lived in the 9th century B.C. Hesiod was the father of Greek poetry and, like Robert Burns, a son of the soil. The Greeks loved his legends and poetry about the gods, accepting all his stories as true and real, as children today believe fairy-tales. He tells his legends of the doings of the gods and goddesses as if they were earth people, with earth desires and passions, the only difference being that he makes everything to happen in an imaginary world. At times the gods are on earth fraternising with the people, and at other times the setting is in the heavens.

It is all very interesting when looked upon as legend, and it gives an insight into the mentality of the time ; but what a commotion it made when the philosophers of Greece, away back in 500 B.C. and onwards, began to throw doubt on their literal accuracy. It reminds one of the excitement and consternation caused in this country when last century some were intelligent enough to suggest that the stories in the Bible should be treated in like manner. Words of contempt were thrown on their heads. They were called atheists, infidels and so on, just as were the Greek philosophers when they took up a similar attitude to their legends, which were considered sacred and true.

Prometheus, the subject of this story, was one of the hero-gods of Greek mythology. He was looked upon as the Mediator and Redeemer, as the one who had brought immortality to mankind through suffering, chained to a crag, in the Caucasus mountains.

Before the legends were spun, Prometheus, who became a saviour-god, was doubtless sacrificed to the gods and reappeared after death. Because of this, legends were told about him and a religion developed. The beliefs, which circled round his name, were similar to those which were evolved round the name of Bel and the other saviour-gods. As there was the same cause, it brought about the same effects, and the priests told symbolic stories about him relating to the sun. Dramatic representations took place in Greece concerning his arrest, crucifixion, death and resurrection, similar to those relating to the other saviour-gods. Seneca, the Roman historian, refers to the fact that these dramas were produced five hundred years before the Christian era, but before we consider this aspect, and the beliefs surrounding the death and resurrection of Prometheus, I shall relate the legend as told by Hesiod.

The story begins with the creation of the world

and of man. The original pair, he tells us, were made from the dust of the earth, and lived in Paradise, where there was no sickness, no work, no trouble and no evil. Though the race had been created by the gods, yet the first inhabitants of the world were always doing wrong and angering the gods, so much so that all were drowned except a chosen few who were spared to carry on the race. Then comes the story of the flood which was probably copied from Babylon. The Greeks were very proficient at this, and wherever they went they always managed to find something new to add to their literature.

In spite of the gods drowning mankind, which one would think was sufficient revenge, they still remained angry, and when mankind asked for fire, which symbolised knowledge, Zeus, the principal god, refused it, saying that fire belonged to the gods and not to man. This is very much the same idea as we find in other mythologies, that knowledge belonged to the gods and that it was a sin to try and obtain what they had decreed was theirs alone. In Genesis the reason given why the gods turned Adam and Eve out of the Garden of Eden was because they had discovered the knowledge of good and evil, and would next be trying to learn how to live for ever.

The Greeks believed that if it had not been for Prometheus fire would never have come to earth, but, taking pity on the poverty of mankind, he stole it by a trick from Zeus and brought it to earth. Prometheus was one of the titans of earth, the race which the Greeks believed inhabited the world in primitive times. In Genesis we read of the days "When the sons of God (or, as it should be translated, 'the sons of the gods') came in unto the daughters of men and they bear children to them, the same were the mighty men which were of old, the men of renown". Prometheus was one of these mighty men, and, in the eyes of the Greeks, he stood for their Saviour, who acted as the mediator between the gods and men after the unfortunate mistake Epimetheus made in opening Pandora's box.

It will be remembered that in Chapter II reference was made to all the troubles which afflicted mankind coming as the result of the curiosity of Epimetheus. Because Prometheus stole the fire from heaven, Zeus gave Epimetheus a wife called Pandora, a woman of divine beauty, who tempted him to open the box she brought with her. Out came all the troubles which have since pursued mankind and only Hope remained inside. After that, woman was looked upon as the cause of all man's misfortunes, and Prometheus as the one who brought knowledge from heaven. He planted in humanity the power to think, and the fire he brought from heaven turned out to be the origin of art and all the comforts and necessities of humanity. Zeus was so angry with Prometheus for giving mankind all this knowledge, that he condemned him to a cruel and miserable death.

As the result of man obtaining knowledge, evil came into the world, because without knowledge mankind would never have recognised the difference between good and evil. From that time onwards man worked out his own destiny, with the choice of good or evil before him. He had developed out of the nursery stage and started on the road to progress. So the serpent in the Bible story, and Prometheus in this one, seem to have been the benefactors of mankind, and Jehovah and Zeus the reverse. From this time onwards there was continual tension, and bad diplomatic relations existed between mankind and the gods, the latter always trying to thwart man in his attempt to reach a higher status on earth. If it had not been for Prometheus things would have been in a bad way, but his crucifixion, as a punishment, saved the situation.

At the very place where our hero made his theft from Zeus is the extinct volcano of Mosychlus, which was an appropriate situation, because in those days, in all probability, fire issued from its crater. At the foot of this volcano stood a very ancient temple, built on the spot where the theft took place, and where Prometheus was seized and bound by the order of Zeus and carried to a crag on the Caucasus mountains. Here he was crucified to "an upright beam of timber to which was affixed extended arms of wood", in other words a cross. Lucian, the foremost essay writer of the silver age of Greek literature, who lived in the latter part of the 2nd century A.D., expressly states that Prometheus was believed to have been crucified by Zeus. Each day Zeus sent an eagle to gnaw the Saviour's liver, which daily grew afresh, and so Prometheus hung, awaiting death. This sacrificial act for the good of humanity was commemorated in Greece by torch races at the Panathenaic games.

Achilles, hit by a poisoned arrow from the bow of Hercules, and in acute pain, offered to die in place of Prometheus. This offer was accepted by Zeus, but before his death occurred Hercules went off to the Caucasus mountains and set Prometheus free. As the Greeks believed that Prometheus actually died, perhaps we can take this story of Hercules as symbolic of death releasing the Saviour. No matter how one interprets this, and also the tale that Zeus decreed that Prometheus was for ever to wear an iron ring, the fact remains that in the minds of the Greeks he died by crucifixion on a crag in the Caucasus mountains, a victim of the wrath of Zeus, and that from this legend developed the religious doctrines of his death and resurrection.

Instead of being a legendary fire stealer he became to the Greeks their divine Saviour and Redeemer, the one who had died to take on his shoulders man's load of guilt, and to suffer in place of humanity. It is doubtful if there is to be found in the whole range of Greek literature deeper pathos than that of the divine woe of this beneficent god-man who was crucified on a Scythian crag in the Caucasus mountains for his love to mortal man. At his death the earth shook as the result of a great earthquake and nature was convulsed. The rocks were rent, the graves opened and, amid a great tempest, Prometheus gave up the ghost.

His worshippers looked upon him as divine and as having come down from heaven to live the life of a god-man. They believed that he was the creator of the human race, and that on his return to heaven he acted as the mediator between God and man. In their art they represented him as crucified to a rock and wearing a mock crown. A number of instances have come down to us of the sacrificed victim wearing a crown of thorns, which takes us back to the Babylonian festival of the Sacaea, when the victim was dressed in King's robes, crowned, enthroned and given five days licence, after which he was stripped, scourged and crucified.

Æschylus, the father of Greek drama, who lived in the 6th century B.C., dramatised the death and resurrection of the suffering Saviour in these words, which were used by the actor, representing Prometheus, hanging from the cross on the stage :

Who e'er thou art, a hapless god thou see'st.
Nailed to this crag the foe of Zeus thou see'st.
Him thou see'st, whom all the immortals
Whoso tread the Olympian threshold, name with hatred.
Yet thou beholdest man's best friend,
And hated for excessive love.

Soon as Zeus sat on his ancestral throne,
He called the gods together, and assigned
To each his fair allotment and his sphere of sway supreme.
But ah ! for wretched man to him no part or portion fell.
Zeus vowed to blot his memory from earth,
And mould the race anew.

I, Prometheus, only of the gods did thwart his will.
And, but for my strong aid
Hades had overwhelmed and hopeless ruin swamped.
All men that breathe, such were my crimes.
These pains, grievous to suffer, pitiful to behold
Were purchased thus, and mercy's now denied
To him whose crime was mercy to mankind.

And here I hang, in cunning torment stretched,
A spectacle inglorious to Zeus.

In the drama which was added to the end of the Christian gospel legends, we are told that Jesus on the cross called out in a loud voice, "My God, My God, why hast thou forsaken me ?" Five hundred years before this event the dramatist Æschylus attributed to

Prometheus, when represented as hanging on his cross, the foregoing tragic utterance. It is more comprehensive than the one attributed to Jesus, and yet the same idea prompted them both, the belief of the ancients that a suffering Saviour took upon himself the anger of a God, and so saved mankind. Wherever the saviour-god religions are studied we find that, as human sacrifice developed, it produced the same idea on each occasion when a human being, who was sacrificed, appeared again after death and became a saviour-god in the eyes of his worshippers.

We have considered the religious beliefs surrounding the saviour-gods in Greece, Egypt and Babylonia. I want now to relate the beliefs held by the Persians about their god Mithra, and after that to go on to India and consider what was believed on that great continent. As the belief in the Persian saviour-god was adopted by the Romans seventy years before the Christian era, it will be noticed that by the time we have finished our tour of exploration we shall have encircled Palestine before our era commenced. One has only to pick up a map and see how Palestine was surrounded by saviour-god religions before the Christian saviour-god was born. I shall now include Persia and Rome by relating

THE STORY OF THE SAVIOUR-GOD MITHRA.

The study of Mithraism is especially interesting, as between it and Christianity there was a bitter fight for supremacy during the second, third and fourth centuries of the Christian era. The beliefs of both religions were so similar that they ultimately fused.

Christianity did not conquer Mithraism but absorbed it.

The worship of Mithra was nearly universal in the western world at the height of the Roman Empire, and appealed to both bondmen and freemen. As I have said, it was the great rival to the Christian Faith and, if the policy of the Emperor Julian had been successful, instead of that of Constantine, the religious history of Europe would have been quite different. Mithra, quite possibly, would have been the Saviour and Redeemer of the people who now call themselves Christians, and, what is now called Christendom, would not have had a religion mixed up with Judaism. Moreover, the Jews would doubtless have had Palestine as their home, which was denied them by the early Christians, as we shall discover as we proceed. Instead of Jehovah being the Father God, Ormazd would have had that honour, and Mithra would have been the second member of a trinity of gods, consisting of Ormazd, Mithra and Ahriman.

Constantine, however, came into power first and, since he reigned for twelve years after the Council of Nicæa defined the Christian Faith, it gave this religion time to consolidate its position, whereas Julian, who favoured Mithraism, did not commence to rule till 361, or twenty-four years after the death of Constantine. He only reigned two years and, as he met his death in Persia, the home of Mithraism, this was taken to mean that Christ had conquered Mithra.

In spite of his short reign he made considerable progress in re-establishing the old religion, and, had he reigned some years longer, would probably have succeeded in doing so. His hatred of Christianity was intense, as, in his childhood, he had witnessed the massacre by the Christians of all his relations, friends and many believers in the old faith, while he himself was kept in captivity till twenty-five years of age, his life often being in jeopardy. However, the story of how Christianity, by butchery and massacre, won its way to power will be told in greater detail when we come to this period of the history of the Christian Faith in Chapter X.

What we are now considering are the beliefs surrounding the Saviour-god Mithra. Unfortunately, when the Christian Church became supreme at the close of the fourth century, it obliterated, as far as possible, all reference to these beliefs, because it did not wish later generations to know that what was being believed under the name of Christianity had previously been believed under the name of Mithraism. Like a conqueror of old who, after a long war, destroyed his enemy root and branch, so the Christians destroyed every trace of this religion, exterminated all believers, and thought that nothing more would ever be heard of it. They forgot, however, that monumental remains were still scattered throughout Europe, and that from them later generations would discover what the early Church was so anxious should be forgotten.

In Great Britain, Mithra was worshipped by the Romans for the first three hundred years of the Christian era. They have left no trace that they ever worshipped Christ, but many indications remain that they worshipped Mithra. A sculpture has been found in Northumberland which contains the inscription 'To the God, best and greatest, invincible Mithra, Lord of Ages". Similar texts have been discovered on sculptures and monuments both in England and throughout Europe. Many exist in France, Germany and Italy. A fine sculpture of Mithra slaying a bull is in the British Museum. On most of these monuments we find two figures beside Mithra, one holding a raised and one a lowered torch, which are the ancient symbols for death and life, signifying the death and resurrection of mankind. Elsewhere Mithra is imaged with his arms stretched out to eternity and as having two keys representing life and death. Besides these monuments there is still preserved a collection of Persian legends, known as the Zendavesta, in which we find what remains of the beliefs which surrounded Mithra.

Mithraism was the religion of Persia for hundreds of years before the Christian era and its roots can be traced to India and Babylon. It was brought to Rome about 70 B.C. by her soldiers who had been fighting in Persia, and it was later adopted as the State religion. Mithra was definitely associated with the sun, but before we begin to consider all the terms of adoration and respect with which his followers endowed him, let us start at the beginning and not at the end. Mithra, his worshippers believed, died as a sacrificial victim, but as to how his death took place we have no information to guide us.

He may have been a reformer, or one endowed with psychic power, or both. We do not know, so there is nothing to be gained by guessing, but we do know that the teaching assigned to him contains very lofty ideals. His followers believed that he reappeared after death and then ascended to heaven. Because of this everything which follows came to surround the person of this man who has come down to us under the name of Mithra. On one occasion he found water by shooting an arrow at a rock. Water gushed out where the arrow hit the rock, which reminds us of the story of Moses obtaining water by striking a rock with his rod. This may have been a divining-rod used by Moses, similar to what water-diviners use today to find water. On another occasion Mithra fasted and was tempted by the Devil.

As happened with all the other saviour-gods, stories and legends associated with the sun or vegetation, or both, gradually wove themselves round his name. He became known as the Light of Heaven, The Light of the World and The Lord of Luminous Space. He was given the name of Mithra, which is derived from Mirr, the Persian for the sun. In other places he is called The Lord of Wide Pastures, which suggests that, like other gods, he was associated both with the sun and with vegetation. Besides these terms his worshippers called him The God of Truth and Faith and The True One, and looked on him as co-equal with the Supreme Deity. Like Osiris, he was judge of the underworld. He was the god of battles, swift to assail and slay all enemies of truth. He was known as The Supreme God, and also as The Logos and Incarnate Word. He was termed The Mediator, and also The Saviour and Redeemer. He was believed to be The Son of the Most High, and The Preserver of Mankind from Satan. He was known as The Alpha and The Omega, The First and The Last, The Maker and Father of All

Things, and The Creator of the World. Other terms of worship were The Lamb of God, The Lord and Father, The Lord of All, God of the Skies, The Purity of The Eternal Light, King of Glory, The Son of Justice, The God of Strength, The Father of The Ages to Come, The Angel of Great Council, The Good Shepherd, The Most Beloved by Men, and The Lamb Slain for the Sins of The World.

In the early days of his worship he was ranked lower than the great Persian God Ormazd, but by the time of Darius, in the 5th century B.C., he held equal place with the older god. In the 4th century B.C. the beliefs of Mithraism were much the same as those which were brought to Rome. After the incorporation of Mithraism with the philosophy of Zoroaster, Mithra became the second member of the Persian Trinity, and then we find him coming more and more to the front. Ormazd, on the other hand, gradually took second place, as happened with Rā and Jehovah. This also happened to Indra, as we shall find when we come to the beliefs surrounding Krishna. Just as Christianity borrowed from previous religions, so did Mithraism, and we can trace without difficulty what the Persians borrowed from Egypt and Babylon.

All the saviour-god religions interchanged their ideas. One cannot go back and say that here originated this belief and here originated that. What took place at the beginning of the Christian era, with regard to Jesus, likewise took place in the earlier centuries. The borrowing process which went on then, and which ultimately produced the Christian religion, took place in every instance, and so ideas were passed on from one religion to another. The gods changed their names, but the beliefs which surrounded a new god were just those which surrounded the old ones.

Bel in Babylon gave place to Murdock, who took over all the beliefs surrounding Bel, and when the Greeks went to Egypt they borrowed the beliefs surrounding Osiris and draped them round a new god, whom they called Serapis. Each god had his day, but the beliefs, being intimately related to man's death and resurrection to a less material existence, remained, and were carried on from age to age. After a sacrificial, or martyred, victim, who had impressed the people with his words or deeds, reappeared, the cloak of many colours, made up of myths and legends, was lifted from off his predecessor and laid on his shoulders.

Mithra was hailed as The Rising Sun and each morning special prayers were offered for his return. Just as the sun sinks into the darkness of night, so it was believed that Mithra after death went to Hades to reappear and ascend to Heaven. What we now call Sunday was the day on which he was specially worshipped as the Lord of Light. Long before the Christian era Sunday was a holy day, and, to the worshippers of Mithra, it was known as "The Lord's Day". Mithra was born at Christmas, and his birthday was celebrated as a festival, because on this day the sun enters the winter solstice. Easter, the day the sun enters the vernal equinox, was celebrated as the date of his sacrifice and resurrection. At Easter certain formalities and ceremonies took place and his body, imaged in his likeness, was laid in a rock tomb. When his followers returned to the tomb they could not find it, and so mourned for the lost god. When the body was found some days later the people rejoiced, the priest announcing "Be of good courage, you have been initiated into the mysteries, and you shall have salvation from your sorrows".

This again is symbolism, drawn from the sun being out of sight at night, and then returning in the morning, when the people rejoice at the new day. Vegetation is also apparently lost during the Winter and returns in the Spring. Thus, by associating Mithra with the sun and vegetation his worshippers received all the elevation in thought they were mentally capable of appreciating, as to them the sun represented the creator, the very life of the universe. Its setting and rising represented death and resurrection, and quite possibly, from its going and coming, there also arose the belief that the Saviour would return to earth.

The Mithraists believed in happiness in heaven for all believers after death, and that they had been saved through the death and resurrection of Mithra, who was worshipped as a humane and beneficent god. After death they anticipated that the human spirit, which had been separated from God by sin, would be re-united through the propitiatory power of Mithra. They symbolised this reunion by saying that they would each receive a Crown of Glory. The rites and ceremonies performed by the worshippers of Mithra were, for all practical purposes, the same as have been preserved by the Christian religion. Admission to his Church was obtained through baptism by water, and his death and resurrection were kept in remembrance by the celebration of the Eucharist.

Justin, one of the Christian fathers, who was just as foolish in the things he wrote as the other early Church worthies, after describing the institution of the Christian Eucharist remarks, "which the wicked devils have imitated in the mysteries of Mithra, commanding the same thing to be done". Tertullian, another Christian father, remarked that "the Devil, by the mysteries of his idols, imitates even the main parts of the Divine mysteries. He also baptises his worshippers in water and makes them believe that this purifies them of their crimes. There Mithra sets his mark on the forehead of his soldiers, he celebrates the oblation of bread, he offers an image of the resurrection. The Devil has gone about to apply to the worship of idols those very things in which consists the administration of Christ's sacrament".

Paul also shows his annoyance towards the Mithraists when he remarks, "But I say, that the things which the Gentiles sacrifice, they sacrifice to devils, and not to God : and I would not that ye should have fellowship with devils. Ye cannot drink the cup of the Lord, and the cup of devils : ye cannot partake of the table of the Lord, and of the table of devils". (1 Cor. x, 20.) When it is remembered that Paul and all other Christian apologists were waging a bitter war against Mithra, the expressions they use can be understood, but we are not permitted to know what the Mithraists thought of the Christians, as all their literature was destroyed.

One thing Paul, Justin and Tertullian make clear is the similarity between the Christian and the Mithraic ceremonies and, as it is well known that the Mithraic Eucharist is hundreds of years older than the Christian

Eucharist, the only conclusion to draw from this is that the Christians, in the first place, copied from the Mithraists. The mark on the forehead, referred to by Tertullian, refers to the ancient Mithraic practice of marking on the forehead of the Initiate the form of the cross, and this is still done figuratively in Christian churches at baptism. The Mithraic use of the symbol of the cross is confirmed by the discovery of a bas-relief representing the Mithraic sacrament. On a small tripod is to be seen the bread in the form of wafers, each marked with a cross. A photograph of this will be found in *Les Mystères de Mithra* by Professor Franz Cumont.

Sir James Frazer, in his monumental work of twelve volumes *The Golden Bough*, makes the following comment on what we have just been considering : "Among the gods of eastern origin who, in the decline of the ancient world, competed against each other for the allegiance of the West was the old Persian deity Mithra. The immense popularity of his worship is attested by the monuments, illustrative of it, which have been found scattered in profusion all over the Roman Empire. In respect both of doctrines and of rites the cult of Mithra appears to have presented many points of resemblance to Christianity. The similarity struck the Christians themselves, and was explained by them as a work of the devil who sought to seduce the souls of men from the true faith by a false and insidious imitation of it. However that may be, there can be no doubt that the Mithraic religion proved a formidable rival to Christianity, combining as it did a solemn ritual with aspirations after moral purity, and a hope of immortality. Indeed, the issue of the conflict between the two faiths appears for a time to have hung in the balance."

From Mithraism, Christianity borrowed the festival of Christmas and also its ritual surrounding the nativity. The Mithraists retired into an inner shrine from which at midnight they issued with a loud cry, "The virgin has brought forth ! The light is waxing !" Mithra, it was believed, was born the son of a virgin mother on the 25th day of December. She was known as the Heavenly virgin. For some centuries the Christian Church made no celebration of the birthday of its Saviour. At the beginning of the fourth century the Western Church adopted the 25th day of December as the birthday of Jesus and in 375 the Eastern Church did likewise.

The reason why the 25th of December was adopted is best given in the words of a Syrian Christian of the time who has left a record of it in writing as follows : "It was a custom of the heathen to celebrate on the 25th day of December the birthday of the sun, at which they kindled lights in token of festivity. In these solemnities and festivities the Christians also took part. Accordingly, when the doctors of the Church perceived that the Christians had a leaning to this festival, they took counsel and resolved that the true nativity should be solemnised on that day". Augustine exhorted his fellow Christians not to celebrate the birthday of Jesus on the 25th December because of the birthday of the sun but on account of him who made the sun.

Likewise, because the "heathen" observed Easter to celebrate the rising from the dead of Adonis, Mithra and other saviour-gods, so the Christian Church adopted the same date for its celebrations in connection with the death and resurrection of Jesus. In this connection Sir James Frazer remarks : "Taken altogether the coincidences of the Christian with the heathen festivals are too close and too numerous to be accidental. They mark the compromise which the Church, in the hour of its triumph, was compelled to make with its vanquished and yet still dangerous rivals", which exemplifies what has already been pointed out, that each new religion copied from the one which preceded it.

There is really nothing new in any of the saviour-god religions, in fact, under different names, the Christian religion goes back to the beginning of the worship of saviour-gods. As the belief in saviour-gods developed out of the belief in human sacrifice, so Christianity can be traced back to the beginning of sacrifice. As its legends and stories were taken from the earlier religions, and as these were associated with the sun and vegetation, so we can trace Christianity back to the days of nature worship when everything on earth and in the heavens was believed to be animated by a god or a spirit.

The following is taken from fragments of the Mithraic ritual which have been discovered.

How hast thou come to us, thou Holy One from that decaying world into this undecaying one,

are words which are supposed to be addressed by some heavenly being to a new arrival from earth ; and again we read,

Gladly pass the souls of the righteous to the Golden Seat, the abode of all other Holy Beings.

As to the godly man who has been cleansed, the wicked evil-doing Daevas (Devils) tremble at the perfume of his soul after death as doth a sheep on which a wolf is pouncing.

The souls of the righteous are gathered together there.

He has gained nothing who has not gained his soul.

He shall not gain a place in Paradise who has not gained his soul.

Mithra, it was believed, was born in a cave, which is the kind of birthplace in which two Christian fathers, Justin and Origen, say that Jesus was born, and, at his birth, shepherds came to offer him presents. Many of the ceremonials now in use in the Christian Church were taken from Mithraic worship, in fact this was the source from which it took its rites and ceremonials, and its priests their vestments. As John M. Robertson remarks in his able review of this religion in his book, *Pagan Christs*, "the higher mysteries of communion, divine sacrifice and resurrection, as we have seen, were as much Mithraic as Christian. So that a Mithraist could turn to the Christian worship and find his main rites unimpaired".

Mithra is represented as carrying a lamb on his shoulders, and the Mithraic places of worship faced towards the East. The Mithraist believed in Purgatory, which must have been taken over by the Christians, since nowhere in the gospels or epistles is such a place mentioned. The mother of Mithra was honoured by the Mithraists in the same way as other religions honoured the virgin mothers of their virgin born gods. The ecclesiastical structure of the Catholic Church was based on that of the Mithraic Church. The Mithraic Pope, the Father of the Mysteries and the Father of the Fathers, had his seat at Rome. Where St. Peter's now stands was a Mithraic temple, and there also it is believed the Pope had his residence. A number of the ancient legends which are associated with the early Christian Church are obviously of Mithraic origin.

The special interest that this religion has for us is that we know that it was the accepted faith in Persia from 500 B.C. onwards, that it was brought to Rome seventy years before the Christian era and lived side by side with the Christian Faith. First of all it was its superior, to become later on its equal, and finally to be absorbed by it owing to the fact that Constantine was more attracted by the claims made by the Christians than by those made by the Mithraists. This is not the place to consider this side of the question as here we are only concerned with the beliefs of its worshippers, but later on, when we come to the 4th century A.D., I shall have more to say as to the causes which brought about the absorption of an older religion by one of younger growth. In the chapter which follows we shall also read more about this Persian saviour-god when we consider the ceremonials surrounding the Mystery Cults.

I have kept for the last, one of the most interesting accounts of the life and death of a saviour-god. It is especially interesting because the beliefs surrounding him are still held by millions inhabiting the earth at the present time. Of the many saviour-god religions this one and Christianity are the only two of any importance which now remain. What follows does not refer to some insignificant cult of some little known people, but to the Saviour of a religion embracing one hundred and forty million worshippers, who look up to him for salvation as fervently as does the Christian to Christ.

We now cross over from Persia to India, to the home of mysticism, the garden of religion. In this great country, where mystical speculation has had such free play, we find a story of the Hindu saviour-god which supplied Christianity with many of its legends and ideas. For that reason it must be included in this chapter devoted to the relations of the Christian Faith. What I have to relate is

THE STORY OF THE SAVIOUR-GOD KRISHNA.

He succeeded the god Indra in the affections of the people. Just as Indra declined, so Krishna rose in their esteem. Before, however, considering the beliefs surrounding Krishna, let me briefly refer to those held regarding Indra, who, in his time, was one of the great deities of India.

Indra, it was believed, suffered death as a victim by crucifixion, more than 1500 years B.C., and his death on the cross is still celebrated in Tibet and Nepal. There, it is the custom in the month of August to raise to his honour crosses wreathed with abrotonus and to represent him as crucified, with his hands and feet pierced and the foreheard bearing a mark. This crucified figure is still carried about certain towns and villages in those parts. We must therefore assume that this god, who lived several thousand years ago as a man, died the death of a sacrificial victim. He re-appeared after death and ascended to heaven. This is all that we can gather about his life and death. What follows is the sequence.

Because of this reappearance he was looked upon as the saviour of his people since he had broken the curse of death. Marvellous stories were told about his birth. His mother was a virgin and it was believed that he had descended from heaven to incarnate on earth for the purpose of taking the punishment which the gods had inflicted on mankind. Because of his reappearance, which turned him into a god in the eyes of his worshippers, it was believed that he lived as a god-man on earth. He led a life of strict celibacy, taught the virtues, and stressed the necessity of holiness. Towards all living things he showed kindness and tenderness. He could walk upon the water and be carried through the air. He had the power of telling future events with great accuracy. He practised the most devout contemplation and disciplined both his body and mind. Thus he acquired complete subjection of his passions. He was worshipped as a god who had existed as a spirit from all eternity, and his immediate followers were termed "Heavenly teachers".

This much-beloved god, who gave and received love, was also, like so many others, represented as slaying the serpent of evil. At one time he had a large following in India, but gradually, just as happened with other gods, the people gave up their old love for a new one. In the case of Indra, he declined in the affection of the people, as his rival Krishna increased, and so we find today that Indra is now a little known god while Krishna is still the much-beloved god of that widespread religion known as Hinduism.

We have to go back a long way to find the source of the myths and legends which have come to surround Krishna, and even when we have got there we know that there are sources further back from which the compilers obtained their ideas. At least 1000 years B.C. a child was born at Mathura between Delhi and Agra. He came to be known as Krishna and it was believed that he was a prince invincible in love and war. He died and reappeared. In consequence he became, in the eyes of his followers, a god who fought against evil, and the representative of all that was good. Unfortunately the Indian climate is such that papyri cannot be long preserved, with the result that the sources of our information are copies of many previous copies, whereas in Egypt we have the well-preserved hieroglyphics and in Babylon the indelible writings on tablets of clay.

The sources of Krishnaism are first the Mahabhârata, a great epic poem, the events of which were laid long anterior to our era. Many of its contents probably relate to beliefs before the time of Buddha, who lived in the fifth century before the Christian era. Another source is the Bhagavat Gitâ, or Song of the Most High, one of the masterpieces of Indian literature, and lastly, the tenth book of the Puranas, a great work of legendary tales and theological literature comprising the entire Krishna saga. Besides this literature one finds all over India religious sculptures and monuments illustrating the beliefs of the people.

In outline the legend about this god is as follows. A couple named Vasudeva and Devaki were his parents. They lived at Mathura, referred to in one of the early non-canonical gospels as the place where Joseph and Mary took Jesus to escape from the massacre of the infants by Herod. On the night of his birth they had to remove Krishna beyond the reach of his uncle, King Kamsa, who sought his life, because the king had been warned by a voice from heaven that this son of Devaki would put him to death. Krishna escaped, but many other children of a tender age were killed by the king in his cruel attempt to safeguard his throne. This is an ancient legend, and is attached to the birth story of other god-men. It is perhaps symbolic of the seed that is scattered, much of which dies and never fructifies, and of the sun which kills the stars by its brilliance.

Krishna was conveyed by his parents across a river and put under the care of a shepherd called Nanda and his wife Yacoda. There, with his brother, he was brought up in the woods as their son. The two brothers grew up and became valiant men, slaying monsters and spending their time with the female cowherds. These scenes of his birth and infancy became in the course of time the most celebrated centres of his worship.

When adolescence was reached the two brothers put to death King Kamsa, their persecutor, and Krishna became king in his place. He continued to clear the land of great beasts, waged war against wicked kings, and performed other noble deeds. He transferred the seat of his government to the city of Dvaraka, the site of which has since been located. There he was overtaken by catastrophe. His brother perished and then he himself was wounded in the heel, like Achilles, by the arrow of a hunter, from which wound he died. The piercing of the heel or side of a saviour-god is a relic from human sacrifice on the altar, when the priest pierced the victim so as to release his spirit for the gods.

How much of all this is true and how much is

false no one can say, at least the Hindus declare it to be just legend and not part of their beliefs. They no more believe that Krishna was a murderer than Christians believe that Jesus was, because *The First Gospel of the Infancy of Jesus Christ*, published in the 2nd century A.D., tells us how he killed a boy who had annoyed him. This legend about Krishna may be just a story about the sun, woven round the name of Krishna when he came to be looked upon as a god. King Kamsa can be interpreted as the god of darkness killed by the god of light, or the god of evil killed by the god of good. The story of Krishna being valorous in love and war can likewise be applied to the sun on a calm summer day and in a thunder-storm.

What, however, is interesting are the developments from the belief that Krishna reappeared after his death. The legends came later, as they always did. He evidently died as a sacrificial victim, or as a martyr, because, from the time of his reappearance, stories began to grow round his name. Hindus have told me that they believe that he was crucified for their sins. This, they tell me, is part of their belief, but I can find no confirmation of it anywhere.

The stories surrounding Krishna are so like those which surround Jesus, that Christian missionaries, when they went to India in the eighteenth century, very naturally thought that they had been copied from the Christian gospels. This question has, however, received very careful consideration from expert Sanskrit scholars, but no evidence has come to light to make them think that this occurred. John M. Robertson, so well known for his work on Comparative Religion, weighs up the whole problem in his book

Christianity and Mythology, considering every side of the question and the opinions of all the leading authorities. His conclusion is that "His name and story were current in India long before the Christian legends, as such, were heard of, and the series of mutually supporting testimonies puts this beyond doubt", and "that the most conservative Sanskrit scholarship on the Continent, not only admits, but insists on the pre-Christian character of the Krishna myths".

This being the case let me now tell the story of the earth life of this much-beloved Hindu saviour-god, as it is recorded in their sacred literature. His birth was miraculously foretold. He was born the son of a virgin mother named Devaki, which means divine lady, and yet he is given a human father. His mother was a pious woman, who was overshadowed by a god when an angelic voice said, "In thy delivery, O favoured amongst women, all nations shall have cause to rejoice". Like the mother of Jesus she had a special woman friend. Both the mother of Krishna and her friend went through the rites of purification before the expected child of each was born. Devaki had other children besides Krishna.

At his birth there was great rejoicing in heaven and on earth. A choir of angels sang praises to the new-born Saviour. He was placed in a manger amongst cattle and was visited at his birth by wise men, who brought him valuable gifts. Shepherds also visited the new-born child. He was hailed as the God of Gods, The Holy One and The Living God. An angel warned his father that a tyrannical king was about to kill his son, and to escape from this the parents took the child away from Mathura across a river, the waters of which parted to permit them to pass on dry ground. It is claimed that he was born under the star Rohini, and from calculations made, his birthday was about the 25th December, a favourite birthday for saviour-gods, as on this date the new year is born, the days begin to lengthen and the sun to strengthen. What better day could the ancients have chosen to celebrate the coming to earth of the one "who brought immortality to light"?

From infancy he was a child prodigy. Even his bath water had miraculous power. At birth he stood up and declared himself to be the Son of God. This story is also told of Jesus in the *First Gospel of the Infancy of Jesus Christ*. I shall be referring to this gospel in Chapter VII, when I shall give certain extracts. Those things, which were told of Jesus as a child, were also reported of Krishna, which makes scholars believe that this gospel, relating to the doings of the child Jesus, is a copy of the stories which were written about Krishna.

Before his mission Krishna had a fore-runner. As a child he disputed and argued with his teachers and was blessed by an aged saint who remarked that he could now die in peace as he had seen the Saviour of the world. He was lost and his parents looked for him. He preached a sermon on moral precepts, went from place to place, talking in parables, healing the sick, casting out devils, and was often engaged in prayer and fasting. He could remove sin and disease by a look. He went into the wilderness to contemplate and was there tempted by the Devil, whom he overcame. Therefore he is represented as crushing the serpent under his feet. He is also portrayed as a child in the arms of his mother. This representation of a suckling child and his mother appears in other religions and is symbolic of the earth producing life. We also have Krishna pictured as being carried across a river, which is similar to the legend we have of Saint Christopher carrying the child Jesus across a river.

At times Krishna called himself divine and at others he claimed to be human, just as did Jesus. He was baptised in the Ganges, when the Holy Spirit descended upon him. He claimed to have come from heaven to suffer for the sins of mankind, saying on one occasion, "I am come to reject evil and restore the reign of good, to redeem man from the consequence of the fall and deliver the oppressed earth from its load of sin and suffering". He performed many miracles, one of the first being the cure of a leper, and we are told that, "Wherever he went he was moved with compassion for the down-trodden and the suffering".

On one occasion he was responsible for a miraculous catch of fishes and on another he went up to a fig tree and said, "Blessed are those that bear pain themselves and show kindness to others". We are told that he healed all manner of diseases, cast out devils and raised the dead. He was looked upon as the Messiah and the son of God. He said that he had come to save sinners and cried out, "I am the resurrection and the way to the Father", and again, on another occasion, "I will deliver thee from sin, have faith in me". Turning to a follower, he said, "I am animated with equal benevolence towards all beings, no one who worships me can perish. Those who love me are in me and I in them." On another occasion he said, "Those who love me shall never suffer death", and once, when his disciples rebuked him because of his friendship with sinners, he replied, "My law is a law of mercy to all". He lived the life of a god-man who had come from heaven to suffer voluntarily for the sins of humanity.

Krishna went about from place to place gaining converts and had many followers who were attracted by his miracles and preaching. "This is indeed the Redeemer promised to our fathers", they cried aloud when following him. He could read the thoughts of the people. He criticised the orthodox religious teaching of his day, advocated its reform and criticised the priesthood. Consequently he had enemies who conspired against him. He lived a life of purity, tenderness, holiness, meekness, humility and poverty ; he denounced riches and never married. He preached mercy, philanthropy, the coming Kingdom of God, the need of repentance and prophesied wars and rumours of wars. Krishna associated with sinners and the poor ; in one case a poor widow received especial attention, while another time he conversed with a woman at a well. He was transfigured, appearing with a "face like the moon and wearing a diadem", and assured his disciples that "Present or absent I am always with you", to which they replied, "Indeed thou art the Son of God". He sent his twelve disciples on a mission to preach the gospel and gave them power to forgive sins, to perform miracles, to cure the lame, the blind and the sick, handle poisonous reptiles, swallow deadly poison, eject devils and raise the dead.

The most pertinent saying of Krishna is to be found in the Bhagavat Gîtâ and reads as follows :

Although I am Lord of all created beings, I am made evident by my own power, and as often as there is a decline of virtue and an insurrection of vice and injustice in the world,

I made myself evident. Thus I appear from age to age for the preservation of the just, the destruction of the wicked and the establishment of virtue. I am animated with equal benevolence towards all beings, I know neither hatred nor predilection ; but those who adore me devoutly are in me, and I in them. Even he who has sinned, if he adore me only, is reputed virtuous. He will immediately have a just soul and obtain eternal peace. Have faith in me. No one who worships me can perish. Forgetting all else, address thyself to me. I will deliver thee from all sin.

Krishna, we are told, went to a city during his wanderings, followed by the multitude who scattered palm leaves before him. He entered it as a king in royal apparel. He was met by a deformed woman, who anointed him with oil. He cured her and said that what she had done for him would never be forgotten. On another occasion Krishna restored the son of a widow to life, and the method he adopted is reported as follows : "And Krishna laid hold of the dead man's hands and said 'Arise' and by the will of the Almighty the dead man immediately arose". To show his humility he washed the feet of those present.

At another time he was anointed with oil by a woman, and when his disciples objected to the waste, he replied "Better is a little given with a humble hand than much given with great ostentation". He submitted to insults and injuries without reply and forgave all his enemies. He had a supper with his disciples before he died and had one special disciple whom he greatly loved. Before his death he went to the bank of the river Ganges, performed three ablutions and then knelt down and prayed to Brahma. The treasurer, who carried the bag with the money, turned out to be a traitor.

Krishna claimed to be one with his father in Heaven and lived the life of a mystic, a healer and a moralist. He was put to death by wicked hands and died, pierced by arrows, with the prayer on his lips, "Father, forgive them for their ignorance". At the time of his death the sky became black and the earth was convulsed. His body was thrown upon a pyre, where it was burned. Two women followers threw themselves on the pyre. The people present declared that when death came to their Saviour they saw his spirit ascending to heaven and that the spirits of the two women were seen accompanying him to glory. This was taken as a sign from heaven to mean that the prophecy that he had made before death, that he must die before his sayings would be believed, had been fulfilled, because he had thus proved to all his saving power.

He descended to Hades to help the dead and then reappeared to his disciples as a spirit "in all his divine majesty". This reappearance is commemorated by a special festival. He was then seen to ascend to heaven in the presence of many people. From that time onwards he was looked upon as a reincarnation of the god Vishnu and so became the second member of the Hindu Trinity, comprising Brahma, Krishna and Siva. He was honoured as one of the highest amongst the gods, as one who had become incarnate to suffer for the transgressions of humanity. These beliefs, which I have related, were the subjects of dramatic representation on the Hindu stage.

The second coming of Krishna, when the millennium is expected to commence, is awaited by all Hindus, and their sacred literature tells us that "He shall come crowned with lights and the heavens and the earth shall be joyous, the stars shall pale before his splendour, the earth will be too small to contain him, for he is infinite, he is almighty, he is wisdom, he is beauty, he is all in all to all men. All animated beings, beasts, birds, trees and plants will chant his praises. He will regenerate all bodies and purify all souls. He will be as sweet as honey and ambrosia, and as pure as a lamb, without spot, and as the lips of a virgin. All hearts shall be transported with joy. From the rising to the setting of the sun it will be a day of joy and exultation, when our God will manifest his power and his glory and reconcile the world to himself".

This anticipation of the coming day of gladness, combined with the belief that Krishna has gone before to prepare the way, has been the means of bringing untold comfort to countless millions who found the road of life heavy and the burden hard to bear. For them Krishna has borne their sorrows and been their friend and comforter on their weary pilgrimage from the cradle to the grave. On the other hand, the creeds, dogmas and doctrines which have been woven round his name have been the cause of sects, divisions, disunion and the accompanying intolerance which such things always bring in their train.

The Hindu religion is based on salvation by faith in the doctrine that Krishna came to save the world from sin. The worship of Krishna is one of the most popular of the many faiths in India and has been so since long before the Christian era. Sir William Jones, in his great work *Asiatic Researches*, published at the end of the eighteenth century, remarks that, "The name of Krishna and the general outline of his story were long anterior to the birth of our Saviour and probably to the time of Homer (850 B.C.) we know very certainly. In the Sanskrit dictionary, compiled more than two thousand years ago, we have the whole history of this incarnate deity".

We know that communication existed between India and Egypt and it is probable that these two countries exchanged religious ideas in the pre-Christian era. In fact, it is quite reasonable to believe that the pre-Christian beliefs in saviour-gods, prevalent in Egypt, Persia, India and Babylonia, were moulded by the exchange of thought between these countries in the same way as Greece fashioned its saviour-gods on what is learned from them. We know that Buddhism evolved out of Brahminism, copying also from Krishnaism, and that borrowing from one country by another was a very common practice in these days, especially after the conquests by Alexander the Great, when he established everywhere a common Greek language which made easy the interchange of thought.

Let me in conclusion summarise some of the beliefs and doctrines of this religion. The fallen and degenerate of the human race can only be raised by the realisation that sin is atoned for by the death of Krishna, who is the incarnate Saviour of man, the Redeemer and the Shepherd of the Flock. He was, and still is, believed to have been the creator of the world, to have been from all time, and to have brought everlasting life or immortality to mankind. He is the light of the world and the dispenser of grace, the beginning, the middle and the end, the son of righteousness, the all and in all, a being without sin, whose mission was to deliver the world from sin. He came as the Lord from Heaven to destroy the Devil and his works. He is omnipotent and omniscient, the Lord of Lords, who embodied all the power and the wisdom of God. All power was committed to him and he had the keys of death.

The doctrine taught by the priesthood includes punishment in Hell for all unbelievers, where there is a never dying worm, and where the Devil makes free use of brimstone and other inflammable substances. Heaven with Krishna is reserved for believers. The Hindu Heaven corresponds with Christian beliefs, including a belief in Purgatory and a great and final day of judgement, when there will be a general resurrection, presided over by Krishna, the judge of the dead. The dimensions of the Holy City are also given.

The followers of Krishna are taught to strive against sin and to believe that for each sin there should be repentance. All believers at death reach a beautiful city, which constitutes Paradise, and they are told that here on earth there is no continuing city. The spirits of the dead are carried to heaven by angels, and it is believed that there are good and fallen angels, that evil spirits obsess people, and that sickness and disease are caused by evil spirits. Great stress is laid on sin, and we find in the sacred books of this religion discussions on the doctrine of free will and predestination. The Devil and evil spirits are the cause of all evil, but true believers are saints who receive white robes.

Here also we find reference to the Logos. God is personified as wisdom and is known by his works. Emphasis is laid on one supreme God, veneration for truth, the fact that where one's treasure is there the

heart is also, that as you seek you shall find, besides
other well-known maxims. The door of salvation is
open to all, but only through belief in Krishna is
salvation possible. We find reference to the blind
leading the blind, a new heaven and a new earth,
Living Water, Baptism, Fasting, and Krishna now
taking the place of sacrifice. As Hinduism has always
had an organised priesthood, we are not surprised to
find that everything contrary to the foregoing is
blasphemy.

The Hindus revere what is equivalent to our Bible,
which has an Old and New Testament, the latter advocating a new and reformed system of religion. They
believe that all scripture is given by inspiration from
God and that their writings are the work of inspired
men. Their Bible is supposed to contain all that is
necessary for life and salvation, and should be studied
from youth to old age. They also hold that all scripture
is profitable for doctrine and that their Bible is an
infallible guide for life and salvation. It teaches that to
be carnally minded is death, whereas the law of the
spirit is written on the heart, and God is within you.
Man is made up of body, spirit and mind. God dwells
in the heart of each one who is guided by the divine
law. Each can have the indwelling Comforter and
all must be born again. We, however, need not be
surprised at the similarity between all these tenets and
Christianity, as the psychic stream nourished both
religions. How they originated will be discovered
when we come to analyse the beliefs surrounding
Jesus the Christ.

The Hindu Bible teaches that there is only one
supreme God, who is Brahma, and that Krishna is his

son. It then tells us that etheric matters are incomprehensible to the natural man, although stressing the fact that each one of us is an etheric being. Self denial is taught, and also the duty of renouncing the pleasures of this world so as to enjoy in full those of the world to come. Withdrawal, or seclusion from society, and that bodily suffering benefits the spirit, are also taught, as is voluntary suffering for righteousness' sake. Earthly pleasures are regarded as evil and the greater the cross so the greater is the crown. The spirit is more than the body and retirement for religious contemplation is advocated. Spiritual relationship is superior to that of earth relationship and the forsaking of relations, if they encumber the spirit, is advocated. The road to heaven is a narrow one, but to die is great gain. The subjugation of the passions is necessary. Faith is extolled and heresy is one of the greatest of sins.

No occasion should be lost to confess the redeeming power of the Saviour. Belief in the creeds of Hinduism is all important for salvation, and unbelievers are the chief of sinners. Faith can remove mountains, but it must be accompanied by works. Private or secret prayer is recommended, and so much stress is laid on this that one would say that the maxim is to pray without ceasing, in sickness and in health and also for the departed. All enemies must be treated kindly and all injuries accepted passively. Enemies must be prayed for, fed and loved.

The Kingdom of Heaven is to be sought before all else, to love God is the first obligation, and to worship God is an essential in the life of everyone. Cease to do evil and learn to do good is an essential precept. Each one should have an inward knowledge of God but must not rely on works for salvation. Each must be pure of heart, speak and think no evil and love every living thing. All must live lives of virtue, moderation and temperance, show patience, control the thoughts, practise charity and take special care of the poor.

The faithful must be hospitable to each other, humble and pure, not indulging in light conversation. Almsgiving is a virtue and it is more blessed to give than to receive. Respect for those in power is enjoined and each one must honour his father and mother. Children must be brought up in the knowledge of the scripture. Chastity is essential, while lying and falsehood are amongst the worst of sins. To swear or steal is condemned and so also is war. Slavery, drunkenness, covetousness, adultery and fornication are heinous transgressions. Anger must be avoided and the passions controlled.

The foregoing is a brief outline of the beliefs held by the Hindus, but there are many precepts, believed to have been uttered by Krishna, which cannot be abbreviated and should be read as they have come down to us. What follows is taken from the selection made by Kersey Graves, who collected all the sayings he could find which are attributed to the Hindu Saviour. The following are only a few out of hundreds which he collected :

Those who do not control their passions cannot act properly towards others.

The evils we inflict upon others follow us as our shadows follow our bodies.

Only the humble are beloved of God.

Virtue sustains the spirit as the muscles sustain the body.

When the poor man knocks at your door take him in and administer to his wants, for the poor are the chosen of God.

Let your hand be always open to the unfortunate.

Look not upon a woman with unchaste desires.

Avoid envy, covetousness, falsehood, imposture, slander and sexual desires.

Above all things cultivate love for your neighbour.

When you die you leave your worldly wealth behind you, but your virtues and vices go with you.

Kill not, steal not, lie not, swear not, revenge not, avoid all impure words and never testify falsely.

Show mercy and sympathy to all living things and avoid all cruelty to men and animals.

Shun riches and worldly honour.

Seek the company of the wicked in order to reform them.

Do good for its own sake and expect not your reward for it on earth.

The mind is immortal, but must be pure and free from all sin and stain before it can return to him who gave it.

The mind is inclined to good when it follows the inward light. The mind is responsible to God for its actions and he has established rewards and punishments.

Cultivate that inner knowledge which teaches what is right and what is wrong.

Never take delight in another's misfortunes.

It is better to forgive an injury than to avenge it.

You can accomplish by kindness what you cannot do by force.

A noble spirit finds a cure for injustice by forgetting it.

Pardon the offences of others but not your own.

What you blame in others do not practise yourself.

By forgiving an enemy you make many friends.

Do right from hatred of evil and not from fear of punishment.

A wise man corrects his own errors by observing those of others.

He who rules his temper conquers his greatest enemy.

The wise man governs his passions but the fool obeys them.

Be at war with men's vices but at peace with their persons.

There should be no disagreement between your lives and your beliefs.

Spend every day as though it is your last on earth.

Lead not one life in public and another in private.

Anger in trying to torture others punishes itself.

A disgraceful death is honourable when you die in a good cause.

By growing familiar with vices we learn to tolerate them too easily.

We must master our evil propensities or they will master us.

He who conquers his passions rules over a kingdom.

Protect, love and assist others if you would serve God.

From thought springs the will and from the will the action, true or false, just or unjust.

As the sandal tree perfumes the axe which fells it, so the good man sheds fragrance on his enemies.

To love the virtues of others is to brighten your own.

Spend a portion of each day in quiet devotion.

He who gives to the needy loses nothing himself.

A good, wise and benevolent man cannot be rich.

Much riches is a curse to the possessor.

The wounds of the mind are more important than those of the body.

The virtuous man is like the banyan tree which shelters and protects all around it.

Money does not satisfy the love of gain but only stimulates it.

Your greatest enemy is in your own bosom.

To flee when charged is to confess your guilt.

The wounds of conscience leave a scar.

He who is cursed by a woman is cursed by God.

God will punish him who laughs at woman's suffering.

When woman is honoured God is honoured.

The virtuous woman will have but one husband and the right minded man but one wife.

It is the highest crime to take advantage of the weakness of a woman.

Women should be loved, respected and protected by husbands, fathers and brothers.

These moralisings bring the story of Krishna to an end, and with it I conclude this chapter regarding some of Christianity's most important relations. It would be wearisome to consider in detail the beliefs surrounding all the other known saviour-gods, as the same ideas run through them all. At least thirty saviour-gods are known to history, who were believed by their followers to have suffered death as a sacrifice for sin, and who were elevated by them to be godmen on earth and saviours and mediators in heaven.

What Bel, Osiris, Prometheus, Mithra and Krishna were to their worshippers so was Devatat to the Siamese. Æsculapius and Ixion were the saviours to those who worshipped them, just as was Thor to our Nordic ancestors, with his hammer, in the form of a cross, symbolically breaking the rock of sin. Hermes, with the cross as his symbol, was the Logos, and Hercules, after suffering death on a pyre, was seen to rise to heaven, as was Krishna. Quexalcote was the Christ to the Aztecs in Mexico, and died, so legend says, preaching against human sacrifice.

The Eucharist was celebrated in Mexico before the Christian era, with the same ceremonies and rites as accompanied the feast elsewhere. The Aztecs believed in transubstantiation and fasted before partaking of the body and blood of the sacrificed victim, using purgatives beforehand to ensure cleanliness inside the body. Prescott, in his *History of the Conquest of Mexico*, tells us that when the Spaniards landed in Mexico they found a religion very similar to Christianity. The people there were awaiting the return to earth of Quexalcote and thought that Cortez, the Spanish leader, was their long-awaited Saviour returned to earth.

In Mexico the Spaniards found an organised religious community with a dominating ecclesiastical organisation, on the same lines as in Europe. The people practised confession to the priests and did penance. They worshipped a trinity of gods and believed that their saviour-god, Quexalcote, was a virgin-born god who had died for their sins. At the Eucharist service of the Aztecs the invaders found that they could partake of it without noticing much difference between it and their own. Before their eyes was the cross, the sacred symbol of the Aztecs, and they were offered bread and wine, which had been consecrated by the priests who declared that they had turned it into the body and blood of the slain god.

With the same feelings they witnessed the ceremony of baptism, the infant being baptised and named as in the Christian Church. Prayers were said expressing the belief that the child, by becoming a member of the Aztec Church, through its baptism, would be cleansed of its natural sin, which had been handed down from the time of its first parents who had sinned. The Spaniards discovered that the Aztecs had their own story of the creation, the Garden of Eden, the Tower of Babel, the Flood, and of the Saviour who had come to redeem them from the wrath of God or the gods.

It is interesting to try to account for this great resemblance between the worship of Quexalcote and

Christ. Two explanations are possible. One is that the same causes which produced the saviour-god religions, in what is termed the old world, also produced the same beliefs in Mexico. Another is that the old world saviour-god religions found their way to Mexico by way of Greenland. Dr. W. J. Perry, in his book *Gods and Men*, analysed and tabulated the folklore of a North American Indian Tribe (The Pawnee), and discovered that its religious conceptions were founded on early Egyptian speculations. Not only was this the case, but he claims that in many outlying parts of the world, far remote from the original home of civilisation, the distinctive features of Egyptian belief are to be found in places where they can have had no intrinsic local significance.

However it came about that the Mexican people obtained their beliefs, the fact remains that the Christian missionaries, when they arrived in Mexico from Spain in the sixteenth century, were more than surprised to find such a similarity between their religion and that of the people they had conquered. Their surprise, however, was no greater than that of the Christian missionaries to India when they discovered the similarity between the beliefs of the Hindus and their own. The stories these missionaries from India and Mexico brought home to Europe so interested some scholars that a start was made in the science of Comparative Religion. The beliefs of all the world's religions have now been investigated and compared. This has proved that no one religion can claim to be the only revelation from God, or be in possession of the only Saviour of mankind, that the longings and aspirations of humanity are the same the world over, and that the psychic stream is responsible for all the religious beliefs of mankind.

Up to the beginning of the Christian era the people in all the countries surrounding Palestine had, for over two thousand years, been worshippers of saviour-gods. The Jews alone had withstood this influence and continued to sacrifice as of old, awaiting the one promised to their forefathers. In the pages which follow we shall find how the promise was fulfilled, but, in these concluding pages of this chapter, it is perhaps fitting to say that in view of our greater knowledge many false ideas must now be abandoned, including one still very prevalent, that all moralisings and injunctions for leading better and more virtuous lives came from Christianity.

In truth, Christianity is only a reflection of the great, noble and wise precepts which were uttered long before its birth by the sages, prophets and philosophers who lived in the centuries before the opening of the Christian era. In John's gospel (vii, 46) we are told that Jesus on one occasion was not arrested because the officers said that they could not do so owing to the fact that "Never man spake like this man". To this remark the Pharisees replied, "Are ye also led astray?" After a gap of nineteen hundred years we are now realising the meaning behind this answer. The ignorant soldiers did not know about the moralisings of the past as did the Pharisees.

Ignorance, of course, is behind most of the mistakes of the past, and ignorance leads to cruelty, bigotry and intolerance. Light gleamed into a dark and savage Christian world only when man developed sufficiently to admit that everyone had the right to investigate and express freely his own opinions. As this only came about in this country in the middle of last century there is little wonder that the great majority are still quite ignorant of ancient philosophic and ethical thought, and of the beliefs of other religions. Up till the middle of last century the laws of this country did not permit free investigation, or discussion, of subjects relating to the Christian religion, and thus the Church kept its power, and its followers their beliefs. Since the change came about the Church has been steadily losing its power and influence, because the people are learning the truth, and are now realising how they and their ancestors have been deluded by the preaching of false doctrines.

Everything contained in the Christian Faith is to be found in religions which were old before it was born. This was known to the early Church fathers, some of whom wrote about it quite openly. Eusebius, Bishop of Caesarea, born in Palestine in A.D. 265, and called the Father of Ecclesiastical History, when referring to the Therapeutæ, an ancient cult, wrote these words, "Those ancient Therapeutæ were Christians, and their writings were our gospels and epistles. The religion published by Jesus Christ to all nations is neither new nor strange", and expressed the view that what is called Christianity was borrowed from them.

Augustine, born in A.D. 354, probably the best known of all the Christian fathers, is equally definite on the subject. He wrote as follows; "For the thing itself which is now called the Christian religion was known to the ancients, and was not wanting at any time from the beginning of the human race until the time that Christ came in the flesh, from whence the true religion that had existed previously began to be called Christian, and this in our day is the Christian religion, not as having been wanting in former times but as having in later times received the name".

The beliefs delineated in the foregoing pages were preserved in the Mystery Cults, which will be considered in the next chapter. Thus throughout the first four centuries of the Christian era, the theologians, who were responsible for manufacturing the Christian faith out of the material within that great depository of religious knowledge, the Theological College at Alexandria, had ample data on which to work. There was nothing new for their imagination to invent as the beliefs and legends were all at hand and already accepted by the masses. They had only to make the most suitable selections of the legends of the past, and with these construct the story of the life of the new-found Messiah.

As one old belief after another was draped round the name of Jesus over the first four centuries of our era, so the new religion grew up in the likeness of the old. The age-old beliefs were hung on a new peg, called by a different name, and the educated people were quite familiar with the sources whence they came. They were not asked to change their beliefs, only the name of the god. This had happened before with other gods, who had evolved, in consequence of sacrificed victims appearing after death, and so it happened once again.

In concluding this chapter I should like to quote from what James H. Baxter, Professor of Ecclesiastical History at St. Andrews University, says in *Christianity in the Light of Modern Knowledge.*

Upon the popular interpretation and practice of Christianity, the effect of its establishment as the State religion had been profound. If Paganism had been destroyed, it was less through annihilation than through absorption. Almost all that was Pagan was carried over to survive under a Christian name. Deprived of demi-gods and heroes, men easily and half unconsciously invested a local martyr with their attributes, and labelled the local statue with his name, transferring to him the cult and mythology associated with the Pagan Deity. Before the fourth century was over the martyr-cult was universal. . . . Pagan festivals were adopted and renamed, and Christmas Day, the ancient festival of the sun, was transformed into the birthday of Jesus.

As time passed the sources from which the new religion was derived were forgotten, and, by the fifth century, Christianity assumed the character which it has since borne, the one and only revelation received from God, with its central figure, Jesus the Christ, as the Saviour, Mediator and Redeemer. How all this came about we shall discover in the chapters which follow.

CHAPTER IV.

CHRISTIANITY—ITS PARENTS.

THE saviour-gods, who received particular attention in the previous chapter, were, what might be termed, National Celebrities. In their day they each commanded the allegiance, respect and worship of a nation. Krishna is the spiritual ruler of the Hindus, Bel was of the Babylonians, Mithra of the Persians and Osiris of the Egyptians. Besides these, reference was made to other gods, who, in comparison with the others, were but minor potentates.

In the Graeco-Roman world there were also other saviour-gods who were worshipped with the same devotion as those about whom we have been reading. These were the gods of the Mystery Cults, who went under the names of Orpheus, Attis, Adonis and Dionysus. Mithra and Osiris, both national gods, as time went on, were also included under the gods of the Mystery Cults, as was Isis, the Egyptian goddess. So we find in Egypt, Greece and Rome the above-mentioned seven deities having their own particular worshippers who met together and, in the form of rites and ceremonies, perpetuated the memory of their love for mankind.

In cities like Athens, Rome, Antioch, Tarsus and Alexandria, these various religious communities lived together, each individual worshipping the god his parents had worshipped, or to whom he was especially attracted. As this was the form of religious thought prevalent at the time of the birth and development of the Christian religion, the beliefs, rites and ceremonies, surrounding the worship of these Mystery Cult gods, require our consideration.

We realise by now that there is nothing new in Christianity except its saviour-god, who was called Christ, by which name the new religion came to be known. This calling of old ideas by a new name could not have happened without a specific cause, which was the entrance of Jesus on the scene, who, without any intention on his part, became the central figure, and the much-beloved saviour-god, of those who heretofore had received their comfort and consolation through the rites and ceremonies performed by the Mystery Cults. What then was the cause which produced an effect, which effect produced the Christian religion ? Let me put it another way to make the matter even clearer.

Just as the Mystery Cults, of themselves, could not have produced the Christian religion, so Jesus, of himself, could not have done so either. Jesus was born and lived like other men. There was nothing about him personally which would make the people turn him into a god-man on earth, a god in heaven, change his name from Jesus to Christ, and make him the head cornerstone of a new religion.

Jesus had to be acted upon by some outside influence. He had to be picked up, so to speak, from amongst the crowd in the street, and given a unique position. People can become great in life in many ways, none of which Jesus pursued. During his life he was an ordinary individual like the rest of us. He did nothing to cause his posthumous greatness. He did not influence the imagination by being a great soldier, a great legislator or an outstanding philosopher, and, if he had been left to himself, he would have lived, died and been forgotten like the people amongst whom he was born.

We must, therefore, find the cause which brought Jesus to the notice of the people who were ready, with their already established beliefs, to accept the Christ when they were satisfied that this Christ conformed to their expectations. Nothing miraculous happened to produce the opinion that Jesus was the Christ. What happened had happened before, and the previous chapter is a record of similar transformation scenes. Jesus, like Krishna and the other saviour-gods, only became great after death.

Why, for example, did Krishna become a saviour-god? What was the cause of his being transformed from a man to a god? The answer we have already found to be his reappearance after death. But there are two other questions which we must ask, and, when these are correctly answered, we shall then have the whole case before us clear and distinct. The origin of the Christian Faith will then have been discovered, and every cause which brought it into being will be found to dovetail together to make a complete and finished picture.

Who killed Krishna? Why was Krishna killed? For that matter why were all the saviour-gods victims before their deification and who were their murderers? We have now advanced sufficiently in our study of the saviour-god religions to consider seriously these two questions, and when we have answered them, and then only, can we get down to the correct explanation of the origin of the Christian Faith, for which all the information so far brought together has been but a preparation.

We require an answer to four questions. If these are answered correctly, we have reached our goal. The first two questions as to who were the saviour-gods and why they were deified we answered in the previous chapter. The answer to the first was that they were human beings like ourselves. The answer to the second was because they appeared after death. Now we want to know how and why they met their deaths. With these four questions correctly answered we shall then be able to arrive at the origin of the Christian Faith.

Who, then, killed these men who reappeared after death, and so gave rise to all that came to surround their names? The answer is—The Priests. The next question which follows naturally, and to which we must find an answer, is—Why did the priests kill these men? The answer is—Because of fear of rivalry. This is not difficult to appreciate when we realise how important the priesthood had become in the eyes, not only of the people, but of the priests themselves. They were specially endowed for the purpose of performing the sacred rites to the gods, they alone knew their habits, wishes and peculiarities. Slowly prescriptions had arisen, customs and rituals had developed, and the priests, in their own estimation and in that of the people, had become the only bridge between earth and heaven.

The priests alone retained the divine traditions, they alone knew how to approach the gods, they alone could read the hidden signs, their pleasures and displeasures. They considered themselves sacred and so did the people. Without them no votary could approach the shrine, the place appointed for the priests and the gods to meet. Thus they rose in importance far above their origin. The holy office of priesthood became an established institution, and the more its members magnified their god, or gods, the more they magnified themselves. As the national gods increased in importance, the priesthood of each nation was intent on glorifying its own special god or gods, to the disadvantage of those of rival nations.

Uneasy always lies the head that wears the mitre, and the fear, always present in the minds of the great lest they fall, has always been present with the priesthood. Out of fear, the greatest of all human emotions, developed the saviour-god religions, as this chapter will make clear. On the one hand it was fear of man for man, on the other fear of man for the gods. The priests were jealous of their organisation and wished no rival. The people were afraid of death, which was a mystery, and which they believed ushered them into the presence of an angry god or a company of angry gods.

These two classes of fear were the parents of the Christian Faith. On the one hand it was fear by the priesthood, on the other it was fear by the people, combined with their natural religious emotions and the mystical tendencies of the human mind. Man's developing conscience, making him realise more clearly right from wrong, and his growing belief in his own unworthiness, increased his fear of punishment hereafter, just as the same cause increased his conviction of the gods hating wickedness.

The problem before us therefore resolves itself into this. Down the ages the people have been anxious as to the safety of their spirits after death. There was a natural demand and the priesthood was formed to meet it. The people wanted to keep on friendly terms with the gods and the priesthood undertook to supply the demand. It took as a slogan "Prepare to meet thy God", which always kept the flocks in mind of the necessity of an ecclesiastical organisation, and, moreover, the people were comforted with the thought that, if they did what the priests told them, all arrangements would be made in heaven for each believer meeting the gods on friendly terms when at death he was ushered into their presence.

So we find that some were always prepared to come forward to join the organisation which was formed to allay the natural fear of death in the minds of the people, and to help them to exercise their religious emotions. This huge expensive organisation, called the priesthood, which mankind has maintained down the ages, is one of the best and greatest arguments, apart from an actual psychic experience, in favour of the existence of a spirit in man that survives death. It is an argument based on first causes, and is such a potent one that one might say that in itself it is conclusive evidence of survival after death. The awareness of the spirit within each one produced priests, and so priests are the evidence of the existence of the spirit. If man had not possessed a spirit he would never have produced the priesthood. Each effect in life has a cause. The priesthood was the effect and the spirit in man was the cause.

The priests, being human like other people, very

naturally, once their organisation was started, resented interference by others outside the established order. They were naturally fearful lest the people should be led away into other channels of thought not represented by their organisation. So we have the priests, with their emotions on the one hand, and the people with theirs on the other. Both types were necessary to produce a saviour-god like Krishna, provided the soil was ready, and the seed, in the form of his appearance after death, was planted.

These two types of emotion were the parents of the Christian Faith, but before giving them specific attention let us turn our minds to the political and social history of the times in which they developed. If we do so we shall be in a much better position to understand how it was that the Christian Faith originated, grew and spread. In the pages which follow we shall make ourselves conversant with the conditions prevailing from

THE 4TH CENTURY B.C. TO THE 4th CENTURY A.D.

What I shall now try to do is to give a conspectus of the history of these eight centuries, the course of which had such an effect on the growth and evolution of the Christian religion.

What Philip of Macedonia dreamed and planned, his son, Alexander the Great, accomplished. Philip of Macedonia, who became king in 359 B.C., was a man of outstanding ability and foresight. He engaged Aristotle as the tutor of his son, who, in consequence, was educated in a way no young prince had ever been before. Philip's ambition was to conquer Persia and he built up an army for this purpose. However, he was murdered before his plan materialised, and, in the year 335 B.C., at the age of 21, Alexander took over the responsibilities carried by his father. Philip was a man of fearless courage and sound judgement, which his son inherited, besides being endowed by his mother with her savage energy and fierce superstition.

Equipped by his training, Alexander started his new career with knowledge of unprecedented value. He was a great soldier and, by adopting superior methods, managed to inflict heavy defeats on his enemies. He was, moreover, merciless towards his enemies and exceedingly vain. Without delay he started off on his conquests, bringing Greece to subjection by utterly destroying Thebes and massacring its inhabitants. As the Persians had command of the sea he started on his great journey of conquests by marching along the coast of Asia Minor, capturing port after port, until all the Persian sea bases were in his hands. In a great battle he destroyed the Persian host and then turned south, capturing Tyre and Sidon. Finally he reached Egypt in 332 B.C. Here he built the city of Alexandria, the principal building being the Serapeum, or Temple dedicated to Serapis, the name the Greeks gave to Osiris. Then he conceived the idea that he himself must be a god, as no human father could have produced such a being. He consulted the Egyptian priests and was very gratified to discover that he was no mere mortal but the virgin-born son of the god Rā-Amen, the producer of all the Pharaohs.

However, Darius, the King of Persia, was still at large, and in spite of his previous defeat, he again collected a great army which Alexander encountered at Nineveh in 331 B.C. on his way to India. Here Darius was defeated, and though he escaped he died soon afterwards. So Alexander marched on till he reached the river Indus and entered India. Having accomplished this he returned home, somewhat like Napoleon from Moscow, as his army was poorly clad and starving, but, unlike Napoleon, a conqueror and anxious for more lands to subdue.

He next turned his attention to Arabia, but before this invasion was undertaken he died in 323 B.C., after a debauch. He was only thirty-three and had reigned thirteen years. So ended the career of this cruel and ambitious man, who made slaughter his life-work, and yet he gave those he conquered their national liberty, and in no way tried to suppress them. After his death his empire broke up into four parts. Greece tried but failed to gain her freedom, and Egypt, under Ptolemy, one of Alexander's generals, assumed its old-time greatness. Thrace became a separate country and much of the old Persian Empire was taken over by Seleucus, another of Alexander's generals.

From now onwards the history of the world that interests us centres round five great cities, Jerusalem, Alexandria, Athens, Rome and Carthage. Ptolemy will always be remembered because, under him, Alexandria grew to rival all the other cities of her time. For three hundred years it was the centre of Greek culture and intellectual activity. Eastward it had a great overseas trade through the Red Sea with Arabia and India, and westward it was a great competitor of Carthage. Egypt was now well governed and Ptolemy decided that Alexandria should be the centre of all learning and knowledge. Greek had now become the established language of Egypt and the common language of the trader between East and West. From Palestine flocked large numbers of Jews, who settled in Alexandria and became so much a part of the rest of the community that their Book of the Law was translated into the Greek language. By 50 B.C. its population numbered three hundred thousand freemen and about the same number of slaves.

Behind the decision of Ptolemy to make Alexandria the centre of knowledge we can trace the mind of Aristotle, who must have influenced him when they were together at the Court of Philip of Macedonia. The Museum he set up in Alexandria was the first University in the world. He dedicated it to the service of the Muses, but, as in those days nothing in Egypt could be done without priests, it was a religiously endowed institution and this ultimately brought about its ruin. For the first hundred years or so knowledge accumulated, and men of erudition gathered in Alexandria to exchange views and make use of its great library.

Men like Euclid, the great mathematician; Eratosthenes, who measured the size of the earth, and found its diameter with an error of only fifty miles; Hipparchus, the first to map out the stars in the heavens; Hero, who devised the first steam engine; and Archimedes, one of the world's great inventors, found their way to Alexandria, as did Herophilus, the first anatomist; Aristarchus, the founder of the science of grammar, or correct speech and writing, and many other men who added lustre to their age. In 30 B.C. the city submitted to Augustus, though since 80 B.C.

it had been Roman in all but name. Here it was that
Julius Caesar, and then Anthony, found the fascination of Cleopatra irresistible.

During the reigns of Ptolemy I and II the original
idea remained, but after their time the University
passed into the hands of the priests, who turned the
seat of learning into a Theological College. Only the
library remained, to be destroyed by fire by the
Mohammedans in A.D. 630 because they believed that
the Koran contained everything worth knowing. So
ended this noble attempt to bring knowledge to mankind. While the University remained students came
from all parts, but these were comparatively few in
number. The great majority in every land was quite
ignorant, with no education, a prey to superstition,
priests, sorcerers and fortune-tellers. Diseases were
believed to be caused by devils. Miracles, worked by
magicians, were accepted as the acts of the gods, who
lived above a flat earth, round which the sun circled
each day.

To understand our subject we must get back to
this mental atmosphere. When we think of the lack
of communication prior to the establishment of the
Roman Empire, the difficulty with money, the danger
of robbers on land, of pirates at sea, and realise that
the nearest book shop was in Athens or Alexandria,
there is little wonder that few could read or write and
so spent their lives in mental darkness.

What is still called Religion flourished in this
abyss. Alexandria ceased producing knowledge and
became an exchange for religious ideas. With the
opening of the gate to the East by Alexander, Persians
and Indians passed through it to Alexandria, bringing

with them their mystical lore. Buddhists, Hindus, Brahmins and Mithraists met with Jews, Egyptians, Greeks, Carthaginians and Romans, each with their different religious concepts. By comparing these the idea developed that each one was evidently approaching the Infinite from a different aspect. Out of this melting-pot came the belief that God, the Infinite, had many names, each of which conveyed the same idea. This interchange of religious ideas greatly helped at a future date the spread of Christianity as Jews and Greeks, Romans, Egyptians and Persians were, in these centuries prior to the opening of our era, developing along a line of thought which made it easier for a new saviour-god to take the place of the old ones, and gather into the fold people of different races, religions and languages.

Here we must leave Alexandria, the great world trade centre, the home of the first great Library, University and Theological School, and pass on to another important influence which was developing and which, when at its height, did more than anything to make possible the spread of the Christian Faith.

From 1000 B.C. the Aryans were finding their way from the north to the shores of the Mediterranean, and penetrating into Greece and Italy, to become known as Greeks and Italians. By 750 B.C. the Greeks had flowed over to the south of Italy and Sicily, the Etruscans occupied north Italy, and the Latins the centre. Here the Latins in 753 B.C. started a township on the bank of the Tiber, which became known as Rome. It was separated from the Etruscans by the Tiber only, and it is therefore not surprising that it was captured by this northern race, to return

again to the Latins in the 6th century B.C.　In 509 B.C.
Rome became a Republic, the Latins prior to this
being ruled by kings.

The Etruscans, weakened by their war at sea with
the Greeks, and an invasion by Gauls from the north,
gave the Latins an opportunity to press north. Here
the Latins encountered the Gauls, who drove them
south, sacked Rome and penetrated to the south of the
peninsula. Suffering from disease and poor equipment,
the Gauls departed north again, being satisfied with
a ransom. For the next fifty years Rome worked hard
to establish itself as the head of the Latin tribes, and by
290 B.C. we find this city master of all central Italy. Its
inhabitants had conquered the Etruscans and extended
the Roman boundary as far north as where Genoa is
now.

The Greeks in Sicily and Southern Italy, alarmed
at the increasing power of their northerly neighbour,
invited the King of Epirus, on the other side of the
Adriatic, to come across and help them to settle the
Latins once and for all. Defeating the Romans, as
they were now called, he occupied Sicily and thus
brought Carthage, across the Mediterranean, against
him. With the help of Carthage the Romans defeated
the King of Epirus, who returned home, leaving as
his farewell remark the observation that he now
left Sicily to be the battleground of Rome and
Carthage.

Rome was now the master of Italy, from the
Arno southwards, and for the next hundred years its
history revolved round what are known as the three
Punic wars. With two combatants, Rome and Carthage,
fairly evenly matched, and each determined to become

master of the seas, the history of this long drawn out struggle is one of the most terrible in history.

Carthage, like Rome, was a Republic, and, like Athens, had tributary states. The Carthaginians were Semites and came from Phoenicia at the eastern end of the Mediterranean, the land of the people who gave the Hebrews their language and the Greeks their Alphabet. They came from the same stock as the Canaanites, and worshipped the saviour-god Bel. Carthage was older than Rome, being founded about the middle of the 9th century B.C., and its name means new city. Like the Phoenicians, the Carthaginians were a deeply religious people, religion entering into every important action of their lives, and their priests were held in the highest honour. Aristotle praises the Carthaginians for their sound government, on the score of its stability, and its success in securing the happiness and contentment of the nation. It is indeed inconceivable that this people could have secured such wealth and prosperity except under the good government he describes.

Sicily was the cause of the trouble between the two cities. Rome resented this fertile island being in the possession of the Carthaginians and commenced war in 264 B.C. against Carthage because the Carthaginians put a garrison at Messina. This was the beginning of three of the most wasteful and prolonged wars in history, all for the purpose of obtaining the command of the Mediterranean. By adding a drawbridge to each ship, which enabled the crew to board the Carthaginian vessels, Rome won the first battle at sea, a total of eight hundred ships being engaged. After a series of victories and defeats on land and sea, lasting seven years, this war came to an end with the defeat of Carthage, Sicily becoming a province of Rome. For twenty-two years peace reigned, both combatants trying to heal their wounds, but Rome was always hungry and wanted more. She annexed Sardinia and Corsica, which belonged to Carthage, and so the stage was set for another war, which lasted from 218 to 201 B.C.

Hannibal, the Carthaginian leader, reached Italy from Spain via France, and held his position there for fifteen years, the victor but never the conqueror, because Rome cut off his supplies from Spain. He always defeated the Romans but could never follow up his successes by capturing Rome and thus ending the war. Rome meantime was nibbling up Spain at the expense of the Carthaginians, until in the end Hannibal returned to Carthage to be defeated, just outside the city, by the great Roman general Scipio in 202 B.C.

The third and last war started in 153 B.C. and lasted until 146 B.C. Rome was determined to destroy Carthage and have no rival in the Mediterranean, and in this last war it succeeded. Rome was victorious and beseiged Carthage, which surrendered when only fifty thousand out of a population of half a million remained. These were sent to slavery, the entire city was burnt, no stone being left standing on another, and a curse was invoked on anyone attempting its reconstruction. This, however, did not prevent the city being rebuilt, only to be destroyed by the Arabs in A.D. 638 and it is now only a wilderness. In 146 B.C. Rome also destroyed Corinth, and so became master of Greece, its legions overrunning Macedonia and

Epirus. From now onwards, for the next four centuries, Greece was merged in the Roman Empire and ceased to have a history of its own.

With no enemy at its heels Rome ate up all the countries bordering the Mediterranean, and by 50 B.C., in spite of civil wars and internal unrest, was master of Spain, Gaul, Italy, Greece, Asia Minor, Palestine and Egypt. In 45 B.C. Rome ceased to be a Republic, Julius Caesar becoming dictator. He consolidated the foundation on which Rome built up her great empire over the next hundred years. His successes abroad and his administrative work at home made the people worship him, his image being carried in procession, along with those of the other gods. A statue was set up to him in a temple with the inscription, "To the unconquerable god", priests being appointed to regulate his worship.

Even a god-man must die, and this he did in 44 B.C. For the next seventeen years Rome was governed by three consuls, and then came the Emperors, beginning with Octavius in 27 B.C. He was given the title of Augustus, meaning Illustrious, and reigned till 14 A.D., so that during his reign the Christian era began. Two great institutions, the Roman Empire and Christianity, which vitally affected the lives of millions, thus commenced about the same time. He was followed by Tiberius, Caligula, Claudius, Nero and Vespasian, which is as far as we need go at present.

By the beginning of the 1st century A.D. Rome was master of the Mediterranean world, later to extend its dominions as far as the Forth and Clyde in Britain on the one hand, and the Persian Gulf on the other. Everywhere round the Mediterranean it had pushed further landwards, so much so that, instead of just commanding the ports as it did one hundred years earlier, its power was felt inland, from Egypt across the north of Africa to the Atlantic. From Egypt the Empire extended to Palestine, Syria, Assyria, Persia and Armenia, and thence westwards along the Black Sea up the Danube and the Rhine to Germany and the North Sea. From Britain it proceeded southwards to France and Spain, embracing all the islands of the Mediterranean. Rome was in command of all Europe, except what is now called Russia and Ireland, all Asia Minor to the Persian Gulf and all North Africa. Between 27 B.C. and A.D. 180 Roman civilisation and the Roman Empire were at their height, and Christianity was born and developed when they were at the peak of their greatness.

It was an age of culture, an age of literature, an age when people could travel about from land to land and see what was known of the Mediterranean world. Ships of five thousand tons and upwards traded on this inland lake. Commerce was active and riches increased. Large and beautiful towns were built everywhere. In the north York sprang up, and throughout England cities were built, with well laid out streets, temples, theatres, public baths, markets and all the refinements of the age. They were well drained and well watered. Good roads connected these new towns and the countryside was well cultivated. What happened in England took place wherever the Roman legions set foot. Everywhere they were the pioneers of a new civilisation on which our own has been built.

Rome was a magnificent city ; its walls extended over twenty miles and were pierced by thirty gates.

It had a population of over two millions, its streets were spacious and its buildings magnificent. Augustus boasted that he found it brick and left it marble. The population of the Empire at this time was about a hundred million, of whom five million were Roman citizens, but to all the same law applied and there was no unjust taxation. The civilised world at the opening of the Christian era was at peace, there was no war anywhere, and pirates and brigands everywhere had been suppressed.

In Rome the people were given over to luxurious living on a civilisation built up largely of slave labour. Books became more plentiful and libraries were opened in the different cities. The Romans prided themselves on their private libraries and the newly-rich patrician learned Greek so as to be considered cultured. Art, like education, was encouraged. Women held a high position and the Roman matron was looked upon with esteem.

This time is called the Golden Age of Literature, as writings of high worth came from the pens of men like Livy, Cicero, Virgil, Ovid and Horace. Though the art of printing was unknown yet many scribes were employed copying books, without which no rich man's house was complete. Plutarch was the great biographer of this time and Pliny put all he could discover about natural history into thirty-seven books. Nothing approaching this was again attempted till Humboldt last century published his great work, *Cosmos*. For eighteen hundred years the deadening effect of the Christian Church dried up and stultified the human intellect.

In *The Decline and Fall of the Roman Empire* Edward

Gibbon sums up this age, into which Christianity was born, and in which it developed. "Under the Roman Empire the labour of an industrious and ingenious people was variously but increasingly employed in the service of the rich. In their dress, their table, their houses, and their furniture, the favourites of fortune united every refinement of convenience, of elegance and of splendour".

Such then was the position in this great empire where freedom reigned, but freedom only for the rich and well-to-do. Little attempt was made to improve the lot of the slave or of the poor, and education was confined to the wealthy. By the time Constantine became emperor in A.D. 313 the Empire was beginning to show signs of cracking, which was the reason for his transferring the capital from Rome to Byzantium, and for adopting Christianity as the State religion, in order to solidify his Empire.

Upon the death of Alexander, the Athenians claimed their liberty, but it was not to be. The period of somewhat less than two centuries which intervened between the death of Alexander and the conquest of Greece by the Romans, was a sort of twilight between liberty and subjection. In 322 B.C. Antipater, one of Alexander's immediate successors in Macedonia, placed a garrison in Athens and in 318 B.C. Demetrius, the Phalerean, became its governor. Its history from this date to 146 B.C., when Greece became a Roman province, is one of sieges and bad government. The country became a bone of contention between the neighbouring potentates in Macedonia, Asia Minor, Syria and Egypt.

From the date of the Roman occupation, Athens

enjoyed good government and submitted peacefully to her conquerors. The Romans placed no garrison in the city, no tribute was paid and the constitution remained unaltered. Athens for the first time for many years was safe and had no need to fear her once powerful neighbour Macedonia. The Romans shewed great respect for the national pride of the Athenians, and their attitude is exemplified by the warm expressions of admiration which fell from the pens of Cicero and Horace. A visit to Athens was regarded by the Romans as a pilgrimage and an education.

From the vivid and minute description given of Athens by Pausanias, who visited the city in A.D. 170, we gather how delightful and beautiful it was in those days. The munificence of the Romans now left nothing more to be added to its embellishment. Masterpieces in art were to be seen everywhere, and in detail he describes them all, the city's great buildings, the Acropolis, the Academy, the arches, streets and harbour.

The period during which the greatest injury was inflicted on Greece was in 86 B.C., when the country rose in revolt against the Roman rule. Much of Athens was destroyed and the majority of its citizens were put to death. Delphi, and the other principal shrines, were plundered and an immense amount of property ruined. Much of the wealth which Greece had obtained from the accumulated treasures of the Persian Empire was appropriated by the Romans, and Greece, from being a land of great wealth, became comparatively poor.

As the power of Rome declined Athens became the prey of her barbaric neighbours. At the beginning of the 4th century A.D. Constantine gloried in the title of "General of Athens", but, by its end, in the reign of Theodosius I, the Goths had laid waste Thessaly and Epirus, overrunning all Greece as they did Italy, sacking, pillaging and destroying with a fury fiercer than a desolating tempest. The invaluable treasures of antiquity were stolen, stately and magnificent buildings and statues reduced to heaps of ruins, and Athens, stripped of the monuments of ancient splendour, became a skeleton.

Jerusalem, under the Persians, enjoyed little prosperity, but Alexander, on his way to Egypt, spared the city. Its situation was unfortunate in that it stood on the highway between the east and the west, which in those days were not long at peace. A period of comparative prosperity followed, Alexander's conquest culminating in the High Priesthood of Simon 2 (219-199 B.C.) who repaired the Temple and strengthened its defences. Its walls were again destroyed and the city burnt by the Syrians in 168 B.C. When Judas Maccabaeus reconsecrated the Temple in 165 B.C. he fortified the holy mountain of Zion. Then the Greeks razed the city. Again it was besieged in 65 B.C. by the Romans under Pompey, and also in 37 B.C. by the Romans. On at least two occasions the city was captured because the Jews would not fight on the Sabbath.

Herod, under the authority of Rome, then became King and so greatly restored the city that Josephus described it as a new town. It was built on four hills, the Temple crowning the steep crest of Moriah with white and gold. To the south-west towered the rocky Zion, bearing on its shoulders the citadel and the royal palace. Northwards, behind the Temple, the Hill of Acra was covered with terraces and gardens. On the slope of the other hill the new town stretched further towards the open country. Three walls surrounded the city. After the siege under Titus (A.D. 70), which was the result of the Jews revolting against Roman rule, the Romans entered the city. The Temple was destroyed and only then did the Jews give up hope in the saving power of Jehovah. Over a million Jews perished and the Golden Table, the Golden Candlesticks and the Book of the Law were carried off to Rome. From that date the Jews have been homeless, yet always preserving their nationality.

Hadrian (A.D. 76–138), who did so much to restore Athens, rebuilt Jerusalem, but not the Temple. The city became a Pagan town and only by the spread of Christianity did its fame return. After Constantine announced his discovery of the Holy Sepulchre, pilgrims started to visit the city as the scene of the crucifixion and resurrection. The erection of the magnificent Church of the Anastasis, dedicated in A.D. 336, again made Jerusalem a great religious centre. Under Julian (A.D. 362), an attempt was made to rebuild the Temple, but this came to nothing. Such is the chequered history of the city made holy and sacred by the reappearance of Jesus. Its importance to Christians is solely due to this fact. To the Jew and the Christian it is a holy city, like other cities looked upon as holy by other religions, because each is associated with a god-man or a great religious leader.

One of the greatest events in world history was the invasion of the East by Alexander in the year 334 B.C. As the result of his thus opening the gates to Eastern ideas, two civilisations were brought together, that of the East and that of the West. In consequence of the interchange of thought which followed, new ideas developed, productive of both good and evil in the history of the race. The East had been conquered by the West physically, if one might put it so, but, on the other hand, the religions of the East flowed westwards. From the East came the mysticism which had hitherto been absent in the West, and from now onwards we find the influence of Osiris, Mithra, Bel, Krishna, and Buddha pervading western thought more and more.

Under this influence arose everywhere in the western world those voluntary associations, devoted to religious ceremonial and contemplation, known as the Mystery Cults, which were the Greek Church of the time we are considering. They were the foundation stone on which the Christian Church was built, and the Christian Greek Church of the present day is the direct descendant of this pre-Christian Greek Church, with similar beliefs and ritual, the only important difference being the change in the name of the god worshipped. The Greek Church still calls itself the Orthodox Church and it has every right to this name.

Besides these associations there arose a new development, one of greater freedom of thought and expression, made possible by the more liberal and enlightened policy of Alexander, which was later adopted by Rome. Under the Empire of Alexander all races had common rights, no attempt being made to crush nationalism. The commercial and industrial spirit was encouraged, the result being an influx of Asiatics who spread along the shores of the Mediterranean.

From the east came also what is termed the oriental system of monarchical government, as Alexander adopted the idea that monarchs were the representatives of God on earth, if not actually gods themselves. In our country the belief in the divine right of kings, the descendant of this idea which Alexander brought to the west, was finally abolished with the dethronement of the Stuarts, but it prevailed in Germany until the abdication of the Kaiser at the close of the Great War.

During the period we are considering, religious interests took first place in the lives of the people, and though from our histories we read of battles and conquests, of nations being subdued first by Macedonia and then later by Rome, yet it was from neither the soldiers nor the politicians that Christianity arose. Its growth came from the people themselves, who went about their everyday life like other people, giving thoughts to their own welfare and destiny. It was the ordinary man and woman of these times who planted their ideas on the new faith, who showed the same enthusiasm for the new Christ as their parents and grandparents had for the saviour of the particular cult they favoured.

The people in Greece and Rome, who were those mostly responsible for the adoption and propagation of the Christian religion, were losing faith in the gods of their forefathers, Zeus, Apollo, and a host of others. We have already seen how the philosophers and thinkers of Greece had come to the conclusion that the gods of their mythology had once been men, and that the stories told about them were imaginative fiction. With the opening up of the East, the beliefs relating to the saviour-gods Bel, Osiris, Mithra, and Krishna acted as a stimulus to the growing interest now being taken in the saviour-gods, and these beliefs greatly influenced the Mystery Religions of Greece and Rome, about which more will be said presently. From the east also came the philosophic teaching of Gautama, who was styled Buddha, meaning the enlightened one, as Jesus was styled the Christ, meaning the anointed one.

Within the six hundred years prior to the Christian era lived men like Buddha, Confucius, Lao-Tsze, Socrates, Plato and Pythagoras, who all taught the immortality of the spirit and how all people on earth should live to fit themselves for the life hereafter. By now the great thinkers were coming to realise the unity in nature, how everything hung together, each phenomenon being but a link in an endless chain, that cause was followed by effect, which in turn produced a cause. From this developed the idea that there was one supreme Being behind everything. Though the other gods were still accepted, yet they occupied more the place of demi-gods, and later that of archangels and angels. In fact the hierarchy of heaven, as carried down to us by the Christian tradition, was much in vogue in the time we are considering.

It would be well to give some attention to three great Eastern thinkers who lived two centuries earlier than the time covered by this outline, because, within the period we are now reviewing, the influence of their thoughts and teachings was becoming marked. The opening up of the East by Alexander made way for the thoughts of Buddha, Confucius and Lao-Tsze to come to the West, and there they found a natural home in Alexandria at the Theological College. Let us therefore give some thought to these men and to their teachings.

Here we come to an entirely new intellectual life, hitherto cut off from the civilisations of the west by mountain barriers and desert regions. The Aryan tribes, who settled in India, came from the same stock as those who found their home in Greece and Italy, but they soon lost touch with their kinsmen and developed upon lines of their own. The Indian Aryans found a warm climate, a prolific soil, and nature gave them all they needed. There was plenty for everyone and so they developed into contemplators and not fighters. They had everything they wanted and there was nothing for which to fight. There was no need for robbers on land or pirates at sea, and so we find their legends composed of love stories. How different from the turbulent life of their kinsfolk who found their way to the shores of the Mediterranean.

About 560 B.C. the founder of Buddhism was born in India. We are told that he was a good-looking, energetic young Prince and up to the age of twenty-nine he lived a life of ease, comfort and luxury. He had a beautiful wife and everything that he could possibly desire. Amidst plenty and beauty he passed from gratification to gratification and yet he was not satisfied. He felt that there was something real which he had not yet found, and that all he had grasped so far was the shadow. One day, when out driving, he encountered a poor, bent, miserable creature. His driver remarked, "Such is the way of life and to that we must all come". Next he came upon a man suffering from some horrible disease, about whom his driver passed the same remark, and lastly he saw the unburied body of a man which had been mauled by an animal. Again his driver made the same remark.

The insecurity of life, its passing pleasures on the one hand, and its miseries on the other, struck the sensitive mind of this young aristocrat so forcibly that the idea came to him that if happiness could be obtained with poverty then there would be nothing to lose. Was it not a question of mental exercise which, when correctly carried out, obviated the need of material things to produce happiness? In other words, Buddha argued that by contemplation, and the ignoring of what this earth has to offer, one can attain happiness. He was one of many who had formed the same opinion, but he turned his thoughts into a philosophy which he preached to those who became his disciples.

On his return from the drive he heard that his first son was born and now Gautama made his great decision. His life was either to be spent with his wife and son amidst his luxurious surroundings, or, apart from them all, devoid of every comfort and luxury. He chose the latter and, amid the great rejoicings his son's birth aroused, he called his servant, and told him to prepare his horse. Taking a passing look at his wife and child, he resisted a last embrace in case he awoke her and she prevented him from carrying out his decision. He thus turned his back on everything he loved, on all his possessions, and went off into the night alone, changing his costly clothes for the rags of the first poor man he met. Again and again he was tempted to return, but never yielded, and pursued the path he had so unwillingly chosen, gathering round him pupils to whom he taught his philosophy.

All the misery of life he traced to selfishness. Suffering, he said, is due to the craving for individuality and the torment of greed. Man must overcome every sort of personal craving, and until he does so trouble and sorrow will follow humanity. Craving is noticeable in three different ways, the first through sensuality, the desire to gratify the senses ; secondly, by the desire to penetrate beyond death ; and thirdly, by the wish for prosperity, the accumulation of wealth and the love of the things of this world. These desires must be abolished before life can become serene, but when they are overcome, and man has conquered desire, then he has reached the highest state of wisdom, Nirvana, the mental state in which the mind is at peace. Nirvana does not mean the extinction of self but the extinction of earthly desires, which bring in their train trouble and misery.

Buddha practised what he preached. He, like all monks and nuns, withdrew himself from the world, and to those who followed him he taught that there was something greater than ourselves, something beyond earth's desires and that, by renouncing these, reality could be found in contemplation. Though he was doubtless influenced by Brahmanic philosophy he comes down to us as one of the world's greatest religious pioneers. We may not agree with all his conclusions, but there is no doubt that he laid down a code of ethics of as high an order as any before or after his time. He is credited with more moralising and ethical wisdom than any other religious teacher.

He produced for the benefit of humanity his eightfold way of right thinking and right acting, known as the Aryan Path. First he insisted on truth and the abandonment of all superstitions. Next came the holding of right views and right aspirations. As base cravings are to be expelled, love for the service of others and desire to do and to secure justice must take their place. From this it is evident that Buddha taught a change of desire and not the annihilation of desire. Then came devotion to knowledge, to right speech, right conduct, right living, right effort (because no one must be lazy), and, lastly, right rapture, which is aimed against the ecstasies of the devout.

He was the first to declare the universal brotherhood of man, and his followers, though they have degraded much of his teaching, and turned it into creeds and dogmas, have at least made an attempt to follow his precept of peace and love to all men. He insisted that reason, based on evidence, is our only guide to truth and that only through knowledge can mankind attain happiness. Only when greed, covetousness and all selfish desires are annihilated and when justice, mercy and goodness remain, will human happiness be obtained. Buddhism, which is accepted by four hundred and fifty million people, can proudly claim that it has never been the cause of war and strife, and that its founder was the first to proclaim, so far as we know, that knowledge and wisdom are the only two levers capable of raising mankind.

Buddha taught that all men and women should enjoy equal rights. He denounced the priests of his day and fortunately escaped their wrath. He inculcated a pure system of morality, and advocated kindness and love towards all men. If mankind only could live up to his teachings, to his principles of peace and love, oppression and tyranny would be known no more. He taught no cruel doctrine of sacrifice, he believed in no angry God, nor in that most immoral of all religious doctrines, that a Saviour took the punishment for the transgressions of believers. Life to Buddha was a preparation, something which should be lived aright, by the elimination of worldly desires, so that we prepare ourselves properly for the life hereafter. His was a religion of conduct and service, not of sacrifice or observance. He propounded no creeds or dogmas and advocated no rites and ceremonies. To him the life lived was everything.

As round all the great in those days, legends grew about his name after his death. He was looked upon as having been a god-man and was credited with a virgin birth and numerous miracles. It was said that at his birth the celestial choir sang, "This day is born for the good of men, Buddha, and to dispel the darkness of ignorance, to give joy and peace to the world". To him at birth came wise men with rich gifts who proclaimed him the Saviour of the world. He lived to be an old man and continued his teaching to the last. Though he was rich, yet, for the sake of others, he became poor so that they, through his poverty, might become rich. His teachings made rapid headway and, by the 3rd century B.C., the new cult was gaining wealth and power, the teaching of the master now having been consolidated into dogmas and doctrines.

King Asoka (264–227 B.C.), one of the greatest and noblest kings of history, still revered by millions, whose kingdom extended from Afghanistan to Madras, adopted the faith and, influenced by the teachings of Buddha, gave up his contemplated conquest of the Indian peninsula. Instead of conquering by force he set out to conquer by love, sending missionaries everywhere to spread the teachings of Buddha. He erected monuments all over his kingdom on which were inscribed Buddha's simple precepts. His missionaries found their way to Alexandria, where they influenced the west, their principal contribution to Christianity being the Monastic system, with its orders of monks and nuns. In turn, the Buddhists were influenced by some of the beliefs and teachings surrounding Osiris, which found their way into the religion of Buddha. They copied what is now known as the Madonna and child from Isis with Horus in her arms, and we find Buddha pictured in the arms of the goddess Hariti.

Those who were known in Palestine as Essenes were supposed to be the western offshoot of the Buddhist community. They were known in Egypt as Therapeutae, about whom it will be remembered a quotation was given from the writings of Eusebius in the previous chapter. There they had dwelt for two hundred years before the birth of Jésus. They divested themselves of all worldly goods and thus relieved themselves of all cares and anxieties.

Going further east we come to China, and there we find another great teacher, who also lived in the 6th century B.C. Confucius, the founder of Confucianism. He was of good birth but poor, and, after occupying various official positions, like Plato, he set up an Academy for the purpose of discovering and imparting wisdom. After all these years the Chinese still say :

> Confucius ! Confucius ! How great was Confucius !
> Before him there was no Confucius.
> Since him there has been no other.
> Confucius ! Confucius ! How great was Confucius !

His teachings centred round a high standard of living, and he personally presented to the people of his time the ideal man of whom he preached. From him came the admonition, "Do not do to others what you would not that they do to you". He was more constructive in his thoughts than Buddha, and conceived a new order of society in which his ideal type of man could live. He was too practical to advocate withdrawing from the world, and recommended instead associating with others for the purpose of raising them. Only by effort, he said, could disorder be banished from the world, only by establishing right principles could men and women be honestly and justly governed. He was appointed a magistrate and, with this authority, he sought to regulate life in every direction. Everything became subject to rigid rule and was carefully ordered. Though such methods do not appeal to people who value freedom, yet they did

to the Chinese, and there can be no doubt that Confucius has had a greater influence on the development
of the Chinese national character than any other man,
with perhaps the exception of Lao-Tsze, whose
teaching also greatly influenced his countrymen.

Lao-Tsze was the founder of Taoism, which
occupies a place close to Buddhism, and his teachings,
like those of Buddha, have been debased by his
followers. Confucius had a philosophic mind and
Lao-Tsze that of a mystic. For many years Lao-Tsze
was in charge of the Imperial Library. He preached
a stoical indifference to the pleasures and powers of
the world and advocated simplicity. He pleaded for
modesty, selflessness and the subjection of all desires.
Like most mystics his meanings are very obscure, of
which the following is an example :

All things originate from Taou, conform to Taou and to
Taou they at last return. Formless, it is the cause of form,
It is an eternal road, along it all beings and all things walk, but
no being made it, for it is being itself, and yet nothing. It is
the path, and also the path goers, and everything and nothing
and the cause and effect of all.

Because of the indefiniteness of his teaching, it
was overlaid, as time went on, with legends, and had
grafted upon it complex and extraordinary observances. This was not so with Confucianism because
Confucius was definite and explicit in all he taught.
His name is still cherished by a third of the human
race and, like Socrates, Plato and Aristotle, he advanced a philosophy which has profoundly influenced
the thinking portion of the human race for two
thousand four hundred years. As Confucius influ-

enced the east so these three great Greeks influenced the west.

Socrates (470–399 B.C.) was a martyr and suffered because he was courageous enough to advocate the speaking of one's honest thoughts, which in his day did not always appeal to the State authorities. He received the ordinary education common to a son of an Athenian freeman. He grew up short and sturdy in figure and ungainly of movement. From his face appeared two protruding eyes, between which was a broad flat nose, and below this two thick lips. His brow was a dome of intellect. After starting life as a sculptor he soon abandoned his chisel and devoted himself to the study of philosophy.

He did not travel much, but once at Delphi he saw inscribed on one of the doors of the temple the words, "Know thyself". He then set about the great task of learning to know himself and this he did by dissecting the minds of others through questioning. By the same method he set about finding out the qualities that made for goodness, happiness, bravery and justice. To him the greatest virtue was pure knowledge and he would accept nothing that would not pass the acid test of reason.

He fought as a common soldier during the Peloponnesian War, which lasted almost a generation. One of the greatest philosophers of that age thus fought side by side with the ordinary man and the slave, because service was the debt he owed to his beloved Athens. When this war was over he set about seriously instructing his fellows. He spent his days in the market-place, at the street corners, and wherever he could challenge the people to give heed to his thoughts. His theme was the attainment of justice and wisdom, and he was rigid in extracting absolute truth and applying it to all concerns of life. Virtue is wisdom, he taught, and when men know how to think aright they will do right. When men know how to think justly they will act justly.

We only know Socrates through the writings of his two devoted disciples, Xenophon and Plato, the latter pouring out all his marvellous genius into his account of the conversations which he records. Socrates was a man given to long trance-like periods of abstraction. He was clairaudient and, like others so constituted, was guided by a voice which he said never misled him. He was too outspoken not to have enemies who accused him of not believing in the national gods, of introducing new ideas and thus corrupting the youths of Athens.

The penalty was death, but, before drinking the poison, he was asked by his friend Crito, "How shall we bury you?" to which he answered, "Wherever you will, if only you can catch me", for he was assured that whatever would happen to his body his spirit went marching on. When death came Crito remarked, "This is the end of our friend, a man we may say, the best of all of his time that we have known and, moreover, the most wise and just".

Plato (427–347 B.C.) was a king of thought, and the age into which he was born was unique for men of greatness. He was born just after Pericles, the great soldier and statesman, who lifted Athens to the pinnacle of her fame, had passed on. In his day lived Sophocles, known as the best of all the Greek tragic poets ; Euripides, the great Greek dramatist ;

Thucydides, the greatest historian of antiquity ; and Isocrates, the orator, and one of the most remarkable men in the literary history of Greece. Socrates taught Plato, who in turn taught Aristotle.

Plato served as a soldier, as did all Athenians, and fortunately escaped capture and death when the Spartans overran Athens and razed the city walls to the ground. The result of his intercourse with Socrates taught him to think clearly, and he left, as a memorial to his teacher, the dialogues in which he makes Socrates the conductor of the discussions, and the world's cleverest and wittiest cross-examiner. His description of the last talk, and the last scene before Socrates drank the poison, is one of the greatest discourses to be found in world literature.

Broken by the tragedy of his teacher's death, Plato, while all men were flocking to Athens to learn from him, went forth abroad to study philosophy. From Egypt he went to Palestine and returned home by way of Italy and Sicily. Wherever he went he discoursed on philosophy, emphasising the need of virtue, fortitude and justice. He denounced tyranny as cowardice and taught that happiness could only come through justice. Speaking thus before Dionysus, the tyrant king of Sicily, he was arrested and sold as a slave. Happily this was to an admirer, who restored his liberty, and so he returned safely to Athens.

With his accumulated experiences he started writing and teaching. He opened a school of philosophy which was to radiate light in a dark world. Demosthenes, the great orator, was amongst his pupils, as was Aristotle. In this school Plato taught for forty years, and after that he spent his life amidst his friends and pupils at Athens, teaching and writing his philosophy which has influenced mankind for two thousand three hundred years. He was the first man to make men understand that things were not always what they seemed to be.

He propounded a philosophy to prove that ideas are more real than material things, which in themselves are only passing and imperfect imitations of the ideas they represent. Virtue, he taught, followed from knowledge and wisdom, and, when these are mastered, then good quite naturally took the place of evil. He envisaged a Republic embracing the Utopias imagined by idealists, and, in this flight of imagination, he expressed superb thoughts. He was the first outstanding Communist, the first school-master, one of the first to emphasise the need of knowledge to raise humanity and bring about human progress. He was one of the first to tell man to rely on himself and not on the gods. He loved everything that was beautiful, and whatever he wrote was full of rich and noble thoughts, which he handed down to his successor, Aristotle.

Aristotle (384–322 B.C.) was the supreme thinker of his time, and takes his place as the one who has most influenced the thought of Europe. He was sane and luminous in all he wrote. His influence brought about the foundation of the University of Alexandria and, while this lasted, he, though dead, yet spoke through the mouths of the philosophers who attended that first seat of learning. When, in the second century, the University became a Theological College, the light of knowledge was extinguished by the darkness of superstition, and priests took the place of teachers.

A thousand years after his death the writings of Aristotle stimulated the germ of thought in the eighth century, which, eight hundred years later, in the sixteenth century, developed sufficiently to produce the Renaissance. A faint light broke through the night of the dark ages, to increase sufficiently to illumine the middle ages, and flood the world of today in places with intellectual light. He was the last of the immortal three, Socrates, Plato and Aristotle, and his influence on European thought was greater than that of Socrates and Plato, because his line of approach appealed more to the practical men who produced the Renaissance. Plato was too much of a metaphysician; as to him, what seemed real in time and space was not real, but only the reflection of the real.

Aristotle taught the opposite, that the only reality is that which is actual in space and time. The sun, the earth, the planets, the passage of time, all are real and the thought which registers them is transient. Aristotle was a natural philosopher, and anticipated Bacon and modern science by ordering and classifying the knowledge of his time. He collected and classified plants and animals, and was the first biologist, groping for the idea of evolution. With the wealth of Alexander behind him he had at one time a thousand men in different parts of the known world collecting material for his natural history. His writings found their way to Alexandria and thence seven hundred years later to Constantinople. Fortunately, before this city was captured by the Turks in 1453, these reached Venice. Their translation from

Greek into Italian determined the whole course of mediæval and modern culture. Thomas Aquinas spread Aristotle's teaching and it was later taken up by Erasmus and Thomas Moore.

Like Plato, Aristotle had his own school, known as the Lyceum. Here he expounded his own philosophic system, and it is said that his pupils discussed everything in heaven and on earth. His method of teaching was similar to the one adopted by Socrates and Plato, as he did not dogmatise, but instructed in the form of question and answer, which was greatly preferred to continuous exposition. He, and his students under him, made an encyclopedia of philosophy, which was the first attempt to bring all knowledge within two covers. He was the first to lay down the principles of logic, the first physicist, biologist and psychologist. This tremendous intellectual force, fearing that his fate would be like that of Socrates, when an old man, shook the dust of Athens from his feet, lest, as he said, "The Athenians should sin twice against philosophy". The year after leaving his native city he died.

Besides this trio of intellect, which greatly influenced not only their own time but all succeeding ages, we must not in this resumé forget the influence exerted by men like Pythagoras, who lived towards the end of the 6th century B.C. Religion in his time had become corrupt in Greece, the ennobling influence of Orpheus having waned. Pythagoras was an ethical and religious reformer and founded a system of esoteric philosophy. He was the connecting link between Orpheus, who, seven hundred years earlier, founded the sacred mysteries, and Plato.

Pythagoras translated the thought of his predecessor into the intellectual requirements of his day. He taught purity of living and the need of lofty aims and ideals. His philosophy was an appeal to the intellect. From his childhood he had a love of learning, and conferred freely from an early age with all who could satisfy his longings. He was always searching for unity so as to obtain a rational explanation of the universe. He visited Egypt and Babylon in his search, gleaned all he could from their wise men, and then returned to Greece to teach what he had learned.

From what we are told of him he evidently had considerable psychic power and, with the knowledge this brought him, he expounded a psychic philosophy, which was handed on till it was taken up by Plato, to be carried on in turn by Plotinus in the second century of the Christian era. About Plotinus I shall have more to say later on in Chapter IX.

The Aristotelian age was not to last. It burned itself out as our scientific age would have done if none had been found to follow Copernicus, Galileo and Kepler. The wealth of Alexander had made the accumulation of knowledge possible, but his early death brought this to an end before its benefits to mankind were realised. If Aristotle had not had this means at his disposal he might never have become the first great scientist. So the world had to wait for nearly two thousand years before some were mentally ready to resume the task he had commenced. Meantime the thinkers returned to their philosophic contemplations, and the accumulation of facts came to an end.

For only fifty years after his death was any scientific research carried on, and that was at Alexandria, after which time it dwindled away to nothing. There seemed to be no desire for ordered knowledge, it was so much easier to contemplate and speculate than to adopt the laborious methods entailed by collecting, comparison and classification. The human mind had not yet reached the state of constructing knowledge by logical reasoning and observation.

It was still in the state of what Professor Jung, in his *Psychology of the Unconscious*, terms Undirected Thinking, as compared with our modern method of Direct Thinking. The former is thinking as we do in dreams, the latter is by means of words used as pegs to define our meaning, which we move from place to place as our reasoning directs.

Indirect thinking produced mythology ; direct thinking, knowledge. Indirect thinking produced what is called Religion, embracing the saviour-gods and all the mythology which surrounds them. "Myths," says Jung, "are the mass-dreams of humanity, and dreams the myths of individuals." So the people, after Aristotle's time, went on dreaming, till they dreamed the old legends, which surrounded their saviour-gods, round a new saviour-god whom they called Christ.

I shall now conclude this historical interlude, which has been only too brief, but I trust long enough for the purpose intended. This glance at the times in which our subject is set, though cursory, may nevertheless have helped to focus in the mind of the reader a picture of the conditions, and the thoughts, in which the Christian Faith came into being, a period in world history which was fruitful of vast and profound changes.

We now come to the stage when we can give special consideration to the parents of the Christian Faith, beginning with the priesthood. If there had been no priesthood there would have been no Christianity. Likewise, if the old beliefs surrounding the saviour-gods had not been carried on by the Mystery Cults, under which name these old ideas were the prevailing beliefs of the time, in which Christianity was conceived and formed, there would have been no Christ and no Christian Faith.

The priesthood was the cause of the effect, namely the apparition of Jesus, and can be termed the father of the religion. The Mystery Cults were its mother, as, from the effect caused by the priests, Christianity was conceived in the womb of the Mystery Cults, where it grew, till it was born as a new religion, having absorbed from its mother everything she had to give. So, first of all, let us now learn something of

THE PRIESTHOOD

One must study the history of priestcraft to understand the priestly mind. It is an extraordinary history and it is unfortunate that so few know much about it. Some day, when the grip of priestcraft has been entirely broken, the history of this craft will be taught in our schools and become part of our general knowledge. Meantime it is only available to the student who has access to the volumes relating to the history of the different religions throughout the world. No matter which religion is studied, the same type of mind is always evident.

In the days when man was a child he could only be governed by his emotions. All government, religion and knowledge were in the hands of the priesthood, which was able, by its organisation, to keep the people in order and govern their lives, just as a parent directs the life of a child. It had the defects of its limited intelligence, just as had those it governed. Its long term of office enabled it to acquire vested interests and a tradition which the three hundred years of Science has not yet been able to break down. During the last three centuries history relates a battle between the forces of progress and that of past tradition. Mankind, with the mind of a child, received that for which he was fitted from. his masters, but, as his mind grew, he rebelled, as a youth does if his parents are not wise enough to appreciate his mental development.

The history of priestcraft, up to the middle ages, is one of both good and bad government. From that date it is one of warfare with the growing mentality of the race, winning where this was weak and losing where it was strong, but never retreating from its age-long position without a fight, and the infliction of cruelty on all those who challenged its authority. It is not an order devoted to the social advancement of the race, to education, or to healing the sick. Its one and only object is to act as an intermediary between the gods and man, to reveal their instructions to mankind, to keep them on the best possible terms with humanity, and to pass on to the gods the desires and needs of the human race.

Let me briefly summarise the history of priest-craft, its ideas and its policy, which are the same today as they always were. What I shall relate about the past is equally true about the present and recent times, the only difference between the past and the present being that it has not now the power it had, owing to the increase in education. Priestcraft can be summarised under the following twelve headings :

(1) The priesthood of the saviour-god religions has always considered itself an organisation specially endowed by the gods, or a god, to preserve a revelation which they claimed was made by a god, or the gods, to its organisation. Its members, the priests, took a solemn vow at their ordination to keep intact its regulations throughout their lives and always to believe its creeds, doctrines and dogmas, as handed down by ancient tradition.

Though the names of the gods it represented changed down the ages nothing else has, and its ideas are the same today as when the order was first instituted. Though the different orders of priesthood throughout the world claimed to represent different gods, which each claimed to be the only true god, and though the members of one order were not on speaking terms with the members of any other, yet the organisation, its ideas and policy, are still the same today as they have always been from the beginning.

(2) The priests, at ordination, agreed to perform

the rites and ceremonies of the religion their organisation had been endowed by the gods to preserve for all time.

(3) The priests have always maintained that everything that is contrary to the creeds, doctrines, dogmas and sacred literature of their organisation is sinful, and that it was their duty to use every means within their power to stifle and abolish anything of such a nature.

(4) They agreed to be trained in special colleges, maintained by the organisation for the purpose, which training fitted them to perform these ceremonies and rites, to believe the creeds, doctrines and dogmas of their order, and to expound the meaning of the sacred literature which the gods had given into its keeping.

(5) They believed that they belonged to a Holy Order instituted by the gods, and that only through the acceptance of the beliefs held by this organisation could happiness be attained in the life after death.

(6) At their ordination they made a solemn declaration that they believed that all who thought differently from the way laid down by their organisation passed into Hell at death, which was a state of everlasting torment.

(7) They believed that their organisation was instituted by the gods for the purpose of protecting and managing their Church on earth, which Church consisted of all who were prepared to abide by the rules and regulations laid down by the organisation. No one could become a member of the Church who had not been first baptised at infancy, or later in life, and certain preparations were necessary

before the applicant could be admitted to membership of the Church.

(8) They were also trained to administer the
sacrament to members of the Church, and perform a
ceremony over the dead body according to the
prescribed wording and ritual. No one except a
priest had the sanction of the gods to perform any of
the rites and ceremonies connected with the religion.

(9) The priests believed that they had the power
to purify women after childbirth. This they held
was necessary as each child was born in sin, which
means that each child was born with the stigma of
wickedness implanted in his mind, and was thus a
potential victim of the anger of the gods. Consequently the child had to be baptised to give him
entry into the Church, whose members, by their
beliefs, had secured their salvation through the
mitigation of the wrath of the gods, by having associated themselves with the institution the gods had
set up on earth.

If the child were not baptised it was not a
member of the Church and so went to Hell. An
advertisement slogan of the organisation was "The
streets of Hell are paved with the bones of unbaptised children". This was for the purpose of
getting new members to take the place of those who
died. Besides the necessity of the child being baptised, the mother had to be cleansed, by some magical
words pronounced by the priest, because she had given
birth to a child which had contaminated her.

(10) They believed that a marriage undertaken
without the prescribed religious rites was contrary to
the will of the gods, that those who married under

the law of the State and did not also avail themselves of the rites of the Church, or took the vows the priests had prepared, were "living in sin". The first priest who thought of this prescription was a genius and it was the most profitable idea that ever entered a cunning mind. Marriage, in itself, does not interest the priesthood. What has always interested them is the children, the more the better, and, by marrying the parents, they obtained a grip on the children, their future supporters, because the parents at marriage were made to vow to bring up the children on the doctrines prescribed by the priests. What a child is taught it never forgets and such beliefs become fixed ideas. Thus the priests made certain of the future of their organisation and have always opposed birth control.

(11) The business side of the organisation has always received careful attention from the heads of the order, who invariably arranged that the first fruits of the fields were handed over to maintain the members of the organisation. This business acumen resulted in every order of priesthood amassing colossal wealth, the revenue of which the order divided amongst its members. In Egypt, Babylon and India, thousands of years ago, we find from records that the order of priesthood was the largest landowner, the largest owner of cattle and the largest owner of slaves. This business side received equal attention from the Christian priesthood, with the result that the Roman and Anglican Orders are the wealthiest organisations in the world.

(12) The Chief Priests also so worked affairs that their order took chief control in the government

of the nation in which the order was situated. They dictated to kings and governments and controlled the policy of the nation. What happened in pre-Christian days has also happened throughout the Christian era.

This is a brief summary of the history and mental outlook of the priesthood since the order was instituted thousands of years ago, and it embraces what the word Priestcraft stands for. It does not just refer to the present day. It does not only refer to one religion. It does not only refer to one epoch in world history. It embraces the history and aims of priestcraft since the craft first began, up to the present day. It embraces every religion employing priests, and the policy and the mental outlook of the Holy Order is the same today as it was six thousand years ago, the same when Krishna rose up against it, and the same when Jesus did likewise at a later date.

The only difference between a priest in civilised countries today and a priest of the past is that he, like the rest of us, must conform to modern laws and customs. He has ceased being a murderer, a butcher and a torturer as he does not now slaughter human beings or animals, and torture or imprison heretics. Education has so developed the minds of the people that such things are not now allowed, though in certain countries in Europe priests still persecute those who oppose their organisation, and laws are still in force which prevent any expression of opinion contrary to that held by the priesthood.

The foregoing is an analysis of what priestcraft stands for, and there is only one conclusion to be drawn from it. This is that those who have belonged to it, or now do, whether they called themselves, or still call themselves, Pongyis or Mullahs, Rabbis, Priests, Pastors, Ministers of the Gospel, or any other name they have adopted to differentiate themselves from the rest of mankind, must have had, or have, minds which were, or are, (1) ignorant and intolerant, (2) narrow in their outlook, (3) patrimonial, and (4) individually entirely lacking in experience of worldly affairs.

From youth upwards priests have been trained in only one line of thought. When they reached manhood, and entered the order, they made a solemn declaration that they believed in, and would use their strength to further, the objects for which their organisation was established. It therefore stands to reason that those capable of this must always have been against (1) education, (2) progress, and (3) reform. There was nothing to reform because their organisation held the entire and only revelation from the gods. Progress was a word they could never understand because the gods had revealed to their organisation all that man should ever know. The gods had, moreover, decreed that the people were to carry out the laws prescribed by the King, who, as the gods' chief representative on earth, was the head of the priestly order and consequently the Head of the Church, just as it still is today in our own country. Education was quite contrary to the spirit of their caste. The only thing the people needed to know was how to be saved through the means the gods had revealed to the priests on earth.

Consequently the priestly mind was always, and still is, intolerant of any opinion apart from the opinions formed by their order. Consequently it was also narrow in its outlook and, as priests never mixed with others on an equal footing, or exchanged with others opinions about the things of everyday life, or came up against the rough and tumble of life, they were generally quite ignorant of the practical world in which they lived, but of which they were not. Lastly, the priestly mind was patrimonial because every priest was an initiate, one of an exclusive caste which none could enter but those who had been initiated.

In the days when men were cruel and brutal we can readily understand how such ignorant and intolerant minds could be more cruel and brutal than any others. The exclusiveness of their training, which was voluntary, meant that they absorbed what they were taught in a way which no ordinary individual could do. Their minds so ran in the direction of their teaching that there was no exertion needed to make them think as the organisation wanted them to think. In a word, they were naturally intolerant and were nurtured in intolerance. Intolerance is one cause of cruelty, it prevents progress, creates hatred, and causes misery and suffering to all who come up against it.

History tells us that the priests have been both good and bad. There have been many good priests and there have been many bad priests. As they were drawn from the people, they represented the moral, mental and religious outlook of the people of their day. Those who could accept their teaching received comfort, while those who could not were persecuted and made miserable. It is questionable whether the

Heaven they held out to believers comforted more people than were made miserable by the Hell they preached. In the Order were to be found all types of minds. Those with the lust for power generally attained their ambition, and gained control, while the rest, who were mostly simple-minded and ignorant men, accepted the policy of their leaders and supported their deeds.

Many men entered the profession in order to get power or to live a life of ease, while many others became members with the sincere wish to do good and so help their fellow creatures. Outside the order, however, many people, without payment or recognition, have done much more than the priests to relieve suffering and poverty. This, as civilisation advanced, has increased, with the result that today there is a great army of voluntary workers doing deeds of charity and kindness, which army vastly outnumbers the paid priests. Besides these there is another huge army of doctors, nurses and social workers, attached to no religious order, who are spending their lives relieving pain and helping in the uplifting of humanity. For every priest there are now half a dozen school-teachers who are inculcating knowledge into the minds of their pupils, teaching them how best to live and how to make the most of life.

When the world was ruled by the order of priesthood there was no education ; disease, filth, misery and cruelty prevailed everywhere, and man went from the cradle to the grave under its direction. Its intolerance led to numerous wars, and the history of Christendom shows us that nearly every war up to the eighteenth century was a religious war and instigated by the priesthood.

Besides this, its policy towards women was most demoralising. It considered a woman as the cause of all the wickedness in the world, treating her sex as an inferior order of existence, and yet it was from women down the ages that the order received its principal support. During the centuries, when Greece and Rome were at their height, the priesthood took an inferior place, and then women were treated with respect in the community. When the Christian priests obtained control of affairs in Europe, as the result of the decree of the Emperor Constantine, women were degraded and remained so until within recent years, when, in consequence of the decline in power of the priesthood, they have re-established the position they occupied in Greece and Rome.

If the people were overridden and tyrannised it was the fault of the people, who were so ignorant that they allowed themselves to be dictated to by those whom they considered to be their superiors. From what has been said we can now understand why, down the ages, priestcraft has opposed all progress and reform. There was nothing to reform because the priests were in the favoured position of receiving the first tenth of all the produce of the fields, and so no one could come before them. They were so safe that it was impossible to improve their position.

To the priesthood there was no need for reform, and so to talk of progress was absurd. Science, and all it stood for, was the work of the Devil, who wished to make the people dissatisfied with existing conditions. Education was consequently always opposed because, if the people thought more clearly, and knew more, then the organisation was weakened. Healing was never encouraged because disease was either caused by devils or sent as a punishment. As slavery was supported by the gods, who had ordained that some should be freemen and others bondmen, every effort to abolish it was always opposed with vigour.

Human sacrifice was ordained by the gods, and therefore the priests opposed its abolition until they were forced to stop it because of the united opposition of the people. For the same reason they had to give up animal sacrifice, but, so long as a sacrifice of some kind or another could be laid on the altar it justified the necessity of the organisation. Consequently they turned bread and wine into the body and blood of the slain victim, and considered that he had been slain afresh every time they celebrated the Eucharist.

It will be seen from the foregoing what a stranglehold such an organisation had on all progress, on all reform, and on the development of mediumship, especially when it terrorised an ignorant multitude which it could frighten and fleece. The priesthood wished no progress, no reform, no mediums, and their will was law because the people followed them blindly, knowing no better, and never getting a chance to know better, because education was banned, and every reformer and medium, as he appeared, was murdered.

The priesthood has now lost its power in all countries where schools exist, provided such schools are not controlled by the Church. Church schools were instituted, not from a desire to educate the people, but in self defence, when other schools were being started, so that Church doctrines could be taught and instilled into the minds of the children at an age when they were most receptive.

Evolution, however, could not be suppressed for ever and a time had to come when the people, over the dead bodies of the martyrs, forced the priesthood to give them their rights so long denied. This happened in Greece when she overthrew the power of the priesthood, it happened in Rome when she did likewise, and it happened again in this country last century when the people were allowed to express their opinions on religious subjects, without fear of imprisonment. This was followed in 1870 by their being taught how to read and write. Thus the standard of intelligence is rising as the result of the freedom for which the reformers laid down their lives, endured imprisonment, torture and banishment.

The foregoing must not be taken to mean that the evils which priestcraft represents : tyranny, ignorance and all that goes with it, are peculiar to this profession. Many kings and dictators have been equal tyrants, and we are today witnessing the same type of mind in Germany, Italy, Russia, Spain, and elsewhere where dictators rule. In each of these countries an organisation has been formed to protect and propagate a political creed, and all who oppose it are either shot or imprisoned.

The difference, however, between political tyranny and that of priestcraft is that the former refers to the affairs of this world, about which people know something, and the other has worked on the ignorance of the people concerning the life after death, thus torturing the minds of the living by the pictures drawn of their sufferings after death, and the condition of their dead friends and relations. Priestcraft has always thrived on ignorance and fear ; the more ignorant and fearful the people, the more it prospered and the larger was its revenue. The greater the ignorance of the people the more it was paid to pray the dead out of Hell. As the people became more intelligent and less fearful, so its revenue declined, as we are witnessing in our own country at the present time.

Some of us are not unfamiliar with the history of the Christian Church's attitude towards all liberty and reform. It is a terrible history, but one that is quite typical of priestcraft from the earliest times. We need not, therefore, be surprised that no reformer, like Krishna and others, escaped the clutches of the priests when he tried to raise the people to a higher level of thought. Progress has taken place in spite of every effort of the world's ecclesiastical order to prevent it. The watchword of each was "Semper Idem", not only in their politics but also in their beliefs and ceremonies, which are much the same today as they were thousands of years ago.

Savage man, feeling that his life's comforts and necessities were determined by the gods, worshipped them, prayed to them and fed them. As he believed that they were immaterial beings the only food he could offer them was the spirits of human beings and animals, which he did in the way he thought they desired. He served their meal in an orderly manner by going through its preparation, and serving it, in the same way as he prepared and served his own food. He ate his own food on a table of some kind or another and the womenfolk were responsible for its preparation and serving. Today we prepare our food, have it served in a certain way, and eat it in a certain way. Our primitive ancestors did likewise, the only difference between us and them being that they had not reached the fork and spoon stage, or attained to the refinements of civilised man.

Apart from this there is little difference. Savage man thought that the gods enjoyed what he did, that they ate as he did, and that they wished to be served with the food he offered them in the same way as he was served. So when offering a spirit to the gods he put the body of the one whose spirit was to be released by death on a table, which he called an altar, and believed that the gods came down and ate the spirit of the victim on the altar. Paul, for this reason, terms the altar, or communion table, "The Table of the Lord" (1 Cor. x, 21), and Presbyterian Christians call it "The Lord's Table". The Pagans called it "The Table of the gods". The butcher who killed the victim was known as the Chief Priest, and the Cook, who cooked it into a burnt offering, was called a High Priest, which was a title corresponding to our word Bishop. The Servers, or minor priests, were those who arranged everything beforehand and who cleared up the refuse when the meal was over. The name "Server" is still used at the Eucharist celebrations of the Anglican and Roman Churches for those who perform the same duties.

On the site of the ancient city of Oxyrhynchus, Doctors Grenfell and Hunt discovered a papyrus of the 2nd century A.D. which reads as follows : "Chaeremon invites thee to dine at the table of the Lord Serapis in the Serapeum tomorrow, the fifteenth, at nine o'clock". Serapis was the Greek name for Osiris and the Serapeum was the name of the temple dedicated to him at Alexandria. Aristides (A.D. 117–189), the distinguished Greek sophist, moreover, tells us that the worshippers of Serapis enjoyed a real communion with him in his sacrifice for them, that he met them at the altar during the Communion service where he partook with them of the sacrament.

Porphyry (A.D. 233–306), the Neo-platonist, remarks that the spirits sit beside the worshippers, and we find from an inscription to the god Hercules, discovered in Kos, a description of the ritual performed at the Eucharist to his memory. Herein we find it mentioned that the communicants sit down at the "Table of God". Paul confirms that this was the prevailing belief in those days amongst the Pagans, but in his enthusiasm for Christ he terms the Lord's Table of the Pagans "The Table of Demons" and refers to them being in communion with devils (1 Cor. x, 21).

The record which has come down to us of how the body of the Greek saviour-god Dionysus, as represented by an animal, was broken for, and eaten by, his worshippers, so as to fortify them with his immortality, differs only slightly from a Presbyterian communion service, where the body of the victim is represented by a loaf of bread, placed on the table, and his blood by wine in a flagon. The priest, who is called a minister, runs the sacrificial knife into this loaf and divides it amongst the minor priests sitting round. The minor priests, or servers, who are called elders, after consuming some of the symbolic body of the victim, round the Lord's Table, in the belief that the Lord is present, as a spirit, then drink some of the wine, which symbolises the victim's blood. When this is done they rise and take the remains of the symbolic flesh and blood to the waiting descendants of the savage cannibals who instituted this ceremony, but who ate the actual body and drank the actual blood of the victim. The elders hand round the bread and the wine, which each communicant partakes of, as representing the victim's body and blood which was sacrificed on their behalf.

The Anglican and Roman services correspond more to the one performed by the Mystery Cults. Here the participant goes up to the altar to receive the symbolic flesh and blood direct from the priest and not from the server. In this case also the communicant believes that the sacrificed victim is present as a spirit. It is all just refined cannibalism, the only change being in the food eaten, not in the idea, which is the same now as it was then.

In order to feed the gods, and serve them in an orderly way, the priesthood became established, and out of this meal developed the rites and ceremonies of religion. When our ancestors ceased being nomads and built houses in which to live, they also provided houses for the gods, in different centres, where they could eat the spirits, and the people could gather at the same time to partake of the body and blood. A Church or Temple to begin with was a common eating house for the gods and mankind. Here they met, and sat down together, and this is still the primary use of churches, though, as time went on, preaching and hymn-singing were added. So commenced Temples and Churches, and the priests, owing to their privileged position of being the food providers for the gods, became the care-takers of these eating houses.

Thus the gods had their banqueting halls on earth, with their butchers, cooks and servants, who provided them with human spirits for food. If the priests were obtaining sufficient in the way of offer-ings from the people, then they told them that the gods were satisfied. If they were not, then the gods were angry and the people must give more. Besides human victims the gods wanted animals and the fruits of the field, the spirits of which they also relished. The cooked remains of all these food-stuffs appealed to the palates of the priests and when they obtained enough the gods were satisfied.

The priests, in order to keep up supplies, had to adopt the methods of modern dictators. They had to keep the people in a perpetual state of alarm, to make certain that their services would be required. If the people ceased fearing the gods, and became indifferent as to what happened to them after death, then their work would naturally cease. So they taught that "The fear of the Lord is the beginning of wisdom" (Psalm cxi, 10). Thus they kept the people on tenterhooks by their stories about the wickedness of humanity, and its sins of omission and commission, how death had come as a curse because of man's sins and wickedness, and how the regular flow of victims must continue to keep the gods in a good humour. Besides this they invented a new method of raising money by telling people that in return for money, or produce, they would pray to the gods and make arrangements for those spirits in Hades, for whom they prayed, to be released. This method of raising money is practised in half the Christian churches of the present day.

Then somewhere, and at some place, someone was brave enough to rise up and lead the people to a truer conception of death and a higher idea of the gods. He, of course, was immediately seized by the priests and offered up as a sacrifice to the gods. He was the first martyr to priestly intolerance, the first of a very long line, and, if he had been the last, human sacrifice would still be with us today. The human race has progressed over the bodies of those reformers, who, in spite of all opposition from tyrants, both political and religious, were braver, saw further, and had a deeper insight into the mysteries of life than the rest of the people. By their leadership the human race slowly rose to a higher range of thought, and more and more supported those who advocated progress and reform. The more this came about the fiercer became the opposition from the dictators in their attempt to continue the old order.

Just as the people on earth were advancing, so were those in the etheric world, which comprises all who lived on earth. Earth fills this other world and, as we are on earth, so are we there. On the lower planes of that other world of finer vibrations the inhabitants differ little from those on earth. Here we are in a nursery, preparing for a fuller life in the other world, but even when we get there it unfolds only in proportion to our mental development. As children leave the nursery in a more advanced state, so they reach the schoolroom in a more developed state. As the schoolroom is thus supplied by this more developed type so is the other world. As mankind advances on earth so he likewise advances in the etheric world. The effect of this was that in bygone days the gods developed as man developed, because the gods are just men and women, with the same minds as they had on earth, and this is equally true in times present as in times past.

Our enquiry into the part played by the priesthood in the origin of the saviour-god religions would not be complete without some further consideration of the prevalence everywhere, and at all times, of psychic phenomena produced in the presence of those we now term mediums, those endowed with psychic power. That psychic phenomena are the cause behind every religion must some day be accepted by all, however much their present materialistic outlook may hide from them the truth. Like the priesthood, the majority are suffering from having their minds directed into a wrong channel in early life. Never having experienced anything supernormal throughout their lives, and never having read about what others have experienced, or, having read and disbelieved, they ignore this first cause behind all religious development, and the beliefs which accompanied it.

Priests have always said that the religion they represent started by a miraculous interference with nature, performed by the god they worshipped. Scholars, who have made religion and mythology a study, believe that every religion started from hallucination, magic or dreams, in fact anything that they can think of except the supernormal explanation. It is interesting to read the number of different explanations they give to explain the origin of the Christian Faith. Each one is different and each one is equally absurd. Some day the mists will roll away and the sun of knowledge will clear their outlook, and so balance their judgement.

From the information given earlier in this book it is evident that the origin of every religion is psychic phenomena of one kind or another. In order to make clear how this was the cause of the Christian Faith we must consider the attitude of the priesthood towards those called mediums, in whose presence these phenomena occurred. Towards them the priesthood has for ever shown the most bitter hostility. This is one of the outstanding features of the craft; not its fight against materialism, but its fight against mediumship.

In every religion, in every age, from the time the order of the priesthood was instituted, this hatred of everything to do with mediumship is apparent. It runs through the Laws of Moses and it prevailed in Egypt, Babylon and India. In fact, it is found everywhere in literature written by priests. The Laws of Moses are typical of the attitude of the priesthood everywhere towards mankind getting into touch with those who have passed on, and who come back to us through the channel nature has provided. On the other hand, the Epistles of Paul, which were not written by priests, openly support and encourage mediumship, and, until the priests gained control of the Christian Church in the fourth century, mediums were the instruments used to link up earth with heaven.

True, amongst ignorant people mediumship can be abused. Undesirable spirits can possess mediums who permit them to come. They slip through the guard on their side which protects all mediums, but they are soon warned off. Mediumship can degenerate into fortune-telling, but, if so, it ceases to be mediumship, since mediumship relates only to the use of a human being, by people in the other world, as a channel for passing their messages through to the inhabitants of the earth.

The casting of spells, and the frightening of people by magical arts and other fraudulent practices, are all things which sensible people have always disregarded. Only the ignorant and foolish take such things seriously, but, as the world is mostly composed of the foolish and the simple, rogues can always find profitable employment. The fake is only the imitation of the real which the faker copies, and, so long as stupid people exist, the earth will never be cleansed of fraudulent priests or of fraudulent mediums, who usurp the place of the genuine mediums endowed by nature with psychic gifts.

Mediumship has brought untold comfort to humanity, and millions, past and present, have been assured of the happiness of their loved ones who have passed on. Besides this they have obtained assurance as to their own destiny, and been strengthened to live better and more useful lives. The happiness mediumship has brought to those who have made use of the channel nature has provided is impossible to calculate.

Sorcerers have frightened the foolish by their tricks, spells and divinations, but, however much they are to be blamed for this, when their record is compared with that of the priesthood they appear as shining angels. No other body of human beings have to face the charge which history lays against the priests of having frightened millions of millions of people for thousands of years with the prospect of everlasting torment in Hell. If we take only the Christian era, and go no further back than fifteen hundred years, when the priests captured Christianity, the mountain of misery this Christian doctrine has produced would reach such a height as to defy human computation.

Compare the insignificant number of fake mediums or sorcerers with the millions of priests who have preached the everlasting torments of Hell every week for fifteen hundred years. What an out-cry there is when a fraudulent medium is discovered, and yet not a word of protest is ever raised against the mass teaching and mass preaching of Hell, which is one of the foundation-stones of the Christian Faith, and is found prominently expressed in its sacred literature, liturgy and beliefs. One is aware that an illiterate and ignorant people must be ruled by their emotions. The priesthood were the ruling class and this was one of the methods it adopted, but those who rule should try to lift the people under them to a higher level of intelligence. This the priesthood never did, and this neglect of its responsibilities will be for ever remembered against it.

Instead of the priests taking charge of the mediums and cultivating mediumship in an intelligent and regular manner, instead of educating the people to understand the difference between good and bad mediumship, genuine and false communications, or how the best conditions could be obtained to secure the most satisfactory results, they have always adopted an attitude of hostility towards all mediumship. All mediums, good or bad, were denounced. All mediums were branded the servants of the Devil, and all communications through them were classed as coming from the Devil and his angels, for the purpose of undermining everything that was good in humanity.

Through no fault of their own, the lives of all mediums, speaking generally, have always been full of peril. Anyone who was endowed by nature with what the Greeks called psychic gifts, one who was used by men and women in the other world as their medium for the purpose of sending communications to their friends on earth, lived, in consequence, a life which was both intolerable and dangerous. Those who entered the state of trance and were controlled by these discarnate beings, those who had the power of seeing and hearing them in a normal state, those in whose presence the movement of objects occurred, without apparent contact, or a materialisation was built up, those in whose presence the Direct Voice was heard, or who were used by healers on the other side to heal the sick, were marked out and pursued to their death.

They were given names which were considered ignominious, such as wizards and witches. They were called Servants of the Devil, and are still called this by Christian priests of every denomination in our own country and throughout Christendom. The people were warned, and still are, to avoid them, and if they did not, and brought to them the sick to be healed by their psychic power, then the organisation lifted one of its mighty paws and crushed them.

For thousands of years there has been everywhere this cruel persecution of mediums by the priests. They burned them, harried them, defamed them, mutilated them, tortured them by every means that their cruel minds could invent, and this continued till public opinion rose up against this savagery and stopped the slaughter in the eighteenth century. Now the priests can only tell lies about them, and warn the people never to seek their dead through the agency of these servants of the Devil. From earliest times the priests influenced the passing of cruel and unjust laws against these harmless people, and, throughout the Christian era, the Church everywhere in Christendom influenced legislation designed to exterminate anyone with psychic gifts.

These laws are still on the Statute Book in this country and are applied contrary to all justice and fair play. The lot of the medium has only been improved in so far as he or she cannot now be burned or tortured, but mediums are still imprisoned and fined, and the influence of the Church prevents these unjust laws being repealed. It produced these laws, has guarded them, and has always obstructed their repeal. Mediums are termed vagabonds and rogues in the law of Great Britain, and everything to do with mediumship is illegal. When we come to find how high the medium stood in the opinion of the early Christians we shall better appreciate the evil effect of the priesthood over the past fifteen hundred years.

The Church is so bitter against communication with the departed that the denouncing of mediumship is still one of the themes of Sunday sermons. From bishops downwards, the priests pursue this well-conceived plan to frighten their flocks against this contact with the Devil. Few Church publications will insert an advertisement of a book dealing with this subject, and if it is ever mentioned in such publications it is for the purpose of condemning it. Since priestcraft came into existence millions of mediums have been tortured and murdered under its direction. This persecution of mediums is a history in itself and can be found in all standard books devoted to the subject.

The reason is obvious. Mediumship has from all times been the greatest competitor of the priesthood. If the people could get into contact with the other world through mediums then the priesthood would be unnecessary. It would go out of business. So it adopted from the first a war of extermination towards mediums, and yet, if there had been no mediums, there would never have been any psychic phenomena. Without this there would have been no religion and without religion there would have been no priests. They thus derive their position and sustenance from what they have always denounced and exterminated whenever possible.

Can this anomaly be explained? It was because the people lost their way in the early days of religion when the priest-magician was clever enough to imitate the genuine phenomena. As he was able to repeat the performance at will, which was something the genuine medium could not do, the people followed the false and neglected the true. The wonder is that mediums were not entirely exterminated. If it had not been for the priesthood, communication with the other world would now be much more general than it is, because mediumship is an hereditary gift and, if left to develop, increases generation by generation, as we have discovered since the burning of mediums ceased.

On the basis of psychic phenomena the priesthood built up its entire ecclesiastical structure and, though the basis was sound, the erection was rotten, built of deception and maintained by fraud. So murder, force and cunning, in conjunction with a determination to keep the people ignorant, have always been necessary to keep it from collapsing. Mediumship and education are the two forces which are demolishing the erection of lies and misrepresentation on which the Order of Priesthood has always thrived and still thrives. The fight between truth and falsehood will continue till this evil organisation has ceased to function, but it will remain so long as it is allowed to retain the wealth it has accumulated from the weak and fearful.

All those who arose to denounce the priesthood for its false claims, as we are led to think Krishna, Bel and Osiris did, were sacrificed to the gods and, by their appearance after death, became god-men on earth and gods in heaven. It is the bitterness shown by the priesthood towards those who became saviour-gods which is the best proof that these men were reformers or mediums, possibly both, who were leading the people away from the orthodox worship of the day.

When one finds bitter hatred shown everywhere for thousands of years by a certain caste towards the people who possess psychic gifts, it is not difficult to deduce the reason why those whom the people claimed did wonderful things, and spoke as never man spoke, became victims and died violent deaths. Their deeds and sayings were impressing the people to turn away from sacrifice, and in consequence the priesthood was obtaining reduced supplies to offer to the gods. The priests talked much of the coming Messiah but had no desire that he would come in their day. Yet, as in the case of Krishna and the others, their very eagerness to avoid such a change of outlook brought it about.

The history of the priesthood for thousands of years gives an answer so clear and so unequivocal, as to how and why those who became saviour-gods died, that there is no other possible to imagine. We can imagine that those who became saviours were against sacrifice, on which the priests lived, and their exclusiveness, bigotry and intolerance. Probably they also spoke against the cruelty which accompanied all creeds and dogmas, and resented the neglect of the poor and needy. The continuous overriding by the priesthood of the ethical code, if it interfered with their own vested interests, doubtless also raised the anger of these reformers.

They were against the love of wealth, power and position, so sought after by the priests, and the latter's neglect of the welfare of the people. The concentration of the priesthood on the altar, instead of on helping the people to reach out to higher things, aroused the wrath of these more ethically-minded men who saw further, and thought more deeply, than the rest of the people.   In a word, these reformers, like Buddha, taught that religion did not consist of creeds, rites and ceremonies, but in the contemplation of the deeper things of life.

Krishna, we can imagine, preached against all this priestly wickedness, and perhaps demonstrated the workings of the spirit world through mediumship. He told the people that the Kingdom of God was in each one, and that it resided in the mind when directed along the channel of right and honest thinking. This kingdom could never be obtained by creeds, by ceremonies or by sacrifices, but by the cultivation of kind and pure thoughts, by unselfishness and love for all.   Because of this the priests, fearful of losing their regular offerings for sacrifice, the support of the people, and the wealth they contributed, murdered those reformers so as to stamp out all opposition to the orthodox form of worship.

It was so natural for the people to look on the appearing after death of the victimised reformer as a sign from heaven, that a change in outlook was necessary.   The martyred victim, hung on a cross, or a tree, or stoned, or sacrificed on the altar, was to them a victim offered to the gods.   His return proved that death had lost its sting and that he had gone before to prepare the way for his people.   Someone braver than the rest, like Paul of Tarsus, then led the people forward on this new line of thought, and it is also possible that the victim sent messages through trance mediums or clairaudients, encouraging the people to continue the fight he had begun.

However it happened, and happen it did, a new conception entered into the religious life of the people, the belief in a saviour-god. This development came about slowly, and, on each occasion after the victim reappeared, the idea attracted more and more of those endowed with the priestly mind, who surrounded it with symbolic ideas, so loved by the mystic, till in the end the victim became a god in heaven and a god-man on earth, surrounded by legends and symbolism.

For the sake of understanding the problem better I shall now enumerate the stages of development, already referred to in the previous chapter, between the human reformer and his translation into a god-man on earth and a god in heaven.

(1) Someone with reforming zeal, and probably with psychic power, revolts against the orthodox religion of his time.

(2) He goes about preaching a reformed religion. He perhaps looks upon himself in the light of a Messiah, or prophet, ushering in a new order of religious thought. If he does not think so then the people do. One or other of these suppositions must be true because of what happens after his reappearance. Probably, in most cases, he regards himself as a Messiah and so also do his followers. He may have had healing powers, been guided clairaudiently and have had other mediumistic powers.

(3) He angers the orthodox, is arrested by the priests, tried and condemned to death, which sentence is carried out according to the custom prevailing.

The earliest reformers were probably sacrificed to the gods on the altar.

(4) He is seen and recognised after death, which means that he has survived the sacrifice and that the gods have not eaten him.

(5) This event has considerable effect on those who had been his followers, who read into it that he has conquered death and come back to prove that he has done so. This meant that sacrifice had come to an end, and that the gods no more wished to eat the spirits of the victims. Consequently the spirits of the people on earth would not be eaten by the gods when they passed over into their presence. Our ancestors were cannibals and thought only in terms of eating human flesh, and of the gods eating the spirits of the dead. Consequently it is not difficult to imagine the fear each one had as to his fate after death. The return of a sacrificed victim, therefore, set in train a new set of ideas, which in time gave rise to the belief in the saviour-god. Out of these thoughts arose the idea that the teaching the victim had delivered, while on earth, was a god-sent revelation, and that he must have been a messenger sent from the gods to usher in a new era.

(6) This idea developed till the victim was finally looked upon as the Saviour who had conquered death, and reappeared as a sign to his followers that he had gone before to prepare a place for them.

(7) In time, under the influence of the mystically minded, he was imagined as a god in heaven, whose status was next to the chief of all the gods, while his earth life was pictured as that of a god-man, born of a virgin, who went about doing marvellous things

and uttering the wisest sayings his worshippers could find to put into his mouth.

(8) Some of the less conservative priests of the orthodox faith also accepted these new ideas and became the leaders in the new religion.

Priests were always the constructors of the beliefs surrounding all religions and not merely their interpreters. Paul was not a priest ; he evolved no new ideas, as all he did was to adopt old beliefs and relate them to Jesus. All religions with a priesthood were evolved by priests. The people had nothing to do with their construction except in so far as the priests built round the people's thoughts. They could not produce a religion that the people could not understand. The priests did the building but the bricks were the people's ideas. The priesthood was the custodian of the mythology, the symbolism and astrology of its times. From the real and apparent life in nature they spun their stories and speculations, symbolising everything connected with those they turned into god-men on earth and gods in heaven. So we find that all the legendary tales, which were their own production, came to be considered as sacred and a revelation from the gods.

(9) The ecclesiastical mind built up creeds and doctrines surrounding the one now looked upon as the saviour-god, always borrowing from the surrounding religions. So we find the doctrines, dogmas, creeds, ceremonies and rites the same in all the saviour-god religions.

(10) Then a Church organisation was formed to protect the foregoing, and perpetuate the memory of

the saviour-god, by its members eating the flesh and drinking the blood of men or animals in the belief that the Saviour had transmigrated into the creature killed and eaten. The then prevailing belief in the transmigration of the spirit of man from one body to another was probably the origin of the doctrine of transubstantiation, and is best exemplified in the beliefs of the Mystery Cults which we are about to consider. The origin of the belief in the transmigration of spirits is doubtless to be found in a misconception of the meaning of mediumship.

(11) Thus the participants partook of the body and blood of the creature, believing that they were fortifying themselves by partaking of a body inhabited by their Saviour. Sacrifice thus continued, though the religion had as one of its beliefs that it had come to an end through the reappearance of the victim, and this very same anomaly is to be found in the Christian religion.

(12) Bread and wine in time took the place of the slain victim. As the spirit of the Saviour could not enter into these, the priests claimed that by magic they turned them into the actual body and blood of the victim. So the participants believed that in this way they were fortified by taking within themselves part of the body and blood of their saviour-god.

(13) Sacrifice, however, still continued and the priesthood remained corrupt. A reformer again arises, is killed and reappears, and the wheel starts once more on the same round, each cause having the same effect, because the new copied from the old, until the new, which supplanted the old, only differed from the old in the name of the new god worshipped.

So we have many saviour-gods in religious history, one following the other, till we reach the time we are now considering, which is those centuries prior to the opening of the Christian era, when Krishna was worshipped in India, Mithra in Persia, Osiris in Egypt and Dionysus in Greece. Bel alone amongst the saviour-gods had lost his worshippers, the beliefs surrounding him having been taken over by his successor, Murdock. Everywhere there were Mystery Cults, into which the worshippers were initiated for the performance of the ceremonies surrounding the god of the Cult.

So we have now obtained the answers to our four questions which we had to answer before we could attempt to understand the origin of the Christian Faith. These were :

(1) Who were the saviour-gods ?—Men like ourselves.

(2) Why were they deified ?—Because they appeared after death.

(3) Why were they killed ?—Because the priests feared them.

(4) How were they killed ?—By the priests according to the prevailing custom.

These answers cover the questions, not only as regards Krishna but also as regards Bel, Osiris, Mithra, Prometheus and all the others, Jesus included, as we shall discover in the next chapter. They were all the victims of a jealous, cruel and fearful priesthood. Their teaching and deeds on earth, and their appearance after death, were the reasons why the people elevated them to the rank of gods in heaven and god-men on earth. It is strange to think that ideas set out at length in this and the previous chapters produced Christianity, and yet in truth they did.

Before, however, giving our undivided attention to the Christian Faith, we must consider the beliefs prevailing when this religion was conceived. We now know what the Jewish priesthood was like and what its opinions were. It was as exclusive and as cruel as any before or after its time. Its priests were the criminals in the tragedy which will be discussed in the next chapter ; they were the cause of the death of an innocent man. This crime, and the victim's reappearance, would not, however, have been sufficient to have produced a new faith. The people had to be ready for the change, prepared to abandon the worship of their old god and go over to the new one. Two factors were, therefore, necessary to start what came to be known as the Christian Faith : (1) the Priesthood, who sacrificed the victim, and (2) the People, whose religious ideas are best exemplified by those held by the worshippers attached to

THE MYSTERY RELIGIONS.

The centuries prior to the Christian era were a period of great religious speculation and contemplation. In Egypt, Greece and Rome a new conception of life was evolving, and this, from the Apocryphal literature, was also apparent in Palestine. An intense desire is noticeable for greater at-one-ment with God, and with it the people felt the sense of their own weakness and unrighteousness. More and more the belief was growing that the universe was governed by one supreme being, and that the gods were demigods with no part in the ordering of nature. The longings and aspirations of the people found expression in the Mystery religions, through which they dedicated themselves to God and a higher life. Those who sought initiation underwent severe bodily discomfort in the belief that by punishing the body they purified their spirit.

Legge, in his book *Forerunners and Rivals of Christianity*, remarks that in the six centuries from Alexander to Constantine, "There has probably been no time in the history of mankind when all classes were more given up to thoughts of religion or when they strained more fervently after high ethical ideals". The world, in fact, was experiencing a religious revival and eagerly seeking after a new sign from Heaven. In this atmosphere the Mystery religions spread rapidly, and gave comfort and satisfaction to the deeper longings and aspirations of the Greek and Roman people. The longing after righteousness was eased by the satisfaction obtained through the individual casting every sin and wickedness on to the saviour-god. This gave to each one the content and happiness desired.

In *The Acts of the Apostles* and the Epistles we get a very one-sided view of the position which prevailed in this age. Christians think of Paul journeying and preaching through a heathen world whose gods were idols and whose prayers were offered to images of wood and stone. This misunderstanding, due to ignorance and prejudice, came about through the obsession on the part of early Christian writers that Christianity was the only true faith and that those who worshipped any other god but Christ worshipped devils.

Paul sounds the warning note about the danger of "Some giving heed to the doctrines of devils" and says that "The Gentiles sacrifice to devils, and not to God, and I would not that ye have fellowship with devils". It is well known that proselytes are the most fanatical and rabid in the religious community. A Protestant who becomes a Catholic is much more zealous than one who is born a Catholic, and vice-versa. So the leaders of the new faith, who adopted the god Christ in place of their old one, considered that the gods their contemporaries worshipped were devils because the only true god was the one they now worshipped.

This explains why it is that Christians hold, and always have held, such erroneous views about the religious beliefs of the Pagans who were contemporary with the early Christians. The Pagans were deeply religious people, and to think of them in any other way shows entire lack of knowledge of the times. It is one thing to term as Pagans those who worshipped other saviour-gods, in order to differentiate them from those who worshipped Christ, but to think that these Pagans had different religious views and aspirations from the Christians is quite wrong. The word Pagan means countryman, as the country people were the last to accept Christianity. For want of another word I have used the word Pagan to cover all saviour-god worshippers apart from those who worshipped Christ. We appreciate the religious enthusiasm of Paul but we must also remember that there were thousands of Pagans with thoughts equally elevated, with ideals equally immaterial, and with aspirations as lofty as those which have come down to us under the name of Paul and the other apostles.

Dr. Angus, the Professor of New Testament and Historical Theology of St. Andrew's College, Sydney, in his book, *The Mystery Religions and Christianity*, is equally definite on this subject, remarking that

> From the days of Aristotle onwards numerous treatises were written on prayer as e.g. by Persius, Juvenal and Maximus of Tyre. Practically every moralist of later Paganism—Cicero, Seneca, Epictetus, Lucian, Marcus Aurelius, Porphyry, Plotinus —devoted attention to this expression of the religious life. Many of their declarations upon this topic are marked by deep spiritual insight. Some of the language is of supreme beauty and might be used by Christian hearts. The many endeavours made by statesmen, poets and philosophers to bring about a revival of religion indicate that religion was viewed as the imperative necessity of society.

Alexander the Great was not slow to take advantage of this religious atmosphere and instituted himself as the one on whom the gods had placed the divine cloak. This cloak was handed down to his successors and no one made greater use of it than did Julius Caesar. Constantine was the first to discard it and place it on the back of the Bishop of Rome of the Christian Church, whose successors, the Popes, have worn it throughout the Christian era. Kings and priests in the Western world have, from the time of Alexander, made use of this appeal to the religious emotions of the people, and we have already noticed how useful it was to the Egyptian kings. The idea goes back for thousands of years and is in its origin essentially oriental. With its introduction into Europe by Alexander it gave the ruling power additional authority. As Christianity spread amongst the barbarians the idea undoubtedly helped to strengthen the link between the people and the Church, so much so that by the 8th century A.D. the Pope was wielding a power over Europe equalled only by that of an eastern potentate.

The religious emotions of the people, in the age to which this chapter refers, were perhaps due to some extent to the feeling that the mythology which had comforted their forefathers was no longer tenable. From the time when Evemerus, in the 4th century B.C., had expressed his opinion that the gods of mythology had once been men, a slow but steady awakening had taken place. The people were coming to realise the folly and absurdity of the beliefs of their ancestors. Evemerus did to Greek mythology very much what Thomas Paine and Voltaire did to Christian theology when they startled the religious world, at the end of the eighteenth century, with the assertion that Jesus had never been more than a human being, a man like other men. Evemerus ushered in the age of scepticism to Pagan mythology as did Voltaire and Paine to Christian theology. He put a check on god-making, so much so that after his time we find only two new gods, Apollonius and Christ, both produced in the first century of the Christian era.

We remember in our own childhood days how real the heroes of our fairy stories were to us and how, without effort, we left behind the belief that Cinderella or Jack the Giant Killer were real people. The Mediterranean world, in the days we are considering, was just at the stage we were in when six years old, and the majority today, so far as religion is concerned, are as simple and believing as they were as children. In religion, the majority are like Peter Pan, they never grow up, and they have the same superstitious beliefs as the Greeks and Romans. Christianity acts like a sedative, it keeps people from thinking. It keeps them quiet and contented, like the expected return of Santa Claus does children, who look forward to his visit next Christmas just as Christians anticipate the second coming of Christ.

Like all the men and women of mythology, Santa Claus actually lived in Myra in Asia sixteen hundred years ago, and his mortal remains lie buried in the Cathedral of San Nicola in Bari in Italy. His name was Nhka and, after death, he was known as San Nicola. Most people think of Santa Claus as a mythical being, but there was a real man behind the name just as there was a real man behind the story of Robinson Crusoe. Likewise there was someone real behind each religious and nursery myth and legend spun to please the people of the past who had the minds of children. What are now considered to be nursery stories were believed to be true by our ancestors in the same way as were the religious myths and legends. We are only now realising that our ancestors had not only the minds but also the imagination of children, and that what they have passed on to us were the products of their childlike imaginations. Some of these were taken up by the Christian Church and hedged round by a fence too holy and sacred to pass through, which kept them from rational examination.

For a thousand years the Greeks had guarded their mythology by sacred tradition, and only by more rational thinking in the days of the philosophers, beginning about 600 B.C., was a breach made in long-cherished ideas. The people, however, could not go all the way with them because, as Cicero said, they wished to "live with joy and die with better hope". In the place of the legends of the wonderful exploits of their gods in heaven, and on earth, they turned to the saviour-gods for comfort and hope of salvation. In the ceremonies surrounding this worship they obtained their happiness and received their comfort, very much as Greek, Roman, Anglican and Lutheran Christians receive them by the performance of the ritual surrounding their worship.

Last century in this country we experienced much the same development. The publication of Darwin's *Origin of Species*, and the Rationalist literature of the times, threw some into a state of agnosticism and others into an intensification of religious ceremonial and ritual. The scepticism which developed with regard to the Christian legends followed much the same course as it did with the Greek legends in Greece and Rome, some becoming agnostics and others ritualists. When old cherished beliefs go, the reaction seems to be this intensification of ceremony and ritual on the part of some. They feel that the mere doing of something gives them the satisfaction that the believing of something used to give.

So what happened in the Graeco-Roman world does not astonish us and, as the edifice of myth and legend built up by Homer and Hesiod declined, so the popularity of the Mystery Cults increased.

Though, in the minds of the educated Greeks, the gods had flown from High Olympus, yet in their place they found others, and their saviour-gods became very dear to them. They communed with them in their homes and in their churches. As the old legends went so did the old polytheism. A higher idealism also developed, the morality attributed to their old gods being that of a much earlier age. The people had advanced beyond their old religion, just as most Christians have advanced beyond the morality of the Old Testament. Their philosophers had led them to higher and nobler thoughts. Thus, in this age of transition, a new conception of the Infinite developed along with a purer and higher morality. The people yearned for a closer at-one-ment with God, and strove to lead more holy lives in order to please the divine being pictured by their more cultured minds.

As in Greece so in Rome. Though Rome had gained the then known world, she found her religious satisfaction, not at home, but in the East. During and after the three Punic wars, religion was neglected and the gods forgotten. Did not Appius Claudius Pulcher throw the sacred fowls overboard before the sea battle of Drepanum, and Flaminus go into battle without propitiating the gods? From Egypt and Persia the Romans now found their religious comfort. Though they officially took over from Greece in 217 B.C. twelve of her gods, and gave them Latin names, it was the saviour-gods from the East who outlasted those taken from Mount Olympus.

One by one the old myths were repudiated, or interpreted symbolically, and, in their place, came philosophy and an ethical system combined with contemplative mysticism. From the time of Plato, amongst the educated, the old Greek religion ceased to be, and from the 4th century B.C. onwards religion and philosophy blended. Some followed Epicurus in believing that the gods took no interest in the affairs of men, that it was useless waste to sacrifice to them, and folly to fear them. On the other hand, we find an intensification of the desire for greater harmony with the Infinite through ritual and ceremony. It was so like the state of affairs today, with the agnostic on the one hand, the ritualist on the other, and, between these extremes, those who are loath to give up the mythology of their forefathers on which has centred their hope and comfort.

In the 10th century B.C. there commenced in Greece the worship of the saviour-god Dionysus. Surrounding his name were the beliefs which encircled all the other gods of this class. In reality he lived as an ordinary human being, being born in Thebes and buried in Delphi. On his tomb was inscribed, "Here lies Dionysus dead, the son of Semele". His worshippers, however, believed that he came to earth a virgin-born child, died a violent death, was seen after death, and returned to heaven to sit by the side of his father Zeus on a kingly throne. Quite probably he died the violent death reported of him, and it is also possible that he went about, as reported, as a teacher uttering wise and noble thoughts, with the people following after him. This is quite natural, as is the report that he taught his generation how to tend the vine, for which knowledge he was called the greatest benefactor of mankind.

His followers also believed that after his death his body was broken, to symbolise the end of the earth body, and that, when he returned to heaven, Zeus placed a sceptre in his hand and made him the judge of all the earth. Zeus was brought into the picture by the belief that he overshadowed Semele, the mother of Dionysus. Dionysus became the most beloved god of his time in the entire Greek pantheon, and his worshippers believed that in heaven he took only second place to Zeus, all the other gods being his inferiors.

As time went on these other gods, in the people's imagination, became demi-gods and then angels, the Father and the Son remaining as the two principal gods. Dionysus was known as the Vine, the Saviour, the Judge of the Dead, the Deliverer, the Born Again, the Only Begotten Son of God, and his followers believed that, as he himself stated "I am one with my father in Heaven".

His worshippers on earth celebrated his death by enacting it in the form of a passion play, similar to that performed in connection with the death and resurrection of the Babylonian god Bel, the priests impressing the people with the beliefs that as Dionysus lived after death so would they. The following saying relating to his powers has come down to us : "Trust ye in God, for out of his loins salvation has come to us, Dionysus has risen from the dead for the salvation of the world". At the drama, before the resurrection of the god from the tomb, doleful music was played, but after his resurrection it became bright and cheerful. His etheric body could not be shown as freed from his material body, so the people had to be content with seeing the resurrection depicted by one of the actors coming bodily out of the grave.

This dramatic representation gave the people quite a wrong idea of death, and what follows death, and may have been the cause of the belief, held by so many in those days, particularly the Egyptians, that at the resurrection of the dead the spirit returned to its earth body which it re-animated. We find this idea running through Christian eschatology, and can now understand why it was believed that those who were dead could rise from their graves, and walk about Jerusalem when Jesus died. How this story originated will be referred to later on. This literal interpretation of what took place at the drama has caused much confusion of thought throughout the Christian era.

The Eucharistic service was similar to those already described. In the early days of the Mystery Cults an animal represented the victim who was worshipped, the people eating its flesh and drinking its blood, but, by the time Christianity adopted the Eucharist from the Mystery Cults, bread and wine were as often as not consumed to represent symbolically the body and blood of the Saviour.

To show how the people in those days received the same comfort from the belief in the resurrection of their Lord and Saviour as have Christians, it is interesting to read what Plutarch, the great Greek writer in the 1st century A.D., wrote to his wife after the death of their daughter in infancy. His wife was feeling the tragic loss acutely, and so he wrote to her reminding her how Dionysus had conquered death and opened the gates of heaven to those who loved him. Then he goes on to say that the death and resurrection of Dionysus teaches us that "the soul is immortal, so why trouble unduly about our daughter, as her soul is with Our Lord, and, when our turn comes, we shall be with her again".

Here is an instance of the comfort this belief gave to the Greeks, as it did to the Romans, the Egyptians, the Persians, the Babylonians and the Hindus for hundreds of years before the birth of Jesus and, not only before, but right up to and beyond his birth, because the worship of Dionysus and other saviour-gods continued until Constantine decreed that Christ was to take their place. Tarsus, the home of Paul, was one of the principal centres of this form of worship, and so the creator of the new Christ had all the material at hand to drape round Jesus, when he became convinced that Jesus had come to replace Dionysus and the other saviour-gods.

Dionysus, it was believed, descended to Hades after his death, as did all the gods who were associated with vegetation, because the ancients believed that under the surface of the earth was the source of all life. How otherwise could vegetation grow ? So, like Jesus, they all visited the underworld, the idea being perhaps that there their spirits were revitalised before ascending to Heaven. However, Dionysus, when he got to Hades, found his mother Semele awaiting him, and, like a dutiful son, he took her with him to Heaven. The principal festival held in his honour occurred in Spring when new life was coming to vegetation, and, in the processions in his honour at this time of the year, he was represented as an infant in a basket to symbolise young life.

Herodotus (484–424 B.C.) tells us that he looked on Osiris as standing for the same beliefs to the Egyptians as Dionysus did to the Greeks, and this is true of all these saviour-gods. What is said of one refers to the others in all important details, and, as the beliefs surrounding them have been given so fully in the previous chapter, all that will now be mentioned are the facts of outstanding interest. There is no necessity to refer separately to the cults of Orpheus, Apollo, or to the Eleusinian Mysteries, comprising the worship of Demeter and Persephone, as these were all ultimately absorbed into the worship of Dionysus, but something should be said about another much-beloved god, known as Adonis.

Adonis was originally worshipped in Babylon and Syria under the name of Tammuz, which means the Son of Life. He was also known as The Only Son of God. Adonis is another saviour-god, whom his followers believed died for them more than one thousand years B.C. Like all the others he was a human being. He was the son of Cinyras, the King of Syria, the land of the Phoenicians. Ctesias (400 B.C.) perpetuated his memory in the following verse :

> Trust, ye saints, your Lord restored.
> Trust ye in your risen Lord.
> For the pains Tammuz endured,
> Our salvation have procured.

Adonis, we are told, was crucified, but whether as a sacrificial victim, or as a martyr, we know not.

Crucifixion sometimes took place on the altar, the cross being laid thereon with the victim nailed or bound to it. Two days after his death he was seen in his etheric body and, in the presence of his disciples, he rose to heaven. In consequence he came to be looked upon as a god-man on earth and a god and saviour in heaven. In the 7th century B.C. his worship was brought to Greece and the saviour was given the name of Adonis, from the Greek Adon, meaning Lord. To begin with he was called Adonis Tammuz, but in time this was shortened to Adonis. As Christ and Jesus have come to mean the same, so Adonis and Tammuz meant the same to the Greeks. Adonis, like Christ, is not a proper name, but a title like Buddha, which was bestowed on Gautama.

Because of the death and reappearance of Adonis he was looked upon as the giver of eternal life to his followers and the usual stories accumulated around his name. He was related to the reproductive power in nature, and, at his death, it was believed that he passed into the underworld, as it was thought the sun did at night, and the life of vegetation did in winter. The story consequently was spun that his divine mistress, the goddess Aphrodite, went to fetch him back each spring, and that during his absence love died and only returned with him. He was consequently mourned annually and some will remember that Ezekiel says that he saw the women of Jerusalem weeping for Tammuz at the north gate of the Temple.

The Greeks pictured Adonis as a handsome youth, much beloved by the women. Aphrodite (Venus), the goddess of love, and Persephone, the goddess of the underworld, whence came all life, fought for him until Zeus declared that he was to live half the year, during the summer, with Aphrodite and half the year, during the winter, with Persephone. His cult had in pre-Christian times a cave in Bethlehem (The House of Bread) which it used for his worship. This same cave is now shown to visitors as the birthplace of Jesus. The chief temple of his worship was at Byblus, in Syria, where there was a great sanctuary dedicated to his name, and to his followers Byblus was considered a holy city.

Regular festivals were held in Western Asia, Athens and Antioch, and there the drama took place of his death, his coming to life and ascending to heaven. Antioch, it will be remembered, was one of the earliest centres of the worship of the new god, Christ, destined ultimately to supersede Adonis. As happened at the drama performed to other saviour-gods the body of Adonis was represented as being lost and then searched for. When it was found there was great rejoicing. The followers of Adonis observed a Eucharistic service, similar to those of the other Mystery Cults and of the Christian Faith.

Though Adonis had a human father, yet, when he became a god, his mother, who was called Myrrha, was believed to have been a virgin when he was born. It is interesting to notice how some of the saviour-gods have as their mothers women with names like Mary, which means the mother of life. So we have the month of May, when life returns, the French *mère* for mother, and *mer* for sea, in which the first life developed, and many other adaptations of the word for the same idea. In Athens, the death of

Adonis was commemorated in the middle of March each Spring, and the celebration was called The Festival of Flowers. This festival was carried right into the third century of the Christian era.

Sir James Frazer, in *The Golden Bough*, aptly remarks in connection with the many parallels found between the beliefs attached to the Mystery Cults and Christianity : "When we reflect how often the Church has skilfully contrived to plant the seeds of the new faith on the old stock of Paganism, we may surmise that the Easter celebration of the dead and risen Christ was grafted upon a similar celebration of the dead and risen Adonis, which, as we have seen reason to believe, was celebrated in Syria at the same season". He then goes on to show how Christians copied their pictures of Christ and the Virgin Mary from Greek art relating to Adonis and his mother.

The saviour-god Attis was originally worshipped in Phrygia, and what Adonis was to Syria Attis was to Western Asia. The centre of his worship was Hierapolis. Before his deification he was believed to have been a young shepherd who lived about 1200 B.C., but, when he became a god, in consequence of his death and reappearance, he was elevated to the rank of a god-man and his mother, Nana by name, became a virgin. The legend about Attis found its way from Asia to Greece and Rome.

His followers kept an effigy of a man bound to a tree in remembrance of his sacrifice. This was the sacred symbol of the cult, which was carried through the streets on all feast days. After the procession the people assembled for the Passion Drama, depicting his arrest, death and burial. During the ceremony his effigy was taken down from the tree and laid in a sepulchre. Then the people mourned and fasted for three days. On the third day, which was called The Day of Blood, which meant the Day of Life, there was great rejoicing, with clashing of cymbals, the beating of drums and the sounding of horns, for had not the weeping women gone to his tomb and found it empty, a bright light shining where the body had been laid?

When it was discovered that the Lord's body was not in the tomb the priests declared that, "Our Lord has risen and our salvation is assured", and, "Because Attis lives so shall we live". What we now call Easter Sunday was to them a festival of great joy, being known as The Festival of Joy. Then the image of Attis was again carried through the streets, washed and cleansed from its contact with the earth and, covered in garlands, laid on a cart drawn by oxen. Mirth and gaiety prevailed everywhere and the priests put on their finest robes.

This resurrection festival was held throughout Greece and in Rome. His worship preceded that of Mithra in Rome, because we read of a festival in his honour held in 204 B.C. It is also thought that his temple stood on the Vatican Mount, a spot believed to have been a sacred place for at least three thousand years. When St. Peter's was being enlarged in 1608 some very interesting discoveries were made, all pointing in this direction. Attis was worshipped throughout the Roman Empire, and inscriptions in his honour are to be found in France and Germany, where sanctuaries dedicated to him have been discovered.

His worshippers met together at regular intervals to partake of the Eucharistic service, common to all these saviour-god religions. In the early days a lamb, or some other animal, was killed, divided up, and handed round to the worshippers, but before the Christian era opened bread and wine were substituted, and a greater refinement developed in the rites and ceremonies. With the higher level of intelligence the people were evolving out of the age-long custom of partaking of a sacrificed animal. So, instead of a lamb being killed on the altar, its place was taken by bread and wine.

Attis had many terms of affection bestowed on him, but he was usually called The Lord. He was also termed the Very Fruitful and associated with vegetation. The tree became his symbol because the people believed that he was originally hanged on a tree, which was a very common method in those days of carrying out the death sentence. The victim's arms were drawn above his head, and we have several references to god-men being slain in this way. Odin, the Nordic saviour-god, is supposed to have suffered thus and so did Jesus, if Peter is correctly reported in *The Acts of the Apostles*. The effigy of the Greek goddess Artemis was hanged annually and she was known to her followers as "The Crucified One".

Hercules was also a saviour-god but, except for one interesting fact, there is nothing particular about his worship to make it necessary to give it detailed notice. Everyone knows that in St. Peter's in Rome stands St. Peter's Chair, which is possibly the chair of the Pater Patrum, the supreme Pontiff of Mithra at Rome. In 1867 it was examined by the eminent archæologist, de Rossi, and found to be made up of inlaid ivory panels representing the twelve labours of Hercules. It may be that these labours gave Christians the idea of the fourteen Stations of the Cross. On Mithraic monuments we also find representations of twelve episodes, so that the Mithraists may, in the first place, have copied the idea from the Hercules myth.

In the Mystery religions the Greeks and Romans continued the beliefs held sacred for thousands of years relating to the saviour-gods. They took over from surrounding countries all the essentials in these old beliefs and we find them focused in Greece and Rome, the tendency being, as time went on, for one cult to absorb another because of the similarity of views. The Christian cult in its turn grew up and developed, gathering its beliefs from its neighbours, by continuing the absorption process till, with the help of Constantine and later Emperors, it had absorbed them all.

The Mystery religions were the chief stronghold of all those who were opposed to the new Christian Faith, the Pagan controversialists always maintaining that everything advocated by the Christian writers was contained in the orthodox religions of the time, that Christology was the product of Christian imagination, and that Christians were bringing forward nothing new and nothing that was not already believed.

Our information about the Mystery religions comes from the writings of the early Church fathers, and from contemporary writers, from whom we find how Christianity grew out of the old beliefs quite naturally, the new god taking the place of the old ones without anything dramatic happening. It was a process of absorption, as had happened so often before. Osiris became Serapis to the Greeks without any effort, and Serapis, and the rest, became Christ in the same way. No upheaval paved the way, but, when Christ came to be worshipped throughout the Roman Empire by Christian communities everywhere, Constantine (A.D. 325) proclaimed that he was to be the future god of the Empire. It took another century, however, before Christ had taken the place of all the other gods, and this was the time when bitterness and hatred prevailed, when Christian persecution commenced, as the believers in the old saviour-gods did not relinquish their faith without a struggle.

The saviour-god religions, termed the Mystery Religions, to which I shall refer as the Mysteries for the sake of brevity, took greater and greater hold on the imagination of the Greeks and Romans from the 4th century B.C. onwards. By the time the Christian era opened they were the accepted religion of the people and remained so till the Christian Faith took their place. Each city and town had a temple, church or meeting-place dedicated to the god its members worshipped. In these, on Sunday, matins and vespers, or morning and evening services, were held, the people turning out in their best Sunday clothes and proceeding to their places of worship in the same decorous manner as that to which we are still accustomed in our own days. The service consisted of hymns, prayers and ceremonial, very much as occurs today in Italy and Greece. Apart from the regular services there were baptisms, confirmations and the celebration of the Eucharist or Holy Communion.

Christianity brought about little change, no more than occurs today when a new king's name is substituted for that of a dead one in the Book of Common Prayer of the Church of England. A new king is prayed for and when the new Christ took the place of the old Christs a new god was prayed to. They were, however, the same prayers and the new god meant the same to the people as did the old one, as does a new king. Under a new king things go on the same as before and so we proclaim the change of a king by announcing "The King is dead. Long live the King". Constantine's decree was, in effect, a proclamation to the Greeks and Romans, "Dionysus the Christ is dead. Long live Jesus the Christ".

The only change was one of unity, as if today, by Royal Proclamation, all Christian denominations became one and harmonious. Constantine did not bring about this unity and harmony, but he paved the way for it, and his successor Theodosius (A.D. 379–395) accomplished what Constantine attempted. Before this date the old saviour-gods were still worshipped ; after it there was only one, namely Jesus the Christ. With the authority conferred by Theodosius on the Bishop of Rome, the Christian priests made certain by the sword, by persecution and by suppression, that Jesus would have no rival. They destroyed the Pagan shrines, overturned the altars and burned all the old literature and liturgy.

What was it then that took place in the Mystery churches ? There was regular congregational worship, a strong bond of fellowship amongst the members, and they often had their cemetery beside the church. The words of cheerful hope on the tombstones made them indistinguishable from those in the Christian burial grounds. The Mysteries, over the preceding thousand years, had shed the cruder rites and ceremonies, and what Christianity absorbed were the purer forms of worship prevailing in the second, third and fourth centuries of our era. In its youth the new faith had also many crudities, some of which were shed as time went on, but in Russia the Greek Church, and elsewhere the Roman Church, still retain many primitive beliefs and ceremonies taken over from the Mystery religions. In these pre-Christian days much depended upon the mentality of the worshippers just as it has done during the Christian era. The Mystery churches would certainly compare very favourably with the Christian Church of the middle ages, in fact it is doubtful if the Mysteries ever fell to such a depth.

We have learned from this study of religious evolution how, through the ages, man has slowly, and by stages, attained a greater and greater appreciation of the Infinite. We have traced down the ages the golden thread of developing mind which has guided mankind from savagery to civilisation ; from magic, through worship and sacrifice, to philosophic contemplation. From a lowly and simple origin, the Mysteries developed and, at their best, could claim the adherence of men of profound thought who found in them satisfaction for their longings and aspirations.

Through the symbolism of the Mysteries, men and women felt that they were born into a new life, that they had cast their sins upon their Saviour and Mediator, through whose sacrifice they had been redeemed. Then they could say with fervour, "As truly as Osiris lives, shall I live, as truly as Osiris is not dead, shall I not die. Thus am I born again for Eternity".

The Mysteries taught that the body was the tomb of the spirit and, that by overcoming the desires of the flesh, the mind was stimulated to perceive things etheric, which were of God. By allegory this idea was simplified, and is best expounded by Philo in his numerous works, which supplied Paul with the allegory upon which Christian theology is based. The Mystery religion was essentially one of redemption, which professed to bring believers to at-one-ment with God through the death of the saviour-god. Belief in the saving power of the one who had suffered secured forgiveness of sins. "According to your faith" was the burden of their teaching, and this runs through their hymns and prayers.

Of the different cults which existed in Greece and elsewhere the Eleusinian was the most famous, and it will be remembered that this merged into the worship of Dionysus, who was a representative saviour-god of the times, Sophocles describing him as "The God who rules Italy". The cult of Orpheus, whose teaching is described as so lofty that it is doubtful whether any faith, ancient or modern, has surpassed it, likewise fused with the beliefs surrounding Dionysus. So what refers to the worship of Dionysus is applicable, in all its essentials, to the other saviour-god religions in the years just prior to, and after, the opening of the Christian era.

Philo, the great Hellenised Jew, expressed the thoughts surrounding the Mysteries in various writings. He was a large-minded, benevolent and dignified man, one of the leading men of his day in Alexandria. His brother was the Rothschild of Alexandria, and his niece by marriage was Bernice, who, with her brother King Agrippa II, we are told in Acts xxvi, listened to Paul telling of his vision and conversation with Jesus on his way to Damascus. As Philo was born about 30 B.C., his writings must have been known to Paul, and those associated with him, when weaving the current beliefs round Jesus.

Philo is recognised as the most important exponent of philosophic and mystical thought of his day, and represents what was taught at the Theological College in Alexandria. His philosophy was founded on the Hebrew law, Plato, Pythagoras and the philosophy of the Stoics, but he absorbed the teaching of the Greeks so thoroughly that he is regarded rather as a Greek than a Jewish philosopher. His writings can be briefly summarised as follows.

Philo attributed to God absolute sovereignty over the world, to be worshipped, not as an individual, but as representing the essence of perfection, goodness, truth and purity. God fills and encompasses all things with his being. God is made manifest to mankind by divine beings which are identical with those we today call spirits, or etherians, or etheric beings. To Philo these were the messengers of God to earth. God, in his opinion, is revealed to man by what he calls ideas, the totality of which is the reason of God, or Logos. In other words, God is mind, or the sum total of the thoughts of the universe.

The Logos reveals God to mankind and is called the first-born Son of God, the Archangel, who is the vehicle of all revelation, and the High Priest who stands before God on behalf of the world. Again this can be understood as meaning that in mind the divine is made manifest. Through the Logos the world was created, and he terms this divine being The Word of God, The Mediator between God and man, which can be understood by accepting the theory that mind is the first principle out of which all has evolved.

Philo's doctrine of man is dualistic and mainly derived from Plato. Man is a twofold being with a higher and a lower nature. The higher is due to his being a spirit, whereas the lower is due to his fleshly desires and passions. The body is therefore a prison of the incarnated spirit which seeks to return whence it came. Consequently man must free himself from all carnal lusts and reach out to God, who will help all those who make the effort. Without God's help man is a captive and unable of himself to reach true wisdom and virtue. His duty is to reach fellowship with God and this is the goal he should set before him. Thus the truly wise and virtuous seeker is lifted above his earth desires and enjoys in ecstasy the vision of God, his own consciousness sinking and disappearing in the Divine Light. Then to the righteous at death comes the entire liberation from the body, and the return of the spirit to its original condition. It came from God and to God it must return.

Philo's teaching, the sources of which can be traced to India and Persia, represents the link between

Jewish and Pagan thought. It was made use of by Paul and others, in a crude way, to bring about the combination of ideas which emerged under the name of Christianity. Alexandria was the great melting-pot of Jewish and Hellenic culture, and this mystical form of thought, of which Philo was the leading exponent, was known under the name of Gnosticism, which was to exert such an influence in the time to come in producing the Christian Faith. Philo so influenced the Hellenised Jews that they gave greater heed to Paul than perhaps they would otherwise have done.

The aim of all the Mystery believers was to know and understand God better, which desire developed into this mystical philosophy termed Gnosticism, from the Greek word gnosis, meaning knowledge. Those who adopted it were called Gnostics. The Gnostics one might term the intellectuals of the Mystery religions, much as the Jesuits claim to be in the Roman Catholic section of the Christian Faith, and the Modernists amongst the Protestants. The Gnostics desired further knowledge of God, and this fact became pronounced from the 2nd century B.C., if not earlier, increasing in intensity till their mystical philosophy helped to produce the Christian Faith. By initiation, which corresponded in those days to what one experiences when entering one of the Christian Orders, the Initiate believed that he obtained a supernatural revelation which gave him a new outlook on life and God. In other words, he was born again, having been rendered superior to the trials and dangers of this earth life.

Gnosticism, which might be termed the Paulinism of the Mystery Religions, because Paulinism is based on Gnosticism, spread throughout them all, so much so that by the 2nd century B.C. the difference between the various Mysteries was so slight as to be unimportant. This mystic teaching had also the effect of purifying these religions, till animal sacrifice became a thing of the past, and believers commemorated the death of their god by the Eucharistic service, similar to the one now prevailing in the Christian Church.

The influence of the East had a great effect in producing Gnosticism, besides the belief that God manifested himself to each by means of a special revelation. Otherwise he is unknown, and is so far above man that he defies comprehension. This is essentially Eastern, where it is still held that only through a passive attitude of the mind can God be reached. "Be still, and know that I am God" (Psalm xlvi, 10) was the Hebrew expression of the same idea. Prior to this Eastern influence, the gods were very well known and very intimate with the people of the West. This idea gradually gave way to the belief that the gods previously worshipped had once been men. Gnosticism was the outcome of this reaction. One God, in place of the gods, was then accepted, the knowledge of whom only came as a gift by grace to a mind conscious of its sinfulness.

Philo, Posidonius and Plato were the three men who stood out conspicuously in bringing into effect this great transition from western to eastern religious conceptions, Plato asserting that "To discover the Maker and Father of this universe is both an arduous task, and, having discovered him, it is impossible to speak of him at all". What is known as Neo-platonism developed from these contemplations and will be referred to later on. Towards this endeavour for greater knowledge of the Infinite no one did more than Posidonius, whose influence affected Lucretius, Seneca, Virgil, Cicero and Philo.

This quest for the knowledge of God, combined with the longing to secure salvation, became the principal occupation of that intensely religious age. Only through union, or at-one-ment, with God could the people find peace and comfort, but as the majority could not be satisfied with contemplation only, they, like the orthodox of today, obtained their desires, and received their comfort, through the Passion Plays, the Eucharist, and the rites and ceremonies of their religion.

To see before their eyes joy triumphing over suffering, and life over death, in their seasonal Passion Plays, gave the Greeks and Romans the same comfort as it gave the people of those countries who had supplied them with their saviour-gods. The influence of the East abolished the gods of Greek mythology and put in their place the saviour-gods, to whom we have already given so much consideration. The Mysteries stimulated the emotions of the Greeks and Romans, from the 2nd century B.C. onwards, in a way the old mythology could not do. The saviour-god idea found a new soil, in which it grew and flourished, as it comforted the people because they had grown out of their old mythology. One might say that what is today called Christianity came to Europe from the East when Alexander opened the door and let it in. If Jesus had never been born the

world would still have had Christianity in everything
but the name. Jesus reappearing, and becoming the
Christ, consolidated the prevailing opinions under the
name of Christianity, but the new name brought no
new ideas and no new beliefs to humanity.

The Mysteries certainly helped to strengthen and
comfort all believers entering the Valley of Death.
To be with their Lord in glory was something to be
looked forward to with great joy. The other world
was illuminated to Europeans by these beliefs in a
way that it had never been before. The mystical
speculations of the East had brought in a new range
of ideas which pictured the hereafter as a very glorified
earth, and is best represented to us by *The Revelation
of John*, which expresses the beliefs of the Mysteries
regarding the hereafter. Literature of this kind was
much in vogue in those days, and the speculations of
the writers were largely drawn from the Hindu
religion, which painted the other world in the same
colours as those used by John.

The people looked forward to walking along the
golden streets of the heavenly Athens and the
heavenly Rome, where all things were made of the
most precious substances. This idea made the next
world intensely real, but, besides this, the belief prevailed that the believer at death cast off all worry and
left behind him all the troubles of this world, finding
his pleasure in singing praises to his Saviour and
Redeemer. On the other hand, a terrible future after
death was foretold to those who were not believers
in the redemptive power of the Saviour.

Like all saviour-god religions the Mysteries gave
hope to believers and preached the damnation of all

unbelievers. "He that believeth, and is baptised, shall be saved ; but he that believeth not, shall be damned" (Mark xvi, 16), sums up the Mystery teaching on this subject, and the Christian priests did not forget to take over this doctrine with the rest of the Pagan beliefs, doctrines, dogmas, rites and ceremonies.

It is possible to give only the outstanding beliefs and ceremonies which surrounded the Mysteries, leaving aside the variations which were quite unimportant. One can obtain a true picture of the Christian Faith without going into all the details relating to the different divisions and sects. Its main principles are the same throughout, and its beliefs, except for some differences in forms and ceremonies, are in all important respects the same. This is likewise true of the Mystery religions.

In each one, the initiate went through different stages of initiation, just as they do today in the Roman and Greek churches. There were the preparation and probation stages, then came initiation and communion, ending in the stages of blessedness and salvation. "Only the pure in heart can see God" was ever before the candidate, and only those who lived exemplary lives were permitted to apply for initiation. Celsus (2nd century A.D.), the first to expose in writing the false claims made by the Christians, tells us that in calling the initiates from the congregation the proclamation read as follows : "Whosoever has clean hands and an intelligible tongue ; whosoever is holy from every defilement, and whose soul is conscious of no evil ; whosoever has lived a righteous life" can come forward for initiation, and that "no one should approach unless he is conscious of his innocence".

Those uneasy in their conscience could always fall back on the confessional, and emerge from it with the knowledge of what penance must be done to clear the conscience. We find an interesting discussion between two men, one in favour of confession and one against. The argument of the one against is, that from God no secrets are hid and that his sins were already known to God without his having to communicate them to the priest.

Baptism was by water and sometimes also by blood. That by water was for the purpose of purification, and that by blood for the purpose of obtaining at-one-ment with the Saviour. "Without the shedding of blood is no remission of sins" (Heb. ix, 22) is what the Mysteries taught, and each initiate went through a solemn initiation service comprising much ritualistic ceremony. What is now called Confirmation, in Protestant countries, in those days was an elaborate ceremony including a baptism of blood. On the roof of the enclosure, where stood the altar, there was a grating under which the new member stood while a priest above would kill a lamb and allow its blood to fall through the grating and cover the head and body of the initiate. This ceremony was called "The washing in the Blood of the Lamb", which phrase was adopted by the New Testament writers to refer to Jesus.

Throughout the New Testament Jesus is called The Lamb, an expression which came from the lamb killed at this ceremony to symbolise the death of the saviour-god. The initiate, standing underneath the grating, believed that being washed in the blood of the lamb removed his sins on to the shoulders of the Saviour, who had suffered for him, and who, by his death, had opened the gates of heaven to all cleansed by the precious blood. This initiation was for the purpose of bringing the initiate into at-one-ment with his Lord so that he personally would be identified with his Saviour, and with all that his Saviour had gained by his death and suffering for humanity.

We also read much in the New Testament about blood being necessary to cleanse sin. Here are a few quotations about the Lamb slain, the Blood of the Lamb, and the Blood shed by Christ.

> Unto Him that loved us, and washed us from our sins in his own blood. (Rev. i, 5.)
> Thou wast slain, and hast redeemed us to God by thy blood. (Rev. v, 9.)
> And made them white in the blood of the Lamb. (Rev. vii, 14.)
> Elect . . . through . . . sprinkling of the blood of Jesus Christ. (1 Peter i, 2.)
> The blood of Jesus Christ his Son cleanseth us from all sin. (1 John i, 7.)
> But ye are washed, but ye are sanctified. (1 Cor. vi, 11.)
> How much more shall the blood of Christ . . . purge your conscience from dead works to serve the living God. (Heb. ix, 14.)

As a matter of fact, crucifixion does not cause much shedding of blood, so we must look elsewhere for the source of so much attention being given to the shedding of blood, and being washed in blood. All such expressions were in use for centuries before the Christian era and are found in the initiation ceremony of a new member into the Greek Church.

Plato condemns this ritualistic ceremony because he says that salvation is promised in return for mere ritualistic acts of purification and initiation, and not because of the life of goodness of the one initiated. In these pre-Christian centuries quite a controversy went on as to whether salvation could be secured only by faith, or if works also were needed. The pre-Christian Greek Church, like the Christian Church, said, "Thy faith hath made thee whole" (Mark v, 34), and on this topic some of the greatest men of the age gave their opinion.

Isocrates (5th century B.C.), to whom I have already referred, expressly states that salvation in the future life, which is the reward of the initiated, is gained by all who live pious and just lives. Diodorus (1st century B.C.), the Greek historian, who, in thirty years, wrote forty volumes devoted to his country's history, said that the initiated are believed to grow better because of their faith. Andocides (5th century B.C.), the Greek diplomatist who was for a time in command of the Athenian Fleet, held the same opinion. According to Sopater, the Greek commentator, initiation established a kinship of the soul with the divine nature, while Theon (2nd century A.D.), the Smyrnan mathematician, said that the final stage of initiation is the state of bliss and divine favour which results from it.

It is interesting to discover the same diversity of thought running through the New Testament, where two diametrically opposed opinions are also expressed on the way salvation can be reached. In places we read that salvation is the result of faith and in others that it comes from works. Here are a few quotations taken at random :

IN FAVOUR OF FAITH

By what Law ? of works ? Nay, but by the law of Faith. (Rom. iii, 27.)

God imputeth righteousness without Works. (Rom. iv, 6.)

Knowing that a man is not justified by the Works of the Law. (Gal. ii, 16.)

Not by Works of righteousness which we have done . . . he saved us by the washing of regeneration. (Titus iii, 5.)

How much more shall the blood of Christ . . . purge your conscience from dead Works. (Heb. ix, 14.)

IN FAVOUR OF WORKS

Wherefore ? Because they sought it not by Faith, but as it were by the Works of the Law. (Rom. ix, 32.)

What doth it profit, my brethren, though a man say he hath Faith and have not Works ? Can Faith save him ? (James ii, 14.)

Faith, if it hath not Works is dead, being alone. (James ii, 17.)

Show me thy Faith without thy Works and I will show thee my Faith by my Works. (James ii, 18.)

Was not Abraham our father justified by Works ? (James ii, 21.)

You see then how that by Works a man is justified and not by Faith only. (James ii, 24.)

The dead were judged, according to their Works. (Rev. xx, 12.)

Whose end shall be according to their Works. (2 Cor. xi, 15.)

This question of salvation by Faith or by Works has been the cause of much confused and anxious thought from the time the Greek philosophers put virtue before belief. This comes about from ignorance, which produces fear. Fear produces Religion, under which name we find all the beliefs, rites and ceremonies of mankind. Fear of what ? What have we to fear ? The Unknown. When man is ignorant he fears. He stands on earth, a minute object, and yet he has a mind which is acted upon and is influenced by matter and forces millions of millions of miles away in space. Distance impresses him with his own insignificance and ignorance, as do Storm, Thunder, Lightning, Death, Life, Pain and Suffering. All these and many other things make him realise his weakness and ignorance.

So man is a fearful being. Religion is the scheme he has invented to make him less fearful. He has built up out of what he has experienced a system of thought to make him more comfortable and happy on earth. If he had reasoned this out in a logical way he never could have produced it, but it was because he could not reason logically that he needed this illogical system to comfort him. Religion, then, is an illogical, unreasoned scheme, produced by fear and ignorance, as a buffer to soothe man's nerves and make him less fearful. In a few words, Religion is a method, which has developed over the ages, of obtaining mental peace by doing or thinking something.

The great void, called space, he filled with gods and devils because he saw movement everywhere. He knew by the observance of psychic phenomena that invisible beings were around him, and he felt by instinct that he survived death. Where or how he knew not. These factors were ever in his mind, and, through fear and ignorance, knowing how insecure was life on earth, how he could not even trust his brother man, he imagined all kinds of horrible things befalling him after death. So he sacrificed to feed the gods, and this culminated in the belief in one big sacrifice, the greatest possible he could imagine, that of a god-man, for the benefit of all who believed.

To those who believed not, this mountain of imagination meant nothing and was of no comfort. So those who believed told those who believed not that the sacrifice was for all believers. To this the non-believers replied that they were not fearful because they did not feel the need of a sacrifice, and that if they did what was right no punishment could befall them. These two types of mind have always been in evidence, the fearful, those who lived by faith, and the others who lived by works, the religious man and the philosophical man. Each represents an opposite type of thought, Religion and Philosophy.

So in the age of Religion and Philosophy, which we are now considering, it is natural that the question of Salvation by Faith or by Works should continually be coming to the surface. Socrates, Plato, Aristotle, Confucius, Buddha and others led men to realise that fear was the cause of religion, and that by an ethical philosophy, by striving for virtue, would come comfort and contentment. They were the first to break the fear of man, the first to put something in place of Religion. The birth and growth of the Christian Faith, which came after their time, proved that mankind was not ready for their philosophy. Philosophy has, however, stood the test of time, and, as religion decays, so philosophy increases.

Every religion, no matter what it is called, is an illogical structure of thought produced to calm the human mind and make it less fearful. Philosophy is a logical, reasoned, constructive effort to determine

man's place in the universe, and how he should live
to obtain the greatest happiness for himself and
others. Religion brings comfort to all who do not
think deeply. Philosophy comforts those who do think.
The more people think the less religion appeals, and
the more philosophy attracts. The more we think
the more we realise that neither Faith nor Works are
needed for salvation, because salvation is a figment
of the imagination.

As we live here on earth so shall we live hereafter, because each individual is no more and no less
than Mind. It is mind, and its covering, which we
term the etheric body, which survives death, and as
our mind is on earth so it will be in the etheric world.
If we are selfish, cruel, crooked and in every way dis-
agreeable here on earth, so shall we be there. If we
have been lonely on earth through selfishness, so shall
we be lonely there. If, on the other hand, we are
unselfish, kind, and generous, we get our reward here
by being happy and contented, and by making others
likewise. What happens here happens there, because,
as we are here, we shall be there, and as we sow we
reap. The reaping is continuous and does not commence when we die.

Believing in saviours, and all the paraphernalia
of religion, only helps weak creatures on earth to
bear their trials, and face the unknown, but, as we
become better educated and less fearful, these things
appeal less and less. What really counts is character,
what we are, and what are our ideals and aspirations.
These are what we carry with us on our journey
towards the Infinite. Death is only a change of
appreciation of the vibrations which make up the

Universe. In our earth bodies our mind appreciates physical vibrations. When each mind sheds the physical body, it appreciates etheric vibrations, which constitute a world very much like this earth, though it is more refined and beautiful for those who can appreciate beauty and refinement.

As the mind is, so are our surroundings. We make our place there by our thoughts much more than we do here, because, in the finer vibrations of the etheric world, mind is influenced by, and can influence its surroundings to a greater extent than it can do here. Each one, therefore, makes his own heaven or hell there to a more marked degree than here, but the happiness or misery of everyone is his own making. Nature has decreed that as we think so we are. We are saved, in the theological sense, neither by Faith nor Works. Death is no break in the mental pattern, and as we are here so shall we be there.

In the times we are considering, the people were struggling to find a solution of these problems which, with our psychic knowledge of today, become so simple, freed from all the entanglements of theology and religious beliefs. The New Testament is just a reflection of the beliefs of those times, and so we find religion and philosophy mixed up together, the early Christians discussing and questioning just as did their Pagan contemporaries. The human mind was not yet ready for philosophy alone. The majority needed a saviour and the beliefs and ritual surrounding his worship.

Much thought was therefore given to baptism, and washing, and white robes, as if such physical things could make a bad man good. They soothed the conscience, but religious history proves that Faith and Belief have never produced virtue, and that often the most faithful, and the greatest believers, were the most disreputable. A saviour made things so easy for sinners who cast their sins on to his shoulders. There was no limit in time or quantity, anything and everything up to the last gasp could be placed on the saviour's shoulders. Flesh, however, has always been weak, and the repeating of fine phrases has never deterred the evil-doer, or made the selfish and cruel unselfish and kind.

After being washed in the blood of the lamb the one initiated was allowed to handle and kiss the sacred objects laid on the altar, when he then received the Holy Sacrament. The ceremonial and ritual were remarkable for their magnificence. On special occasions sacred things were exposed in a peculiarly impressive manner to the worshippers. Painting, sculpture, architecture and music were combined with lavish skill to form one grand and impressive spectacle. Here centred all that art and wealth could do, to impress those partaking, of the greatness and solemnity of the occasion.

The aim of these Mystery religions was certainly high, however it may have been abused. A 5th century B.C. inscription over the temple at Lindus reads as follows : "All who enter this sacred place must be pure in heart and not conscious of any crime". The churches were open to all, male and female, rich and poor, freeman and slave. All were welcome who could believe the doctrines preached, and all could share in the rites and ceremonies, the only disqualifying crime being murder, which exception the Christian Church also adopted.

The *Encyclopædia Britannica*, under MYSTERIES, describes an initiation service in the following graphic words : "Then came the actual Mysteries. The Initiates were admitted to the holy building; the splendid illumination seemed dazzlingly bright after the darkness outside ; the strange apparitions, the impressive voices, the gorgeous dresses of the actors, the magnificence of the sacred drama, to which the highly suggestive and symbolic art of Greece no doubt contributed largely ; all these they saw and heard in awesome silence. Then came the crowning act of the ceremony . . . They were admitted one by one to touch, to kiss the holy things, to lift them from the cist, to put them into the basket, to taste them, to replace them in the cist, and to pronounce the sacred formula. The scene that takes place in every modern Greek church on the eve of Easter Sunday gives some faint idea of the character of this ceremony". The hymns sung at these ceremonies referred to the Holy Child who had come from Heaven, lived amongst men, died for their sins and risen for their salvation.

In the Hall of Initiation of the Temple of Mên at Pisidian Antioch, an oblong depression has been discovered which was obviously used for water for baptismal purposes, and elsewhere similar discoveries have been made. Firmicus Maternus (4th century A.D.), the Latin author, a Pagan, in referring to baptism, writes, "There is another water

whereby men are renewed and reborn", which reminds us of the verse in Mark (i, 8), attributed to
John the Baptist, "I indeed have baptised you with
water but he shall baptise you with the Holy Ghost".
When we come to Titus (iii, 5) we find the Mystery
idea expressed in the following : "Not by works of
righteousness which we have done, but according
to his mercy he saved us, by the washing of regeneration, and renewing of the Holy Ghost".

Juvenal (2nd century A.D.), a worshipper of Isis,
who is looked upon as the most descriptive of all the
Latin poets, tells us of a form of penance a devotee
of Isis had to undergo. "She will break the ice and
descend into the water ; thrice a morning she will
bathe in the Tiber and lave her tumid head in its
very depths, then, with bleeding knees, she will
creep, naked and shivering, over the whole length of
the Campus Martius". When reading this one thinks
of Luther, in A.D. 1512, going up Pilate's staircase at
St. Peter's, on his knees, repeating, "The Just shall
live by Faith". Pilgrimages were also made by the
Pagans to Egypt, Persia and elsewhere, to pay homage
at the shrines of the gods worshipped.

Tertullian (2nd century A.D.), one of the
greatest exponents of Christianity, tells us that the
neophite, on attaining the degree of Soldier of Mithra,
was offered a crown or a garland. This was not
accepted but was thrust away, the initiate remarking,
"Mithra is my crown", from which the idea doubtless
occurred to the writer of 1 Peter (v, 4), "Ye shall
receive a crown of glory that fadeth not away".

White robes were worn during initiation ceremonies as the initiate was entering into a state of holy

matrimony with his saviour-god. This marriage state idea was also adopted by the Christians, and also the use of white robes, from which came the text in *The Revelation* (iii, 5), "He that overcometh, the same shall be clothed in white raiment". The candidate for initiation into the Mysteries was seated on a throne during one of the stages of initiation, when it was believed that he sat with the Deity, and so in *The Revelation* (iii, 21), we find the following, "To him that overcometh will I grant to sit with me in my throne".

Many people are familiar with Paul's belief that he caught a glimpse of the third heaven. Anyone who reads this in 2 Corinthians, chapter 12, will realise how alike it is to the following account given by an initiate of his feeling during initiation : "Hear therefore but believe what is true, I approached the confines of death and trod the threshold of Proserpina. I was carried through all the elements and returned again. In the middle of the night I saw the sun gleaming in radiant splendour. I approached into the presence of the gods below and the gods celestial and worshipped before their face. Behold I have told you things which, although you have heard them, you must not understand", or, as Paul puts it, "It is not lawful for man to utter", because all initiates were under a solemn vow of secrecy.

By rites and ceremonies, the ordinary members of the Mysteries found the means of greater at-one-ment with the divine, but others, like Paul, found it through ecstasy and trance, in which state the devotee lost consciousness of earth and attained contact with a higher range of vibrations, now termed etheric.

Plotinus (3rd century A.D.), the most outstanding Neoplatonist, tells us that he was favoured with this beatific vision only four times during the years Porphyry lived with him, and Porphyry, who was another well-known Neoplatonist, tells us that he experienced it only once. Plotinus describes the experience as one in which the spirit was elevated above earth shadows and "returns to its father and enjoys possession of the heavenly love". Philo had also similar experiences, as well as the gift of inspirational writing, being able to write for hours at great speed with little or no effort or thought. He has left us an interesting record of this inspirational state, which he often experienced, but, when it was not active, he found writing sometimes almost impossible.

Another act of initiation was the burial of the initiate in a grave, with only sufficient ventilation for him to be able to breathe, the idea being that when he was unearthed he would rise a new creature and be born again for eternity. This was part of the rites of purification, and symbolically represented the death of the old self and the resurrection of the new self, to a new life. The initiate arose from the grave with the words, "The spirit in us is divine and a veritable image of Dionysus". This remark enables us to realise how an apparition could be taken to be a god, as in these days such a being was looked upon as a god. Today he would be termed an etheric being, one who had lived on earth and died, to return and be seen by those with clairvoyant vision.

The Greek and Roman churches of the Mystery religions, as we have already read, were open to all, bondmen and freemen, who could enter them on equal terms, membership being quite unrestricted. Only the Jews kept aloof and, by their zeal, took from but never gave anything to the religion of their adopted countries. As religion had ceased to be a State affair this rivalry was tolerated, since, under Roman rule, all had equal liberty to worship as and how they pleased.

The Mysteries discarded the hereditary principle which had been common to all western religious systems. People came to look upon religion as a personal matter between themselves and their God, not as something to do with the State, or the class into which they were born. The members were bound together by ties of fellowship, and the obligation of common vows. They experienced the enthusiasm of revivals and all such emotionalism which accompanies individualistic religion. Religious frenzy occurred at their festivals, when all personal control vanished, but this state is known to all religions when the enraptured one becomes insensible to pain and can endure torture and suffering.

Besides this, the Mysteries were free of nationalism. Everyone could join this common Brotherhood. It was not confined to the Romans or the Greeks but was open to the Jews, Syrians, Persians and the Egyptians, who were all equally welcome. So the Church of Dionysus, or the Church of Mithra, was to be found in all lands comprising the Roman Empire, and there men and women worshipped for the purpose of obtaining greater at-one-ment with their God and not, as it used to be, collectively for the good of all.

So these Mysteries were in no way State churches ;

they preached a universal religion, and the brother-hood of man, quite apart from nationalism. To all the choice was free, and, like religious communities of the past, they suffered persecution and so venerated their martyrs besides their saints and ascetics. The numerous skeletons which have been discovered in the Mithraic chapels testify to the slaughter which took place when Christianity became the State religion of the Roman Empire and obliterated by death all its rivals.

There is abundant proof in ancient literature that the effect of the Mysteries was not dependent on any dogmatic instruction. The old Greek writers expressed the view that these mystery ceremonies were for the purpose of keeping the people in mind of their risen Lord and Saviour, who had proved by his resurrection that their salvation was now secure.

How like times were then to what they are now. Religion and Science could then no more meet than they can today. The human mind, then as now, was just in different states of development. Galen (2nd century A.D.), the most celebrated of ancient medical writers, maintained that "the study of nature, if prosecuted with the concentrated attention given to the Mysteries, is even more fitted than they are to reveal the power and wisdom of God, inasmuch as these truths are more obscurely expressed in the Mysteries than in nature".

From this, and other similar writings, it is evident that these writers wished to impress the people with the belief that nature itself, if properly understood, could satisfy their longings without resorting to the beliefs, the symbolism and the ritual of the saviour-god religions. When reading these writings one is tempted to compare them with those of our present-day Deists, who state their case in much the same way.

Running concurrently with these beliefs came the development of Greek philosophy, now called Platonism, Stoicism and then later Neo-Pythagoreanism, and Neo-Platonism, with their high ideals, which can be condensed into the words used by Epicurus (342-270 B.C.), the founder of the famous School of Philosophy which is known as Epicurean, "God is not to be feared ; Death cannot be felt ; The Good can be won : All that we dread can be borne and conquered". The blending of these philosophies with the Mysteries raised the level of religion to a height never before attained, and, in its presence, the old Greek mythology was put aside. It disappeared without much of a struggle, as the new conception of religion dawned upon the world.

From Greece went out missionaries, carrying their new mystic philosophy. Converts, in their enthusiasm, discussed religious matters on all occasions. It was the principal subject of conversation in the shops, in the streets and in the market squares. The main topic was how man could attain closer union with his God. A stranger entering a shop would be met by this question when making a purchase. In this atmosphere the Christian religion was born, grew and developed when the seed took root. The Mysteries can therefore be fairly claimed as the

Mother of Christianity, in whose womb it was conceived.

Alexander had brought to Greece the mysticism of the East, which the Greeks mingled with their philosophy. The new product, which, in form and essence, corresponded to what became known four centuries later as the Christian Faith, they exported to the lands under their dominion, and later on to those countries comprising the Roman Empire. So it is evident that the conquests of Alexander were a great event in history. In religious history they were to the Western world quite as important as Constantine's decision to make Christianity the State religion of his Empire, or the setting up of the Holy Roman Empire, or the Reformation.

Alexander was not only the pioneer of Hellenic culture but made the universality of Christianity possible because the Roman Empire took over those parts that he had conquered, and over which Greek culture had spread. When Christianity became the State religion it had a wide area to cover without having to change the people's basic beliefs. India alone, of all the Eastern countries which worshipped a saviour-god, escaped its influence, though this country played a large part in its formation.

Paul claimed that Christianity had made as one every race of men, for "There is neither Jew nor Greek, there is neither bond nor free, there is neither male nor female : for ye are all one in Christ Jesus" (Gal. iii, 28), but it was Greek culture, philosophy and religion which had made this possible long before Christianity was born. Alexander, apart from his butcheries, was not only a great soldier and a great ruler, but also a great reconciler. By his conquests, and his policy, he brought together nations who had been strangers and foreigners to each other, and made them friends.

Between nations that never traded together, goods were now interchanged. Customs, different in each country, were blended, and so Scythian and Jew, Greek and Macedonian, Egyptian and Persian met together at this marriage of the East and West. There was no bitterness felt by the conquered towards the conqueror, because he allowed them to retain their individual nationality. All were treated alike and severe punishment was inflicted on any who oppressed his brother man. Greek thought, oriental mysticism, and Hebrew theology, mixed together for the first time under one language, Greek, which the educated of every country spoke as the universal language.

The more the contact with the East increased, the more were the Romans influenced by the thousands of orientals who travelled westward, bringing with them their wares for sale and proselytising from place to place as they went. Missionaries came from Egypt carrying with them the gospel tidings of the saving power of Osiris, just as they came from Persia with the good news that through the resurrection of Mithra all could now be born again to an immortal life throughout eternity.

The saviour-god religions appealed to the slaves, who in turn influenced their masters and mistresses. All this occurred at a time of reaction from unbelief, when the idea was gaining ground that the universe was an ordered cosmos, and not a chaos at the mercy of the caprices of the gods. So monotheism made progress, and the universe became intimately related with the saviour-god who was worshipped.

Thus we find a creator becoming understood through the saviour-god who was credited with the act of creation. This idea was likewise taken over by Christianity because we read, "God, who created all things by Jesus Christ" (Eph. iii, 9). The power given to understand the Father and the Son was attributed to a separate agency known as the Holy Spirit. Thus the three gods of what is now called the Christian Trinity, comprising the Father, Son and Holy Spirit, were believed in and accepted by the Pagans long before Christianity was born. From Paganism they were taken over by this religion in the 4th century A.D., at the Council of Nicaea, but how the Trinity originated first of all in men's minds will be explained as we go on.

The creator of the universe was termed the Father of mankind, the Saviour and Redeemer was termed the Son, both of whom were brought into close relationship with mankind through the Holy Spirit. We read in the Liturgy of Mithra that the devotee prays, "Abide with me in my soul, leave me not, that I may be initiated, and that the Holy Spirit may breathe within me. So that I am thou and thou art I". God was believed to be the All in All, and the First and the Last. Knowledge of him increased through grace, which brought about at-one-ment (atonement) by belief in the Son. This was the message these oriental missionaries brought to the West. They preached the need of a Saviour from sin and followed this up by telling the people of the death of their Saviour and Redeemer. Along with them Greeks came to Rome, bringing with them their Mystery beliefs, and preaching that everyone must be saved, that everyone must be born again and washed from sin in the blood of the lamb.

The Romans, during this religious revival, were evidently feeling their own unrighteousness, and, as they had no saviour-god of their own, were converted in large numbers to this new belief. They had no rich mythology like the Greeks on which to fall back ; their own gods were falling into disrepute, in fact, a pre-Christian Pope, the Pontifex Maximus, questioned their very existence. From Egypt, Persia and Greece the Romans obtained their religious comfort, the result being that the Eastern religions rapidly gained in prestige throughout the Roman Empire, and saviour-gods were worshipped wherever the Roman Eagle flew, with one exception, Judea.

In this new world the Jews found a place equal with the others, and, as they play a large part in the origin of the Christian Faith, it is well that they should receive some special consideration. Here was a race, notorious for its exclusiveness, passionate in its monotheism, with a thirst for righteousness, and a message believed to have been given to it by God to deliver to mankind. In spite of captivity, and being repeatedly conquered, it had retained its nationality and religion in a way no other nation had done. Its centre was Jerusalem, the Holy City, where stood the sacred Temple, the only place on earth that Jehovah, the only true God, condescended to visit.

Previous to Macedonian domination under Alexander, the Hebrews had been subject to Egypt,

Babylonia, Assyria, Persia and Syria, but none of these had altered their faith. However much it may have been interfered with it was never broken. Though the Temple had been destroyed, and Jerusalem sacked, when the opportunity recurred it was rebuilt and the worship restored. Their trials and vicissitudes seemed to strengthen rather than weaken their beliefs. The more they were hammered the harder they became.

Palestine itself was certainly fenced in by the law and looked askance on Hellenistic missionary efforts, but, after the time of Alexander, though this exclusiveness was not broken down at home, it was considerably weakened abroad. The Jew is known for his ubiquitousness, as he is famed as a trader. Though looking to Jerusalem as the centre of his faith, yet he went far and wide seeking after worldly gain. His genius as a trader enabled him to establish himself in all parts of the Roman Empire. Everywhere there were large or small colonies of Jews and in each city was to be found one or more synagogues. Greek culture and thought could not break through the fence of the law around Jerusalem, but it had a very decided effect on those Jews who settled outside their native land, so much so that they became known as Hellenised Jews and their faith became a mixture of Gnosticism and Judaism.

Though they attended the synagogue on the Sabbath they were still coming in contact with the beliefs surrounding the Mysteries on the other six days of the week. This made them more tolerant, it widened their outlook, and they became interested in the new mystical theology. The ground, it will be noticed, was being prepared outside of Palestine to

receive the seed which Paul believed he was ordained
to sow. The Hellenised Jew acted as the connecting
link between the Christian Faith—which, to begin with,
was an offshoot from Judaism—and the citizens of the
Roman Empire, under the control of Roman legions,
but dominated by the culture and philosophy of Greece.

One of the keynotes of the Jewish faith was the
belief in the coming deliverer or Messiah. One can
understand how much this meant to a people who
were never long out of bondage. For a stubborn,
proud race, which believed that it had the one and
only revelation from heaven, and worshipped the
only true God, to be under the heel of a conqueror
must have been like drinking gall and wormwood. In
333 B.C. they were conquered by Alexander the Great.
In 323 B.C. they were under subjection to Egypt.
In 167 B.C. they were under Syria. In 65 B.C. they
were conquered by Rome, under whose rule they
lived, ever restless and anxious to be free. This was
surely enough to make them long for some deliverer
who would lead them forth to conquer their enemies.

The Jews of the dispersion, as those were called,
who spread abroad after the conquest of Palestine
by Alexander, became a great power outside their
own country. They formed a large part of the population of Alexandria, where they enjoyed equal rights
with the Greeks and the Romans. They became a
link between the East and the West. They were neither
one nor the other, but they understood both. Their
Septuagint, the Greek name for the Book of the Law,
because it was translated into Greek by seventy men,
was read by those who came from the east and from
the west, and this tended to strengthen the belief in

monotheism. There was one or more synagogues in every large town around the eastern borders of the Mediterranean, which were opened every Sabbath. Thus the Pagans were ever reminded of this pious people who religiously kept the Sabbath and attended the synagogue, wherein could be heard the singing of psalms and the solemn intonation of prayers.

The Jews were disliked for many reasons, and anti-Semitism has been in evidence since the time they were driven out of Egypt, but it became pronounced from the 4th century B.C. onwards. Some of the reasons for the dislike of the Jews were : (1) their success in trade ; (2) they were unsociable because religious scruples made them unable to enter into the amusements of their neighbours ; (3) they could not be present at public banquets because they feared contamination and there the Pagan gods were honoured ; (4) they were averse to public games, and the theatre, because these spectacles contained so much "heathen" mythology ; (5) they turned every political issue to their own advantage and, by their continual plotting, brought on themselves the hatred of the authorities ; (6) they were ardent proselytisers, attracting the women to the synagogues, much to the disgust of their Pagan husbands. It was only in the market that they were willing to deal with other people on an equal basis.

Some Pagans were attracted to the synagogues, where they heard about the promises made by Jehovah to his people Israel. They became interested in the coming Messiah, and, when it was announced that the long awaited one had really come, died and reappeared, they were the first to join the Christian

Church, which accepted all and made no distinction between Jew and Gentile. Those who became the first Christians knew about the saviour-gods of the past, but were more attracted to a religion which preached a new Messiah than to one whose Saviour had lived and died in the by-gone ages. The time was ripe for a new Christ, one who had performed his sacrificial mission within their own times and not at a much earlier date. There was, therefore, a body of opinion, from the very start of the Christian Faith, ready to accept the new Christ and give him both love and devotion.

The Jews were not only conquered at home but continually being expelled from the countries in which they settled. The first expulsion of Jews from Rome occurred in 139 B.C., because of their proselytising zeal. Their reply to all persecution was always that Jehovah, through the expected Messiah, would intervene on their behalf and, after showing signs and wonders, establish them as the chosen race over their hated conquerors. This did not improve matters, and, by the Romans, they were always distrusted and regarded with suspicion.

If Jesus had not been born to become the seed that produced the Christian Faith, with its three gods, monotheism would probably have developed further under the proselytising zeal of the Jews, and thus the teaching of Mohammet might have been anticipated by several centuries. Nature, however, ruled otherwise, and the spread of monotheism was delayed for another seven centuries, when the Prophet took half of Christendom unto himself.

Independent thinking, in those times, was without

doubt the order of the day. The democratic religious organisations, and the freedom of expression of thought, were certainly conducive to religious speculation. This did not always appeal to the rulers of the Roman Empire, some of whom felt that the people were giving too little concern to the State, and confining their thoughts too much to themselves individually. Little was done, however, to prevent this freedom of expression until Christianity came into power in the 4th century A.D., when an entire change took place, and suppression took the place of liberty. During the reign of the Emperors priestcraft had little political power, as philosophy had, for the time being, crippled its malignant influence.

For at least six centuries prior to the opening of the Christian era the political power of the priests had been waning in Greece. As it waned so mediumship increased, just as it has done in this country since the eighteenth century, when the priests lost their political power and witch burning ceased. Mediumship increases when mediums are allowed to live, because it is an hereditary gift and very often passes from parents to children. Consequently mediumship and psychic phenomena increased, with the result that from the 6th century B.C. to the 4th century A.D. there was a display of what Paul calls "spiritual gifts" such as had never previously been recorded.

The psychic stream then flowed strongly, and the Christian Faith was the effect of this return to nature's revelation, as we shall soon discover. In those days the dead in Greece were termed "the Blest" and the people did not believe that they were in Hades, or Purgatory, or Sheol, awaiting the last Judgement, an idea taken over by Christianity from Judaism. To the Greeks the dead were in the etheric world, about and around this earth, and they came back to communicate with those they had left behind.

From Delphi, in Greece, psychic knowledge spread throughout the Mediterranean world, and did not subside until the Christian Church stamped it out in the 4th century A.D., when everyone with psychic gifts was murdered. Mediums, in that age of psychic phenomena, were respected, honoured and visited by the greatest men in the Empire, some of whom have left on record their experiences. In the reign of Theodosius I, who became Emperor in A.D. 379, slaughter began and continued till everyone having mediumistic powers, upon whom the Church could lay its hands, was exterminated. A century later the philosophers suffered the same fate. All schools were closed and then came the night of ignorance. The dark ages set in, to last for fourteen hundred years, but when we come to this stage in our history there will be much more to tell.

We are interested at the moment in the conditions during, and the beliefs of, those centuries just prior to, and just after the opening of the Christian era, when for about eight hundred years, under Paganism, it was possible for mediums to live and function. Since then there has not been such close contact with the other order of existence till we come to the present time. Between then and now nature's method of revealing the after life was blotted out by the Christian Church, which based its authority on the Law of Moses, produced by Hebrew priests, that no medium was to be allowed to live.

The age into which Christianity was born was one, not only of philosophy, but of psychic development, when philosophers and mediums were allowed to live and express themselves without hindrance from the priesthood. Under Roman rule the Jewish priests could not destroy mediums, the result being that during the first four centuries of our era mediumship flourished, and at no time more than in the first Christian century. The Jewish priesthood hated mediums with a bitter hatred, but they had to find other charges to lodge against Jesus in order to bring about his death.

From the psychic knowledge gained during this time of liberty, philosophers built up their philosophy. They were finding unity everywhere, and the connecting link between the two worlds. Marcus Aurelius (A.D. 121-180), the Roman Emperor, known as "the noblest of the Pagans and the crown and flower of Stoicism", expressed the Pagan philosophy in these words : "All things are intertwined the one with the other. There is practically nothing alien the one to the other, for all things have been marshalled in and constitute the one cosmos. For there is both one cosmos of all things and one God through all. There is one substance, one law, and one common order of intelligent beings, and one truth". In other words, he had come to realise what psychic students have discovered in our own times, that the two worlds, the physical and the etheric, are one, differing only in vibrational activity, and that the inhabitants of the etheric are of the same genus as ourselves, being neither gods nor demons.

Plotinus believed that by reverent contemplation the mind could grasp the cosmos, but only a few were ready for these deeper thoughts, and the majority could no more appreciate their meaning than they can understand the full implication of psychic phenomena, as expounded today in the philosophy of Spiritualism. It was through the Mysteries that the people obtained their happiness and comfort. These oriental religions met the requirements of the prevailing higher morality now so noticeable in the West, they made the people feel more comfortable and at ease, which is the reason why Christianity, with an up-to-date saviour-god, made the headway it did in the first four centuries of its existence. A man's religion consists of his outlook on life and death, and when a crutch is provided it is eagerly seized upon by weaklings, as were the vast majority of people in those days. Philosophy appealed to the mentally strong, who then, as now, constituted the minority.

The Apocalyptic hope, which was so strong in the Mystery religions, was preserved in Christianity. The beliefs of the Mysteries that the Saviour God had reconciled the Father God, and would some day return to gather to himself the faithful elect on earth, had as powerful an influence amongst all religiously minded people in those days as it has had throughout the Christian era. Such symbolism, taken from what one experiences in nature, appeals to the ignorant multitude in a way philosophy and psychic phenomena cannot do, because the masses have not the mentality to grasp their meaning.

Christianity became a universal religion by breaking the bounds of Judaism, by challenging the Mysteries in open conflict, and guaranteeing to its supporters as much as did the Mysteries. This included the claim, held both by the Christians and the Pagans, that the saviour-god had subdued the Devil and his angels, which was certainly a comforting thought, because everyone in those days was haunted by the fear of devils and their agents, the sorcerers. The belief in a saviour-god enabled them to live comfortably and die happily and this has continued up to our own age. Most of us can remember how, till within recent years, the belief existed in the reality of the Devil, his demons, and Hell as their place of abode. In our present more enlightened age we do not realise how fearful were our ancestors of evil spirits, and in the dark ages this was so pronounced that life to many must have been intolerable.

The Devil was continually interfering in human affairs and he had his agents everywhere. These received the names of witches and wizards, people who were quite inoffensive in themselves but were endowed with psychic gifts and had powers beyond the normal. Just as illness and disease were attributed to devils, so were psychic gifts. Both these opinions were encouraged by the priests, who were paid to pray the evil spirits out of those who were considered as possessed by them. Everything, which was not understood in the pre-scientific age, was attributed either to a god or a devil, and, because of this mistake, the people had to counter it by the manufacture of religious medicine to soothe their troubled minds.

Let us now in imagination go back to these pre-Christian days in Greece and Rome. Let us imagine that we are in Athens on a Sunday morning,

the first day of the week, which the people termed
The Lord's Day. We go out after breakfast for a
walk and see the people streaming to the various
churches in the city. We join up with the rest and
walk on till we come to a magnificent building which
we notice is called "The Temple of the Trinity". In
architectural design it embodies all that the artistic
mind can create. Inside there are beautiful statues
and paintings, the decorations are lavish, enriched by
fine carvings, mosaics and decorative colouring. At
the far end stands an altar on which are lighted
candles, and in different parts of the church are
shrines, also illuminated by candles. As we enter
the priest is chanting these words :

Let all nature hear the hymn,
I will hymn the Lord of Creation, the All and One.
Let the Heavens open, let the immortal cycle of God receive
my praise.
Let us altogether give praise to him.
He is the life of my spirit.
His be the blessing of my powers.
Ye powers of mine, hymn the One and All.
Join all of ye in song with my will.
Holy knowledge, enlightened from thee, and by thee, the
spiritual light.
I rejoice as I raise my hymn in spiritual joy.
O Truth, the truth.
O Goodness, the good.
Life and light, from you comes, as to you returns our
thanksgiving.
I give thee thanks O Father, thou potency of my powers.
I give thee thanks O God, the power of my potencies.
Thine own word through me hymns Thee.
Through me receive the all, by Thy word my reasonable
spiritual sacrifice.

Accept from all, reasonable sacrifice.
O life, save us, O life, enlighten us.
O God, make us spiritual.
Thou art God and Thy man thus cries to thee.
From the eternal I receive blessing and what I seek.
By thy will have I found rest.

Another priest now takes up the chant :

By thy spirit, O Father, I declare what I perceive.
To thee, author of my new birth, I offer reasonable spiritual
sacrifices.
O God and Father, thou art the Lord, thou art the Spirit.
Accept from me the reasonable sacrifices which thou
requirest.
For by thy will all things are accomplished.

And then the congregation breaks into this hymn of praise :

Holy is God, the Father of all the universe ;
Holy is God, whose will is accomplished by its own
energies ;
Holy is God, who wills to be known and is known by His
own :
Holy art Thou, of whom all Nature was made an image.
Holy art Thou, whom Nature did not form.
Holy art Thou, more potent than all power.
Holy art Thou, transcending all excellence ;
Holy art Thou, who surpassest all praises.

Then follows this prayer :

We give thee thanks, O Most High, for, by thy grace, we
obtained this light of knowledge.   Name ineffable, honoured in
addressing thee as God and blessed in the invocation of thee
as Father, because thou didst reveal to all men and women a
father's pity, and love and affection and thy most benign working.
Thou hast bestowed upon us feeling and reason and knowledge

—feeling that we may apprehend thee, reason that we may reflect upon thee, knowledge that by the knowledge of thee we may be glad. Saved by thee, we rejoice that thou didst show thyself to us completely : we rejoice that even in our mortal bodies thou didst deify us by the vision of thyself. Man's sole thanksgiving to thee is to know thy majesty. We have come to know thee, O thou Light, perceptible alone to our feeling; We have come to know thee, thou Light of the life of man; We have come to know thee, thou fruitful Womb of all; We have come to know thee, thou eternal Principle of that which brings forth by the Father's agency. Thus, having worshipped thee, we have requested no favour from thy goodness, but grant to our entreaty that we may be preserved in the knowledge, so that we may not fail to attain to this higher life.

After this prayer a priest delivers the following sermon :

By the paternal gods, my sons, respect one another if you care to please me. For you surely do not imagine that you know clearly that I shall be nothing, when I have finished with my human life. For even now you never saw my soul, but you knew its existence from what it did. And you have not seen what terrors the souls of those who have suffered injustice bring upon the criminals ; what avenging spirits they send to the evil-doers. And do you believe that the honours paid to the dead would continue, if their souls had no longer any power ?

I, indeed, O sons, have never believed that the soul, while it is in a mortal body, lives, and is dead when it is free from it ; for I see that even these mortal bodies live only so long as the soul is in them. Nor can I believe that the soul will be without reason, after it has been separated from this unreasoning body ; then it is likely that it will be most rational. When man is dissolved, it is clear that everything has gone to what is homogeneous, except the soul, which alone, whether present or absent, is never seen. Consider also that nothing is nearer to human death than sleep, and that the soul of man seems then most divine, and sees then something of the future, because it is then most free. If then these things are as I believe, and the soul leaves the body, do what I ask from reverence for my soul.

Those who have been pre-eminent for holiness of life are released from this earthly prison, and go to their pure home, which is above, and dwell in the purer earth ; and those who have duly purified themselves with philosophy, live henceforth altogether without the body, in mansions fairer far than these, which may not be described, and of which the time would fail me to tell.

What would not a man give if he might converse with Orpheus and Musaeus and Hesiod and Homer ? Nay, if this be true, let me die again and again. Above all, I shall then be able to continue my search into true and false knowledge ; as in this world, so also in that ; and I shall find out who is wise, and who pretends to be wise, and is not. Besides being happier in that world than in this, they will be immortal, if what is said is true.

Strive for that and know that not thou art mortal, but this thy body. For thou art not what this bodily form shows, but the soul is what everybody really is, and not the figure which can be shown with the finger. Know therefore that thou art a spirit, for it is God who lives, perceives, remembers, judges, and who governs, leads, and moves this body, over which he is placed as the principal. God governs, leads and rules this world. As God himself moves this world, which is partially mortal, thus eternal mind moves this frail body.

It is clear that that is eternal which is moved by itself. Who would deny that this nature belongs to the mind ? For mindless is everything which is moved by an external impulse, but what is living, that is impelled by an inner movement which is its own, and this is the proper nature and power of the mind. If then the soul alone of all things is moved by itself, it is certainly not born, and it is eternal.

Thus ends the sermon and now follows the celebration of the Holy Communion.

After another hymn is sung the service concludes with the following prayer :

I beseech Thee, O Lord, the Father and Guide of our reason, to make us mindful of the noble origin Thou hast thought worthy to confer upon us ; and to assist us to act as becomes free agents ; that we may be cleansed from the irrational passions of the body and may subdue and govern the same, using them as instruments in a fitting manner ; and to assist us to the right direction of the reason that is in us and to its participation in what is real by the light of truth. And lastly I beseech Thee, my Saviour, entirely to remove the darkness from the eyes of our souls in order that we may learn to know aright both God and man. Amen.

Now that the service is over we walk outside and wander through the churchyard, glancing at the inscriptions carved on the tombstones. Here is one inscription :

> The body here beneath the earth, the soul high above the heaven.

A daughter killed by lightning has evidently returned and communicated with her mother, who has put her communication on the tombstone :

> Mother, leave thy grief, remembering the soul which Zeus has rendered immortal and undecaying to me for all time, and has carried now into the starry sky.

Over there is a fine monument to the soldiers fallen in the battle of Potidæa in 431 B.C., and we read the inscription :

> The etheric world has received their souls but the earth the bodies of these men. They fell round the gates of Potidæa.

Next to it is another stone on which we read :

> The soul dwells in the etheric of the immortals.

These words of hope and comfort are all around us, for we read on another tombstone :

Even if thou hurriest by, stop a moment, dear traveller. The fate of death seized me and the earth covers my body, taking back the gift which she had once bestowed. But my soul went to the Etheric World and to the halls of Zeus. The unchanging law took my bones only into Hades.

On the tomb of a sailor drowned at sea we read :

Breakers have broken my bones and flesh, but the soul inhabits the Etheric roof.

Beside this grave there is another gravestone on which the following is printed :

My soul is at home with the stars and dwells in the sacred place of the blest.

A funeral service is just concluding as we pass by and we hear the priest's final words : "Let now the dead body be covered by the earth and each part go away whence it came into the body ; the soul to the Etheric World and the body to the earth".

So we turn away with the feeling that those who have died have died not without some knowledge of their destiny, but, just as we are passing out of the churchyard, the following epitaph strikes our attention :

Dying thou art not dead !
Thou art gone to a happier country,
And in the isles of the blest
Thou rejoicest in weal and abundance.
There, Prote, (the person's name) is thy home,
In the peace of Elysian Meadows.
Meadows with Asphodel strewn,
And peace unblighted with sorrow.

Winter molests thee no longer, nor heat nor disease.
And thou shalt not hunger or thirst any more.
But unholpen of man and unheedful,
Spotless and fearless of sin,
Thou exultest in view of Olympus,
Yea and the gods are thy light
And their glory is ever upon thee. *

Now that our imaginary journey is over, we return to the present time, better informed as to what our Pagan ancestors really believed. We now find that the claim made throughout our era by Christian priests that Jesus was the first to bring light into a dark heathen world is untrue. Increased knowledge teaches us that the words Pagan and Christian are interchangeable and that, morally and religiously, there was nothing to choose between those who bore them.

In the atmosphere created by the Mysteries lived the Hellenised Jews, coming in daily contact with these Pagan beliefs. When it was reported that their own Christ had come it does not surprise us that the idea spread to every Jewish community, to be slowly absorbed and accepted by many. After the fall of Jerusalem, and the destruction of the Temple, which meant the break up of their own religion, how natural it was for some of the less rigid Jews outside of Palestine to turn to worship the new god, the

---

* The original Greek of the quotations copied from the tombstones, and the committal remarks of the priest, will be found in *Anthropological Religion*, by Max Müller. The Greek text of the chant, hymn and prayer was discovered by Reitzenstein in a papyrus of the third century A.D. and this will be found in the *Mystery Religions and Christianity*, by Dr. Angus. The sermon is made up from sayings of Xenophon, Plato, Socrates, and Cicero, and the Benediction is a prayer used by the Roman philosopher Simplicius.

In Rome, in 493 B.C., a temple was dedicated to the Greek Trinity, Demeter, Dionysus, and Persephone, and called The Temple of the Trinity.

Messiah, who had come only to be rejected by the orthodox through lack of understanding.

Thus we find this new competitive religion which, though similar to the Mysteries, had a saviour much nearer in time and one, moreover, who had come in the fulness of time, before the dispersion of the Jewish nation. Thus it was believed that the prophesies of Hebrew scripture had been fulfilled, which gave the new Faith a tradition right back to Adam. From its start it was able to claim equality with its rivals and to attribute to its Messiah all that was attributed by the Mysteries to their gods. So the Hellenised Jew, whose language was Greek, gave to the new god the name of Christ and thus put him on the same level with the Christs of the Mystery religions.

The prophetic messages in their Book of the Law, some argued, had been misunderstood, but there was much disputing on this question, some holding that the Messiah was still to come to deliver the Jews from their enemies, while others accepted the argument of Paul that the Christ had come to earth in the person of Jesus. His return to heaven was only a temporary visit, and he would come back in great glory to bring the age to an end and judge the people on earth. Then the Jewish race would at last come into its own and its hated enemies receive their deserts. Those who adopted this line of reasoning became Christians and received the comfort engendered by this flight of the imagination. On the other hand, the descendants of those who refused to abandon Jehovah in their hour of national sorrow, and believed that he would still send an earthly deliverer, have continued to expect this event these last nineteen centuries, homeless, with no king or country, receiving what comfort they could from the prophesies and promises contained in their scriptures.

If all the Jews, instead of some, had gone over to Christ, how much happier would have been their history, but in those days who could have foreseen that Christ would supersede Jehovah, and obtain the worship and affection of a third of the human race, within which community the Jews would live, to be treated, not as equals, but as inferiors? In every period of history we see these lost opportunities, but here we are considering only the source and growth of the Christian Faith, and so we must avoid side issues.

This chapter has taken us considerably further on in our quest : it has described the soil out of which grew the Christian Faith, and, if my descriptive efforts have been successful, what follows will be understood and appreciated. This would have been impossible without a knowledge of the pre-Christian religious background, which so protruded itself into the Christian picture that finally it became the picture.

We have now reached, in our study, the time when the parents of the Christian Faith are about to give it life. All that has been written in the previous pages has been leading up to this great event. Everything so far said has been for the purpose of preparing the reader to understand the prevailing religious ideas, which brought the new faith into being when the psychic spark, in the form of an apparition of a slain reformer, once again set men's minds on fire with age-old ideas relating to the saviour-gods.

To some all that the next chapter will relate is a mystery, to others it was the result of a miracle, while to many it came about in consequence of hallucination. When properly understood, however, the origin of the Christian Faith will be found to be a natural psychic event, and the maze will be discovered to be no maze at all when the light of knowledge and logical thinking is directed at the right angle on to the problem. So let us proceed with our task of disentangling what seems to be such a tangled skein.

CHAPTER V.

CHRISTIANITY—ITS CONCEPTION.

THE three previous chapters have been devoted to a consideration of the religious ideas which produced the beliefs we associate with Christianity. Our problem now is to discover how it was that certain religiously minded Jews, a generation or so before the fall of Jerusalem in A.D. 70, changed over from Judaism and commenced to worship a saviour-god. That they did so is an historical fact, however unhistorical the god worshipped may be.

With the information accumulated in the previous chapters we are now in a much better position than most people to arrive at a correct solution of this very intriguing problem, so intriguing that it has stimulated scholars by the thousand to attempt its solution. Let me in a few words state the case.

History is made up of recorded events which have been handed down to us in writing from generation to generation. To take a case in point, the Battle of Waterloo was recorded in *The Times* on 22nd June, 1815, or four days after it occurred, and copies of this newspaper have been preserved so that they can be seen and read at the present time. There is no reason to doubt the trustworthiness of this report, because it contains the Duke of Wellington's dispatch, dated 19th June, 1815. We are, therefore, in a position to say that it is an historical fact that the Battle of Waterloo was fought on the 18th June of the year 1815. Besides this we know the details ; who were the combatants on each side, how long it lasted, and approximately the number of men involved.

If everything that has happened on earth in the past were thus recorded, our knowledge of past events would be so complete that nothing more would be desired. Unfortunately it is not so. We know that last century some could read and write and transfer their thoughts into the printed word, but four centuries earlier printing in Europe was unknown and, though a few could read and write, the majority could not. Printing was invented in China in A.D. 593, but this art did not become known in Europe till nine hundred years later.

Paper is a comparatively modern discovery and does not last for ever. The Babylonians certainly hit on the way to preserve their thoughts when they implanted their writing in clay tablets. This was, however, a cumbersome method, and, as the tablets were heavy to carry about, other nations preferred to put a record of their deeds in writing on papyrus made from the papyrus reed. This was the ancestor of paper which, as we know it today, came to Europe in A.D. 704. The manufacture of paper from cotton was then begun in Spain by the Moors, but this was practised in China as early as the 2nd century B.C.

Climatic conditions make it impossible for papyrus or paper to last for very long. A copy of *The Times*, which is before me as I write, giving a report of the Battle of Waterloo, is already in such a dilapidated state that if it were not preserved in a frame with glass on either side it would crumble into dust. This being so, in order to preserve the thoughts contained in the written word, copies have to be made from time to time, and, before the art of printing was discovered, there were people whose business in life it was to copy documents for the purpose of their preservation and increased circulation.

The further back we go the more uncertain becomes our source of knowledge, and the copies we have of many previous copies less likely to be accurate. We know that our ancestors had childish minds and that they would accept as true things which were obviously false. Being simple in the extreme they were neither accurate nor thorough, and so would set down on paper records of current events without the care which would be devoted today to making certain of their accuracy. So our sources of information are unreliable because the one who wrote was not accurate, and the one who copied his writings suffered from the same failing. All history suffers from this defect and the more ancient it is the greater the defect becomes.

Besides this, the further back we go the less are we able to check one writer with the other. We can be almost certain of what happened last century in this country, but, for every century we go back, the certainty becomes less, because the number of people who put their thoughts in writing was fewer. When we get back to the time of Herodotus, the Father of History, who was born about 484 B.C., we have only his word to rely on for much of what he records. Knowledge of the past, therefore, consists of the evidence which has come down to us. Some of the evidence is good because it is supported by various writers of the times, but other evidence is not so good because an event referred to by one writer is not mentioned by others.

Besides what we term history, there are legends, which refer to people and events without giving dates, or any particulars to enable us to relate them to any specific time. Not only are they vague as to the information they contain, but we are unaware of their authorship, or the place where they were written. We do not know where, or when, or by whom, legends were written and it is because of this that they are called legends and not history. It is on legends that religious stories are based, and in the early days of the Christian era innumerable legends concerning one called Jesus found their way on to papyrus.

By the time the legends had obtained such a grip of the people that they wished to have them recorded on papyrus, this Jesus, whoever he was, had become in the minds of his worshippers the most wonderful being who had ever trodden this earth. He had been born, they believed, without the necessity of a human father and, when still a child, he did the most remarkable and miraculous things. He had only to look at people and they would drop dead. He had only to touch things and they lived and moved. About these, and other wonders, we shall discover more as we proceed. As he grew up to be a man he attracted the people in greater and greater numbers by his sayings and his miracles. He had the power to heal by touch. He could make the dead come back to life, and produce enormous quantities of food from next to nothing. He could walk on water and do other such marvellous things that one of the story-tellers in his enthusiasm states that if everything he did was recorded, "the world itself could not contain the books that should be written" (John xxi, 25).

Yet this man, according to the same legends, was arrested, tried and crucified as a common criminal between two thieves; but three days later he reappeared and went about with his disciples, sometimes as a spirit, and at others as a human being, without any attempt on the part of the authorities to rearrest him. After forty days of this kind of thing he soared up to heaven like a balloon and was lost to sight.

This is the story that passed from one to another and was much talked about, and thought about, in the second century of the Christian era, a hundred years or so after the events recorded were supposed to have happened. If this story had not had such momentous consequences it could easily be placed in the only category for which it is fitted, amongst all the other legends and stories which have come down to us from a childish past. Because, however, this legend grew and developed into a systematic form of belief, till it came to be accepted as true by the whole Roman Empire, and ultimately by a third of the human race, its origin is of special interest both from an historical and religious standpoint.

To the Christian, who is not concerned with doubts as to its truthfulness, it has been a source of comfort and satisfaction, and has made life happy and comfortable for millions. On the other hand, it has been the cause of bigotry, hatred, persecution, murder, wars and incalculable suffering and misery. To the historian it is a fascinating problem which calls for solution. As there is an increasing body of opinion to whom its acceptance is no longer possible, historians have endeavoured to put forward an explanation of what occurred to bring into being the Christian era and the worship of a new god, but, as there is no reliable evidence, their attempts have always ended in theories and not in history.

Something happened, about forty years before the destruction of Jerusalem, under Titus, the Roman general and future Emperor, which, as the centuries passed, detached increasing numbers of religiously minded Jews from Judaism, and Gentiles from the Mystery religions, to the belief that a god had suffered and died in Palestine for the sins of humanity. Those who were detached from the old beliefs by the new idea formed a new cult which revered and worshipped this new god. The doctrines which it taught developed from the beliefs surrounding this god who, it was believed, was born seventy years and died about forty years prior to the destruction of Jerusalem. This addition to the main stream of religious thought in the Roman Empire was slight to begin with and only by degrees did it increase in strength.

What began as a new religious outlook, amongst a small number of Jews, who were considered to be heretics, ended after three hundred years as the State religion of Rome, having in its progress absorbed the main beliefs of the Mystery religions, and adopted the Jewish Jehovah as the Father god of the new saviour-god. The new cult had grown by adopting year by year some new idea, some new doctrine, and some fresh dogma from its Jewish and Pagan neighbours, and when it became a fully established religion it was a composition of Judaism and the Mystery religions.

During the centuries of its growth the old stream of religious thought contributed everything to the new stream which, in consequence, increased in volume as it flowed on. Finally, all that remained of the original stream was Judaism, because the new stream had absorbed so much from Paganism that there was little left to enable the Pagan religions to hold together and pursue an independent existence. Under a new name the river flowed on. The ideas for which the new name stood were not new. What was new was the name.

What was it that occurred to cause this diversion of thought? Does history come to our aid? Unfortunately it does not. History only records that the diversion took place, but gives us no facts to enable us to understand the cause. We are confronted with only a mass of legend, myth, tradition and dogma which poured forth in the first three centuries of the Christian era. These give us no facts but tell us only what each writer believed. This legend and tradition is, however, sufficient to enable us to realise that something important happened, eventually to dry up the old stream of Paganism and start a new one, which in time gained adherents far greater in number than the parent stream from which it had sprung.

What caused the religious minded in those days to express their aspirations under a new name? Why did they change their god and retain the old beliefs?

Why did the new idea appeal to the Greeks and the Hellenised, or Greek-speaking, Jews living outside of Palestine ? These, and many other questions, can be asked, and over the last two hundred years scholars have tried to give the answer. Theories of all kinds have been put forward, but none have gained general acceptance. This subject is one which has attracted numerous learned men, but no solution satisfactory to all has yet been reached. The Christian orthodox explanation never receives their consideration because it is so obviously false.

The large number of earnest enquirers into the origin of the Christian Faith, ignoring, as they do, the psychic thread which runs so prominently through the New Testament, will never be able to complete the pattern. Scholars approach the subject solely from an historical point of view, and the faithful from the aspect encouraged by the organisation which came into being to protect the beliefs and ceremonials adopted by the various Church councils in the third and fourth centuries.

The remembrance of the real origin of the religion probably did not outlive the generation following the one contemporary with Jesus. Those who followed consequently attributed its origin to supernatural causes and, by so doing, covered over the source from which the new stream had sprung. A critical study of the documents which have come down to us, professing to give us the origin of the religion, leaves the student bewildered unless he possesses the key to open the secret. To make it possible to understand the mystery, as well as scholarship, the knowledge is required that apparitions are seen occasionally

by those with clairvoyant vision, and that those called
dead can appear after death in a finer and more
radiant body. The Christian dogma that the dead
are awaiting the Judgement Day to return to their
earth bodies must be abandoned, as it is untrue.
Without this key of psychic knowledge the quest for
the origin of the Christian Faith is hopeless.

I consider that it is only possible to discover the
mysterious origin of this religion by applying to it
our present-day knowledge of psychic phenomena,
together with the conclusion scholars have come to
as to how the gospels and the epistles were pieced
together. The orthodox belief that Jesus was, and
still is, one of three gods, who came from heaven, was
miraculously born on earth, performed miracles, was
crucified as the victim for the sins of humanity, rose
again from the dead in his physical body and with
it ascended to heaven, can be put aside as only suitable
for those who have not the capacity for rational
thinking.

The origin of Christianity can be discovered and
understood by all logically minded people, if they are
prepared to accept the fact that the individual mind
passes at once from earth to another order of existence,
surrounding and interpenetrating this earth, and that
it uses as a vehicle a finer, or etheric body, which
can be seen at times by those endowed with psychic
sight. This etheric body, which interpenetrates our
physical body, passes from it at death, and this
accounts for the decomposition of the physical body.
It is the etheric body which holds the physical particles
together. We appear to our friends in the etheric
world as we did on earth, but freed from the agedness

brought about by the weakness of the flesh. Consequently, if we are seen by earth people after death, we can be recognised. This is all important if we are to understand what follows.

So long as the mental attitude is maintained that such ideas are due to hallucination, the origin of the Christian religion is impossible to understand. The Church fathers, ignorant of psychic knowledge, when they codified the dogmas and doctrines of the religion, explained everything by means of the supernatural. As the supernatural cannot exist, because nature comprises the entire cosmos, etheric as well as physical, the Christian religion, from the time the supernatural was introduced, has been based on a pedestal of sand.

In those far-off days, when the Christian beliefs were being systematised and organised, the supernatural and the supernormal, in the minds of our ignorant ancestors, were one and the same. Once the idea took root that a new god had come to earth, the supernormal and the supernatural became interlocked to such an extent that only those who have psychic knowledge can now separate them. Before proceeding on this line of thought, however, let us look round and see what help we can get from history and tradition in our attempt to explain the origin of the religion which has been such a power in the lives of countless millions throughout the Christian era.

The first thing to be emphasised is that the gospels and the epistles, as we now have them, represent what was believed of Jesus in the 4th century A.D., not what was believed of him by his original followers. These documents now represent Jesus as a god but, as they were put together over three centuries, only traces can be discovered of Jesus the man. To find him we have to dig down to the natural rock, and in our digging we have to throw aside all the soil which accumulated during all these years. Once we get down to Jesus the man, our next endeavour will be to reach the cause of his deification. This cause has been almost as much obliterated as has Jesus the man, but there are still some traces left.

By critical analysis we find three stages represented in the New Testament. The first is Jesus, the man; the second is Jesus, the apparition; and the third and last is Jesus, the god. We shall first of all consider

JESUS, THE MAN.

We commence with history. Has history anything whatever to tell us in support of the Christian assertion that a god-man named Jesus lived on earth ? History tells us nothing of any value on this subject, though there were several Jewish historians who lived in Palestine at the time when Christian tradition asserts that Jesus lived. Moreover, Eusebius, the Father of Church history, about whom we shall hear much later on, is equally silent. This great Christian writer, though he lived in Palestine in the third century, and had at his disposal every book pertaining to Christianity, tells us, in the preface to his *Ecclesiastical History*, that in trying to trace out the history of Jesus he found that he had entered "on a desert and untrodden path".

Though Jesus is not mentioned in history it does not follow that, because of this, he did not live. Like the vast majority, both before and after his time, he was passed over by historians, and the only reason why people think that he should have been mentioned in history is because of the marvellous stories told about him in Christian literature. To the believer in these stories it is certainly extraordinary that the historian of his time should have passed him by. This, however, only emphasises the reasonableness of the opinion that the unnatural stories told about him are untrue, but it in no way proves that a man, about whom these false stories were told, did not live. Josephus, for instance, makes no reference to Gamaliel or Hillel who, when Jesus lived, would be considered by the Jews of greater importance than a poor wandering teacher and yet, in spite of this, we do not doubt that they lived.

Certain historians of the second century mention the fact that, in their time, Christians existed. Pliny the younger, in a letter written by him in A.D. 112 to the Emperor Trajan, mentions that when performing his duties as governor of Bithynia he had a certain number of Christians arrested, and that they had confessed that they held meetings before daybreak to sing a hymn to Christ as God. This does not prove that Jesus was an historical character, but only that the Christians of the second century worshipped God under the name of Christ.

Tacitus, in his *Annals*, tells us that Nero, disturbed by the rumours which charged him with the burning of Rome in July, A.D. 64, tried to attribute the responsibility for the catastrophe to the common people called Christians. "Their name," he continues, "comes from Christ, who, in the reign of Tiberius, was condemned to death by Pontius Pilate." The authenticity of this passage is doubted by some but not by all. What is doubted by most is not its authenticity but its reliability. At the time this was written, in A.D. 115, Christians believed that their god, when on earth, had been condemned to death by Pontius Pilate, so the statement by Tacitus may be no more than an echo of Christian belief. It is strange that neither Clement nor Ignatius, writing in the second century, refers to this persecution by Nero.

What we are trying to do is to find out about Jesus apart from the Christians themselves, and, as there is no reason to believe that Tacitus obtained his information from any other source, his testimony does not help us in our quest for the historical Jesus.

Suetonius, a second-century Roman author and secretary of the Emperor Hadrian, wrote as follows in Chapter XXV of his *Life of Claudius*, "He drove out of Rome the Jews who were perpetually stirring up trouble at the instigation of Chrestus". From this passage one would take the view that Chrestus was a leader of the Jews in Rome who were giving trouble to the Emperor. Chrestus cannot refer to Christ as the Jews in those days would not stir up trouble at the instigation of Christ. Suetonius was writing with reference to the year A.D. 50, when it is most unlikely that the Jews in Rome would have become Christians.

Chrest was also another name for Osiris, who in Greek was called Chrestos (Χρηστός), meaning "good, excellent, gracious". This word was also used in epitaphs on tombstones. The difference

between Chrest and Christ (Χριστός), "the anointed",
is very slight and in pronunciation there was little
perceptible difference. It is quite possible that the
early Christians made use of this similarity to justify
their beliefs. "Christ was Chrest" (The anointed
one was good, excellent, gracious), is euphonius in
Greek and also impressive. From this it was just a
step to say that Christians were likewise. This self-
praise was practised by at least five of the most
eminent of the Church fathers, covering a period of
two hundred and fifty years.

About the year A.D. 180, Celsus, the Roman
writer, wrote a book against the beliefs of the Christians and showed his knowledge of the Christian
Faith, but this again does not help us, as, like Tacitus,
his references are to the beliefs of the Christians, not
to historical facts.

Justin, the early Church father, who lived in the
second century, set down his belief that Pilate had
sent a report to Rome about Jesus addressed to
Tiberius. Tertullian, at a later date, also mentions
this, but in such a way as to indicate that his knowledge of the report came from Justin. There is no
proof that Justin knew anything about this report, in
fact everything points to the fact that he assumed
that there was such a report, and that Tertullian took
this on trust from Justin without verification. The
report, which has come down to us as the one Pilate
sent to Tiberius, is of much later date, and is believed
by those who have studied the question to be a forged
document which made its appearance in the fourth
or fifth century.

The Pagans of the first and second centuries had

no reason whatever to be interested in Jesus, so why should we expect them to write about him ? A man who lived in a small Galilean town, one of the despised Jews, who, for a year or so, went about with some followers within a small area and suffered the death of a criminal, would live and die quite unknown to historians. It was only as his fame grew that Christians began to wonder why no contemporary historian had mentioned his name, forgetting that to these historians Jesus meant nothing, however much he may have meant to the Christians of the second and third centuries. Consequently we come across the obvious attempt to get over the difficulty by a Christian enthusiast interpolating the writings of Josephus (A.D. 37–105). The most flagrant interpolation, so often referred to, appears in his book entitled *Jewish Antiquities* as follows :

Now about this time came Jesus, a wise man, if indeed one may call him a man, for he was a doer of wonderful works, a teacher of such men as receive what is true with pleasure, and he attracted many Jews and many of the Greeks : this was the Christ. And when, on the accusation of the principal men among us, Pilate had condemned him to the cross, they did not desist, who had formerly loved him, (for he appeared to them on the third day alive again, the divine prophets having foretold both this and a myriad other wonderful things about him), and even now the race of those called Christians after him has not died out.

Is this passage accepted by historians and critics as genuine ? No. With a very few exceptions, they believe that it is an interpolation. It is not even found in all the manuscripts. It is out of its setting, as it interrupts an indecent tale of Roman society.

Origen, the early Christian father, states that Josephus did not believe Jesus to be the Christ. Origen, and the early fathers, moreover, were unaware of this passage. Josephus was a Jew, not a Christian, and never became a Christian. Consequently the passage above referred to is inappropriate coming from anyone who was not a Christian. Gibbon, the historian, believed it to be an interpolation, added in the fourth century, and this opinion has been shared by most scholars since his time.

It is the opinion of most critics that Josephus did not mention Jesus anywhere in his writings and that the foregoing, and the other reference to "The brother of Jesus called Christ", are interpolations, having been added by someone who believed forgery was justified in the interests of his faith. Justus of Tiberias, who was himself born in Galilee about the supposed date of the crucifixion, in his two great works on the history of the Jews, from the time of Moses to Agrippa II (A.D. 100), makes no mention of Jesus anywhere.

Another historian of the time was Philo, to whom I have already referred. He was born in 30 B.C. and died in A.D. 54. He lived in Alexandria and took a great interest in Jewish affairs, contributing over a hundred books on the history and thought of his time. He was particularly interested in Jewish religious thought, and yet he makes not a single mention of Jesus or any of his followers. This silence of Philo is proof, if such is needed, that the gospel stories are composed mostly of myths and legends which were evolved at a later date. If they had been history, Philo would have been sure to have referred to Jesus, because what the gospels say Jesus preached would have greatly interested him, and he would have been enthusiastic to have found that the Messiah he was awaiting had actually come to earth.

The three great Jewish historians of the time of Jesus thus entirely ignore him and his followers, which is really not strange considering how insignificant was the Christian cult in their time. It was in no way influencing Jewish history or religious thought. Only the unimportance of Jesus can account for his being ignored by contemporary historians, and we must accept this as the reason, because Josephus mentions other Messianic claimants.

Most people think that it was through the preaching of Jesus that Christianity was founded. There is no evidence for this whatever, and the silence of these three prolific writers, who were contemporary with the time of Jesus or the apostles, proves conclusively that in their time either the fame of Jesus had not reached them, or the opinion of his followers that he was the Messiah did not deserve special notice.

The last evidence to consider on this subject is to be found in the Talmud. Here we find a story of the adultery of Mary with a soldier called Pandera, and it is obviously inserted for the purpose of confounding the Christian assertion that Jesus was the son of a virgin. This Talmudic story, which, up to the fifth century, was still growing, only began after Christianity became a religion apart from Judaism. Its purpose was defamatory and from an historical point of view quite valueless. Especially is this so when we remember that the historical parts of the

Talmud do not go further back than the second century of our era and can in no way be looked upon as history contemporary with Jesus.

As this is all that we can glean from history, let us now turn to the traditional documents which have been revered and treasured by the Church throughout the Christian era. The business of the historian is to separate fact from fiction. When there are no facts he must candidly say so, and account for results by making what he can of tradition and legend. Since the end of the eighteenth century scholars have been at work endeavouring to obtain an ounce of fact about Jesus from the enormous load of fiction which grew up round his name during the first, second and third centuries of the Christian era. When exactly did Jesus live? Who was he? How did he live? And what happened to him? We do not know, as we have a mass of myths which are not only fiction but lack even the merit of originality. What these report about Jesus was recorded of other god-men of the past, about whom history is as silent as it is about Jesus.

The gospel stories are a wilderness of legend, and nowhere in them can we find history. The Christian Faith rests on no historical facts; solely on legend and myth, and the historian can only record what was believed, not what actually happened. The numerous documents which came into existence between the fall of Jerusalem and the end of the second century prove one thing only, that certain people, who came to be called Christians, believed certain things about one they called Jesus. These beliefs brought them comfort and consolation, acted as a stimulus to religious enthusiasm, and changed the outlook of believers so greatly that some were ready to die rather than renounce them.

When, however, we try to find the basis for these beliefs, the reason for them, we enter a fogbound region, because the documents which purport to give us the origin of, and reason for, these beliefs are filled with myths and legends, contradict each other, and are so obviously untrue that the historian gives up in despair his search in them for facts and something tangible. The most he can do is to find a nucleus common to them all so that a basis, on which the mass of legend grew, can be established.

Out of this research two schools of thought have evolved, one holding the view that no such person as Jesus ever lived, and that the early Christians took over the legends and myths from neighbouring religions. These they wove into a story about a moralising teacher, similar to the one told about Krishna. As very much of what was told about Jesus was told about Krishna, and other gods as well, including the story of their coming to earth and being sacrificed for the sins of humanity, this school of thought, believing that these gods never lived on earth, considers that the Christian story must be placed in the category of a religious myth, with no earth basis whatever. Dr. Drews, the German scholar, is the leader of this school of thought, and his two principal works, *Die Christusmythe* and *Die Entstehung des Christentums*, put forward a seemingly convincing case if looked at only from his angle of thought. Those who sponsor it, however, forget that an equally good case can be made out against this line of thought, based on circumstantial evidence which is difficult to put aside.

Another and much larger body of scholarly opinion, however, adopts the view that there must be a nucleus of fact around which the fiction has been draped. They admit the legends and myths but see behind them all a real man who lived on earth. They cannot, however, give a reason which generally satisfies, as to why one whom they look upon as a religious teacher only, produced the effects which followed his life on earth.

I take a new line of thought, which, as a basis, accepts a real man as the centre round which the myths and legends collected, as otherwise no rational explanation can be given to account for the origin and development of the Christian Faith. By arguing backwards from effect to cause I hope to prove that there must have been a victim, whom we call Jesus, and that there must have been a propagandist of the new idea, whom we call Paul. Moreover, my deductions will give a convincing reason to account for all which followed the life of this unknown Jesus. I believe that some day the logical deductions, which I have set out in the following pages, will be accepted by all who are in any way interested in the origin of the Christian Faith, and that only by such reasoning will the centre of the theological and mythological maze be reached.

The only facts we have to guide us are the Christian beliefs as they developed, the beliefs of the non-Christians, and the accepted history of the time. On this foundation I propose to work back from effect to cause and thus build up the structure of the

Christian religion. By this method it will be possible to get to its very source which, when discovered, will make clear all that followed.

The belief that Jesus was the Christ, the world Saviour, came to be believed by Christians within the first century of our era, and this belief was the cause of the Christian Faith. This belief, first of all, produced legends concerning him, which were finally translated into creeds, dogmas, doctrines, rites and ceremonies during the three following centuries.

The evolution of Christian beliefs can be discovered by examining critically the traditional documents which have come down to us, and observing how they have been pieced together. By stripping these of their accretions the residue which remains gives us the earliest Christian beliefs of which there is a record. These beliefs were the cause of the Christian religion. It is probable that they germinated about nineteen hundred years ago, but it is an historical fact that eighteen hundred years ago a primitive form of Christianity was spreading and gaining converts throughout the Roman Empire.

Though Christian beliefs do not enter the region of history till early in the second century, yet prior to this we have the epistles of Paul, the Quelle document, the earliest stratum of evangelic tradition, to which reference will soon be made, the Revelation of John, the Acts of the Apostles, the First Epistle of Clement of Rome and The Epistles of Ignatius, which are sufficient to enable us to know what Christians believed at the end of the first century.

The books which now make up the New Testament, like the religion of whose origin and doctrine they are a record, were a matter of slow growth. Oral tradition came first and this was passed on from generation to generation. These stories were ultimately put into writing and were probably inaccurate and exaggerated. Copies were then made, and to each edition, as it was written by the scribes, was added something new as the beliefs developed. These writings did not take final shape till the Council of Carthage in 397. This Council was called to decide on the Canon, or the authorised books which the Church authorities decided to adopt, as some had, by that time, been added to and altered sufficiently to conform to the then prevailing beliefs as to what the Christian Faith really constituted. The other gospels and epistles which did not come up to this standard were rejected.

Many stories, it must be remembered, were in circulation about Jesus from early times and, as his fame grew, so were these stories elaborated. Those which found their way into writing followed the same course, with the result that many and varied were the gospels and epistles which appeared under different titles. The four gospels attributed to Matthew, Mark, Luke and John were the ones officially adopted in the fourth century at the Council of Carthage.

The New Testament is an accumulation of various documents showing the development of Christian beliefs. They are not the work of one mind, as is a history, but the outcome of many minds, not one of whom is known to history. They are not written as a history. The desire of the authors of the four gospels was to portray a short period in the life of a man whom they looked upon as a god and wrote of as such. Many opinions have been expressed as to who these authors were but they are just surmise. These writings, moreover, show a complete indifference to history and geography.

For instance Jesus, the principal character, the one of all the characters about whom there should have been accuracy, is reported as being born during the reign of Herod the Great. This king, however, had been dead at least four years before it was possible for Jesus to be born, according to the data given throughout the gospels relating to his age, and the historical events which are reported to have coincided with his birth, the dates of which are known. We know the date of the death of Herod as Josephus tells us "That very night there was an eclipse of the moon". Astronomers have worked back and found that this eclipse took place on 12th April in the year four before Christ. Different accounts are given as to the birthplace of Jesus, as Matthew and Luke say that he was born in Bethlehem and Mark and John imply that it was in Nazareth.

A comparison of the accounts given in the four gospels reveals the fact that in not one story are they in complete agreement, and that in many they are at complete variance. To the historian they are of no value as history and their only value lies in their records of the beliefs which grew around an unknown man whom the writers called Jesus. It is evident that the early Church did not look upon the gospels as history but as theological treatises, or otherwise these glaring contradictions would have been adjusted to make them correspond one with the other. These records are just an accumulation of dogma and impossible stories. It was for the dogma they were treasured, not for their history and geography.

It is an undisputed fact that Pontius Pilate was Procurator of Judea from A.D. 26 to 36. The fifteenth year of the reign of Tiberius, who became Emperor in August of the year A.D. 14, began on the 19th of August, A.D. 28, and ended on the 18th of August, A.D. 29. The census of Quirinius, mentioned in Luke, took place in the year A.D. 6 to 7, or six or seven years after the date given in Luke as the date of the birth of Jesus. These are the historical dates critics work on, but they do not find that they agree with the other statements in the gospels. These constitute grave difficulties, and they are increased by the astronomical calculations which exclude the possibility of the heavenly occurrences recorded at the birth and death of Jesus.

We evidently cannot make the gospels agree with historical and astronomical facts. Are they therefore of no interest to us ? They are valueless as history, but the four gospels are of interest to students, as, by critical examination, they reveal the birth and development of Christian dogma. If we cannot find history we at least find beliefs, and the only history we have of early Christianity is that of the development of the beliefs which ultimately coalesced into fixed and rigid creeds.

Besides the gospels there have come down to us epistles, or letters. Whatever their original form may have been, they are documents which, in attaining the form in which they have now reached us, have gone through different hands and reveal that their editors were men of diverse thought. So much is this the case that some of these epistles express diametrically divergent views and opinions about the very essence of Christian beliefs.

We have already noticed in the previous chapter the opposite opinions expressed on the question of Salvation by Faith or Works. Dogma, these epistles contain in plenty, but certainly not history, and it is dogma of a contradictory and incoherent nature. So much is this the case that we find at least three different doctrines taught. These differences centre round Christ the Divine Being, evolved by different minds, in different ways, according to the manner in which they assumed redemption was to be secured by the death of Jesus, all of which divergent conceptions can be traced back to pre-Christian beliefs.

We do not know, moreover, when, where, or by whom these epistles were written. They are neither signed nor dated. Most scholars believe that they are the earliest Christian documents. In their first form they were probably written before the gospels and may be placed at a date prior to the fall of Jerusalem. This is especially so with regard to the Gnostic doctrines, which were probably the first Christian doctrines to be taught.

Do these epistles help us in any way in our quest for the historical Jesus ? What they say about the earth life of Jesus is very meagre as they dwell almost entirely on Christ the Heavenly Being. Paul, to whom most of the epistles are attributed, refers to the Last Supper, the Crucifixion, the fact that Jesus was naturally born of the seed of David under the law, thus necessitating a human father and mother, that he was an orthodox Jew sharing human weaknesses, and was obedient unto death. Paul tells us "Though we have known Christ after the flesh, yet now henceforth know we him no more" (2 Cor. v, 16). This may either mean that Jesus the man was of no further interest to him or it is simply a reference to Jesus being no longer on earth.

Apparently the various writers, who elaborated the epistles from the original letters, knew next to nothing of the earth life of Jesus, or, if they did so, it did not interest them. It was the dogma which followed after, and which came into being as a result of his death, that really concerned them. The earth life of Jesus was consequently passed over as of little importance. The epistles dwell on the Heavenly Being, the Redeemer, the Sacrificed Saviour and Mediator who is continually making intercession for all believers.

The account of Paul's first introduction to Jesus after his death, and all that followed, may be a much exaggerated account of the cause of his conversion. Something like this may have occurred with one who seems to have been well endowed with psychic gifts. It is possible to believe that he may have had a particularly vivid psychic experience which changed him from being a bitter enemy of the new Messianic cult to being its most ardent advocate.

These psychic experiences, right down the ages, have changed the outlook of those who have experienced them, and nothing I am aware of creates more enthusiasm than the experience a novice has at his first séance, when evidence of an overpowering nature comes through to prove to him that someone in whom he is specially interested still lives, retains earth memories and affections, and awaits the reunion. A novice of an enthusiastic and emotional type wishes at once to proclaim it all from the house-tops, just as Paul did.   The story *The Acts* and the Epistles tell us about Paul, when stripped of the theological elaborations, can become natural and believable to those with psychic knowledge.

These statements about Jesus attributed to Paul are not history but rather what was believed at the time they were written.   To judge the validity of a statement we must first of all know who said it, what authority he had for saying it, and when he said it. In the case of the stray remarks in the epistles about Jesus, they do not come under this category as we do not know who wrote them, what their qualifications were, or the date on which they were written.   Whoever wrote them evidently did not believe in the virgin birth, and in all probability they were written before this idea took root.

Another deduction we can draw from a critical examination of the gospels is that the early believers considered Jesus, when on earth, to have been a man with human weaknesses, though endowed with divine qualities not possessed by other human beings. Only stage by stage was the man transformed into a god, the equal to Jehovah.   The reason why we know this is because so much that is human is brought into the story of Jesus, so many human touches, just the very things that would never have been mentioned if the original writers had held the beliefs about Jesus which were accepted by all Christians in the fourth century.

These early Christians believed without a doubt that Jesus had a human mother and father, brothers and sisters, that he shewed anger and sorrow, had human frailties, experienced hunger and thirst, endured poverty, and wandered about as an itinerant teacher having at times no place on which to lay his head. From the records it is evident that his mission lasted about a year. Because of his disappointments and sufferings he is contrasted with the man of sorrows and the one acquainted with grief, as written about in Isaiah. Sixty-six times he is referred to in the gospels as the Son of Man, which in the original Aramaic means a "Human Being", though, as related to Jesus, this expression has a Messianic significance. He is reported as denying that he was a god, in fact his last despairing utterance was believed to be, "My God, My God, why hast thou forsaken me ?"

Those who were responsible for the later editions of the gospels believed that Jesus was the Christ, the Saviour, Redeemer, Mediator and the Son of God, but the early writers did not picture him in such a comprehensive and elaborate manner. No present-day scholar accepts the man Jesus as presented to us in the four gospels of the New Testament. It is too clearly realised that over the life of the real Jesus has been laid layer after layer of interpolations, which makes the quest extremely difficult but not impossible. In fact, it is now accepted that a very satisfactory reconstruction has been made of the source from which much of the material given in Matthew and Luke was obtained, but this needs some explanation.

No scholar takes the gospel according to John seriously. It inverts the sequence of the ministry of

Jesus, as given in the other three gospels, and it changes his teaching beyond recognition. Further, it pictures Jesus in an entirely different light, as the Logos, which developed from the speculations of Paul.

The *Encyclopædia Britannica*, under "Gospels", says that either the Gospel of John is inaccurate or the synoptic gospels are, as both cannot be correct, and remarks on the former's "accumulation of obviously inconsistent statements" and how "contradictions" meet the reader. Dr. F. C. Conybeare, who made the subject a life study, describes this gospel as a romance, full of exaggerations, and not worthy of any consideration by those who wish to find the true Jesus. Dr. F. C. Burkitt, late Professor of Divinity at Cambridge University, in his book published in 1932, entitled *Jesus Christ, An Historical Outline*, remarked as follows about this gospel : "The contents of the Gospel of John do not seem historical at all. . . . I do not think the writer distinguished in his own consciousness between what he remembered, or had derived from the reminiscences of others, and what he felt must have been true, and I greatly doubt whether we can distinguish often in that Gospel what is derived from tradition and what is derived from imagination."

This, then, is the opinion of one who, in his day, was one of the greatest authorities on the subject, and it must be respected. If the fourth gospel is derived from the imagination of the writer, it seems a waste of time to consider it, as it does not help us to get back to the real Jesus. This being so, we shall give our attention only to the first three gospels.

The first three agree more or less in style and contents, embodying as they do traditional stories of the life of Jesus. Further, it will be found that Matthew and Luke are so much in general verbal agreement with Mark, that if you strike out from Mark every verse repeated in Matthew and Luke very little will be left in Mark. Matthew and Luke, in other words, independently copied from Mark, abridging and altering here and there. This was the common practice in those days.

Let us now take the next step. After eliminating all the matter Matthew and Luke copied from Mark, there is much left over in these two gospels which is not included in Mark. Here again Matthew and Luke copied from another source to obtain this information, as Matthew and Luke tell the same stories and repeat sayings in much the same words. They must therefore have obtained this information from a common source. Unfortunately this source is lost, but it can be reconstructed from what Matthew and Luke have preserved. The name given to this lost document is "Quelle", from the German meaning "source". The following diagram will simplify the problem :

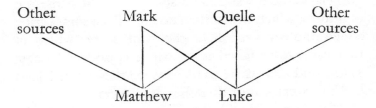

Other sources   Mark   Quelle   Other sources

Matthew   Luke

We therefore find that Matthew and Luke compiled their narratives mainly from two sources, the one being Mark, which we know, and the other called "Quelle", which is lost. By eliminating all that Matthew and Luke copied from Mark, which was, in fact, most of

Mark, we have this residue left over, and Professor Harnack, one of the greatest of Biblical scholars, reconstructed this residue in the form of a narrative, omitting some portions which were not common to Matthew and Luke. The orthodox view that the gospels are independent records, written under inspiration, finds no confirmation, and it is evident that they were put together bit by bit over a considerable period of time.

It is now important that we should give some consideration to Mark, as it formed, with "Quelle", the basis of Matthew and Luke. One of the first things to strike the careful reader is how the writer repeats himself. If Mark were an original gospel these repetitions would not occur, so the conclusion is that the writer, like Matthew and Luke, used earlier documents. As Mark is full of Aramaic phrases and idioms, it is now accepted that the documents from which the writer of this gospel copied were translations into Greek from Aramaic originals. Mark is composed of different layers, and, like the other gospels, stratum was laid on stratum. First came the oral story, which was written down. Then some scribe added another version of the same story, which in time came to be taken as a separate episode. As new stories and ideas came to be believed these were added and this went on for three hundred years.

In his careful analysis of the historical value of the gospel narratives, Guignebert, the Professor of the History of Christianity in the Sorbonne, Paris, in his work entitled *Jésus*, published in 1935, remarks "All that can legitimately be sought for in the gospels is the material of the earliest history of Christian dogma, not that of the life of Jesus. Of the latter they can tell us absolutely nothing, for all that they relate concerning it is obviously incredible."

No scholar believes that the gospels are correct copies of the first accounts of the life of Jesus, or that he said all that is reported of him. As Professor Guignebert remarks, "There is not the slightest doubt that Jesus never uttered the discourses attributed to him by the gospels. They are artificial compositions. . . . Even the Sermon on the Mount is no exception to this rule."

Just as Matthew and Luke copied from an earlier source, so also did Mark. Scholars have deduced this from a critical study of the gospel, from which they have been able to discover how it has been built up. The name they give to this source is Urmarcus, which was a patchwork of traditions of varying authenticity. *The Gospel of Mark,* as we now know it, though the oldest of the Synoptic Gospels, is no more reliable as history than the others. All three gospels are copies of two or more earlier sources which have been lost. These two sources were of doubtful value, but it is better to have this described in the words of one who has made the subject a life study. Professor Guignebert writes as follows :

One important fact is certain, the synoptic tradition still presents Jesus as a living person. It does not translate him into the realms of divinity, as the Pauline writings go on to do. But if it vouches for the actuality of his life, it does not reveal the truth of it. On the contrary, it conceals it under accretions which have no connection with the actual facts. We are confronted by the problem of distinguishing between genuine tradition and apologetic figments. There are liberal critics who maintain that the legendary figure of the Lord is always animated by the vivid experience of Jesus. This optimistic conviction is based on the belief that Urmarcus and Quelle were originally trustworthy documents, which is precisely what we have endeavoured to show they were not. Even had they really been so, it would help us little, because they have been so mishandled by the gospel redactors.

In the last analysis these two primitive originals may have come from the immediate disciples of Jesus. If they were the first two documents, in which reference was made to Jesus, Professor Guignebert thinks that their earliest possible date of origin would be about the year 50, which means that the oral tradition had by then been in circulation for about twenty years. This was a long time in which to preserve the truth amongst people with childlike minds who were intent on glorifying their Lord. Between the time of the Master and the first record in writing is a gap in which much could be forgotten, much added and much altered.

The Quelle document, as reconstructed by Professor Harnack and others, gives us a record of sayings attributed to Jesus. It carries us back to as near to the real Jesus as we possibly can get, and gives us an idea of what the first stratum of tradition had to say about him. On this groundwork we can now trace how, piece by piece, the supernatural erection was built up over the next three centuries. Before we can appreciate how the gospels, as we now have them, came into being, this basis or source should be studied, and, as it will be referred to from time to time as we go on, I now give it as reconstructed by Adolf Harnack.

All the region round about Jordan . . . John saw many . . . coming to baptism and said of them, Offspring of vipers, who warned you to flee from the impending wrath ? Produce therefore fruit worthy of repentance. And think not to say in yourselves, We have as father Abraham. For I tell you, that God is able out of these stones to raise up children to Abraham. And already the axe is laid at the root of the trees.

Every tree then not producing good fruit is cut down and thrown into the fire. I indeed baptise you in water unto repentance ; but he that comes after me is stronger than I, whose shoes I am not worthy to carry. He shall baptise you in fire, whose winnowing fan is in his hand, and he shall purge out his threshing-floor, and shall gather his grain into his barn ; but the chaff he will burn up in fire unquenchable.

Jesus was led up into the desert by the Spirit to be tempted by the devil ; and, having fasted forty days and forty nights, he afterwards hungered. And the tempter said to him, An thou art Son of God, bid these stones to become bread. And he answered, It is written, Not upon bread alone shall man live. So he taketh him with him to Jerusalem, and he stood him on the pinnacle of the temple ; and saith he to him, An thou art Son of God, throw thyself down ; for it is written that he will give his angels charge concerning thee, and on their hands they shall bear thee up, lest ever thou dash against a stone thy foot.

Jesus said to him, Likewise is it written, Thou shalt not tempt the Lord thy God. Again he taketh him with him into a mountain exceedingly high, and shows him all the kingdoms of the world and their glory. And he said to him, All this I will give thee, if thou wilt fall down and worship me. And Jesus says to him : It is written, The Lord thy God shalt thou worship, and him alone shalt thou serve. And the devil leaveth him.

. . . Multitudes . . . he taught the disciples, saying . . . Blessed are the poor, for theirs is the kingdom of God.

Blessed are the sorrowers, for they shall be comforted.

Blessed are the hungry, for they shall be filled.

Blessed are ye, whenever

they revile and persecute you, and say all that is evil against you falsely.

Rejoice and exult, because your reward is great in heaven; for even so they persecuted the prophets who were before you.

Whoever smites thee on thy cheek, turn to him also the other. And to one who would go to law with thee and take thy shirt, give up to him also thy coat.

To one who asks of thee, give; and from one who would borrow of thee, turn not away.

I say to you, Love your enemies and pray for them that persecute you, in order that ye may become sons of your father, for he causes his sun to rise upon the wicked and the good. For if ye love those who love you, what reward have ye? Do not the tax-farmers do this very thing? And if ye love your brethren alone, what that is extraordinary do ye do? Do not the Gentiles also do as much? Ye shall therefore be merciful as your father is merciful.

All things whatsoever ye desire that men should do unto you, even so do ye unto them.

Judge not, that ye be not judged; for with whatsoever judgment ye judge, shall ye be judged; and with that measure wherewith ye measure shall it be measured unto you. And why markest thou the mote in thy brother's eye, but perceivest not the beam in thine own eye? or how shalt thou say to thy brother, Let me cast the mote out of thine eye, while the beam is in thine own eye? Hypocrite, first cast the beam out of thine own eye, and then shalt thou see clearly how to cast the mote out of thy brother's eye.

If a blind man lead a blind, they will both fall into a ditch.

A disciple is not above his teacher, nor a servant above his master. Let it suffice for the disciple to be as his teacher, and for the servant to be as his master.

By its fruit the tree is known. They surely do not gather grapes off thorns or figs off thistles? Even so, every good tree produces good fruit, but the rotten tree produces bad fruit. A good tree cannot bear bad fruit, nor a rotten tree produce good fruit.

Not everyone who saith to me, Lord, Lord, shall enter

the kingdom of God, but he who doeth the will of my father. Everyone then that listens to these words and doeth them shall be likened to a man who builded his house on the rock. And the rain came down, and the rivers came, and the winds blew, and fell upon that house, and it fell not ; for it was founded on the rock. And everyone who listens to these my words, but doeth them not, shall be likened to a man who builded his house on the sand. And the rain came down, and the rivers came, and the winds blew, and smote upon that house, and it fell, and great was the fall thereof.

He entered Capernaum, and there approached him a centurion, calling on him and saying, Master, my child lies at home struck down by paralysis, suffering dreadfully. He said to him, I will come and heal him. But the centurion answered and said, Lord, I am not worthy that you should enter under my roof ; but only say a word, and my child will be healed.

For I am a man in authority, having under me soldiers ; and I say to this one, Go, and he goeth, and to another,

Come, and he cometh ; and to my servant, Do this, and he doeth it. But Jesus heard and wondered, and said to them who followed, Verily, I tell you, not even in Israel have I found so much faith.

But John, hearing in the prison the works of Jesus, sent by his disciples and said to him, Art thou he that is to come, or must we expect another ? And he answered and said to them, Go ye, and report to John what ye hear and see. The blind see anew and the lame walk, lepers are cleansed and deaf hear, and dead men are raised and poor receive good tidings.

And blessed is he who is not scandalised in me. But as they walked along he began to talk to the multitudes about John : What went ye out into the wilderness to see ? A reed shaken by the wind ? But what went ye out to see ? A man clothed in soft raiment ? Lo, they who wear soft raiment are in the houses of kings. Then why went ye out ? To see a prophet. Nay, I tell you, one even greater than a prophet. For he it is of whom it is written, Lo, I send my angel before thy face, who shall prepare thy path before thee. Verily, I tell you that among those born of women there hath been raised up none greater than John the Baptist; yet the least in the kingdom of God is greater than he.

To what shall I liken this generation, and what is it like? It is like to children sitting in the public square, which address the others and say: We have piped to you, and ye danced not. We sang dirges, and ye mourned not. For John came neither eating nor drinking, and they say, He hath a devil. The Son of Man came eating and drinking, and they say, Behold a man, a glutton and a wine-bibber, friend of publicans and sinners. And wisdom is justified of her children.

Go ye and proclaim, saying that the kingdom of God is at hand.

One said to him, I will follow thee whithersoever thou goest. And Jesus answered him: The foxes have burrows and the birds of heaven nests; but the Son of Man hath not where to lay his head. But another one said to him: Permit me first to go away and bury my father. But he answered him: Follow me, and let the dead bury their dead.

He saith to his disciples: The harvest is abundant, but the workers few. Beseech, then, the lord of the harvest to send forth workers for his harvest.

Behold, I send you forth as sheep amidst wolves.

But when ye enter into the house, give it greeting. And if the house be worthy, let your peace descend upon it. But if it be not worthy, let your peace return unto you.

For the worker is worthy of his food.

Verily, I tell you, it shall be more tolerable for the land of Sodom and Gomorrah in that day than for that city.

Woe to thee, Chorazin; woe to thee, Bethsaida. For had the works of power which have been wrought in you been wrought in Tyre and Sidon, they would long ago have repented in sackcloth and ashes. But I tell you, it shall be more tolerable for Tyre and Sidon in the day of judgment than for you. And thou, Capernaum, instead of being exalted to heaven, shall go down unto hell.

In that season he said: I give thee thanks, Father, Lord of heaven and earth, that thou hast hidden these things from the wise and clever, and hast revealed them to infants. Yea, O Father, for so it was thy good will, before thee. All things have been made over to me by the father, and no one hath known.

Blessed are your eyes, because they see, and your ears, because they hear. For verily I say to you, that many prophets and kings desired to see what ye see, and saw not, and to hear what you hear, and heard not.

Father, give us this day our daily bread, and forgive us our debts, even as we have forgiven our debtors, and lead us not into temptation.

Ask, and it shall be given to you; seek, and ye shall find; knock, and it shall be opened to you. For everyone who asks receiveth; and who seeks finds; and to the knocker it shall be opened. Or is there any one of you, of whom his son shall ask for bread, he will surely not give him a stone? Or if he ask for a fish, he will surely not tender him a viper? If, then, ye, being sinners, know how to give good gifts to your children, how much more shall your father from heaven give good things to them that ask him?

He healed one possessed by a devil, dumb, so that the dumb one spake, and all the multitudes were astonished . . . Every kingdom divided against itself is made desolate . . . And if I through Beelzebub cast out devils, through whom do your own sons cast them out? Therefore shall they be your judges. But if I by the spirit of God cast out demons, then indeed hath the kingdom of God hastened to come upon you. . . . Unless a man is with me, he is against me; and he who gathers not in with me, scatters . . . Whensoever the unclean spirit quits a man, he passes through dry places seeking rest, and finds none. Then he says, I will return into the house whence I went forth. And he goes, and finds it vacant and swept and adorned. Then he goes and takes with him seven spirits more evil than himself, and they enter and dwell there. And the last state of that man is worse than the first.

They said, We wish to see a sign wrought by thee. But he said, An evil and adulterous generation seeks for a sign, and sign shall not be given to it, except the sign of Jonah.

For as Jonah was a sign to the Ninevites, so shall be the Son of Man to this generation. The men of Nineveh shall rise up in the judgment with this generation, and shall condemn it; for they repented at the preaching of Jonah, and behold more than Jonah is here. The Queen of the South shall rise up in judgment with this generation and condemn it, for she came from the ends of the earth to listen to the wisdom of Solomon, and behold more than Solomon is here.

They light not a candle and set it under the bushel but on the candlestick, and it lights all who are in the house.

The light of the body is thine eye; if, then, thine eye be simple, thine whole body will be full of light. But if thine eye be wicked, thy whole body will be dark. If, then, the light within thee is darkness, how great the darkness!

They bind up heavy burdens, and lay them on the shoulders of men; but they themselves would not move them with their little finger.

Woe to you Pharisees, because ye shut up the kingdom of God before men's faces. For ye enter not yourselves, nor permit them to enter who would do so.

Woe to you Pharisees, for ye tithe mint and anise and cummin; but have left undone the weightier parts of the law, judgment and mercy.

Now, ye Pharisees, ye cleanse the outside of the cup and platter, but within they are full of robbery and licence.

Woe to you, for ye are like graves unseen, and men who walk over them recognise them not.

Woe to you, because ye build the tombs of the prophets and say, Had we been in the days of our fathers, we would not have been sharers with them in the blood of the prophets. So that ye bear witness that ye are sons of them that slew the prophets. And ye fill up the measure of your fathers.

Therefore the Wisdom of God said: I send unto you prophets and wise men and scribes. Some of them ye will slay and persecute, that there may come on you all the blood shed on earth, from that of Abel until that of Zacharias, whom ye slew between the shrine and the altar. Verily I say to you, All these things shall come on this generation.

Nothing is hidden which shall not be revealed, or secret which shall not be known. What I speak to you in darkness, do ye speak in the light; and what ye hear in a whisper, proclaim ye on the house-tops. And fear ye not them that slay the body, but have no power to slay the soul. But fear rather him that is able to destroy soul and body in Gehenna. Are not two sparrows sold for one penny? And one of them shall not fall to the ground without God's will.

And of your heads the very hairs are numbered. Fear not then. Ye are of far more account than sparrows. Everyone then who shall make confession of me before men shall the Son of Man also make confession of before the angels of God. But whosoever denies me before men, I also will deny him before the angels of God.

And whoever speaketh ill of the Son of Man, it shall be forgiven him; but whoever speaketh ill of the Holy Spirit it shall not be forgiven him.

Therefore I say unto you, feel no concern for your life, what ye shall eat, nor for your body, what ye shall put on. Is not the life more than food, and the body than raiment? Look at the crows, how they sow not nor reap nor gather into barns, yet God feedeth them. Are ye not of more account than they? And who of you by fussing can add to his stature one cubit? And about raiment why fuss thee? Mark the lilies how they grow. They labour not, nor do they spin. Yet I say to you, not even Solomon in all his glory was clad as one of these.

But if God so dresses the weed which is today in the field and tomorrow is cast into a furnace, how much more you, O ye of little faith? Therefore ye shall not worry and say: What shall we eat? or what shall we drink? or what shall we wear? For all these things are in quest for the Gentiles. For your father knows that ye are in need of all these. But seek ye his kingdom, and all these things shall be added to you.

Treasure not up for yourselves treasures on earth, where the moth and rust deform, and where thieves break through and steal. But treasure up for yourselves treasures in heaven, where neither moth nor rust deform, and where thieves neither break through nor steal. For wherever your treasure is, there will be also your heart.

But this know ye, that if the householder knew in what hour the thief cometh, he would keep awake and not allow his house to be broken into. Who, then, is the faithful servant and thoughtful, whom the master set over his household to give its members food in season? Blessed is that servant whom the master shall find so doing when he comes.

Verily I tell you that he will set him over all that belong to him. But if that servant say in his heart: My master delays, and begins to beat his fellow-servants, and eats and drinks with drunkards, the master of that servant shall come in a day when he expects him not and in an hour of which he is not aware, and shall cut him in two and set his portion together with the hypocrites.

Think ye that I came to shed peace upon the land? I came not to shed peace, but a sword. For I came to part asunder a man against his father and a daughter against her mother, and a daughter-in-law against her mother-in-law. And a man's foes are those of his own household.

Be reconciled with thine adversary quickly, whilst thou art still with him in the street; lest the adversary deliver thee to the judge, and the judge to the officer, and thou be cast into prison. Verily, I tell you, thou shalt not depart thence until thou hast paid the last farthing.

And again he said: To what shall I liken the kingdom of God? It is like leaven which a woman took and hid in three measures of meal, until the whole was leavened.

Enter ye through the narrow gate. For wide and broad the road, which leads to ruin, and many are they that pass in along it. For narrow is the gate and worn the road which leads unto life, and few are they who find it.

I tell you that from East and West they shall come and lie down with Abraham and Isaac and Jacob in the kingdom of God, but the children of the kingdom shall be cast out. There shall be wailing and gnashing of teeth.

Jerusalem, Jerusalem, thou that killest the prophets and stonest them that have been sent unto thee! How many times have I wished to gather together thy children, as a bird gathers her nestlings under her wings, and ye would not have it. Behold, your house is abandoned unto you desolate. For I tell you, ye shall not see me henceforth until you shall say: Blessed is he who cometh in the name of the Lord.

Whosoever shall lift himself up shall be abased, and whosoever shall abase himself shall be lifted up.

He that takes not up his cross and follows me is not worthy of me.

Ye are the salt; but if the salt be spoiled, wherewith shall it be salted? It is useful for nothing any more, except to be cast outside and trodden under foot by men.

What think ye? If a man should have a hundred sheep, and one of them lose its way, would he not leave the ninety-nine on the mountains, and go and seek the lost one? And if so be it he find it, I say unto you that he rejoiceth over it more than over the ninety-nine that lost not their way.

No one can serve two masters. For either he will hate the one and love the other, or he will adhere to the one and despise the other. Ye cannot serve God and mammon.

The prophets and the law lasted until John. From then till now the kingdom of God is being wrested by force, and men of violence snatch at it.

Verily I tell you, until heaven and earth pass away not one jot or tittle shall pass away of the law.

I tell you, everyone who divorces his wife causes her to commit adultery; and whoever shall marry a divorced woman commits adultery.

It must be that scandals come, but woe to the man through whom the scandal comes.

If thy brother sin, rebuke him; if he listens to thee, thou hast won thy brother to thy gain . . . How often shall my brother sin against me and I forgive him? Until seven times? Jesus said to him: I tell thee, not until seven times, but until seventy times seven.

If ye have faith as a grain of mustard, ye shall say to this mountain, Get thee hence, and it shall be removed.

If, then, they say to you, Lo, he is in the wilderness, go ye not out. Lo, in the store-rooms, believe them not. For as the lightning quits the east and flashes across to the west, so shall be the coming of the Son of Man. Wheresoever is the corpse, there shall the eagles be gathered together.

As were the days of Noah, so shall be the coming of the Son of Man. For as they were, in those days which preceded the flood, eating and drinking, marrying and giving in marriage, until the day when Noah entered the ark, and as they knew not until the flood came and swept them all away, so shall be the coming of the Son of Man. There shall be two in the field, one is taken and the other left; two women grinding in the mill, the one is taken and the other left.

He that finds his life shall lose it, and he that loses his life shall find it.

To everyone who has shall be given, and in abundance; but from him who has not, even what he has shall be taken from him.

Ye who have followed me shall sit upon twelve thrones, judging the twelve tribes of Israel.

A probable explanation of the Quelle manuscript is that the writer of it was familiar with the oral story surrounding the name of Jesus, and, to substantiate the belief that he was the Messiah, he put together what he thought a Messiah would have said. As time went on, in order to convince the Jews and strengthen the faith of the Christians, the early biographers made use of everything which could be related to the Messiah in the Old Testament, for the sole purpose of showing that prophesy had been fulfilled. What they were anxious to do was to prove that the Messiah had come, and the best method of convincing the people was to depict his life in accordance with the assumed prophesies relating to the Messiah.

Consequently Jesus was made to speak as it was expected that a Messiah would have spoken, the basis of their effort centering on Jesus as a teaching Messiah. If the writer of the Quelle document knew anything of his life, it was ignored to give place to the development of the belief that Jesus was a wonder worker, and an utterer of wise sayings which were taken from the writings of Hebrew and Pagan literature. As his fame grew, imagination supplanted ignorance, and miracles and supernatural stories accumulated to such an extent that we are forced to conclude that the Jesus portrayed in the gospel records, as they have come down to us in their final form, never lived.

This means that we cannot write his biography, in fact every scholar of distinction is of the opinion that nothing has survived to enable us to say who Jesus was, how he lived, or what he said and did. The infatuation which some express for him is stimulated by the idea that he is the Redeemer who, for the love of humanity, sacrificed himself so that all might be saved. To some he is the most revered being who ever trod this earth. To others he is the greatest and the wisest teacher, who lived the most sublime life ever recorded. To some Spirtualists he is the greatest medium and psychic healer the world has ever known, while to Unitarians he is perfect man, and came to earth as an example to show us how we all should live. However much these enthusiasts may resent the truth being told, the fact remains that the historian has no evidence for any such claims. He can find nothing to establish a foundation on which to form an opinion as to who Jesus was, how he lived or what he did.

He is such a dim figure in history that the most that can be said of him is that those who followed after him endowed him with such superhuman qualities that one is tempted to wonder if he did not possess psychic faculties which gave rise to the marvellous stories told about him. There is never smoke without fire, and, when a religious blaze up takes place, something non-material should be looked for. Though the majority of Christian people will deny any connection between psychic phenomena and their religion it is nevertheless the case that psychic phenomena, in one form or another, are the basis of all religion. Only through these manifestations can the other world be appreciated by mankind, and it is because of the other world that there is such a thing as religion.

Psychic phenomena can be termed the link between heaven and earth because they are the manifestations of etheric beings. It is because each one of us is a spirit that we are related to the spirits in heaven. The spirit is the common denominator between the two worlds and only through spirits on earth can spirits in heaven make their presence felt. One psychically endowed, to whom the name medium is given, can be made use of by those living in this different order of vibration from ourselves to impress us with the reality of their order of existence. Knowing the effect the manifestations of a powerful medium have on the emotions of people today, one can easily understand why religious outbursts have been recorded down the ages.

Was Jesus a medium? No one can definitely answer this question. It is quite a possible theory, but if, later on, we arrive at the conclusion that he probably was, it will be by the method of arguing from effect to cause and not from any facts we have to guide us. The only facts we have are that the people believed that the priests arrested him, that he performed miracles and healed the sick. From these facts we can imagine that the priests arrested and killed him because of his psychic gifts, as we know that they believed that they had instructions from Jehovah which read, "Thou shall not suffer a witch (medium) to live" (Exod. xxii, 18), "There shall not be found among you . . . a witch" (Deut. xviii, 10), and that a man or woman with a familiar spirit shall be put to death (Lev. xx, 27). We can also imagine that what at a later date were called miracles originated in psychic phenomena, and that what was termed casting out devils, and healing by touch, were based on what is now called psychic healing.

All this is possible because we know that at the present time some are used by healers in the etheric world as instruments through whom they pass healing rays ; that some have the power to enter trance and be used by etheric beings who speak through them, and that in the presence of some, those called dead can materialise, and also produce the direct voice. All this can happen with a person endowed with mediumistic gifts who, more- over, can also be clairvoyant and clairaudient. A well-developed medium can have all these powers, as I can attest from my own experiences, which have covered every range of psychic phenomena.

How easy it is for those who have had such experiences to say that Jesus was a well developed- medium, and that all that is recorded in the gospel stories is the residue of what has come down of the doings of a man with remarkable psychic power.

And yet on what have we to base this opinion? Absolutely nothing. No thinking person today would accept a report on mediumistic phenomena of such a nature as the gospel narratives. We do not know when they were written or by whom. We have no reliable, or connected, account of anything Jesus did to enable us to relate it to psychic phenomena. Turning water into wine, or making five loaves and two fishes into a meal for five thousand, has no more to do with psychic phenomena than it has to do with the truth, as each evangelist, in telling the story, contradicts the other. Raising the dead has nothing to do with psychic healing, and the other stories of Jesus healing the sick are either associated with devils, or are altogether too vague to enable us to form any conclusion as to what really happened.

Remembering, however, how the gospels were put together, first from oral tradition and then by the addition of stories taken from the lives of other god-men, as we shall learn in the chapters which follow, it would be wise to form no opinion from the gospel records, and adopt instead the method of arguing from effect to cause. The effect produced on those who lived after Jesus was that he was a wonder worker. Because of this tradition the compilers of the gospels attributed to him wonderful deeds, just as they attributed to him wonderful utterances.

Was there a basis for both these being attributed to Jesus? Had he the power to heal by touch, to produce psychic phenomena, to speak in trance, and are the gospel records but the garbled accounts of a later age which knew the tradition and produced the embroidered story? Knowing, as we do, the drawing power of a good medium, all that the gospels tell us about Jesus could be explained as just mutilated stories of a man with strong psychic power, who angered the priests because he was influencing the people along a line of thought which was abhorrent to them.

On the other hand, he may have been a clever magician. That is possible, but a magician would not anger the priesthood. Magicians have not been burned and tortured down the ages by the priests, because they were not afraid of them, but they were evidently afraid of Jesus. The wrath of the priests points to Jesus being a medium rather than a magician.

Was he just a religious reformer, and were the miracles added because the people turned him into a god-man in consequence of his reappearance after death ? This is also possible. He may have criticised the priesthood and denounced sacrifice and so angered the priests. Here again it is just as rational to accept the psychic explanation, which covers all the facts, whereas this explanation does not. The New Testament, from the beginning of Matthew to the end of the Revelation of John, is on a plane quite apart from the normal and material. As it has come down to us it is a series of supernatural legends which makes it unbelievable. These, however, might be based on supernormal occurrences which caused later generations to elevate them to the region of the impossible, the supernatural. To believe that what ended as impossible supernatural legends originated as supernormal psychic events is more logical than to believe that Jesus was a reformer devoid of any supernormal gifts.

We know that the people believed that he

performed miracles, and that, as miracles never happen, what has been handed down to us must, at the most, be only a garbled account of what he said and did, and of how he died and was seen again. None of these stories taken literally can be accepted as true. But it is at least reasonable to say that though these stories are garbled they may contain, as a basis, a tradition of a man who had strong psychic power. This perhaps gave rise to the supernatural stories told about him, just as the story of his body not being in the tomb, and the belief that he had risen in his physical body, could have come into being by his appearing after death as an etheric being. Stories of people being seen after death do not grow out of nothing. If they did, why are they so rare? Because they are so uncommon we must seek for a reason when they become attached to someone after death.

Some might ask why it was that this psychic power manifested through Jesus for only about a year, when he was about thirty years of age, and why we are told nothing about his wonderful deeds in earlier life? Marvellous stories were, however, told about Jesus from infancy, which made him out to be a wonder worker from childhood upwards. The gospels, in which these stories occurred, were not included in the canon at the Council of Carthage, as they were only stories and unrelated to the dogma which had developed in the fourth century. These uncanonical gospels might conceivably be the result of stories handed down about Jesus which, by the time they were put in writing, were so garbled and fantastic as to be quite unbelievable.

Everything about Jesus is a matter of inference,

of arguing from effect to cause. To assume that Jesus was a powerful medium would make clear much that is dark in the gospel story of his life on earth. It is because of this, that some, who have witnessed psychic phenomena in the presence of a well-developed medium, assume that Jesus, to produce the profound effect he did, was highly gifted psychically and, by his supernormal deeds and utterances, laid the seed of the marvellous stories which came to be told of him.

However, these so-called miracles were not the cause of the Christian Faith, as it was from the speculations which followed the appearance after death, that the new religion developed. "Because Jesus lives, so shall I live", was the natural deduction drawn from the reappearance, and whether Jesus was arrested because he was a medium, or a reformer, or claimed to be the Messiah, is a point we cannot determine from history as we have not the information to enable us to do so. The most that can be said is that the theory that he exercised mediumistic gifts explains much which is otherwise impossible to understand, and gives a reasonable explanation to account for the fantastic stories which came to be told about him.

Fortunately, the lack of information we have about Jesus in no way prevents us from understanding the origin of the Christian Faith, as it was not from what Jesus said or did that the new religion developed, but because of what those, who claimed him to be the Messiah and their Saviour, attributed to him as the result of his reappearance. He gave them the idea, after his death, that he was a god, and they did

the rest. From the speculations which followed,
creeds, dogmas, doctrines and sacred rites came to be
established and consolidated under the authority of
the Church in the fourth century, after they had been
in a state of flux for three hundred years.

If the early gospel writers had believed from the
first that Jesus was a god or a god-man, we would
not be able to find the traces of the man beneath the
picture of the god. Fortunately, these traces remain,
which enable us to realise that what became the
supernatural originated in the natural. It is understandable how, in those bygone days, when the belief
in god-men was general, a man could in time be
looked upon as a god. It happened with others
before and after the time we are considering. The
Greek god Attis was believed to have been a shepherd,
the Hindu Krishna the nephew of a king, Jesus the
son of a carpenter and so on. However their followers
may have pictured them in heaven, at least it was
believed that they all started off on earth as men. We
must, therefore, accept the fact that to the early
disciples, who came face to face with the natural
Jesus, he was looked upon as a human being like
themselves, but that was before his appearance after
death, which entirely altered their outlook.

This book is not an attempt to write a biography
of Jesus. Many have made this effort based on no
foundation of facts. What is here attempted is to
find the origin of the Christian Faith. Some say that
Jesus was an afterthought and put into an already
existing system of beliefs, others that he was born a
god. Neither of these explanations covers all the
facts we know concerning the early beliefs of the new

Faith, and so we must find a better and more rational explanation, or fail in the task attempted.

From the first Church father, beginning with Clement of Rome, who was followed by Marcion, the belief that Jesus lived runs through all their works, and, if he had been worked into the story, as some declare, they would have had knowledge of it and not accepted his life on earth. In *The Epistle of Clement* to the Church of Corinth, which tradition ascribes to Clement of Rome and which was written about A.D. 96, the following is to be found: "The apostles preached the gospel to us from the Lord Jesus Christ. Jesus Christ was sent from God. Christ then is from God and the apostles from Christ. Our apostles knew through our Lord Jesus Christ that there would be strife". This is the earliest reference to Jesus outside the Gospels and Epistles. Marcion, in A.D. 140, wrote that "The God of Love and Goodness had never before been revealed till the coming of Jesus, who began his mission at Capernaum in the fifteenth year of the reign of the Emperor Tiberius".

We are forced to accept one of three alternatives regarding Jesus: (1) the orthodox belief that he always was and still is a god; or (2) that he never lived, and the story and dogma have been woven round an imaginary creation; or lastly (3) that he was a man like other men. We pass over the orthodox belief as it is impossible to accept without evidence. The second alternative that he never lived is not so absurd as it may seem, in fact it is possible to make out quite a plausible case for the existence of a pre-Christian Jesus cult in Palestine, out of which developed the Christian beliefs, and some learned and thoughtful men have been forced to adopt this view from the facts they have accumulated.

Its weakness lies in the fact that this theory does not explain how this cult, which worshipped a saviour-god called Jesus, took hold of the imagination of the people. What caused it to blaze up and produce a man who has come down to us under the name of Paul, and all the numerous gospels and epistles with their assertions that the Christ had come and gone, shortly to return? The gospels and epistles are certainly not history, but it is inconceivable that an old established Jesus cult could have produced all that these convey, with never a hint of the existence of the old cult. These Christian gospels tell of an entirely new god-man, sacrificed in the time of Pontius Pilate. We need not go to such an extreme if a more rational cause can be found which is based on facts, in accordance with our present-day knowledge. It is wiser to keep to the region of the natural if all the facts point that way.

The last alternative, that Jesus lived like other men, is eminently rational and sane, and, unless the facts compel us to adopt an alternative line of reasoning, we have no other option than to keep to the natural, especially when this natural path explains everything, whereas the unnatural one does not. Accepting, then, what is reasonable, we proceed by a logical and critical elimination to withdraw the clothes of myth and legend from the body of fact. Once we get down to the human being we can then start to reclothe him, and, by logical deduction, find out why each garment was wrapped round him.

By first of all eliminating the various myths and

dogmas which were added, we reach the fact that the first disciples looked on Jesus as a man. Having reached down to the man we shall in later chapters rebuild the structure of myth and legend, as it accumulated during the centuries, till it reached heaven at Nicaea with Jesus, once the man, now the Christ, the second person of a trinity of gods. This process of deification was slow and can be divided into three stages :

(1) Jesus, a man, came to be looked upon after his death as the Messiah by certain Jews. They believed that he was "a man approved of God" (Acts ii, 22), and that he suffered a martyr's death, after which he appeared on one or more occasions in his etheric body. The first written record probably consisted of stories and sayings relating to Jesus for the purpose of making him appear as the Messiah, because the religious minded in those days were continually thinking and pondering on this subject. When the wish found its expression in the visible survival of Jesus the idea took root that the long awaited event had at last become an accomplished fact.

(2) This belief was accepted at an early date by the Gnostics amongst the Hellenised Jews who were awaiting the Messiah, whom they termed the Christos or Logos, and who, in pre-Christian days, had attributed to him many of the ideas which were eventually draped round Jesus. The belief, held by the followers of Jesus, that he had been seen after death, appealed to the Gnostics, who, because of his power over death, looked upon him as the Christos. They incorporated Jesus into their teaching, terming him

the Christ and Logos, and those who accepted him as such, Christians. The Messianic idea, for those who anticipated a Spiritual Messiah, easily fused with the belief concerning the Christos and the Logos, since they were alike. The fragment in the fifty-third chapter of Isaiah, relating to the suffering saviour-god, which was probably an excerpt from a scene in the Passion Play surrounding the death and resurrection of the Babylonian god Bel, was applied to Jesus and constituted an early draping, taken from the beliefs surrounding a Pagan god.

The first Christians were Jewish Gnostics living outside Palestine, and their beliefs were the foundation on which was built up the Christian Faith. Because there were communities of Jewish Gnostics scattered throughout the cities of Asia-Minor, Greece and Egypt, the belief spread that the Messiah had come. Consequently, we are told that Paul found believers in places to which no Christian missionary had ever been.

The Gospel as given by John is Gnostic in origin, and, though it may have been the last to be written, yet its doctrines are of a date prior to the Christian era, and similar to those held by the Mandaeans, a pre-Christian Gnostic sect. Rudolf Bultmann traced out this relationship and remarked that, "We cannot overlook the possibility that the Johnine Christianity represents a type more ancient than the Synoptic". Gnosticism, which was considered at some length in the previous chapter, can also be traced in Hebrew literature which circulated within the two hundred years prior to the opening of the Christian era, and is not included in the Old Testament.

As Hellenised Jews were converted to the new faith, so also were Gentile Gnostics, as the result of the efforts of Paul, but it was not till the fall of Jerusalem that much progress was anywhere apparent. This catastrophe convulsed the Jewish nation, broke down the barriers raised by Jewish exclusiveness, and caused the conversion of large numbers of Jewish Gnostics to the belief that the Logos or Christ had conquered death as a sacrificial victim. From now onwards Christianity appealed more and more to the Gentiles and Hellenised Jews, while the orthodox Jews, living mostly in Palestine, remained loyal to Jehovah. As the Gentile influence grew, so the doctrines of the Mystery Cults were absorbed into Christianity. The fall of Jerusalem can be taken as the date when Christianity, as a recognised new cult, commenced. This was the birthday of the Christian Faith, since prior to this date it was only in the embryo stage.

(3) Gnosticism developed into Paulinism, the name given to the doctrines attributed to Paul, a Hellenist Jew, about whom nothing is known outside of the New Testament. The writings which go under his name are composite documents and have been through different hands. They propound various contradictory doctrines but in the main they elaborate the Gnostic belief about the Logos or Christ. *The Revelation of John* and *The Epistle to the Hebrews* represent this belief in its most advanced form.

When this last stage was reached, the man Jesus in the beliefs of the Christian community disappeared. Christ became the all and in all. The earth life of Jesus consequently received scant notice, as it was the glorious Heavenly Being who was worshipped, and on whom rested the destiny of the human race. Nothing in words could encompass the worshipful respect and adoration this divine being received, and his name came to be regarded as above every name, at which every knee must bow. He became The Lord of Lords, The King of Kings, The Saviour, The Redeemer, The Mediator who made intercession for all believers, and The Judge of the human race.

All this glory and reverence, like everything connected with Christianity, was of slow growth. First of all we find the original Messianic Gnostic community. These later on became known as Christians, which name, by the second century, was used to cover the beliefs of different groups, with many and varied opinions, but all centering round Jesus in one form or another.

However they differed in other respects these early Christians believed that Jesus had lived on earth, that he was the Messiah, that he was arrested and killed by the priests, and appeared as a heavenly being after his death. Consequently he was associated, in their minds, with the divine victims of the Pagans, whom they believed had been sacrificed and had returned to assure mankind that the curse of death was a thing of the past. From this association of events all that developed can be understood and explained from our present-day knowledge. On this basis the origin and evolution of the Christian beliefs become a natural development, and this will be appreciated by those who have read the preceding pages of this book.

I lay no emphasis whatever on anything except

the fact that it was believed that Jesus died a victim, and was seen as a spirit after his death. In that superstitious age this was enough to produce all that followed. Christian propaganda did the rest. It surrounded this human being with all that had been woven round the previous saviour-gods, but one thing we can rule out, it did not invent Jesus and put into the story someone who never lived. The facts do not lend themselves to the idea that the beliefs arose from a blaze up of enthusiasm for an old Palestine god. The pre-Christian beliefs surrounding the saviour-gods had to be lit afresh for them to burn with the fierceness they did around Jesus. At the back of all the myths and legends there was a real man, but what he was like, what he did, and what he said we have no means of knowing because there is nothing to tell us. All we can do is to surmise from the effects produced.

The belief that the priests seized Jesus, and killed him, made the people associate Jesus with a sacrificed victim, but this association would never have taken root in their minds if he had not appeared after death, and thus given them cause to believe that through this sacrifice he had broken the curse of death. There is no necessity to accept more than the fact that the people believed such things about Jesus. We know that they did so and because they did the Christian Faith came into being.

In Matthew xxvi (3–4) we are introduced to the priests hatching their plot to kill Jesus : "Then assembled together the chief priests and the scribes, and the elders of the people, unto the palace of the High Priest who was called Caiaphas, and consulted that they might take Jesus by subtlety and kill him."

Let us now read the story of the trial of Jesus before the Chief Priest as it is contained in Mark chapters xiv and xv :

And they led Jesus away to the High Priest : and with him were assembled all the chief priests and the elders and the scribes.

And Peter followed him afar off, even into the palace of the High Priest : and he sat with the servants, and warmed himself at the fire.

And the chief priests and all the council sought for witness against Jesus to put him to death ; and found none :

For many bare false witness against him, but their witness agreed not together.

And there arose certain, and bare false witness against him, saying :

We heard him say, I will destroy this temple that is made with hands, and within three days I will build another made without hands.

But neither so did their witness agree together.

And the High Priest stood up in the midst, and asked Jesus, saying, Answerest thou nothing ?　What is it which these witness against thee ?

But he held his peace, and answered nothing.　Again the High Priest asked him, and said unto him, Art thou the Christ, the son of the Blessed ?

And Jesus said, I am : and ye shall see the Son of Man sitting on the right hand of power, and coming in the clouds of heaven.

Then the High Priest rent his clothes, and saith, What need we any further witnesses ?

Ye have heard the blasphemy : what think ye ?　And they all condemned him to be guilty of death.

And some began to spit on him, and to cover his face, and to buffet him, and to say unto him, Prophesy : and the servants did strike him with the palms of their hands. . . .

And straightway in the morning the Chief Priest held a consultation with the elders and scribes and the whole Council, and bound Jesus, and carried him away, and delivered him to Pilate.

And Pilate asked him, Art thou the King of the Jews ? And he, answering, saith unto him, Thou sayest it.

And the chief priests accused him of many things : but he answered nothing.

And Pilate asked him again, saying, Answerest thou nothing ? Behold how many things they witness against thee.

But Jesus yet answered nothing ; so that Pilate marvelled. . . .

For he knew that the chief priests had delivered him for envy.

But the chief priests moved the people, that he should rather release Barabbas unto them.

And Pilate answered, and said again unto them, What will ye then that I shall do unto him whom ye call the King of the Jews ?

And they cried out again, Crucify him.

Then Pilate said unto them. Why, what evil hath he done ? And they cried out the more exceedingly, Crucify him.

And so Pilate, willing to content the people, released Barabbas unto them, and delivered Jesus, when he had scourged him, to be crucified.

And the soldiers led him away into the Hall called Præ-torium ; and they called together the whole band.

And they clothed him with purple, and platted a crown of thorns, and put it about his head.

And began to salute him, Hail, King of the Jews !

And they smote him upon the head with a reed, and did spit upon him, and bowing their knees, worshipped him.

And when they had mocked him, they took off the purple from him and put his own clothes on him, and led him out to crucify him. . . .

And when they had crucified him, they parted his garments, casting lots upon them, what every man should take.

And it was the third hour, and they crucified him. . . .

And when the sixth hour was come, there was darkness over the whole land until the ninth hour.

And at the ninth hour Jesus cried with a loud voice, saying, Eloi, Eloi, lama sabachthani ? which is, being interpreted, My God ! My God ! Why hast thou forsaken me ? . . .

And Jesus cried with a loud voice, and gave up the ghost.

Such is the story as it came to be written many years after the tragedy had occurred. What is important is not its assertions but the association of the priests with the death of Jesus. It was believed that they arrested him and that on their accusations he was killed. He had committed no crime against the law and his offence was a religious one. It may have been that he claimed to be the Messiah, or that he was a medium, or that he denounced the priests ; it is quite possible that one or all of these things caused the anger of the priests, and brought about his arrest.

Josephus tells us that in these days twenty thousand priests found a comfortable livelihood in Jerusalem at the expense of the people. This army of parasites spent their time performing sacrifices and holding services in the Temple. Each day there was a morning service at daybreak, and an evening service, when sacrifices were offered up to feed Jehovah. On the Sabbaths and Festivals the sacrifices were doubled. These priests wanted no Messiah to appear to disturb their comfortable existence, no one with psychic power to divert the people from the regular orthodox worship, and no criticism. All who crossed their path met with a violent death, if they could find an accusation which would come within the Roman law, and Jesus was no exception.

So it does not surprise us to learn that Jesus was believed to have been arrested by the priests and hanged on a tree, which was the means of his death as told in *The Acts of the Apostles, The Epistle to the Galatians* and in *The First Epistle of Peter*. After this, his body would be taken down and thrown into the pit reserved for criminals, which brings us to the end of the story of Jesus the man, and if what follows had not happened nothing more would ever have been heard of him. Some days afterwards, so his followers believed, Jesus reappeared and was seen as an etheric being. So we shall now give some consideration to this new phase, brought about by

JESUS, THE APPARITION.

The writers of the New Testament documents make clear to us that the belief prevailed that certain disciples of Jesus saw him at different times, and in different places, after his death. As, however, much stress is laid in the gospel records on the fact that Jesus rose from the dead in his material body, and was then seen as a spirit, we have a confused account of the occurrence. Was he seen as an apparition or as a physical being? The gospel records report that eighteen different people saw him after his death, but Paul tells us that he was seen by five hundred at the same time. Ghost stories tend to become exaggerated, and this statement is more than probably very much exaggerated!

Visions figured prominently in the experiences of the early Christians, and the belief that Jesus was seen after his death receives prominence in the gospels and epistles. This is possible, as the seeing of a person after death, by those with psychic sight, is not contrary to nature, apparitions having been seen since early times. As the seeing of Jesus after death was believed, from earliest times, to be the reason for the urge to spread the gospel message, this is a reasonable explanation, though quite unhistorical. Yet all stories of apparitions and ghosts are unhistorical and outside the scope of history. Nevertheless, apparitions are seen from time to time, and the fact that this is so has affected the course of history.

All religious experiences are unhistorical as they are intimately related to the individual, but they come within the range of history because the individual, as a result of his experience, has changed his opinions and then his deeds. Consequently, if an apparition were the cause of the Christian religion it can never be proved by history. All that can be said is that an individual believed that he had such an experience, and we can then record the effect it had on him and on others. This is what we find in the New Testament, the effect of the visit to earth of an etheric visitor, and, to understand this effect, we must be acquainted with what was then believed about other previous heavenly visitors who returned after having died under similar circumstances.

We need only apply our present-day knowledge to the problem to realise how easily an apparition could set a body of people on to an entirely new line of thought, if it were recognised to be that of one who had just been a priestly victim. It is a well known fact that what was believed to be a vision of the Virgin Mary to a girl in 1858 was responsible for Lourdes becoming a holy place to Roman Catholics. Similar visions have been the cause of other places, where visions have been seen, becoming holy, and, as I write, I notice in a newspaper the story of a French girl who claims to have seen the Virgin Mary on various occasions, and at various places, at Lozère, near Lyons. The newspaper's correspondent reported that thousands have visited the places where the vision was seen, three thousand people going to the village in one day. Catholics are so brought up on visions of the Virgin Mary that any female spirit seen is always called by this name.

Now this vision is not history, but the fact that the girl believed she saw this apparition is history, and that is all we need in the case of Jesus. Visions, apparitions and ghosts are just different names for those who return to earth, as did the gods of old. They are the result of clairvoyant sight sensing the other order of existence, and now and always this extra sensorial perception has caused interest to the thoughtful, and religious emotion to the emotional. This French girl, like so many others possessing psychic sight, claims to have heard the apparition speak to her and, if this is so, she is clairaudient as well as clairvoyant.

It is quite easy to believe that the vision, or the seeing, of Jesus set a body of people off on the Messianic idea, which was then in the air, so to speak, when we know that time and again apparitions of male and female spirits have been the cause of towns springing up, places becoming holy and sacred, and churches being built. As I have stated earlier, I believe that some day this psychic link betwixt the two worlds will become the accepted cause of all the saviour-god religions.

Arguing back from effect to cause, it is evident that something did happen to change a band of orthodox Jews from their rigid faith to a new outlook of life and death, and I know of no other event more likely to do so than one or more of the band seeing Jesus in his etheric body, or someone they took to be Jesus. There was a seed which germinated the child called Christianity, and, in my search, I can find only this one, the appearance after death of one believed to be Jesus. From this experience all that now comprises the Christian Faith developed. What evolved could only have done so from an apparition, as we shall see as we go on. Therefore, on this assumption, arguing from the effect to the cause, we come to the conclusion that an apparition, believed to be Jesus, was seen after his death, because we cannot account for the effect by any other cause.

That an apparition was seen is quite a natural explanation. Apparitions are seen today. Why should they not have been seen then ? If a natural event is recorded, even if it is mixed up with the absurd, it is reasonable to accept it if the consequences which followed can be logically linked up with the natural occurrence, as they can be on this occasion.

Apparitions, I repeat, occur today, and are attested by men and women of veracity and judgement, which fact rules out the theory of fraud or hallucination. Many standard books record such happenings, which are reported as occurring, not only in our own times, but down the ages. I repeat that the reports we have of the appearance of Jesus after death are not history, and that the insistence in the gospels on the material body having escaped the tomb makes the whole story appear ridiculous. Certain consequences, however, followed his death, which can only be attributed to some supernormal occurrence, some psychic event, but they were not due to the re-appearance of Jesus as described in the gospels.

To understand the divergent opinions expressed in the gospel story of the resurrection and that of the Pauline epistles, which are based on Jesus returning as a spirit, requires some explanation. The first Christians were Gnostics, which name covered a system of thought adopted in pre-Christian days by both Pagans and Hellenised Jews. These Gnostics believed that Jesus had returned as an apparition, and this gave rise to the Christian Faith because this event was worked into the Gnostic theology, which is expressed in the Pauline epistles. Gnosticism was not a religion, or a sect, or a cult, but a mystical theology which could be held by both Pagans and Jews. Some of those who accepted this mysticism became Christians and were known as Christian Gnostics.

As the Christian Church developed, it absorbed more and more the teachings and beliefs surrounding the Pagan saviour-gods, until eventually Jesus was transformed into a god such as they were. As this came about the beliefs surrounding Jesus resembled more and more those surrounding his Pagan proto-types, with the result that, when the story of the resurrection, as we now have it, was added to the original account of his appearing as a spirit after death, the first story was nearly blotted out by the final one. Consequently, we are left with an account of Jesus leaving the tomb in his physical body and yet appearing to, and disappearing from, his disciples like a spirit. Just as the original birth story was spoiled by superimposing the Holy Ghost episode, so the appearance of Jesus after death was spoiled by the later addition of the story of the tomb being empty, and Jesus being depicted, on some occasions as a spirit, and at other times as a man, finally to ascend to heaven in human form.

The original psychic event was painted over, but not painted out, by the later addition based on the passion plays annually performed in memory of the Pagan saviour-gods. It will be remembered that in Chapter III we found how an actor took the place of the god and went through the passion drama, being carried into the tomb apparently dead, and then coming out to represent the risen saviour. Because the actor was a man he could not reappear otherwise than as a man. He could not turn himself into a spirit, and because he could not a psychic event was materialised. This gave the people the impression that the god had risen in his material body and ascended with it to heaven.

The Gnostic Christian, on the other hand, held to the original belief that Jesus had appeared as a spirit, and that he never ascended to heaven with his earth body, because, as a spirit, he had reached the etheric world at death. This divergence of opinion was the cause of one of many disputes as to doctrine which took place in the early Church, but we shall hear more about this as we go on. The Gnostic beliefs, which were the basis of the Pauline epistles, the earliest record of Christian belief, were the original Christian beliefs, and the gospel account of the resurrection was a later addition. This addition materialised a psychic event and cut the link between this world and the next. What took place at the passion dramas explains how the gospels' report of the physical resurrection of Jesus came to be believed, and how the early Christian belief was smothered by this idea.

Only the orthodox Christian accepts the story of the tomb being empty as being due to the fact that Jesus reappeared in his physical body. Those who believe that he never lived place this story on the same level as all else told about Jesus, and describe it as fiction. The other school of thought, which believes that Jesus was a man like other men, adopts the view that everything reported about his after death appearances was due to hallucination.

Those scholars who adopt the hallucination explanation say that it was caused by minds excited as the result of the experience they had gone through in losing their master. This may be so ; no one can be certain of such an inaccurately recorded supernormal occurrence, but it seems a far-fetched theory and one not in accordance with experience. Sorrow and the upset caused by a death do not produce imaginary visions of the one recently dead. Bereaved people do not get comfort from illusions ; if they did, there would be less sorrow than there is after a death.

It is not unreasonable, however, to accept the belief of the early Christians that Jesus did appear after death, knowing as we do that apparitions are seen today. To believe that an apparition of Jesus was seen is more reasonable, in view of what followed, than to think that it was due to hallucination.

Ernest Renan, the celebrated French scholar and writer, who was relieved of his professorship of Hebrew at the Sorbonne in Paris because he created a scandal in his opening lecture by referring to Jesus as "an incomparable man", wrote as follows in his book, *Saint Paul,* which was published in 1869 : "The group that pressed round him (Jesus) upon the banks of the Lake of Tiberias believed in spectres and spirits. Great spiritual manifestations were frequent. All believed themselves to be inspired in different ways."

Renan, who might be termed the father of the modern school of Christian thought, deduced from the gospel records that in those days unusual occurrences were believed to have taken place, and we know, from what happens in our own times, that these unusual occurrences do occur and are occurring at the present day. The psychic stream was evidently flowing strongly in those days, and was the cause of real psychic experiences because these, and these only, could be the cause of what followed.

Could hallucination cause such comfort and joy, or such strength of purpose ? We are told that those who held this belief risked death, and that one termed Stephen died for it. Those early followers of Jesus had the strength of will to strike out on a new line of thought, and one quite contrary to what they had been brought up to believe. Their religion held very definite opinions about what would happen in the last days when the dead would come to life. To imagine Jesus alive and active was then just as unorthodox as is the teaching of Spiritualism today, and those who held that view had not even the freedom which exists in our time. The Jewish priests, in spite of Roman tolerance to such matters, were then in control in Palestine, and, from what we read in *The Acts*, they did not hesitate to use every possible method to stamp out the new belief.

The orthodox Jews believed in the coming of the Kingdom of the Lord, which would be ruled over by the Messiah, the descendant of David, who would drive out the Roman conquerors and reign in Jerusalem. This would be an earthly Jewish Kingdom, but others looked for a Messiah who would come to judge the world and set up a Kingdom of Righteousness, known as the Kingdom of Heaven, which would be world wide. These were known as the Apocalyptists, who called the anticipated Messiah by the name of The Son of Man, and we find this expression and anticipation in *The Book of Daniel* (vii, 13–14), and the first *Book of Enoch* (xxxvii, 71). It was from these sources that the writers of the Gospels and the Revelation obtained the name and applied it to Jesus.

The Apocalyptical teaching believed that the end of the age would be ushered in by signs and wonders. Then would come the Messiah to set up his kingdom, when he would judge the world, the wicked being sent to Gehenna and the righteous to Paradise. After the earth people were thus disposed of, there came the general resurrection of the dead, who had been awaiting this event in Hades, or Purgatory. They, too, were judged and dispatched to Heaven or Hell, to eternal bliss or eternal misery. This is the doctrine to be found in the gospels and is the doctrine of the Christian Church. The Christians adopted it from the Jews, who had previously obtained it from the

Egyptians. Palestine was, therefore, the last place on earth one would expect a body of people, surrounded by such opinions, to assert that a dead man had returned from the grave to be seen and spoken to. Nature, as often before, once again confounded the foolishness of man.

Could hallucination be the cause of the development of such a revolutionary idea, that some humble individual was the Messiah, one, moreover, who was a complete failure, and whose death had brought about the entire collapse of what he was reputed to have envisaged ? This idea might conceivably have become accepted during his lifetime, but not by those who lived after his arrest, failure and death. Nevertheless it was after his death, not before, that the idea that he was the Messiah took root and developed. Something very real must have happened after his death to make people think of him as such. A humble priestly victim was certainly the last person to be transformed into the Messiah by people, under the yoke of Rome, who were looking for the Messiah in the person of a great leader, who would free their land from the hated invaders, and then act as the Judge of all mankind.

Could hallucination produce characters like Paul, Peter and others, with the enthusiasm to preach doctrines based on the reappearance of Jesus after death ? How long would illusion have kept the original band together after the Master had left them ? It may have been hallucination but it is much more probable that it was something more, that it was something alive, that it was something which they knew to be true, and in which they could find comfort.

Something acted as the inspiration for the enthusiasm which was necessary to enable a band of simple, humble men to preach beliefs diametrically contrary to those by which they were surrounded, and to proclaim a humble teacher as the Messiah against the orthodox belief in a conquering King who would put all the enemies of Israel under his feet.

An hallucination would never have been the cause of the deification of Jesus, but seeing him alive in his etheric body could have been the cause, when consideration is given to the mentality of the times. I have previously remarked that hallucination is unknown to medical science amongst normal healthy people. It is this deification of Jesus which makes necessary the belief that he, or someone taken to be him, was really seen after death ; in fact we cannot account for it by any other means. Disciples would not deify one who had never lived, and so it follows that whether the apparition was that of Jesus, or of someone else, the fact that it was taken to be Jesus proves that he lived.

If he had been a great king or emperor, a man like Plato or Aristotle, his deification could have been understood, as many of the great in those days were looked upon as gods, but here again there is a marked difference, as round the names of those outstanding men there was never woven all the religious beliefs which surround the name of Jesus. Jesus, a quite unknown man, one of the people, never noticed by a contemporary historian, was turned into a god. Jesus became great after his death, which adequately explains the silence of history as to his life on earth, and the beliefs which followed can only be explained by the fact that he was seen again after death.

Where education exists minds are now more developed. We do not allow our imagination to run riot. We keep to facts and accept only what can be proved. When an etheric being speaks to us on earth, or is seen by a clairvoyant, he is likened to ourselves and we do not call him either a god or a devil. Intelligent people have come to realise that we need no passport into the other world, which we enter just as naturally as we entered this world. Its inhabitants are human beings who once lived on earth. They are like ourselves because they still have the same minds as they had on earth, though they function in a finer body, which, however, is to them just as solid as was their earth body.

Just as we attribute physical phenomena to natural law, so likewise we attribute psychical phenomena to natural law. Just as physical phenomena have ceased to be looked upon as the manifestation of a god or gods, so psychic phenomena are now regarded as natural events, and not translated into the activities of angels or demons, gods and saviours. The study of mythology, moreover, impresses us with the fact that psychic phenomena, as they occur today, have occurred throughout the ages, the only difference being that we now interpret them in a rational way.

The belief on which Christianity is based, namely, the physical reappearance of Jesus, is not only absurd, but quite contrary to nature. So it is termed a miracle, to be believed as an act of faith. An individual appearing as a man after death, as we are told Jesus did, could never have been the cause of what followed, as, if this had happened, everyone would have said that he had recovered and had not died. On the other hand,

Jesus, seen as a spirit after his death, which was brought about by the priests, could have been the cause of all the beliefs which followed, just as similar events had caused them in the case of previous saviour-gods.

These etheric appearances happen today, and there is no necessity to go to extremes to find another explanation for the origin of the Christian belief. The original Christian belief was a natural one, and, when stripped of the absurdities laid over it by the Christian Church, the corner-stone of Christianity, the resurrection, ceases to be a mystery, or a miracle, and becomes a natural event.

When something which has been looked upon as mysterious becomes understood it ceases to appeal to the imagination, but this natural explanation will be appreciated by those faithful unto truth, even if they cannot be faithful to the orthodox tradition. Once the mysterious is understood, and reduced to the level of the natural, the priest has nothing further with which to mystify the people. A human Jesus does not interest the Church, or believers, any more than it interested Paul. The supernatural Christ keeps the Church and priests in being, and comforts the faithful who support the organisation which teaches the doctrines surrounding this idea.

It will be remembered how the saviour-god idea germinated in the mind of primitive man when he was evolving out of the stage of eating human flesh. At some place, at some time or other, the return of a sacrificed victim was taken to mean that the gods had given up eating human spirits. The next step was to look on the victim as the first to break the gods of the

habit of eating human spirits, the first to return to tell
mankind that the gods, like man himself, were tiring of
this diet.   For this work of mercy on the part of the
victim he was deified and worshipped as a god in
heaven. He received the title of Saviour, to be followed
later by that of Mediator, when the idea of right and
wrong developed, and man felt increasingly the
weakness of the flesh.   The original cause of the
victim's deification would then be forgotten and he
would come to be looked upon as one who had died
so that man might live.

From this belief the next stages came naturally.
He was first the Saviour, and then the Mediator
because he had appeased the gods.   Next came the
belief that he was the Judge because the wicked and the
unbelievers must be divided from the good and the
believers, the sheep from the goats, as the Bible puts
it.   As he had bought back mankind at the price of his
suffering he was also the Redeemer, and so we can now
understand why all these terms were bestowed on the
sacrificed victim, as well as many others associated with
the gods of nature.   The steps in this evolution of the
victim can be tabulated as follows :

(1) The victim returned and it was thought
that the gods had given up eating human sacrificed
spirits.

(2) This meant that human sacrifice was now at an
end.

(3) The victim had brought about this decision of
the gods to refrain from the further eating of human
spirits, and because of this he was worshipped as the
Saviour.

(4) As the idea of right and wrong developed he

came to be looked upon not only as the Saviour, but also as the Redeemer, Mediator and Judge. Consequently, he received all the adoration and worship which could be bestowed upon him, and, in the minds of his worshippers, was elevated to a position in heaven alongside the chief of all the gods.

By the time Jesus came to be looked upon as the sacrificed victim, morality had developed to such an extent that the people had ceased to eat human flesh and were trying to please Jehovah by keeping his taboos and forsaking wickedness. So Jehovah was no longer looked upon as a cannibal, as he was in the time when he ate the spirit of Jephthah's daughter. Human spirits were no longer appetising meals to Jehovah, or "sweet savours", as sacrifices are called in numerous places throughout the Old Testament, and what refers to Jehovah likewise relates to the gods of Greece and Rome.

Consequently, the return of Jesus was not looked upon as a sign that Jehovah did not wish to eat his spirit. Instead, the ideas which surrounded the return of Jesus developed from those which were currently believed about the Pagan saviour-gods, who, in their own times, had evolved out of this belief that the gods had sanctioned their return to earth, after dying as victims, to prove to mankind that they had given up eating the spirits of human beings.

The return of Jesus was, therefore, looked upon as a sign that he had been accepted by Jehovah as a sacrifice for the sins of the people and that the curse of death had been removed. He had redeemed mankind from the punishment placed on humanity in consequence of Adam's sin, and he received the titles given to the other saviour-gods who had preceded him, and also the beliefs which surrounded them.

How closely related this return of Jesus was to the idea that Jehovah had now finished eating human spirits, and that the appearance of Jesus after death was the sign to this effect, can be seen from the following, "Christ hath given himself for us an offering and a sacrifice to God for a sweet-smelling savour" (Eph. v, 2), and Paul refers to, "A sweet savour of Christ" (2 Cor. ii, 15). The early Christians were so steeped in the idea of sacrifice, and that one god, or the gods in general, ate the spirits of their sacrifices, that they easily associated the atoning work of Christ to the idea, on which they had been reared, that every animal sacrificed was a savoury dish or a sweet savour which was relished by a god or the gods.

The fact that the spirit of Jesus was believed to have returned may have been thought of by some as due to the fact that Jehovah had now ceased eating human spirits, but the much more general belief was that Jesus had been accepted as the final sacrifice which was to end animal sacrifice. When Jesus reappeared this event was therefore looked upon as a sign that animal sacrifice was at an end as the gods had gone off animal diet. Jesus was regarded as the last and final sacrifice Jehovah required to settle the differences which had existed since the time of Adam between him and mankind.

Here we seem to be at the source of the Christian belief, the very core of our subject. From now onwards it is not what really happened that matters, but what was believed to have happened, and the very fact that opinion, which had been suppressed by an organised Jewish priesthood, was loosened, in consequence of the destruction of Jerusalem, and the break up of the Jewish Church, tended to exaggerate what in its essence was a natural event. It may have been the Master in his etheric body who was seen or it may have been someone else. That matters little. What matters is that his followers believed that it was Jesus, the sacrificial victim for the sins of humanity, who had returned as a spirit, as a sign that he had conquered death, from which all mankind suffered because of sin, "And if Christ be not raised your faith is vain; ye are yet in your sins". (1 Cor. xv, 17.)

Like Osiris he became to his followers the deliverer of all who believed that he had broken the bonds of death and opened heaven to all believers. Little wonder that his name became to believers above every other name, and that nothing more was asked by those about to die than that they should join Christ who had gone before to prepare a place for all who loved him. Death to them was not now the curse of God because of sin, Christ having conquered the grave, broken the curse and thus become the Saviour of the world.

It is not history that an apparition of Jesus was seen, but it is certainly a fact that the early Christians believed that this happened, and this event they made the foundation of their faith. It follows, therefore, that if Jesus had not lived as a man on earth he could not have died. Therefore he could not have conquered death. The belief that he conquered death necessitates that he died, which means that he lived. Because he lived, died a victim of the priests, and then proved that he had conquered death, he was deified. This deification is history.

Arguing back therefore from effect to cause we find that Jesus, to be deified, must have lived on earth and died. This belief in Jesus as the conqueror of death inspired believers, and gave courage to the early disciples to break away from Judaism and evolve a faith with which Judaism has nothing in common. Some supernormal occurrence must have been at the back of it all because Palestine is the last place where one would expect to find a deified man. To deify a man was hateful to the Jewish mind, and the Roman Emperors had to abolish the law in Judaea, observed elsewhere in the Roman Empire, that they were to be regarded as divine beings.

Having now considered the effect of Jesus, the apparition, on the minds of his followers, we shall take the next step and see what happened when he became

JESUS, THE GOD.

No student of the origin of Christianity has been able to put forward a theory, acceptable to all, as to why this unknown Jesus was evolved from a man into a saviour-god. Solve this riddle and the rest is easy, because we know whence all the godlike drapings came. The first problem is to explain why it was that the appropriate figure was there who could carry the mythology. To accept the idea that Jesus was an ordinary man, who considered himself the Messiah, does not explain his eventual transformation into a god who suffered for the sins of the world. Messiahs had appeared before, and after, the time attributed to Jesus, but their fame did not outlast their own lifetime.

We must dig deeper to find the causes which

turned a wandering teacher into the very God of very Gods. This came about stage by stage. There was no preconceived plan about it ; events just made it happen. Let us try to realise it better by means of an imaginary conversation between two Hellenised Jews which took place before the fall of Jerusalem. We can imagine a conversation on the following lines when Hellenised Jews met, and, let us say, that it took place in Alexandria.

FIRST HELLENISED JEW: "There are strange reports coming from Jerusalem about a religious teacher, by name of Jesus, who was arrested by the priests and hanged on a tree. Some of his disciples claim that he was seen after death, and are telling people that he must have been the Messiah."

SECOND HELLENISED JEW: "Palestine has always been afflicted by wandering fanatics, and this Jesus I would have put down as one like the rest, but for this story you tell me of his being seen after death, which may be a sign from heaven that he was a man of God. Can you tell me anything more about him ?"

FIRST HELLENISED JEW : "There is not much to tell, but my brother arrived here yesterday from Jerusalem with the news that the followers of Jesus have gathered themselves into a band and meet together regularly. They are encouraged to do so by certain among them who claim to have seen him since he died and to have received messages from him. In fact one of them goes into trance and, when in this state, is taken control of by a spirit who claims to be the Jesus they followed. He encourages them to keep together and spread the message he delivered when on earth, that regeneration must come from within each one and that when this comes about the Kingdom of God will then come on earth."

Second Hellenised Jew: "That is indeed interesting. We have been expecting, as you know, an earthly deliverer to turn out these hated Romans from our beloved land, but it may be that the prophets meant that a deliverer would be one to teach us to look beyond this earth to a life hereafter for which we must prepare ourselves here. Perhaps this Jesus was the one they meant and the priests have killed a man sent by God."

First Hellenised Jew: "Well! Time will tell, but one thing is certain, that these people, who were the followers of Jesus, are interesting others so much that the priests are again frightened and trying to round up any who are taking too great an interest in what the disciples of Jesus are preaching. The priests arranged with the authorities for a man called Paul to go out and harry them, but he did nothing, as he himself claims to have seen the spirit of Jesus on his way to Damascus."

Second Hellenised Jew: "If all this be true, the Lord is fulfilling his promise that in the last days there will be signs and wonders. Perhaps what you are telling me is the fulfilment of the prophesies. It is a strange story and may lead to something or to nothing. Only time will tell."

Time went on, Jerusalem was captured in A.D. 70 by the Romans, the temple was burned, the priesthood was overthrown and scattered, and the Jews as a nation ceased to exist. Jehovah, it was believed, had abandoned his people, and so several millions of dispirited Jews, without a god, without a temple, without a king, without a government, and with a scattered priesthood, had to live on as a minority amongst other races who despised and hated them. Surely this was enough to make them think, and think deeply, about their traditional beliefs. Sorrow, suffering and affliction have the effect of changing the mental outlook.

At this point it would be well to give some thought to the foregoing remark, made by the second Hellenised Jew, that all that was happening was the fulfilment of prophecy, as this belief had a very marked effect on the minds of the Hellenised Jews, and on the process of changing Jesus into the Christ. To understand conditions in those days it is necessary to know something of the methods adopted to calculate time. When we do so it will be much easier to understand the mentality of the people who worked Jesus into a network of ideas which they claimed had been foretold in their scriptures.

Chronology is the science which deals with time. Before the art of writing existed a systematic and correct calendar was impossible, but writing was in vogue for many centuries before historians began to assign dates to the events they narrated. The masterpieces of Thucydides and Herodotus are stories without dates, and, for this reason, the history of the early ages of the world is involved in almost impenetrable obscurity.

The earliest written annals of the Greeks, Etruscans and Romans are irretrievably lost, and those of the Druids have perished with them. Fragments have been preserved of the attempts made by the Egyptians and Babylonians to produce a chronological list of kings.

The father of chronology was a Greek named Eratosthenes, keeper of the library at Alexandria, who, in the latter half of the 2nd century B.C., attempted the chronology of events from the fall of Troy to his own day. He was the first European to date events on the basis of years. Before his time it had never occurred to a European to calculate time by years or months. The Chinese were more intelligent, and from as far back as 200 B.C. the dating of events was regulated by the moon and the sun. Their year consisted of twelve months and the method adopted in India was similar.

The great difficulty all the ancient chronologists had to face was the selection of a starting-point, but, as time went on, nations and cities west of India decided on some event on which to base their calculations, reckoning, not by years, but by epochs, each given the name of a King, Governor or Chief Priest who had reigned during that period. This method was a step forward, as a fixed point of departure was established. The Babylonians started off with the era of Nabonassar, the Greeks from the time it was believed the first hero of the Olympic Games carried off the contests of the Stadium, and the Romans from the foundation of Rome. Chronologists have worked hard to piece together the approximate dates of ancient history from the records preserved on the monuments and tablets discovered in Babylonia, Persia, Greece and Italy, and, from these sources, they have achieved a considerable measure of success.

It was not until the time of Julius Caesar that the Romans began to measure time by the apparent annual journey of the sun and the monthly journey of the moon round the earth, taking as their fixed point the foundation of Rome and calculating how many years had elapsed since then. In the sixth century of our era commenced the calculation of the years from the supposed date of the birth of Jesus, but not until 1752 was it definitely settled that the year began on the first of January. Up till the twelfth century it began at Christmas, and after that on the twenty-fifth of March.

From the foregoing we can realise better the difficulties of our ancestors. First of all they had no fixed point from which to start off, and secondly, they could not hit on a fixed method of calculation which would never vary. So it does not surprise us that beyond three thousand years the dates given to events are largely a matter of guess-work.

The Jews calculated time from the events recorded in their Book of the Law, dating everything back to the creation of the world, an idea they got when they were in Babylon. They, however, adopted three different methods, with the result that the Hebrew Book of the Law contains one, the Samaritan another, and the Greek Septuagint another. Between the shortest and longest calculation was a span of three thousand five hundred years, enough to make the soundest fundamentalist wonder how Divine inspiration could go so far astray !

When people were in such a simple state that they were unable to calculate time, when they had to rely on ages, epochs and kings' reigns, nothing reliable was possible. So we find that when they thought back they had extraordinary ideas as to when events happened in the past and as to the length of time people lived. Methuselah is a good example. They also believed that time was composed of different cycles, and so they looked forward and anticipated the future based on the cycles of the past.

Each nation believed in different periods of uncertain duration and some thought that when the age reached its end a god would come to earth. This kept the prophets and astrologers well occupied and gave the people something to think about. In the history of Christianity one of the main forces which acted as an auxiliary to the gospel message was the anticipated return of Christ, which elicited the ardent enthusiasm of many who have found comfort from the early days of this religion in thus anticipating the future. Prophecy and fortune-telling have an extraordinary fascination for certain minds.

The Jews anticipated a deliverer, but other nations, like the Greeks and Romans, believed that the new age would be a time of peace and righteousness. When the Jews were dispersed in A.D. 70 the Hellenised Jews gave up the orthodox idea of a deliverer and adopted the apocalyptical outlook, which was brought over to the new Faith by those who became Christians.

The converts to the Christian Faith preached that Jesus had manifested on earth as the Saviour and Redeemer, but that this was only the beginning of things as he would soon return to usher in a reign of righteousness. These dreams and hopes were just a continuation of those conjured up by the religiously minded who lived before our era and found their happiness in day dreams about the future.

The roots of this belief, so far as it concerns the Christian Christ, lie in the Jewish Apocalyptic literature, the books of *Jeremiah, Ezekiel, Joel, Daniel, Enoch* and *The Wisdom of Solomon,* which expressed this hope, and the gospel writers, especially Matthew, lost no chance to prove that the prophesies had been fulfilled. In this literature we find references which were made to refer to the Messiah who would suffer and die, and a passage from one of these books will indicate what was written in the others. In *The Wisdom of Solomon,* written about the 2nd century B.C. by a Hellenised Jew in Alexandria, and included in the Apocrypha, we find the following passage :

> The ungodly say . . . let us defraud the righteous man ; for he is not for our profit, and he is contrary to our doings. . . . He maketh his boast to have the knowledge of God ; and he calleth himself the Son of the Lord. . . . Let us see then if his words be true ; let us prove what end he shall have. For if the righteous man be the Son of God, he will help him and deliver him from the hands of his enemies. Let us examine him with rebukes and torments that we may know his meekness and prove his patience. Let us condemn him to a shameful death ; for he shall be preserved as he himself saith.

This is just a reflection of what Plato wrote two centuries earlier when he pictured the "just man" who was crucified at the hands of his enemies. This belief in the coming Christ, which was so prevalent in the pre-Christian world, also included the anticipation that the Christ, after he had suffered, would return to judge the world. All the ideas surrounding the anticipated Messiah were taken from the saviour-god religions, each of which looked forward to the return of the Saviour-god as Judge and righteous ruler.

This was expressed about seven hundred years before Paul adopted this belief in relation to Jesus, when the allegorical character called Job was reported as saying : "For I know that my Redeemer liveth, and that he shall stand at the latter days upon the earth : And though, after my skin, worms destroy this body, yet in my flesh shall I see God." (Job xix, 25.) No one knows who Job was, or who wrote this ancient story, but there is no reason to think that his anticipation represented only the Jewish outlook concerning the coming Christ ; in fact the expressions in the gospels, relating to the end of the age, are to be found in the Persian sacred book, the *Avesta*, which is at least a thousand years older than Christianity.

The Jews believed that the Messiah, on his return after his suffering on earth, would reign for a thousand years on earth, after which the world would be destroyed, the righteous being taken to live in bliss with the Redeemer. As they had such hazy notions as to time all differed regarding the period when these things would be, which is one reason why those who study Biblical prophesies are always being confounded and never can get their dates to agree. The number of people is legion who have fixed the date of the Lord's return from these ancient prophesies, based on the speculations of those to whom time was as shifting sand.

When Jesus was being transformed into the Christ, a prevalent belief amongst the Hellenised Jews was that past time could be divided into six epochs of a thousand years each, each millennium corresponding to a day in the world's creation. This idea they got from the Psalmist who tells us that a day to the Lord is equivalent to a thousand years. Basing their calculations on the creation of the world in six days, and assuming each day to represent a thousand years, it followed that the era of work was nearing an end, and that the millennium of Sabbath peace was approaching.

The general belief that the age was coming to an end was made good use of by those who had become convinced that the Christ had come to suffer and die. This was, however, but the preliminary to the coming thousand years of peace and righteousness, which his return would usher in, when he would rule the world with justice through his faithful followers. This is how some Hellenised Jews looked upon the the matter and, as they were the first Christians, this idea was eventually taken up by the entire Christian community. In consequence, we find it reflected in the New Testament writings, of which the following are a few examples :

If I (Jesus) will that he tarry till I come, what is that to thee ? (John xxi, 22.)

Jesus . . . shall so come in like manner as ye have seen him go into heaven. (Acts i, 11.)

Keep this commandment . . . until the appearing of our Lord. (1 Tim. vi, 14.)

Who shall judge the quick and the dead at his appearing. (2 Tim. iv, 1.)

Looking for the . . . glorious appearing of the Great God. (Tit. ii, 13.)

He hath appointed a day, in the which he will judge. (Acts xvii, 31.)

But this I say, brethren, the time is short. (1 Cor. vii, 29.)

For the time is at hand. (Rev. i, 3.)

These remarks were a reflection of the Christian opinion of the time. The Gentile Christians had their own reason for adopting the view that Christ would shortly return, because it did not clash with the Pagan opinion in which they had been nurtured. In Luke (xxi, 24) we find reference to this anticipation of the Gentiles in these words, "Until the times of the Gentiles be fulfilled". Ovid (43 B.C.-A.D. 17), Lucian (2nd century A.D.), and Virgil (70 B.C.-A.D. 21) wrote about the coming age of righteousness and judgement, when peace and happiness would take the place of war and misery.

The destruction of Jerusalem and the Temple, and the idea that the Messiah had come, combined with the state of despondency in which the Jewish mind was at that time, were quite sufficient to turn the Hellenised Jews by the thousand (and some Hellenised Jewish priests) over to the new conception preached, and written about, by those who believed that the Christ had come, and would soon return to usher in a new age. So we read, "And a great company of the priests were obedient to the faith". (Acts vi, 7.)

The end of the Temple was a sign that God had manifested in his Son, as the Gnostics had foretold he would, and that the age of sacrifice was over, the Son having taken the people's sins by his own sacrifice. Christianity, therefore, did not take over animal sacrifice from Judaism, the Hellenised Jews having lost their faith in this method of propitiating Jehovah, and the Gentile Christians supplanted the old Jewish traditional belief that a sacrifice was necessary to satisfy Jehovah by introducing the Eucharist in its place.

So the Jewish converts to Christianity obtained a new comfort and hope which helped them to forget the disaster which had overwhelmed their race and religion. As Christians they retained their old god, and also found a new one, whom they ranked as his Son. Thus the new faith was attached to an old one, which had behind it an age-old tradition. This gave it a status amongst the Pagans, and attracted the Gentiles, in a way an entirely new one could not have done. No other saviour-god religion outside of India had such a tradition, or sacred literature, from which it could claim that Christ had fulfilled the prophesies and that Christianity was the fore-ordained successor to Judaism.

Christianity was a break away from Judaism, just as Protestantism was from Catholicism, but the fact that some Catholic priests became Protestants, and some Catholic churches became Protestant churches, enabled the new ideas to become established in a way they never otherwise could have done. Paul, like Luther, found the organisation at hand ; all each had to do was to adjust things to the changed outlook. Those who remained loyal to the old outlook naturally resented this interference with the established order, and so we find the same bitterness displayed by the orthodox Jews against the Christians as the Catholics shewed towards the Protestants for disrupting their organisation.

Again we listen to the conversation of two Hellenised Jews, which takes place just after the destruction of Jerusalem in A.D. 70. The reference made to the rebuilding of Jerusalem refers to this work undertaken in the reign of Herod the Great, (40-4 B.C.), of which mention was made in the fourth chapter.

FIRST HELLENISED JEW : "Jehovah has abandoned us, my friend. We have done some evil in the sight of the Lord, but what it is I cannot say. We have kept the Law to the best of our ability, we have kept the fasts and the Sabbaths and done everything that the Lord has commanded."

SECOND HELLENISED JEW : "My opinion is that our priests killed the Lord's anointed. Are we not told in Daniel (ix, 25) that the Christ would come after the rebuilding of Jerusalem ? My belief is that he did come and because we killed him instead of making him our King, the Lord has again destroyed our city and his Holy Temple. Jesus was none other than the Christ promised of old, and, if we had only believed his message, the Lord would not have abandoned us. Instead of which our priests arrested him and killed him, just as they would a sacrificial victim. This slaughtering by the priests of sacrifices has not reconciled Jehovah. Jesus, an innocent man, was killed just like a human sacrifice. If the reports are true, our priests, when occasion permits, still offer up human sacrifices. There have been some strange reports coming to my ears of what they do in country districts."

FIRST HELLENISED JEW : "And so you believe that Jesus was the Messiah ? How interesting, because I am coming to think that way myself. His reappearance after death was certainly a sign from heaven. To think that the priests took a man of God and sacrificed him ! Paul, during his lifetime, went about telling the people that Jesus was none other than the Son of God, whom the Gnostics have been telling us would some day come to earth and suffer for our sins. Why should we Jews be the only nation without a Saviour when all the others have one ? All I have heard about Jesus makes me think of the "righteous man" we have been expecting, and of whom we read about in *The Wisdom of Solomon,* who showed his meekness and patience under the insults of the priests. He proved himself to be the Son of God, my friend, and his shameful death has fulfilled the prophesies. You remember the passage, 'For if the righteous man be the Son of God he will help him and' after death 'he shall be preserved'. Does his appearance after death not prove that Jesus was the Son of God because it showed that the Lord had delivered him from death?"

SECOND HELLENISED JEW: "I think Paul was right, and many others who go to the synagogues think likewise. Jesus proved that he was no ordinary man when he returned, after death, to his disciples. I was talking to one of our rabbis about him the other day, and he tells me that he thinks that Jesus was the Christ. In fact, he intends to preach about him on the Sabbath, and tell us that his coming before the dispersion of our race was the fulfilment of prophecy, that we rejected him because we had not the eyes to see, or a true understanding of the Scriptures, 'Truly the Lord worketh signs in heaven and in earth'."

How very natural something mysterious can become when one has the facts and applies them in a logical and sensible way. It is so easy to understand how rapidly a stone can roll down a hill. What interests the student of religion is the first impulse which caused the movement. For this we have now accounted. To discover this secret has been the quest of scholars since, in the middle of last century, the Bible ceased to be looked upon as too sacred to receive rational thought. The draping process is not difficult to reconstruct, but what has always been uncertain is how the god idea started. To discover this source in the dim and distant past, and explain, in a logical and rational way, something of peculiar and intimate interest to most people, is surely worthy of effort and research, especially when the people are daily misled by a subsidised Christian priesthood, whose aim is not the discovery of truth but the maintenance of tradition.

These two imaginary conversations which I have given, one before and the other after the destruction of Jerusalem, show the growth of an idea. They were not isolated conversations but took place wherever Hellenised Jews met together. An idea which might have flickered out was blown into flame by the fall of Jerusalem, and all that this meant to the Jewish race. If there had been no Hellenised Jews nothing might ever have come of it, so Alexander, who dispersed the Jews to Greece, Syria and Egypt, was a primary cause of Christianity. The orthodox Jews, fenced in by the Law, would never have been able to conceive the idea of Jesus being the Christ. The priests would never have sanctioned such an idea, and we can imagine that the Jews in Palestine, who became Christians in the early days, could only have been those who knew Jesus and were impressed by his words and deeds.

Outside Palestine, where the Hellenised Jew was less rigidly priest-ridden, he was coming in daily contact with the beliefs surrounding the saviour-gods of the Mysteries, and it is not difficult to see how he could work in the story of Jesus, his death and reappearance, so as to make himself believe that the Messiah had really come and suffered. How could Jesus be other than a god when he was actually seen after death? To the Jewish mind all the dead Hebrews were in Hades awaiting the general resurrection and their judgement by the coming Messiah. Jesus, however, by his appearance, had proved himself to be a god, for if he had been a man he would have been in Hades with the others and could never have been seen in a glorified body like unto a god.

Did not everything fit in exactly with what the prophet Isaiah had foretold? The Messiah would come unknown to all, be despised, rejected and led like a lamb to the slaughter. Was his death at the hands of the priests not the sacrifice foretold by this prophet, "Thou shalt make his soul an offering for sin"? The ways of God are past our understanding, says the Psalmist, and if God chose to reveal himself in his Son, by his appearance after death, thus giving his people a sign that the age-old feud between heaven and earth had ended, it was not for mankind to question his wisdom or his power.

By such thoughts the Hellenised Jew soothed his mind, troubled because of the catastrophe to his nation, while the Christian zealots pounded away with the idea that the Christ had come, and, by his death and sacrifice, had opened the gate of Heaven for all believers. The disciples, who had known Jesus, had found it difficult to embrace this more universal outlook and so held to the idea that Jesus was the Messiah for the Jews only, and not for the Greeks. With the fall of Jerusalem this isolated outlook was shattered, and the teaching initiated by Paul made headway, so much so that we now find the early idea of Jesus, the Messiah, changing into the belief that he was The Saviour of the World.

Everything that was necessary had combined to produce a new saviour-god. Here we find all the necessary ingredients :

(1) The victim,
(2) Killed by the priests on the great day of sacrifice, the Pass-over. If he were not actually killed then, the connection of the priests with his death made the gospel writers settle on this date as the most suitable time.
(3) He appeared after death,
(4) and consequently proved that he had conquered death.
(5) Because of all this he was considered a god who had come to earth,
(6) to suffer as a sacrificial victim,
(7) which made his worshippers regard him as the Saviour, Redeemer and Mediator.

So throughout the epistles we find this idea of sacrifice expressed over and over again. The following are a few examples :

And walk in love, as Christ also hath loved us, and hath given himself for us an offering and a sacrifice to God for a sweet smelling savour. (Eph. v, 2.)

For then must he often have suffered since the foundation of the world : but now once in the end of the world hath he appeared, to put away sin by the sacrifice of himself. (Heb. ix, 26.) (This pagan idea originally came from India with its rein-carnated Saviours who suffered, to return after long intervals.)

But this man, after he had offered one sacrifice for sins for ever sat down on the right hand of God. (Heb. x, 12.)

For if we sin wilfully after that we have received the knowledge of the truth, there remaineth no more sacrifice for sins. (Heb. x, 26.)

For even Christ our passover is sacrificed for us. (1 Cor. v, 7.)

For every high priest is ordained to offer gifts and sacrifices : wherefore it is of necessity that this man (Jesus) have somewhat also to offer. (Heb. viii, 3.)

By the which will we are sanctified, through the offering of the body of Jesus Christ once for all.   (Heb. x, 10.)

Who needeth not daily, as those high priests, to offer up sacrifice, first for his own sins, and then for the peoples' : for this he (Jesus) did once, when he offered himself.   (Heb. vii, 27.)

How much more shall the blood of Christ, who through the eternal spirit offered himself without spot to God.   (Heb. ix, 14.)

So Christ was once offered to bear the sins of many ; and unto them that look for him shall he appear the second time, without sin, unto salvation.   (Heb. ix, 28.)

In this idea of Christ as a sacrificed victim we have theology in one of its great flights of imagination. Only theology could turn a human being into an offering producing a sweet smell, and relished by a god, but the depths and heights to which the human mind can reach are past understanding.   This man Jesus, a wandering medium, let us imagine, thus became a sweet-smelling savoury, a sacrifice acceptable, well pleasing to God !

Every Easter Christians sing, "Christ, our passover is sacrificed", because Christ became related to the sun, which, at Easter, enters the Spring equinox, when life returns to earth, as it was believed that Christ had brought the life hereafter to mankind.   The name Easter is derived from the Anglo-Saxon goddess of Spring, who was known as Eostre, and, as we proceed, we shall discover how all the Pagan rites, ceremonies and beliefs were taken over and applied to Jesus, who was thus transformed into a Pagan god.

The disciples of Jesus were not the only ones to conclude that an apparition was a visitation by one of the gods.   They only represent the mentality of the time.   Others besides those early believers, who thought that Jesus was a god, because he appeared after death, believed that an apparition was a visitation of a god to earth.   Cicero (106-43 B.C.), in the following passage in his book, *The Nature of the Gods*, makes it quite clear that an apparition was looked upon as a god at the time of Jesus.   He wrote as follows : "Those whose minds scorn the limitations of the body are honoured with the frequent appearance of the gods", in other words, those with clairvoyant vision can see etheric beings.

Many other old quotations, similar to the above, could be given to prove that when the Jews, Romans, Greeks and others saw an apparition they termed it a god.   As, however, we are dealing with those who were nurtured in a Jewish atmosphere, we shall only consider a few taken at random from the Old Testament, instead of quoting classical instances :

"The Lord appeared to Abraham, and said" (Gen. xii, 7).

"The Lord appeared to him, and said" (Gen. xxvi, 2.)

"I have seen God face to face."   (Gen. xxxii, 30.)

"Jacob said, God Almighty appeared unto me at Luz." (Gen. xlviii, 3.)

"They will say, The Lord hath not appeared to thee." (Exod. iv, 1.)

"I appeared to Abraham by name of God Almighty." (Exod. vi, 3.)

"The Lord hath appeared of old to me, saying" (Jeremiah xxxi, 3.)

"The God of glory appeared to our father Abraham." (Acts vii, 2.)

Paul confirms what I have been trying to emphasise, namely that the apparition of Jesus was the cause of his deification.   Writing of Jesus he says :

"Who, being in the form of God, thought it not robbery to be equal with God." (Phil. ii, 6.)

In Second Corinthians (iv, 4) he refers again to

"Christ, who is the image of God";

but in Romans i, 3, he is even more explicit when he writes :

"Jesus Christ . . . declared to be the Son of God . . . by the resurrection from the dead."

When we remember that in those days God was believed to be an etheric man, shaped like other men, with all the characteristics and passions of man whom he had made in his own image (Gen. i, 27), it is not so difficult to understand how it was that an apparition was believed to be God by the monotheistic Jews, or one of the gods by the polytheistic Gentiles. When not taken to be a god an apparition was looked upon as an angel, which means a messenger of god. Jesus went through the apotheosis, finally to end as equal to Jehovah himself, and the reason for this deification can be traced to his reappearance and to this only. The following quotations are taken from the earliest Christian writings :

"Even Jesus, that appeared to thee in the way." (Acts ix, 17.)

"I (Jesus) have appeared to thee for this purpose." (Acts xxvi, 16.)

"In the end . . . hath he appeared to put away sin." (Heb. ix, 26.)

"But is now made manifest by the appearing of our Saviour Jesus Christ, who hath abolished death, and hath brought life and immortality to light." (2 Tim. i, 10.)

"After that he appeared in another form to two of them."
(Mark xvi, 12.)

"Afterward he appeared to the eleven as they sat at meat."
(Mark xvi, 14.)

"This Jesus hath God raised up, whereof we all are witnesses." (Acts ii, 32.)

"The Lord is risen indeed, and hath appeared to Simon."
(Luke xxiv, 34.)

"Have I not seen Jesus Christ our Lord ?" (1 Cor. ix, 1.)

"And last of all he was seen of me also." (1 Cor. xv, 8.)

Many other instances could be given, but the
foregoing are sufficient for my purpose. Once the
idea became rooted in the minds of the leaders of the
new movement that Jesus had proved himself to be a
god by his appearing, and that by his sacrifice he had
released all the dead from Hades, where they were
awaiting this atoning deed to enable them to proceed
to Paradise, there was no end to the flights the imagination could reach. All the pent up ideas of an intensely
religious age burst the banks of reason and carried
the people forward in an onward rush, so much so
that nearly every theological and mystical idea, at one
time or another, has been connected with Jesus.

Paul tells us how Jesus humbled himself by becoming man and dying on the cross, and that God
has highly exalted him and given him a name above
every name, at which every knee shall bow. If we
ignore this theological way of putting it, and come
down to facts, we could put it thus. Jesus was a
man like other men, he died, reached the etheric
world and so was exalted. One or more of his
followers got a glimpse of him thus exalted, and
concluded that he could have been none other than
a god. On this god idea, combined with his death

at the instigation of the priests, it was argued that he was a victim sacrificed for the sins of the world, and was now glorified as a god in heaven. Consequently, he was adored by a grateful humanity for thus removing the curse of death.

This idea is behind all the Pauline theological rhetoric which, by adopting the language of the mystical theology of the times, uses ambiguous words and phrases difficult to understand. On this foundation of mystic and Gnostic theology arose the Christian Faith, which appealed first of all to the Hellenised Jews brought up to believe that "Your iniquities have separated between you and your God". (Isaiah lix, 2.) Sin had brought about this separation, and so death meant quarantine in Hades, till the redeeming work of the Messiah had been accomplished. The dead were contaminated with sin and had to be kept in isolation till they had been purified and made fit to reach the presence of God.

Only by ourselves becoming imbued with the mentality of those days is it possible to understand how Christianity developed out of Judaism and Paganism. This can only be done by reading the Pagan and Jewish literature of the times. When we thus transport ourselves back to that superstitious age we have no difficulty in coming to the conclusion that nothing was too impossible to be believed in that mental atmosphere. Given the necessary conditions, and these evidently prevailed, it is simple to understand how the return of Jesus after death was the cause of his being considered a god.

Unfortunately our ancestors were not as careful in recording supernormal phenomena as we are today, and mixed up with them their theological beliefs. This mixture we term Mythology. Consequently, we find that Mythology is a combination of psychic phenomena and the religious speculations of the times. The ancients peopled the heavens with angels and demons, with gods and devils. They had minds like those of children and, instead of giving a natural interpretation to psychic phenomena, they surrounded these supernormal events with myths and legends. What was natural in the return of Jesus after death was elaborated by later writers, who cared nothing for fact and were only interested in making Jesus appear as a god. A god could do anything, so he could without difficulty return to his earth body, to be seen in it, and thus ascend to heaven.

There was a long period during which the Christ myth evolved from a germ to full stature. This chapter relates only to its conception, its germination, which took place prior to the fall of Jerusalem in A.D. 70. In the next century history comes to our aid and enables us, from the writings of the early fathers, to understand something of the growth of the new religion. The conception period lasted from the reappearance of Jesus till A.D. 70 and its birth followed when the opinions of Paul became accepted. This birth period will be considered in the next chapter, where we shall find an account of the manufacturing process which set to work to produce a new god, and one whom these Christian enthusiasts considered was above and beyond all the gods of the Pagans.

During the conception period Paul was hard at work and, with his powerful personality and strong will, can rightly be termed the founder of the Christian

Faith, which to him was to bring joy and comfort
to believers everywhere—Greek and Roman, Master
and Slave. He met the Mysteries on their own level
and excluded no one from the joy and felicity which
accompanied the belief in the new saviour-god. He
became so enthusiastic on the subject that he exclaimed, "O death, where is thy sting? O grave,
where is thy victory?". . . "Thanks be to God who
giveth us the victory through our Lord Jesus Christ."
(1 Cor. xv, 55.)

If Jesus had not been a man on earth before his
death this belief would have been no comfort. A
god surviving death would not prove that man did
so, and his rising in his physical body could not prove
the survival of the spirit of man after death. The
comfort came because Jesus was a man and proved,
by appearing as a spirit, that he had survived death,
as "By man came death, by man came also the resurrection of the dead". (1 Cor. xv, 21.)

The theologians spoiled the comforting knowledge nature gave, by turning Jesus into a god-man,
as, whenever this happened, and the man Jesus was
obliterated, the satisfaction derived from the natural
revelation disappeared, and the people had to rely
for their comfort on creeds, dogmas and ceremonies.
This was man's way of dulling the fear of death, but
when we come to Chapter X some may think that it
was unfortunate that the priesthood obliterated
mediumship, and thus closed nature's own channel
of revelation, which brings more comfort and satisfaction than man-made dogmas and ceremonies.

Catch phrases such as, "The blood of Jesus Christ
his Son cleanseth us from all sin" (1 John i, 7), were

used by those who could only think in terms of blood and sacrifice. In consequence, the people came to regard the new religion as comprising theological phrases, rites and ceremonies, and not as the revelation nature itself gave in the first instance. They were not mentally ready for psychic knowledge, and all that it implies, just as they were not ready for physical science. A saviour-god and sacrifice suited the mentality of the masses then, just as it does today, and until people become educated, and increase in psychic knowledge, they will lack the satisfaction which can be obtained from nature's own revelation through mediumship.

By the time Jesus had reached the god stage, when it came to be believed that because he was a god he could reanimate the physical body he inhabited while on earth, and return with it to heaven, all logical deductions from his appearance as a spirit had ceased. The theologians were now in possession and built up on the original psychic event their theological structure, obliterating what was true, and adding piece by piece their false conceptions and mysterious phrases which impressed the unthinking multitude.

When Jesus became accepted as the world's saviour the idea was passed on from generation to generation, because the priests taught the people from childhood upwards that he had suffered for their sins. What is taught to a child is never forgotten. All that was necessary to secure a place in Heaven was to believe in the salvation effected by Christ, perform the ceremonies of the Church, and support its organisation, including the priests. This is made definitely clear in the Church of England prayer book, but will be more fully discussed further on.

A superstitious and uneducated people adopted these suggestions quite naturally. They felt their sinfulness and weakness, but, as all their failings had been settled for them by a Saviour before they were born, they had no cause to worry, and this belief made them able to face with courage life's trials and temptations. If they did sin it mattered not as the account had been settled for all time regardless of its magnitude.

This raises the question as to whether in the years to come the knowledge of survival, which will in time become general, will not end all organised religion. Some day the fear of what follows after death will vanish from this earth. Under the name of Religion has been built up an enormous structure, produced by the mind of man under the emotion of fear. With the knowledge psychic science now brings to humanity this fear will depart and with it will go religion associated with priests of all denominations and sects. Through mediumship each one of us can discover his destiny after death, and receive the satisfaction that his friends are alive and well. Those who have made the change called death, can satisfy the enquirer as to the destiny of the human race, and that is enough.

The belief in one God or a dozen gods will not keep a creedal Religion in being. The gods have always been intimately related in the past, by the ignorant, to our happiness or misery after death, but now that they are known to be human beings who lived on earth, and that there is no theological Heaven or Hell, no place exists in the minds of those with psychic knowledge for what is today called Religion. Its purpose has been served now that the mystery has been cleared away. When each one is taught that his destiny is known, and that each can satisfy himself, and receive proof, by a visit to a reputable, well-developed medium, theology, called by the priests the Queen of Science, will be dethroned. This elimination of what should be more correctly termed the Queen of Ignorance will come by the increase of psychic knowledge, and with it will depart orthodox Religion accompanied by its exponents the priests.

A sound philosophy based on physical and psychic science will take their place, and give mankind knowledge instead of mystery, and evidence instead of hope. We have so long been fed on unnatural doctrines for the purpose of calming our fears that we cannot bring ourselves to realise that knowledge is the best remedy for fear and that the more we know the less we fear. Many will be unable to follow the reasoning in this book because it makes natural what has always been regarded as supernatural, but, as everything in the universe is natural and subject to natural law, it is only a matter of time till the Christian Faith is regarded from a natural and not a super-natural standpoint.

Whatever the future may have in store, the fact remains that Christians have received their comfort because they believed that a god-man died a victim's death as a sacrifice to Jehovah. The theologians at an early date cut the psychic link, and materialised the religion to such an extent that Christians through-out the Christian era have had no idea as to how it was that the religion they believe came into being. Paul built up a mystical theology which, when it found its way into the hands of the Church theologians, became so materialised that the after life in Christian theology is some doubtful existence, after an equally doubtful general resurrection of the physical body, anticipated to take place at some equally doubtful date. What we are to do, and where we are to live, when our spirits return to their old earth bodies, after dwelling in the limbo of Hades, no Christian can say. It is one of the Christian mysteries, and is relegated, with many other like mysteries, to the region of Faith, in which the true believer perpetually dwells.

Paul, we imagine, was on the scene shortly after the death of Jesus. The writings which have come down to us under his name claim that he was both clairaudient and clairvoyant, and that he had seen and talked with Jesus as an etheric being. Consequently, on the claims made by the disciples that some of them had seen the risen Lord, and on what Paul himself experienced, he propounded the idea that as Jesus appeared as a spirit he had proved his power over death. Thus, Paul saved for all time the true story of what really happened. The gospel editors who, at a later period, added the story of the empty tomb, thus spoiling the account of the original psychic event, had by then lost all contact with the psychic basis from which the Christian Faith developed, and their mistake has been carried down the centuries to the present day.

Jesus was either seen after his death as an etheric being or he was never seen at all. If he were never

seen then the origin of the Christian Faith is an enigma
which will never be solved.　What followed his death
can only be explained by his reappearance, in fact there
is no other explanation.　He was still interested in
those he had left behind, and his earth memories
attracted him back to the scenes of his life and death,
just as they attracted back others before and after his
time.　There is nothing surprising in the thought that
after death we should still be interested in our friends
on earth and the scenes of our earth life, which we
can appreciate by lowering our etheric vibrations by
thought until they come within the range of earth
vibrations.

When this desire is very intense the vibrations of
the etheric body are reduced to a point where they can
be seen by someone with psychic sight, and this must
have happened in the case of Jesus.　He was seen
because someone was looking in his direction.　This
may have happened more than once to the same person, or there may have been several people with this
higher range of sight who saw him.　Such things
happen so often today that there is no reason to
believe they did not happen in the days we are considering.

To those who have not had this experience it is
difficult to put in words how impressive it all is.　On
hundreds of occasions I have experienced in others
the working of this supernormal gift of clairaudience
and clairvoyance.　Women have this gift more developed than men but, in the presence of both men
and women who have psychic sight and hearing, I
have received from them descriptions of etheric beings,
whom they see, of such a vivid and lifelike nature

that I have never had any difficulty in recognising my departed friends. Besides this, by means of clair-audience, I have received messages from the people described which were so accurate and so intimate that they could only have come from the minds of those who, when on earth, were known by the names they gave to the medium. The medium in each instance was previously quite unaware of the information given, knew nothing, and had never seen or heard of these friends of mine who gave me particulars of such an intimate nature concerning both myself and themselves.

With these experiences in mind one can better appreciate what really occurred when Jesus returned to his disciples after his death. Besides this, one can appreciate, when allowance is made for the fact that these disciples were not only very simple people, but deeply religious and emotional, what a staggering effect the reappearance of their Master must have had on minds so plastic. Paul, at a later date, claims to have had a similar vision, and it does not surprise me, as one who has had many experiences of the return to earth of those called dead, that it gave them all the necessary courage, and acted as the strength and inspiration of the work they performed in laying the foundation of the Christian Faith.

Everything hinged on this vision of the risen master. Because of it the people argued backwards that he was a sacrificial victim, and then forwards that because of the reappearance he had proved that he had conquered death, and that God was now satisfied with the last sacrifice the priests had offered up. No further sacrifices were needed as the greatest one of all had been made for all time for all mankind. This process of thinking has probably been applied to all sacrificial victims who appeared after death, and it gave rise to all the saviour-god religions.

Why should Christians be the only people to produce this form of thought or to need the comfort it has given ? All men and women have like feelings, and these produce similar results. The Bible, if understood aright, is just the reflection of the religious aspirations and speculations of the whole race of mankind. The value of the Bible is not in its history or science, as it contains neither ; it is not in its morality, because only the morally backward sink to its low level of moral teaching that, "the righteous shall rejoice when he seeth the vengeance ; he shall wash his feet in the blood of the wicked" (Psalm lviii, 10), and many other such degrading thoughts. Its value lies in the fact that within its pages are preserved the religious aspirations and beliefs of the Jews and Christians for a period covering about a thousand years, and that from these we can gather what were the thoughts of the other races during that age.

No small race like the Jews could stand apart and not be influenced by prevailing opinions, especially a race which had been conquered so often during the five hundred years prior to the Christian era. By these conquests the Jews naturally absorbed some of the prevailing opinions of the times. Their mono-theism enabled them to withstand the surrounding beliefs regarding saviour-gods but, though they did not adopt one in pre-Christian days, they were suffic-iently interested and influenced to anticipate one, and, when the opportunity occurred, the Jews outside the bounds of Palestine soon produced a saviour-god along the lines of their Pagan neighbours.

In this way they obtained the comfort their Pagan fellow townsmen received from the belief that death had been conquered and that the powers of evil had been overthrown. To have a god to worship who had conquered death, and emerged victorious, had this potent meaning, because the belief in the gods of evil had a tremendous influence on the lives of the people of those days. The fact that man was considered as a fallen being contributed much to the fear of death, and it is not difficult for us to realise how the Hellenised Jews would look with longing on the Pagans with their comforting belief that this curse had been removed by their god's death and resurrection. It must have been a tremendous relief to these dispersed Jews when they came to believe that the new Saviour was the son of Jehovah, and that they could maintain their old traditional beliefs, while receiving the comfort which came from belief in a saviour-god.

The words of Paul must have rung out glad tidings to all the Jewish Christians, "But now is Christ risen from the dead, and become the first-fruits of them that slept. For since by man came death, by man came also the resurrection of the dead. For as in Adam all die, even so in Christ shall all be made alive." (1 Cor. xv, 21.) Thus Christ meant to his worshippers all that the saviour-gods of the Pagans meant to them. Satan was now conquered and Hades would evacuate its population when Christ returned at an early date to separate the good from the evil.

If Jesus had been killed by the Romans for a civil

offence he would never have come to be looked upon as a sacrificial victim. He angered the priests because, in their opinion, he had committed a religious offence, and so, after his death, he was looked upon as a sacrifice. The people came to believe that Jesus was a sacrificial victim of the priests, whose spirit had been accepted by Jehovah as an offering in their place. Because of this he became the Saviour and Redeemer. Jesus, they believed, had opened the door of heaven which Jehovah had barred and bolted against Adam and his descendants. The age-old warfare between the gods and the devils was over, and, when the millennium opened, Satan would be bound and thrown into the bottomless pit with all his demons and all unbelievers. Then Hell would be closed up for a thousand years and humanity would be safe from the Prince of Evil and his entourage.

This all came about because of the prevailing belief that Adam was originally an immortal being, but that, in consequence of his disobedience, all mankind had lost the right to eternal life till a Saviour was accepted by Jehovah as a sacrifice. Then all the dead would be released from the underworld, known as Sheol to the Jews and Hades to the Greeks. When Christ conquered Satan, who presided over Hades, he became the god of the underworld, as did Osiris when he conquered Set. Both Christ and Osiris were looked upon by their respective worshippers as the liberators and judges of the dead, who were awaiting the day of Judgement for their release. Then the good would live with Osiris, if they had been his followers on earth, or with Christ if they had been Christians before their death. Those who were then judged to be wicked were handed over to Set or Satan to receive everlasting punishment.

As flesh is weak and of the earth, so Adam is compared to the earth, "The first man is of the earth, earthy ; the second man is the Lord from heaven". (1 Cor. xv, 47.) This is a variation of the same theme that Adam's sin was the cause of death and that Christ's sacrifice had been the means whereby man's heritage, eternal life, was restored to mankind. Consequently we find various expressions coupling these two events together, and much of Chapter V of *The Epistle to the Romans* is given over to Adam's sin for which the death of Christ had atoned.

In the preceding pages we have dug through the theology to the natural event, the apparition, and, when we got down to it, we followed the process the early Christians adopted of wrapping round this psychic link between the two worlds the Gnostic theology prevalent in those days. By stripping off the dogma and theology, and exposing to the light of day the psychic cause, which brought all this about, what was difficult to understand becomes easy. It is the theological dogma, so loved by the priestly mind, which strains our reason to breaking-point, and makes Christianity so mysterious that it can be believed only by those who have been trained in the school of faith. The priests, of course, do not wish their subject clarified, because, when it is made understandable to the people, their work is done. As the interpreters of the mysteries they must maintain the mystery of the Christian Faith so long as possible, because, if there were no mystery, there would be no need of priests.

When Jesus became transformed into the Saviour and Redeemer he was invested with the power over death, besides being considered the conqueror of evil and the judge of all mankind. In the first chapter of *The Revelation of John* we read that John saw standing before him "One like unto Jesus", who said to him, "I am he that liveth, and was dead, and behold I am alive for evermore, Amen, and have the keys of hell and of death".

These keys, with which his followers on earth had invested him, were duly taken over by his Church on earth, which constituted itself as the jailer of Christendom, deciding before even the Judgement Day had arrived as to who were the saved and who were the damned. All the comfort the atoning work of the Saviour had accomplished was thus withdrawn from humanity by the Church, which claims to have been instituted by him and to represent him on earth. The Church proclaimed a coming day of Judgement, but that was a hollow farce as it made clear to all that only those who accepted its creeds and performed its ceremonies would reach Heaven, and that all others were destined for Hell.

So the Church possessed the keys of life and death, and became the Judge of mankind, while all this time the Lord has delayed his return, and the Judgement Day has been postponed times without number. There is, however, nothing now for the Judge to do, as his Church on earth has settled everything beforehand ; it has been the Judge of mankind throughout the Christian era, and has decided the fate of believers and unbelievers.

The great work of redeeming mercy performed

by Christ in opening heaven to all believers was commemorated by ceremonial and ritual, the chief of which was the Eucharist, which we have already discovered was part of the ceremonial which accompanied the beliefs surrounding all the saviour-gods. It is one of the oldest religious ceremonials known to history and was adopted by the Christians from their Pagan neighbours. By eating the god's body and drinking his blood all partakers in this ceremony believed that they shared in the god's immortality.

Hence the enthusiasm of Christians to obtain converts to the belief that a god-man had once again proved his power over death. True, it had all happened before. Fear had previously forced the imagination to produce the comforting belief in the saving power of one who had conquered death. There was nothing new about it all, but the belief in the old gods was wearing thin, and the time had come when a place was ready for a new god in the minds of many of the inhabitants of the Roman Empire. The transition was, however, gradual, as we are told by Paul that Christians continued to partake of the Eucharist at the table of the Pagan gods as well as at the table of Christ (1 Cor. x, 21). Before the complete change over took place, this partaking of the Eucharist by Christians at the table of Attis, Dionysus, Osiris or Mithra and also of Christ was quite natural. A new god takes time to become known.

To protect Christian ceremonies became the duty of the Christian Church, and those Jewish and Pagan priests who became Christian priests, assumed in time the custodianship of the Christian Eucharist, just as did the Pagan priests the Pagan Eucharist.

Instead of sacrificing an animal as did the Jews, they went through the process, as did the Pagans, of slaying the saviour-god symbolically, and consuming bread and wine which by magic they had turned into his body and blood.   Those Pagan priests who became Christians brought with them all the necessary cere-monial and ritual from the Pagan Church.   Chris-tianity thus became materialised and symbolised. What was originally a psychic experience became as-sociated with forms and ceremonies till the cause of the new religion was ultimately obliterated by the sacerdotal clothes with which it was covered.

Because of the belief that Jesus had become a god his earth life had to be unique and different from that of ordinary men.   Consequently all the wise sayings which could be gathered together were attributed to him.   He could not go about as do ordinary men, but whatever he did had to be turned into a miracle, so that the more extraordinary the reported deed the greater did the god Christ become.   Besides this, he had to be born as a god should be born, and return to heaven in a way different from that of mortal man.

When Jesus was on earth he was looked upon as a man like other men and it was only after his death, when he became a god in heaven, that his earth life was made to resemble the life of a god-man.   All this developed in an age of ignorance and super-stition, but such beliefs could not today find a footing in any Protestant country if they were something new.   It is only the age-old tradition behind Christian beliefs which keeps the Church together in this more intelligent age.

The gradual deification of Jesus, as we can also

infer from a study of the Christian documents, brought about by degrees the ignoring of his earth life and the concentration on him as a heavenly being. This, as we have seen, was a gradual process. As the idea evolved the man by degrees became merged into the god. Believers were quite uninterested in such a natural event as the date and place of his birth or the identity of his parents. No one by this time knew anything about such details and they were of no importance so long as they knew that he had lived, died and conquered death.

The gospel writers were not troubled as to when exactly he was born, so they fixed the time as nearly as possible to fit in with the time of his death. As they did not know his age at death, they imagined that he must have been born sometime in the reign of Herod the Great. John's gospel (viii, 57) tells us that the Jews asked Jesus "Thou art not yet fifty years old and hast thou seen Abraham?" which ironical question might imply that Jesus was nearly that age, and the divergence of Christian opinion is exemplified in the statement of Irenaeus, Bishop of Lyons (A.D. 130–202), that Jesus was fifty-four years old when he died.

The only time likely to be remembered was that Jesus died when Pilate was governor. We are told that Jesus was baptised by John the Baptist in the fifteenth year of the reign of Tiberius, but, as there was uncertainty as to his age when this took place, his birthday had to be imagined. In that uncritical age this was passed by as unimportant. It is unlikely that his birth was ever registered, and no one had any means of finding out where or when he was born. It was only a hundred years or so after his birth that he became sufficiently famous to make this event interesting, by which time all who knew him had died, and his biographers had no means of obtaining the information. In any case, it was his death and what followed it which was of interest.

Tradition had handed down the names of his parents, but as this god-man had to be born like all other god-men, the later idea of his father being a god was intertwined with their names, making the affair ridiculous, as both stories could not be true. Because of all this uncertainty about Jesus and of the mist which, as the years passed, enveloped him more and more, it became easier to believe all the legends and myths which were slowly but surely gathering round his name. Some held that prophecy had decreed that the Messiah was to be born in Bethlehem, others that it had decreed Nazareth as his birthplace, so on account of this there is confusion as to his exact birthplace. Probably it was somewhere in Galilee, but no one knows.

Thus a man, in the minds of his followers, became a virgin-born god who was conceived by the interaction of another god with a virgin, as was believed about the other saviour-gods. The story grew by borrowing from other Pagan beliefs, so that at birth the god-child, we are told, was visited by illustrious visitors and the heavens declared the advent of the Saviour of Mankind. The human father, described in earlier published documents, and believed in by the early Christians, was pushed aside by the Holy Ghost who, quite against the moral code, was given the place which really belonged to the human father. The principal beliefs surrounding Jesus everyone wished to remember were that he was miraculously born, lived as a god-man on earth, was crucified for the sins of humanity, and that after his death and resurrection he became a member of a Holy Trinity of gods, and so equal to Horus the Son in the Trinity of a rival faith.

Strangely enough, parts of the early birth narratives were allowed to remain, and, in consequence, we have the paradoxical position of an account of an unnatural conception and at the same time the genealogy of his father Joseph back to David. It is evident that it was the earlier belief that Jesus was descended from David, because of the prophesies that the Messiah would be born of the House of David. This remained part of the story, the Holy Ghost story being added later when Jesus had evolved out of the Messiah stage to that of the Saviour of the World, the Redeemer and Mediator, the co-equal of Jehovah in Heaven.

It was natural that, on such a foundation, opinions should be varied, and we are not surprised that the traditional accounts emphasise quarrelling and disputes amongst the early Christians. The Greeks were, however, the people responsible for the saviour-god idea becoming established and spreading throughout the Roman Empire, and they finally overcame the opinion of the Hellenised Gnostic Jews who believed that Jesus was the Christ for the Jews only.

The saviour-god idea, preached by Paul to the Gentiles, appealed to the Greeks, and the surrounding nations, because it was one in which they had been nurtured. A Jewish Christ might suit the Jewish mind, but he was not enough for the Greeks, who consequently erected, on the basis prepared by the Messianic Jews, the superstructure of beliefs appertaining to the other saviour-gods worshipped in Greece. By lifting Christianity out of its Jewish cradle they withdrew it from the exclusiveness of the Jewish atmosphere, and so gave it a character which made it appeal to the other nations of the Roman Empire.

A Messiah, for the Jews only, did not interest the Greeks, but Dionysus coming to earth again under another name certainly did appeal to them. So we are told that Paul made headway amongst the Greeks because he preached salvation for all through Christ, whereas the other disciples remained in Jerusalem to propagate the Messiah idea. The belief in the new saviour-god finally took hold everywhere, except amongst the orthodox Jews, who remained loyal to Jehovah, and became the greatest critics and enemies of the new faith. They never lost a chance to assert that the Christians had transformed one who was born a Jew, lived as a Jew and died as a Jew, into a Pagan Christ.

On Greek soil, therefore, and not on Jewish, the new saviour-god idea grew and flourished, and under the name of Christ all the old religious ideas were perpetuated. Orthodox Israel alone, of all the nations comprising the Roman Empire, was never brought into the fold. It has never accepted the belief that Jesus was the Messiah, and, as he evolved more and more into a Pagan Saviour, the entire Christian belief became repugnant to them. Thus the Pagans, and many Hellenised Jews, were converted to Christianity, but not the orthodox Jews. The Jewish outlook on the whole subject is aptly summed up by Justin, (A.D. 100–160), the Christian father, in the record he has left of his argument at Ephesus with a Jew named Trypho. He tells us that Trypho told him, "You follow an empty rumour and make a Christ for yourselves. If he were born and lived somewhere he is entirely unknown."

Knowing as we do now how Jesus evolved into the Glorified Christ, the Jew's remark was both apt and true. Trypho typifies the Jewish outlook of the time when both myth and legend were being wrapped round Jesus, and a man was being dressed in the robes of the world's saviour. Is it not true that to ease the ache and longing for knowledge of the hereafter humanity has made its Christs, and this imaginative effort is in no way peculiar to the Christians?

The belief that Christ has gone before has given comfort to those who needed comfort, and were ignorant of the vital knowledge that happiness after death is a certainty, and perfectly natural, to those who have lived aright. Death is not a curse, but a change into another and better order of existence, and there is no God waiting to judge humanity on the other side of the grave. What is called Heaven is not the habitation only of Christians, as there will be found those of other faiths and of all shades of opinions. As we sow on earth we reap hereafter and each person's conscience acts as judge.

This chapter has concentrated on the conception of the idea which caused the Christian Faith. It has been written to disclose the mentality of the times. Out of this Christianity was born and grew into a healthy child under the direction of a vigorous man by the name of Paul. We have found the reason why a man, who was a victim of the priests, was given a place in heaven beyond which human imagination could not extend. Unfortunately, our information is greatly mutilated, but, by patient research, scientific study and psychic knowledge, we have been able to expose the false and disclose the true.

Whatever the aim of Jesus was in life it was not realised ; if he announced a kingdom it did not appear, and one who believed he had a message to deliver died a victim instead of living to see his effort bear fruit. By his life he was not able to accomplish what he desired, and at his death he left a few dispirited and dejected disciples who had no other alternative but to return to their ordinary work.

If it had not been for his appearance after death this would have been the end. Instead, however, of his death being the end, his reappearance roused the enthusiasm of some of his contemporaries to the belief that he had returned as a sign that the curse of death had been broken by his sacrificial death at the hands of the priests. If this idea had not developed the local fame and affection engendered in the minds of the inhabitants of a small tract of territory would not have outlived his generation. It was the enthusiasm of the followers of Jesus which brought Christianity into being, and this enthusiasm was the result of the psychic stream once again bringing the two worlds together.

What Jesus taught, if he taught anything in particular, never survived him, and, although Christianity may be said to have its origin in him, since the new faith grew out of speculations concerning the meaning of his reappearance, yet, though the cause, he was not the founder of the religion. Such an idea as the Christian religion never entered his mind, but, on the other hand, if there had been no Jesus there would have been no Christianity.

CHAPTER VI.

CHRISTIANITY—ITS BIRTH.

So JESUS died, a priestly victim, like many both before and after his time. Force had again overcome the weak. Ideals can never stand up to overmastering brutality produced by fear, ignorance, prejudice or greed. If things had followed their normal course, Jesus would have remained a memory to those who had learned to love him, but it so happened that matters did not work out like this. His affection for his followers brought him back and one or more of them caught a glimpse of him, but there may have been another reason which made him return.

It is well known to those who study psychic phenomena that hauntings occur, particularly after a violent death. For a time the mind of the victim cannot think of anything but the misery he has experienced. This brings him back to the place where his sufferings were endured. Earth memories, in such cases, are particularly vivid, and it is quite possible that Jesus remained near the scene of the tragedy for some considerable time after his death.

From the accounts which have come down to us it is evident that the early Christians believed that some of the immediate followers of Jesus had psychic gifts, and this is just what we would expect, working back as we are doing, from the consequences which have become history. We have no history to guide us as to the causes of the events which followed the death of Jesus, but at least we can deduce from the effects that certain causes must have been present. One deduction is that one or more of the followers of Jesus had clairvoyant sight.

This combination of circumstances, the urge Jesus had to return to earth after his death, and the clairvoyance of one or more of his disciples, changed the outlook of the dejected band he had left behind. Rejoicing took the place of sorrow, and, instead of the earth life of the Master ending in apparent failure, his disciples came to realise and believe that it had ended in a glorious triumph. The scattered band reunited to discuss the meaning of it all, and we can be sure that whoever had seen him glorified, as Paul puts it, would be the centre of attraction.

After this, Jesus may have been seen on other occasions. This is quite a reasonable supposition, considering the fact that the indications are that there were some amongst his followers who had medium- . istic qualities. It is quite possible that Jesus was not only seen but heard, and that he also communicated through any who were trance mediums or in whose presence the Direct Voice could be heard. From the accounts which have been given to us it seems as if several of his followers had this gift of trance.

Quite unconsciously, therefore, Jesus laid the seed of the mighty organisation which developed under the title his followers bestowed upon him. During his lifetime such an idea as being the founder of a world religion had never occurred to him, just as it never occurred to him that being seen by one or more who mourned him would be the spark needed to set the world on fire with a new idea.

Jesus, when the remembrance of what he had suffered faded from his mind, would cease being earth-bound and reach out for pastures new. Like most other people, he would have friends on the other side who would help him to adjust his outlook to the new order into which he had just arrived. This would help him to forget his earth sufferings, he would gradually realise that his troubles were over, and that all he had gone through would never happen again. Gradually these vivid earth memories would fade and he would become interested in the affairs of the etheric world, which he would find in many respects similar to the one he had left, but more beautiful. Life would become easier and happier and soon all earth troubles would be forgotten, though this does not mean that he would lose his interest in this world, in fact, from what Paul tells us, he evidently retained it throughout Paul's lifetime.

We now come back from heaven to earth and shall follow out the consequences of the visible return of Jesus to earth. Jesus had performed his part, quite unconsciously it is true, in the establishment of the Christian religion. What follows is the work of his worshippers, who, as generation succeeded generation, added to and embellished the story, till a simple psychic event was transformed into a code of dogmas and doctrines which have affected the lives of a large section of the human race since the fourth century.

We now return to the little band assembled somewhere in Palestine. They evidently met together at stated intervals and the writer of *The Acts* tells us of a séance, "when they were all with one accord in one place".

After these séances, or gatherings, we can be sure that those who had been present would talk and probably exaggerate what had taken place. Those who had seen Jesus on earth, and known him, would probably be much more interested than those who had never known him. There would be much scoffing and jeering. What they had to tell would be derided by those who looked upon themselves as intellectually superior. It all happens today, the supernaturalist on the one side, and the materialist on the other. Both are quite ignorant of what takes place at séances, and yet are ever ready with their opinions that it is all due to fraud and hallucination.

Under the leadership of Peter, or perhaps someone else, this early Jesuist community conceived the idea that Jesus was none other than the Messiah which all were awaiting. This idea bound them even more closely together, so much so that in the course of time there was a large enough body to form a Church in Jerusalem which would doubtless follow the orthodox lines of the time, with the additional belief that Jesus, their master, was the Messiah, and that he had come to prepare the way for the millennium they were all awaiting.

Not content to accept the simple fact that the Master had been a man like other men, with perhaps psychic gifts, they flew off at a tangent and built up ideas regarding him which could have been caused by no other reason than the fact that he had appeared to them after death. It was probably a generation before any definite opinion came to be formed as to the meaning of it all. We must not expect that Peter, for instance, said to John, "I have just seen Jesus ; this means that he has conquered death, which consequently means that he was a god-man, and it likewise follows that because he has conquered death he is the saviour of the Jewish race, and has settled once and for all the estrangement between us and God, which was the result of Adam's disobedience."

Things do not happen like this. New ideas evolve slowly and take a long time before they are accepted. Besides this, the people themselves are never capable of forming new ideas. These have to be forced into their heads by constant repetition, and, even then, owing to the conservative nature of the human mind, it takes years for opinions to change. The great ones on earth are not only the mighty warriors, or the great statesmen, but those who have the power by speech or writing to change ideas either for good or ill.

A great mental change came about in the first century of our era and this could only have been possible as the result of the forceful personality of a master mind. We cannot understand the mentality of the time unless we remember that the Jews had been brought up to believe that the dead only returned to earth on the resurrection day, the great day of judgement, which was to usher in the millennium.

The belief in our consciousness and personality surviving death, as it is understood today by those with psychic knowledge, was quite foreign to the Jews in the time we are considering. The Jewish religion, though it acknowledged one God, had very hazy opinions as to what succeeded death. The idea of our surviving in an etheric body, a duplicate of our physical body, in a world of finer vibrations surrounding and interpenetrating this earth, was not understood, and could never have been appreciated by the Jewish orthodox mind of those days. To the Jews, the resurrection was a material event, when the spirits of the dead, resting in Hades, would return and reanimate their earth bodies. The great majority even today cannot understand this subject of vibrations and until they do they are unable to visualise the reality of an etheric world, an etheric body, or psychic phenomena.

After the reappearance of Jesus his followers began to have a glimmer of reality, but it was only a glimmer and very quickly the light was extinguished. Even Paul, with all his mediumistic gifts, could not deduce from what he experienced the real meaning of it all, and had to surround his experiences with the prevailing dogmas and doctrines relating to the saviour-gods worshipped in Tarsus and elsewhere.

We have nothing reliable to tell us how things fared with the original followers of Jesus. *The Acts of the Apostles* is of little help, as it is a late first-century compilation by an unknown author, which has gone through various mutilations and received so many interpolations that its historical value, if it ever had any, has gone beyond recall. We, however, can obtain some idea from the writings of Paul, which most critics believe are the earliest Christian documents, as in them scattered references are made to the early Church in Jerusalem, which will be noticed as we go on.

Anything we can glean of the activities and beliefs of the early Messiahists, most of whom became

Christians, is taken from these writings of Paul which, though not history, are yet generally accepted, if we exclude the interpolations and additions. This being so, it is well to hear the opinion of one who made their study a life-work and who is accepted by most New Testament scholars as a leading authority on the subject.

Dr. Frederick Cornwallis Conybeare, late Fellow and Praelector of University College, Oxford, in his work on Christian Origins entitled *Myth, Magic and Morals*, gives it as his opinion that : "Of the Epistles of Paul, very few are now disputed by competent critics. I am disposed to accept as authentic all of them, not excepting the ones addressed to Timothy and Titus. *The Epistle to the Hebrews* has never been seriously attributed to Paul, but it is clearly anterior to A.D. 70 and Tertullian was probably right in attributing it to Barnabas."

On the other hand, First and Second Timothy and Titus are definitely considered by other competent critics as non-Pauline, and many express doubts as to the authorship of Ephesians. So we may say that excepting Hebrews, Titus, Timothy and Ephesians it is generally held that the others in the original came from the hand of Paul. In the pages which follow I quote from these as if they were Pauline, as here we are concerned more with early Christian beliefs, and not so much with authorship.

Opinions differ as to what has been added and altered since the original letters were written, but this much is true, that these epistles represent the foundation of Christian beliefs in the first century. They can be taken as representing early Christian thought and that is all we need, namely the knowledge that in these early days a victim was believed to have suffered and been seen after death. Of that we can be sure and, with that as our basis, everything else follows naturally. This is just what we would expect with our knowledge of what took place when previous victims returned after death.

Before, however, we begin to dwell on the groundwork laid down by Paul, let us first of all give some detailed consideration to the life and work of this great master mind and founder of the Christian Faith, who, from what he himself tells us, can correctly be described as

PAUL, THE MEDIUM.

Originally called Saul, he used the name of Paul for no known reason. He may have had two names, like John Mark and Simon Peter, but the only one he himself uses in his letters is Paul. He termed himself a "Hebrew of the Hebrews". In *The Acts of the Apostles* it is stated that he was born in Tarsus and that he was a Roman citizen by birth, but there is no clue as to what this claim to Roman citizenship is based upon.

That he received part of his education at Tarsus, which was a great seat of learning, is a possible inference from his use of some of the technical terms which were current in the Greek schools of rhetoric and philosophy, but his imperfect command of Greek points to his education in this direction being limited. His family were Pharisees and it is more probable that his main education came from Jewish sources.

In *The Acts* we are told that his teacher was Gamaliel, who was the head of the moderate school of Jewish theologians. Like all Jewish boys he learned a trade, the one he adopted being that of a tent maker, but nothing more is related of his private life. It is not known whether or not he was married, as he has left us only this ambiguous remark which conveys nothing one way or the other: "I say therefore to the un-married and widows, It is good for them if they abide even as I." (1 Cor. vii, 8.)

Paul, from what he himself tells us, was a trance and clairvoyant medium. In *The Acts* he is also referred to as a healing medium, and we are also told that on one occasion when praying in the Temple he became entranced. A careful reading of his writings, and of what is written about him, will make this quite clear. If anyone is sufficiently interested to study this matter more deeply I would suggest the reading of that very interesting book, *My Life in Two Worlds*, by Mrs. Osborne Leonard, so as to compare her experi-ences with what I have to tell in the pages which follow.

Mrs. Leonard is accepted by everyone who knows her, and has sat with her, as one of this country's leading trance, clairaudient and clairvoyant mediums, or, to adopt the Biblical phraseology, she has the gift of speaking with tongues, of discerning spirits, of interpretation and of prophecy. Often in her presence the Direct Voice is heard. No one who has sat with her doubts her honesty and great mediumistic qualities. Consequently, a number of books have been written by those who have had séances with her, detailing the evidence for survival obtained through her. The reason I have singled out this lady to compare with Paul is not because of her genuineness or great medium- istic qualities, as many other mediums come within this category, but because she, like Paul, has put down her experiences in writing, thus making the comparison similar.

In her book she tells of happenings which come within the same category as those recorded by Paul nearly nineteen hundred years ago. Just as the physical phenomena of nature were the same then as now, so were psychic phenomena. As they were in Paul's days so they were seven hundred years earlier in the time of Job, because we read, "Then a spirit passed before my face; the hair of my flesh stood up: It stood still, but I could not discern the form thereof: an image was before mine eyes; there was silence, and I heard a voice saying, Shall mortal man be more just than God?" (Job iv, 15.) There is no difference between this psychic occurrence and the one experienced by Paul or those recorded by Mrs. Leonard. They relate to another order of life, which surrounds us, but is unseen and unfelt by all on earth, except a small number of people who are sufficiently sensitive to be able to do so.

What happened then happens now, the only difference being that we now understand and ap- preciate physical and psychic laws in a way they were not then understood. If Paul had been less theologically inclined, and had lived in our days of greater knowledge, he could have compiled a book on much the same lines as the one written by Mrs. Leonard. Instead of this he turned all his psychic experiences round to fit in with his conviction that Jesus, who appeared to him, was none other than the

Christ, the Saviour of the World. In the previous chapter we discovered how and why this great assumption came about. Let us now concentrate on what Paul himself has to tell us about his mediumistic gifts.

These remarks are scattered right through his epistles and I shall gather them together in the following pages. The first introduction we have to Paul, outside of his own writings, is in *The Acts*, where in Chapter ix we are told about his experience on the way to Damascus, and again in Chapter xxvi, in practically the same words, he is represented as telling King Agrippa what made him turn over from being a persecutor to become the ardent worker for the cause of Christ. The words he is reported as having used before the king are as follows :

> At midday, O King, I saw in the way a light from heaven, above the brightness of the sun, shining round about me and them which journeyed with me. And when we were all fallen to the earth, I heard a voice speaking unto me, and saying in the Hebrew tongue, Saul, Saul, why persecutest thou me ? it is hard for thee to kick against the pricks. And I said, Who art thou, Lord ? And he said, I am Jesus, whom thou persecutest.

Paul, like others of his time, took this supernormal experience to be a visitation by a god, as obviously, when he was on the way to persecute the followers of Jesus, he would not call Jesus, "Lord". It was the bright light that made Paul fall to the ground in worship, and though he makes no direct reference to this event in any of his epistles, yet he does so indirectly when he says that after he had seen Jesus as a spirit he went to Arabia and returned again to Damascus. (Gal. i, 17.) He tells us that his conversion came about through seeing Jesus after his death, but exactly where it happened does not so much matter, since what is of interest to us is the fact that up to the very last he declared that he had seen the risen Lord.

He writes to the Galatians that, "it pleased God to reveal his son in me", and he is evidently referring to the above-mentioned experience on the way to Damascus. Otherwise we would be at a loss to know what happened, as all we are told in *The Acts* is that he saw a light from heaven above the brightness of the sun and then heard a voice. Evidently more than this actually happened, as from what he says in his writings he saw an apparition whom he believed to be Jesus, a vision so bright that he ever afterwards referred to the etheric visitor as a glorified being.

This is more easily believed when we know that similar visions are seen in our own times by people with psychic sight, and that the impressions those leave on them are the same as the impression left on Paul, that of a glorified etheric being. The German word for an apparition is *"eine Erscheinung"*, or a shining one, which is much more expressive than the English word, and conveys exactly what a German wishes his hearer or reader to understand was seen—a shining being.

Much more impressive, from an evidential point of view, than anything else Paul says are his constant references to Jesus now being a glorified spirit in heaven. Something of the nature of an apparition (*eine Erscheinung*), of a being more radiant than anything on earth must have been seen by him to have produced this oft repeated remark. His entire life was changed as a result, because Jesus was now to him a shining, glorified, glorious creature, just as Jehovah was to Moses, as we are told that the "sight of the glory of the Lord was like devouring fire". (Exodus xxiv, 17.) Why did Paul become imbued with this idea of the risen Lord? Only those with psychic knowledge can possibly answer this question, but before doing so let me tabulate Paul's references to the heavenly Christ:

Beholding the glory of the Lord. (2 Cor. iii, 18.)

Raised up from the dead by the glory of the Father. (Rom. vi, 4.)

They would not have crucified the Lord of glory. (1 Cor. ii, 8.)

The Father of glory . . . set him at his own right hand in heavenly places. (Eph. i, 17.)

The glory of the celestial is one. (1 Cor. xv, 40.)

The last Adam (Jesus) was made a living spirit. (1 Cor. xv, 45.)

The glory of Christ. (2 Cor. viii, 23.)

God was manifest in the flesh, justified in the Spirit, seen of angels, received up into glory. (1 Tim. iii, 16.)

Besides this, he is constantly bringing into his writings such expressions as:

That it may be fashioned like unto his glorious body. (Phil. iii, 21.)

The Lord shall . . . destroy with the brightness of his coming. (2 Thess. ii, 8.)

We shall also bear the image of the heavenly. (1 Cor. xv, 49.)

We are the children of God . . . and joint heirs with Christ that we may be also glorified together. (Rom. viii, 16.)

The sufferings of this present time are not worthy to be compared with the glory which shall be revealed in us. (Rom. viii, 18.)

How shall not the ministration of the spirit be rather glorious? (2 Cor. iii, 8.)

When Christ . . . shall appear then shall ye also appear with him in glory. (Col. iii, 4.)

He called you . . . to the obtaining of the glory of our Lord Jesus Christ. (2 Thess. ii, 14.)

In Christ Jesus with eternal glory. (2 Tim. ii, 10.)

Strengthened . . . according to his glorious power. (Col. i, 11.)

Looking for . . . the glorious appearing of the great God and our Saviour Jesus Christ. (Titus ii, 13.)

In consequence of the deep impression this vision had made on him, Paul envisaged Jesus as the Christ returning in all his glory, when those awaiting him would be changed into his glory and become his ministering angels. The psychic stream, as we have already noticed, was running very strongly in those days, and this can be discovered by the numerous references to etheric matters in the Christian literature of the time. So strong was it that it turned a Jew, brought up in the dismal eschatology of his race, into a Spiritualist with a vivid realisation of the other world, its inhabitants and the fact that our resurrection takes place at death. The idea of the resurrection of the physical body he no longer accepts and emphasises this by these words, "Now this I say, brethren, that flesh and blood cannot inherit the kingdom of God; neither doth corruption inherit incorruption". (I Cor. xv, 50.)

It is inconceivable that anyone could have written in the way Paul did without having had some dynamic psychic experience behind him. Those who have been privileged to have such experiences in our own times can understand and fully sympathise with the ardent, emotional, enthusiastic Paul, who deduced from his vision that Jesus was the Christ, soon to return to gather his elect, as etheric beings, into his presence to be with him in glory for evermore. Our earthly tabernacle, he tells us, will then be dissolved, but we shall receive in its place a divine eternal body (2 Cor. v, 1). Everything to him was in a world beyond this earth, and the idea, in which he was nurtured, of the Messiah coming to earth as a physical being, and setting up his kingdom in Jerusalem, had by this time passed out of his mind for ever.

I know men and women of the same ardent temperament who have been changed from a materialistic outlook on life to one which made them enthusiastic to go out and tell the world all about their psychic experiences. If they had been brought up in the theological atmosphere which surrounded Paul, and had been awaiting the Messiah, nothing is easier to understand than how they would have followed in his footsteps and produced the same ideas. A strong, deeply religious character like Paul only needed such an experience, as we are told he had, to make everything he did and said understandable. Without such an experience we would be at a complete loss to know why he wrote as he did, and why he employed the words he used.

Dr. Abraham Wallace once told me that on different occasions he had witnessed the materialisation of etheric beings which he could only describe in words resembling those used by Paul. Their shining presence dazzled him. His experiences made him so enthusiastic that he reminded me of the great apostle in his ardent desire to preach the return to earth conditions of those etheric beings who had manifested in his presence. So much was this the case that one could say of him, as Paul said of himself, that neither height nor depth was able to prevent him expounding the revelation which had come to him. Sir Arthur Conan Doyle was another such enthusiast, and one could not be in his company without realising that to him, like Paul, the return of the departed had lit within him an unquenchable desire to spread the gospel of Spiritualism.

Baron Schrenck Notzing, in his profound study on this subject, which he put before the public under the title *Materialisation Phenomena,* wrote as follows : "On December 15th, 1921, we saw a complete phantom appear in the doorway of the bedroom. It projected flashes which lit it up. This was repeated ten times. Dematerialisation could be observed by the same light. The phantom became smaller, diminished and melted away. Dr. Auer could see from time to time objects behind the phantom, through its substance, by the light of these flashes."

Dr. Gustave Geley tells us that at a séance with the medium Franck Kluski, on May 15th, 1921, he observed similar phenomena to those experienced by Schrenck Notzing. He writes : "A moment later magnificent luminous phenomena occurred." On another occasion, with the same medium, he tells us of his seeing "a large luminous trail like a nebulous comet and about half a metre long formed above his (Kluski's) head". Professor Pawlowski, who sat with the same medium, writes about his observing "the appearance of a completely luminous figure of a man, who illuminated all the sitters and even the more distant objects in the room. His hands and the region of the heart were much more strongly luminous than the rest of his body".

Sir William Crookes writes in his book, *Researches into the Phenomena of Spiritualism* : "I have seen a solid luminous body . . . which was visible for more than ten minutes. During this time the medium was lying back apparently insensible in an easy chair."

Quotations from the writings of other men of science could be given in such volume that the question can no longer remain in doubt. In the case of luminous materialisations the drapery is usually white in colour, sometimes of dazzling whiteness, its luminosity pervading the room even after the features of the form have disappeared. On other occasions a mist is seen, which in the New Testament is termed a cloud. This gives off no luminosity, as in the case described by Mrs. Leonard in one of the opening chapters of her book, already referred to, relating to an early experience which proved to her that she had psychic power. This is what she says :

The atmosphere was very psychic and peaceful. We three sat listening to the music, when suddenly I became aware that the centre of our part of the room seemed filled with a grey mist. I blinked my eyes, closed and opened them, but the mist was still there, and it grew thicker. Then in the centre of it there gradually built up the form of a man, young and dark. He was in uniform. His face was pale and distraught. He held something in his hand, a round object which I could not see clearly. All at once I realised that he was the young King Alexander of Serbia, who had been murdered a few years previously. He seemed to sense my unspoken recognition of him, for he looked fixedly and sadly in my direction, and extended his hands so that I could clearly distinguish the object he held. It was a small cannon ball covered with blood . . .

He repeated several times over in English the words, "My poor country", after he had spoken in a foreign language which those present could not understand.

Besides Mrs. Leonard the other two who were present also saw the vision and heard the words spoken. It, therefore, could not have been a subjective experience relating to Mrs. Leonard alone, and, as the others heard what she heard, the apparition must have been sufficiently materialised to vibrate our atmosphere so that all could hear normally and not clairaudiently what was said. In other words, the etherian she took to be King Alexander had drawn from her sufficient ectoplasm to enable him to materialise sufficiently to be both seen and heard.

If the foregoing were an isolated incident I would be the last person to refer to it. Because I have seen such things myself, in the presence of mediums, and know Mrs. Leonard personally, her scrupulous honesty and caution in all that she claims to have experienced, I give it as an example of what happens in our own time in the presence of those endowed with psychic power. Thousands of sane, normal and honest people can witness to having seen in the presence of a medium just what Paul, Mrs. Leonard and numerous other people say they have seen, an apparition of one called dead, and for that reason it is quite reasonable to believe what Paul tells us he experienced, especially when we know that this experience altered his entire life.

Six weeks after the vision seen by Mrs. Leonard, the Great War started, and she was used by many who passed over to the other side, in consequence of this tragedy, as the medium for their messages to their

friends on earth. Mrs. Leonard looks on the above-
mentioned experience as a sign from the other world
that the Great War was approaching, and that it would
originate in Serbia, just as Paul looked upon his
experience as a sign from heaven that Christ had
come and suffered for the sins of humanity.

Both had similar experiences and both looked
upon them as a revelation from heaven. With such
things happening today one can appreciate better what
the ancients meant when they wrote about signs and
wonders, apparitions and visions, seeing a god or the
gods and so on. If we adjust ourselves to their state of
limited knowledge, and their inability to express themselves as clearly as we can today, it is quite easy to
understand that their experiences were just the same as
our own at the present time.

Let me give one more of Mrs. Leonard's experiences. She had not seen or heard from her father for
some weeks. What she now tells was the first inti-
mation she had that he had passed on :

I was resting on my bed in the afternoon, reading, when
my attention was drawn by a movement of some kind near the
side of the bed. I looked up and was astonished to see my
father standing in front of me. I saw him just as distinctly as
one can see an ordinary earthly person. He stood between my
bed and the fireplace, facing the bright winter sunshine that
streamed in upon him from the window. I noticed that his
body was solid and it completely blocked out part of the mantle-
piece and fireplace. He appeared to be several years younger
than on my last meeting with him—bright, alert and upright,
his face wreathed in smiles. I could see he was delighted to be
able to show himself to me. I could have touched him by
stretching out my hand. I managed to whisper, "O Dad !" He
smiled even more, nodded his head and vanished.

Mrs. Leonard remarks that her father died away from home and that his brief visit to her was the first news she had that he had passed on. She did not even know that he was ill. Her father had died three days prior to his thus appearing to her as an etheric being.

With all this in mind, the similarity of Paul's experiences with those related is obvious to everyone. What is important is that Paul confirms in his own writings that he saw Jesus after his death, when he says, "Last of all he was seen of me also." (1 Cor. xv, 8); "Have I not seen Jesus Christ our Lord?" (1 Cor. ix, 1); and again, "It pleased God . . . to reveal his Son in me." (Gal. i, 15).

Throughout his writings, Paul is continually referring to his own mediumship and psychic gifts, especially in his letters to the Corinthians. This was quite natural when we remember how near Corinth is to Delphi, the ancient home of mediumship, where the best medium in Greece, termed the Pythia, could always be consulted. At Delphi dwelt the first universally recognised mediums, and to this sacred spot travelled kings and governors, statesmen and great warriors, philosophers and men of letters, to find strength, comfort and advice in the affairs of life. In the 6th century B.C. the Pythia, known also as the Delphic oracle, was at the pinnacle of her fame, which continued for almost a thousand years, as up till A.D. 360 the renown of the one holding this position still extended throughout all the civilised world. Plutarch (A.D. 50-100) tells us that no instance is on record of her ever being accused of fraudulent practices, and he writes of the Pythia in these words:

When Kings and States consulted the oracles on weighty matters that might do harm if made public, the replies were couched in enigmatical language, but when private persons asked about their own private affairs, they got direct answers in the plainest terms, so that some people complained of their simplicity, and as being unworthy of their divine origin. Her answers, though submitted to the severest scrutiny, have never proved false or incorrect. On the contrary, the verification of them has filled the Temple with gifts from all parts of Greece and foreign countries. . . . The answers of Pythoness proceed to the very truth without diversion, circuit, fraud, or ambiguity. She has never yet, in any single instance, been convicted of falsehood.

Paul could, therefore, better express himself on his mediumistic qualities to the Corinthians than to those other people with whom he kept up a correspondence. So he tells them that they must not be ignorant of psychic gifts, meaning that they were to use them correctly and in an intelligent manner. In other words, he writes to them as an expert to tell them how those members of the early Christian Church in Corinth, who were considered to be mediumistic, were to exercise their mediumship. So he writes, "Now there are diversities of gifts, but the same spirit (1 Cor. xii, 4), meaning that the same controlling spirit can produce through one who is psychic various types of phenomena, and he goes on to say that there are differences of administrations, diversities of operation, but the manifestation of the spirit is given to every man to profit withal. Some therefore, he says, when in trance speak words of wisdom, others words of knowledge, while others can exercise the gift of healing. Some can work miracles, some foretell the future, and some can discern spirits, while others speak in tongues.

Throughout these epistles we are continually coming across reference to prophecy and speaking in tongues. When we consider the number of centuries which separate the time of Paul from us, how the meaning of words has changed, and how his letters are translations from ancient Greek into seventeenth-century English, we cannot expect to find in them the same terminology as we now use for the various phases of psychic phenomena. One must take the context and from it gather the meaning of the words used. By "miracles" Paul doubtless means what is today called telekinesis, or the movement of objects without physical contact. He also refers to "speaking in tongues", and to speaking in "an unknown tongue".

An account of this phenomenon is given in Acts ii, when the disciples were in Jerusalem for the feast of rejoicing at the in-gathering of the harvest, known as Pentecost. This appears to be an exaggerated account of what may have taken place, but at least it gives one a clue as to what is meant by speaking in tongues. Obviously it refers to trance utterances. The writer of this story had evidently heard that some spoke in "an unknown tongue", which in Paul's day was the phraseology for what we today call speaking in trance, as what was said through the mouth of the medium was unknown to the medium. He therefore puts together the story of everyone on that day of Pentecost speaking in a foreign language because, writing a long time after the event, he was ignorant of what was meant by speaking in "an unknown tongue".

The story reported in *The Acts* is quite evidently an account of a séance, when one or more trance mediums were present. On such an occasion the temperature drops considerably, especially at the time phenomena occur. Many tests have been made of this phenomenon and it has been discovered that the fall amounts to as much as twenty degrees Fahrenheit. This fall in the temperature causes a draught of wind which corresponds to "the rushing mighty wind", to which reference is made at the Pentecostal séance. The reference to the "cloven tongues like as of fire" which appeared to those present, and "sat upon each of them", is a description of what are called "spirit lights", which move about the room, touching those present. They are phosphorescent in appearance, each about the size of a half-crown, and by their repeated change of shape could be likened to tongues of fire. On many occasions I have tried to catch them but they have always eluded me, thus showing that there are intelligences present who can see in our darkness. Another explanation of their meaning is given on page 736.

Then we are told that those present at this séance were all filled with the Holy Ghost, or, as we would say, everyone present became entranced. In other words, it was a séance composed entirely of mediums, who spoke in trance "as the spirit gave them utterance". It is certainly surprising that so many mediums should be together at one time, but we are not accepting the details of the affair as accurate. This extraordinary exhibition attracted the multitude, who were confounded because every man heard his own language spoken. No date is given and so we are left in the dark as to when all this took place, but it seems strange that so many foreigners should be in the company "when the multitude came together" to listen to what was being said, as the account goes on to say that those present represented fifteen different nationalities, each of whom heard their own language spoken.

It is very rare in psychic science to discover a medium who, when in trance, can speak a language different from the one to which he has been accustomed. A control can influence a medium to speak as he wishes in the language the medium knows, but it is only on rare occasions that a medium in trance can speak an unknown language. I have heard different foreign languages spoken by the Direct Voice but this is something quite apart from the medium's vocal organs. A clairaudient medium can always hear and repeat foreign names, words, and sentences which he does not understand, and on various occasions I have heard this done. But the medium is not then in trance and to have fifteen languages spoken on one occasion would certainly constitute a record in mediumship.

This being so one can only imagine that the reporter of this séance was misinformed or drew a wrong conclusion from the expression "speaking with other tongues". The expression is misleading, though quite accurate, as those in trance really do speak a language which is not their own because it is the language of their control. Nevertheless this does not mean that they speak in a language which is foreign to them. However this may be, and whether what is recorded did or did not actually happen, the whole story is evidently founded on what we today would call a séance, which was by no means confined to those days, because the writer of *The Acts* tells us that this Pentecostal séance was only carrying out what the prophet Joel knew all about when he said, "It shall come to pass afterward, that I will pour out my spirit upon all flesh ; and your sons and your daughters shall prophesy, your old men shall dream dreams, your young men shall see visions." (Joel ii, 28.)

From now onwards I shall have much to say on the subject of the medium's control, in fact Christian beliefs and controlling spirits are so bound up together that it is impossible to give serious consideration to the religion without continually bringing them in to explain the origin of Christian beliefs. It is therefore important that the reader should clearly understand how the controlling spirit influences his earth medium, and I cannot do better than quote the questions and answers relating to this subject, as they are to be found in *On the Edge of the Etheric*. The following answers were given to me by one of the spirit controls of John C. Sloan when speaking to me by the direct voice. My first question was, "When you control the medium and use his vocal organs what really happens ?"

To this I received the following answer, "When the medium is controlled, and we wish to speak through his vocal organs, we get him into a passive condition. This is the condition he is in when in trance. His spirit has left his body for the time being, and is outside. When he is in this condition we are able to work on his larynx and vocal cords, his tongue and throat muscles. We do not go inside him, however, but stand behind him. We are able to get ourselves into a condition, or in tune with the medium, to such an extent that when we move our voice organs the medium's move likewise. There is a connecting link, etheric or psychic, whichever you like to call it, which has the same action on the medium's muscles as a tuning fork on another tuning fork if they are both tuned to the same pitch. Thus the two sets of vocal organs work in harmony. There is no question of the messages in any way being influenced by the medium's mind, as his mind does not come into the question at all. We do not work through his mind, but directly on his vocal organs. Everything that comes through is exactly as it originates in the mind of the controlling spirit. The medium's mind and brain are switched off for the time being, and the spirit operator controls the muscles of the medium's vocal organs."

To the foregoing I replied by another question : "The medium is still in trance ; where has his spirit been since we started ?" To this I received the following reply : "When the trance state comes on it means that the medium's spirit has moved out of his body. His spirit is at present exactly on his right, not far from his body."

I then asked, "Can you tell me more about your controlling the medium during trance ?" To this question I received the following reply : "I take on earth conditions, slow down my vibrations and stand behind him. Ectoplasm is found everywhere in the human body. When I stand behind him it is similar to standing behind the mask, only in this case it is the medium's own vocal organs which I move to form the words. They move in company with my organs, whereas, when we speak directly, apart from the medium, we enter the mask and form the words by our own tongues, which are temporarily materialised."

The reference to the mask relates to information previously given as to how the direct voice is produced. Otherwise the foregoing is sufficiently clear and distinct to enable anyone with only a slight knowledge of psychic phenomena to understand what takes place when a medium enters the trance state, and speaks under the control of an entirely different personality. When in this condition the medium is quite unconscious of his surroundings and entirely unaware of what is uttered through his mouth.

Paul, when writing to the Corinthians, introduces us into this realm of mediumship and enables us to appreciate how, in the days of the early Church, mediumship, and its accompanying psychic phenomena, were not only common occurrences but were accepted as a natural adjunct to the worship, prayers and hymn singing which made up the service. This continued after his time and we find the Church fathers writing about the psychic gifts of the mediums employed in the Christian churches.

Paul refers to the "gift of prophecy", which was the expression used in those days for clairaudience. He also refers to the "discerning of spirits", which was just his name for clairvoyance. The Greek word for prophet, in Paul's time, meant a medium, and in *The Revelation* we find the prophet and clairaudient referred to as one and the same person, because we read, "The voice which I heard from heaven spake to me again" (Rev. x, 8), "And he said unto me, Thou must prophesy again." (Rev. x, 11). There is no doubt about this, but if further proof is needed it is to be found in these words : "Believe not every spirit, but try the spirits whether they are of God : because many false prophets are gone out into the world." (1 John iv, 1.)

If we go back to the Old Testament we gain further light when we read, "When a man went to enquire of God, thus he spake, Come and let us go to the seer : for he that is now called a Prophet was before-time called a Seer." (1 Sam. ix, 9.) In the next chapter we read, "The Spirit of the Lord will come upon thee, and thou shalt prophesy . . . and shalt be turned into another man." (1 Sam. x, 6.) Nothing could describe in fewer words what occurs to a medium when he enters the trance state.

The Hebrew word for prophet is *nābi* and for seer *rôeh*, which in the time of Samuel had come to refer to the same person. Like many mediums of the present day, and times past, Samuel could foretell the future, and several instances are given of his accurate predictions. Throughout the Bible, and ancient literature, the gift of anticipating the future is associated with medium-ship, just as it is in our own times. We are also told, "God spake by the mouth of his holy prophets". (Luke i, 70.) From this and other statements we discover that trance utterances were looked on as "the voice of God", that mediums were known as "men of God" and that to "enquire of the Lord" was their way of expressing questions put to a medium's spirit control.

Samuel is called "the seer" throughout *The Book of Samuel*, and we know from what we are told that he was clairaudient, in fact he appears to have heard the Direct Voice which he mistook for the voice of Eli. (1 Sam. iii.) We also read that Iddo, the Seer, saw visions (2 Chron. ix, 29), and so we have clairaudience and clairvoyance thus linked up with seership. Through-out *Chronicles* various Seers are referred to, and in *The Book of Amos* we find the king telling the prophet to leave the country, in these words, "Amos, O thou seer, go, flee thee away into the land of Judah . . . and prophesy there." (Amos vii, 12.)

In *The Encyclopædia Britannica* we find that "Prophet (προφήτης) is a word taken from the vocabulary of the ancient Greek religion which passed into the language of Christianity, and so into the modern tongues of Europe, because it was adopted by the Hellenistic Jews as the rendering of the Hebrew *nābi*. The word, therefore, as we use it is meant to convey an idea which belongs to Hebrew and not to Hellenic belief". Thus the word prophet, meaning a medium, was adopted by Christians, but its meaning was forgotten when they lost touch with the etheric world. In the fourth century mediumship was abolished and priests took the place of mediums. Since that time no Christian theologian has understood what Paul and the other early Christians meant when using the words prophet and prophesy. The foregoing, however, makes it clear that a prophet was a medium, that a seer was also a medium, and that a prophet and a seer referred to the same individual, namely a medium.

Another expression for a prophet and a seer was "a man of God", but if we bring it down to present-day English, Samuel, Gad, Amos, and the others referred to in the Old Testament as prophets and seers, were mediums who, owing to their psychic gifts, acted as intermediaries between the inhabitants of the etheric world and this earth. It does not follow, of course, that these prophets and seers necessarily interpreted correctly the messages they received or that the people understood them. The interest to us lies in the fact that the psychic stream is to be found running through, and watering, the religious ideas of the Hebrews, just as it has done those of all other nations.

Saul was evidently chosen to be King of Israel

because he prophesied when "the Spirit of God", or literally "The Divine Spirit" possessed him. (1 Sam. x, 10.) The holy spirit also possessed David, and these two Kings of Israel were anointed when each became King, or, to use the Greek word, they were each a Christ, the anointed one. An inhabitant of the etheric world, who has come down to us under the name of "Holy Spirit", also possessed Jesus, but this will receive consideration in the next chapter. Yaweh, the God of Israel, who is now known to us as Jehovah, and is also referred to in the Old Testament as The Lord, was evidently the spirit control of Moses.

He was adopted as the God of Israel, just as the Holy Spirit, the spirit control of Jesus, was adopted as one of the Christian gods. Yaweh must have been a strong personality as he so impressed the Israelites that they put him above all the other gods, and finally, after the captivity, decided that he was the only God. By following what they believed he delivered through his mediums, whom he is believed to have controlled, the Hebrew religion developed, based upon mediumship and psychic phenomena, without which there would have been no Judaism, no Christianity and no religion of any description in the world.

Mediums are the primary cause of religion, which in time grows into a form of belief comprising doctrines, dogmas and rites requiring priests to protect and perform. Mediums always created the original idea, and thus Moses, the medium, was the cause behind Judaism, and Paul, the medium, the cause behind Christianity. We can have no better example of the truth of this assertion than noting what has taken place within the past twelve years in French

Indo-China. Within this short period a new religion has come to life and developed so rapidly that it now claims to have adherents numbering three millions. It goes under the name of Caodaism, which means in the Annamese language Supreme Being.

In 1927 some Europeans living in Indo-China, mostly Government officials and their wives, met together for the purpose of having séances, as one of them was found to be a well-developed medium. These séances attracted the educated natives, and from this nucleus the teaching, claimed to come from etheric beings, spread amongst the natives by means of public meetings which were held to demonstrate the super-normal powers of the medium in trance. Churches sprang up everywhere, and a priesthood came into being because the people adopted something from Buddhism, Taoism and Confucianism, just as Christianity adopted its beliefs from neighbouring religions.

Today, beliefs have come to surround the original psychic manifestations, rites and ceremonies are performed, and a creed has been drawn up placing stress on the importance of human affection, the unimportance of material wealth, and belief in the survival of the spirit. The French authorities state that they have no cause to complain about these new beliefs as they find that they secure social stability and keep the people contented. Thus in our own times we can follow the birth and growth of a new religion which has pursued similar lines to those travelled by Christianity, as we shall discover as we proceed.

In the days of Paul some had the gift of prophecy, which can be traced down the ages, and in the Apostolic churches (which is the name given to the

Christian churches during the first three centuries of our era), anyone having this gift stood up before the congregation and gave a message thought to be from God, but which was in reality from some etherian in the other world. Except that we now know that these voices come from beings living in another order of existence, and are not "the voice of God" as was thought in those days, what happened in the first Christian centuries in Christian churches corresponds with what happens today in Spiritualist churches in this country, and throughout the world, when some part of the service is occupied by the congregation hearing clairaudient messages received through the etheric duplicate of the medium's hearing organs.

This early form of Christian worship continued for some centuries, until the priesthood became strong enough to obliterate all mediums by wholesale slaughter, and thus abolish the psychic element out of which their religion had grown. Throughout the entire New Testament we can trace, underneath all the legends and incomprehensible doctrines it contains, a strong psychic stream of thought, which was diverted into legends, doctrines and dogmas through being misunderstood and misinterpreted. The influences which produced the New Testament must undoubtedly have originated in an unusual expression of psychic power, due to a number of people being endowed with the faculties of clairvoyance, clairaudience and the other gifts associated with mediumship.

Unfortunately we are unable to relate this outburst to previous or later times, until we come to the present day. Prior to the date we are considering, writing was not common enough to leave on record any previous occasion when this occurred, and, after the Church of Christ obtained control of the Roman Empire, there was no possibility for it to happen, as any recurrence was immediately stamped out by the mediums being murdered. So we have no history to guide us as to whether these psychic outbursts occurred from time to time, but the record of the last two hundred years, since the Church was prohibited from destroying mediums, reveals the fact that when the priests lose power mediumship increases.

The history of Greece also points in the same direction, and so it seems fairly safe to conclude that mediumship waxes and wanes in inverse ratio to the power of the priesthood. It is, moreover, evident that the people, in the days when the Christian religion was in the making, lived in a psychic atmosphere different from any which prevailed in Palestine after the captivity. This coincided with the decline in the power of the Jewish priesthood outside Jerusalem and their final overthrow when this city was captured by the Romans.

Unlike the Hebrews, the Greeks encouraged the idea that discarnate intelligences surround us, who can see us and are interested in us, even though they are unseen. To the Greeks, at the time we are considering, the gods or spirits were their friends and companions, and the etheric world a real place where the people on earth foregathered after death. If it had not been for Greece, the psychic happenings in Palestine, surrounding Jesus, would never have survived to reach the world at large.

The Hebrews refused to believe in the gods and remained devoted to Jehovah, whom they feared and honoured as a being far apart from man, both in his person and dwelling-place. Paul transported to Greek soil what was the outcome of the psychic events in Palestine, as there he found their interpretation, by associating them with the beliefs of the Mystery Cults. His work coincided with the break up of the power of the Jewish priesthood, which gave the Hellenised Jews the opportunity to adopt the Greek outlook. Thus many Jews became Christians and abandoned the materialistic philosophy of Judaism.

From what Paul tells us the entire range of mediumistic gifts was used in the early Christian churches in Greece, and so, when he writes to the Corinthians, he tells them how they should order their Church service so that everything is carried on decently and in order. The fourteenth Chapter of First Corinthians is devoted to observations on the exercising of mediumistic gifts, from which the following are extracts :

He that prophesieth speaketh unto men to edification, and exhortation and comfort.

He that speaketh in an unknown tongue edifieth himself; but he that prophesieth edifieth the church.

I would that ye all spake with tongues, but rather that ye prophesied, for greater is he that prophesieth than he that speaketh with tongues, except he interpret, that the church may receive edifying.

Now, brethren, if I come unto you speaking with tongues, what shall I profit you, except I shall speak to you either by revelation, or by knowledge, or by prophesying, or by doctrine. . . .

Wherefore tongues are for a sign, not to them that believe, but to them that believe not ; but prophesying serveth not for them that believe not, but for them which believe.

If therefore the whole church be come together into one place, and all speak with tongues, and there come in those that are unlearned, or unbelievers, will they not say that ye are mad ? . . .

If any man speak in an unknown tongue let it be by two,
or at the most three, and that in turn, and let one interpret. . . .

If anything be revealed to another that sitteth by, let the
first hold his peace.

For ye may all prophesy one by one, that all may learn, and
all may be comforted.

And so Paul goes on with his warnings, advice and
encouragement, and then he advises each to exercise
the gifts for which each is fitted by nature. "Have all
the gifts of healing ? Do all speak with tongues ? Do
all interpret ?" (1 Cor. xii, 30.)

Paul makes many references to his own psychic
power : "I thank my God, I speak with tongues more
than ye all. Yet in the church I had rather speak
five words with my understanding, that by my voice I
might teach others also, than ten thousand words in an
unknown tongue." (1 Cor. xiv, 18.) He much preferred
to use his own mind than allow his body to be the
instrument of a spirit, but this verse proves that he was
a trance medium and so had a controlling spirit, just as
all mediums have today. A man with his forceful
personality had evidently no wish to be looked upon
by the Corinthians as only the mouthpiece of some
etheric being, though at other times he seems to glory
in being so. In fact, his writings are often very involved and contradictory on all the many topics in
which he indulges.

The next time he writes to the Corinthians he
strikes a rather more humble attitude and does not
claim to be a greater medium than them all, as he says,
"It is not expedient for me doubtless to glory. I will
come to visions and revelations of the Lord", remarking
how he was taken in trance to the third heaven, where

he saw and heard things in Paradise which it is not lawful for man to utter. (2 Cor. xii, 1.) Then he reminds the Corinthians of his psychic exploits when he was last with them, forgetting his earlier observation that it was not expedient for him to glory. "Truly the signs of an apostle were wrought among you in all patience, in signs, and wonders, and mighty deeds." (2 Cor. xii, 12.)

When writing to the Romans he tells them much the same as he told the Corinthians, how "Through mighty signs and wonders, by the power of the spirit of God" (Rom. xv, 19) he had brought converts amongst the Gentiles to the faith. Everywhere throughout his writings he reveals his psychic gifts in expressions such as the following :

Though I speak with the tongues of angels. (1 Cor. xiii, 1.)

Though I have the gift of prophecy. (1 Cor. xiii, 2.)

Lest I should be exalted above measure through the abundance of the revelations. (2 Cor. xii, 7.)

Whether in the body, I cannot tell; or whether out of the body, I cannot tell. (2 Cor. xii, 2.)

In consequence of the revelations which he believed he was receiving from Jesus direct, he adopted the rôle of chief spokesman and quite ignored the opinions of the other apostles, as we shall see as we go on. His revelations had come direct from Jesus in heaven whereas they had only known Jesus when on earth. Paul therefore, as the mouthpiece of Jesus, had no need of an earthly Jesus when he was the chosen instrument of the heavenly Christ. So he emphasises his independence of the disciples who knew Jesus.

The gospel which was preached by me is not after man, for I neither received it of man . . . but by the revelation of Jesus Christ. (Gal. i, 11.)

How that by revelation he made known unto me the mystery. (Eph. iii, 3.)

For I received of the Lord that which also I delivered unto you. (1 Cor. xi, 23.)

I conferred not with flesh and blood, neither went I up to Jerusalem. (Gal. i, 16.)

And I went up by revelation and communicated unto them [the other apostles at Jerusalem] that gospel which I preached among the Gentiles. (Gal. ii, 2.)

Evidently Paul greatly valued his mediumship and desired that others should develop their psychic gifts, because he tells those to whom he writes that they must :

Follow after charity, and desire spiritual gifts, but rather that ye may prophesy. (1 Cor. xiv, 1.)

He therefore that ministereth to you the Spirit, and worketh miracles among you, doeth he it by the works of the law, or by the hearing of faith ? (Gal. iii, 5.)

Quench not the spirit. Despise not prophesyings. Prove all things ; hold fast that which is good. (1 Thess. v, 19.)

Neglect not the gift that is in thee, which was given thee by prophecy, with the laying on of the hands. (1 Tim. iv, 14.)

Covet to prophesy, and forbid not to speak with tongues." (1 Cor. xiv, 39.)

How shall not the ministration of the Spirit be rather glorious ? (2 Cor. iii, 8.)

For the invisible things of him from the creation of the world are clearly seen, being understood. (Rom. i, 20.)

While we look not at the things which are seen, but at the things which are not seen : for the things which are seen are temporal ; but the things which are not seen are eternal. 2 Cor. iv, 18.)

Paul makes no special reference to his own healing powers, but in Acts xix, 11 we find a very significant remark: "And God wrought special miracles by the hands of Paul : So that from his body were brought unto the sick handkerchiefs or aprons, and the diseases departed from them, and the evil spirits went out of them."

When the Church authorities in the fourth century banished the mediums from the churches, and then destroyed them, Christian people lost all contact with psychic matters, and, in consequence, with the origin of their religion. Only within the last fifty years has psychic healing received any serious consideration, and consequently, until our own day, this verse, relating to the healing properties of handkerchiefs, held by a healing medium, has been meaningless. The use of handkerchiefs to heal the sick takes place today and we are able to relate this verse to our present-day psychic knowledge. From it we are able to realise that in the time of the early Christian Church its mediums had healing powers like our present-day mediums, and that they adopted the same methods to heal the sick as psychic healers do today.

To confirm this statement I could give records of many interesting cases of cures by psychic healing, which have come within my own personal knowledge, but I shall give only one relating to healing by handkerchiefs, so as to make clear the meaning of the verse relating to the healing power of Paul.

In 1932 a girl of four years of age, named Doreen, had measles. On May 16th the doctor said that pneumonia had set in and four days later she developed meningitis. Her parents were told that she might die at any minute. The doctor called in a specialist on May 25th and he confirmed the diagnosis of meningitis. He agreed that there was no hope of the child living until the end of the week. The parents called in another doctor, who also agreed that there was no hope and that nothing further could be done.

When all hope was abandoned the child's grand-mother, who herself had received great benefit from psychic healing, decided that at least no harm could be done by calling in the psychic healer F. J. Jones, who conducted a healing circle at Marylebone House in Russell Square, London. As Jones dealt with dozens of cases a day he could not go to see the child, but he held in his hand for some time a handkerchief which was taken immediately and placed over Doreen's head. Whenever the handkerchief was so placed Doreen stopped screaming. The next day her temperature was down and another handkerchief, which had been held by Jones, was placed on her head.

Thinking the case was hopeless, the doctor did not call again till May 27th and was very mystified at the child's improvement. He was not told the reason. On the next day, May 28th, he said her recovery was marvellous. That same afternoon Jones called to see the child for the first time. He went into a trance and his spirit control treated her by keeping Jones' hands on her neck. The control, through the mouth of Jones, then said that he would draw the disease from the head through the back of the skull, and, as there would be much pus discharged, he asked that the hair be shaved from the back of the head and that, when suppuration started, the wounds should be treated with a mixture of olive oil and chalk.

That evening the discharge commenced from eighteen places on the part of the skull which had been treated by the spirit control. The doctor, when he called on May 30th, was told that the grandmother was treating the child with an African remedy. The spirit control claimed to have been an African medicine man on earth. As the earth doctor could do nothing himself he did not interfere. On June 3rd the doctor said it was a miracle Doreen was still alive. On June 8th and 9th Jones, in trance, again treated the child. On June 17th Doreen was able to speak for the first time since her illness, and on June 23rd she went out for a walk with her grandmother and soon became quite strong and well again.

When such things can happen today, it is quite reasonable to believe that they happened in the days gone by, and all that is doubtful is whether what has been told of Paul was directly related to him or to someone else. The writer of *The Acts* is so inaccurate in all he tells us about Paul that one hesitates to accept anything he has to say about him and his mission to the Gentiles. Most of what he writes is contradicted by what Paul himself has to say, and, besides this, his accounts of the miracles, and other impossible deeds performed by Paul and the other apostles, put the book on the same level as the gospels.

Every medium has what is called "a control", an etheric being who protects his medium from interference by other spirits. The Bible name for this is "familiar spirit". One can understand the necessity for this as otherwise the medium might be constantly interfered with by spirits anxious to manifest on earth. For this reason those who take up this work of controlling mediums have also the task of protecting their mediums from all harm. Besides this, they become very proficient, owing to constant practice, in communicating through their respective mediums. Consequently controls often pass through their mediums messages from etherians who have not had practice in communicating with earth.

Mediums and their controls become great friends. When one considers that a medium can at times see the controlling spirit, and at other times sense his presence, as well as hear him speak, one can understand how this is possible. There is, therefore, a strong inclination for each medium to glorify his own control and to imagine him as a highly gifted heavenly being. Because of this close attachment between the control and his medium those who make a special study of mediumship always associate the name of the control with the medium. So Mrs. Leonard is always linked with her control Feda, that wonderful personality who manifests when Mrs. Leonard goes into trance.

There was evidently a close psychic relationship between Paul on earth and Jesus in heaven. What it was exactly is difficult to discover. There is not enough evidence to prove that the spirit of Jesus controlled Paul in trance, as Feda controls Mrs. Leonard in trance, and yet from Paul's phraseology he was evidently vividly aware of the presence of Jesus from time to time. When writing to the Galatians he tells them that "God has sent forth the spirit of his Son", who lived in him, a remark which might be taken to mean that Jesus was his control. He is quite emphatic that Jesus was the source of his teachings and mentions this several times. He also tells the

Ephesians that he received his revelation from the Spirit, and this belief runs through all his writings.

This awareness undoubtedly inspired and encouraged him. Also it influenced his phraseology and was the cause of his considering that his teachings were inspired by Jesus. This gave him the courage to make claims that no sane man would otherwise have made. Jesus was perhaps a source of inspiration to Paul, rather than a control, and this is quite in accordance with what mediums experience today when they sense at intervals the presence of some particular spirit, in whom they are specially interested, and for whom they have a special affection.

When we bear this in mind we see how naturally it all reads in the epistles when Paul is continually associating himself with Christ. Just as the earth life of Feda does not specially interest Mrs. Leonard, so the earth life of Jesus did not specially interest Paul. Why should it ? Mrs. Leonard today knows Feda as a living, intelligent, etheric, or heavenly being, and that interests her much more than to think of Feda as a woman on earth. We can now understand why Paul so ignored the earth Jesus and so glorified the heavenly Christ.

If Paul had not been a medium the only inference one could draw from his writings is that he was mentally unbalanced. He was either a medium or suffered from religious hysteria. However, when we accept the fact that he was a medium everything becomes clear and understandable, as what he tells us he actually experienced. The fact that he wound round his psychic experiences the Gnostic and Mystery theology of the times is not a reflection on his sanity, but on his wisdom, though we must be charitable and remember that his knowledge was not on the level of ours of today. He lived in an atmosphere of theological ignorance and stupidity which it is difficult for some of us to imagine in our time of greater enlightenment.

Paul evidently often felt conscious of the near presence of Jesus, whom he termed Christ, and so he writes :

> Christ liveth in me. (Gal. ii, 20.)
> It pleased God . . . to reveal his Son in me, that I might preach him. (Gal. i, 15.)
> Since ye seek a proof of Christ speaking in me. (2 Cor. xiii, 3.)

Christians have copied Paul's phraseology in reference to themselves, and used his expressions relating to Christ and the Holy Spirit, being quite unaware that their origin is to be found in mediumship. The day will come when this will be recognised, but until then the Christian phraseology will continue without being understood. Christ being "immanent in each believer", his being "nearer than hands or feet", "the living presence of Christ", and all such expressions are inexplicable apart from mediumship, though through the influence of Paul many imagine that they experience what he did. If this is not due to imagination then the cause is due to their own mediumistic qualities which can sense some etheric presence.

This intimate study of the medium Paul of Tarsus will make what follows much clearer and more understandable. With his psychic power, vivid imagination, gift of phraseology, combined with his mystical and theological speculations and extreme enthusiasm, he could work wonders amongst a simple religiously minded people. Whatever he believed to be right he would push to the utmost extreme. He was a combination of a sensitive medium and a fanatical zealot. In religious history we know of other similar characters, and in politics we need not go far back to find one, as Hitler, the clairaudient zealot, is moulding German and European history in our own time.

Now that we have come to understand the temperament of the man Paul, let us give some consideration to his doctrines, which go under the name of

PAULINISM.

A careful reading of the Pauline epistles makes it evident that in the early days of the Christian cult there were disputes and acrimonious discussions between the leaders of the early Church, which is not surprising, considering all that happened. The position, as it existed in those early years, was difficult enough for the leaders at Jerusalem without the complications caused by Paul's entry on the scene, with his opinions which were quite at variance with those held by the disciples who had known Jesus.

A company of men and women, under the leadership of three men called Peter, James and John, who were disciples of Jesus, were definitely of the opinion that their master, who had died a violent death, was now alive in his etheric body and had appeared in this to some of them. From this they concluded that he was the Messiah whom every Jew was expecting. This band gathered adherents to this view and they met together, with the result that gradually a Church organisation was formed at Jerusalem under the leadership of Peter. To them, however, Jesus was no other than a Jewish Messiah whose appearance on earth was but a preliminary to his reappearance as their judge, when he would divide the righteous from the unrighteous and then usher in the millennium.

So convinced were they that Jesus had left them for only a short time, that those who had wealth divided it amongst those who lacked it. A communist society consequently came into being, but this did not last long, though since their time others, who believed in the imminence of the Lord's return, have followed their example and lived to regret their miscalculations. But for Paul this new Messianic cult might never have exerted any influence, or gained converts, outside the Jewish race. Paul, however, not only changed everything but he also caused Peter, James and John an enormous amount of worry and trouble, so much so that they must often have wished that he had never been born.

The new Jesus cult was entirely Judaic in its outlook. The members of the new Church were Jews and any new adherents were also Jews. As it enlarged its bounds beyond Palestine and embraced the Hellenised Jews, its limited vision was somewhat enlarged, but it was still Jewish in its outlook. Things went on like this for some years till the orthodox Jewish priesthood commenced persecuting and harrying this young Messianic community, so much so that we hear of one called Stephen who was stoned to death. Paul, we are told, was present at his martyrdom, and then went off to Damascus to dislodge some more of these heretics, so that they likewise could receive the punishment due to them for daring to ignore the authority of the priests.

On his way to Damascus, Paul, according to the account in *The Acts*, saw a bright light and heard the voice of Jesus. Instead of arriving at his destination breathing out fury against the heretics, he arrived there a changed man. We are told that he was blind for three days, after which he received his sight, which may be symbolical of a changed mental outlook. A man by name of Ananias heard clairaudiently of Paul's arrival, his etheric communicator also telling him that he was to go out to Straight Street, where he would find him. Ananias went to the place mentioned and met Paul. We are told that he laid his hands on him and his sight returned, which again may be symbolical of the fact that Ananias gave Paul a new idea of things, so much so that Paul saw that he was pursuing wrong methods and decided to think things over preparatory to turning over a new leaf.

When dealing with Eastern stories one must remember the hyperbole always in use. An Easterner can never call a spade a spade, and if he wants to talk about someone's changed beliefs he says that he was blind and then received his sight. Another interesting point in connection with this story is the introduction of the clairaudient message given to Ananias. Many similar instances have come under my own personal notice, and it is undoubtedly a fact that clairaudients do receive messages to go to people and give them messages from Etheria, or the etheric world, about things of which they are entirely ignorant. Many cases such as the following I have proved to be true.

For instance, a clairaudient will receive a message

from an etheric communicator, coupled with the fact
that he is the son of a lady living at an address which he
gives. The speaker's name is given in full, and, to
prove that he is the person he says he is, he asks the
clairaudient to tell his mother something intimate
which only he himself and his mother had known.
The clairaudient gets into touch with the lady, either
by telephone or letter, and gives her the message from
her son, and also the intimate and private key message
to prove that he is the person he represents himself to
be. When identity is thus established one is more
inclined to accept the message as coming from the
person who on earth went under the name given.

Let me mention a personal experience which happened to me a year after my mother died, one of many
of a similar nature that I have experienced over the
past twenty years. Just after her death I took her
wedding-ring from her finger and put it in my pocket.
Later I had it attached to the end of my watch-chain
and kept it in my right-hand waistcoat pocket. One
day, about a year after her death, I received a letter
from a friend who knew my mother and who, the
previous day, had had a sitting with a medium, during
which my mother had sent him messages clairaudiently
through the medium. One of these was to tell me
that she was so pleased that I had taken her wedding-
ring off her finger, after her death, and kept it in my
right-hand waistcoat pocket attached to my watch-
chain. Neither my friend, nor the medium, nor anyone
else on earth, knew anything about the matter except
myself.

With such things happening today it was quite
a possibility that Ananias did receive a message

clairaudiently to get in touch with Paul and that, by the experiences which befell Paul, Jesus in the etheric world, or someone else, put a stop to Paul's persecution of the followers of Jesus on earth. These psychic events must have happened to people in those days, because no one could imagine such things being possible if they had not experienced them, or heard about them. Knowing that they happen today enables us to accept as reasonably probable a story incorporating mediumistic phenomena, which otherwise would be treated as quite impossible ever to have happened. On the other hand, when miracles are reported, and we are told that things happened which could not possibly have happened without the laws of nature being broken, we have either to assume that the story is untrue or that the writer is giving us a late vitiated version of something which, to begin with, was quite a natural psychic occurrence.

Take, for instance, the story just related of how Jones cured Doreen. If this had happened nineteen hundred years ago, and had been passed on from one to another for twenty or thirty years, by which time Jones had come to be looked upon as a god-man, it is not difficult to believe, considering the mentality of the times, that by then it had been enlarged to such an extent that the people then believed he had raised Doreen from the dead. Thus the story of Lazarus, and other similar legends, may have had their origin in some cure as remarkable as the one which happened to Doreen, and which, as the years went on, became so exaggerated as to make them impossible to believe. All the miracles told about all god-men may, to begin with, have had quite a natural psychic origin, and

Paul's claim to work "wonders and mighty deeds", doubtless refers to nothing more than the effects of his psychic power, which he did not understand and so attributed to God.

After Paul met Ananias he went off to Arabia to get peace to think things over. He then returned to Damascus with his mind made up that he had been appointed by Jesus as his representative on earth to preach to the Gentiles that he had come to suffer and die for the sins of humanity. This momentous decision to which Paul came greatly upset Peter, James and John, who objected to the Gentiles being included in their scheme. Consequently, Paul to them was a source of great annoyance, and they heartily wished that he would keep away and not meddle in affairs which were not his business.

Here was a man who had not even known Jesus, who had persecuted his followers, and then had the presumption to tell them what the reappearance of Jesus really meant. He had the impudence, so they thought, to tell the immediate disciples of Jesus, that they were wrong in their assumptions, and that he was right, because he had had a special revelation of his own from Jesus in heaven, which had convinced him that the disciples Jesus had left on earth were on the wrong road, and were drawing entirely erroneous conclusions from their master's reappearance.

As happens under such conditions, a quarrel developed between Paul and Peter, James and John, who looked upon Paul as an upstart and impudent busybody, who was interfering with something about which he knew nothing. The only belief they held in common was that Jesus had appeared after death and had returned to heaven, but with Paul's further speculations they were in profound disagreement. To those who had known him, Jesus was a man sent from God, who had met with a cruel death on this his first appearance on earth, and their duty was to await his second appearance. In their eyes he was not a Saviour who had died to save sinners. There is no trace of this idea in the first stratum of evangelic tradition.

Paul, on the other hand, went about teaching that Jesus was none other than an ideal and eternal being who had condescended to leave the right hand of God, enter sinful flesh, die the death of a malefactor on a cursed tree for the purpose of appeasing the wrath of an angry God, thus bringing about the salvation of all mankind. "For I delivered unto you first of all that which I also received, how that Christ died for our sins", he wrote to the Corinthians. And when the missionaries of Peter penetrated to Galatia he wrote to the Galatians, "I marvel that ye are so soon removed from him that called you into the grace of Christ unto another gospel . . . but there be some that trouble you, and would pervert the gospel of Christ. . . . As we said before, so say I now again, If any man preach any other gospel unto you than that ye have received, let him be accursed." (Gal. i, 6.) In those days Christian competition seems to have been very keen, and Paul gave the lead to those who followed him as to how to deal with people who preached false doctrines, which, when the Church became established, were termed heresy.

This ideal superhuman saviour of Paul had, as the result of his resurrection, left behind in the grave all that had appertained to him in the flesh. As the dead did not rise till the great resurrection day, Jesus, having appeared immediately after death, had proved himself superior to the flesh. Therefore Paul calls him the "firstborn from the dead", and the "firstborn of many brethren". Elsewhere he terms him the "first fruits of them that slept". Though he had died a Jew he had left behind on earth all that pertained to Judaism, so much so that Paul tells the Galatians, "Ye are all the children of God by faith in Christ Jesus. . . . There is neither male nor female, for ye are all one in Christ Jesus". (Gal. iii, 26.)

This being so, why should the Gentiles bother about accepting the Jewish law? Why should they undergo circumcision, or keep the Sabbath, or observe the taboos peculiar to the Jews? On these subjects Paul and Peter had diametrically opposite opinions. Paul sneers at the exclusive pretensions of Peter and makes no attempt to hide from the Galatians, in his letter to them, that he has a very poor opinion of the apostles in Jerusalem. They, on the other hand, are horrified at the idea of a Gentile securing salvation without conforming to all the ritual and taboos of Judaism.

On what ground, they asked, had Paul built up his conception of Christ? His reply was that what he preached he received by revelation, and that it was not necessary to know the Jesus who had lived on earth when he was in touch with Jesus in heaven. He had seen Jesus in his glorified body, and on this peg he hung his speculations as to what this meant for humanity.

His mind went round like this : Jesus "was made in the likeness of men and became obedient unto death." (Phil. ii, 7.) Then Paul saw him in his glorified etheric body, a bright and shining being, who could not be other than a god. Consequently, Jesus "thought it not robbery to be equal with God" (Phil. ii, 6), who to Paul was also a glorified being like the Jesus he had seen. Paul, therefore, was quite independent of any knowledge he could receive from the disciples, and never in any of his letters does he quote a saying of Jesus on earth. Why should he, when he believed that he was the chosen instrument to receive from heaven the instructions of Jesus whom he called Christ ?

Paul, therefore, makes it quite plain to the Galatians "that the gospel which was preached of me" had not come from the disciples of Jesus but from Christ in heaven. "For I neither received it of man, neither was I taught it but by revelation of Jesus Christ." He tells the Galatians that after Jesus had revealed himself to him in the first instance he "conferred not with flesh and blood" but went off to Arabia. Then he goes on to say, "Neither went I up to Jerusalem to them which were apostles before me", but instead he returned to Damascus. He evidently did not wish to face the disciples after all the bitterness he had shown towards the followers of Jesus. It was only after three years that he went to Jerusalem to see Peter "and abode with him fifteen days", but, strangely enough, he saw none of the other apostles, "save James, the Lord's brother".

This was his first meeting with Peter and James, and he did not return to Jerusalem after that for fourteen years, when he took Barnabas and Titus with him. He was influenced to make this second visit to Jerusalem, "by revelation" and communicated to them "the gospel which I preach among the Gentiles", but he did not dare to do so openly because of the opposition he knew his gospel would receive. So he tells us that he only communicated it privately to them which were of reputation. He feared a general revolt which would have deprived him of his "liberty wherewith Christ hath made us free", and that he "should run or had run in vain".

He remarks that Titus, being a Greek, managed to escape circumcision, and that though "false brethren" were brought in to spy privately on "our liberty which we have in Christ Jesus, that they might bring us into bondage", he held his own and would in no way compromise on what he taught. So he asks, "To whom gave we place by subjection?" to which he replies, "No, not for an hour, that the truth of the gospel might continue with you". Then he continues with these words which show how lightly he held the opinion of the disciples in Jerusalem: "But of those who seem to be somewhat, whatsoever they were, it maketh no matter to me. God accepteth no man's person, for they who seem to be somewhat in conference added nothing to me, but contrary when they saw that the gospel of the uncircumcision was committed unto me, as the gospel of the circumcision was unto Peter".

Paul evidently felt that he came out of the discussion the victor, because, after a sneer at James, Peter and John, "who were reputed to be pillars", he tells the Galatians that they "perceived the grace that was given unto me", and gave him and Barnabas the right hand of fellowship. So Paul returned to resume his missionary work amongst those he termed the heathen, while Peter and the rest reserved their mission for the circumcised, Paul's name for the Jews, who, by their adoption of this unnatural custom, became a peculiar people. By this foolish religious rite they set themselves apart from the rest of humanity because it acted as a deterrent to intermarrying with other tribes and nations. How bitterly they have suffered because of this exclusive rite which in ancient times they borrowed from an early Egyptian custom.

So the apostles managed to get Paul away from Jerusalem, but the quarrel did not end there, and he tells the Galatians that when he was in Antioch, which was the headquarters of the Gentile Christians who rejected the Law of Moses, he "withstood Peter face to face, because he was to be blamed". Peter evidently adopted as his motto, that when one is in Rome one should do as the Romans do, because at Antioch "he did eat with the Gentiles". James arrived later, and when this happened Peter took fright and "withdrew and separated himself, fearing them which were of the circumcision". This was too much for Paul, who challenged Peter to his face and asked him the following straight question : "I said unto Peter before them all, if thou being a Jew livest after the manner of the Gentiles and not as do the Jews, why compellest thou the Gentiles to live as do the Jews ?"

We are not given Peter's reply, but whatever he said would not have mattered to Paul, who ignored the views of the disciples at Jerusalem and continued to preach salvation "by Jesus Christ according to my gospel", to the Roman Empire. His experience at Antioch had widened his horizon, and the years which followed were almost wholly spent among its great cities, "preaching among the Gentiles the unsearchable riches of Christ". He became the inspiration of a number of communities and watched over them with a father's constant care. He gathered round him a company of faithful disciples who shared with him his missionary work, and these he sent out, some to break new ground, some to settle disputes, or to report progress and gather contributions.

Only a man of great courage, iron will, and strength of purpose could have endured what Paul suffered in order to accomplish his task of bringing the Gentiles to the knowledge of Christ. His missionary zeal made for him enemies everywhere, so much so that he was able to bring together a record of his adventures which few could equal. "Are they ministers of Christ? (I speak as a fool) I am more; in labours more abundant, in stripes above measure, in prisons more frequent, in deaths oft. Of the Jews five times received I forty stripes save one. Thrice was I beaten with rods, once was I stoned, thrice I suffered shipwreck, a night and a day I have been in the deep; in journeyings often, in perils of waters, in perils of robbers, in perils by mine own countrymen, in perils by the heathen, in perils in the city, in perils in the wilderness, in perils in the sea, in perils among false brethren; in weariness and painfulness, in watchings often, in hunger and thirst, in fastings often, in cold and nakedness." (2 Cor. xi, 23.)

And besides this he writes, "What cometh upon me daily, the care of all the churches." What an outstanding character he must have been, and how unfortunate it is that there was no Plato ready at hand to tell us something about him on the same lines as his record of Socrates. Paul was all enthusiasm, while Socrates was all wisdom, and Plato would doubtless have been repelled by his lack of logic and reasoning power. The picture Paul paints of himself reveals to us a man at times harsh and domineering, while on other occasions he is overflowing with love. At other times he is arrogant and boastful and then he becomes modest and retiring. All this is quite natural and true to certain types. Intensely hated by those he made his enemies, he was greatly beloved by his friends and admirers. One is not surprised, therefore, that the disciples at Jerusalem heartily disliked this volcanic character and had as little as possible to do with him.

According to *The Acts*, Peter came into line with Paul, though Paul's epistles give us no indication of this, and, if he had done so, one would think that Paul would have been proud to say so. For him it would have been a great victory. The story in *The Acts* is more likely to have come into being because those who succeeded the apostles saw how their case was weakened by these two divergent opinions, which gave an opening to the Jews and Pagans to scoff and deride the early Christians.

The early Jewish Christians looked on Peter as the champion and hero of their faith and never forgave Paul for including the Gentiles as "fellow heirs" of the "children of the promise". Peter to them was what Paul was to the Gentiles. When *The Acts* was written the writer evidently attempted to show that Paul and Peter had from the first adopted the same doctrine. This was done for the purpose of bringing together the Christian Jews and Gentiles, so as to present a unified Church before the Jews and Pagans. Peter's work, so far as our evidence goes, never extended beyond Antioch, and there is nothing whatever to connect him with the founding of the Church at Rome.

The unfortunate quarrel between Paul, the dauntless, and those who had known "Christ after the flesh", seems never to have been healed during the lifetime of their generation, and neither side knew who had won in the contest, as all had passed away before public opinion decided whether to accept the doctrines of Peter or Paul. After the fall of Jerusalem Paul's doctrines made headway until ultimately they swamped the exclusive teachings of the other disciples. Had Paul known "Christ after the flesh", he would have had more sympathy with the opinions of Peter, James and John, and it is difficult to imagine that one who had talked to and lived with the master on earth could, even in his wildest dreams, have turned him into the being imagined by Paul.

Just because Paul had never known Jesus, it was possible for him to imagine him as the glorious heavenly Christ before whom all the angels and demons in Heaven and Hell must prostrate themselves. If Paul had known Jesus would Christianity ever have been born? Who can say? Similar beliefs had come to surround other priestly victims before his time, so why not Jesus because of his appearance after death? If there had been no one to drive the idea home to the people the seed might have fallen on stony ground and died for want of nourishment. Paul, however, supplied the nourishment needed and because of the doctrines he preached, and the picture he painted of Jesus in heaven, the simple oral traditions relating to the master's life on earth were gradually elaborated and embellished, finally to end as the gospels as we now have them.

During the time of Paul's preaching of the "gospel of Christ", these stories of Jesus, and his simple natural life on earth, were handed down to the next generation. Paul ignored them all and never made use of a single remark or episode attributed to Jesus. If he ever heard reports of what the followers of Jesus remembered Jesus had said and done he ignored them as they were not in accordance with his revelation. Consequently, we have running concurrently amongst the Jews the story of Jesus as a man on earth, and what he was reported to have said and done, and the preaching of Paul about Jesus who was none other than the God of all the gods.

When Paul's teaching won general acceptance, the one who had been represented by his followers as "a man of God", the term in those days for a medium, was turned into an incarnate god, so that everything he did became a miracle. We shall see later on how this happened, but this is as much as we can glean from Paul's epistles about the early Church. It is all so natural and understandable, human nature being the same then as it is now. When a red-hot iron is placed in water it creates a commotion. Paul can be likened to such in the early Church at Jerusalem, and we notice throughout his epistles that he felt himself to be estranged from many, since, up to the last, certain churches would not receive him.

It is very unfortunate that we can gain so little information about the early Church and its leaders from *The Acts.* This book has been attributed to Luke, who, according to tradition, wrote the gospel which has come down to us under this name. Whoever wrote *The Acts* was either very badly informed, or careless to a degree, if the information given in the epistles is correct. One or other must be wrong, and scholars prefer to accept the facts in the epistles to those given in *The Acts.* Luke's distortion of facts is so blatant, and his ignorance of Paul's beliefs so pronounced, that one wonders wherever it was he obtained his information. It seems very improbable that he either attended the preaching of Paul or ever read his epistles. Clayton Dove devotes one hundred and sixty-three pages of his book *Paul of Tarsus* to the contradictions between Paul and *The Acts.* No argument or explanation is necessary as he wisely puts Paul's statements on the one side of the page and the account, as given in *The Acts,* on the other side.

The following two accounts of what succeeded Paul's conversion are typical examples of the differences which are revealed by such a comparison.

ACCORDING TO PAUL	ACCORDING TO ACTS
"When it pleased God to reveal his Son in me . . . immediately I conferred not with flesh and blood, neither went I up to Jerusalem to them which were apostles before me, but I went into Arabia and returned again unto Damascus." (Gal. i, 15.)	"Then was Saul certain days with the disciples which were at Damascus. And straightway he preached Christ in the synagogues, that he is the Son of God . . . Then the disciples took him by night, and let him down by the wall in a basket. And when Saul was come to Jerusalem he assayed to join himself to the disciples." (Acts ix, 19.)

The aim of this book is constructive, and it is written for the purpose of making use of every available piece of trustworthy evidence to build up a rational explanation of the origin of the Christian Faith. The contradictions, mis-statements, errors, unfulfilled prophesies, absurd and impossible stories to be found in the Bible, I pass by if they do not come within the scope of this book, as such matters are a study in themselves and quite apart from the subjects dealt with in these pages.

Just as I have had to ignore the gospels because they are of no evidential value, so I must also ignore *The Acts* for the same reason. This being so we are left with the meagre information to be found in Paul's epistles relating to the early Christian Church. These epistles must be looked at from a broad aspect, and not in detail, as they have been subject to much textual criticism, and many opinions have been expressed as to exactly what Paul wrote and what Paul meant. At one time or another every one of these epistles has been denounced as a forgery and much ink has been used to prove that this or that passage is an interpolation. A large book in itself is necessary to do this subject justice and any passing reference to these criticisms could not make clear the intricacies of the whole question. The textual criticism of the Pauline epistles is much too involved to be treated in this casual fashion.

Fortunately, such matters do not affect the theme of this book. We are not concerned with textual criticism or with the differences between what Paul told the Corinthians, and what he told the Romans. Neither are we concerned, for example, with the ridi-

culous story in *The Acts* (xxi, 18) that Paul became
humbly subservient to the disciples at Jerusalem and,
on their instructions, went through the rites of purification, to be nearly killed for his trouble. This
tale is impossible to believe of one whose doctrine
was that Christ had come to supersede the Law of
Moses, and the only reason we can imagine why this
story of Paul's humiliation was inserted was to humi-
liate him and elevate the other disciples.

All these factions and disputes, all the hatred
shewn by the Jewish Christians to Paul, are only
interesting as shewing that we are dealing with human
beings and live issues. When human nature is revealed to us at its worst and best, as it is in *The Acts*
and the epistles, we can be sure that real live men were
at work, and that Christianity is the outcome of human
experiences and human emotions, and is not the
result of the development of an old pre-Christian
Jesus cult. If the Christian Jesus, on this assumption,
never existed, why all this quarrelling and hatred over
a form of worship that had been going on for centuries
around an ancient Palestine deity of this name ? It
is always something new, which has not become
consolidated, that causes disputes and friction till the
beliefs become established. Then a tradition becomes
established which everyone accepts and about which
they do not quarrel.

What interests us at the moment is the fact that
a man called Paul really lived, and was the principal
propagator of the idea that Jesus, by his appearance
after death, had revealed to mankind that he had
conquered death. This event, in association with his
being a priestly victim, gave Paul the idea that he was

the awaited Saviour, who had propitiated the Father God and brought to an end the curse laid on humanity as the result of Adam's sin. There is no need to accept more than that this was the substance of Paul's doctrine, and on this question few today will be brave enough to cast a doubt.

This being so, the interpolations and inconsistencies between the different Pauline epistles and between them and *The Acts* do not specially interest us. Those who make a study of textual criticism have done an important work in emphasising these anomalies, but for us, who have discovered in the foregoing pages the clue to the origin of the Christian Faith, these details are unimportant. All I am anxious to do is to explain the origin of what has been an age-long mystery, and get down to the basic facts which are really essential.

Ernest Renan, to whom reference has already been made, in his treatise, *The Future of Science*, wrote : "I envy the man who shall evoke from the past the origin of Christianity. Such a writer would compose the most important book of the century." With this expression of opinion most thinking people will agree, but when dealing with religion one cannot expect the same unanimous opinion as when dealing with an accepted historical fact, or something material and concrete. The student of religion is always confronted by prejudice and ignorance, as his subject is one which influences the emotions of the people. Consequently, he does not expect to have his opinions received as they would be received about most other everyday affairs. The Supernaturalist has his own opinion as to the origin of the Christian Faith, and the Rationalist and the Materialist have their opinions. These have received full expression in the past, but, so far as I know, the Spiritualist explanation of its origin has never received serious consideration.

This book, therefore, breaks entirely new ground, and resolves the Christian Faith into something quite understandable by those who accept the reality of psychic phenomena. So far we have only discovered the germ which brought the religion into being, but there is much yet to be learned about the doctrines and dogmas to which this germ gave life. These, likewise, owe their origin to psychic phenomena, as will be discovered in the following pages. I, therefore, make the claim that *The Psychic Stream* reveals the true origin of the Christian Faith, and I believe that this will be accepted when prejudice and ignorance give place to knowledge and rational thought. Only time is now required for the claims made in this book to be admitted, and, when this happens, what has been a mystery for nineteen hundred years will become as clear as daylight.

Textual criticism, in itself, will never disclose the origin of the Faith, though it is invaluable in throwing light on how the beliefs were laid down stratum upon stratum. Thus we find that all the accretions and interpolations, which were added to the gospels and epistles during the course of Christianity's early development, are but the natural outcome of the growing belief in the truth of Paul's doctrines. These additions are mostly all symbolic, with hidden meanings, and each has an ancestor who did service to the glorification of some earlier saviour-god.

Before, however, we pass on to consider these additions which gathered round the original oral stories about Jesus, it is important that some reference should be made to Paul's claims concerning the Eucharist, which read as follows :

For I have received of the Lord that which also I delivered unto you. That the Lord Jesus the same night in which he was betrayed took bread : And when he had given thanks he brake it and said, Take, eat : this is my body, which is broken for you this do in remembrance of me. After the same manner also he took the cup, when he had supped, saying, This cup is the New Testament in my blood : this do ye as oft as ye drink it, in remem brance of me. For as often as ye eat this bread, and drink this cup, ye do shew the Lord's death till he come. (1 Cor. xi, 23.)

Some think that this is an interpolation of a date later than the time of Paul, but whether it is or not, does not alter the fact that it is based on the Pagan Eucharist and not on the words of Jesus. This being so, Paul may as well be made responsible for it as anyone else. The subject will be further discussed in Chapter VIII when further light will be thrown on how the words attributed to Jesus originated. What Paul reports is recorded by Matthew, Mark and Luke in very much the same way, and some sentences are almost word for word the same.

These gospels were, however, written at a much later date than the epistle to the Corinthians, and it is possible that the gospel writers copied the particulars from Paul, and added them to the story of the Last Supper. If this supper ever did take place it was probably nothing more than the Essene custom, observed when taking leave of a brother about to depart on a journey. Another interesting point is that Paul did not get his information from the disciples themselves, who had been present, but from the Lord direct. Peter, James and John, who, we are told, were present at the Last Supper, evidently never mentioned the matter to Paul, who says that he heard about it from heaven by a special revelation.

It must not be thought that because a person is a medium, he is wise, good and truthful, or that he follows the promptings of his control. What refers to the medium also refers to the control. Because a being has discarded the flesh body he is not necessarily good or wise. Consequently mediums have the failings of the ordinary run of people. A medium is only a human instrument of discarnate intelligences, nothing more or less, and everyone must use his own judgement on what is passed through from the other side. The mind of every medium is a citadel, which cannot be captured unless with his permission, and, when in a normal state, he is no different from any other person. His mind is thus always himself, and under his command, except when he is in the trance state.

Paul, from his writings and doctrines, shows only too clearly that the revelations which he claimed to be receiving from heaven were none other than the workings of his own mind. He doubtless sensed psychic influences and at times saw clairvoyantly and heard clairaudiently, but from these supernormal experiences he formed his own conclusions. So, with regard to this revelation which he claims to have received from the Lord, nothing is clearer than the fact that Paul applied to Christ the Pagan custom of Communion with the slain saviour-god. In spite of what he says, he may have heard from the disciples of a farewell meal to Jesus, and that they commemorated the master's memory by its repetition, in the belief that the Lord was also present. If this be so, then he Christologised it just as he did everything else.

Paul must have learned in Tarsus of the Eucharist ceremony performed by the worshippers of Dionysus, as in that city this saviour-god was widely worshipped. A similar ceremony was also observed in Tarsus to the saviour-god Mithra. Going about, as Paul did from one Pagan city to another, it is quite natural that he was influenced by the mystical symbolism surrounding this solemn ceremony. If Jesus had a farewell meal, Paul would have had no difficulty in developing this into the Pagan Eucharist ceremonial. If, on the other hand, he had heard nothing about a final meal which Jesus had with his disciples, it would also be quite natural for him to adopt the rites and ceremony surrounding the Pagan Eucharist and apply them to Jesus. As it was from Paganism that Paul obtained the idea of Jesus being a saviour-god it is very natural that he should copy the Pagan service of Communion from the same source.

Paul, therefore, was the originator of the Christian Eucharist, if this reference to it came from him, and the Gospel writers, at a much later date, copied what Paul recounted, and incorporated it in their story of the Passion. In those days, when copies were made by scribes, and accuracy was not important, the copies made from Paul's original were inaccurately done, with the result that Matthew, Mark and Luke each give different accounts of what took place at the last supper, and the words that were used by Jesus.

These accounts, however, correspond closely enough to relate them to the letter to the Corinthians. Whoever wrote John's gospel did not think that the event was worth more than a passing reference, as he passes it off with the words, "And the supper being ended". Evidently the writer of this gospel had only heard that a supper had taken place before the death of Jesus, but he knew no details, or, if he did, he did not think them worth reporting.

Paul evidently believed that the Eucharist ceremony he produced through his revelation was superior to the Pagan ceremony, but where the difference lay no one can discover. Doubtless he thought that it was quite in order to consume the bread which had become the body of Christ and drink the wine which had become his blood, but that it was entirely wrong to do so if the god in question were Dionysus, or any other Pagan deity.

Where religion is concerned feelings always run high, and Paul is typical of religious intolerance because he tells the Corinthians that eating Christ's body and drinking his blood are pleasing to the Lord, but that partaking of the body and blood of any other saviour-god is eating and drinking to a devil.

In Paul's mind the Eucharist service is a sacrifice, so he wrote to the Corinthians: "But I say that the things which the Gentiles sacrifice, they sacrifice to devils, and not to God: and I would not that ye should have communion with devils. Ye cannot drink the cup of the Lord, and the cup of devils: ye cannot partake of the table of the Lord, and of the table of devils. Or do we provoke the Lord to jealousy?" (1 Cor. x, 20.)

It is quite evident that to Paul the bread that was eaten was the actual body of Jesus and the blood that was drunk was his blood. At least, if he did not think so, he should have worded his account differently, but here again he followed the Pagan belief which has brought about endless discord in the Christian Church and came to a crisis at the Reformation.

It is well, however, here to emphasise that Paul was in exactly the same state of religious and mental development as were the Pagans and the Jews, and that Christianity, based on Paul's teaching, is in no way superior to Paganism. The eating of the body of the god, and the drinking of his blood, was a custom adopted by the Pagans from their cannibal ancestors which the Christians continued quite naturally.

The Christian outlook in the time of Paul was in every way similar to the Pagan outlook. In both cases the worshippers believed that they fortified themselves by this act of communion. In *The Odyssey* we even read that the shades of the departed had to be strengthened by drinking the blood of Ulysses before they were able to converse with him. This was the mentality of the early Church fathers, who believed that because Jehovah fed on the spirits of the burnt offerings, so likewise the other gods fed on the sacrifices made by the Pagans.

The early Christians had no doubts whatever about the existence of these other deities, as their conversion to the new Faith meant nothing more than changing over to a new god, round whom all the old beliefs had been woven, while their old gods still lived on. This change over was for no other reason than the fact that Christ meant more to them than their old gods, because his was a recent appearance on earth, which was but the prelude to his return within their generation, when he would then usher in the millennium.

This belief in the end of the age, and that Christ would shortly return to separate those who accepted him from those who rejected him, did more than anything else to establish the new belief. It brought in converts from Paganism, who evidently regarded religion in much the same light as do some people today, who consider it as a progressive revelation. Many, moreover, looked on Jesus as the incarnation of the god they had previously worshipped, and to them there was no disloyalty to the old god who was still being worshipped under a new name.

The soil was ready for the seed Paul had to plant, and his genius lay in the fact that he saw the need of the times. He supplied the Pagans with religious beliefs based on the saving power of Christ, who had recently visited this earth, had returned to heaven, and would soon be back again to judge the world. This doctrine, based on old beliefs and brought up to date, appealed to his age and, with his forceful personality, he pushed it home. Men are not regarded as great for their wisdom, or because they make fewer mistakes than others of their time, or because of their accuracy, or correct anticipation of events, but because of what they accomplish. Paul, on this generally accepted conception of greatness, was a great man, in fact one of the most outstanding men of all times. He ranks with the greatest because of his achievements, and the ultimate successful accomplishment of a great ideal, which he conceived, and of which he laid the foundation, to convert the Roman Empire from Paganism to Christianity.

Another idea which we find in Paul's epistles is the one relating to the magical value attached to the Eucharist, as he tells us that "Whosoever shall eat this bread, and drink this cup of the Lord, unworthily, shall be guilty of the body and blood of the Lord." (1 Cor. xi, 27.) This, and other warnings, are thrown out, and we find that he tells the Corinthians that because the Eucharist service in their churches has not been carried out with sufficient solemnity many are weak and sickly and not a few have died. So, in his mind, as in the minds of the Pagans of his day, this Eucharist rite acted as a charm against sickness, ill-health and death. Ignatius, the Bishop of Antioch who died in Rome about A.D. 115, said that the partaking of the Eucharist is the medicine to ensure immortality, which again suggests the idea of its having some magical effect on the communicant.

Paul believed that in some magical manner the sacrament of bread and wine became the actual body and blood of the sacrificed victim. This idea became part of the Christian doctrine when the Pagan priests brought with them, on their conversion to Christianity, the Eucharist rite which had been for thousands of years the principal ceremony in all the Pagan saviour-god religions. It was essential for Paul to accept this rite, as otherwise he could not have obtained converts to his gospel. After this happened he had to keep them from also partaking of this ceremony to their old saviour-gods. Consequently he used strong language, reminding them that the old gods had now become devils and that Christian believers "have been all made to drink into one spirit" (I Cor. xii, 13), namely Christ.

If the same belief did not prevail today in Christian churches, one could hardly credit the possibility of anyone believing that the bread and wine became the body and blood of the victim sacrificed nineteen hundred years ago, which endowed the communicant with his immortality. Even today, however, the belief is widely prevalent that the bread and wine are transformed into the Saviour's actual body and blood by reason of some magical words mumbled over the elements by the performing priest.

This idea has a long pedigree and came from people who were not only cannibals and savages, but believed that by making an image in dough of an enemy, the enemy's death could be effected if they cursed this dough image and used the correct magical form of words. There is a close connection between these two beliefs, but the actual belief in transubstantiation originated in the priests making an image of the saviour-god, which they placed on the altar. Over this they said some magical words, and then told the people that it had become the Saviour's body. This Christian belief originated in the magic age, when people believed that the priests were magicians. When superstition can reach to such depths it is not difficult to understand how, for many centuries prior to the Christian era, the catholic belief prevailed in the magical properties of the bread and wine, as representing the body and blood of a slain god, and that each time the ceremony was performed the god was slain afresh.

So when we read "Except ye eat the flesh of the

Son of Man, and drink his blood, ye have no life in you" (John vi, 53), we are not reading the words of Jesus but those of an age-old superstition, which Paul copied from Paganism, and which the writer of John's gospel copied from Paul, and put into the mouth of Jesus. Thus, by careful research and logical thought, can the mysteries of the Christian religion become understood. Only by getting down to the mentality of the days in which it was born can we appreciate the reason for its forms and ceremonies, its dogmas and doctrines. In an age of darkness they were taken over from Paganism, and nothing was ever done to adorn them since they are the same today as they were then. Besides being an age of religious superstition, it was also an age of dishonesty. It was a time when plagiarism was rife and dishonesty a virtue, if practised for the glorification of Christ. We must consequently walk within narrow limits and be prepared to accept only what links on to our chain of cause and effect, the first link of which was the appearance of Jesus after death.

Only the conclusions which follow need be accepted, as, from what has already been written, enough circumstantial evidence is available to make them not only possible but highly probable. These conclusions are that Jesus lived and died a martyr's death, the victim of the priests. At his death his etheric body parted from his physical body and entered the finer vibrations of the etheric world. Like many others who have died, he returned to earth conditions and on various occasions was seen in his etheric body. One of those who saw him was a man called Paul, who was clairvoyant and clairaudient.

From that time onwards he felt the presence of Jesus, or one he took to be Jesus, and this gave him the idea that he was the chosen instrument of the living and risen Christ. This feeling of an etheric presence, moreover, inspired him throughout all his tribulations to "preach Christ crucified", for the sins of humanity.

This influence of the spirit of Jesus so impressed his sensitive nature that he tells the Corinthians in his second letter, "Ye are an epistle of Christ, ministered by us, written not with ink, but with the spirit of the living God". (2 Cor. iii, 3.) Only a medium who felt the presence of his controlling spirit could write like this, just as only a mind living in the psychic atmosphere peculiar to mediums could write.

But God hath revealed them unto us by his Spirit. (1 Cor. ii, 10.)

Howbeit in the spirit he speaketh mysteries. (1 Cor. xiv, 2.)

God hath sent forth the Spirit of his Son. (Gal. iv, 6.)

If we live in the Spirit, let us also walk in the Spirit. (Gal. v, 25.)

We both have access by one Spirit unto the Father. (Eph. ii, 18.)

As it is now revealed unto his holy apostles and prophets by the Spirit. (Eph. iii, 5.)

Through . . . the supply of the spirit of Jesus Christ. (Phil. i, 19.)

When we recollect that to Paul the sensing of a spirit at once made him think of God we can understand why he also wrote:

Mighty signs . . . by the power of the Spirit of God. (Rom. xv, 19.)

Knoweth no man, but the Spirit of God. (1 Cor. ii, 11.)

Paul shows all the symptoms of mediumship, but in ignorance he has quite unintentionally misled people, who had no psychic knowledge, into thinking that Jehovah himself and his son (known to the Gnostics as the Logos, to the Jews as the Messiah, and to the Greeks as the Christ), had used him as their mouthpiece for the purpose of giving a new revelation to mankind. So when Paul says, "I think also that I have the spirit of God" (1 Cor. vii, 40), he is informing us of his mediumship, about which there is no doubt, and at the same time exposing his ignorance of the source of his inspiration.

Much of the language used by Paul could not have been invented or forged, it comes spontaneously from a medium who has a theological and mystical mind. The psychic atmosphere necessary to produce it surrounds the medium who feels himself in as close a touch with a higher range of vibrations as we ordinary people feel towards physical vibrations.

What Paul wrote was the outcome of his belief in the return of Jesus to earth vibrations and the impression he created on him. The one who felt it all had to write about it, and only the one who felt thus could use such language. It was Paul, inspired by the presence, but not the words, of some etheric being whom he took to be Jesus, who, with his forceful mind, laid the foundation for the new faith. He was not the mouthpiece of a controlling spirit, and what he wrote were his own ideas. Accept this and the key is in hand to unlock the mysterious door which, for nineteen hundred years, has kept the Christian Faith from facing the light of day and becoming understood.

How wanting it all is of mystery can be better understood if what Paul wrote were put into present-day phraseology. I can imagine that if Paul were present with us today, freed from the theology in which he was nurtured, he would express himself in this fashion :

I rejoice exceedingly in that I have discovered that the mystery of death is the result of psychic ignorance, due to humanity accepting conditions on earth just as they appeal to the senses. Thanks be to God that he has created some with finer senses than the majority, of which I am one. Thus I am a privileged instrument, chosen by God to convey to mankind, bound in material chains, the joyful message that there is no death. Have I not seen those called dead clothed in bright apparel, which has made me realise how we on earth live in a world within a world, quite unconscious of the teeming life beyond our clouded senses ? Have I not heard their voices proclaim that death is but a milestone on the road of infinite progression, that it is nature's greatest delusion because the fabric of human destiny is being woven on the loom of eternity, and we on earth only see the underside.

The mantle of death of which we see only the material aspect has also its etheric counterpart, and what seems the end is but the beginning of a life freed from the cares, suffering and sorrows appertaining to the carnal body. In the etheric body the one who has cast aside his contact with the physical finds the tired lines caused by the frailty of the flesh smoothed away, and age left behind, as it pertains only to the earth body. Grieve not then, my brethren, but think of the welcome which has been accorded to the one who has passed out of his material shell to join the great majority, of which we, when our turn comes, will form a part. As you sow so will you reap. Only what you are counts when you make the change, and as you fashion your mind on earth so will your place be hereafter.

Freed of the theological drapings, which mean nothing to the intelligent individual of today, this is the substance of Paul's preaching. If the Paul of the first century, with his psychic and mystical outlook, had been nurtured in present-day psychic knowledge, he could have found ample scope for his forceful pen in the psychic facts and philosophy of today, without the necessity of introducing theology into his great discovery that there is no death, no lying in Hades till some future resurrection day when life would again continue in the old material body.

By introducing Jesus, as the Christ, into his argument, and making the return of Jesus after death the touchstone, or criterion of his theology, he set alight the imagination of the Pagan world as no amount of preaching of psychic philosophy could have done in these days. The uneducated masses always require something bizarre, in order to make them think, and Paul struck the very chord for which their minds were waiting. Catholic Christianity in the third century unfortunately discarded the substance of truth revealed by Paul's mediumship, and materialised it all as the following chapters will make clear.

Mediums, like other people, have different temperaments. The majority are calm and placid and not endowed with any outstanding energy. On the other hand, a medium can have a strong, forceful personality and hold decided opinions of his own, construed from what he considers are the revelations he obtains from his controlling spirit, but which he moulds into his own opinions. Swedenborg (1689–1772), the great Swedish medium and mystic, who claimed divine authority for his revelation, is an outstanding example. Paul was also such an individual, and from the psychic and mystical knowledge he acquired during his lifetime he built up a system of thought which was the basis of Christianity.

When a medium acts as an instrument for messages from the other world he allows his own mind to become subservient to that of his etheric communicator, and thus provides a channel through which messages can be passed from heaven to earth. On the other hand, when he takes upon himself the rôle of a religious leader his own mentality comes first instead of last, he ceases to be an instrument and becomes a dynamo charged with inspiration, which he discharges in his own words, produced by his own thoughts.

When one such as this comes to the conclusion that he is the chosen instrument to impart a revelation to mankind, he ceases to be a medium in the true sense of the word. His own mind dominates the situation, but still he feels the psychic influence which affects his conclusions. Plutarch, a generation after Paul, when discussing such a condition, wrote that "The soul is an instrument for God. But this instrument is very imperfect. The thought of God must reveal itself in a form which is not its own, and in producing it through an intermediary it is filled with and interpreted by the nature of this intermediary." If he had been writing this about Paul he could not have used more appropriate words.

The "presence of our Lord Jesus Christ" (1 Thess. ii, 19), which so influenced Paul, produced speculations beyond all human reason. To consider all his mystical and theological theories is a subject in itself. They are very involved and contradictory but, when analysed, they are found to be the current gnostic and apocalyptic beliefs of the times, into which he threaded the heavenly Christ, whom he believed had actually come to earth and revealed the Father.

Paul's moral teaching was in no way superior to that of the Pagans. Plato, Aristotle, Zeno, Seneca, Plutarch, Epictetus and Marcus Aurelius produced as high a moral philosophy as did Paul. His attitude towards women was reactionary and had unfortunate effects throughout the Christian era. It was so contrary to the beautiful sentiments he expressed about love and charity that it is difficult to believe that both were written by the same hand.

Many of the mystical speculations and phrases, which he related to Christ, can be traced to the mysteries of Eleusis, the oldest and most popular of the Grecian Mysteries, "claimed to be the highest and most holy" of all the religions of Greece. The centre of this worship was at Eleusis, near Megara, close to Corinth, which Paul visited. To Demeter, "the Universal mother", "the Mother of Gods", the most ancient of Grecian divinities, the Greeks applied mystical phrases similar to those Paul applied to Christ. At her name the deepest emotions were produced. From her all things came on earth and in heaven. From her the mind and spirit of man had come, and to her it returned.

The secret wisdom connected with this form of belief, combined as it was with the death and resurrection of Dionysus, and his being seen after death, comprised the doctrines associated with the mysteries of Eleusis. The initiate was taught to "know that the Supreme Spirit sacrifices itself to manifest itself. It lives, suffers, and breathes in you and others. Look deeply within thyself; seek him and thou wilt find him".

When Paul was at Corinth he surely visited Eleusis and saw above the statue to Demeter, at the entrance to the temple, "I am the celestial light and source of souls", while above the statue to Persephone, represented as a gleaner, was written, "I am Death and hold the secret of Life". A star was in her forehead and a sheaf of wheat in her arms to symbolise her purpose. From the myth surrounding this goddess the Christian Church took over its idea of purgatory, the part of the under-world from which it was possible to reach to higher realms, as it was not a permanent abode of the departed. Persephone was the goddess of this region, and so her statue represented Hope. Another statue symbolised Love and to these Paul added Faith. Between the statues of these two goddesses was the statue of Dionysus, who was depicted as radiant, triumphant and glorious. Above his head were the words, "I am Life, Death and Resurrection, I hold the winged crown", the crown perhaps which Paul at the end of his career believed he would receive from Christ, who to him had become the resurrection and the life.

Dionysus, this heavenly being, born on earth to suffer and die for mankind, a divine creation from all eternity, humbled himself to save humanity. Through him only could one arrive at the fullness of knowledge, could one hear the inner voice, and some day become like unto this heavenly being of transcendental beauty, the divine model of humanity. "One day perhaps thou wilt resemble him" was told to believers. This, and much more in a similar strain, was what was believed in the days of Paul in Tarsus and through-out Greece.

Perhaps Paul, when in Corinth, witnessed the Festival of Eleusis, when the image of the child Dionysus was carried solemnly through the assembled crowds. His mysterious birth, life and resurrection were enacted on the stage of the amphitheatre, con-cluding with the chorus singing, "You who have contemplated the holy mystery in which the gods and man have taken part, take with you its remembrance on earth. Let it console you during life, but keep it locked in your heart like a diamond in a rock. You can receive the truth in this Sanctuary and carry its rays in the world, but whoever betrays its sublime origin will lose it forever."

Thus concluded a moving drama, witnessed by the spectators sitting on seats cut into the rock, each episode in the drama being announced before it began. The performance was gorgeously staged and was referred to as "the most beautiful sight in the world" and as "divine visions", Plato comparing it with the sights happy souls will enjoy after death. Then followed clairvoyant demonstrations by the carefully tended mediums, who were specially chosen because of their psychic power, "when a window was opened showing the fullness of the living Light suffused with divine love".

After this were seen materialisations of "fluidic figures", or etheric beings, who made use of the ectoplasm from a specially selected band of mediums who sat on the stage. So deep was the impression caused that it acted as an inspiration to men like Solon, who made the laws of ancient Greece; Themistocles, who won for Europe the greatest sea battle ever fought; Pericles, who set Athens on the pinnacle of her fame; Sophocles and Æschylus, the two greatest of Greek tragic poets; Praxiteles, who chiselled marble into human shape; Plato and Aristotle, the master minds of the ancient world; Phidias, who gave Athens the sacred Parthenon, and to countless more whose names are not to be found in history.

Paul, a man of culture, must have been steeped in this psychic and mystical thought, which he applied to Christ, who to him had fulfilled all the aspirations and speculations of the Greeks. Little wonder that his doctrine appealed more to them than to the Jews, and that he became the great apostle of Christ to the Gentiles. The times produced such a one as Paul, and he in turn produced his theories which, three centuries later, in a more material form, became the basis of the Christian creed. Given similar conditions it would all happen again; the law of cause and effect would repeat everything, so there was nothing miraculous or supernatural about it all. Everything was natural, and minds on earth, and in heaven, would again react in the same way to the same causes and effects.

These causes and effects, and these only, are necessary to explain the origin of the Christian Faith. We need nothing more but we must have nothing less. No act of faith is necessary for their acceptance. They could not have been invented in the first half of the first century of the Christian era, or at a later date. They are all too subtle to be the outcome of an intentional deception. We know that the Christian Faith germinated some time in the first century of the

Christian era, and it is generally accepted that this happened before the fall of Jerusalem. The acceptance of the foregoing essentials explains what happened subsequently, but we must have Jesus and Paul in the picture, or otherwise no rational explanation of what caused this great mental upheaval is possible.

Towards the end of his life Paul wrote to Timothy, "I have fought a good fight, I have finished my course, I have kept the faith. Henceforth there is laid up for me a crown of righteousness, which the Lord, the righteous judge, shall give me at that day : and not me only, but unto all them also that love his appearing." (2 Tim. iv, 7-9.) Here was the swan song of one who had had the satisfaction of living to see the work to which he had given his life firmly established. This is what he felt before his death, but whether he obtained the crown he desired, through the Faith and by the Grace he preached, is another matter. He would suffer disappointment to find that the Jesus he had, when on earth, turned into a god, was in reality just a human being like himself, with no power or wish to return to earth to judge humanity.

In time Paul would adjust his outlook to his new conditions, but not without some regrets for his unfortunate misconceptions on earth. Doubtless he would remember how limited is human vision and that he himself had emphasised this when he told the Corinthians that on earth we see through a glass darkly. His mistaken idea with regard to Jesus, which he left behind him on earth, continued to develop till it reached world-wide proportions, and from succeeding generations of Christians he received unbounded gratitude. Cathedrals and churches were called after him, and, in the greatest city in the world, there stands its principal church known by his name.

His doctrines have given comfort to millions who could not think out for themselves the deeper problems of life, while those who felt able to do so without his help were often killed and mutilated, tortured and persecuted, imprisoned, cursed and maligned by those who believed the doctrines of the principal apostle and ambassador of Jesus the Christ. Christians adopted his theology but forgot "whatsoever things are true, whatsoever things are honest, whatsoever things are just, whatsoever things are pure, whatsoever things are lovely, whatsoever things are of good report . . . think on these things". (Phil. iv, 8.) Christianity, however, has never been an ethical religion, but one of personal salvation through Faith in Christ.

The doctrines produced by Paul in consequence of (1) his seeing Jesus as a spirit, (2) the prevailing Gnostic and Apocalyptic beliefs, and (3) his knowledge of the Greek religion, into which he worked his heavenly Christ, ultimately overcame the opinions held by the original disciples in Jerusalem, and they are nowhere more tersely expressed than in the following passage :

Who [Jesus Christ], being in the form of God [an apparition • being looked upon in those days as a god], thought it not robbery to be equal with God : But made himself of no reputation, and took upon him the form of a servant, and was made in the likeness of men : And being found in fashion as a man, he humbled himself, and became obedient unto death, even the death of the cross. Wherefore God also hath highly exalted him, and given him a name which is above every name : That at the name of

Jesus every knee should bow, of things in heaven, and things in earth, and things under the earth ; And that every tongue should confess that Jesus Christ is Lord, to the glory of God the Father. (Phil. ii, 6-11.)

Jesus thus came to be accepted by Christians as a divine being and the saviour of the human race, equal in power and glory to Jehovah. Therefore it followed, quite naturally, that the story of the earth life of Jesus, as it was handed down, tended more and more to picture him as a god-man on earth. So much was this the case that by the time the first tradition about him found its way into print his biographers recorded what the people in their day believed, and not what had been believed by the contemporaries of Jesus.

As the years passed, and these stories were re-written and rewritten, additions were made which had the effect of slowly but surely concealing the human, and emphasising the superhuman god-man. From the time of the fall of Jerusalem this influence increased and his biographers did not cease the adorning process for some three hundred years, when the gospels, as we now have them, were finally completed.

We have now reached the Christian age, succeeding the fall of Jerusalem, and our next step forward is to consider the compilation of the gospel records, to find whence the stories came and why they were added to the original oral tradition. Paul had laid the foundation of the new faith, and the gospels represent the earth life of the man Paul had persuaded Christians to believe was now a god in heaven. From this viewpoint his biographers depicted his life on earth as that of a god-man, who, after suffering for the sins of mankind, had gone to heaven as a preliminary to his return to earth to usher in the millennium.

The psychic stream lifted Paul up from the bank of Judaic materialism, and carried him along a certain distance, but he became stranded before he realised the true meaning of his psychic experiences. Consequently, he could only think in terms of doctrine and dogma, and these were taken up by later generations to become fixed creeds, quite unrelated to what he had experienced. What the pages which follow will record are the result of his great misinterpretation of nature's revelation, as succeeding generations continued to travel along the wrong path into which he had directed them. In consequence of this wandering from the path of truth they produced legends of such an extraordinary nature that it will require the next two chapters to explain their origin and meaning. This is what I now propose to do.

CHAPTER VII

CHRISTIANITY—ITS CHILDHOOD

PART ONE

In the previous chapter we discovered the reason for the idea which gave birth to the Christian Faith. Paul, its inventor and exponent, is believed to have died about the year A.D. 68, two years prior to the fall of Jerusalem, which event resulted in the break up of the Jewish Church, the destruction of the Temple and the dispersion of the Jews. The date and place of his birth and death are quite uncertain; no one knows, so the foregoing date should be taken as only approximate.

Paul had used to the full the material at his disposal to drape round the priestly victim who had appeared to him after death as a glorified etheric being. From his deductions, evolved from the mystical speculations of the age, he produced the Christian Faith, which was tended and nursed by theologians and mystics until, two hundred years later, it became a strong and vigorous youthful personality.

Having considered its birth, our next step forward is to give some thought to its childhood, during which were produced the stories and legends relating to the man whom Paul had convinced so many people was now a god in heaven. The disruption of the Jewish Church greatly favoured the new belief, so much so that by the end of the first century quite a number of Jews had become Christians, and they, together with those Gentiles who had been converted by Paul, continued his missionary effort and so gained more converts to the new faith.

The fall of Jerusalem in A.D. 70 may reasonably be taken as the cause which firmly planted Paul's idea of Jesus in men's minds. Up till this date the Hellenised Jews, who had been influenced by the apostles, looked upon him as they looked upon other Messiahs who had preceded him. To the Jews he was just one of themselves who had been born in a natural way, lived a natural life and died a violent death. According to the gospels they looked on him as a prophet (a medium) who was able to work miracles, or, as we would say today, in whose presence psychic phenomena occurred. Consequently he received no attention from the historians, for the very obvious reason that the historians in those days considered that they had more important things about which to write.

We have already noticed two divergent lines of thought which we might term the Petrine and the Pauline. The Petrine interested only those Jews who accepted Jesus as the Messiah. Paul tells us that Jesus was seen after death by Peter, who interpreted this experience as a sign that Jesus was without doubt the Messiah who had gone to heaven preparatory to his return to earth to judge the Jewish race. Thus we find in one of the oldest references to Jesus the conjecture this idea raised in the minds of his disciples : "Ye who have followed me shall sit upon twelve thrones, judging the twelve tribes of Israel" which is the concluding sentence in *The Quelle*, to which reference has already been made.

This idea spread, and the members of the early Jesuist community seem to have lost all interest in worldly affairs, spending their time gazing into heaven so as to be the first to welcome the Lord when he returned. Consequently they distributed their property and became a communist community. Quite an intersting story is told of a couple named Ananias and Sapphira, who evidently wished to have one foot on earth and one in heaven, as they joined up with the rest but retained some of their money secretly, in order to have a nest egg in case the Lord tarried longer than anticipated. This worldly wisdom was, however, discovered by Peter, who chided them for their want of honesty. Both Ananias and his wife denied the charge and fell dead in consequence !

These ancient story-tellers always resorted to the supernatural and the dramatic to make their stories interesting to those who wanted novelty and were quite indifferent to truth. We must never forget that the people of the age with which we are dealing had minds like children, and legendary stories appealed to them much more than the facts of everyday life. They had no reasoning capacity, as we understand it, and allowed their imagination to run wild, accepting everything just as it appeared to be, without looking for the causes behind it. So the earth to them was flat, circled by the sun, moon and planets which, because they moved, were considered to be animated by the gods. For religious fervour and lack of knowledge they can be compared with the American negro, without even his advantage of living within a more intelligent community.

In a region "beyond the stars" were the principalities and powers referred to by Paul, the thrones, the seas and rivers of crystal, the cities composed of precious stones, with streets of gold, imagined by the writer of *The Revelation*. In the abyss under the earth lived another order of beings, the demons and devils, who disputed the authority of the divinities in heaven. These demons produced all the disease to which mankind was subject : blindness, deafness, insanity, as well as all the other ills of mankind, and it was one of the functions of the Messiah to subdue and reduce the demons to impotence.

These ideas, held by the early Christians, came from Egypt, Persia, Babylonia and India, whose literature displays the same ignorance of astronomy, biology, anthropology, and the other sciences, as that displayed by Jesus and his contemporaries. It is only within the last fifty years that people generally have abandoned the mistaken science of the Bible, and adopted the knowledge accumulated as the result of modern research and investigation.

Beyond the stars, whose distance from the earth was quite unrealised, there was a land of pure delight known as Heaven, where lived the gods, the archangels and the angels. It was to this abode that the Christians believed that Jesus had ascended in his physical body, and, on this flat earth, these early Messiahists anxiously awaited his return, when the law of gravity would cease to operate, to enable them all to soar upwards to meet the Lord in the air.

This was the opinion held by those primitive

Christians after Paul had hurried from land to land to spread the warning that "The Lord is at hand." (Phil. iv, 5.) In his eagerness to spread the news he made four journeys after his conversion. The first took him to Cyprus, Pamphylia, Pisidia, Iconium, Lystra, Derbe, Perga and then to Syrian Antioch, after which he visited Jerusalem. His second journey was to Galatia, across Asia Minor to Troas, Philippi, Thessalonica, Berœa, Athens, Corinth, Gallio and Syria. No sooner was this journey over than he started out again to Galatia, Ephesus, Troas, Macedonia, Achaia, Philippi and Jerusalem. After suffering imprisonment at Cæsarea he set out for Rome, where it is believed that he died.

Wherever he went he told the Gentiles that the Christ had actually come on his preliminary visit to earth, and that the age was about to end. Christ had performed his sacrifice for their salvation and was now sitting at the right hand of God, preparatory to his return, when he would judge the world and divide the believers from the unbelievers. Paul thus broke the bounds of Judaism and presented Christ to the Gentiles, not as a Jewish Messiah, but as a saviour-god who had taken the place of Dionysus, Mithra, Serapis (= Osiris), Attis, Adonis and all the rest. In order to press home his new idea he called these much revered gods demons, though, in the minds of their worshippers, they had performed the same atoning sacrifice as he applied to Christ. In place of the Pagan gods, Christians at a later date prayed to the saints, who received as much worship as ever the Pagans gave to their deities.

The general belief in the end of the age greatly

helped to spread the Pauline mystical theology, and Paul obtained converts wherever he went, so much so that he established Christian communities throughout the Roman Empire. After the fall of Jerusalem, the Jews, who had been influenced by Peter, continued to look upon him as the instrument God had appointed to lay the foundation of the Christian Church, while those who had been converted by Paul gave him this place of honour. It took many years before these two branches of the Christian Faith merged into one and produced Catholic Christianity. Before this happened, divisions and dissensions occurred, and many were the wranglings and disputes which arose amongst this youthful community which, year by year, grew in strength, becoming first a cult and finally a religion, to take its place alongside the other old-established faiths of its time.

It is not difficult to understand how in those days of vivid imagination and mystical lore, when books were not circulating and printing was unknown, the wildest stories about Jesus and his life on earth were passed round. Reading these, especially those given in the non-canonical gospels, one obtains the idea that the writers felt that nothing was too impossible to associate with the name of Jesus. It seems as if they believed that they were glorifying God by spinning the most absurd and impossible yarns about the one they looked upon as a god incarnate. Paul had so worked on their imagination that these story-tellers had no bounds to their imagination.

Consequently the stories told about Jesus after the fall of Jerusalem were vastly different from those told about him after his appearance. The forty odd

years which had elapsed from the time of his tragic
death had, as the result of Paul's enthusiasm, produced
an entirely new picture of the hero of their faith. It
was in this atmosphere of heightened imagination that
the oral stories, which had come down about Jesus,
and which had become more and more exaggerated
year by year, came to be written down. From now
until the writings of the first Christian father, Clement
of Rome, in the closing years of the first century, we
have to rely on the imaginative efforts of these early
gospel writers, and so our next step is to give serious
consideration to

THE GOSPEL LEGENDS.

The Gospels are not history or a biography, but
rather a picture produced by each succeeding generation plastering on some new scene. A bit was added
here, and a bit there, over three centuries ; thus we can
often see through what has been superimposed, and
observe what was there before. We must ever keep
in mind the time factor, and think as the Christians
thought when the part was added. To take the
gospels as history or biography is much the easier
course and to most people it is the obvious thing to
do. When reading history or biography, we are
accustomed to accept what we read as true, and to
assume that each event is chronologically arranged.

Though, to the non-critical mind, the gospels
appear as such, it is quite a delusion, which we can
only overcome by thinking as the writers thought
when adding each new piece. Thus, piece by piece,
we can tear off what has been added and so reach the

original. This we have already done, but now we are about to consider the plastering process and so we must attune ourselves to the mentality of those who performed it.

Much thought and study has been given by scholars to determine when the first records of the life of Jesus were committed to writing. Obviously it is impossible to determine this with any exactness, because, in those days, documents were not dated and it is only by internal evidence that an estimate can be made. The generally accepted opinion of critics, comprising the moderate school, is that *The Gospel of Mark* came into existence about A.D. 70, *The Gospel of Luke* some time between A.D. 80 and 95, *The Gospel of Matthew* about A.D. 100, and *The Gospel of John* about A.D. 110.

These dates, however, must be looked upon very much in the light of guesses, but the matter is of no very great importance. What we can say is that within the thirty years from the fall of Jerusalem, which brings us to the beginning of the second century of our era, various documents came into circulation relating to the earth life of Jesus, who was believed to have died, either by crucifixion or by being hanged on a tree, at the time when Pontius Pilate was Governor of Judaea, some forty years prior to the fall of Jerusalem. Most students of Christian tradition would be willing to endorse such a statement, and this is enough for our purpose.

As to the authors of these four gospels, tradition assigns *The Gospel of Mark* to the John Mark who is mentioned in *The Acts* and *The Epistle to Timothy*. Irenaeus (130–202), who was Bishop of Lyons, tells us that John Mark, some time after the death of Peter, laid the foundation for the gospel which goes under his name, but as Irenaeus was relying on tradition, and as a century is quite long enough for tradition to become valueless, his opinion must be taken for what each one thinks it is worth. Tradition has assigned *The Gospel of Luke* to Luke, the companion of Paul, referred to by him as "the beloved physician", but no one has the slightest idea as to who wrote the gospels of Matthew and John.

The first tradition concerning Jesus was written down in Aramaic and later translated into Greek. The sources used by Matthew and Luke we have already discussed in Chapter V. Neither Mark, which is considered to be the oldest gospel, Matthew, nor Luke are original documents, the writers having relied upon previous written sources of information. Many people think erroneously that the gospels were written for the purpose of establishing a permanent record of the life of Jesus, and that everything recorded in them is accurate, having been, so to speak, dictated by God to those under whose names the gospels have come down to us.

For this belief there is no evidence whatever. For one thing a revelation from heaven can only come to the one who receives it. After he writes down his revelation it ceases to be a revelation to those who read it, because they have only his word that what was written came by revelation or under inspiration. The writer may have been mistaken in making such a claim, or may have made a false claim to deceive his readers.

No claim, however, is made in the gospels that

their writers were in any way different from other biographers, and the text, "All scripture is given by inspiration of God" (2 Tim. iii, 16), was an opinion expressed by Paul in reference to the Jewish Book of the Law, and had no reference whatever to what is now called the New Testament, which was not in existence when this was written. Only very slowly did the books which now comprise the New Testament come to be looked upon as documents different from other literature, and, in the days in which they were written, and for three centuries later, they did not receive the reverence which Christians, in the centuries which followed, bestowed upon them.

For this reason great liberties were taken with the original documents, so much so that the scribes, when a new story became current about Jesus, included it in the copy they were making, or used it to embellish an already existing story. Besides this want of reverence for the gospel records it must be remembered that they were not written for the purpose of enlightening or edifying future generations of Christians. When they were written the Christians were daily awaiting the return of their Lord. They took little interest in the past, and for that reason were quite indifferent as to the accuracy of what was being told about the earth life of the one they were daily expecting to appear as their judge, surrounded by a glorious heavenly host. These Christians gave no thought to future generations, because they believed that at any time Christ would return and usher in the millennium.

What, then, was the reason behind the publication of the first gospel, known as *The Gospel according to Mark*? Obviously it was written for no other purpose than to prove to the Jews that Jesus was the Messiah and the Son of God. Quite possibly, prior to the fall of Jerusalem, there were in circulation certain sayings attributed to Jesus, which formed the basis of what is now called *The Quelle*, but, if this were so, their purpose was only for moral edification and preparation for his return. No attempt was made in this early document to give any facts about the career of Jesus, and, only as controversy with the Jews increased, was it felt necessary by the Christians to have some apologetic literature beside them to enable them to counter the criticisms of their Jewish neighbours. *The Gospel of Mark* was the result of this necessity.

Evidently this gospel was not considered sufficient, and, for two hundred years after the fall of Jerusalem, a regular deluge of gospels appeared, written by Christians for the purpose of glorifying their Lord in a world where critics, both Jewish and Gentile, were seizing every opportunity to disparage and make light of their claims. Besides the canonical gospels according to Matthew, Mark, Luke and John, which were officially adopted at the Council of Carthage in A.D. 397 as those most suitable for inclusion in the canon of the New Testament, there were many other gospels and epistles which were rejected as not conforming to the then orthodox opinion. Those rejected are too numerous to mention by name as their number comes to over eighty, but the majority are not now extant.

When reading these non-canonical gospels, acts and epistles, one feels as if one were reading the books which comprise the New Testament, with this difference : that new stories are told, and the old stories are greatly improved upon by being made even more supernatural than those which have come down to us. In *The Gospel of the Birth of Mary* we find that she, like Jesus, was miraculously born of a barren mother, who was told by an angel that this would come about. This gospel gave the impulse to the veneration of Mary, which ended in her adoration as the Queen of Heaven. Here we have an example of a goddess created because she produced a child who became a god after death. From what is reported of her she seems to have been an infant prodigy like her son, about whom we shall learn more from the apocryphal gospel relating to his infancy, which will be quoted later on in this chapter.

The Gospel of Nicodemus gives us many new details about the trial and death of Jesus, and a long description of what he experienced when he descended into Hades. Conversations are recorded between different devils, and what Jesus said to them and they said to him. Its interest to us lies in its vivid description of the conquest of the Devil and his angels, which ends with these words : "Then the King of Glory, trampling upon death, seized the prince of Hell, deprived him of all his power, and took our earthly father Adam with him to his glory." In its twenty-two chapters one realises the fear the curse on Adam had on our Christian ancestors, and the tremendous relief they felt in the belief that Christ had conquered and subdued the Devil and his angels, thereby returning once and for all man's original birthright—everlasting life. It should be read by those who today whittle down the Christian Faith to one of ethics, and believe that Jesus came to earth as an example to teach us how to live.

Nothing is clearer than the fact that the Christian religion rests on the foundation laid for it by Paul, that "As in Adam all die so in Christ shall all be made alive." This sums up Christianity in as few words as possible and nothing less can be Christianity. Those who do not believe this are not Christians and have no right to bear the name. The creed mentions the descent of Jesus to Hell (which should read Hades) because of this all-important belief, and *The Gospel of Nicodemus* makes it clear why it does so.

The various apocryphal epistles are after the style and wording of the epistles in the New Testament, and contain moralising and admonitions to the churches and people to whom they are addressed, together with similar mystical and theological expressions. In the *Epistle of Barnabas* we discover a new expression which likens Jesus to a cow: "This heifer is Jesus Christ the wicked men were to offer to death". We are accustomed to his being called a lamb because he took the place of the lamb on the altar and, as heifers were also slain as sacrifices, there is no reason why he should not be likened to a cow, or a bull, or a goat. We find mythology full of gods being likened to animals and Christian mythology is no different from any other.

In this epistle we also find that Jesus abolished the rite of circumcision. "It is abolished" as it came through "Abraham looking forward in the spirit to Jesus circumcised". So, with the arrival of Jesus it "was not of the flesh" any more. This must have been a great relief to believers and it prepared the way for the adoption of the new faith by the Gentiles. Many Jews must also have been influenced to become

Christians for the same reason, as they doubtless felt that this rite made them a peculiar people and apart from the rest of mankind.

In the early Christian centuries all these apocryphal gospels and epistles were in circulation alongside those which are now included in the New Testament. The ordinary use of the word apocryphal means fictitious, but that meaning is secondary, as originally it was used in the first Christian centuries as an honourable title and had no such meaning as is now attached to it. In its preliminary significance the word was used to describe certain highly esteemed writings containing esoteric doctrines which were kept secret by the initiated in select circles. These apocryphal books were believed to contain the true contents and meaning of the Christian revelation and some were looked upon as coming direct from God.

Dr. Wake, Archbishop of Canterbury, in his book, *The Apostolical Fathers*, published in 1817, states that there cannot be any doubt that these epistles deliver to us the gospel of Christ and that they ought to be received, if not with equal veneration, at least with little less respect than the sacred writings contained in the New Testament. These writings were read in the early Christian churches and commanded as much respect as those now termed canonical. Eventually, however, in the fourth century, a list was drawn up by the ecclesiastical authorities in which there was a clear-cut distinction between books which were to be read and those which were not to be read. Those we now call apocryphal were then given the term heretical and gradually their use as Church literature terminated.

Looking back, we can clearly realise how, when a central authority came into being, it was found necessary to codify and organise the Christian Faith. Prior to this everyone was at liberty to conceive the meaning of the death of Jesus as he pleased. The early Christian community was a heterogeneous body of opinion, their one and only point of connection being their belief in the death and resurrection of Jesus.

From the second century the gospels of Matthew, Mark, Luke and John received greater respect generally than any of the other publications. As time went on they were altered and interpolated, so that they thus continued to represent the main stream of Christian doctrine. Consequently, when a final decision was made at the Council of Carthage, as to what books should be accepted as canonical, these were adopted. The four gospels, accepted by the Church, therefore represent the orthodox opinion at the end of the fourth century, but they were then very different from the earlier editions, as alterations and additions had been made in the interval to conform with changing doctrine, a prominent example being found in the First Epistle of John (v, 7). This is the only reference in the New Testament to the unity of the Trinity and is only to be found in late copies of this epistle, no reference being made to it in any Greek manuscript.

The dogma of the Trinity was, however, not allowed to pass without causing such discord as nearly split the early Church in two. In consequence, the Council of Nicaea was convened in 325 to settle the controversy as to its meaning. Because more priests at this Council voted for than against, the present orthodox definition of the Trinity was finally adopted as part of the Christian Faith, but we shall read more about this question in Chapter X.

For three centuries after the fall of Jerusalem, Christian beliefs were in a state of flux, and many were the different sects which emerged with their own views about Christianity, and for what it really stood. We shall discover in Chapter IX how a central authority gradually developed to become the orthodox Church, with the power to decide which doctrines and dogmas were to be accepted and which rejected.

After Paul laid the foundation of the Christian Faith it took three centuries to build the structure. Many and varied were the views of the different architects who made it their business to add to this crazy erection. Till the fourth century there was no central authority and one church would accept something from one quarter and reject it from another. There was no settled opinion and an assembly of bishops revealed very divergent opinions.

From the foregoing it will be realised how unstable was the erection of myth and legend, dogma and doctrine, during the first four Christian centuries, as the beliefs which were to lead to salvation were quite as fluid as were the stories told about Jesus. With no central authority to edit these tales, and reject what was doubtful, almost everything miraculous that could be imagined about Jesus, from the time of birth to his death, was believed. Only a portion has been preserved to us in the four canonical gospels, and that portion covers his birth, an episode when he was twelve years of age, about a year of his missionary life, his death, resurrection and ascension. The apocryphal gospels and epistles consequently convey to us a more extensive picture of the beliefs held in these early Christian centuries.

From what we read of the views of the Church fathers in the fourth century, they evidently did not consider that Jesus had obtained his full godhead until his baptism, after which he was a fully developed god-man. So they selected the gospels of Matthew, Mark, Luke and John, which were mostly devoted to his career after his baptism. This was the best material they had at hand, as the Christian outlook in the first century, when the information was available, was not conducive to history making. The eyes of the faithful were so directed towards heaven, in anticipation of the Lord's return, that interest in what had previously happened was very slight. So much was this the case that when the information about Jesus was really wanted it was not available, and had to be imagined.

The early Christians were insistent that before their generation passed Christ would return to judge the world. Their adversaries scoffed at them and, as Justin Martyr tells us, accused them of imagining a Christ to suit their desires. Christ did not come, and so the Christians were wrong, and the heathen, whom they so despised, were right. This delusion, one of the principal planks in the Christian system of belief, has gone on during every generation throughout the Christian era.

Till the Renaissance few, if any, in Christendom doubted the return of Christ in great glory within their lifetime. This extraordinary idea, prevalent from the first century onwards, obtained such a grip of people's minds that it became a regular part of their religious food, in fact it was nothing less than an obsession. In the new age, which was to succeed the general resurrection and the judgement, there was to be no marriage or work, and so celebacy and idleness became fashionable. Century after century this delusion continued, and expressed itself from time to time by a kind of mass hysteria when the ultra-credulous sold or parted with their worldly possessions, and set out to some spot in order to be the first to welcome the Lord on his return to earth.

In the second century we read of a certain bishop making the announcement that on a specified Sunday the Lord would come to gather together his elect. Hundreds parted with everything they possessed, marriage ceased, and, when the appointed day arrived, there was gathered together a large company at the selected place, without food or water, so great was their faith. Nothing happened, large numbers starved, and those who had sufficient strength to return had nowhere to go as they had parted with their houses and everything they possessed.

This is but an example of what has happened time and time again over the last nineteen centuries, up to the present day. In our own lifetime everyone can call to mind some instances of its continued existence. The other day two women in my neighbourhood, in comfortable circumstances, parted with everything they had, because they believed, in spite of all these disappointments of the past, that, like the inveterate gambler, they had found the system to enable them to calculate correctly the exact day for this great event. They are now in poverty and dependent for their existence upon their relations.

Let us, however, return to the first century which set Europe ablaze with an illusion such as has never before afflicted mankind. The glorification of the new-found Saviour and Redeemer, in the eyes of a hostile world, was the reason behind the publication of the numerous gospels written about Jesus. That is about the only thing of which we can be certain. They were written about Jesus, but they were certainly not biographies of his life. A biographer wishing to write a biography of Alexander the Great, of Plato, of Charlemagne, and all the historical figures of the past, can do so because he has the materials at his disposal, in the form of more or less authentic documents, which enable him to paint a picture in words of his subject. With Jesus, however, his greatness came about after his death, not because of his life on earth, and for that reason there are no authentic documents to enable us to write his biography. His followers did not even know when or where he was born.

His interest to believers lies in the beliefs which came to surround him after his death, not in the facts of his life. Cut out the supernatural part regarding Jesus and the whole story falls flat, it becomes devoid of interest, and everyone would become quite indifferent as to whether he ever lived or not. A story of a Jew going about healing the sick and speaking platitudes is of no interest to anyone, but if it is believed that this Jew is really a divine being who lived on earth as a god-man, died to reconcile man with God, and appeared after death as a sign that the reconciliation was complete, then it becomes a very personal matter, and one of intense interest to everyone. That is the hold Jesus has over Christians, not his life on earth, which is really of secondary interest.

He had to live on earth in order to suffer and die. If he had not lived he could not have died, and if he had not died he could not have reappeared. If he had not reappeared after death he never would have been heard of, and Christianity would never have been born. Herein lies the difference between Jesus and the historical characters of the past. If he had not re-appeared, what is now called Christendom would be thinking that all believers had been saved from the curse of God, or the gods, by a previous Saviour, assuming, of course, that intelligence had not in-creased at any greater rate than it has done over the past nineteen hundred years.

We need not speculate as to whether, if Christi-anity had never been born, science would have developed more rapidly than it did. A case can be made out that it would. There would have been no incentive to abolish learning as it would not have been thought that everything that should be known was in the Bible, and that the age was at an end. On the other hand, those who broke away from Christianity and became Mohammedans adopted towards their holy book, *The Koran*, the same narrow attitude as the Christians adopted towards their Bible, claiming that outside *The Koran* nothing was worth knowing. Therefore it would perhaps be safer to say that every religion is the outcome of the mentality of the people, and that, as the religion is, so are the people mentally.

Delusions, however, have a retarding effect, and the Christian delusion that there was nothing further to strive for on earth certainly did not make for better homes and the making of the most of what nature puts at our disposal. When the people were almost daily expecting the second advent, why should they strive, especially when their Lord had told them to take no thought for the morrow ? So Christendom slipped into the dark ages when the people lived in hovels and gave their money and time to building Cathedrals and Churches. Europe became a vast camp of monasteries and convents, in which the holy idle were supported by a peasantry living like animals in filth, serfdom and degradation.

Mankind, after giving thought to his material needs and pleasures, devotes a great amount of his time to thinking about his destiny. Just as of old, he still yearns to pierce the veil, and yet so few realise that during the past hundred years enough evidence has accumulated to solve the mystery which has forever kept mankind in fear and bondage. Though the fear of death still keeps a mighty organisation of priests in being, it really need not if all were intelligent enough to absorb the psychic knowledge of our times.

From over the seemingly wide unending sea have come floating on its waves twigs and branches, to show that life exists beyond the horizon and that the seemingly cruel sea is just a channel, a span from life to life. Where the dead have gone reason now can go, and from the further shore the revelation has come. There is now no need to feel that life is but a narrow vale between two bleak eternities. No longer need we strive in vain to look beyond the heights, nor cry aloud and hear only the echo of our wailing cry. No longer need we say that from the lips of the unreplying dead there comes no word to calm our fears. The mystery of death is ended for those who take the trouble to enquire.

Because of this fear of death mankind has endowed his religious beliefs with a sacredness so holy that it has been a crime for anyone even to attempt to prick the bubble. The veil which hangs between the two worlds has only been lifted to the few, and so the great majority are in considerable doubt as to what really exists on the other side, though they feel instinctively that something is there which intimately concerns them. If everyone had been endowed with the gift of clairvoyance and clairaudience, and could see and hear the other order of existence which surrounds us, organised religion would never have been. Nature, however, has ordained that we live on one plane of existence at a time, but to some it has given the power to sense what is beyond the ken of ordinary people, while it has endowed most with the feeling that something lies on the other side of the boundary called death.

Only those with deficient sight require spectacles, just as those with deficient hearing require an ear trumpet. The spectacles and the ear trumpet are the aids invented to remedy what nature withholds from us, and can be likened to the world's man-made organised religions. If everyone had good sight and hearing, spectacles and ear trumpets would be unnecessary, just as organised religion would be unnecessary if everyone were clairvoyant and clairaudient. Mediums, however, are nature's aids for the psychic deficiencies of ordinary people, and, when they increase sufficiently, what nature reveals through them will take the place of religious doctrines.

We are, however, so constituted that everything about us is relative and not absolute. Normally our hearing and sight are relative, appertaining only to the range of vibrations into which we were born. Our sight is limited to the physical range of vibrations having a frequency between thirty-four thousand and sixty-four thousand waves to the inch, or between four hundred and seven hundred and fifty billion waves to the second. This, of all the innumerable etheric waves making up the universe, is what impinges on our eyes. The warp and woof of an infinite number of etheric waves make up the universe. Where they begin and where they end we know not, but our sense of sight can only catch so minute a fraction that it might be compared with what an inch is to a mile. This leaves ample accommodation in the universe for other worlds and orders of existence. The order which can be seen by clairvoyance is the one next in the scale of vibrations beyond the physical world.

Each physical body is just an open network of electrons and protons. What is between we term space. If this space were eliminated and all the electrons and protons in the body were brought together they would not occupy a greater space than does a dot made by the sharpest pencil. Our bodies are, therefore, mostly made up of space, just as is the universe to our physical eyes. Consequently there is ample room for an etheric body, vibrating at a higher frequency than the physical, to find its place in company with our physical body. We know that this duplicate body exists and parts from the physical body at death, as clairvoyants can see the etheric body separating from the physical and becoming a separate entity. When this takes place the physical commences to decompose, as the mind, which is the individual, and the etheric body have withdrawn the support which kept the physical particles together.

To our eyes the vibrations composing the physical body seem to occupy all the space available, but we now know that each body is capable of accommodating numerous other ranges of vibration besides the physical. Paul believed that each one of us had what he termed a spiritual body, as he tells us "So also is the resurrection of the dead. It is sown in corruption ; it is raised in incorruption : It is sown in dishonour ; it is raised in glory : It is sown in weakness ; it is raised in power : It is sown a natural body ; it is raised a spiritual body. There is a natural body, and there is a spiritual body." (1 Cor. xv, 42.)

As this word spiritual is also used by Christians when expressing their religious emotions, it is better to use the Greek word and term this finer duplicate body our etheric body, and then there is no chance of misunderstanding. Those who have passed on, and come back, tell us that each physical cell of our body is held together by an etheric duplicate, and that this etheric counterpart is the real body which parts from the physical body at death.

Clairvoyants can see the radiation which the etheric structure produces. This radiation is termed the aura and surrounds every living body. Every living thing has an etheric body and an aura of different degrees. The etheric body, composed of these etheric cells, is, therefore, a counterpart of the physical body, and, when death takes place, the individual slips out of his physical sheath and functions in this duplicate body, which is controlled by the same mind as controlled the physical body. The mind accompanies the etheric body to its new abode, composed of vibrations in harmony with the etheric body. Those who have lost arms, legs, or have other defects, find these remedied when they become separated from the physical body, as it was only the physical that was imperfect, not the etheric. When mind first begins, in the embryo stage, to gather round it physical matter, it works through the etheric duplicate as it requires this link in order to make contact with the physical.

Thus we are all etheric beings, and, because of this, the earth is but the nursery stage in our career. We are but at the beginning of a journey, and most people need some guide to tell them where they are going and how best to get there. These guides are known as religion and philosophy. Every one of us is relatively a child, going through our earth life for the purpose of preparing us for a fuller life hereafter. This can all be put in much greater detail and with more elaboration. It is something apart from the subject of this book, though intimately related to it. In my trilogy *On the Edge of the Etheric*, *The Rock of Truth* and *The Unfolding Universe* I have set out the Spiritualist philosophy which, in the light of our greater knowledge, enables us now to understand our origin and destiny, and the reason for existence, besides making it possible to understand the cause and history of the world's religious ideas.

In the times we are considering, our ancestors had not the capacity, or the necessary knowledge, to enable them in a rational way to explain the mysteries of existence. True, the philosophers attempted to do so but even they fell short of reality. Just as to-day the masses prefer religion to philosophy, so, in those old days, only the minority were influenced by philosophy. Symbolic legends, magical occurrences and supernatural stories gave them the comfort for which they were mentally fitted. In our own day philosophy still appeals only to the few, and the great majority are religiously, not philosophically, inclined. Those to whom neither religion nor philosophy appeals are indifferent to both because they have advanced beyond the orthodox religion of our times but not sufficiently to be helped by philosophy. Thus they lack a guide to life, and, without one or the other, they are adrift without a compass to enable them to set their course.

Nineteen centuries ago philosophy was reserved for the minority and the great majority were wedded to religion. They had behind them the stories of the gods and their doings on earth and in heaven. Just like children in the nursery, who appreciate fairy-tales instead of stories true to life, they loved these tales about the doings of the gods, and, when it came to be believed that Jesus was also a god, it was natural that what was told of the other gods should also be told of him. All the material was at the disposal of the gospel narrators, stored up in the Theological College at Alexandria.

Between the true Jesus and ourselves there therefore rises up this thick mist of legend, and but for Paul we would have nothing of any value to enable us to form an idea as to his identity. Paul created this supernatural being out of the natural man he tells us was born a Jew, and those who followed after Paul adorned and glorified his creation till the original man ceased to be human and became a god-man.

In the gospels we have only echoes of the real Jesus, but, from what Paul tells us, it is evident that he was born like other human beings (Rom. i, 3), and received the rite of circumcision as did all other Jewish boys (Rom. xv, 8). His parents, whom the gospels tell us were Joseph and Mary, evidently had other children, and in their time they were all looked upon simply as ordinary human beings like the rest of us. We are also told that Joseph was a carpenter, but, whatever he was, it is evident that he was a man of the people, and that Jesus was brought up like most other Jewish boys.

Evidently Jesus, on reaching manhood, was burdened, like so many others of his time, with the weight of sin, as we are informed that he received baptism at the hands of a religious zealot called John, later to be known as John the Baptist. Quite probably Jesus had the gift of healing and also psychic power, and this in a way set him apart from the common run of humanity. In any case, for some reason or other, he felt himself compelled to adopt a line different from his contemporaries, and came to be looked upon in the light of a teacher and healer.

In those days, as in our own times, anyone with psychic power, and with something new to say, could always attract followers ; so Jesus wandered from place to place accompanied by those who looked upon him as a wonder-worker. The atmosphere was loaded with anticipation of the coming Messiah, and he may have adopted the idea that he was the only one who could save Israel, if the people would but follow his teaching. However, this state of affairs did not last long, and, after a year of wandering throughout the country, he was arrested and put to death.

There is nothing unreasonable or impossible in this, as it is all quite natural and in keeping with the times. We have already discovered why Jesus was arrested and what happened after his death. What now concerns us are the stories and legends which gathered round his name, in the latter part of the first century, many of which will be found to contain the bones of psychic truth. This psychic basis it will be our business to discover.

In a previous chapter it was remarked that all the stories about Jesus, and the earlier saviour-gods, had been told the wrong way round, that the writers should have commenced by telling of their re-appearance and then how, because of this, they had come to be looked upon as gods, when wonderful stories about their lives on earth were woven round their names. It will be noticed that this mistake of commencing at the wrong end is not repeated here. Because of what is related in Chapters V and VI the gospel legends came into being, and these we shall now consider in detail, in the order in which the various stories occur in the gospels, beginning with

THE BIRTH LEGEND.

The New Testament opens with the words, "The book of the generation of Jesus Christ, the son of David, the son of Abraham", and then follows the pedigree of Jesus from Abraham to Joseph. When we reach the end we find to our surprise that the fifteen verses we have read have not given us the genealogy of Jesus, because Joseph was not his father, and so we have been led down a blind alley for no purpose whatever. Then starts quite a new story about one called Mary, who, we are told, was the wife of Joseph, but a few verses on she is referred to as only his espoused wife, which quite alters matters as he found out before he married her that she was about to have a child.

This gave him some concern but, as he dreamed that an angel came and told him that all was well, because the father was the Holy Ghost, he decided to marry the woman, but did not treat her as his wife until the child was born. In this dream Joseph was told to call the child "Jesus", so that the prophecy that a virgin would produce a child and call his name "Emmanuel" might be fulfilled, which contradiction is not explained. So much for what Matthew has to tell us. We now pass on to read what Mark has to say on this subject and note with some surprise that this very important episode is not referred to and that he starts the life of Jesus from his baptism.

The third gospel by Luke does not commence with the pedigree but brings it in later on, as he has something to tell which the other three gospel writers either did not know about or did not believe : the story of the miraculous birth of John, who came into being after his mother Elizabeth was an old woman. His father Zacharias, a priest, was struck dumb for nine months until the child was born because he asked the angel Gabriel how such an event was possible.

Six months later Gabriel visited Mary and announced to her the news that the Lord had highly favoured her, which, instead of pleasing her, greatly troubled her because it meant that she would be an unmarried mother. Gabriel also told her that this would come about by her being impregnated by the Holy Ghost, who would overshadow her, and that she would give birth to one to be called "Jesus", who would occupy the throne of his father David and reign for ever. Joseph, who, we are told, was descended from David, was not the father of Jesus, but no explanation is given as to how Jesus could be descended from David when his mother was of the house of Aaron, and, in any case, the Jews never considered their descent on the female line. Gabriel's description of the coming Messiah, as he delivered it from Jehovah, in no way resembles the Christian Christ, and, moreover, Jesus never occupied the throne of David and, instead of being a king, he died a criminal.

Mary then starts off to tell her cousin Elizabeth the news, but no mention is made of her telling her future husband Joseph, who is brought into the story when we are told that Joseph and Mary set off for Bethlehem to be taxed. The writer of *The Gospel of John*, like the writer of Mark, either did not know this story, or did not believe it, as he makes no reference to the birth of Jesus and commences his life-story at his baptism.

The two accounts in Matthew and Luke, it is well to remember, were added to quite a different story, certainly not earlier than a hundred years after the supposed event happened, very much as if we started the story today of someone born in 1839 without a father and, when asked to explain how this came about, we reply that his mother had been over-shadowed by the Holy Ghost. No one would believe us and yet Christians have tenaciously believed the story of the unnatural birth of Jesus for eighteen centuries. This anomaly therefore requires some explanation.

When Jesus, in the minds of his worshippers, became a god it is obvious that he could not be the natural child of his father and mother. From the time his followers believed him to be the Messiah, which was shortly after his death, the tendency developed to think of him more as a heavenly being than as a man, and so gradually the details of his earth life were forgotten and had to be imagined. So these second-century Christians, because they had by that time come to the conclusion that Jesus was a god from conception, and not from baptism, as had been believed up till then, adopted the story which in those days was attributed to the Pagan saviour-gods, of how their mothers had become miraculously impreg-nated by a god.

The childish simplicity of those who manufac-tured the gospels is apparent to all who study the matter carefully because, in an earlier stratum of tradition, we read that the father and mother of Jesus did not understand what he meant by saying, "I must be about my Father's business." (Luke ii, 49.) We even read that his friends on one occasion thought that he was insane (Mark iii, 21), and yet his mother, who seems to have been present, never revealed on this golden opportunity that he was in reality a divine being. His contemporaries believed that he had a

human father and mother, brothers and sisters (Matt.
xiii, 55), and, in accordance with Eastern custom,
"James the Lord's brother" became the President of
the first church in Jerusalem because he was the
brother of Jesus, and for that reason alone.

All this, which comes from the oldest and therefore the most reliable tradition about Jesus, has been
allowed to remain, while on to later editions the story
was added that the mother of Jesus was a virgin.
Consequently Joseph, hitherto accepted as his father,
had no participation in his birth, though the earlier
account of his lineage through Joseph to David
remains. Neither Peter nor Paul knew anything of the
virgin-birth story, and it was not added until they, and
all the other apostles and contemporaries of Jesus,
had passed away. During the lifetime of Jesus he
was known as the son of Joseph, and this was accepted
by everyone for several generations after his death.

Christians, in accepting the story of the virgin
birth, reject Paul, the creator of their faith, because he
tells us that Jesus was born "of the seed of David
according to the flesh" (Rom. i, 3), and again that he
was "of the seed of David . . . according to my gospel"
(2 Tim. ii, 8). This conclusively proves that the
genealogy of Jesus, through his father Joseph back
to David was the belief current in the time of Paul,
and that the story of the Holy Ghost overshadowing
Mary was a later addition. Nowhere in the New
Testament, except in the birth narratives of Matthew
and Luke, is the virgin birth of Jesus referred to, his
descent from David through Joseph always being
accepted.

We are therefore not surprised to find that in the

earliest Greek and Syrian manuscripts the pedigree of Jesus in the gospel of Matthew ended with these words, "Jacob begat Joseph and Joseph begat Jesus". Later versions altered this to read, "and Jacob begat Joseph, the husband of Mary, of whom was born Jesus, who is called Christ", and added the story about the Holy Ghost. In any case the genealogical table in Matthew, giving twenty-six names, is quite different from the one given in Luke, with forty-two names between David and Joseph, even down to the father of Joseph, Matthew stating that his father was Jacob (Matt. i, 16), and Luke that his name was Heli (Luke iii, 23).

When these two gospels do not agree as to the grandfather of Jesus, few thinking people will be prepared to accept what they say of his pedigree to David, especially when it omits various kings in the direct line from David, and also states that Josias begat Jechonias, when he was his grandfather, not his father. This family tree, which says one thing in Matthew and another in Luke, was a fabrication for the purpose of relating the new-found Messiah to David, quite regardless of the truth, so that prophecy might be fulfilled. Luke traces the descent right back to Adam, "who was the son of God", for the evident purpose of linking up Jesus with Adam, the two names on which the entire Christian Faith rests.

The Gospel of John, produced in the second century, shows that the belief in Jesus's descent from David still existed when it was written, because we read, "Hath not the scripture said, that Christ cometh of the seed of David and . . . of Bethlehem" (John vii, 42). Another second-century document, *The Acts of*

Judas Thomas, refers to Judas Thomas as a twin brother of Jesus, and *The Acts of Pilate*, of the same century, categorically states that Jesus was the natural and legitimate son of Joseph and Mary. Jesus himself, however, is reported as denying any descent from David (Matt. xxii, 42), just as he denied that he was God (Matt. xix, 17).

Jesus was therefore either wrongly reported, which means that the gospels do not record what is true, or he said what is reported and those parts of the gospels which make out that he was descended from David, and was also a god-man, are not stating what is true. This is just another instance of how the Messiah and the god idea came to be added to the original record of a naturally born man. If it had been done with a deliberate attempt to deceive, surely the editors would not have been so simple as to leave in passages which directly contradicted the later additions. In their days minds were not critical, and the gospels were just plastered with one new belief after another as each developed, not for the purpose of convincing future generations, but to strengthen the faith of contemporary Christians and give them new ammunition to hurl against their opponents. Their thoughts centred on the latest invention and ignored what had gone before.

We can trace this development in the gospels without difficulty as Jesus, during his lifetime, was accepted by everyone as the son of Joseph and Mary and he himself is never reported as doubting this fact. When, after his death, he came to be regarded as the Messiah in the eyes of his followers, he had to become related to King David, because prophecy had decreed that the Messiah would be of the seed of David. The third and last stage was the addition of the story of the Holy Ghost being his father, which was added for the purpose of enhancing his status as a god-man, and also to satisfy the Gentiles, who were not interested in their Saviour's Jewish descent. What interested them was his divinity and such a being could only be born in the same way as the Pagan gods they had abandoned.

It does not surprise us, therefore, to find that in the second century the Jews accused the Christians of adding to the birth story of their Christ the same mythology as was believed about the other Pagan deities who had come to earth, and lived as god-men. So the early Christian fathers boldly faced their critics by the ingenious argument that if the Pagans felt it necessary to commence their legends of their gods coming to earth by a story of them being born the sons of virgins, the Christians were equally at liberty to tell the same story about their god.

Justin the Martyr (A.D. 100–166), one of the early Christian fathers, states his case as follows :

> Why are we Christians alone of men hated for Christ's name when we do but relate of him stories similar to what the Greeks relate of their gods, Hermes and Perseus ? Even if we assert, and we do, that Jesus was born of a virgin, we contend that this too is a feature shared by him with Perseus, and when we tell you that Jesus healed the halt and paralytic and the maimed from birth, and that he raised the dead, you will see that here too we merely repeat things said to have been done by Æsculapius.

Elsewhere Justin writes that the claim made by Christians that Jesus Christ was born of a virgin mother, was crucified, died, rose again and ascended to heaven, was in no way new or strange to those familiar with Pagan mythology, and he then enumerates some of the gods to whom we have already given our attention in the earlier chapters of this book. This being so, can we wonder that the Christians were hated by the Pagans and Jews? They were arrogant, boastful and deluded, and when their false claims were exposed they resorted to insults and abuse, calling the gods of their neighbours devils.

When Christianity later dominated its rivals all controversy was silenced, and in time the exposure of its errors was forgotten. In the days we are now considering it was, however, fighting for its existence and could not stifle criticism and exposure. Some of the writings of its critics still remain, though most were destroyed when it became triumphant, but what the Church fathers tell us is sufficient to enable us to know the line of attack the critics adopted. Though the early Christians believed that their ideas were approved by God, and some suffered death for their delusion, yet this was not sufficient to make them liked by those whose religious beliefs they attacked and denounced, and for whose future they predicted eternal torment in Hell.

The writings of Justin make it possible for us to visualise the divergent opinions of those days, and they are of special interest when it is remembered that he was one of the ablest of all the Christian apologists, suffering martyrdom for his beliefs. Tradition records his martyrdom for his faith at the hands of a Roman magistrate who was a Stoic, and because of this he is always known as Justin Martyr to distinguish him from others of that name.

The virgin birth story crept in slowly during the second century, arousing controversy and argument, of which the passage written by Justin is a reflection. As the idea that Jesus was a god-man on earth spread, and became more firmly believed, so the story of the virgin birth was more widely accepted, till, ultimately, the early controversy was forgotten. By the third century the belief was generally accepted and finally, at the Council of Nicaea, it was incorporated into the creed of the Christian Church. From that day to this the faithful on countless occasions have asserted their belief in this event.

In passing, attention should also be drawn to the other admission by Justin, that the stories about Jesus healing the sick and raising the dead were just repetitions of what was told of the saviour-god Æsculapius. What follows in this chapter will make it quite obvious that the legends of the miracles performed by Jesus, as given in the gospels, were manufactured by early Christians out of the Pagan material they had at hand, and that they were neither new nor strange to the Pagans of those days.

No sooner was the belief in the virgin birth accepted than the attempt was also made to relate it to Hebrew prophecy. The Jews were, however, quick enough to show that the writer of Matthew's gospel had made his own interpretation of the passage in Isaiah, which in the original Hebrew text reads, "a young woman shall conceive and bear a son" (Isaiah vii, 14), and that it rightly referred to King Hezekiah. This exposure did not deter the Christian

Church from perpetuating the falsehood, as it continued to mistranslate the words "young woman", as used by Isaiah, by the word "virgin" till the revised version of the English Bible was published in 1884, when the translators, too fearful to alter the text, added a marginal note to the effect that the word "maiden" could be substituted for the word "virgin".

Many and bitter were the controversies caused by the adoption of the belief in the virgin birth of Jesus. The Ebonite Christians in Palestine stood out boldly and would be no party to the inclusion of the travesty about their Lord's birth. They insisted that he was born in a natural and non-miraculous manner, and none should have known better, as they were the direct descendants of the first Jewish Christians.

The Pagan atmosphere which surrounded the growth of the budding faith made their stand fruitless, since it was naturally contended that, as Jesus was the Son of God, he must have been born in a supernatural manner. The Ebonite Christians argued against this and contended that his birth was no more wonderful than Sarah producing Isaac because "the Lord visited Sarah . . . and the Lord did unto Sarah as he had spoken. For Sarah conceived and bear Abraham a son". (Gen. xxi, 1.) A compromise was attempted by putting forward the suggestion that the humanity of Jesus came from the flesh he absorbed from his mother, his divinity coming from the Holy Ghost, his father, and this became the accepted explanation by those who wanted their god to rank in every way as high as the gods of their Pagan neighbours.

For the next few centuries Christians occupied their time speculating as to how the virgin became impregnated, and various ideas were believed at one time or another. Tertullian thought it came about by means of "a divine ray", which was the explanation the Egyptians gave to account for the miraculous birth of Apis. Augustine, and other fathers of the Church, stated that the Holy Ghost entered through her ears, and ancient Christian art depicts this idea in various aspects.

While the Christians were adopting desperate measures to preserve the belief in the miracle of the creation of Jesus, both Pagans and Jews were throwing at them the most scurrilous suggestions. One extreme bred another, and so it is not surprising that the enemies of the new Faith made assertions for no other reason than to anger those who had stolen their thunder. One was that Jesus was the son of a Roman soldier called Pandera, while others tried to prove that Mary was a harlot or an adultress, another even asserting that she had committed incest with her own brother.

Because Christians have gone to one extreme is no reason why we should think that Jesus was other than the legitimate child of his parents. So let me put the matter thus. After sifting out the accretions, which came to surround Jesus, when he became a god in the minds of his worshippers, we find a consistent remnant of tradition that he was born somewhere in Galilee, in the reign of the Emperor Augustus, of a humble family, which included several children besides himself, and that nothing more than this about his birth and parentage can be accepted as probably true. Anything additional is simply Christian adornment, engendered by the belief that the appearance of

Jesus after death was a sign that he was the Christ, whose birth had to correspond with prophecy, as interpreted by Christians, and the legends surrounding his prototypes who had preceded him.

The belief that the Holy Ghost entered Mary through her ears raises another line of thought. Dr. Conybeare puts forward the interesting observation that because some women were prophetesses, or, to adopt the more modern term, clairaudientes, so the idea evolved that when prophesying in church they had to have their heads covered, to keep away spirit communicators who were not likely to impart to them edifying doctrine. This, in his opinion, is the origin of the taboo against women entering a church without a head-covering as one was necessary to protect their ears. So in time such a covering came to be looked upon as a protection against evil and was consequently adopted by nuns from early Christian times. Paul gives the reason for his injunction to the Corinthian women, that in church they must keep their heads covered "because of the angels" (1 Cor. xi, 10), or, in order to keep away any meddlesome spirits from interfering with the accepted controlling spirits of the clairaudientes.

It is possible that Paul knew of this ancient taboo, in fact it occurs in the Old Testament (Numbers v, 18), and he believed that by clairaudientes keeping their ears covered they adopted a protection against obtruding spirits. Conybeare further points out that the word "overshadowed", in the original, means to come upon one so as to cause one to prophesy, or, as we would now say, to speak as one hears clairaudiently. The spirit could only operate through the etheric ear of the clairaudient, and for this reason Origen, the Church father of the third century, argued that as spirits used the ear to speak through, so it was by this channel the Holy Ghost entered the Virgin Mary. Thomas Aquinas had also much to say along this line of argument.

Though speculations as to how Jesus was born went on for centuries, the controversy as to whether he was virgin born, or not, was finally settled at the Council of Ephesus in 431, when a resolution was carried that Mary had conceived Jesus as the result of the action of the Holy Ghost and that she was the Mother of God. This decision in time raised another problem as to how Christ could be born without sin from a human mother. So, after various conferences, the Catholic Church pronounced that Mary herself had been conceived and born without sin and was in consequence immaculate. Strangely enough this new dogma did not become the official doctrine of the Church until 1854, when the Pope solemnly announced that the belief in the immaculate conception of Mary was now a new dogma necessary to salvation.

The belief in the virgin birth was of such slow growth, that as late as the fourth century the birthday of Jesus was not observed, and, up to the end of the sixth century, his virgin mother received no special recognition. The Feast of the Annunciation gradually came to be held after the sixth century, but it was centuries before a special day was set apart for this event.

When the virgin became recognised as the Mother of God, the Christians, as with everything else, appropriated the ceremony and ritual surrounding the feasts to the Pagan virgins who were worshipped as the Mothers of God. Isis, who had been adopted by the Romans from Egypt, was thus replaced by Mary, just as were Cybele and Artemis in the East. Hymns in honour of Isis were used without much change to do honour to Mary, while the statues of Isis, with Horus in her arms, were set up in Christian churches and labelled the Virgin and the Christ child. Other religions besides the Egyptian imaged and worshipped the virgin and child, as statues of Madonnas have existed for thousands of years in India and Assyria. Juno was imaged with the child Hercules, as was Devaki with Krishna, Demeter with Dionysus, and so on.

Thus from Paganism came the virgin cult, composed of worshippers of the virgin mother. As the Christians adopted the son of the virgin as their Saviour from the beliefs surrounding the other virgin-born Pagan gods, so they adopted the worship of the virgin from the Pagans who adored Cybele, Demeter, Isis, and the other Mothers of God who had each produced a Saviour. As the produce of mother earth satisfies our material needs, so these mothers of the gods produced divine beings who satisfied the religious needs of their times, and a devout and simple people consequently gave them all the honour possible. This homage Catholic Christendom has continued towards the Virgin Mary for the same reason.

The virgin birth idea certainly did not come from the Jews, and it can be traced in its entirety to the mythology of those religions beyond the confines of Judaea. The Jews had no preconceived ideas that the Messiah should be miraculously born, or that his birth would be signalised by any miracle. The expected Jewish Messiah was to be of the seed of David and born in a natural way. As the Jew Trypho said to Justin, "We all await Christ who will be a man amongst men", and no Jew expected a virgin-born Messiah, but one directly descended from David.

When, however, we turn to Pagan literature, we find ample evidence for the origin of the belief. Perseus was believed to be the son of Zeus and his mother Danaë a virgin. Nana, the virgin mother of Attis, conceived him without human contact ; Leto miraculously conceived Apollo, just as Isis conceived Horus. Demeter likewise conceived Dionysus, and Maya the Buddha. These are only a selection of a number of cases to be found in mythology which are similar to the story about Jesus.

There is little doubt that the Christian version of the virgin birth legend was copied directly from Egypt, because we find in an ancient sculpture on the walls of a temple at Luxor the same story as is given in relation to Christ. Here we see a picture of the Egyptian Holy Spirit announcing to the virgin mother that she would conceive and bring forth a god-child. In the next scene he is represented as holding a cross, the symbol of life, before her mouth, thus miraculously impregnating her. This is followed by a scene depicting her having given birth to a god-child, round whom are standing figures in adoration. We need not go further than this as it would be wearisome to relate all the virgin mothers known to mythology, and the different ways each conceived a god-child.

The Theological College at Alexandria had all

the necessary material at hand by the time Christian opinion had developed sufficiently to make it necessary for Jesus to be elevated to the same status as the other Pagan gods. So there is no need to wander through all the mythology of the past relating to the virgin births of the other saviour-gods. The story was undoubtedly copied from Egypt, and the ancient legend of Isis, the virgin mother of Horus, was adopted by the Christians and related to Mary in the same way as the Christians adopted the portrait and image of Isis with Horus in her arms, and related it to Mary and the child Jesus. The story has further Pagan parallels of fathers being warned in dreams not to have contact with their wives as they had been impregnated by a god and would bear a god-child. The father of Plato was thus warned by Apollo.

Thus, step by step, the virgin birth legends can be traced back till we get to the time when man was so ignorant that he believed that all procreation was the result of intercourse of the gods with women, primitive man being quite unaware as to how child-birth came about. From this mentality came the old Babylonian story of how a god in the form of the wind hovered over the earth and caused it to bear fruit. This developed into the story of the creation as related in Genesis, when "the Spirit of God moved upon the face of the waters" and brought the cosmos into being.

Again, the rising of the constellation Virgo at midnight, at the beginning of the solstitial year, points to the ancients, who gave it this name, associating the new year with a virgin, and regarding what we call Christmas as the date when life returned to earth after the death of autumn. This was an analogy of what the virgin was believed to have accomplished for mankind by giving birth to the Christ.

While concentrating on the Christian plagiarism of the virgin birth, we should not overlook the symbolic meaning it conveyed to those who originally brought the idea into being many thousands of years ago. The ancients believed that the corn fructified in mother earth through the action of a god. So Demeter, the corn goddess, produced a god-child through contact with a god. Christ, "the Bread of Life", likewise fructified by the action of a god. As the corn nourishes the physical body, so the "Bread of Life" nourishes the etheric body and enables it to survive death.

Paul expressed it thus : "That which thou sowest, thou sowest not that body that shall be, but bare grain, it may chance of wheat, or of some other grain. But God giveth it a body as it hath pleased him, and to every seed his own body" (1 Cor. xv, 37). This idea was behind all the virgin birth legends, and the Christian Gnostics, the descendants of the Pagan and Jewish Gnostics, carried it even further, under the name of Docetism, holding that everything relating to Jesus was symbolic and that his earth body was not human but composed of phantasmal or celestial substance. However, in A.D. 160 this way of looking at things was ruled by most churches to be heresy. The symbolic meaning behind the virgin birth legend is, however, interesting as showing that all these ancient mythological stories, which came to be wrapped round the gods, were at their basis related to our life, death and resurrection, the mystery of which was forever present in the minds of our ancestors.

The Christian Church continued to interpret mythology as history and made it a condition of salvation that it should be believed as such. It thus misused mythology and falsified history. Deep down, if we dig far enough, we find that the roots of all religions have been watered by the ancients taking the life, death and resurrection in nature as their analogy of what happens to us. This occurs in summer, winter and spring, with the same unfailing regularity as the life, death and second birth of man into another realm of vibrations interpenetrating the one we now experience. As our ancestors were ignorant of psychic science and could only express the immaterial through an analogy with the material they, like Paul, adopted the evidence obtained year after year from the death and resurrection of vegetation, and used this to symbolise their inmost and deepest feelings.

The people expressed their religious ideas symbolically. Just as the gospel stories are symbolical so were their expressions. Tertullian, for instance, writes, "We little fishes, following the example of our fish Jesus Christ, are born in water, nor otherwise than abiding in the water." The reason Jesus was symbolised as the fish, and called "the divine Fish", was because of his virgin birth, as they could think of nothing in nature more like this form of birth than the method adopted by fishes for propagation. In the third century this symbol applied to Jesus was declared to be heretical and the letters composing the word Ichthus (fish) were used as an anagram : *Iesus Christos Theou Uios Sôtêr* (Jesus Christ, of God son, Saviour). Anyone visiting the catacombs in Rome will see drawings of fishes, which symbolised Jesus to those early Christians.

This brief survey of the story of the virgin birth of Jesus, as told in Matthew and Luke, would, however, not be complete unless we discover how it was that the people in those days could imagine it possible for a spirit to enter a woman and become a child. Something objective, which had been experienced, was necessary to make this belief possible, not only in the case of Jesus but in connection with all those who were believed to have been born in this unnatural way. After reading what will be said on the subject of the baptism of Jesus it will become obvious how it was possible for such an idea to prevail. From mediumship and all that surrounds this supernormal faculty in humanity the ancients evolved their ideas surrounding god-men. To those we today call mediums they gave the name god-men and related them to the gods. A god-man, a man of god, one filled with the holy ghost, and all the other names attached to this type of individual, meant, in our present-day speech, a medium, but this will become clearer as we go on.

We shall pass over, with only a reference, the incredible story of the census of Caesar Augustus, mentioned in Luke, which necessitated a poor man like Joseph travelling with his wife, in her condition, from Nazareth to Bethlehem, about a hundred miles by road, to register their existence. This census, however, Josephus tells us, took place ten years after the death of Herod, in whose reign Matthew and Luke state Jesus was born. Clearly, this story is again an invention to satisfy the prophecy that the Messiah was to be born in Bethlehem. No Roman ruler would register people according to where their ancestors were supposed to have lived a thousand years previously, as this story says, and so make these long journeys necessary. A census is for the purpose of knowing the dwelling-places of the people, and the total population, not their ancestry, which was of no interest to Rome.

Those best able to judge are of the opinion that Jesus was not born in Bethlehem and that it is even doubtful if he were born in Nazareth. This being so, the story of his being born in a stable is also unlikely. Reference has already been made to the cave in Bethlehem, wherein visitors are told Jesus was born, and which from ancient times was associated with the worship of Adonis. If Jesus were born in a stable it is strange that the apocryphal reference to his birth should state that he was born in a cave in Bethlehem, the association doubtless being with this cave.

Sacred caves, associated with the birth or worship of gods, were not uncommon, as Apollo, Hercules, Hermes, Demeter and others had sacred caves associated with their names. The Mithraists were pre-eminently noted for their sacred caves, in which they worshipped, and it is not improbable that Luke, who is the only one to refer to the incident that Jesus, at birth, was laid in a manger "because there was no room in the inn", was influenced in compiling his story by these traditions relating to the birthplace of previous god-men.

Robertson, in his book *Christianity and Mythology*, remarks that in the story related of the birth of the babe-god Dionysus he is referred to as "the child wrapped in swaddling clothes and lying in a manger". The babe-god Hermes was also referred to in similar words. Dionysus in effigy was carried about in procession in a manger basket on feast days. Horus is represented as being born between the sacred cow and the sacred bull. The similarities between the stories of the birth of Jesus and that of Krishna are very striking, including the coming of the shepherds to worship him at his birth. Mithra was believed to have been born in a cave and Mithraic monuments depict him as surrounded by adoring shepherds who offer him the first fruits of the earth. Apocryphal tradition tells us that Jesus spoke immediately after his birth and this was also told of Krishna, Apollo and Hermes.

Besides the similarity between the birthplace of Jesus and that of other pre-Christian god-infants, we find also similar parallels in their being visited at their birth by Magi, who bring presents and worship the new-born children. The object of the writers of all these legends is clear. Believing, as they did, that these infants had grown up to be god-men, it was quite natural, in those days when mythology was accepted as history, to depict their entrance into this world with a certain amount of ceremonial. As it was also thought that the stars influenced the destiny of each individual, and that all the great were born under a special star, so each of these god-infants was believed to have been born under his own particular star.

Thus we read that the Magi stated that they had seen "His star in the east and are come to worship him." The Magi was the name given to the followers of Zoroaster, the Persian prophet and teacher, and the inclusion of them in the story is interesting when the similarity of Zoroaster's teachings with what was attributed to Jesus is considered. The Persians had for over a thousand years anticipated the coming Christ, and nothing was more fitting than that a people, who had greatly influenced the Jewish apocalyptical beliefs, should have been represented when the Christ the Persians had so long anticipated had actually come to earth and fulfilled their prophecies.

Heaven likewise was interested in this great event because "a multitude of the heavenly host praising God" appeared to the shepherds saying, "Glory to God in the highest and on earth peace and goodwill toward men". Buddha was similarly honoured, as the heavenly host, which appeared on his birthday, sang, "This day is born for the good of men Buddha and to dispel the darkness of ignorance, to give joy and peace to the world." Both Buddha and Krishna received a visit and a blessing from an aged saint, which we are told also happened to Jesus when his mother took him to the Temple.

Nothing is known in history of the massacre of the infants by Herod, who is presented to us as believing that the Messiah had been born, because a certain star had appeared. This is strange reading to anyone who is conversant with the utter indifference this king adopted to all Messianic claims. According to Matthew this star moved along with the Magi until it stood over where the young child lay. This was to be the sign which was to guide them to the birthplace of Jesus, and later enable them to return to Herod, to tell him where the young child could be found, so that he also could go and worship him. They were, however, warned by God in a dream not to return to Herod and reveal the birthplace, and because the king "saw that he was mocked of the wise men, was exceeding wroth, and sent forth, and slew all the children that were in Bethlehem, and in all the coasts thereof, from two years old and under." (Matt. ii, 16.)

Only people quite ignorant of Roman rule could believe such an impossible story. Such things did not happen in the Roman Empire in those days, and if Herod had been guilty of such an atrocity he would have been immediately deposed and punished. The idea may have its origin in the universal myth relating to the massacre of the stars by the day, because, when daylight comes, they disappear from sight. The Sun-god is the only one to escape from the slaughter, whereas the others appear to have been massacred or obliterated in the vault of heaven. The story, as it appears in Matthew, probably came from India and was told concerning King Kamsa, the uncle of Krishna, who tried to kill him for the same reason as we are told Herod tried to kill Jesus. Krishna, however, was taken by his parents to Matura, which is the same place, according to one of the non-canonical gospels, as Jesus was taken to in order to escape from Herod.

I have already referred to the fact that the birthday of Jesus was unknown to the early Christians and that the twenty-fifth of December was at a later date adopted by western Christians, it being the day on which it was believed that Mithra was born. In the East the birthday of Jesus was celebrated on the sixth of January, the date of his baptism, as it was believed that Jesus was baptised on his thirtieth birthday. Neither the date of his birth nor death are known but one thing certain is that he could not have been born in the reign of Herod, for the reasons already given.

Scholars, therefore, can come to no other conclusion than that the story of the massacre of the infants by Herod was drawn from surrounding mythology and applied to Jesus. The earliest stratum of tradition gives us no information about his birth, and Mark, the oldest gospel, entirely ignores it. The legends surrounding his birth, when this gospel was first written, either had not begun to circulate or Mark did not believe them. Evidently the writer of John's gospel also did not believe them, because he likewise passes them by in silence.

Like other infants, Jesus grew up to be a child, and so we now pass on to learn what the early Christians had to say about

THE CHILDHOOD OF JESUS.

Luke, alone of the canonical gospels, tells us about Jesus at the age of twelve being lost and later on being found in the Temple, surrounded by savants, who were astonished at his wisdom. An apocryphal gospel gives a much fuller and more elaborate story of the childhood of Jesus. The account given of his wondrous doings in *The First Gospel of the Infancy of Jesus Christ*, produced by the Christian Gnostics in the second century and translated into English in 1697 by Professor Henry Sike, Professor of Oriental Languages at Cambridge, enables us to see how imagination in those days ran riot. The following are a few of the outstanding passages copied from this gospel, which is to be found in the *Apocryphal New Testament.* Thus spoke Jesus just after he was born :

Mary, I am Jesus, the Son of God, that Word which thou didst bring forth according to the declaration of the angel Gabriel to thee, and my Father hath sent me for the salvation of the world.

Coming in their journey to another city, they saw three women going from a certain grave with great weeping, and by them a mule, covered over with silk, and an ebony collar hanging down from his neck, whom they kissed, and were feeding.

And they said, O our Lady Saint Mary, pity your handmaids, for we have no head of our family, no father, no brother. But this mule, which you see, was our brother, which some woman by witchcraft have brought into this condition which you see ; we therefore entreat you to compassionate us.

Hereupon Saint Mary was grieved at their case and, taking the Lord Jesus, put him upon the back of the mule. And said to her son, O Jesus Christ, restore according to thy extraordinary power this mule, and grant him to have again the shape of a man and a rational creature, as he had formerly.

This was scarce said by the Lady Saint Mary, but the mule immediately passed into a human form, and became a young man without any deformity.

Presently they came to that sycamore tree which is now called Matarea. And in Matarea the Lord Jesus caused a well to spring forth, in which Saint Mary washed his coat. And a balsam is produced, or grows, in that country, from the sweat which ran down there from the Lord Jesus.

There were in the same

city two wives of one man, who had each a sick son. One of them was called Mary, and when she put upon Caleb her son a coat made from swaddling cloth of Jesus (received from Saint Mary in exchange for a "handsome carpet") his disease was cured; but the son of the other wife died. Hereupon there arose between them a difference.

And when Mary the mother of Caleb was heating the oven to bake bread, and went away to fetch the meal, she left her son Caleb by the oven; whom her rival, the husband's other wife, took and cast into the oven, which was very hot, and then went away. Mary on her return saw her son Caleb lying in the middle of the oven laughing, and the oven quite as cold as though it had not been before heated.

After this her rival, the other wife, as she was drawing water of the well, and saw Caleb playing nearby, took him and threw him into the well. And when some men came to fetch water from the well they saw Caleb sitting on the superficies of the water, and drew him out with ropes, and were exceedingly sur-

prised at the child, and praised God.

And when Mary the mother of Caleb told the Lady Saint Mary what her rival had done, Saint Mary replied to her, God will vindicate your injured cause. Accordingly, a few days after, when the other wife came to the well to draw water, her foot was entangled in the rope, so that she fell headlong into the well, and they who ran to her assistance found her skull broken and bones bruised. So she came to a bad end.

When the Lord Jesus was seven years of age, he and other boys made clay into several shapes, namely, asses, oxen, birds, and other figures, each boasting of his work and endeavouring to exceed the rest. Then the Lord Jesus said to the boys, I will command these figures to walk. And immediately they moved, and when he commanded them to return they returned. He also made the figures of birds, which, when he commanded to fly, did fly; and if he gave them meat and drink, they did eat and drink.

On a certain day, when passing by a dyer's shop, the Lord Jesus, going into the shop, took all the cloths and threw them into the furnace. And when Salem the dyer on his return began to make a great noise and chide him, the Lord Jesus replied, I will change the colour of every cloth to what colour thou desirest. And then presently he began to take the cloths out of the furnace, and they were all dyed of those same colours which the dyer desired.

And Joseph, wheresoever he went in the city, took the Lord Jesus with him, where he was sent for to work to make gates, or milk-pails, or sieves, or boxes ; the Lord Jesus was with him. And as often as Joseph had anything in his work to make longer or shorter, or wider or narrower, the Lord Jesus would stretch his hand towards it, and presently it became as Joseph would have it. So that he had no need to finish anything with his own hand, for he was not very skilful at his carpenter's trade.

For a certain time Joseph laboured two years on a throne for the palace of the King of Jerusalem, which, when he came to fix it, he found it wanted two spans of the appointed measure. But Jesus said to him, Fear not ; lay hold on one side of the throne, and I will the other, and we will bring it to its just dimensions. And they did so, and the throne obeyed and was brought to its proper dimensions.

On another day Jesus went in search of some boys who had hidden in play, and when he asked some women at the gate of a certain house, they said there was no one there. Then the Lord said, Who are those whom ye see in the furnace ? and they answered, They were kids of three years old. Then Jesus cried out, Come out hither, O ye kids, to your shepherd. And the boys came forth like kids, and leaped about him.

And when the women beseeched mercy, and entreated him that he would restore the boys, Jesus said, Come hither, O boys, that we may go and play ; and immediately, in the presence of these women, the kids were changed, and returned into the shape of boys.

In the month Adar a boy of the city was stung by a poisonous serpent. The Lord calling the serpent, it presently came forth and submitted to him; to whom he said, Go and suck out the poison which thou hast infused into that boy. So the serpent crept to the boy, and took away all its poison again. Then the Lord Jesus cursed the serpent, so that it immediately burst asunder and died.

One Sabbath day the son of Hanani, a Jew, broke down some fishpools which the boys had made by a river, but when he came to the fishpool of Jesus to destroy it, the water vanished away, and the Lord Jesus said to him, In like manner as this water has vanished, so shall thy life vanish; and presently the boy died.

Another time, when the Lord Jesus was coming home in the evening with Joseph, he met a boy who ran so hard against him that he threw him down, to whom the Lord Jesus said, As thou hast thrown me down, so shalt thou fall, nor ever rise. And that moment the boy fell down and died.

And when they brought him to a schoolmaster to learn his letters, and the master lifted up his hand to whip the Lord Jesus, his hand presently withered, and he died.

Then said Joseph to Mary, Henceforth we will not allow him to go out of the house; for everyone who displeases him is killed.

And when he was twelve years old, they brought him to Jerusalem to the feast; and the Lord Jesus continued behind in the Temple, among the doctors and elders and learned men. And he grew in stature and wisdom, and favour with God and man.

Till he arrived to the end of his thirtieth year, at which time the Father publicly owned him at Jordan, sending down his voice from Heaven. "This is my beloved son, in whom I am well pleased. Who for our sakes, took human body, and hath redeemed us, so that he might embrace us with everlasting mercy, and show his free, large bountiful grace and goodness to us. To him be glory, and praise, and power, and dominion, from henceforth and for evermore." Amen.

If this gospel had been included by some council of priests in the New Testament, Christians would have believed that Jesus did all these things reported of him. Because it was not, they feel at liberty to exercise their own judgement and discard these tales as untrue, which emphasises the opinion held by many that religious beliefs come, not as the result of logical thinking but, in consequence of what a child is taught when its mind is receptive. Few can get away from the training of childhood and youth, and the Church has shown great perspicacity in influencing the father and mother at their marriage to train their children in the Christian Faith.

As the parents themselves have been brought up in this faith they thus pass it on to their children, who, in Church and Sunday School, hear only the orthodox version of the Christian Faith, seldom discovering that it rests on a foundation of myth and legend. Thus children from a tender age are taught legends as history, and so accept all their lives these Christian stories as true, many never thinking that they may be otherwise. So the wheel has gone round, each generation passing on what it was taught by its parents, though in Protestant countries for some years past a decided slowing down has been apparent. This is fortunate if the race is to have any future, and emerge from the slough of ignorance in which it has wallowed throughout the reign of the Christian Church.

The canonical and uncanonical gospels must either stand or fall together. They were all produced by the Christians of the first, second and third centuries, who, even in the fourth century, did not cease the adorning process. Because, at a council of priests in the fourth century, four gospels were chosen to be included in the canon of the New Testament, we must not infer that the Christians at that time disbelieved the accounts given about Jesus in the other gospels. Though they are now considered apocryphal they were then believed to record historical episodes in the life of Jesus, and the gospels of Matthew, Mark, Luke and John have no more authority behind them than those now termed apocryphal.

After thus straying from the path of orthodoxy, we shall now return to the official and recognised accounts of the life of Jesus, and take up the next episode in his career, namely

THE BAPTISM OF JESUS.

One of the strongest proofs that the virgin birth legend was a late addition is the account given of the baptism of Jesus. Here we are told that Jesus received the Holy Ghost in the form of "the Spirit like a dove descending upon him". One who was produced by the Holy Ghost surely did not need this second impregnation, as he was endowed with this being, or was this being, from his embryo stage onwards. The inclusion of a dove in the story is probably symbolic, as in Palestine and Syria it was the sacred bird round which circled various religious taboos. It was the symbol of the Logos, Philo stating that the Logos is symbolically called a turtle-dove.

This event in the life of Jesus was magnified as time went on. Mark gives the story with the least embroidery, whereas Matthew and Luke enlarge upon it. When we come to *The Gospel of the Hebrews*, an apocryphal gospel, we find an elaborate story and an amplified account of what was said by the voice from heaven. The idea all these accounts wished to convey was that Jesus was then born again, not of flesh but of the Holy Spirit. This was used as an argument by the Ebonite Christians against the idea, which developed later, of his being the psychical progeny of the Holy Spirit. The early Christians believed that Jesus was born of the Spirit at his baptism when he was thirty years old. Then he began his ministry as a god-man, which is the reason why the canonical gospels relate his deeds from this time only, as before it he was thought of as one of no special repute. When, however, the birth legend was added at a later date, the belief changed, and he was then considered to have been also a god-child. This idea brought *The Gospel of the Infancy*, and others, into being and the interpolation in Luke about his reasoning with the Doctors when twelve years of age.

If we accept what is natural in the story, Jesus, like so many others of his time, felt his own unrighteousness and adopted the method then in vogue of having his sins washed away by water, as if they were something attached to the flesh. For ages the belief has prevailed that water has this cleansing effect, and this corresponds to the old idea, particularly prominent in ancient Greek, Egyptian and Roman religious customs, that a priest could transfer sin from the individual to an animal or human being. Sin, from this aspect, is a movable quantity, and so the Christian dies happily if he has partaken of the Eucharist, which, like baptism, has to him some magical cleansing effect.

The Mystery religions taught the cleansing effect of blood and this belief Christianity also adopted from Paganism. Perhaps Jesus also shared the Messianic anticipations of his time, and wished to purify himself in readiness for the arrival of the longed-for Messiah. So he made his way to that deserted region through which the waters of the Jordan run before they empty themselves into the Dead Sea. Here he met John the Baptist.

The first introduction we have to this character is in *The Gospel of Luke*, where we are told that his foetus leapt with joy in his mother's womb when it heard that Mary had had intercourse with the Holy Spirit, which fabrication is on the same level as what we are told about Jesus in *The Gospel of the Infancy*. After thirty years, from this early period in his life, John and Jesus met face to face, as man to man. We are told that John's costume consisted of camel's hair and a skin girdle, which was the mode of dress adopted by those who withdrew into the wilderness. Elijah adopted a similar apparel. John's food consisted of locusts, the name for a local bean, and wild honey, which is still the diet of those parts. His speech was far from refined as he called the people "a generation of vipers".

Mark tells us that Jesus "was baptised of John in Jordan", which was quite natural and according to the custom of those times. In *The Gospel of John* the story is more elaborate, as the Baptist calls the people's attention to the fact that Jesus is "the Lamb of God who taketh away the sins of the world". All the gospels then relate that Jesus had a wonderful experience. After coming out of the Jordan "he saw the heavens opened, and the Spirit, like a dove, descending upon him. And there came a voice from heaven, saying, Thou art my beloved Son, in whom I am well pleased". (Mark i, 10.) Here we are given in a few words an account of what has been always regarded as a supernatural event, so it deserves our serious consideration.

This story, though differing in detail, is in the main the same in all the four gospels. The hearing of a voice from heaven was in no way peculiar to this occasion, as there are twenty-two instances in the Bible in which it is stated that a voice spoke from the void, in other words, that a voice was heard but no speaker was seen. It is well to remember this in view of what is to be told later on. At the moment we are considering the account as it stands in the four gospels. The fact that this legend is unhistorical goes without saying, and we have not even early tradition to help us. In the first stratum of Christian tradition, though mention is made of John the Baptist preaching and baptising, no reference is made to Jesus being baptised.

John the Baptist is an historical character because he is referred to by Josephus, who tells us that he frightened King Herod by his eloquence and power over the people. Fearing that he would lead a revolutionary movement, the King arrested him and put him in prison, after which he was executed. Josephus states that John was a good man, who tried to raise the people by preaching virtue, piety and fair dealing, but he tells us nothing about Jesus being baptised by John, though this is hardly to be expected as he would be just one in a crowd. In those days there were many fanatics who, like John, went into the wilderness of Judaea, that forbidding region on the edge of the basin in which lies the Dead Sea. No attempt is made by the evangelists to locate the place where John baptised, as they confine themselves to the statement that it was "on the Jordan", a stretch of seventy miles.

Whether Jesus was baptised or not matters little. To understand the meaning lying behind the story it is not necessary to accept its truthfulness. We are dealing with the opinions of Christians in the second half of the first century, who, in order to accommodate their beliefs, required such a story, and for this reason it was added on to the early tradition surrounding Jesus. To understand why this was done we must again go back to the appearance of Jesus as an etheric being, which was the hub round which the entire system of Christian thought revolved. The story of the baptism was written to explain this event and was its natural outcome.

If we put ourselves into the Christian frame of mind of this period we find that their thoughts went round something like this : (1) Jesus was seen after death. (2) So he was a god. (3) How was he seen ? (4) In a glorified body. (5) Yet he lived as a man on earth. (6) So he must have been endowed at some time in his life with this body of a god. (7) But when did this happen ? (8) At his baptism when his body had been cleansed and thus made fit to receive it. So (9) from that time onwards he was a god-man.

In the second century this developed further and instead of the Christians being content with Jesus being a god-man from his baptism they thought of him as one from conception. Nothing reliable was known about his life so, when he became a god from birth, a natural demand arose for accounts of his life from that date. As a divine being all things were possible and the writers of the apocryphal gospels, who met the demand for stories about Jesus, allowed their imagination full play, nothing being too impossible to relate or be believed. So Pagan literature was searched for stories of what other god-men had done from infancy upwards. These were applied to Jesus, but deep down below these borrowed plumes was a basis of fact which it is my business to expose.

If Jesus, as is quite possible, had strong psychic power, everything that has been recorded about him in all the gospels, both canonical and non-canonical, could be traced back to this source. The legends would then be branches which spread out and formed a great tree of myth and legend from an acorn of mediumship. This is all possible, but, as has already been said, we have nothing reliable on which to base this conclusion. It can only be by inference, just as we had to infer from circumstantial evidence that only an apparition could have been the cause of the beliefs which developed in the first half of the first Christian century. So we can only infer, from what is told of Jesus, that there was some basis which gave rise to all these marvellous stories, and, though we cannot be certain of what actually happened, we can form a fairly shrewd idea from our knowledge of what takes place in the presence of a highly developed medium.

What is important, however, is not so much the

actual truth of these stories as the reason which brought them into being. Why was the baptism of a man, which was a natural everyday event in those times, changed into a supernatural event? It is because this story, as it has come down to us, became a necessary corollary to his appearance after death as an etheric being. It was the direct outcome of the general belief, held by all Christians at the time it was written, in the latter part of the first century, that Jesus had thus appeared after his death. We are not concerned at the moment with the fabrication that he appeared in his physical body, as this was a later addition which will be considered when we come to deal with the resurrection.

Those early Christians, Paul and Peter and all the others, knew nothing of the physical resurrection of Jesus. To them it was his etheric appearance, as a glorified etheric being, after he had slipped out of his physical body. This event, the very core of the whole subject, can only be described as having had a staggering effect on the outlook of increasing numbers who lived in those days. No other word can express the effect it had, and it is no exaggeration if we remember that many who became Christians had been brought up to believe that the dead lay in Hades till the Judgement Day.

The early Jewish Christians had no knowledge of the etheric body. Paul learned something of it from the Greeks, but even they could not relate it correctly to the physical body as we can today, though they knew enough to call a butterfly and a moth by the name of *psyche* because both emerged from seeming death in the chrysalis state.

Anything Paul learned of it he failed to understand fully because of the theology and mysticism in which he had been nurtured. So, to the Jews of those days, no mortal man could appear to anyone after death. Only angels, or the messengers of Jehovah, could appear to people, and since Jesus had done so he was a divine being to those who believed.

Consequently he must have been differently constructed from the rest of humanity. He, however, had gone about like other men and was known as the son of Joseph and Mary. How, then, was it possible for this ordinary individual to appear after death and adopt the rôle of a god? Something must have happened in his lifetime to change him from a man into a god-man, and supply him with this glorified body, in which he functioned when he appeared to Peter, Paul and the others.

No more fitting occasion could be found for endowing Jesus with this radiant body than at the ceremony of his baptism, which event, if no tradition had come down about it, would not have been difficult to invent, together with the supernatural story as we now know it. Whether there was any tradition that Jesus had been baptised, or whether there was not, those who wrote up this story assumed that he had been baptised, when he was cleansed from his sins. Jehovah then took this opportunity of filling a freshly washed human body with another body, in the likeness of himself, to which the name "Holy Spirit" was given, thus making Jesus a divine being who used the fleshly vehicle only for the purpose of manifesting on earth.

Though this is all quite irrational, we can see

through it and understand what was in the minds of those early Christians. To them, Jesus, before his baptism, was constructed as they were. At his baptism his body was animated by what they believed was a divine spirit. This naturally means that the Christians believed that before the body of Jesus housed this divine being it was, like other human bodies, devoid of the glorious, radiant body as described by Paul. This story satisfied those who required an explanation of his appearance after death and could only imagine an earthly resurrection of the individual on the last day with the same body he possessed before death.

A body, similar to the one in which he appeared, must therefore have been supplied to Jesus by Jehovah at some time during his life on earth. Otherwise how did he come by it ? His reappearance gave rise to all these speculations which came to surround him. They were an attempt to explain how it was that he was seen after death, as only a god could be seen. By no other process of thought could they understand how it was possible for a human being, who had suffered a violent death and whose body had been buried, to be seen again after death. Every man, and every woman, from the time of Adam, lay in Hades, and would not be disturbed until the great Day of Judgement, when they would rise again in their physical bodies and appear before the judge of all mankind.

On this misconception of a psychic fact is based the story of the baptism of Jesus. The etheric body is a part of everyone. It is not only the structure which supports the physical cells of each body, but it can exist apart from the physical body. The entire Christian Faith was evolved by those who were quite ignorant of this fact and consequently they believed that apparitions were gods and angels. Nature is a great illusionist, and, unless we use our intelligence and apply the facts she puts at our disposal in an intelligent way, we shall always be deceived. Only comparatively recently have we discovered that the blood circulates through the body, that devils are not the cause of disease, that the sun does not circle the earth, and even more recently that death is not what it seems to be.

This misunderstanding of the construction of the human body has given rise to all the saviour-god religions, as the same misconception has been the cause of them all. If this vital knowledge—that each one of us has an etheric body, a duplicate of the physical body—had been correctly understood, neither the Christian religion nor any other saviour-god religion would ever have come into being. Through their ignorance of nature the early Christians thus endowed Jesus at his baptism with something unique, which they thought did not belong to other mortals. That which is not understood is regarded as mysterious, and, if it appertains to religion, it is termed holy. When something which is holy becomes understood it ceases to be holy and the air of sanctity and mystery which surrounds it vanishes.

The use of the words Holy Ghost occurs only in the New Testament, though we find reference to the Holy Spirit in the Old Testament on three occasions, which are : "Take not thy Holy Spirit from me" (Psalm li, 11) and "They rebelled, and vexed his

Holy Spirit" (Isaiah lxiii, 10), followed in the next
verse with "Where is he that put his Holy Spirit
within him?" The Christian Church has never
defined the Holy Ghost and it now remains for those
with psychic knowledge to make the attempt. The
name Holy Ghost occurs on eighty-six occasions in
the New Testament. In the birth legend he is referred
to as if he were a spirit, and elsewhere in the New
Testament the idea is expressed that this being occupied the bodies of others, besides Jesus, because we
read of different people on other occasions being filled
with the Holy Ghost, speaking when moved by the
Holy Ghost, and so on.

It is not difficult to guess that this spirit was
none other than the spirit control of a medium, who,
in those days, was looked upon as a divine being. In
all that we read we find that he fulfilled this vocation
to perfection. When a medium enters the trance
state, or is receiving clairaudient messages, the control
is alongside, though the impression created on those
present, when the medium becomes entranced, is that
he occupies the medium's body. Consequently today
many use the expression that a spirit is in the medium
when in trance. Only when filled with the Holy
Ghost, as the early Christians termed it, can a medium
speak with tongues and exercise the entire range of
psychic phenomena enumerated by Paul.

We read in the New Testament of several individuals being thus endowed and, in consequence, considered as mediums. This being so it will be realised that
to the people in those days the Holy Ghost was not
peculiar to Jesus, except that it came to be believed that
his body housed the Holy Ghost permanently during his

time on earth. Because of this addition to his normal self he was able to perform his miracles and speak and act like a god-child and a god-man.

Fortunately, we are not left in doubt on this question as *The Shepherd of Hermas* tells us exactly who the holy spirit really was in the minds of the early Christians. This book, which was written and published about 135–140, was not included in the canon of scripture at the Council of Carthage in 397, but nevertheless it was held by the early Christians in very high esteem. Hermas was the brother of Pius, Bishop of Rome. Irenaeus tells us that this book ranks alongside all the other books contained in the scriptures. Origen considered that it was divinely inspired. Eusebius and Athanasius say that it was appointed to be read in the churches. We are, therefore, left in no doubt as to the authority and standing of this work in the early Christian Church.

What, then, has this book to tell us about the holy spirit ? First of all it tells us that those we today call mediums were then known as "men of two minds". This is quite an apt description, as a medium is of one mind when normal and another when under control. Mediums received other names in those days, to which reference will be made as we proceed. The writer then discusses at some length as to how to discern a genuine medium from a false medium. His method is too long to quote in full, but this is how he concludes :

The false medium, "being himself void, he gives void answers to the void, he answereth according to the emptiness of the man. For any spirit given of God is not enquired of, but, having the power of the Godhead, it speaketh all things of

itself because it is from above, from the power of the divine
spirit. But the spirit that is enquired of and speaketh according
to the desires of men is earthly".

From this, and what has gone before, it is not
difficult to discover that the writer means that the
genuine medium, who is controlled by the holy spirit,
exercises his gifts without effort on his part. He
therefore cannot give forth revelation whenever
asked to do so, but only when the spirit moveth him.

The writer then goes on to tell about the genuine
medium as follows :

From his life prove thou the man that hath the divine
spirit. First, he that hath the divine spirit, which is from
above, is meek and peaceable and lowly, and refraineth himself
from every wickedness and vain desire of this world, and he
maketh himself more needy than all men, and answereth nothing
to any when enquired of, and speaketh not solitarily. Neither
when a man would speak doth the holy spirit speak, but when
God willeth that he should speak, then he speaketh. Whensoever, therefore, the man, who hath the divine spirit, cometh
into a church of just men who have faith in the divine spirit,
and the congregation of those men make their prayer to God,
then the angel of the prophetic spirit, which besetteth him,
filleth the man, and the man, being filled with the holy spirit,
speaketh to the multitude as the Lord willeth. Thus, then, shall
the spirit of the Godhead be manifest concerning the divine
spirit of the Lord. Such is its power.

The writer then continues to the effect that no
amount of money can influence the divine spirit, as
money is only for the people of this earth. Consequently the divine, or holy spirit, says what he
considers to be the truth, whether it pleases the
congregation or not, and the medium must not be
held responsible.

This should be sufficient proof to anyone that the holy spirit to these early Christians was the spirit who controlled the medium, but we have further confirmation of this in the writings of Athanasius. In his time—the fourth century—creeds, doctrines and dogmas had taken the place of the medium, but he knew enough about what was thought of the holy spirit to be able to write :

My very dear friend, whom I so truly long to see again, you yourself wrote to me, in much grief, and told me that some held similar opinions about the holy spirit, and said that he was not only a creature but one of the ministering spirits, differing in nothing from the angels but in degree.

Here we find that some Christians, even in his day, when the psychic age of Christianity was drawing to its close, believed that the holy spirit was one of the ministering spirits, which was just another name given in those days to the controls of mediums, and is referred to in Hebrews (i, 14).

When Athanasius wrote this it had become a heresy to look on the holy spirit as other than the third person in the Godhead. That was the result of theological development, but, from what Athanasius has to say, it is quite evident that it was not the opinion of all the Christians, even in his time, and, from what we know, it was not the accepted belief of the Christians up to the end of the third century. With this knowledge we can now go back with a better understanding of what was believed to have taken place at the baptism of Jesus.

" The connection between Jesus and what we today could call a medium, in the opinion of the early

Christians, was complete because it was believed that he did what mediums can do when filled with the holy spirit, or when under spirit control. They also believed that the spirit control remained with him throughout his earth life, because they had to account for this divine spirit being seen as Jesus after his death, whereas, with a medium, the control manifests only when he is in trance or is hearing clairaudiently. Mediumistic phenomena to them was a manifestation of God, which Jesus exhibited in the form of miracles, as he was endowed with a spirit control. As this control was a being whose nature and origin they did not understand they applied to it the name of Holy Spirit, spelling Holy with a capital H and spirit with a capital S. From that time to the present Christians have looked on this individual as just another god.

It will make this question more easily understood if we drop the word "holy", and the capital letters, which are only additions made by man to the word spirit because he was dealing with something mysterious, in a realm beyond the material which belonged to a god or the gods. A spirit, whether a control, or one who does not manifest his presence through a medium, is no more holy when he lives in the etheric world than when he lived on earth. They are all very human people just as they were on earth, and would be the first to repudiate the suggestion of holiness.

Divine or holy spirit is not a purely Jewish or Christian term, as other religions also made use of this expression. Let us, therefore, get away from the mysterious, and consequently the sacred, which is the outcome of ignorance, and refer to this individual as a spirit, meaning an etheric being inhabiting an etheric body similar to our physical body. The best word for this being is Etherian, and then we get away from theological terminology and down to something we can understand.

The Bible, in places, terms an Etherian a ghost. Our word ghost comes from the same source as the German *Geist*, which means a spirit or spectre and also mind or intellect. This comprehensive meaning is incorrect, as the mind is something quite apart from the spirit, though it controls it, just as it controls our earth bodies through our spirits or etheric bodies. The name spirit denotes only the etheric body and when we say that a spirit was seen we refer to an etheric body which was seen, controlled by a mind which was unseen. A spirit is an etheric man or woman, shaped just as we are, with character such as we have, as the same mind which controlled the earth body still controls the etheric body when it separates from the flesh.

In many cases, where the word Lord is used in the Bible, the term should have been "spirit", and so we find that these four Biblical words, Ghost, Spirit, Angel and Lord, can all be brought together under the one word Etherian, one who once lived on earth, and has passed on, as we all shall do when our turn comes, to the etheric world interpenetrating and surrounding this earth of ours. In the presence of certain mediumistically endowed people an etherian can make his presence seen, as already explained, and sometimes his voice heard, as will be explained a few pages further on.

This is all so very natural, and devoid of mystery, that many will feel that such an explanation takes them out of the religious atmosphere to which they have been accustomed when considering Biblical events. To arrive at the truth, however, we must keep to facts and not be influenced by early training, prejudice and religious emotion. As the Christian Church has been unable for nineteen centuries to tell us anything about the holy spirit, or holy ghost, except that it is the third person in the godhead, it is fortunate that the mystery can now be solved by applying to it our present-day psychic knowledge. The clearing up of the mystery of the Trinity I shall defer until Chapter X, as at the moment there is quite enough to assimilate.

Whatever mistakes or mis-statements occur in the New Testament, one thing we can be sure of is that the people about whom it tells believed intensely in the reality of angels and spirits. We have already found out that those people were very simple and, like children, could evolve and believe stories which reached to giddy heights of imagination. That these stories were manufactured out of nothing, or for the wilful purpose of deceiving themselves or others, is beyond reason, and need not be considered. A child sees a couple of cats and, by the time the story has gone its round, these have increased to a dozen. It is not wilful deceit on the part of the child which causes this untruth, but childish imagination, which, from two cats, builds up a mental picture of a dozen cats all fighting with one another. As we grow older reason controls our imagination and unreal stories cease to appeal.

The basis of the story was true enough as the child did see the two cats. It was imagination that supplied the rest, and, if the child had been with other children at the time, the desire of one child to go one better than the other in telling the story would be another factor in producing the completed tale. Now the people we are dealing with in those days, when the New Testament writings were in the making, had just such minds, the imaginative minds of children, who, when recording certain mysterious happenings, drew largely on current mythology and psychic phenomena. Consequently, when we find that the word Angel, meaning "a messenger from God", is referred to a hundred and twenty-eight times, and the word Spirit, as meaning an etheric being, two hundred and five times in the New Testament, we must conclude that the people who wrote about them believed that such beings existed. Because they looked upon them as gods, or demi-gods, and borrowed supernatural stories about them, does not mean that they did more than the children with the two cats, which were really there and formed the basis of their story.

When, therefore, we read that at the baptism of Jesus "the holy ghost descended in a bodily shape, like a dove upon him, and a voice came from heaven", we search round for the basis on which the story may be founded. During five years (1919–1924) I sat on many occasions with John C. Sloan, whose wonderful mediumistic gifts caused me to write *On the Edge of the Etheric*. Herein I describe some of my experiences, which are the same as those recorded in the presence of other equally powerful mediums. Hundreds of thousands all over the world have had experiences similar to those I have recorded in *On the Edge of the Etheric*. From almost every country in the world I have received letters from people who have read this book and state that they themselves have had the same experiences. This is surely conclusive and sufficient testimony to support the statements made therein relating to the reality of the phenomena.

In the presence of Sloan I have, on numerous occasions, heard what is called the Direct Voice, the name given to a voice or voices which are heard in the presence of a Direct Voice medium, and which come from the mouth of no human being on earth. The precautions I took to satisfy myself on this point are given in my book and need not be repeated here. Before voices are heard, however, Sloan enters the trance state and becomes quite another personality. This generally happens in the dark, or semi-darkness, but I have heard these voices in daylight and so have many others.

One is aware that he is about to enter the trance state by seeing a bright bluish light approaching him. It comes at different angles, sometimes as if it were coming from the ceiling, and at others from different parts of the room. The light is first seen at a distance of about two or three feet from him and appears to be from six to eight inches across, flat and semi-circular. It is seen to approach him gradually and, when it reaches him, it hovers above his head and appears to become absorbed in him. Then his entire personality changes, and he becomes filled with the holy ghost, to use the old expression. When the light leaves him it rises diagonally from his head and floats up and away, retaining for a few seconds its original brilliance, then fading out of sight.

This light comes from what is called teleplasm, a combination of ectoplasm and psychoplasm, vibrating at a much higher frequency than any earth material. This reflects to earth etheric light vibrations which impinge on our eyes and thus make the object seen. The impression on our eyes of this etheric light, reflected from an etheric substance, is the reason why we can see what we call an apparition if it is intangible, or a materialisation if it is solid. The light which enters Sloan, and which in reality is what has been made visible of his spirit control, floats across to him. In its movement, size and appearance, its being compared with a dove, floating down and alighting on his head, is not out of place. Perhaps its likeness to a dove may be the cause of the dove having been looked upon as sacred in so many countries in the old days.

This light, which the gospel writers compared to a dove, and also the light given off by an apparition, become visible when ectoplasm is drawn from a medium and used by an etherian in combination with the substance termed psychoplasm, supplied by the etheric world. This accounts for the radiant, or glorified, effect which so impressed Paul and remained with him a vivid memory for the rest of his life, just as it remains vivid in the memory of all who have had the same experience in our own times.

This is not the place to give a further detailed explanation of the cause of this occurrence, and of the numerous other bright lights of different shapes seen at a séance when a highly developed medium is present.

Now I only register the fact that I, and hundreds of others, have seen these lights in the presence of John C. Sloan, a man who has devoted some fifty years of his life to allowing his body to be used by those who have passed on, and return to communicate with their friends on earth. The light which was seen to be absorbed by Sloan indicated the presence of his spirit control, who brought about his trance state, in which condition the ectoplasm was drawn from him by other etherians present who used it to materialise their vocal organs and speak so that we could hear them.

Bearing all this in mind, we now turn to the gospels, and when we read that "the holy ghost descended in bodily shape like a dove upon him and a voice came from heaven" we recognise the source of the story. The writers wished to convey the idea that the body of Jesus had become the habitation of an etherian, or what they called a god. Consequently they adopted this psychic event, which accompanies the Direct Voice, to explain how it came about, not because they necessarily knew the source of the story, but because it was the generally accepted opinion of the times that god-men were thus filled with the holy ghost. They may have taken the idea from Philo, or *The Babylonian Talmud*, or from the same story which was related about Zoroaster. What is important is that in those days the people thought one became a god-man, or filled with the holy spirit, in this way.

In his work on *The Ten Oracles*, Philo, the learned Jew, who lived in Alexandria, wrote :

God is not like a man in need of a mouth and tongue and larynx, and he seems to me on this occasion (the giving of the Law to Moses by Jehovah on Mount Sinai) to have worked an august and holy miracle. He bade sound to be created unseen in the air, a perfectly harmonious sound, more wonderful than any instruments give forth, not soulless indeed, yet not com_ posed of body and soul together like a living being, but a rational soul full of clearness and distinctness, which gave a form to the air and distended it and changed it into flamelike fire, and, like breath through a trumpet, sounded forth such an articulate voice as those far off, equally with those who were close by, seemed to hear it address them.

Philo wrote this before even the earliest stratum of Christian tradition was in being, for the purpose of explaining how God could speak to Moses. Doubtless he based his conclusions on his knowledge of the "Bath Koll", the name the Jews gave to the Direct Voice, to explain how it was that Moses heard a voice in the void, or, in Biblical language, from heaven. Philo, who tells us that he was a medium, thus uses his knowledge to explain what happened to Moses, just as I am using my psychic knowledge to explain a similar event connected with Jesus, without, as he did, calling the phenomenon a miracle, as we now understand the cause behind the effect.

Further, we are told in *The Babylonian Talmud* that when Hillel (70 B.C.–10 A.D.), the famous Rabbi—who flourished in the reign of Herod the Great, and was the grandfather of Gamaliel, at whose feet Paul sat (Acts xxii, 3)—was in Jericho, he had the experience of hearing the "Bath Koll". The voice that spoke to him stated that for his righteousness the holy spirit would dwell within him. This is not the only reference to the "Ball Koll", for in the earliest Talmuds it is frequently referred to and instances given of those who heard it. The fact that the Jews had a name for what we call the Direct Voice is proof in itself that it occurred, as people do not give names to things that never happen.

When we turn to Persian literature we also find a similar story about Zoroaster, one of the great teachers of the East. He was the founder of what was the national religion of the Perso-Iranian people, and is believed to have lived about a thousand years B.C. The Persians called the holy spirit the "Vohu Mano", meaning divine spirit, and it is related in *The Avesta*, their sacred book, that in his thirtieth year Zoroaster was enlightened by the descent upon him of the "Vohu Mano", after which he went into the wilderness to be tempted by the Spirit of Evil, known as Ahriman, who offered him all the nations of the world if he would only renounce the worship of Ormuzd, the God of Goodness, Light and Purity, and worship him instead.

Zoroaster replied by quoting Persian scripture, concluding with the words, "Teach me the truth O Lord", just as Jesus answered Satan by quoting Hebrew scripture. Zoroaster, like Jesus, believed that the age was at an end and that the Kingdom of Heaven was at hand, when his followers would witness the good separated from the evil on the Day of Judgement. To read his teaching, hopes and warnings is just like reading the Christian gospels, which latter only repeat what was said and believed a thousand years earlier.

What, therefore, is reported to have happened to Jesus was no different from what was believed to have happened to others before his time. Whether the gospel compilers based their story on a tradition of

Jesus becoming entranced, or believed, from their knowledge of earlier records about other god-men, that this was the accepted method adopted by God to change men into god-men, it is impossible to know. What we have, however, discovered is that what has come down to us as a unique event experienced by Jesus was attributed to others before he lived. The gospel compilers may have copied from the Talmuds but the last thing the Jews would do would be to copy anything from the Christian gospels. The Talmuds are, like Philo, independent witnesses of the fact that the "Bath Koll" occurred in Palestine before the time of Jesus, and that accounts of those who had experienced it were in circulation when the gospels were being compiled.

As the "Bath Koll" was heard in Palestine, and we know that the same phenomenon takes place today under the name of the Direct Voice, there is no reason why it should not have occurred long before the opening of the Christian era. So we are not surprised to find references in ancient literature to voices speaking from heaven, the one in *Deuteronomy* (iv, 36) being a good example, "Out of heaven he made thee to hear his voice". This phenomenon is also referred to in Exodus, Job, Daniel and frequently in the New Testament, in fact there are nineteen instances given in *The Bible* of a voice speaking from the void, which cannot be classed under clairaudience. The difference between the Direct Voice and clairaudience is that the voice is heard by all present, as is implied in the case of the baptism of Jesus, and not by the individual only.

To trace the cause behind the phenomenon of

the Direct Voice occupied much of my time some years ago. During five years I gave careful thought, and much investigation, to this unusual, and yet very real, phenomenon, which occurs in the presence of a medium endowed with the superfluity of ectoplasm necessary to enable the voice to be produced. The conclusions I came to as to how etherians are able to vibrate our atmosphere will be found in my book *On the Edge of the Etheric*, in which I showed conclusively that the voices were not produced by the medium, they being extraneous to him and not caused by any physical vocal organs.

All that need be said here is that the etheric being, wishing to use this method of communication, draws from the medium the substance called ectoplasm, which is treated by chemists in the etheric world so that the ultimate substance formed materialises sufficiently to vibrate our atmosphere. This substance can be operated upon by an etherian present, who can mould it into a temporary vocal apparatus, capable of vibrating our atmosphere, by materialising, by means of this substance, his lungs, throat, larynx, mouth and tongue. Thus he can speak so that all can hear. I have heard a voice speak so loudly that it was heard by people on the other side of the street to the room in which I was sitting with the medium and some friends.

On such occasions, not only one voice speaks, but many, of different tone and calibre, so that one can distinguish a female voice from a male voice and also a child's voice. I have often heard as many as four different voices speaking at the same time to four different people present, so that four separate conversations were being carried on simultaneously. This would go on at intervals for three hours, during which time the medium's hands were held, his right hand by the person on his right and his left hand by the person on his left, and he, in trance, was quite unconscious of what was taking place.

This is not the place to relate the means I adopted to ensure that the voices were not produced by any earth beings, or the evidence I obtained which satisfied me that they could only have come from the minds of those who had once lived on earth under the names they gave. Not just a few such voices have I heard but hundreds, of all tones, of men, women and children, which gave me ample evidence that they belonged to another order of beings who were in contact with us, though normally unseen and unheard. Moreover, this other order of men and women proved themselves to be none other than those who bore the names they gave, as otherwise they could not have conveyed to me the information they did. The evidence I thus received was so overwhelming as to be beyond dispute, but my experiences were by no means unique, as many others have witnessed what I have, though comparatively few have recorded them in writing, being satisfied with the experiences but unable to pass them on to others otherwise than verbally.

Philo, like all in his day, considered such a voice was something supernatural and so attributed it to God who, he says, "bade sound to be created unseen in the air", which sound, he tells us, though not coming from any human being, spoke in a voice "full of clearness and distinctness", so "that those far off, equally with those who were close by seemed to hear it address them". This statement, though over nineteen hundred years old, is a correct account of what is experienced by those who are in the neighbourhood when a supernormal voice is speaking in the presence of a highly developed Direct Voice medium.

If what I have described happens in the presence of those supernormal people whom we today call Direct Voice mediums, there is no reason why it should not have happened in the presence of Jesus, if his body were abnormally constructed, as are the bodies of mediums. If so, then it would have been the cause of his disciples looking upon him as different from other men, especially if he had the power of healing, to which so much reference is made in the gospels. This, however, is just conjecture, as we have no evidence to guide us, though when we find psychic happenings reported as occurring in those far-off days, which are the same as happen to-day, we know that people then experienced what we experience. What they tell us must have been based on actual experience, which could no more be the product of their imagination than is *On the Edge of the Etheric* the product of my imagination. All that we are doubtful about is whether they happened in the presence of Jesus, or were attributed to him when he came to be looked upon as a god-man.

Instead of the words "holy ghost" let us use the word "Etherian", and make the text read, "An Etherian descended in bodily shape, heralding his approach by giving forth a light which could be taken to resemble a dove. This descended on Jesus, and a voice came from the void." This would be quite a correct description of what occurs at a Direct Voice séance, though I would put it like this : "An Etherian, who acted as a spirit control of the medium, manifested and showed himself by a light which could be taken to resemble a dove. This light rested upon the medium's head and seemed to be absorbed by him. Then a voice spoke from the void, which could be heard, but the speaker could not be seen". This is a correct description of what happens today, and it is not difficult to relate it to the story of what occurred at the baptism of Jesus.

At a later date, when theologians took in hand the systematisation of the new faith, this etheric being, whom they thought was a god, who entered the body of Jesus at baptism, and controlled him, became a separate deity and part of the Christian Trinity. Theology is just the mistaken deductions concerning psychic phenomena, as astrology was the mistaken deductions relating to the heavenly bodies and their movements. The vault of heaven, into which man peered, gave him food for much thought, material and immaterial. His physical deductions were classed under the name of astrology and his psychic under the name of theology and mythology. Physical science, under the name of astronomy, has exploded his false deductions in the material realm, while psychic science has done likewise with his theological speculations.

The theologians of the first century, in order to account for the reappearance of Jesus to Paul and Peter in the form of a spirit, produced the story of his receiving at the Jordan that which nature supplies to everyone of us from our parents at the time we are conceived. For the same reason the virgin birth story was added later, because other gods, who had re-appeared, were believed to have received from a god at conception the bodies in which they were seen after death. This idea can be traced back to a female medium becoming controlled by an etherian when she entered the trance state. It is quite possible to understand how in ancient times one who came to be looked upon as a god-man was thought to be the child of a woman who had been controlled by an etheric being. Thus the belief in virgin births probably had its origin in mediumship.

The stories of the virgin birth, and the baptism of Jesus, therefore, seem to be intimately related to mediumship. Our Christian ancestors, ignorant of the causes behind what they experienced, put forward their own theories, which are similar to those found in all sacred literature. These have given rise to creeds, doctrines and dogmas, the product of theologians who spun their theories, based on phenomena which were believed to have been produced by a god or the gods. Today, Christian theologians deny the possibility of psychic phenomena, or attribute them to the Devil, and are in consequence wandering in the wilderness without guide or compass. They have had a very long innings but each year it is coming more and more swiftly to a close. The collapse of Theology is drawing near and, as Astrology was replaced by Astronomy, so Theology will be replaced by Psychic Science.

The words "Holy Ghost", as employed in the New Testament, could in every case be applied to the spirit control of a medium. When we are told, for instance, that "Peter, filled with the Holy Ghost, said unto them" (Acts iv, 8), we are reading of one who is speaking under spirit control. When we turn back to the Old Testament and read, "Thy voice shall be as of one that hath a familiar spirit" (Isaiah xxix, 4), we find the same fact expressed. When we read psychic literature of today, and find the statement that the medium went into trance, and his spirit control spoke, the same meaning is conveyed. There is no difference whatever in the meaning behind these three accounts because they all refer to the same phenomenon. What is remarkable is that over a period of some two thousand seven hundred years we are able to link up what occurs today with what happened then in regard to this little known science.

In the first half of the first Christian century there was this outburst of psychic phenomena, which had the effect of producing the Christian Faith. Because its source was not understood, everything connected with it was looked upon as sacred and holy. Therefore the spirit control of a medium was looked upon as a holy spirit, something sacred, and one of the gods, as someone who was welcomed, and whom it was considered an honour to house in one's body. So we read, "Grieve not the holy spirit of God" (Eph. iv, 30), or, in other words, do nothing that would keep your spirit control from returning and using you as his instrument. Avoid contaminating your body with evil influences or abuse.

How these words holy spirit and holy ghost have been misunderstood ! Think of the controversies they have caused, how from time to time they nearly split the Christian Church in two and how finally, in the eleventh century, the disruption actually took place, when the Greek Church broke away from the Roman Church because they could not agree as to their meaning. The literature that has been poured out, and the sermons that have been preached, in futile attempts to define the holy ghost, are beyond counting. All this has come about as the result of the mistake made by the early Church authorities in believing that an etherian, who acted as a spirit control, was a god, a heavenly creation and not of this earth.

First of all they thought that this god controlled Jesus between his baptism and his death. At a later date, when the virgin birth story was added, this god became the father of Jesus. Then this god was left in charge of the apostles, some of whom he also controlled. Tangling the skein even more, they then believed that the holy ghost was one of three gods, the third person in the Trinity, though he was the father of Jesus and must have existed before him. Jesus was evidently placed above his father because of his work of redeeming mercy, though, curiously enough, he never knew this father as he refers to his Father and the Holy Ghost as separate beings. (John xiv, 26.) Who, then, was this ubiquitous holy ghost, who, after producing Jesus, then controlled Peter, Paul, Stephen, Barnabas and many others (Acts vi, 3) whose names are not given, but who were all filled with this holy being, and, when in this condition, exhibited gifts (Heb. ii, 4), which could be none other than those associated with mediumship ?

Running alongside of this idea we find Jesus referred to by Paul as having existed from all eternity. "For by him were all things created, that are in heaven, and that are in earth, visible and invisible, whether they be thrones, or dominions, or principalities, or powers : all things were created by him, and for him. And he is before all things, and by him all things consist." (Col. i, 16.) This can only be understood by accepting the fact that Paul introduced into his theology the belief that at baptism the holy ghost, whom he thought of as a god from all eternity, occupied the body of Jesus, and that Jesus was the holy ghost. When the virgin birth story was introduced it was believed that the holy ghost took possession of a human body at birth. This is at variance with the creed, which makes out that the holy ghost is a separate person from Jesus, but the difficulty has been overcome by believing that the deity consists of three parts comprising one whole.

This tangled theological skein will never be untangled by the theologians. In the first three centuries of the Christian era the Church authorities planted a maze in which Christians have been wandering ever since. It is a dangerous thing to take the psychic phenomena of nature, spin impossible and contradictory theories and speculations about them till they become a religion, and then cover everything with a mantle of holiness so as to make it all too sacred and too mysterious for anyone to investigate. It was cruel and wicked to invent a word "blasphemy" for all attempts to rationalise the mystery (Matt. xii, 31), and to murder, burn, imprison and torture everyone who attempted to clarify the theological tangle, and prove that there was nothing holy or sacred about it.

The belief that Jesus gave this authority (Matt.

xviii, 7–9) produced the Inquisition, and all the diabolical methods and instruments used by Christians to extinguish the light of reason. Throughout the Christian era the Church has provided many a public holiday, at which the burning and torturing of heretics has been an entertainment, much appreciated by the faithful, who were encouraged in their wickedness by receiving the blessing of those who claimed to be God's chosen representatives on earth.

Pomp and circumstance, when Christianity ruled, were purchased at the price of liberty and happiness. For every cathedral built there was a dungeon. The clang of the fetters filled the air along with the music of the choir, and the hand that lit the taper on the altar lit the faggot at the stake. For every cross there was a sword, for every blessing a curse, and the cries of the damned mingled with the hallelujahs of the saved.

That, in a few words, is the record of the Christian Church throughout the greater part of the Christian era, and, because its speculations were founded on complete ignorance of natural psychic phenomena, there has been nothing but dissension since the religion came into being. The early Church authorities took their ideas from psychic manifestations, which they never understood, and, on this basis, produced their erroneous speculations. Then their successors adopted a policy of extermination of mediumship, and so prevented the people from discovering nature's own revelation, which, whenever understood, always exposes the hollowness of Christian doctrines and dogmas. Little wonder that psychic knowledge is so backward and is still the Cinderella of the sciences.

As intelligence increased, like steam which

accumulates in a boiler, the difficulty of keeping the boiler from bursting became greater every year. The extermination of heretics and mediums kept the explosion from happening for centuries, but the change came about in the eighteenth century, when legislation put a stop to Christian priests burning mediums in Protestant countries. From that date many and various attempts have been made to keep the steam from blowing off. All these met with less and less success, and now the priests are reduced to frightening the faithful, and the fearful, with blood-curdling tales of what happens to those who investigate psychic phenomena, and thus give themselves over to the service of the Devil.

Everywhere, since the Church lost its power at the Reformation, reason has been used to explain natural phenomena. Theology alone has relied on faith, and the forcible stifling of expression, with the result that it is now despised by all men and women of intelligence who love liberty and hate tyranny. It survives today only because it wraps itself round in mystery, uses unintelligible words, and professes that everything with which it deals is holy and sacred. Nothing can progress in this fashion.

The words holy and sacred have often been misapplied and misused. These words have been applied to what is unknown, and they have been used to keep the unknown from being explored. Against the strong opposition of the Church some have studied psychic phenomena and are gradually bringing it to the level of a science. The knowledge thus acquired is revealing the mistaken conjectures on which theology is founded. Consequently the mystery with which it was surrounded is being dispelled, much to the discomfort of the purveyors of superstition.

It is the last remnant of the age of ignorance ; when disease was believed to be produced by devils ; when the gods were supposed to be behind all growth ; when the skies were filled with gods and demi-gods, and the underworld with devils and demons who disputed the possession of man with the gods ; when all natural phenomena, such as thunder, rain and lightning, were the work of the gods who could be prayed to, to bring rain when there was drought, or to stop rain when there was flood. It is the last remains of the days when spirit controls were looked upon as gods or devils.

Theology went from one excess to the other as, on occasions, mediums, called saints after death, were looked upon as god-men or god-women, and as having been filled with some holy being, to whom it gave the name holy ghost. At other times mediums were burned and tortured to drive the Devil out of them. Theology is the last remnant of the age when apparitions were looked upon as gods who appeared to men as signs of some coming great event. The same ignorance which turned Jesus into a god was the cause of the massacre of mediums throughout the Christian era. In spite of being dug into its entrenchments, composed of vast wealth and vested interests, and having thousands of years of ignorant tradition behind it, increasing education and greater knowledge will finally dislodge theology and consign it to those tribes so far untouched by modern civilisation.

When Christianity was in the making, Christians had a large stock of accumulated theology and mystical knowledge behind them in the form of myths and legends, which enabled them to explain to their own satisfaction the mystery they were up against when the reappearance of Jesus caused them seriously to consider the meaning of it all. These legends, which were considered sacred down the ages, became the vested property of god-men, of those who were endowed with psychic powers beyond the attainment of the ordinary run of humanity. The cloak of many colours, which had been put on the backs of previous saviour-gods was all ready, and in good condition, at the Theological College in Alexandria, for the time when a reappearance after death was associated with circumstances already described. Then it was again taken out, brushed up, and put on the back of Jesus, who fulfilled the conditions.

So we now pass on to consider the next patch of which this cloak was composed. From the time that Christians came to believe that Jesus became controlled by the holy spirit at his baptism, he had to follow the path of his predecessors and exhibit his power over the evil one. Thus we are told that Jesus departed into the wilderness, so that the Devil could work his evil purpose on him, to prove that he was now proof against sin. In the opinion of the gospel writers Jesus was now acting as one controlled by a spirit, because we read, "Then was Jesus led up of the spirit". (Matt. iv, 1.) This brings us to a consideration of

THE TEMPTATION IN THE WILDERNESS.

The story of the temptation of Jesus by Satan, when alone in the wilderness, is entirely legendary, the source from which it came not being difficult to trace. Mark passes it off with thirty-three words, but Matthew and Luke tell a more elaborate story of different devices adopted by Satan for the purpose of testing whether Jesus, under the control of the spirit, was in reality sin-proof. John's gospel knows nothing of this sin-testing tale, but tells us that Jesus, after his baptism, was immediately recognised as the Christ, that he gathered together his disciples, and three days later they all attended a marriage at Cana. The earliest stratum of tradition tells us that Jesus retired to the wilderness, and we must therefore assume that whoever wrote John's gospel was either unaware of the story or he did not believe it to be true.

There is nothing unreasonable in the actual account of Jesus withdrawing to some quiet place in order to contemplate after his baptism. His psychic temperament, we imagine, would make him feel in close touch with the reality of the other order of life and substance surrounding and interpenetrating this earth. The people Christians term "spiritually minded" are those who are so made that their psychic senses play a more important part in their lives than is the case with most people. They feel themselves responding to influences not of this earth, and this gives them a different outlook from that of the average man and woman.

Such people turn either to philosophy or religious mysticism, mostly the latter, because so few are endowed with the philosophic mind. Thus today we come across those mystically and religiously minded people who do and say things which the ordinary run of people cannot understand. They do not apply their reason so much as their emotions to their outlook on life, and spin weird phrases which may mean something to them but nothing to other people.

Such individuals are in reality sensitives, which is next to being mediumistic. They feel more keenly than others the fact that they are etheric beings. Thus they are termed religiously minded and find their comfort in the emotionalism of hymn singing and prayer. The majority find that they can combine this with their everyday affairs of earth, but some feel life's worries too much for them and retire to monasteries or convents. In the old days, when life was less secure than it is now, these places of retreat were to be found everywhere in Europe and Asia, and accommodated a larger percentage of the population than they do today.

Turning over the pages of history, we find men and women who, having withdrawn from the turmoil of life, have made themselves prominent because of their unworldliness, or their detachment from the things of this earth. They tried to lead humanity to thoughts and aspirations unconnected with the material, denying themselves the pleasures of earth in the belief that by so doing they would increase their happiness hereafter. These spiritually minded, or deeply religious people, have always existed, and nineteen hundred years ago Palestine, like other places, had its share of those who put this earth behind them and set their desires directly on heaven.

Jesus was evidently one such as they were, and the story of his temptation is a symbolic legend to convey the idea that at this point in his life he was able, as one filled with a spirit sent from God, to renounce the world and the Devil, as since his baptism the old Jesus was no more, the new Jesus being a divine being incapable of sin and wickedness. He was now in close at-one-ment with the etheric realm, where dwelt God, surrounded by angels, all of whom were at war against the Devil and the forces of evil.

Moreover, we find that the story which has been draped round this period of the earth life of Jesus corresponds with stories regarding other outstanding teachers and saviours of the past. Buddha, we are told, was tempted by the Devil, and this story is very similar to the one relating to Jesus. He emerged the victor, as did Zoroaster and Krishna, who had like experiences. As Jesus was offered dominion over the world, if he would but acknowledge the Prince of Evil as its rightful King and Governor, so were they, Krishna being represented as treading on the head of the serpent. The Pagan devil Pan, half man and half beast, with horns, hoof and tail, which the Christians took over from the Pagans, as they did everything else, accompanied Jupiter up to a high mountain and offered him the kingdoms of the world if he would but bow down and worship him, again without success.

Jesus may have been a disciple of John the Baptist, or have belonged to some other Messianic sect. We do not know, but the impression with which the synoptic gospels leave us is that after Jesus heard of the Baptist's death he decided that the imminence of the coming of the Kingdom necessitated that someone should take up the work cut short by Herod. So he stepped into John's shoes and carried on his work. References to Jesus advocating baptism are very contradictory in the gospels. Those passages, in which he is reported as preaching it, are believed by scholars to be interpolations, added later so as to obtain the Lord's support for this rite.

The early Church adopted adult baptism from the prevailing belief in its efficacy, but when the Church became established amongst the Gentiles it adopted infant baptism from Paganism. The Pagan rite goes back into antiquity. The newly born infant was presented to the father, who poured water over it and gave the child a name. If the child were killed before this rite was performed it was not considered murder, but it was a crime to kill a child after the ceremony was performed. The Christians adopted a similar idea, and so we find that the Church proclaimed that only after an infant was baptised could it reach Heaven, and that all unbaptised children went to Hell. By such means the Church obtained a stranglehold over the people who were bound to it from birth to death.

The wilderness was the home of the god Pan. It was into the wilderness that the Jews sent an animal, on which had been laid the sins of the people. So the wilderness was the dumping ground of sin, which was an appropriate place for the setting of the story of the temptation of Jesus, as here the god of evil held sway. Originally the wilderness was some deserted place apart from the people, but in mythology it came to be the imaginary earth home of the gods and spirits of evil.

As it was believed that fasting developed the psychic qualities, so these old stories tell us how those who were tempted fasted in the wilderness, but the proof of Jesus now being a god was further demonstrated by his refusal to turn stones into bread, as no god needed earthly food. Buddha fasted for forty-nine days in the wilderness, and others for different lengths of time. The Yogis, in our own days, fast for the purpose of increasing their psychic powers. So, after forty days, during which he resisted all temptation, Jesus came out of the wilderness the victor. The Spirit of good had proved the superior of the Spirit of evil. That, at least, is the idea the gospel writers wish to convey.

From now onwards, Jesus is represented as uttering wise sayings, and performing miracles, as only one who was a divine being, inhabiting a frame of flesh, could do. We shall consider first of all

THE TEACHING OF JESUS.

We are told that Jesus, after his temptation in the wilderness, gathered together a number of men who were called his disciples. They came from a humble walk in life, some being fishermen. Who they were, and what they were, we have no means of knowing, as we have nothing reliable to tell us. That one, such as Jesus, should influence others religiously minded who, like himself, believed in the coming of the kingdom, is quite natural. If early tradition had not been weakened in every instance by the symbolic legends and interpolations which have gathered round it, what is reasonable would have been accepted as possible by many who today regard everything as myth and legend. There is nothing unreasonable in believing that Jesus surrounded himself with a body of men and women and wandered about the country preaching to the people, doing deeds of kindness, being misunderstood by his family, showing anger and human weakness, and making both wise and foolish utterances.

All this is true to life, and when we find these natural incidents in the life of one who was evolved into a god, we come to the conclusion that what is natural is probably the original stratum of tradition, and what is unnatural came about as the result of his appearance after death. In *The Quelle* document, known also as The Logia, or sayings of Jesus, we have the oldest account of what was believed to be his teaching. As his sayings were not put into writing for more than a generation after his death, it is very unlikely that what he actually did say has been correctly reported. Within that period he had come to be looked upon as the Messiah, and so it is not unreasonable to believe that what is reported of him was what the writers imagined he said, rather than what he actually did say.

Our only source of information is the synoptic gospels. *The Gospel of John* is of little help as it represents Christian thought at the beginning of the second century. Moreover, its entire outlook is mystical and, like Paul's epistles, it tells us little about Jesus. One has only to read what is attributed to Jesus in Mark and then read John's gospel, ending with *The Epistle to the Romans*, to discover the development which took place in Christian thought within the first century of our era. If we go still further back and read *The Quelle* document we find the contrast to be even greater, and the comparison conveys to us the amount of mystical and theological thought which grew up as the result of the appearance of Jesus.

The Quelle, on the one hand, and the Pauline and Johannine writings on the other, present to us two separate pictures. These can be accounted for by the natural development of ideas, and constitute a formidable argument in favour of the natural evolution of the Faith from some specific event, such as the appearance of Jesus. This led to the extravagant beliefs we find prevailing a hundred years after the event, which would never have come into being if a founder had himself laid down the principles of a new religion. They could only be the result of a great dynamic cause which gave the impetus to produce this remarkable development of Christian thought throughout the first century of our era.

The New Testament constitutes a record of this evolution of thought, the source of which can only be traced to some psychic cause as none other could have produced the effect. This being so, what Jesus taught carried little weight with the early Christians. They did not go back beyond his death and re-appearance and study his teaching. Paul entirely ignored what the master had taught and so did the other apostles. He had, by his death and reappearance, wiped it all from their minds, which were full to overflowing with the thought of his immediate return as judge, when those who were ready and awaiting him would be given privileged places in the new kingdom he would inaugurate.

As his return was delayed, and those who had known him had passed away, the wish increased to know something of what he had said and done. So, along with the theological and mystical development, some were interested enough in his life on earth to gather together what tradition had handed down as his sayings and teachings. A collection of these was ultimately put down in writing, the simple nature of which can be appreciated from what has been preserved to us in *The Quelle* document. This, however, must be looked upon as containing nothing more than what those, who thus laid the foundation for the synoptic gospels, thought Jesus said, and not what he actually did say. No one was present when Jesus was speaking, taking notes of what he said, as in those days no one had any desire to preserve the master's words. Each one, Jesus included, was daily awaiting the coming Messiah, and gave no thought to preserving the master's sayings, either for themselves or for future generations.

The indifference of his biographers to historical accuracy produced diverse results, as will be found by a careful analysis of the first three gospels. In these we find that each evangelist made use of his information as he pleased, with the result that no two accounts agree, as each used his material differently, enlarging or condensing it as he thought fit. Besides this, the difficulties of the early Church, and the constant criticism it received from the Jews, are reflected in some of the sayings attributed to Jesus. Furthermore, there is no consistency or connection between one group of ideas and the next, though they appear in the same discourse. Jumping from one subject to another conveys the impression that the writer is stringing together different traditions for the purpose of making a readable story, and not an historical account.

The gospels were written with the idea of

establishing the fact that Jesus was the Messiah, for which purpose the Old Testament was largely drawn upon, and, as this belief developed, they were amended to suit the prevailing trend of thought. So we find Christian beliefs more fully developed in *The Gospel of John*, which was the last to be compiled, with Jesus presented to us as the creator of the universe as "without him was not any thing made that was made". (John i, 3.) What a transformation from the Jesus who uttered as his last despairing cry, "My God, my God, why hast thou forsaken me ?" (Mark xv, 34.)

This being so how can we take seriously anything reported about Jesus ? Can we put our finger on one passage and say that this, without question, was an utterance of the master ? Unfortunately this cannot be done. The paint brush has been too thoroughly at work, touching up first this passage and then the next to suit the ideas of the times. Each editor added something new, which contradicted what was said elsewhere, and so the elaboration went on over the centuries until it all ended in a mass of contradiction and legend.

The Jesus of the gospels is the Jesus of the second, third and fourth centuries, a confused and composite portrait, not the Jesus, who, like others of his time, waited for the long hoped-for Messiah. Pauline and Greek influence, during those centuries, transformed a Jew into a god with all the dogma which now accompanies the Christian Faith. At best we must therefore fall back on the sayings of Jesus, as recorded in *The Quelle*, and feel thankful that even this imperfect account has been preserved to us. Its value lies in our having a record of something which is at least in the main reasonable, if not reliable. It preserves for us the foundation on which was set the erection of myth, legend and dogma during the childhood and youth of the new Faith.

What is known as the Sermon on the Mount is in no way original and its contents are to be found in Jewish and Pagan literature. The remark about the foxes having holes but the son of man having no place to lay his head, is a word for word copy of a lament of Tiberius Gracchus, who lived two hundred years before the time of Jesus, and will be found quoted by Plutarch. One has only to read the Jewish non-canonical books, such as *The Book of Tobit* and *The Book of Sirach*, to realise how the gospel writers have attributed to Jesus the remarks and sentiments expressed therein. The same phraseology, the same ideals, the same outlook on life are all to be found in these writings, which date from 200 B.C. up to the opening of the Christian era.

We have already read in an earlier chapter what the followers of Krishna believed he taught. Similar teachings were attributed to Buddha, Zoroaster and others. *The Talmud*, moreover, contains teachings similar to what was attributed to Jesus, and speaking in parables was the method adopted by the Jewish rabbis. The philosophic and religious discourses of the pre-Christian age were in no way inferior in thought and wisdom to those attributed to Jesus. Everything that is reported of him had been said previously, and it is certainly quite reasonable to believe that many of the wise sayings of the times were attributed to him, because it was thought that such things must have been said by one who had come to be looked upon as the Messiah.

Many of his sayings are to be found in the Old Testament, and there is nothing original even in the Lord's Prayer, which at first was only a few simple lines, as will be discovered by turning back to Chapter V, where they will be found in *The Quelle* manuscript. These were later elaborated in each new edition of the gospels. Compare this prayer with what it became three centuries later and as we still find it preserved for us in the New Testament. Here is an example of elaboration, and what happened in the case of this prayer occurred in regard to everything else originally reported of Jesus.

What all this reveals to us, however, is the probability that Jesus did command attention when he spoke, and made utterances which, because of their aptness, were remembered and handed down to receive the adornment given to everything else related about him. He may even have become entranced at times and have spoken under the influence of his control ; he may have been both clairaudient and clairvoyant, thus making the people think that he was a god-man. Most mediums today, in trance under spirit control, speak on a much higher level of thought than they could do normally, and, in consequence, attract large audiences.

The records, which have come down to us about Jesus, state that never man spoke as he did, and that, when curing the sick, he spoke with such authority that the people were healed. Perhaps the meaning of the original tradition was that in trance he diagnosed correctly and then healed the sick person. This happens today with a healing medium in trance, and would happen then ; in fact, most healing mediums diagnose and then effect their cures in trance, and there is no reason to think that Jesus would have been an exception.

One has only to read the sayings of Zoroaster to realise that what was put into the mouth of Jesus was neither new nor strange, for all attributed to him had been uttered a thousand years earlier by this light of Persia. Buddha followed half a century after Zoroaster, and what was attributed to him was doubtless influenced by what was attributed to Zoroaster. So the wheel went round, and, when Jesus came to be considered the Messiah, the usual accepted sayings of what such a one should utter were attributed to him. He never spoke as the Messiah, and yet his followers came to believe that he did, and supplied him with what they imagined he did say.

When the first stratum of Christian tradition was laid down in writing it was believed that what Jesus had taught was morally elevating, and that he had tried to direct the minds of the people from things material to those of a more immaterial nature. He is depicted as treading the wine press alone and as being neither a zealot nor a dreamer. We might also gather that he did not wish to destroy but rather to bring the Jewish religion into closer relationship with the etheric world, which is what we would expect from one of his evident psychic temperament.

This is quite reasonable to believe though it is based on nothing historical. Everything points to his sayings being adorned, like his deeds, from what were the accepted ideas of the times as to what a god should do and say. The earliest stratum of tradition also reveals that he anticipated the termination of the present age and the near advent of the Messiah, who would come in all his glory to judge Israel. These early beliefs remain and to them have been added, at a later date, the fact that he proclaimed himself the Messiah.

Whether, at the close of his career, he believed that he was the Messiah, is a matter of conjecture, but such a complete transformation as this portrays is unlikely and the first stratum of tradition that he, like his contemporaries, awaited the Messiah seems much more probable. Here, however, we are in a realm of doubt and uncertainty. All that we do know is that after his death Christians came to think of Jesus as the Messiah, and the only explanation we have for this is because he reappeared after death to one or more of those who had known him.

As scholars are of the opinion that Jesus during his lifetime was never known as the Son of God, we must fall back every time on this psychic origin of the belief in his divine relationship with the Father-God. When he became the Son, so Jehovah became the Father of mankind (2 Cor. vi, 18). This was a Pauline development, and not part of the teaching of Jesus, according to the first stratum of tradition, in which he is represented as not being a universalist in his outlook, his teaching being for the Jews of his time, and not for the world, or for future generations. It was for his day and generation only, as he, and all his countrymen, were eagerly awaiting the end of the age and a new order of society.

This outlook was shared by the Christians, Jesus having then become the Messiah whose arrival in the sky was daily expected. For this reason the ethical teaching attributed to him does not form any part of the Christian Faith. These ethics are not incorporated in any creed, doctrine or dogma of the religion, and have never been tabulated by the Church as a guide to life or salvation. Though some individual Christians have tried to follow the ethics attributed to Jesus, the history of Christendom reveals the fact that they have not only been generally ignored but contemptuously rejected. The belief in the creed has always been considered of real importance, and that only through baptism, and faith in the saving power of Christ, could salvation be secured.

A study of the Thirty-nine Articles of Religion, as contained in the Church of England Prayer Book, bears this out. Except for Article 38, upholding the giving of alms to the poor, there is not one single ethical idea to be found in the remaining thirty-eight articles. They outline a religion which is entirely selfish, one related entirely to self and one's own happiness, comfort and safety, here and hereafter. Salvation, and how to live, are entirely dependent on baptism and the belief in the saving power of Christ, as without this "Works are not pleasant to God". Countenance is given to war as "It is lawful for Christian men to wear weapons and serve in the wars". This need not surprise us as the only sin that God will not forgive is unbelief in Christ and non-participation in the sacraments of the Church.

These articles set out Christianity as it has always been presented throughout the Christian era, and a study of them will reveal how it came about that, when Christianity ruled, and was truly and heartily believed by the people, Christendom was the battlefield of continuous religious wars. Besides these it was responsible for persecution, torture and imprisonment to a degree more intense than is to be found anywhere in the history of the world. Heaven became the destiny of all the earth's greatest scoundrels, provided they were ardent believers in the superstitions advanced by the Church. Humanitarianism was unknown, bigotry and intolerance were everywhere, and learning was despised because, according to Article 6, the "Holy Scripture containeth all things necessary to salvation, so that whatsoever is not read therein, nor may be proved thereby, is not to be required of any man."

As the Holy Scripture is overflowing with cruelty, and shews utter disregard for the sanctity of life, it does not, therefore, surprise us to find the Christian era amongst the most cruel in history. The sufferings of human beings, up to within the last hundred years, received scant notice from Christian people, and today the same callousness is shown towards cruelty to animals. The Christian Church has never been their friend, but instead it has countenanced the hunting of foxes, otters, stags and hares, with all its cruelties. Before every bull-fight in Spain, and other Catholic countries where this form of sport is carried on, those who partake in the fight always receive the Eucharist.

I have before me a book entitled *Foxhunter's Philosophy* in which will be found quotations from the sermons of Catholic and Protestant priests, from an English Archbishop downwards, condoning or praising this means of finding pleasure, of which the following is an example :

Is it not in accordance with this great principle of suffering that animals should play their part by sometimes suffering and dying to help in keeping Britons hardy, healthy and brave ? This law is continually seen in operation. The supreme example of it was shown to the world on Calvary. Why should animals be exempted from this law or principle ?

At the celebration of the Feast of Saint Hubert, the patron saint of hunting, a stag hunt takes place each year at The Château Chambord, near Paris. Before the hunt there is a religious service and the priest blesses the hounds. They are then let loose on a defenceless stag in a park from which it is unable to escape because it is fenced in all round. This has taken place annually for hundreds of years, and has always received the blessing of the Church, in the form of a religious service, before the hunt begins.

The mentality which sees nothing wrong in making animals suffer is on a similar level to the mentality that believes in orthodox Christianity, and, just as the belief in Christian creeds and doctrines declines, so does humanitarianism increase. Over the past hundred years there has been a steady drift away from Christian belief on the one hand, and a decided quickening of the human conscience as to its duty towards the human and animal kingdoms. As the mind rises beyond the Christian conception of God, and his doings in the past, so we find more thought given to the welfare of the human being. Much has been done in this direction over the last hundred years, but we have not yet begun to carry through the abolition of all needless cruelty to animals, who have feelings like ourselves.

Jesus is nowhere reported as denouncing cruelty

to animals, but one who spent his short missionary life in healing the sick cannot be imagined as approving of cruelty in any shape or form. However, this has nothing to do with the Christian Faith, one way or another, as Christianity is not an ethical religion and has never claimed to be such. As Christians believed that their sins had been, and always would be, cleansed by the blood of the Lamb, there was no incentive to live good lives. Consequently passions and prejudices were not curbed, so much so that the history of the Christian era is one of unbridled passions, cruelty and misery.

Many individual Christians have lived good, noble and unselfish lives because their characters were such. Many have taken the life of Jesus on earth as their pattern and tried to live as they believed he would have them live. This, however, is something quite apart from the creeds and dogmas of the Christian religion, the belief in which brought about their salvation. Officially, the life of Jesus was only made use of to strengthen the doctrines and dogmas by the insistence that he lived the life of a god-man, and performed miracles which only a god could do. These miracles raised him in Christian estimation, because he was able to raise the dead, heal the sick, and perform other supernatural deeds. Such reported acts must be considered by themselves, and so we shall now deal with them under the heading of

THE MIRACLES OF JESUS.

In order to understand this problem we must divide all the ancient stories of miracles into two categories : (1) those which have a symbolic meaning, told in the form of a story and related to a god-man ; and (2) those which doubtless have as their basis magic or psychic phenomena.

The first miracle that Jesus performed was in Cana in Galilee, where we are told that he attended a marriage. (John ii, 1.) As the wine ran short he obtained some water, turned this into wine and so made up the shortage. This is not more wonderful than the story of Elijah who, during his sojourn with a poor widow, kept up the food supply by the help of Jehovah. Consequently she always found sufficient meal and oil with which to bake her cakes. From a casual perusal we would put this miracle performed by Jesus on the same level as the story of Jack, who sowed a bean one night and found the next morning that it had become an enormous beanstalk, up which he climbed to find another country which was quite new to him. We shall, however, discover that it is more than a fairy tale.

Facts did not interest the ancients so long as their stories had a symbolic meaning. They could not think in an abstract way but only as children do, and their thoughts could only be influenced by parabolic stories having no relation to the laws of nature. So we find that long before the Christian era god-men were credited with doing things which ordinary people could not do, as they had the power, being gods, to alter the laws of nature. Everything in those days was subject to the caprice of the gods. Dionysus was known as the wine-god, and he had the power of changing water into wine. So the story that is told about him is just symbolic of what happens in nature.

Growth and production, the ancients believed, came about as the result of the action of a god, and so they had a god for each fruit of the earth. Today we refer to nature producing growth but it is only a change of word, not an explanation. No one has seen the seed that gives life to earth, but only the physical garment which is warmed and wooed by sun and rain, so that from a tiny speck of dust-like stuff a violet or a rose springs forth. It is not the physical that gave the life but the mind within, which makes us realise that without mind there would be no life. This question of life and growth is a philosophy in itself and is dealt with at length in my books *The Rock of Truth* and *The Unfolding Universe.*

Today, just as in the days of old, we must give a name to the cause which produces growth. Whether we call this cause God, or the gods, or Nature or Mind, we can never get away from the fact that it is something intangible and immaterial and that life is related to the mental order of the universe. We can control this unseen force but never create it or destroy it. All we can do is to force it out of the physical, and from manifesting in the physical.

Because the ancients could not explain the reason for growth, Dionysus was credited with the power belonging to mind, which produces wine from the rain which falls on the soil, by transforming it into sap to become the juice of the grape. This wonderful process of nature, which no one can copy, was to the ancients a miracle which could only be performed by a god, and the one who was made Lord of the Vine was Dionysus, the Saviour of the Greeks.

It becomes evident that the story of the miracle

at Cana was appropriated from Greek mythology by the writer of John's gospel, which is the only one to relate it, when we realise that the Catholic Church celebrates this miracle twelve days after Christmas, the date of the Pagan wine-god festival. At this Pagan festival it was the custom to place three empty flagons in a church and seal the door, the belief being that the next morning they would be found full of wine. Thus did the Greeks symbolise and give thanks for the bounty of nature in producing the grape from which they derived their wine.

The story of Jesus telling a Samaritan woman that she had had five husbands and was now living with a man who was not her husband (John iv, 18) cannot be classed as a miracle. It was a record of a case of clairaudience which can be experienced by anyone today who attends a Spiritualist gathering when a good clairaudient medium is giving messages received from etheric beings. Often I have heard delivered messages of a similar personal nature which could only have come from someone in the other world who knew the person to whom the clairaudient was speaking.

Let me give an example. A woman in the audience is singled out by the medium on the platform to whom she speaks as follows : "Your father is standing beside me and he asks me to tell you that he has met Edward, to whom you were engaged and would have married had he not died. Edward sends you a message, which is that he gave you an engagement ring with three diamonds set in and you are now wearing it. His sister, with whom you were at school, is also here and she asks me to remind you that she introduced you to her brother Edward, who was with her when you met them coming out of your hotel in Paris."

I have heard many messages given to different people at the same gathering, most of them containing even more information and detail than the above. These details are given for the purpose of identifying the etherians who use the clairaudient, as we use a telephone, to send messages to earth people who can only hear what they pass through the medium, but cannot see them. I have heard many hundreds of evidential messages given from public platforms and, as I happened to be the speaker, I was able to look down on the audience, and see from the expressions on the faces of those addressed that what the clairaudient was telling them was correct. It is very seldom that a mistake of any importance is ever made, if the medium is of the first rank.

As this takes place regularly in the Royal Albert Hall, the Queen's Hall, and other large halls throughout the country, the medium cannot often distinguish the people addressed. Recently one of our leading newspapers made a special feature of this phenomenon and, by enquiring of those addressed, discovered that they were all strangers to the medium, that the audience was not packed with accomplices to whom she spoke, and that it was impossible for her to have discovered beforehand the information which was given to each individual.

This fact is in striking contrast to the evidence which was made public in the Law Courts, in London, on March 21st, 1939, during the proceedings of the case of Giddings, the magician, and *Psychic News*.

This newspaper challenged this magician to duplicate the phenomena of clairaudience and clairvoyance, and its report of his attempt brought the affair into Court. During the proceedings it was disclosed that before a magician can give information concerning the dead relatives and friends of people present, he requires to make enquiries beforehand, and the counsel for the magician, in addressing the jury, made the following important statement :

> As to messages from the dead they [magicians] caused enquiries to be made about people going to the performance, and discovered facts about people who had lost relatives, without those people being aware that Giddings, who was completely unknown to them, knew anything about them.

This, once and for all, completely disposes of any similarity between the methods of the medium and the magician. The magician admits quite frankly that he cannot know about the people present without making previous enquiries. On the other hand, the clairaudient medium makes no such enquiries and arrives at a meeting entirely ignorant as to who is to be present. Clairaudient mediums go from place to place all over the country. Considering the large numbers of messages they give, and the great number of people who receive them, they would require an army of spies going about before each meeting finding out about people who intended to be present at their meetings. As Mrs. Estelle Roberts once said to me, "If I had the spy system some people say I must have, my life would be made intolerable, because I would be under constant threat of blackmail from my confederates." A medium only gets one guinea or so for her clairvoyance at each meeting and it may well be asked how it would be possible for a spy system to be maintained, without great expense, enormous risk of blackmail, and danger of conviction of fraudulent practices.

Clairvoyance and clairaudience are definitely established facts, and when we compare what happens today with the story of the Samaritan woman, it becomes evident that the people of the time when the gospels were written had also the knowledge of this gift of clairaudience and clairvoyance. They either attributed to Jesus the story about his knowing the Samaritan woman's past, because they looked upon him as a god-man, or there was a tradition about Jesus having used the gift of clairaudience on such an occasion. This is just another example of psychic gifts being attributed to Jesus, and these can be picked out in the story of his life quite easily by anyone acquainted with psychic manifestations.

The story of Jesus feeding five thousand people with five loaves and two fishes comes under the same category as the turning of water into wine and has no psychic basis. A similar story is told about Elisha. In each gospel this story is told slightly differently, but they are all sufficiently alike to enable us to realise that they refer to the same event, and that it was believed that Jesus, with a few loaves and fishes, was able to feed this large number of people.

A similar story is told about Dionysus who, when passing through the desert with his followers, produced an abundance of wine and so kept a large company alive. The number of parallels between the miracles attributed to Dionysus, the saviour-god of

Greece, who was worshipped at the time of Jesus, and those attributed to Jesus, is worthy of notice and reveals the influence of Greece in those early centuries when Christianity was in the making. When, however, its centre of influence moved to Rome in the third century, we find Christianity being influenced by Mithraism, which at that time had such a hold in the capital of the Roman Empire. So, when Christianity was formulating its ceremonies, and organising its Church worship, it copied from this religion, and, as we proceed, we shall find that many Christian customs and ceremonies were copied from those surrounding the saviour-god Mithra.

The legend of the feeding of the five thousand is really a very apt symbolic story which the Christian Church turned into history and related to Jesus. Just as Dionysus, turning water into wine, was symbolic of the natural process nature adopts in producing wine, so this story of the five thousand being fed by a few loaves and fishes is symbolic of nature's bounty to mankind. A sower puts into his basket, seed, which in bulk is equivalent to five loaves, and he walks up and down the field distributing it right and left. With this basketful of seed he plants enough to produce wheat or barley in sufficient quantities to feed hundreds. Not only does nature supply us with our requirements from the fields but also from the sea, and it is well known that two fishes can produce a very large family.

This is what the ancients meant by such a story, and the reason it was applied by them to the god-men they worshipped was to relate growth to the god, behind the grain and the fishes, who caused the growth and the increase. Paul tells us that he could only plant but "God gave the increase". Thus they recognised what we might term the divinity within everything that grows, and what was more natural than to relate a story about Dionysus producing large quantities of wine, and Jesus producing a great supply of bread and fishes ?

This, and the story of the water being turned into wine, are the only nature legends to be found in the gospels, and are quite unrelated to magic or mediumship. When understood, their meaning becomes clear and their origin appreciated. Thus the ancients gave the gods the credit for producing wine, bread and fishes. It was from such minds that we obtained our nursery fairy tales, which were spun to please their childish minds and are now adapted for our children. What we today call fairy tales were their secular stories, whereas Christians class these old religious legends under the name of sacred literature, if they are associated with Jesus, and believe that they are God-inspired history. If the same stories are told about the Pagan gods, then they are classed under heathen mythology.

Another miracle attributed to Jesus is the story of his walking on water, and that on one occasion he gave Peter this power. This is just a story relating to levitation, and similar accounts are found in mythology of god-men walking in the air and on water. Stories are told of Dionysus and Hercules walking on the sea. Authentic records are preserved of mediums being levitated, one of the best, because it occurred in modern times, being the levitation of D. D. Home. His levitation was witnessed on numerous occasions by many, including Sir William Crookes, and other equally well-known and responsible men, who vouched for the fact that this occurred in their presence when no resort to trickery was possible. *The Encyclopædia of Psychic Science* devotes nine columns to accounts of different levitations from early times. A proportion of those levitated were made saints by the Church, if they happened to be devout Catholics. The rest were termed witches.

In *Die Christliche Mystik* we read of seventy-two saints who were believed to have been levitated, including St. Dunstan, St. Dominic, St. Francis of Assisi, St. Thomas Aquinas, and others well known to history. A study of the history of witchcraft reveals the names and experiences of others who were looked on as possessed by the Devil, because it was believed that their levitation was produced by the help of the evil one. Henry Jones, a twelve years' old English boy of Shepton Mallet, was reported in 1657 to have been carried by invisible means from one room to another, and also raised so that his body hung in the air, his hands touching the ceiling. This is but one of many similar instances which have come down to us from the past.

Recent experiments, by means of photographs, have revealed the presence of psychic rods extending from the medium to the floor, and thence to underneath a table, which were sufficiently materialised, and had behind them sufficient power, to raise it well above the floor level. Levitation is now scientifically understood, and this story of Jesus walking on the Sea of Galilee has doubtless as its basis the phenomenon of levitation. The story may have some tradition behind it, or it may have been adapted from the current belief of the time, that god-men could rise from the ground without apparent physical contact. These three seemingly miraculous episodes, which have been attached to the career of Jesus, are on a plane apart from his healing miracles, which we find running right through the gospel legends. Much of his time was devoted to healing the sick, and for this reason the gift of healing attributed to Jesus must be considered by itself under

THE HEALING POWER OF JESUS.

The teacher, in those far-off days, received greater attention if he could attract the people by his deeds as well as by his words, and in the East it is still the same in our own times. He had to accompany his words by signs and wonders. The magician with a glib tongue could work wonders amongst a simple people, but one thing he could not do by his magic. He could not cure people of their diseases. Livy, who was writing his history of Rome and her greatness a generation before the Christian era commenced, relates in his various works accounts of many miraculous cures. When they were all collected together at the end of the fourth century they formed a ponderous volume. These related principally to the miracles effected by the healing mediums connected with the Mystery Cults of Greece. The healing powers of the god-man Æsculapius were recorded in the temples dedicated to him, which records tell us of the wonderful cures he brought about "through his being endowed by the holy ghost".

The Greeks, for hundreds of years prior to the Christian era, were interested in healing through mediumship. They cultivated and protected their healing mediums, just as they did their trance, clairvoyant, clairaudient, and materialisation mediums. Pergamon, where a great temple was built, known as the Temple of Æsculapius, was the centre of healing mediumship, and Delphi was the centre of all other forms of mediumship. Besides this there were temples for healing dedicated to this god at Epidauros and Cos, in fact we know of two hundred healing temples dedicated to this god in the ancient world, in each of which tablets were displayed giving the names of those he had cured while he lived on earth as a god-man. In these temples healing mediums worked in conjunction with earth doctors and carried on the good work done by Æsculapius when he was on earth. He was a great healing medium and went from place to place healing the sick, just as healing mediums do today.

After his death he came to be looked upon as a god-man when on earth and a god in heaven, the son of Apollo. It was also believed that he came back to earth and controlled the healing mediums, thus helping on the work he inaugurated. Galen, the most celebrated of ancient medical writers, who was born in Pergamon in A.D. 130, wrote on one occasion to one of his patients : "We see again and again people who wish to be healed following the advice of the god, even if he forbids them to drink water for two weeks. The patients would certainly not carry out such strict orders if given by one of us."

The sanctuary of Æsculapius was founded at

Pergamon in the 4th century B.C. in memory of this great healing medium, and we are indebted to Ælius Aristides (A.D. 117–189), a Pergamese writer, for a minute description of what he terms the Asklepieion. According to him no medicines were used and the patients, while undergoing treatment, were encouraged in all forms of bodily exercise. During the day they were expected to run a certain distance, or ride or hunt. Music was played at regular intervals and there were constant theatrical performances.

This famous healing sanctuary has been unearthed within the last ten years and remains still exist of the theatre, which seated three hundred and fifty spectators, the library, the temple for worship and the temple for healing. Attached to these were dormitories, a swimming bath and other amenities. From a recent analysis the water has been discovered to be radio active, which was doubtless the reason for this spot being chosen as a healing sanctuary.

Thus the Greeks, and later the Romans, paid their tribute to this great healing medium whose cult resisted Christianity longer than any other of the Pagan religions. It could not, however, stand out for ever against the Christian barbarians, who overthrew and destroyed all its healing temples, and slaughtered its healing mediums. From that time onwards people paid Christian priests to pray the devils, they believed were causing the disease, out of their bodies.

Lucian of Samosata, one of the principal of Greek essay writers, who flourished about the middle of the 2nd century A.D., recounts in his work *Philopseudes* the psychic cures effected in his day, how the sick on being cured rose up and carried off their beds, or, more correctly, their stretchers, on which they had been carried, how the dead were restored to life, how evil spirits (his name for disease) were dispelled, and how an angel appeared to help in this work of mercy. Other ancient chroniclers could be cited, but the foregoing are sufficient, as they direct our minds into the correct channel, and away from the narrow Christian belief that Jesus alone of all men could perform acts of healing because he was a god-man.

We are told that Jesus on several occasions brought back the dead to life. As the people believed, when the gospels were being written, that Elijah, Elisha and Peter had performed this same miracle of bringing the dead to life, it is not difficult to understand how they imagined that it was also possible for Jesus to do likewise. Æsculapius was believed by the Greeks to have brought the dead back to life. The origin of the story related of Jesus raising the daughter of Jairus may, however, have been copied from a similar episode in the life of Apollonius of Tyana, who lived a generation after Jesus. In this case the story is of a Roman girl, the daughter of a consul. In Matthew she is the daughter of a ruler.

Philostratus (A.D. 175–250), the eminent Greek sophist, in his work, *The Life of Apollonius,* recounts this story of the raising of the Roman consul's daughter from the dead by Apollonius and describes the wonderful healing powers of this god-man. It is just as likely that Philostratus copied it from a current story about Jesus and attached it to Apollonius. Another possibility is that the gospel writers drew from the stock of current beliefs surrounding other previous god-men who were credited with this supernatural power. The resemblances between the stories of the healing powers of Apollonius and Jesus are very striking, as Apollonius cast out devils everywhere he went, and we are told that they talked just in the same way as Mark tells us they spoke to Jesus. Josephus also tells us that the famous rabbi Eliezer once drew a demon through the nostrils of one afflicted, in the presence of the Roman Emperor, and that the demon upset the basin of water prepared for his drowning.

The story about Jairus's daughter in the gospels is a late insertion and is not referred to by Arnobius, the Christian apologist, who described the various miracles performed by Jesus in his treatise in seven volumes entitled *Adversus Gentes*, and published about the year 303. Lactantius, another apologist who wrote in the early part of the fourth century, and recounted the miracles of Jesus, likewise makes no reference to the raising of Jairus's daughter, Lazarus, or the widow's son; and Matthew, Mark and Luke either never heard of the raising of Lazarus, or did not believe the story, as they make no reference to this, the greatest of miracles, John (xi, 1) being the only evangelist to mention it.

What is probably the truth about the raising of dead people by the god-men of the past is that they were in a state of catalepsy, and were thought to be dead. In those days many people must have been buried alive, being thought to be dead. The wife of the Rev. Henry Erskine, in the seventeenth century, was assumed to be dead. She was put in her coffin and duly buried. Fortunately, as it turned out, her husband could not get off her finger a gold ring, and so it was allowed to remain. On the night of the funeral, the family butler dug down to the coffin, opened it and commenced to saw off the finger in order to get the ring. This started the circulation of Mrs. Erskine's blood and she sat up in her coffin, to the amazement of the butler, who fled. She scrambled out of the grave and returned home. Her husband was sitting in his library, when a knock was heard at the window, and he went to the door to find his wife outside in her grave clothes.

After this very unusual experience, which is just as extraordinary as that of Lazarus coming alive out of his tomb, she gave birth to Ebenezer Erskine on June 22nd, 1680, at Dryburgh, Berwickshire, and this is probably the only case of a child being born after his mother had been buried. He was famous as the founder of what became the United Presbyterian Church of Scotland. Erskine was a direct ancestor of my uncle; and my aunt, who has this ring in her possession, naturally treasures it as a family heirloom.

Applying this story to Peter's mother, Jairus's daughter, the son of the widow of Nain, and Lazarus, we find little difficulty in imagining that through massage on the part of a strong psychic healer, such as Jesus may have been, the body would again be made to function, if it were in a state of catalepsy, and the people of those times would naturally think that the dead had been brought back to life. This seems to be the obvious explanation of these miracles performed by Jesus, especially when we know that one thought to be dead was restored to life by W. T. Parish, the present-day well-known psychic healer

who lives in East Sheen, London, of whom more
will be said a few pages further on. To many, Parish
is considered a prophet (medium) raised up by God,
as it is said Peter described Jesus, when speaking to
the Jews (Acts iii, 22).

We are told that Jesus healed by touch, in fact,
except for the foregoing outstanding miracles which
were attributed to him, and which were likewise
attributed to other god-men, his wonder-working
seems to have taken the form of healing rather than
of miracles, which could be related to magic. So
we read :

The men brought unto him all that were diseased and
besought him that they might only touch the hem of his garment, and as many as he touched were made perfectly whole.
(Matt. xiv, 35.)

Jesus put forth his hand and touched him. . . . And immediately his leprosy was cleansed. (Matt. viii, 3.)

And he touched her hand, and the fever left her. (Matt.
viii, 15.)

A woman who was diseased with an issue of blood twelve
years, came behind him and touched the hem of his garment
. . . And the woman was made whole from that hour. (Matt.
ix, 20.)

Then touched he their eyes . . . And their eyes were
opened. (Matt. ix, 29.)

Jesus . . . touched their eyes : and immediately their eyes
received sight. (Matt. xx, 34.)

He laid his hands on a few sick folk, and healed them.
(Mark vi, 5.)

She . . . touched his garment . . . and felt in her body
that she was healed of that plague. (Mark v, 27.)

They laid the sick in the streets, and besought him that
they might touch . . . the border of his garment : and as many
as touched him were made whole. (Mark vi, 56.)

For he healed many; insomuch that they pressed upon him for to touch him, as many as had plagues. (Mark iii, 10.)

They bring a blind man unto him, and besought him to touch him . . . and he put his hands upon him . . . and he was restored and saw every man clearly. (Mark viii, 22.)

Jesus . . . put forth his hand and touched him . . . and immediately the leprosy departed from him. (Mark i, 41.)

Jesus . . . knowing . . . that virtue had gone out of him . . . said, Who touched my clothes? (Mark v, 30.)

He took him aside from the multitude, and put his fingers into his ears . . . touched his tongue . . . And straightway his ears were opened, and the string of his tongue was loosed, and he spake plain. (Mark vii, 33.)

The whole multitude sought to touch him: for there went virtue out of him, and healed them all. (Luke vi, 19.)

They brought unto him also infants, that he would touch them. (Luke xviii, 15.)

He put forth his hand, and touched him, saying . . . Be thou clean. (Luke v, 13.)

A woman . . . came behind him, and touched the border of his garment: and immediately her issue of blood stanched . . . Jesus said, Somebody hath touched me: for I perceive that virtue is gone out of me. (Luke viii, 43.)

He touched the bier . . . and said, Young man, I say unto thee, Arise. (Luke vii, 14.)

And Jesus . . . touched his ear, and healed him. (Luke xxii, 51.)

These quotations from the three synoptic gospels in some instances evidently refer to the same events, but taken all together twenty references are made to Jesus healing by touch. John's gospel is silent on the subject of healing by touch though it refers to certain cures effected by Jesus, without mentioning that they came about as the result of the sick person being touched.

Tradition has thus handed down to us through

the gospels the knowledge that Jesus was believed to have this power of healing, and when we know that today there are mediums in our midst who also have this psychic gift, and effect their cures by touching, or holding their hands on the place affected, or by making passes over it, we can recognise in these stories about Jesus just what is going on today. There was nothing miraculous in what is reported about Jesus. If what we are told about him is true he was endowed with this great gift of healing which the simple people of his day considered miraculous.

We are told that some thought that he did his works with the help of God and that others considered that they were done by the help of the Devil. It is also quite evident that Jesus, like everyone else in those days, believed that he cured people by exorcising the devils who caused the disease. Psychic healers, we now know, work with the aid of etherian doctors, who are able to send rays of psychic force on to the affected part through the hands of their human instruments. This healing ray is sometimes so strong that if a person puts his hand between the hand of the medium and the patient, it has to be drawn away, as it experiences something comparable to an electric shock. A study of psychic healing reveals the fact that what takes place in the presence of these gifted people is caused by some power and intelligence apart from their own. This was evidently realised in the time of Jesus, because the people knew that what he did could not have been done by himself alone.

Those who attributed his work of mercy to the

Devil had the same mentality, due to ignorance and prejudice, which Christians have displayed over the past sixteen hundred years towards this form of healing. Even in our more enlightened age Christian churches close their doors against such healing being performed within their precincts, though we know that in the times of the apostles, and the early Church, psychic healing accompanied the preaching of the Christian Faith.

Reference has already been made to Jones, the psychic healer, who was the means of healing Doreen. Unfortunately he has now passed on, having killed himself with overwork, and no record was ever published of his marvellous cures, a number of which I have personally investigated. In our midst today is another psychic healer of equal eminence, about whose unselfish life for the welfare of humanity an account has now been preserved by the recent appearance of the book entitled *Parish the Healer* by Maurice Barbanell. Therein Parish's healing power is described by one who has had many opportunities to experience his great gift, and when this book is studied it is possible to understand what may underlie all the foregoing references to Jesus healing by touch.

The enthusiasm of those cured by Parish, and of those who know about the work he does, makes us realise how stories about the healing power of Jesus were handed down from generation to generation, and how it was quite possible that during his time on earth the claim was made that he was either the instrument of God or of the Devil. Parish is called by his friends "an instrument of God", but the bigots, and there are still many amongst us, just as there were in the time of Jesus, say that he obtains his power from the Devil.

As I have previously remarked, there is never smoke without fire, and however inaccurately the healing work of Jesus may have been reported, yet through it all there is this emphasis on the fact that the healing came through his hands. If something such as this had not happened, it is unreasonable to think that this method of healing would have been stressed, and that in every case reported in the synoptics the same method would have been reported as being employed. The touching of his garments, and the feeling he had that virtue or power had gone out of him, can again be related to present-day knowledge.

We remember how Doreen was cured by having placed on her head handkerchiefs held by Jones. Jones impregnated those handkerchiefs with some psychic substance which brought about the cure. The very clothes of a powerful psychic healer are impregnated with this psychic plasm. Besides this, when psychic force passes through the body of a healer, he is aware of it. So we find in this ancient account of Jesus a close resemblance to what we know occurs today in the life of a psychic healer. Though we need not take the details surrounding the cures effected by Jesus as accurate, yet, as previously remarked, when these ancient documents refer to something natural, which we know can happen, it is more easily believed than when they report something, such as the virgin birth, which we know is an impossibility.

Healing mediums have also as a rule mediumistic

powers in other directions. Almost invariably they can enter the trance state and be controlled by, amongst others, the etheric doctors operating from the other side. They have also often the gift of clairvoyance and clairaudience, and some can supply the ectoplasm required for spirits who materialise, or produce the Direct Voice. It is, therefore, a reasonable inference that if Jesus had strong psychic healing power he was also a medium for the Direct Voice and Materialisation, besides having the gift of clairvoyance and clairaudience. If this be so, we can understand better certain other episodes in his life, and appreciate the reason for the affection and respect in which he was held by all who claimed to be his disciples.

We remember the story of the two disciples walking to Emmaus shortly after their master had died, and how they told the etheric stranger who walked with them about their loss "concerning Jesus of Nazareth who was a prophet mighty in deed and word before God and all the people". Whoever wrote this believed Jesus to be a medium, or, as we would say today, "a medium strongly endowed with psychic power". This is what we are told was the feeling about him before he became deified ; he was evidently, to his followers, an outstanding medium whom all who knew both loved and respected.

The cures accomplished by psychic healers are in themselves sufficient, definitely to establish this method of healing, but, besides this, a healing medium in trance, under the control of an etheric doctor, can diagnose an illness by looking at the patient. No questions are asked and yet, in the great majority of cases, the seat of the disease is located immediately. I have been present in a room along with twenty sick people whom the medium had never seen before. Without asking a question the medium in trance diagnosed correctly each illness from which those present were suffering. The medium stood before each patient for a few seconds before speaking. Often his eyes were shut, and when he spoke he did so in a voice not his own, but as one speaking with complete knowledge of what was wrong. In no case was a mistake made.

Various methods are adopted by the etheric doctors to locate the trouble, and they tell us that they are guided by the luminosity which comes from our etheric bodies. This luminous atmosphere surrounding everyone is termed the aura, which can be seen by clairvoyants and etheric people. When our body is healthy, certain colours radiate from it which change whenever a part becomes diseased, and so the etheric doctors can locate by its colour the part affected. Sometimes powerful mediums are so surrounded by this aura that it can be seen, which is perhaps the reason why god-men are so often depicted surrounded by a halo of light. The halo round the god-man's head is to be found in religious art down the ages.

Psychic healers have cured so many diseases that it is impossible to say what cures Jesus principally effected. In those days people were so ignorant of disease that they could not describe what was wrong, so all ancient records do nothing more than state the fact that people who were sick and ill were made strong and well again. We are, however, definitely told that Jesus made the blind to see, which reminds me of a case in which I took a personal interest some years ago. A psychic healer, whom I know personally, fully restored the sight of a man who, for all practical purposes, was blind and had been told by his doctors that he would never see again. Consequently he was making arrangements to dispose of his business when he heard of the wonderful cures being carried out by my friend. Within a month his sight was fully restored, and he is today conducting his business completely cured, and thankful to be able to see again.

So when we read in the gospels that Jesus made the blind to see, and when we find recorded on a stone tablet, discovered in a temple in Rome, that Æsculapius restored the sight of two blind men, it is quite rational to say that if by psychic power this can happen today it likewise could happen then. There is no reason why the same cause which operates now did not operate then. Because our ancestors called these psychic healers god-men, and we call them healing mediums, does not alter the fact that a few specially gifted people were then, as they are now, endowed with this power which enabled them to make the blind to see, the lame to walk, and to cure "all sick people that were taken with divers diseases" (Matt. iv, 24).

We read also of Jesus healing people without going near to them, which is likewise a feature of psychic healing. What happens in these cases is well understood by those who study this question. Here I only record the fact, and also remark that many reliable instances are on record of what is termed distant healing. Professor Ernesto Bozzano, the

Italian savant, who has made a study of all phases of psychic phenomena, vouches for the cures effected, but he is only one of a large number of doctors and others who have proved the reality of psychic healing, both by the touch of the medium's hands and by the etheric helpers contacting and curing distant cases by using the medium as a connecting link.

The belief in demons originated in earth-bound spirits of low mentality possessing sensitives, whom we would now term mediums, who were then not blessed with a good etherian as a control. Naturally the demons were allotted a place in which it was believed they lived. This has come down to us as Hell, whereas those termed good were believed to live in Heaven. Owing to the belief in these two types of returning spirits, imagination developed the idea of these two states of existence in the other world. From what we are told by those who today communicate with us from beyond the veil, the division between the good and the evil over there is more determined than here, but there is no impassable gulf fixed between them, and when the evil can bring their thoughts into harmony with those of the good they can come together. Hell and Heaven are not places, but mental states which can be experienced on earth, just as much as in the etheric world.

In the time of Jesus we read much of demons possessing certain people, but this idea was largely due to their ignorance of disease and its cause. Our ancestors magnified unduly the idea that earth-bound spirits took possession of ultra-sensitive people, who lacked the strength of character to set their wills against the intruders. From this developed the idea that all those we now term insane, or who have double personalities, are controlled by demons, and from what we read in the gospels one would think that Palestine was packed with people controlled by these debased entities.

The insane were not then cared for as they are now, and all who were peculiar were looked upon as demon-possessed, so much so that this extended even to illnesses. Demons were blamed for bad health, just as they were for bad crops. The origin of the belief in demonology can be easily understood, as the possession of one psychically endowed by an entity of low mentality is possible, and much more common amongst ignorant and uneducated people than amongst those who understand the meaning of their gift.

Witches and wizards were mediums in various states of development, who, in the days of ignorance, were looked upon, and no doubt often considered themselves, as demon-possessed. Some of our ancestors were, however, sufficiently intelligent to appreciate mediumship in its true sense, so much so that right back in history we find some of those so constituted protected, just as they are today. They received the protection and care of those who were sufficiently influential and intelligent to be able to defy the Church, and prevent them being classed under the term of either witch or wizard.

We have no wizards or witches amongst us today, not because mediumship has changed, but because the subject is now understood, and not related to demons or the supernatural. Mediumship, like disease, is now recognised to be natural to the human being, but in the time of Jesus it was not, and that is why the psychic stream came to be covered over by dogmas and doctrines after it broke out in a flood, as it did in Palestine at the beginning of our era. The priests dammed it back and forced it underground, but not before it set in being what became known as the Christian Faith.

Nothing is clearer from the gospel accounts than that Jesus thought that diseases were caused by evil spirits. When someone was cured by his touch he evidently thought that a demon had gone out of the one afflicted. Such was the belief of the times, and so we have the story of Jesus sending demons into a herd of swine. If, after a cure, a nearby herd of pigs took fright it is easy to understand that the people would think that the demons had entered the herd.

I have experienced the return of what the ancients would have termed a demon. In this instance one who had been a debased criminal returned to earth and controlled a medium. This was allowed by the medium's controls, who took good care that their instrument would come to no real harm. The evil entity was very violent, and threw the medium on the floor, cursing and swearing, his language being of the foulest description. Gradually he was tamed, and, when last I heard of his return, he was a changed being. It is very probable that some people, looked upon as insane, are in reality undeveloped mediums under the influence of etheric earth-bound spirits. By being brought into contact with the more highly developed spirit controls of Jesus, those termed insane in his day may have been cured by the evil spirits being influenced, by these controls, to leave those they were controlling and take up a more natural life.

The one to whom I have referred, who on earth had been a criminal, was tamed by the policy of the controls who protected the medium with whom I sat. They allowed him to make contact with earth and become influenced by the higher mentality with which he was brought into contact, after which they were able to bring him to a better and less embittered outlook on life. Edward C. Randall, of Buffalo, U.S.A., in his day an outstanding lawyer and President of the American Super Power Company, which supplies New York with light, told me, when I stayed with him some fifteen years ago, that he had given up many hours of his busy life to the work of helping to a higher level of thought debased spirits who were permitted to manifest through the medium with whom he sat. What he did others have done, and that being so, Jesus, by his mediumship, could have been the instrument used by his controls to bring them and the so-called demons into touch with each other.

If he cured those called insane it was due to his bringing his controls into contact with the evil spirit controlling the afflicted one. This can only be understood when it is remembered that the good in the etheric world often cannot appreciate the presence of the evil, and vice versa, because of the different vibrations each sets up. Only by using a human instrument, in certain cases, can those spirit missionaries, who wish to help those living in darkness in the other world, get into contact with earth-bound spirits to raise them to a realisation of the fact that they have left this earth and cannot return to it.

This vast subject, about which volumes could be written, can only be touched on here. The literature on the subject is already extensive, and a perusal of Dr. Carl Wickland's *Thirty Years Among the Dead* will bring home to the reader the fact that some phases of insanity are due to possession and can be cured through mediumship. Dr. Wickland's wife was the medium for the numerous cures he obtained, and, during her lifetime, they both gave themselves up to this work of mercy, acting as the instruments of a band of healers on the other side.

In those old days, when doctors were non-existent and little or nothing was known of disease, or the make-up of the human body, it is not to be wondered at that anyone who allowed his body to be used by etheric healers to cure the sick was looked upon as one filled with the holy spirit, and that the belief spread so that "multitudes followed him and he healed them all". If Jesus, during his lifetime, were considered to be so endowed it would make it easier for his followers, after his reappearance, to believe in his divinity. This was definitely established, as the result of his etheric appearance, before the Church went down the wrong road and adopted the belief that he rose from the grave in his physical body, an idea which would never have been thought of if it had not been for his etheric appearance.

The healing power of Jesus evidently attracted some people of importance and wealth. It is a mistake to think that he just lived on what he could pick up as he went along. Luke tells us that certain women of position supported him. He had healed them and this was the way they showed their gratitude.

So we read that they "ministered unto him of their substance". (Luke viii, 3.) Among these women was Mary Magdalene, about whom, due to a misreading of the text, the quite baseless idea has developed that she was a fallen woman, also Joanna the wife of Chuza, who was Steward to King Herod, and Susanna and "many others".

There is something very natural and human about this information and, assuming Jesus to be a healing medium, it so corresponds with what happens today when mediums receive gifts and are often supported by some of those they have healed. What a difference it would have made to our religious outlook, and our knowledge of the psychic framework of the physical body, if this had been allowed to continue throughout the Christian era and mediums had been ministered to by those they had healed. This is what took place in the Apostolic Church, and continued throughout the first three Christian centuries, but the tightening grip of the priesthood strangled it, and, from the fourth century to our own times, the cruel claws of the priesthood have never been withdrawn from the throat of mediumship.

According to the synoptic gospels Jesus had also the power of enabling etheric beings to materialise in his presence. This episode in his life is known as the Transfiguration, so we shall now give some thought to

THE TRANSFIGURATION OF JESUS.

We find the account of this event in the gospels of Matthew, Mark and Luke, but nothing is said about it in *The Gospel of John.* The synoptic gospels, however, agree in that they all tell us that Jesus, accompanied by Peter, James and John, went into a high mountain where he was transfigured before them. Matthew says that his raiment was white as the light. Mark describes it as white as snow and Luke remarks that it was white and glistening. Matthew tells us that the face of Jesus did shine as the sun, whereas Luke says that his countenance was altered. All the three synoptic accounts also refer to a cloud which accompanied this phenomenon, out of which a voice spoke the words which were always associated with visitors to Jesus from the etheric world, "This is my beloved son, hear him." Then out of the cloud appeared Moses and Elias, who talked with Jesus. Luke alone informs us that the three disciples were filled with a deep sleep, out of which they awakened to see Jesus radiant and talking to the two spirits.

Dennis Bradley, in his book, *The Wisdom of the Gods*, describes in the following words an experience he had with Mrs. Scales :

Gradually the whole of the expression of the medium's face changed completely. It was a transformation. Whilst the outline remained, the eyes and the expression became beautiful. . . . At first it was only with great difficulty that a few words were articulated. It was as if they were produced with considerable effort. Within a little while, however, the power strengthened considerably, and the spirit of my sister was able to assume complete control. It was my sister. It was her spirit, using the organism of another physical body, and speaking to me in her own voice.

This quotation is given for the purpose of recording that in our own times a medium's face can become transfigured, in fact I have seen this happen on various occasions, the brightness of the face coming from the ectoplasm covering it, which had been drawn from the medium's body. Many other similar instances could be quoted from accounts received from investigators in all parts of the world, but what has been said is sufficient to emphasise my point that a medium's face can become bright and shining when those on the other side care to take the trouble to produce this phenomenon.

Besides the shining appearance of the face of Jesus, all the synoptic gospels mention Moses and Elias as being seen by everyone present. As these two figures were thus seen we must assume that they had passed out of the range of being visions only and were actual materialisations, something similar to King Alexander of Serbia's materialisation in the presence of Mrs. Leonard and her friends, to which reference was made in Chapter VI.

The full materialisation of an etherian is rare, but has happened often enough, under good test conditions, to make the fact undisputed. A number of books of recent years, written by trustworthy and competent scientific men, testify to this, but the opinions of two who have witnessed it must suffice. Dr. Charles Richet, Professor of Physiology at the Faculty of Medicine, Paris, the most eminent scientist of his day in this branch of knowledge, wrote as follows in his book, *Thirty Years of Psychical Research,* which was published a few years ago :

I shall not waste time in stating the absurdities, almost the impossibilities, from a psycho-physiological point of view, of this phenomenon. A living being, or living matter, formed under our eyes, which has its proper warmth, apparently a circulation of blood, and a physiological respiration, which has also a kind of psychic personality, having a will distinct from the will of the medium, in a word, a new human being! This is surely the climax of marvels! Nevertheless it is a fact.

Another scientist, equally eminent in his line of thought, was Sir William Crookes, one of the greatest physicists of last century, and one time President of the Royal Society, who published his investigations into psychic phenomena in the *Quarterly Journal of Science*. These were reprinted and published under the title of *Researches in the Phenomena of Spiritualism*. Among other things he gives an elaborate and detailed account of a materialised form, who called herself by the name of Katie King, and appeared in the presence of the medium Florence Cook.

Point by point Crookes tabulates what he experienced under conditions which made fraud and trickery impossible. When the medium was in trance, lying on the sofa, the form of Katie King materialised in his presence and then walked about the room fully clothed, in the full view of eight people. Katie carried on conversations with everyone present and played with Crookes' children, telling them stories of her adventures in India when she lived on earth. Crookes reports that she took his arm, that he in turn put his arm round her waist, and that the woman behaved as a normal human being. She appeared and disappeared from sight instantaneously.

So as to make certain that Katie King and the medium were separate individuals he photographed them together, forty separate photographs being obtained. It was impossible for them to be the same individual as they were of different height, Katie being half a head taller, and the colour of their eyes and hair was also different. Katie's hair was rich golden auburn and the medium's almost black. The medium had her ears pierced for earrings, Katie's were unpierced ; the medium had short fingers and Katie had long. The medium had a large blister on her neck while Katie had not. Katie's pulse beat at seventy-five and the medium's at ninety. Their looks and build were also different, Katie being a bigger woman than the medium, in fact they were two unmistakably separate beings. This took place, not once, but on many occasions in different places over three years, but mostly in a prepared room in Crookes' own house, which was locked and barred against intruders.

In 1874, in the *Quarterly Journal of Science*, he wrote as follows :

> To imagine that an innocent schoolgirl of fifteen (the medium) should be able to conceive and then successfully carry out for three years so gigantic an imposture as this, and in that time should submit to any test which might be imposed upon her, should bear the strictest scrutiny, should be willing to be searched at any time, either before or after the séance, and should meet with even better success in my house than at her parents', knowing that she visited me with the express object of submitting to strict scientific tests ; to imagine, I say, the Katie King of the last three years to be the result of imposture, does more violence to one's reason and common sense than to believe what she herself affirms.

The evidence in favour of the contention that in the presence of certain mediums full form materialisations of one or more individuals takes place is now more than sufficient to establish it as a fact. We now can say with scientific certainty that for a short space of time other beings can appear before us who, in conversation, claim to have lived on earth, to have died, and now to be living in a different order of matter surrounding and inter-penetrating this earth of ours. How and where they live is explained at length in *The Unfolding Universe.*

Though they are often in our presence yet they cannot be seen because of their faster vibrations, but, by means of ectoplasm taken from a medium, they can slow down these sufficiently for a limited time in order that they may be seen and handled. Their coming into our view occurs when the ectoplasm takes effect and their disappearance from view when it loses its effect. Though they are thus lost from sight they can still remain in our company, because they are individuals having bodies shaped as ours, which house the same minds as they had when on earth.

Such then, briefly, is the knowledge which we have acquired on this subject over the last hundred years, and when we read that Krishna appeared on one occasion with his "face like the moon and wearing a diadem", we can think of the experience Dennis Bradley had when the medium's face changed com-pletely and her eyes and expression became beautiful. We read also in Exodus of a similar transformation coming over Moses, who was transfigured on a mountain "when the skin of his face shone while he talked to" the Lord. (Exod. xxxiv, 29.) In other words, Moses was a medium and the Lord, or Yaweh, was an etherian who made the face of Moses to shine with ectoplasm while they carried on a conversation.

In the synoptic account of the transfiguration of Jesus, and the materialisation of Moses and Elias, reference is made to a bright cloud overshadowing them, which phenomenon precedes materialisation, it being the cloud of ectoplasm which first appears, to disappear gradually when its place is taken by the materialised figure. By absorbing this cloud of ectoplasm the spirit can make itself seen to our eyes. The reference to the disciples sleeping during this occurrence may mean that they went into trance, as one can hardly imagine anyone falling into natural sleep when such an extraordinary event was being enacted.

Some of the Christian fathers explained the transfiguration as the fulfilment of the promise, which Jesus had made some days previously, that he would let some of his disciples see a glimpse of his glory before his death so as to fortify them for his coming departure, and to prove that he was the Messiah. He had appeared among men humble, poor and despised, but on this occasion he showed himself in the real splendour of his glory, and in his true and natural condition.

Why, if this be so, did he instruct Peter, James and John, after it was all over, to tell no man till the Son of Man be risen from the dead ? If Peter had this experience would he ever have denied his master ? It is impossible to reconcile the story of the transfiguration with the one which follows, relating that Peter denied all knowledge of Jesus. Have the early Fathers, and Christians generally, not reversed the entire order of the proceedings ? The glorification of Jesus came about as the result of his appearance after death and, because of this, we have the story of his transfiguration. Yet the writer of John's gospel never refers to this event, and early tradition is equally silent.

It was quite possible for Jesus to have been transfigured during his lifetime and for him, in the company of his disciples, to have seen the materialised forms of two spirits. As this happens today it could have happened then, provided one of the company was a materialising medium. This, however, is the most that can be said. It is possible that such an event occurred, but the evidence that it did happen, as given in the synoptic gospels, is quite insufficient for our purpose.

To believe in such an unusual episode we must have first-hand evidence from one we know and from one who had made certain that trickery was impossible. No details are given in this case, and Peter, James and John do not witness for it independently on any occasion ; in fact, when Jesus was arrested, they all scattered and were as men without hope. It seems to be just a story thrown into the life of Jesus for the purpose of linking him up with the other world during his time on earth. It had a similar purpose as the miracles, which were added so as to give him the same status in the eyes of the Greeks as had Dionysus, who could turn water into wine and feed thousands in the wilderness with next to nothing.

Outside the sacred Christian literature stories have come down to us of the materialisation of spirits, and in the last chapter we read about this occurring in the presence of mediums at the Eleusinian Mystery drama. We are told that Saul, when he visited the medium of Endor, experienced the return of Samuel to earth conditions. Such happenings bring us more closely into touch with the etheric world than any other phase of psychic phenomena. The story of the transfiguration was eminently suitable for the occasion when it was written, as then it was believed that Jesus had opened the way to heaven for all mankind, and that, while he was on earth, he was intimately in touch with the etheric order of existence.

What could be more appropriate than to relate that two great figures in Jewish history returned to earth and spoke "of his decease which he should accomplish at Jerusalem"? (Luke ix, 31.) Long after the time Jesus was on earth they were thus made to act as heralds of the new era he had ushered in, and the current knowledge of the materialisation of spirits was brought to bear on this belief, out of which the story was evolved. Here, as in the case of every other episode in the life of Jesus, we must think of each originating from the minds of the people who looked back fifty years or more and believed that the heavenly being they called Christ, whom they worshipped, was once a god-man on earth in close touch with Jehovah and his angels.

We must always start from the appearance of Jesus after death and work back, thinking the reverse way from that to which we have been accustomed. As his life is presented to us in the gospels we work up to his death through stories of miracles and records of psychic happenings portraying him as a god-man, whereas these all came to be woven round him after his death because of his reappearance, which, in the minds of his biographers, had proved that he was a god. Consequently his life was portrayed, when written fifty years after his death, as that of a god-man and, in the case of the event we are considering, psychic phenomena were employed to strengthen Christian belief.

Without, therefore, accepting the details, or even the fact that Jesus and his three disciples had this experience, it is sufficient for our purpose to relate it to his reappearance after death, out of which it and all else followed. His reappearance gave the necessary urge to build up the appropriate stories, the truth of which was not important to his biographers, so long as they strengthened Christian belief. What is true, was the intensity of the wish of these early Christians to give Jesus all the honours due to a god, and they could think of nothing more suitable than to tell that he went about performing miracles, calming storms, catching shoals of fish, and that in his presence the dead appeared. All such legends were taken from symbolic nature stories or psychic phenomena, both of which, in their minds, were closely related to the gods of heaven, of which Jesus had proved himself to be one.

The same reasoning was behind the story, told in all four gospels, that towards the end of his ministry the people recognised his divinity, which resulted in his triumphal entry into Jerusalem. As this, however, forms part of the Passion Drama, it will be considered in the next chapter, after reading which we shall find that the gospel stories of the life of Jesus came from two separate sources. So far as we have gone these legends relate to his birth, early life, baptism and ministry, which each evangelist took from the stories circulating at the time of writing. These were enlarged, improved upon, and added to in the succeeding centuries. What follows in the next chapter was compiled in quite a different way, as we shall discover as we go on.

Now we have come to the consideration of what took place in the final week of the life of Jesus, according to the beliefs of Christians towards the end of the first century, and to this we must devote an entire chapter.

CHAPTER VIII

CHRISTIANITY—ITS CHILDHOOD

PART II

THE story of Jesus entering Jerusalem in triumph, as it has come down to us, comprises the beginning of the end of his career. This we shall now consider under the sub-title of

THE MESSIANIC ENTRY INTO JERUSALEM.

We read that Jesus instructed two of his disciples to go to Bethany, at the southern end of the Mount of Olives, to fetch a colt. When this animal arrived the people put their cloaks upon it and Jesus rode triumphantly into Jerusalem. Mark tells us, "Many spread their garments in the way; and others cut down branches off the trees, and strewed them in the way . . . saying, Hosanna! Blessed is he that cometh in the name of the Lord! Blessed be the kingdom of our father David that cometh in the name of the Lord. Hosanna in the highest. And Jesus entered into Jerusalem and into the Temple." (Mark xi, 8.)

This story of the Messianic entry into the city, like much else told about him, was related in order that prophecy might be fulfilled. Therefore Matthew reminds us that Zechariah had anticipated it years before when he had said : "Rejoice greatly, O daughter of Zion ; shout, O daughter of Jerusalem ; behold, thy King cometh unto thee; he is just, and having salvation ; lowly, and riding upon an ass, and upon a colt the foal of an ass." (Zec. ix, 9.)

Anyone reading the chapter of Zechariah, from which the above is taken, will realise at once that the prophet had no such idea in his mind when he wrote it, in fact it is only one verse taken out of an entire chapter dealing with events which could not be related to Jesus by even the greatest stretch of imagination.

Are we to believe that Jesus was thus acclaimed by the people ? If so, we naturally wonder why the account ends so abruptly, to be followed by the statement that the same evening he went to Bethany and the next day was hungry. It is also strange how all the enthusiasm stopped when he reached the door of the Temple and that four days afterwards the people were imploring Pilate to crucify him. Nobody seemed to know anything about the affair the next day, and we are given instead the strange story about Jesus cursing the fig tree because it had no figs, though we are told that "the time of figs was not yet". Evidently the idea behind this story was that even a fig tree should have recognised his divinity and produced fruit for him. Because of its neglect it was made barren for ever. Probably there was some symbolic meaning intended, but it is certainly difficult to appreciate.

A careful reading of the synoptic gospel records of the career of Jesus at this time will make clear that this story of the fig tree has been inserted between the account of his entry into Jerusalem and the cleansing of the Temple. The question naturally arises as to whether or not the original legend has been broken in two. We are told that after this triumphal procession Jesus entered the Temple "and when he had looked round about upon all things" he went to Bethany. Then was surely the time, with the mob behind him, to clear the Temple of the money-changers who were desecrating its precincts. But no, he goes off to Bethany and curses a fig tree. What a strange story !

Originally the tale must surely have continued with the clearing out of the money-changers after the triumphal entry into Jerusalem, and not after Jesus came back from cursing the fig tree. The area covered by the Temple was great, six hundred feet long by six hundred feet broad, and he could not have cleared it alone, as we are told he did, though it might have been possible if he had been backed up by the crowd which had followed him the previous day.

In this story of the cleansing of the Temple we find Jesus represented as at the height of his career, defying the priests in their own domain, so that the prophecy might be fulfilled—"In that day there shall be no more a merchant in the House of the Lord of Hosts." (Zec. xiv, 21.) John's gospel inverts the sequence, as it does most of the events in the life of Jesus, and tells us that he drove out the money-changers shortly after his temptation in the wilderness, and not four days before his death, as related in the other gospels. The writer evidently copied the story from one of the three synoptic gospels and inserted it anywhere, quite regardless of chronology.

How this story of good overcoming evil must have been appreciated by the Christians at the time it was produced, as their most formidable enemies were then the Jewish rabbis, bitter at the loss of their status through the break up of the priesthood, and also because so many Hellenised Jews had adopted the new faith. By then the Temple had been destroyed and Christians could answer all the awkward questions raised by the Jews with the retort that Jesus had warned them of their fate, and that what had happened was their just punishment for all their wickedness.

The three synoptic gospels emphasise that from the time Jesus entered Jerusalem in triumph the priests were determined to kill him, but he did nothing to assuage their anger. Instead, he told them the parable of the wicked husbandman, and argued and debated with the Pharisees and Sadducees on subjects about which they felt keenly. From this time onwards he goes forward to his fate and is portrayed as calmly accepting the destiny he had already foreseen.

To return to the prophecy of Zechariah, it would seem as if the story told in the gospels had grown out of it, because it was thought that it could be made to refer to Jesus. But there was something even behind this. What was it that gave the writers the desire to find something in the Old Testament to support the story of Jesus entering Jerusalem in triumph? Again we find that the prevailing Greek beliefs surrounding Dionysus supply the answer, because we have a story of Dionysus meeting two asses, on one of which he mounted. Thus he crossed a vast morass or river and reached the temple of Dodona.

One of the Greek symbols for Cancer in the Zodiac is two asses and this was the legend with which the sign was associated. The emblem signifies that the sun in Cancer in the Zodiac is passing the period of its greatest heat. Another symbol was a crab. An ass and a crab are appropriate, as their retrograde movements typify, by an easy association of ideas, the retreat of the sun from its furthest northern excursion. So Cancer, which constituted the sign of the summer solstice, was given the emblems of two asses and a crab. Jesus was thus likened to the sun, as from this point in his career he could no longer withstand his enemies. So the legend about Dionysus was related to him and an appropriate text in Hebrew literature was also made to apply to him.

Robertson, in *Christianity and Mythology*, mentions that "There is preserved a Gnostic gem representing an ass suckling its foal, with the figure of the crab (Cancer) above, and the inscription D.N.IHV.XPS. (Dominus Noster Jesus Christus) with the addition of Dei Filius. The Gnostics knew the significance of the symbol well enough." Here then we have Jesus associated with the sign Cancer, which the Greeks associated with Dionysus, and so we find the link connecting the story of Dionysus and two asses going to the temple of Dodona with Matthew's account of Jesus going to the Temple at Jerusalem, seated "on an ass and a colt, the foal of an ass". Professor Burkitt tells us, moreover, that the word Hosanna, which we are told the crowd shouted in welcome to Jesus, is the Aramaic for a green bough which was used at the vintage feast. This again relates this story about Jesus to Dionysus, the god of the vine, who, like Jesus, was the true vine to his worshippers.

I must not omit reference to the method employed by Jesus to clear the Temple. We are told that Jesus used a whip to drive the money-changers from the Temple. Osiris, also known as Serapis and Chrestos, was looked upon not only as the Good Shepherd, but as one who in anger could drive out the evil-doers with a scourge. We are told that Jesus used a "scourge of small cords" to drive out the money-changers. Again we have incidents in the lives of both Dionysus and Osiris corresponding to those told about Jesus entering Jerusalem in triumph and turning out the transgressors. These Greek and Egyptian legends were well known in the days when the gospels were being put together, and were evidently made use of for the purpose of giving Jesus the same status as the god-men worshipped by the Gentile Christians before their conversion. A story has also come down to us of how the god-man Apollonius of Tyana expelled the sorcerers from the left bank of the Hellespont because they were exacting money for sacrifices to prevent earthquakes.

It is interesting to notice how the beliefs surrounding the Greek god Dionysus, who was worshipped at the time the gospels were written, have influenced the stories about Jesus from the beginning to the end of the gospel records. There are few stories told of Jesus which have no parallel in the life of this much beloved god. Furthermore, how similar is this story to the one already told about Krishna in Chapter III. It will be remembered that Krishna was believed to have entered a city amidst the applause of the multitude, who laid palm-leaves on his path. After this experience he was anointed by a woman with oil, just as was Jesus after his triumph.

Surely the rational attitude towards this story of the glorification of Jesus is to adopt the conclusion we have formed on previous occasions that this, like all the others, was produced for the purpose of giving Jesus the same standing as Dionysus or some other saviour-god. We shall realise how natural this was if we think back to the time we are considering and remember that the Gentiles, who became Christians, accepted as a matter of course that Jesus should be credited with deeds and sayings similar to those which, from their childhood upwards, they had been accustomed to attach to Dionysus, Mithra, Osiris and all the other saviour-gods worshipped in their days.

How much more rational it is to think that, in the days when the gospels were being compiled, the people gave Jesus all the glory of which they were capable, because they believed that he was their Saviour and Redeemer. This satisfied their religious emotions, and by this glorification they found their comfort. This is natural, but how seldom do we find that the contemporaries of one who did not run with the prevailing ideas of his time ever recognised or appreciated his qualities. The ideas or deeds of those who laid the foundation of something greater for the generations to come, were only esteemed when the people advanced sufficiently to be able to appreciate the wisdom and foresight their predecessors despised. That appreciation has always come slowly and often it has taken many generations to mature.

Jesus, as such a one, would receive little gratitude in his day and generation. It is much more natural to believe that when the priests stirred up the people against him all his hard work, and all the vital energy he gave out in healing the sick, would be forgotten. He would be killed and his body cast aside with few to lament his end. The base ingratitude of the people of France towards the medium Joan of Arc, after all she did for her country, is a typical example of the fact that mankind has often murdered the great ones of the earth and then, years later, fallen down and worshipped at their graves.

Much as we would like to think that Jesus had been made aware of the gratitude of the people for all his works of mercy and kindness, the underlying thread of what seems to be the truth indicates that he received the same kind of treatment at the hands of the Jews as did Joan, and many others, before and after their times. What follows, therefore, after it is stripped of all its adornment, was the natural dénouement of a life given over to the service of mankind, because it jeopardised vested interests which felt that the people were being led away from the orthodox faith. So we take the next step and consider

THE LAST SUPPER.

From now onwards we are given a day by day account of what followed the cleansing of the Temple. The next day Jesus foretold its destruction (Mark xiii, 2) but, as this account was written after the event, we must come to the conclusion that it is just another instance of giving Jesus credit for prevision, in order to heighten his glory.

Another day passed when, in the house of Simon the leper, a woman anointed his head with precious ointment, which caused some indignation amongst those present because of the waste, but Jesus commended her (Mark xiv, 3). A similar incident occurred in the life of Krishna. Matthew tells this tale in much the same way as does Mark, but Luke and John report it differently. Matthew and Mark say that the anointing was in preparation for his burial and that it took place at Bethany. Luke places it in Galilee in the house of a Pharisee, at the outset of his career. John, like Luke, tells us that the woman anointed his feet but does not mention his head.

When these accounts were written Jesus had become known as the Christ, the anointed one. In the cult of Dionysus anointing was performed by women, whereas to the Jews such a service by a woman was unlikely to appeal. The anointing of Jesus, according to Matthew and Mark, took place at Bethany and after this he left for Jerusalem, about two and a half miles distant, which on this occasion he entered without ceremonial. He and his disciples had decided that in this city they would partake of the Passover, which points to Jesus to the very last maintaining his Jewish principles. It may seem to us a rash step to have taken, as he entered the domain of his enemies. Whether he felt that here he could start on fresh ground and impress the Sadducees and Pharisees with his views, or, on the other hand, he went to the city just in the ordinary course of his wanderings we cannot say. The gospels set the scene of the coming tragedy in Jerusalem, and preface the story by an account of Jesus partaking of a final meal with his disciples.

To make the necessary preparations Jesus sent two of his disciples on before, as it was the eve of the Passover when the Paschal lamb was slain. He is credited with the power of prevision, as he told them that they would meet a man carrying a pitcher of water, whom they were to follow, and he would show them a room where they would keep the Passover. This is a somewhat similar story to what we read about Ananias, who was told that if he went into a certain street he would meet Paul of Tarsus.

The man to whom Jesus referred was duly met, and arrangements were made for the Paschal meal, which consisted of a lamb, with bitter herbs and unleavened bread. It was the custom on these occasions for four cups to be drunk by each participant, in memory of the four words used to describe the deliverance of Israel from Egypt. The first cup was prefaced by a thanksgiving, or Eucharistia, which word is now used by Christians for their principal ceremony of thanksgiving to Christ. Each cup had a name attached to it, and was drunk to mark the symbolic character of the four sections into which the meal was divided. In Mark there is no reference whatever to these ceremonials, and all that we are told is that Jesus took bread and brake it, and handed round one cup of wine. Luke, however, amplifies the original account by mentioning "the cup after supper" being drunk, evidently for the purpose of making his story agree more with common custom and usage.

It is difficult to believe that the Last Supper was

in reality a paschal meal, as after it the disciples went out of Jerusalem to the Mount of Olives (Mark xiv, 26), and so disregarded the Mosaic command that after partaking of this sacred meal no one must leave his house till the morning. If the supper were a paschal meal it would mark the commencement of the feast held the next day on the fourteenth of Nisan, when all work stopped, and yet we are told that on the feast day Jesus was arrested, tried and crucified. Moreover, Simon the Cyrenian was compelled to help Jesus to carry his cross, and fine linen in which his body was wrapped was purchased on this holy day. This points to business continuing as usual, and we are consequently forced to the conclusion that all these things did not happen on the Feast of the Passover.

Evidently Sunday, on which it was believed the resurrection took place, was taken as the date from which the Evangelists adopted their chronology, this day being the one hallowed by time as the resurrection day of previous saviour-gods. The Mithraists termed it "The Lord's Day", which expression the Christians adopted, and is just another reminder of how closely Christian and Pagan thought are intertwined.

The reason the gospels do not all agree as to what occurred on the preceding days is because they interpret differently the meaning of the three days which were to elapse between the time of death and the resurrection, being doubtful whether Jesus was to rise on the third day, according to prophecy, or after three days. Hence we have this divergence of opinion as to what happened prior to his resurrection. The repeated reference in the gospels to Jesus being three days in the tomb has an interesting bearing on his reappearance and will be considered when we come to deal with the resurrection.

Every effort was made to represent Jesus as the paschal lamb, in fact he is called The Lamb of God (John i, 29). Consequently stress is laid on the fact that he died when the Mosaic law determined that the lamb was to be killed (Ex. xii, 6), and that his legs were not broken on the cross. If we turn to the Hebrew scriptures we find the explanation, as the Mosaic law stated that "Neither shall ye break a bone thereof" (Ex. xii, 46), of the paschal lamb. Likewise Jesus was buried where he died because the lamb had to be killed and eaten at the place of sacrifice. (Ex. xii, 46.)

The gospel writers were evidently not concerned with history or facts, and all four accounts of what happened to Jesus during his last few days on earth are very contradictory. When the information was available no one was specially interested in remembering when and how Jesus actually died, because he was not then looked upon as a Suffering Messiah. The belief that Jesus was such only arose when Paul originated the idea. When this took root the Old Testament was searched for prophesies to support this new outlook. Only then was the passage in Isaiah liii taken to refer to Jesus. Before this time all the numerous quotations in the Old Testament, which have been taken out of their setting and made to refer to Jesus, were never considered to relate to the coming Christ. So it came about that when, in after years, the Christians became interested in the passion and death of Jesus, the information as to how he lived and died was not available as there was no source to which to turn in order to obtain it. Jerusalem was destroyed and all who knew Jesus had passed away.

What interested those who put together the gospel legends was the mystical lore and symbolism connected with the Passover which, to them, had been replaced by the Eucharist on this day of the Great Feast of the Passover, hallowed by centuries of anticipation of what it was now believed had materialised. To produce a story to show that everything related had been foretold in Holy Scripture was much more important in their eyes than historical accuracy. They were theologians, not historians, and prophecy, not facts, interested them and their readers.

The energy they displayed in their task corresponds to the same enthusiasm displayed today by some Biblical students who twist and turn every possible passage in the Old Testament in their endeavour to prove that the British race comprises Jehovah's chosen people. Our present-day British Israelites display the same disregard for accuracy as did their Christian ancestors who, when compiling the gospel stories, allowed their ardent zeal to outdistance their reason.

Jesus, by his reappearance, had revealed to mankind that he was the Messiah. When the belief developed that he had replaced the paschal lamb it was quite appropriate that stress should be laid on the fact that he was slain by the priests. So he was regarded as a priestly victim, who had suffered in place of the lamb which had for so long been the symbol of his body, sacrificed for mankind. Such a sacrifice could only happen on the Great Feast day, and for that reason this time was adopted as the date of his death ; otherwise its significance would be lost.

Consequently we are told that Jesus on this day abolished the old and instituted the new testament (Heb. ix, 15) by becoming the victim at the hands of the priests, to satisfy the wrath of God. He had foreseen everything and foretold all that was about to happen, just as had the Hebrew prophets down the ages. This is what was thought years after this event was supposed to have happened, and all that concerned the gospel writers was to associate the Passover with the Eucharist which Paul had introduced to satisfy the Greeks. This they did in such a way as to give the impression that Jesus himself had instituted the rite and then stepped out and laid himself upon the altar of sacrifice.

Thus was rung out the old order and the new order rung in. The cross ceased to be a shame and instead became a throne from which the King announced the eagerly awaited words, "It is finished" (John xix, 30), to a world thirsting for redemption. To Christians the Passover had fulfilled its purpose as a rite instituted in anticipation of the coming of the Christ. The Eucharist, or thanksgiving, took its place, because the atoning deed had been accomplished, as "Christ our passover is sacrificed for us". (1 Cor. v, 7.)

It was only fitting that this great change should be instituted by Christ himself, so we are given the account of the Last Supper with all its historical and chronological inaccuracies. Whether or not Jesus ever had a final meal with his disciples we cannot tell. It is not unreasonable to think that he had, as we know that the Essenes, a sect whose outlook resembled what we imagine was the outlook of the real Jesus, partook of such fraternal meals prior to a brother making his departure.

Tradition may have come down that Jesus, before his death, had such a meal, and, on this basis, Paul may have introduced the Pagan Eucharist as a sacramental communion in the body and blood of the Christ. If Acts (ii, 42) is to be trusted the disciples continued, after the death of Jesus, a purely Jewish custom in the Temple by partaking of a meal together which was quite devoid of any Eucharistic meaning. Assuming that this was so we can quite understand how, as the Lord delayed his return, the tendency would be for the ideas of Paul to appeal more and more to the Christians, until ultimately they became a Christian rite of commemoration of the death of the Saviour until his return.

If Paul had told the truth, and not resorted to misrepresentation in his enthusiasm to gain Greek converts, we might have learned something from him. Instead of doing so, he put into the mouth of Jesus, words which his disciples could not have understood at the time they were supposed to have been spoken, and which could not have been understood by Christians till Paul's ideas had germinated and taken root. A few hours after Jesus is reported by Paul as declaring that he was the Saviour, Peter denied him and, after his death, all his disciples dispersed and fled. Such a situation is difficult to imagine, so we come back to the inevitable conclusion that the words which

Jesus is reported to have uttered have their foundation in the mystical sacramental rites surrounding Dionysus or Mithra, both of whose cults were strongly entrenched in Tarsus and other places visited by Paul.

What is now termed the Christian Eucharist has a long ancestry, going back for thousands of years before the Christian era. The Egyptians ate bread and drank wine as one of the sacred rites in memory of the saviour-god Osiris. This has been for ages the principal rite in all the saviour-god religions. The Chaldeans and Assyrians celebrated this sacred ceremony in memory of the death and resurrection of their saviour Bel. It is to be found in all the mystery religions of Greece, and is incorporated in the worship of Attis and Adonis.

So we have not far to look to find the source whence flowed the ideas to be found in *The Epistle to the Corinthians*, which were later adopted by the Christians, and incorporated in the legend relating to the Passion of the Saviour. Of this we can be certain, just as we are certain of the fact that the gospel story, which has come down to us, is historically inaccurate, and that we have no basis whatever to enable us to form any opinion as to how Jesus spent the last few days before his death.

What we are told about the betrayal of Jesus by Judas is equally difficult to accept. His rascality doubtless rests on nothing more than imagination, due to the attempt to bring in a fulfilment of prophecy, "Yea, my own familiar friend, in whom I trusted, which did eat of my bread, hath lifted up his heel against me." (Psalm xli, 9.) Paul knew nothing about the treachery of Judas, or his violent death, as he tells us that Jesus appeared after death to "the twelve". (1 Cor. xv, 5.)

The various accounts about Judas in the gospels are so contradictory that there is nothing to be discovered from this, our only source of information. Luke, for example, places the announcement of the betrayal after the Last Supper, whereas Matthew and Mark state that this happened before the supper began. John makes no reference to the meal being of a Eucharistic character and refers to Jesus giving Judas a sop, after he had dipped it, but that no one present knew what this meant, though a few verses earlier the narrator of this episode tells us that this was the sign Jesus had just told his disciples he would give to single out his betrayer.

It is quite evident from this, and many other examples, that here we are not dealing with rational thinkers. Those who wrote the gospels were neither rational, logical nor accurate. Out of this maze of inconsistency and contradiction we cannot hope to find history. We have, however, discovered what brought the legends into being, and that underneath them all ran the psychic stream which fertilized human imagination to a degree only experienced at rare intervals in world history. The interest to us is in what is behind the stories, and how they are all related, in one form or another, to the non-material aspect of creation.

Each one of us is related to this other aspect of life and will some day experience it. This being so, we are naturally interested in discovering how our ancestors interpreted this other order and its inter-action with their lives on earth. The fact that they thought about it in the form of legends, which are not historically accurate, should not lessen our interest in their childish efforts to express a great and profound truth which was as vital to them as it is to us.

Much the same can be said of the Bible as a whole. It is not a book we should turn to for instruction in any of the sciences, and to regard it as a divine history book prevents its meaning being understood. In it we are not introduced to facts, but to human emotions in the form of religious beliefs, which were set down from the point of view of each individual scribe, quite regardless of historical accuracy or logical reasoning. All these private diverse opinions, as time went on, came to be looked upon as historical records, to be elevated, still later, to the level of God-inspired accounts of what was to be believed. These scattered writings, covering a period of about a thousand years, were put between two covers and called "The Word of God" in the sixth century of our era, but it was not until the ninth century that we find the Bible in the form approximating our present edition, and even then it contained a number of books omitted at the Reformation. It is well to keep all this in mind if we wish to maintain a true perspective and wise judgement on our subject.

What took place at the final meal Jesus had with his disciples, if he ever had such a meal, we do not know. One thing of which we can be certain is that the words he is reported to have uttered were attributed to him by his biographers only when the Christian Faith came to be centred round Calvary.

The years that intervened, between his reappearance and the time when Christians came to be interested in his life on earth, gave ample time and opportunity for Jesus to become associated with the other Pagan Christs who had preceded him. Before his return after death no one thought of him as the Saviour of the World, least of all himself. In the gospels we are not dealing with a history, based on facts or opinions prevailing when his death took place, but on the Christian outlook as it had developed at a much later date.

This subject of The Last Supper received careful consideration in Chapter VI, as chronologically the time to deal with it was when Paul incorporated his version of it in his letter to the Corinthians. It is here referred to because, at this later date, when the gospels were being constructed, it was incorporated into the life of Jesus. So we shall now follow on with what occurred after the supper came to an end by considering

THE ARREST AND TRIAL.

By going to Jerusalem, Jesus brought about his death. The Temple authorities dominated Jerusalem. The membership of the priesthood consisted mostly, if not entirely, of the Sadducean party, of all the Jewish sects the most antagonistic to Messianic ideas and mediumship. No prophet could hope to be received kindly in such surroundings. The priesthood had at its disposal great material resources, besides being in control of the Temple police. Priests controlled the Sanhedrim, a council which was the custodian of the Jewish religion, and had the power to bring the law into action in its defence. Consequently Jesus entered the worst possible environment for his teaching and, what was even more important, his person. Had he such confidence in his psychic powers, or had his position become so desperate that he stoically accepted his fate, whatever that might be ?

Short as had been his mission, he had said and done enough to make him a marked man to the rabbis, and they could no longer tolerate his existence. They watched his movements and listened to his sayings, knowing that sooner or later he would give them sufficient excuse to enable them to arrest him and bring about his death. In those days, just as before and after, no one with psychic gifts was safe whenever there was a priesthood in control of affairs. Sooner or later this order always found some means or other to destroy the one it accused of witchcraft or demonology.

No genuine medium has ever been able to prove that the gifts with which he was endowed were of God and not of the Devil, because the priests always declared that all supernormal manifestations came from the Devil. When the Jews accused Jesus of being in league with the Devil they ignored his reply, "If I do not the works of my Father, believe me not. But if I do, though ye believe not me, believe the works : that ye may know, and believe, that the Father is in me." (John x, 37.)

Before he said this, the Jews had tried to stone him, and, after he had told them how to test his mediumship, they again tried to stone him, which was their form of punishment for all who exercised mediumistic gifts. (Lev. xx, 27.) Whether all this actually happened or not the statement reflects the prevailing opinion of the time and, it being related to Jesus, discloses that we are dealing with the old story of the antagonism of the priests towards mediumship.

If we consider the betrayal of Jesus in the light of history it is very difficult to understand why Judas was introduced on to the scene. He seems to be quite an unnecessary character, but if the story is looked upon symbolically it can be understood. Judas stands for the Jews, Ioudaios being the Greek for Jew, as it was the Jews who were responsible for the death of Jesus. One who had made a triumphant entry into Jerusalem a few days previously, and who was evidently walking about the streets quite freely, different journeys to Bethany being reported, did not need to be pointed out to the authorities by one of his disciples. On the other hand, if what we are considering constitutes the last days of Jesus in the form of a drama, the introduction of Judas can be understood. Before, however, adopting this latter alternative, as the possible explanation of the story surrounding the last days of Jesus on earth, let us continue our review of the various incidents, one by one.

After the supper Jesus proceeded with his disciples to the Mount of Olives, a ridge about two hundred feet high which overlooks Jerusalem on the east beyond the brook Cedron. Here we are given a moving story of his agony at a place called Gethsemane, where he withdrew from his disciples and prayed alone while they, heavy with sleep, became unconscious of their surroundings. In his prayer Jesus implored his Father in Heaven to spare him the suffering and misery he, foresaw, and, in answer to this, an angel appeared to him from heaven to strengthen him. Being in agony "he prayed more earnestly : and his sweat was as it were great drops of blood falling down to the ground". (Luke xxii, 44.)

This is a very human story, which has moved millions to pity, and redoubled their gratitude to the Saviour for what he endured and suffered on their behalf. And yet did all this really happen as reported ? The disciples were asleep and at some distance from Jesus, so how was it possible for them to know how he prayed and the actual words he used ? How was it possible for them to know that an angel or spirit stood beside Jesus and strengthened him ? There is only one way for them to have known this, and that was by Jesus telling them what he had said, and that he had seen an angel beside him while he was praying. But no, this is not what Jesus said when he returned to his disciples. His words to them were, "Why sleep ye ? rise and pray, lest ye enter into temptation." (Luke xxii, 46.) He got no further than this because "while he yet spake" Judas came up to him with the multitude behind him and attempted to kiss him. After this there was no opportunity for Jesus to tell his disciples anything, as from that moment communication between them ceased.

The story of the agony endured by Jesus in the Garden of Gethsemane is difficult to believe, because we have not a shred of evidence as to how the information was obtained, and the story, as it has come down to us, is not vouched for by any responsible individual. There is no denying that all that is reported could have happened, in fact that something such as this may have happened is quite natural. Even the greatest saint may dread the approach of death. His conscience may be clear, and his faith secure, but nevertheless entering the valley of the shadow of death is an experience which happens only once in a lifetime. One must do so alone, and that which is unknown contains all sorts of possibilities which are intensified by the imagination.

Does all this not reveal what an impossible position the evangelists have reached? They tell us this moving story, so natural and so human, and yet make out that the one who experienced all this was a god, whose home was in heaven, a temporary sojourner on earth, away from his native element. Not content with this, Christianity carries the absurdity even further by stating that Jesus was then, and still is, one of three gods, and that after his death he took up his rightful position in heaven.

Thus we are brought back every time to the fact that the apotheosis of Jesus took place after his death, and that the attempt made in the gospels to present him to us as a god-man is the result of what occurred after his death and not during his lifetime. Evidently nothing happened in his lifetime to make the people think that he was other than, at the most, a wonder-worker, and so we come back once more to the source of the Christian Faith, the appearance of Jesus after death, which produced the effect revealed in the gospels and epistles.

The narrative proceeds with the account of Jesus being taken from Gethsemane to the house of the High Priest, where the Sanhedrim quickly assembled in the middle of the night. Here he was interrogated by the High Priest, confronted by witnesses, and, after ill-treatment, condemned to death on the charge of blasphemy. The Sanhedrim, however, had not the power to carry this through, and why this mock trial was necessary is just one of the many questions which come uppermost when reading this story. The next morning, which was the Feast of the Passover, and the most holy day of the year, Jesus was taken before Pilate, and the trial took place once more.

Here, as elsewhere, glaring contradictions are to be noticed between the reports given in Luke and those given in Matthew and Mark. John's gospel tells quite a different story as in it we find that Jesus was first taken to Annas because he was the father-in-law of Caiaphas, who was the High Priest that year. Annas then questioned Jesus and sent him to Caiaphas, who, strangely enough, sent him away without doing anything, though the synoptic gospels tell us that he, as High Priest, condemned him to death and then sent him on to Pilate. All this time the people were rushing about the streets in great excitement on this holy day, and everything reported was quite contrary to Jewish custom, which prohibited a judgement at night and also one given on the same day as the interrogation.

After reading all these contradictory accounts we find Jesus standing before Pilate, charged by the priests as a criminal, which is equally impossible to imagine at this most holy period of the year. Pilate would never have spent his time performing judiciary work on a public holiday. Then we are told that the real trial commenced, stress being laid on the fact that Jesus was brought to his death by the wicked and malicious accusations of the priests. In the condition of hatred, which prevailed between the Jews and the Christians at the time the story was written, nothing too bad or scurrilous could be said by one side about the other. So, in the report of the trial of Jesus, we find Pilate represented as anxious to set Jesus free, but fearing to do so because of the Jews. Here we are given a dramatic touch by his calling for a basin and water, and washing his hands so as to make it clear that the guilt of Jesus's death did not rest with him.

This was simply an additional thrust at the Jews, as no Roman Governor would so neglect his duty. Jesus was condemned under Roman law and by the Roman Procurator, but whether his name was Pilate or not is an open question. For the same reason the ridiculous story of Barabbas was thrown in. As if a Roman Governor would dare to release a condemned murderer because the Jews he so despised demanded it ! Besides this, the custom of releasing a prisoner at the request of the people is only to be found in the gospels. No other Jewish writer mentions this extraordinary privilege. The idea is not only absurd, but how was all this possible when we are told that only a few days previously these very people were spreading palm-leaves, and according Jesus a triumphant entry into Jerusalem ? The two stories cannot be true, and it is doubtful if originally they were expected to be looked upon as more than symbolic legends. This, however, will be better understood before this chapter ends.

Matthew's gospel tells us that the priests brought three charges against Jesus, namely :

(1) This fellow said, I am able to destroy the Temple of God, and to build it in three days.

(2) Jesus said to the High Priest, "Hereafter shall ye see the Son of Man sitting on the right hand of power, and coming in the clouds of heaven".

(3) And Jesus stood before the Governor : and the Governor asked him, saying, "Art thou the King of the Jews ?" And Jesus said unto him "Thou sayest".

Mark repeats these three so-called crimes in much the same words as those used by Matthew, but Luke's account is somewhat different. Luke omits the first charge about his threatening to destroy the Temple, but confirms the second and third, while adding a new one :

(4) We found this fellow perverting the nation and forbidding to give tribute to Caesar.

John's gospel is silent about the charges brought against Jesus, though it tells us that Pilate asked him if he were the King of the Jews. In every gospel we find the remark that Pilate found him "Not Guilty" and yet he agreed to the demand of the Jews that he be crucified. This does not read like Roman Justice.

It is well to remember that there were no reporters present at this extraordinary trial, if such a word can be used for the tale to be found in the synoptic gospels. The disciples had all fled, and everyone who had been alive when it is supposed to have happened was dead when it was written up. An interval of at least fifty years existed between the time it was supposed to have happened and the time it was put into writing, which was fortunate for those responsible for this travesty of Roman rule. Further, we have no original document relating the occurrence, but only a copy of many copies which, during the process, has been translated from the original language, Aramaic, into Greek and then into English. Neither do we know who wrote the original report, who made the many copies, or who made the first translation. In a few words, we are completely in the dark as to how closely the reports we have resemble the original event and what authority the evangelists had for their statements.

To this we must add the fact that the first three charges mentioned could not have been levelled against Jesus by the priests because no one before his death associated Jesus with such matters. The charge, given only by Luke, that he refused to pay taxes to Caesar, is flatly contradicted in his account of how, a few days earlier, Jesus told the spies, sent by the priests to question him, that they must pay to Caesar that which was due to him.

Thus we are left in the air. We do not know why Jesus was arrested, tried and executed, and, if it were not for Paul's repeated reference to his being crucified, we would be completely in the dark as to how this unknown Galilean prophet met his end. Even the ultra-rationalist school is forced to take cognizance of the fact that Jesus was crucified, because this statement occurs ten times throughout the Pauline epistles, too often to be regarded as the work of a later day interpolator.

We can assume that, to begin with, what we now term the Passion Drama was quite a simple account of the arrest, death and reappearance of Jesus.

That is all we can be sure of, because that was all Paul seems to have known, but he nowhere claims to have been a witness, so at best our evidence is second hand. He was, however, a contemporary of Jesus, and, if he has little to tell us, we can be satisfied that not much was known. If we have no evidence to enable us to believe, the next best thing is to discover how that which has come down to us, as a series of tragic episodes abounding in dramatic acts, came into being.

All we know is that Christians believed that Jesus was a martyr who was unjustly sentenced to death, and appeared again after death, that his death was caused by the priests bringing false charges against him, and that, by his reappearance, he had proved himself to be the Messiah. What the charges were we know not but this is really quite irrelevant. Paul tells us that he was crucified and appeared after death. On that he built up all his speculations. He evidently considered the life of Jesus unimportant as he makes little reference to it and never mentions the trial. It was his reappearance that so influenced him and on it he based his doctrines.

The Christian belief that the priests brought about his death produced the idea that he was a priestly victim, and this was worked up into the belief that he was sacrificed for the sins of mankind. The legend of his trial was written in an atmosphere of hatred towards the Jewish race, which makes us suspect its historical accuracy. What we have been considering is, in reality, later Christian conjecture and not history. How this came to assume the form it did we shall soon discover, but let us for a moment dwell on what we may reasonably accept, that Jesus was a priestly victim.

The history of the policy of the priesthood is sufficient in itself to point to the conclusion that when the priests arrested a man or a woman it was either for heresy or witchcraft. Jesus does not seem to have been a heretic, and even if he had claimed to be the Messiah it is unlikely that this would have brought about his arrest, because others before and after him had made this claim and been unmolested. A man wandering about from place to place, speaking in parables, and either claiming to be the Messiah, or looked upon as one by the people, did not receive the death sentence. Such people were passed over as of no danger, being looked upon more in the light of harmless fanatics who did not affect the regular flow of victims for the altar, and that was what interested the priests.

According to the gospel narratives it was when Jesus was in Jerusalem that the plot was hatched to bring about his arrest, and so the leading priests, that is, those belonging to the great sacerdotal families, set about concocting the charge to bring against him. They could quote to Pilate the words of Jehovah, "A man also or woman that hath a familiar spirit . . . shall surely be put to death : they shall stone them with stones ; their blood shall be upon them" (Lev. xx, 27), and perhaps they did. Matthew may have had this law in mind because it is significant that he tells us that the Jews relieved Pilate of any guilt in condemning an innocent man by declaring that "His blood be on us, and on our children." (Matt. xxvii, 25.)

What, then, can we accept as probably true ? Paul tells us that Jesus was crucified and this was believed by all the early Christians. The Romans were unlikely to crucify a man because he claimed to be the Messiah, and it was under Roman law that Jesus was condemned. If that were not his crime, what was it ? Angering the priests would not bring the law into action. Christians had probably every reason to attach the blame for his death to the priests, but we need not accept as true the charges which were brought against him. The priests doubtless were behind his death, but not because of what we are told in the gospels. The Romans, however, would be indifferent to what the priests wished and Jesus would suffer under their law, not under Jewish law.

What charges could the priests bring against Jesus that would appeal to a Roman Governor ? Two only, that he was inciting the people against the Roman rule and that he was a sorcerer. One or both of these would, if proved against him, bring about his death. Did Jesus say anything against the existing rulers ? He was quite unknown to historians, and if he had been a political agitator the historians of his time would probably have referred to his arrest and death, as they did with others. However, he might easily have been overlooked.

The followers he left behind had evidently no political aspirations, and we might conclude from this that Jesus had none either. The whole atmosphere Jesus left behind him was a religious one, and politicians are not people to be influenced by speculations arising out of an apparition. It would mean nothing to them, whereas if the disciples were quick to seize on a sign from heaven that Jesus was the Messiah their minds must have been religiously, not politically, inclined. Nothing points to politics being the motive behind Jesus in his work and outlook. Even if Jesus had claimed at his trial that he would soon be returning from heaven in great glory, this would have amused, but never frightened, Pilate or any other Roman Governor.

We are, therefore, left with the alternative that the priests worked on the superstitions of the time relating to those people endowed with supernormal powers being the agents of the Devil. If this were so then everything would fit in with the religious atmosphere, with the belief that Jesus was a religious teacher, that he miraculously healed the sick and performed other miracles, and that he was a prophet sent from God. One endowed with psychic powers, and of a deeply religious outlook, could be killed in those days on the charge of being in league with the Devil.

There is no surmise about this, as we are told that the Jews tried to stone him because he claimed to be doing his works with the help of God. (John x, 31.) This shows that at the time this was written it was believed that Jesus had acted in such a way as to bring himself under the Levitical law, which decreed that anyone who had a familiar spirit, or was a medium, deserved death by being stoned. Under Roman law mediums were safe from harm, but there were laws against sorcerers, and mediumship and magic can be easily confused by the ignorant.

Such instances of psychically endowed people, whether they went under the name of mediums, witches or wizards, being put to death, are so common in history that, in the absence of direct knowledge as to why Jesus was crucified, it is the most obvious inference to adopt, when taking everything into consideration. Especially is this so when we know that the penalty in Roman law for being guilty of sorcery was crucifixion.

The references, which are made throughout the gospels, to Jesus performing miracles and healing the people by the help of the Devil are quite in keeping with the beliefs of the age. As this idea was not one which would develop in the years after his death, when he was being evolved into a god, we may have in these references fragments of genuine tradition. It was so contrary to the beliefs prevalent about him, when the gospels were written, that it seems as if this natural and rational explanation is the one which lies nearer the truth than any other. By this process of elimination it seems, therefore, reasonable to claim that because Jesus was endowed with psychic gifts he became a priestly victim. This is the only reason which can be put forward to make the story which has come down to us capable of intelligent comprehension.

The trial of Apuleius in A.D. 150 is an instance, and one close enough to the time of Jesus, to be a guide to us as to what happened to those endowed with psychic powers, and who were looked upon as sorcerers. Apuleius was born in A.D. 125, at Madaura, in Numidia, and was celebrated as a philosopher and writer of romance, his book *The Metamorphoses* being his most famous work. It was directed against a materialistic outlook on life, and reveals, in the form of a legend, the methods employed in his day of depicting religious ideas in the form of legendary stories, such as we find in the gospels. He put forward new ideas based on oriental religious beliefs. He was imbued with Platonic philosophy, and his ideals and moralising were high and elevating. He is described in the *Encyclopædia Britannica*, from which this information about him is derived, as "attractive, vehement and passionate but devoid of rancour, enterprising, munificent, genial and an enthusiast for the beautiful and good". In his work *The God of Socrates* he expounds the Platonic doctrine of beneficent spirits guarding and helping humanity.

From what he tells us he had psychic gifts, including clairvoyance. He was indicted on a charge of exercising his powers over a woman he wished to marry, and who, so her relations said, had become enamoured of this handsome youth "by his magical arts". He conducted his own defence and was pardoned. Had he been poor, with no influence, the result would probably have been different, but this is an example of the dangers those with psychic gifts ran in past times when demons were believed to be at work on earth with agents everywhere.

Up till the age of Science the belief in demons, or evil spirits, working through certain people to the detriment of the human race, was almost universal, and the gospels reveal this only too clearly. On the other hand, good spirits were believed to be at war with the evil ones, which meant that there was perpetual warfare between the good and the evil for the possession of mankind.

It is to this belief that all the saviour-god religions

owe their theological development, because their gods died to redeem mankind from the destructive power of the Devil and his angels, who had gained their power as the result of the fall of man. Now we know that such salvation was unnecessary, as those our ancestors called angels or demons were none other than those who had lived and died on earth, and had carri~d over with them at death all their good and bad characteristics. Instead of being a danger to humanity they were in reality much less capable of effecting either good or evil, in their new order of life, than they were when living as men and women on earth.

If Jesus were condemned because of his psychic gifts he was just one of thousands who have suffered through the ignorance of mankind with regard to the meaning of psychic phenomena. As, however, we have no information to guide us, the reason for his condemnation will for ever remain wrapped in uncertainty. Why he was condemned matters not, that he was killed for some reason or other, and that the priests, in the minds of the Christians, were the perpetrators of the deed, is all that is important.

The origin of the Christian Faith can be taken as discovered, as the result of our new knowledge of psychic phenomena, even though we cannot find any facts relating to the victim, whose reappearance, and not whose death, brought it into being. On the basis of these two beliefs, that he was a priestly victim and that he reappeared after death, all the beliefs which developed from them can be understood, as they were the natural outcome of the religious opinions of that age.

Jesus, we read, suffered the death of a criminal, as one who had broken the Roman law, and so we now come to the story of

THE CRUCIFIXION.

Matthew tells us that after the sentence of death by crucifixion was passed on Jesus he was scourged, then dressed in a scarlet robe, a crown of thorns being placed on his head and a reed in his right hand. This was done by the soldiers of the Governor, who then mocked him by bowing before him, after which they took the reed and smote him. Then they stripped him and led him to the place of crucifixion. Mark tells us the same story, but Luke omits all this and only reports that after the sentence Jesus was led away to be crucified. From Luke's account the victim could not have suffered, as Matthew and Mark tell us he did, because he was able to deliver a homily to the women who accompanied him, which is impossible to imagine if he had been scourged, and if a crown of thorns had been placed on his head.

Matthew, Mark and Luke tell us that the cross was carried by Simon, a Cyrenian, but, when we turn to John's gospel, we find no reference to any of these incidents. He merely states that Jesus, after the sentence, was led away, "and he bearing his cross went forth to the place of a skull called Golgotha", which name has a remarkable likeness to Gilgal, a sacred circle on a hill near to Jericho where sacrified victims in earlier days were slain by the priests (Hosea xii, 11). Matthew and Mark also mention Golgotha, but Luke alone calls it Calvary.

The non-canonical *Gospel of Peter* elaborates the story by stating that, after clothing Jesus in purple, they placed him on Pilate's own seat of judgement and that "the whole Jewish people disown, mock, insult and maltreat the Lord of Glory". Here we find a new note struck. In the canonical gospels the blame is attached to the Roman soldiers, but Peter's gospel throws it on to the Jews, though the synoptics only tell of the Jews insulting Jesus at the house of the High Priest.

If all this happened, as described, how strange it is that Paul never mentions it. He was mixing with people who must have known all about this torture inflicted on Jesus after the trial, and yet either they never mentioned it to him or else he did not think it worth repeating. Another alternative is, of course, that it never happened. Why should Roman soldiers, even if they were at liberty to do such things, which no one can believe, treat a poor wretch in such a fashion just before his crucifixion? People were certainly cruel and callous of suffering in those days, but we cannot imagine that human nature fell to such a level. Soldiers, then as now, had their duties to carry out, which were at times distasteful, but one who had done them no harm, and was not even a criminal in the real sense of the word, would not be treated in such a fashion for the mere pleasure of inflicting suffering. The writer of John's gospel evidently had never heard about it or did not believe it. So we must look about for an explanation.

In the ancient Babylonian festival of the Sacaea a prisoner, sentenced to be scourged and crucified, was given five days to enjoy all the pleasures of life.

He was treated as a king, decked up in the king's robes, allowed to sit on the royal throne, and treated with the ceremony accorded to the King. He was known as the "King of the Sacaea". After this brief spell of luxurious living he had to suffer his punishment. Then he was stripped, scourged and crucified. At the time when Jesus was on earth the Jews carried out a similar farce, the victim being an effigy. This is believed to have been copied from Babylon, probably when they were there in captivity.

On the festival to Apollo at Athens a criminal sentenced to death was crowned and given royal honours before meeting his fate. Philo tells the story of how King Agrippa, when in Alexandria, was insulted by the mob, who took an idiot whom they named Karabbas, dressed him up as a mock king, hailed him as "Lord", and gave him the honour expected by Agrippa. During the Roman feast to Saturn, known as the Saturnalia, one was chosen by lot and presided over the festival. He was given the title of "King of Saturnalia" and received royal honours. When the feast was over he was sacrificed on the altar of Saturn.

Thus, when the gospels were being compiled, there was ample material at hand to supply the writers with what their imagination lacked. They wished to depict Jesus suffering to the very dregs of the cup it was his destiny to drink, and any verse to be found in the scriptures, which could be made to refer to a suffering Messiah, was applied to him. Had Isaiah not anticipated such a being (Isaiah liii) about whom he had written, "I give my back to the smiters, and my cheeks to them . . . I hid not my face from shame and spitting " ? (Isaiah l, 6.) Micah, moreover, had said, "They shall smite the Judge of Israel with a rod upon the cheek". (Micah v, 1.) So they had no difficulty in writing up a moving scene.

Prometheus and Hercules had each worn a mock crown, so why not Jesus ? Whether Jesus underwent scourging or not, its addition to the story heightened the picture they wished to paint of the suffering Messiah who, according to their reading of the scriptures, was, in those tense hours, between his sentence and his death, carrying the load of sin accumulated since Adam's fall. Further on, the reason why Jesus is represented as bearing this additional suffering will be more fully explained.

The statement of Jesus being given the title "The King of the Jews" certainly associates the tale with "The King of the Sacaea" and "The King of Saturnalia", just as the bringing in of Barabbas associates him with what is now thought to have been an ancient Semitic feast known as the Feast of Barabbas. Barabbas means "the son of the father" and up to the time of Origen (185–254) he was referred to in most of the gospel manuscripts as Jesus Barabbas. This is what Origen tells us, but how long this continued after his days we know not. On his testimony, then, the name we now have as Barabbas referred to "Jesus the son of the father". It is curious to find in the same episode such a coincidence as the two criminals having the same names and titles.

This story of Barabbas has some ancient symbolic meaning, as we find similar legends associated with the saviour-gods Bel and Hesus. It will be remembered that at the trial of Bel a malefactor was released.

Sir James Frazer considers it probable that the name of the idiot, who was called Karabbas and took the place of Agrippa, was originally spelt Barabbas and that what Philo wrote has been changed from Barabbas to Karabbas through a scribe's error in copying. He further believes that the name refers to an ancient Semitic rite, the name Barabbas being the figure in a mock sacrifice, which points to the time when the sons of kings and chiefs were sacrificed by, or in place of, their fathers. This is in agreement with the Jewish custom, just referred to, of a victim in effigy being put through the ceremonial surrounding sacrifice, which was in vogue in the time of Jesus.

With this background, we have one reason why Barabbas was introduced into the gospel story, as a substitute, who was released to emphasise the fact that the work of redeeming mercy could only be carried through by the one ordained by God to come to earth to suffer for the sins of mankind. This may or may not be so, as another symbolical meaning we might take from this legend is that Barabbas was released to depict the end of the old form of sacrifice, now that Jesus had himself come as the real sacrifice for which they had all been waiting. Just as Jesus superseded the Feast of Barabbas, when the son of the father was sacrificed, so he abolished the Feast of the Passover, and the paschal lamb, which had for so long taken the son's place.

In the legend of the lamb being provided to take the place of Isaac we have a symbolic story representing the end of human sacrifice. So Jesus took the place of the lamb which was now no longer required to symbolise him, and, though "the son of the father" was applied to both victims, the same title had a different meaning for each. Jesus Barabbas was the son who took his father's place on the altar, and Jesus Christ was the son who was sent by his father to satisfy his anger, not to take his place as a victim.

Thus within those last few dramatic hours, in which the gospels relate the final episodes of the life on earth of the Saviour of the World, the two forms of sacrifice, animal and human, hitherto adopted to still the wrath of an angry god, were brought to an end, the first by Jesus at the Last Supper, when he took the place of the lamb, and the second at his trial when Barabbas was released.

All the gospel writers agree that Jesus died as the result of being crucified, though they differ in respect of the events which centred round the cross. Within twenty-two verses Matthew's gospel reports fourteen incidents to which it would be well to refer briefly in the order of their occurrence.

On the way to Golgotha the cross was carried by one named Simon of Cyrene. Jesus was given vinegar and gall to drink. When he was on the cross they parted his garments, casting lots for each one. Over his head was written, "This is Jesus, the King of the Jews." On either side of him was a crucified thief. The chief priests, the scribes, the elders and others present, including the two thieves, mocked him. From the sixth to the ninth hour there was darkness over all the land. About the ninth hour Jesus cried with a loud voice, "My God, My God, why hast thou forsaken me?" Someone then offered him a sponge filled with gall and vinegar. Jesus cried again with a loud voice and gave up the ghost. The veil of the

Temple was rent in twain from top to bottom, the earth quaked and the rocks were rent. The graves opened and many bodies of saints arose, but not till after his resurrection did they go into Jerusalem and appear unto many.

This may be taken as a fair summary of what this gospel has to say about this eventful occasion. In the Vulgate and Ethiopic versions and the Sinaitic, Vatican and Bezan codices, and many old manuscripts, the word wine takes the place of vinegar, and in the Arabic version myrrh takes the place of gall. Originally a narcotic was evidently intended, as in those days women of rank prepared such a drink to stupefy the victim. Later the wish developed to depict Jesus conscious and suffering to the end, and also as suffering in conformity with prophecy. Consequently, the words gall and vinegar took the place of myrrh and wine, which was drugged. The writer gives the name and address of the man who carried the cross, surely not worth mentioning, and yet not a name is given of those who rose from their graves and walked about Jerusalem in their physical bodies. The names of those they visited are likewise omitted.

Mark's gospel follows in the path laid down by Matthew. Additional information about the unknown Simon is given by the mention of the names of his sons, who are also unknown. Some differences are to be noted, such as the disagreement in the inscription above the head of Jesus which is given as "The King of the Jews." The most remarkable omission, however, is that no mention is made of the earthquake or the saints coming out of their graves. Perhaps the writer had never heard the story or, if he had, did not believe it.

Luke's gospel gives the superscription on the cross as "This is the King of the Jews" and is the only one to tell about the converted thief, the first to be saved by the death of Christ. Surely this was a vital omission on the part of the other evangelists, and one which is all the more marked when we read in Matthew and Mark that instead of one being penitent both the thieves reviled him. Luke, or the source of his information, had perhaps heard of the God Hesus, who was represented as crucified between a lamb and an elephant, one depicting innocence, and the other the sins of the world, which only the largest animal could represent.

Like Mark, Luke omits all reference to the earthquake and the saints coming out of their graves. John's gospel does likewise, omitting also to mention the darkness, but adding the story of Jesus committing the care of his mother to the disciple he loved. This is the only reference anywhere to Mary being present on this tragic day. This gospel gives the wording on the cross as "Jesus of Nazareth, the King of the Jews," and further information not given by the others. It tells that the legs of Jesus were not broken because he was dead, that a soldier pierced his side, out of which came blood and water, that the inscription was written in Hebrew, Latin and Greek, and that the chief priests objected to Pilate about its wording.

This tragic story has probably had a greater influence on humanity than any other in world history. True, this has been confined to only a portion of the human race and to only a comparatively small part of the time the race has been in existence. Nevertheless, the story of the crucifixion of Jesus has doubtless affected the emotions of more people than any other event in history. Since the seventh century, when his death was first represented by the Saviour in effigy hanging from a cross, these lifelike representations have been scattered all over Europe. Prior to the year A.D. 680 veneration was accorded to the Mithraic lamb, but from that date onwards it was ordained that in place of the lamb the figure of a man attached to a cross should be substituted. The crucifix is also to be found in North and South America, Africa and Australasia and wherever Christianity prevails. This emblem, either in the form of a cross or a crucifix, is also to be found in almost every Christian church.

The cross is the symbol of the Christian Faith and has inspired countless millions of Christians for good and evil, in war and in peace. It has been carried before advancing armies, creating havoc and destruction wherever they went. It figured prominently in every trial for heresy and witchcraft. Torquemada, and his brother torturers throughout Europe and America, always carried it prominently on their persons. On the other hand, it has been carried in the hand of the missionary peacefully penetrating unknown regions with the ardent wish to spread the story surrounding this emblem of his faith, just as it has inspired the saints to live lives of greater self-denial.

The origin of the cross as a religious emblem goes back to the days of savagery. The savage found that by rubbing two sticks together he could produce fire by friction. This new wonder he worshipped as a god, and so we find fire an object of worship from early times. It became the symbol of life, and the two crossed sticks, which produced it, came to be looked upon as sacred. Thus the cross became a venerated emblem to be worshipped by millions for thousands of years. It is to be found carved on the stone slabs placed over the graves of some of the most ancient races. In Egypt, Assyria, Persia, India, Mexico and Scandinavia the cross occupied a prominent place in religious worship.

Constantine, we are told, adopted it as the Christian emblem from the solar wheel, the two spokes of which formed a cross. There is, however, some doubt as to this, especially as it is much more likely that the Christian symbol was taken from the Egyptian *crux ansata*, which was to the Egyptians the emblem signifying salvation and eternal life. It is also interesting to remember that the Mithraic symbol, which was placed on the forehead of the initiate, was in all probability in the form of a cross, and this is confirmed by what Tertullian has to say on the subject. Mithra is also imaged with his arms outstretched to the Infinite.

Most of the ceremonials of Christianity were adopted from the worship surrounding Osiris and Mithra, in which the cross had a religious significance, but, though a cross was to be seen in early Christian churches, it was not placed on the altar and it received no special devotion. That this emblem was preserved in Christianity is not surprising when we know that the death of the Saviour on the cross roused Paul to say, "God forbid that I should glory save in the cross of our Lord Jesus Christ." (Gal. vi, 14.) However, not till the seventh century, when the crucifix was introduced, did the Christians adopt an original symbol for their faith, as it is not the cross but the crucifix which is peculiarly Christian and belongs to this faith alone.

The evidence we have that Jesus was crucified rests mainly on Paul, about whom we know only what he himself and *The Acts* tell us. From his writings we gather that he was a contemporary of Jesus, and in these we find him asserting in ten separate places that Jesus was crucified. Besides this, he refers in ten other places to the cross of Christ, and he based his preaching and his doctrines on the death of Jesus. We also know that Christians towards the end of the first century believed that their Lord had suffered death through crucifixion. Whether the crucifixion took the form, as represented in the gospels, is another question.

Evidently some believed that Jesus was hanged on a tree (Acts v, 30 and x, 39, 1 Peter ii, 24), which would mean that his arms were tied up above his head. Whether they were stretched above his head, or at right angles to his body, is of no great importance, and it is quite possible that the reference to his being hanged on a tree referred to crucifixion. So we can say that it was believed that he suffered death by his body being stretched out, in some manner or other, on either a natural tree, or on one with its branches cut off and a cross-piece put along the top. If Jesus died nailed on a cross, the cross would be an upright post with a peg inserted between his legs to support his body, as otherwise it would have fallen off, the weight of the body tearing his hands. The conventional crucifix is the result of Christian imagination, as the Roman cross took the form of a T and was not very high off the ground.

We naturally expect that an event which has had such a profound effect on world history, and human emotions, would have been well known from earliest times, that historians of the time would have written about it, that the place where the cross stood would have been carefully marked and preserved, so that future generations would be able to return and worship at this holy spot. As it is, we do not know where Jesus died. All we know, from contemporary reports, is that Paul said that he was crucified, an unlikely death for a Jew to invent for the Messiah as "He that is hanged is accursed of God." (Deut. xxi, 23.) At a much later date it appeared in writing that he was crucified in Jerusalem.

To understand this peculiar lack of evidence we must remember that all the Christians left Jerusalem in the year 66, after the great Jewish revolt, and that they did not return for many years, as in 70 the city was destroyed. The Jerusalem of the time of Jesus had by then ceased to exist. Titus left it in ruins, and, in place of the Temple, Hadrian in the second century erected two temples, one to Aphrodite and the other to Jupiter. Further, the full significance of the death of Jesus did not dawn upon his followers till the preaching and teaching of Paul had become understood, by which time Jerusalem had been laid waste. So we need not be surprised that no record of the sacred place of the death or burial was preserved. The place now pointed out to sightseers and pilgrims rests on the worthless opinions of the emissaries sent by Constantine to locate the places where the Lord had died and been buried. Eusebius, who tells us of this discovery, does not mention how it all came about, and only that the Emperor felt it to be his duty to find these sacred places.

We have, therefore, no first-hand evidence, and yet, by circumstantial evidence, we have enough to prove that it is probably true that Jesus died a death similar to what has been recorded in the gospels. All the symbolism which surrounds his death, all the prophesies which have been collected to show that he lived and died according to the scriptures, are our evidence that he died a violent death. It is difficult to believe that those Jews, who became Christians, would invent such a death for one they considered the Messiah, as it was quite contrary to their expectations of the end of one they had been brought up to antici-pate as their coming King. When Jesus died it was not believed that his death had been foretold; all these so-called prophesies were discovered years later and adapted to the event. They had to be twisted to conform with something that had actually happened, and in the process much that did not happen was believed to have taken place.

His death was violent because he was believed to be a slain victim. This is probably true, as otherwise the symbolism and prophesies, which grew round his death, would not have been made to fit in. We now know that the stories surrounding his crucifixion are symbolic legends, or have been inserted so as to fit in with prophecy. These were the effects which could only have come about as the result of a cause. If Jesus had died in his bed, from an ordinary illness, it is quite impossible to imagine that the stories which gathered round his death would ever have come into being. Such things do not happen, and, because they never happen, we can come to the conclusion that Jesus did not die in his bed. There must be a cause to give rise to stories, however exaggerated they become at a later date.

By inference, and picking the stories to pieces, we find that the Christian belief of Paul and others, that Jesus was a victim, was probably the right one. This, coupled with his reappearance, which would have had no religious significance had he not been a victim, turned him into a sacrificial victim, and makes it more than probable that the priests had something, if not everything, to do with his death. Thus he became a priestly sacrificial victim in the eyes of his worshippers, but before this was possible he had to die by being killed. He had to give, by his death, to all those who came to believe in him, a cause on which to build up their symbolic legends, just as he gave the urge to those who searched through the scriptures, in order to associate him with what the prophets had foretold.

Though we do not know where Jesus died his violent death, the actual place was of vital importance to those engaged in constructing the beliefs surrounding his name. It was essential to the early believers that it should have taken place at Jerusalem, where stood the Holy Temple and where was centred the Order of the Priesthood, because his death had changed the old order by abolishing the Temple and the priesthood.

It is strange that Paul does not tell us where Jesus died, but, when we go back in thought to those days, we realise that it would then be so well known that there would be no necessity for him to mention the fact. Unfortunately no early tradition remains to

guide us in our search, as *The Quelle* is silent about the
last tragic week of Jesus on earth.

Jesus lived.   He died somewhere a violent death
at the hands of the priests.   His body was buried
somewhere, and he was seen again at some place as
a spirit by one or more people.   Everything else that
we read about him is later elaboration which could
not have come about without this fundamental basis
primarily existing.   The New Testament, we might
say, is ninety-nine per cent. Christian speculation
regarding Jesus and one per cent. fact.   The one per
cent., however, was necessary, just as the seed is
necessary before a great tree can come into being,
with its numerous branches spreading out in all
directions.   The art in New Testament scholarship
lies in discovering the facts and separating them from
Christian speculation.

Nowhere else did this speculation reach to such
heights as when consideration was given to the effect
of the death of Jesus on those already dead.   We have
previously noted the lack of information about those
who rose from their graves on that unique occasion.
We would have liked much more information on the
subject, and also about the damage done by the earthquake, but only forty words are devoted to it by the
writer of Matthew's gospel.

Even when we turn to *The Gospel of Nicodemus*,
a non-canonical work, which devotes twenty-four
verses to the attempt made to find out from two who
had risen from the dead what things were like in
Sheol, we learn nothing new.   Eleven of these verses
are devoted to recounting the efforts made in per-
suading them to go to the Temple.   There they wrote

down what occupies the remaining thirteen verses. Before doing so they groaned and were greatly troubled at the idea of giving away secrets. Then, making "the sign of the cross with their fingers on their tongues" they start off writing their account.

Most of this consists of a thanksgiving to Christ for allowing them to reveal the mysteries of death. Only two verses deal with the real issue, the one in which everyone is interested, and these read :

When we were placed by our fathers in the depth of Sheol, in the blackness of darkness, on a sudden there appeared the colour of the sun like gold, and a substantial purple coloured light enlightening the place. Presently upon this Adam, the father of all mankind, with all the patriarchs and prophets rejoiced and said, "That light is the author of everlasting light who hath promised to translate us to everlasting light". Then Isaiah the prophet cried out . . . [Here follow quotations from Isaiah.]

How disappointing to have obtained only this after all the questioning. But if we can learn nothing from this gospel about the life after death its story exemplifies the simplicity of the minds of those who wrote the gospel stories and those who, during the Christian era, have believed them and still believe them. Its interest to us lies in the fact that Christians, just as did the Jews, believed that all the heroes of the Old Testament were "in the depth of Sheol, in the blackness of darkness". Abraham, Isaac, Moses, David and all the rest, down to the most insignificant Jew, were treated in this fashion in spite of all the food they had produced for Jehovah to eat, and all the millions of lambs, sheep and oxen they had roasted for his benefit.

Light, this gospel tells us, came only to them when

Jesus said on the cross "It is finished", and then David, and the host of saints, were taken by him out of Sheol to Heaven, to the accompaniment of "Lift up your gates, O ye princes, and be lift up, O everlasting gates, and the King of Glory shall come in". Thus this gospel identifies Jesus with Osiris, who released the dead from the underworld and took them to heaven. This plundering of Sheol by the Saviour produced a literature of its own, and reminds one of the Greek tales surrounding Orpheus, who invaded Hades for the same reason.

Fortunately, today we are not dependent for our knowledge as to what happens after death on what is called by Christians "the only revealed religion", which tells us nothing except bliss for believers and damnation for unbelievers. In the century after the Christian Faith was brought into being by the return of Jesus from the other life, which he had entered at death, the people were so engrossed in the prospect of his immediate return in the flesh, as a god-man to judge the world, that little use was made of mediumship to discover what the other world was like, and how those who had reached it lived. By the time this expectation had ebbed somewhat the Church was in control and mediumship abolished.

The only way to know about conditions after death is to ask those who have died, and return to us, in the presence of a medium. By asking these visitors from that other land, to which we all are bound, we now find that it is a world very like our own, though, since its vibrations are more rapid, it is more beautiful and life is more intense, varied and full of vitality. A study of the literature on the subject will make this better understood but this is not the place to enlarge further on the matter.

So we now proceed to examine the symbolic legends surrounding the death of the Saviour, in order to discover their meaning. Jesus died at Easter. This was necessary after he came to be looked upon as a saviour-god. We have already discussed in Chapter III the connection between saviour-gods and sun-worship. All that need be repeated here is that for thousands of years Easter has been a festival dedicated to the sun, and, when it came about that people began to believe in saviour-gods, it was natural that this date should be allocated to their resurrection. Just as the saviour-god had waned in influence through death and burial, and returned a glorious etheric being, so did the sun, the influence of which had waned during winter to return in spring. Christmas was the sun's birthday, when the days began to lengthen, but Easter was its resurrection day when it again shone with sufficient power to heat and stimulate life in Mother Earth. So the saviour-gods were associated with the sun in the minds of our ancestors.

As it was believed that Jesus was tried at Jerusalem before the Roman Governor, it was also thought that he was crucified at the Holy City. Another way to look at it is that, as Jesus had abolished the Temple, the priesthood and sacrifice, Jerusalem was the only fitting place where his death could take place. It, therefore, came to be believed that there he died under the sentence of Pilate, the Roman Governor, who was believed to have been in office at the time Jesus was crucified but, as explained in a previous chapter, when this idea came into being there was considerable uncertainty as to the period of time Pilate had held the office.

At the death of Jesus an earthquake occurred, which phenomenon also accompanied the death of other saviour-gods. Nature could not be indifferent to an event which affected the happiness of the human race, and she likewise had to respond in the most fitting manner the minds of Christians could imagine. The dead rose from their graves in the flesh, and, after the resurrection of Jesus, they entered Jerusalem. The reason for this was because Jesus by his death had freed mankind from the curse of death. No longer was it necessary for the saints to remain in Sheol now that he had opened the gates leading to eternal life. This story is therefore symbolic of the general resurrection of the dead which, at the time it was written, was anticipated at any moment, when the Lord would come and separate the good from the evil.

The sun was also darkened for the space of three hours, as this phenomenon had also to accompany the death of a saviour-god. What we have already described in previous chapters about the belief and efficacy of sacrifice can now be linked up with this greatest of all sacrifices, which was to bring the old method of placating the deity to an end. The study of Hebrew, Babylonian and Egyptian religious history shows us that an eclipse was considered an evil omen. Then the gods were angry and revealed this by withdrawing their light from mankind. Even when the time came when the ancients had reached the point of not regarding the sun itself as a god, they yet believed that a god was behind it, it being the outward manifestation of his divinity. To them an eclipse was one of the most potent signs that the god was angry, and so we read in Amos (viii, 9), "And it shall come to pass in that day, saith the Lord God, that I will cause the sun to go down at noon, and I will darken the earth in the clear day." In Joel (iii, 14) we also read that, "The day of the Lord is near . . . The sun and the moon shall be darkened, and the stars shall withdraw their shining."

The best way to soothe the anger of a man is to put before him the best food possible, and the ancients believed that the gods were always hungry and smelling about for human and animal spirits to eat. A hungry god was always an angry god. Thus on special occasions when a god was very angry, and showed it by withdrawing the light of the sun from the earth, the king or chief came forward with his son and offered him as a sacrifice, or a meal, to the god. The more royal the blood the more tasty the morsel and so the god came down and smelt the sweet savour of the royal offering. He then ate the spirit as it parted from the body and became contented and joyful once more. Consequently the eclipse passed, the god was satisfied, and the people, less fearful, were able once again to resume their ordinary occupations. They had given their god the best they could produce and now they expected to be left in peace for a time.

The ritual practised by the priests, before the sacrifice, included the anointing of the victim's body. In some places the body was placed on a cross and then lifted on to the altar. As the spear pierced the body of Jesus, so the High Priest released the spirit for the god to eat by piercing the body with the sacrificial knife. The reason why we are told that the body of Jesus was pierced by a spear was to identify him with a human sacrifice on the altar, and for the same reason he was anointed and his legs were not broken. The piercing of his side, from which flowed water and blood, conveyed symbolically the idea that his body produced the water of baptism, and the blood which ensured salvation.

The story of the death of Jesus came into being when he came to be looked upon as a priestly victim, and it was based on the customs surrounding human sacrifice. There was no more important event in the history of sacrifice than the ceremony which took place during an eclipse of the sun. So, naturally, this was associated with Jesus. Though no eclipse of the sun took place when he died, yet it was necessary that this should be related to him as a further proof that he was a sacrificial victim of the highest order. When Jesus died the sun shone again because Jehovah had been appeased by the sweet savour. He was again reconciled to mankind, as, on this occasion, he refused the food, and Jesus returned as a sign that he wished no further sacrifices.

With all nature standing in awe and reverence before this great spectacle, the greatest event in the world's history, when mankind was on the point of having access to heaven, Jesus died. And, at the moment of his death, the earth spoke, the sun shone again, and mankind was free for the first time since Adam's ejection from the Garden of Eden. Thus "through the offering of the body of Jesus Christ once for all" (Heb. x, 10) "an odour of a sweet smell, a sacrifice acceptable, wellpleasing to God (Phil. iv, 18), "Christ . . . hath given himself for us an offering and a sacrifice to God for a sweet smelling savour" (Eph. v, 2). While the eclipse lasted, in the case of those sacrifices offered to the gods prior to this greatest of all sacrifices, the people knelt round the altar and prayed to the sun in heaven that he would again make his face to shine upon them (Psalm xxxi, 16), just as the Christians prayed "that the offering up of the Gentiles might be acceptable" (Rom. xv, 16).

A very striking fact with regard to the various reports the evangelists give about the crucifixion is the constant reference to Old Testament prophecy. This is so much the case that some hold the opinion that the whole story has been built up on these quotations and that Jesus was never crucified. This is a plausible argument, but unsound. Without the event itself there would have been no incentive to gather all these prophesies together. A more rational way of thinking is to believe that the event occurred, and that those who reported it built up an elaborate story from the so-called prophesies because, at the time they wrote, they were entirely devoid of any details concerning the event. This is what seems to have happened and is the explanation of much of the elaboration surrounding it.

Psalm xxii seems to have had a considerable influence on the compilation of the crucifixion story. In verse 16 we read, "For dogs have compassed me ; the assembly of the wicked have inclosed me : they pierced my hands and my feet." Following this, we read in verse 18, "They part my garments among them, and cast lots upon my vesture." Psalm 69 was also used, as therein we are told that, "They gave me also gall for my meat ; and in my thirst they gave me vinegar to drink." If we turn to Isaiah liii, 12 we read,

"Therefore will I divide him a portion with the great, and he shall divide the spoil with the strong ; because he hath poured out his soul unto death : and he was numbered with the transgressors ; and he bare the sin of many, and made intercession for the transgressors."

Various remarks which are quoted as having been made at the trial and crucifixion have evidently also been influenced by the Hebrew scriptures. The jeering remark, made to Jesus on the cross by those present, that he trusted in God, and that now it would be interesting to see if God would deliver him, is just an adapted quotation from Psalm xxii, 7, "All they that see me laugh me to scorn : they shoot out the lip, they shake the head, saying, He trusted on the Lord that he would deliver him . . . seeing he delighted in him."

The remark of the dying thief can be found in Genesis (xl, 14) : "But think on me when it shall be well with thee", just as the cry of Jesus, as given by Mark, comes from Psalm xxii, "My God, my God, why hast thou forsaken me ?" Luke, on the other hand, makes Jesus say, "Father, into thy hands I commend my spirit", which is a quotation from Psalm xxxi, 5. The quotation from Zechariah (xii, 10) evidently gave the idea of the sorrow and mourning described by Luke after Jesus expired on the cross, as it ran as follows : "And they shall look upon me whom they have pierced, and they shall mourn for him, as one mourneth for his only son, and shall be in bitterness for him, as one that is in bitterness for his firstborn. In that day shall there be a great mourning in Jerusalem".

It is very improbable that the evangelists could have known the private conversation which took place between the members of the Sanhedrim at the foot of the cross, and it is equally improbable that these leaders of Jewish thought would be there on the great Feast Day. It was also very improbable that Jesus, before he expired, would have strength enough to give the loud cry of which we are told, but it was necessary that he should do so, as it had been foretold that "The Lord also shall roar out of Zion, and utter his voice from Jerusalem; and the heavens and the earth shall shake." (Joel iii, 16.)

It was also impossible for Jesus to have been on the cross at the sixth hour, as the synoptic gospels tell us, when, according to John's gospel, he was standing before Pilate at the sixth hour. One or other of these accounts must be wrong. Here, however, we are not dealing with history, but with accounts written at a very much later date, at different times, in different places, and influenced by different ideas. These were afterwards collected together to form what the Church claimed was a history of the life and death of Jesus, which claim is clearly false, and is only possible to maintain amongst those who do not think when they read.

When Jesus cried, "It is finished", the veil of the Temple was torn in two as a further sign that Jehovah had again come face to face with his people, and abolished the order of the priesthood, because now there was but "one mediator between God and men, the man Christ Jesus". (1 Tim. ii, 5.) Prior to this great sacrifice the veil of the Temple had hidden the Holy of Holies, where Jehovah dwelt. Only through the priesthood could he be approached as only they had access to this holy spot. Now, however, the old order had ended and the new one had commenced. The veil was rent in two, the Holy of Holies was opened to the people, and Christ took the place of Jehovah as "the living presence" in place of the altar, (Heb. xiii, 10) as mediator between God and man, "now to appear in the presence of God for us." Because, "now once in the end of the world hath he appeared, to put away sin by the sacrifice of himself", and "so Christ was once offered to bear the sins of many ; and unto them that look for him shall he appear the second time without sin unto salvation". (Heb. ix, 24–28).

So at the Eucharist service it is believed that the communicant and Christ reach what is called "a spiritual fellowship" as to each one he is the mediator and redeemer. Therefore, the communicants partake of the bread transformed into his body and the wine into his blood, in order to bring themselves into closer at-one-ment with the great sacrifice he accomplished for them.

Though in the time of the Temple the worshippers could not enter the Holy of Holies, yet, from the date of his death onwards, this spot, now known as the Sanctuary, where stands the altar, was open to every believer, who could enter it and commune directly with his God.

That was what was intended by the early Christians and is clearly expressed in *The Epistle to the Hebrews*. In the early Christian churches there was no altar, as sacrifice was now no more and the altar was therefore unnecessary. When the priests captured Christianity the altar became part of each church, on which lay the bread and wine which had been transformed into the body and blood of the sacrificed victim. Thus the table of the gods, at which they fed, returned to become part of the Christian church furniture, though this was quite at variance with the gospel message and apostolic teaching.

Looking back, how clearly we can realise that the destruction of the Temple inspired this apostolic outlook. This ancient institution was now no more, so naturally the Christian Jews put Christ in its place. The Jewish priesthood was scattered and Christ also replaced the priests. The destruction of the Temple added new ideas to Christian imagination, and did much to stimulate the thoughts surrounding the new testament which the death and resurrection of Jesus had given to mankind. So the symbolical tearing of the veil in the Temple at Jerusalem was intended to convey the belief in the opening of a new era, with the priesthood abolished, because there was now no further need of altars or priests as "Christ washed us from our sins in his own blood". (Rev. i, 5.) This blood-sacrifice satisfied Jehovah, and Christ now took the place of the paschal lamb.

As the blood symbolised life, so his life was sacrificed for mankind and thus we read :

Christ being come an High Priest of good things to come, by a greater and more perfect Tabernacle, not made with hands, that is to say, not of this building; Neither by the blood of goats and calves, but by his own blood he entered in once into the holy place, having obtained eternal redemption for us. . . . How much more shall the blood of Christ, who through the eternal Spirit offered himself without spot to God. . . . And for this cause he is the mediator of the new testament, that by means of death, for the redemption of the transgressions that were under the first testament, they which are called might receive the promise of eternal inheritance. (Heb. ix, 11.)

Besides reconciling God to the world, Jesus abolished the priesthood by himself becoming the only priest or mediator between God and man, "For the priesthood being changed" (Heb. vii, 12), the old order of Melchizedek came to an end, another Priest having taken its place (Heb. vii, 15), because "the Son of God abideth a priest continually" (Heb. vii, 3), "and Christ himself, as the high priest, entereth into the holy place". (Heb. ix, 25.) Here "he offered up himself" (Heb. vii, 27) and so "we have such a high priest, who is set on the right hand of the Majesty in the heavens". (Heb. viii, 1.) Consequently, the strained relationship between Jehovah and his people came to an end and friendly relations were once more established, as the "veil is done away in Christ". (2 Cor. iii, 14.)

Keeping all this in mind we can now also understand the meaning of the words, "Then the soldiers . . . took his garments, and made four parts, to every soldier a part; and also his coat: now the coat was without seam, woven from the top throughout". (John xix, 23.) Why did the evangelist feel it necessary to tell his readers this fact, and that the soldiers decided not to rend the coat into four parts but to cast lots for it? It seems at first glance that he was just passing on something he believed had happened, but this is unlikely. The seamless robe was peculiar to the priesthood. The Jewish High Priest, so Josephus tells us, always wore a seamless robe and Jesus, the new High Priest, was given this robe as part of his clothing. Going further back, we find that this idea developed out of sun-worship, the light given off by the sun being termed its robe, without break or parts, which extended north, south, east and west. So we find the origin of the seamless robe and its four parts in nature worship. Apollo and the other sun-gods had their seamless robes, some having purple ones, such as we are told was put on Jesus after his trial.

The extraordinary thing about it all is that the Jews, themselves, did not believe that Jesus ushered in a new order and abolished the old. They still disbelieve, and they are even now waiting for it to happen. They are still waiting for the Messiah, for the veil of the Temple to be torn in two, for the Messiah to become the High Priest, and for the millennium, which Christians believed was coming immediately after the resurrection of Jesus. The very people who originally, in pre-Christian days, produced the idea of the coming Messiah, said, when Christianity was born, as they say now, that Christians went off on the wrong track, and surely the Jews of all people should have known how to recognise the Messiah when he came.

We have no proof of the historical truth of all these symbolic legends, written by Christian hands sometime about the end of the first century of our era, but we do know that the Lord never returned, and for this great event Christians are still waiting, though many are disheartened and have become indifferent because he has tarried so long.

He has tarried so long, in fact, that many are now asking if the Christian Church has not blown up an enormous bubble of speculative fancy which can be burst by a mere pin-prick of intelligent thought. The Lord has tarried so long that the churches dedicated to him are generally almost empty. The weekday services in our Cathedrals comprise as worshippers the priests and choir boys, the congregation being practically non-existent. The early Christians, because of their intense belief in the saving power, and early return of the Saviour, believed that priests had become unnecessary. Today the people are beginning to feel the same, but for quite another reason. Then faith was intense, but in our own times education and increased knowledge have revealed the mistakes and miscalculations of those who were the first to proclaim Jesus as Saviour, Mediator and Redeemer. Priests, of all the innumerable Christian sects, are therefore becoming looked upon more and more as useless burdens, because only the simple are now interested in their preaching, their doctrines and their ceremonials.

The early Christians evidently believed that Jesus, as Christ, took the place of the priesthood as the mediator between God and man, thus making the priesthood unnecessary, there being no further sacrifices to be offered up. As the Lord delayed his coming, doctrines and dogmas began to form round his death. A Church organisation was formed to protect the Eucharist ceremony, which was incorporated into a solemn service held in remembrance of his death. For the first three centuries laymen celebrated this rite, but when the priesthood, in the third century, captured the Church, only priests were employed to perform this sacrificial memorial rite. The Christian priesthood had no part in the constitution of the early Christian Church, but the next chapter will disclose how it built up an organisation, for which there was no place, or provision, and how it abolished nature's mediums, who were acting under the inspiration of what the Christians in these early centuries called the holy spirit.

From this time onwards Christianity ceased to be a religion closely related to psychic manifestations, and became one of doctrines and dogmas, emphasis only being laid on beliefs and ceremonials. If Jesus had remained Jesus, and not become Christ, and if his reappearance had been remembered as a natural psychic event, there would have been no need of a priesthood, but, when he became Christologised and theologised, these theological experts were needed to explain the mysteries which Paul was the first to introduce. Consequently the Christian priesthood came into being, and, from the third century onwards, its influence is increasingly noticed, as, by then, the religion had absorbed Paul's doctrines and dogmas, and grown out of the simple faith of the Apostolic Church.

Just as the Jews foretold, the Lord did not come, which means that they were right and the Christians were wrong. At times it pays better to be wrong than right, and in this case it would certainly have been better for the Jews to have fallen in with the beliefs of the Christians and become Christians. Instead of which they held out, and argued with the Christians that they were all wrong in building up this enormous edifice of theological speculation just because Peter and Paul saw an apparition of Jesus after his death. Paul, they argued, had gone down the wrong path, which would lead to a blind alley.

The apparition of Jesus to these Jews was no more than an angel, such as had been seen many times and often by the prophets of old, and Paul, so they said, had put on his experience an entirely wrong construction. In this the Jews were perfectly right. Paul did make a mistake, and the Christian Faith has been built up on erroneous speculations, arising out of an apparition being seen by one or more Jewish clairvoyants, who formed the belief that this experience was a sign from heaven that the Messiah had come, suffered and was due to return at any moment.

Over the centuries this delusion was woven into a system of thought, and threaded backwards and forwards with theological doctrines and dogmas, drawn from all the religions in and around Palestine. It appealed to the Greeks and, because they were looked upon by the Romans as the intellectuals of those days, it was taken up by the Romans, who would never have looked at it if it had come direct from Palestine. As they were the dictators of the world of those days, the world accepted it. But this does not alter the fact that the Jews were right and the Christians were wrong. The Jews thus became a minority, scattered within a great Christian community whose religion had sprung from Judaism, but was not Judaism.

There was, however, sufficient connection between the two to bring about constant bickering and ill-feeling. The Jews jeered at the Christians because of their mistaken speculations, and the Christians hated the Jews because they had killed the Lord of Glory, and cast aside the one and only chance Jehovah had given to humanity to find salvation. If Jehovah required such a sacrifice before he could again become friendly, someone had to kill the victim, and so the Christians should have been thankful to the Jews for exercising this priestly office and thus appeasing the angry deity. In religion, however, one does not find logic or rational thought, and where the emotions are concerned sanity is usually lacking. So this book is, I fear, but a record of the follies and stupidities of the human race, from which failings it has obtained its religious comfort.

However, when Christianity was in its childhood, everything was vastly different from the intelligent outlook of today. The Christians, with Greek and Roman support, won the day and treated the Jews with the contempt their opinions did not deserve. From Mark, the earliest gospel, right through Matthew, Luke and John to the end of the non-canonical *Gospel of Peter* we observe an increasing volume of abuse against the Jews, with the obvious intention of relieving Pilate, and his Gentile soldiers, of the guilt of the death of the Saviour, and laying it all on the backs of this unfortunate race.

So as to relieve the Gentiles of all blame, with regard to the death of Jesus, the writer of Peter's gospel, like the writer of Luke and Acts, tells us that Pilate sent Jesus to be tried by Herod Antipas. Peter's gospel, however, goes even further than Luke and Acts, because it tells us that it was Herod who condemned and sentenced Jesus to death, his judgement concluding with these words, "All that I have commanded you to do to him, do it".

With the symbolic rending of the Temple veil the old era was ended and a new one commenced. The promise of a Saviour to Adam opened the old book of the Covenant which Christ closed, to open in turn the book of the New Testament. There was no further need now of human or animal sacrifice, which was one great blessing Christianity conferred on mankind. All that was of the past. What was now necessary for salvation was belief in the saving grace of the Lord Jesus Christ who, when this belief came to be first accepted, was sitting at the right hand of God, and making arrangements to return to earth at any moment to separate believers from unbelievers.

Then he would reign for a thousand years over a people purged from all iniquity, in a world of peace and righteousness. The Devil and his angels had been conquered. The age-long war between the gods and the demons was over, and, when the millennium opened, Satan would be bound and thrown into the lake of fire (the same as the Egyptians reserved for Set) along with his demons and all unbelievers in the Christian doctrine. Hell would then be closed for at least a thousand years, and humanity would be safe from the Prince of Evil and his entourage.

All this speculation came into being because of what happened after Jesus died. The veil between the two worlds is but a cloud and at death one passes through it imperceptibly. Whatever else is told of Jesus which is legend, this is true, that Jesus at death, like all before his time and after it, entered the etheric realm, which was his destination as it is of all mankind. His earth memories evidently brought him back to earth to be seen of some with clairvoyant vision. Sorrow amongst the friends he had left on earth was thus turned to joy, and mourning to gladness. That is what we can reasonably believe actually happened.

We are not now, however, considering what

really happened, but what, a hundred years or so later, was believed to have occurred. With this clearly in mind I shall now review the next episode in this great drama, namely

THE ROCK TOMB.

According to the gospel accounts, the body of Jesus was taken from the cross and reverently placed in a prepared tomb. Matthew tells us that Joseph of Arimathea, who was a rich man, came forward and begged of Pilate the body of Jesus, which, when received, he wrapped in a clean linen cloth and laid in his own new tomb, hewn out of the rock. After having done this he rolled a great stone to the door of the sepulchre and departed.

Because Jesus, by his reappearance, had convinced some of those who survived him that he was the Christ, it was necessary that a legend should be spun telling how his body received a burial fitting the rank he attained after his death. So, when we read the account in Mark, we find this endeavour to impress readers with the high standing of the one whose tomb the body of Jesus occupied. Mark tells us that Joseph was an honourable councillor, which is thought to mean a member of the Sanhedrim. Mark, like Matthew, emphasises the fact that after the body had been prepared, it was left in the rock tomb, against which a stone had been rolled, and that there were witnesses to this event.

Luke tells us that Joseph was a good man and had not consented to the Council which decided that Jesus was to die. For the benefit of the Gentiles Luke mentions that Arimathea is a city of the Jews. The sepulchre had never before been used, which was fitting for the holy purpose to which it was now being dedicated. John's gospel tells the story of Joseph obtaining the body from Pilate, but brings in the story of Nicodemus, who brought a mixture of myrrh and aloes for the purpose of preserving the body. In this account no reference is made to the tomb belonging to Joseph.

Thus the four gospel writers tell more or less the same story, but it is nowhere else confirmed, as in *The Acts* we are simply told that "They took him down from the tree, and laid him in a sepulchre". (Acts xiii, 29.) Paul also refers to the Lord's burial with the remark that after Christ died "he was buried". (1 Cor. xv, 4.) According to these two latter accounts Jesus received an ordinary burial which required no special mention. If he had been buried in a rock tomb, never before used, which was the property of a man of note, it is more than likely that Paul would have heard of it, and referred to it.

The earth life and death of Jesus in Paul's eyes resembled that of any other human being, which is just what we would expect from one writing, as he did, within some thirty years of the time Jesus lived. Had Paul written of Jesus as if he were a god-man, as the evangelists do, we would know that Paul was not a contemporary of Jesus, or that his writings had been interpolated at a later date. The human Jesus depicted by Paul is natural and possible to accept, just as we can understand how, as the result of his psychic experiences and temperament, he produced his Heavenly Christ.

Though this story of the burial of Jesus seems to be unknown to Paul, yet his transformation of Jesus into the Christ was the cause of the belief that Jesus was buried in a rock tomb. Moreover, prophecy had decreed that "He made his grave with the wicked and with the rich in his death." (Isaiah liii, 9.) Other saviour-gods received such a burial, so why not Jesus? Mithra and Osiris are outstanding examples of saviour-gods being associated with a rock tomb. Mithra was known as "The God out of the Rock" and was termed "The Rock-born God", which is what Jesus was. In the eyes of his worshippers Jesus went into the rock tomb a god-man and came out of it a god. He went in Jesus and came out Christ. That is how it was conceived many years later, when the story of his burial came to be written down.

He was then believed to have reanimated his physical body, rolled away the stone, and walked out of the tomb the conqueror of the grave. That belief was the outcome of his being seen as a spirit after death, which event turned him into a god. After that happened the theologians set to work to spoil the natural story and spin the one given in the gospels, as, in their opinion, a god should be able to return to his earth body, roll away a heavy stone, appear and disappear at will and ascend to heaven in the sight of the people. The Christian theologians were well aware of the association of a rock tomb with Mithra, as in those days the cult of Mithra was a strong rival to the Christian cult, and Jesus could not be in any way inferior to this god who was much beloved by the Romans.

Christians first of all believed that Jesus was born in a rock cave, just as was Mithra. In those days caves were consecrated to the gods, and had been down the ages, long before temples were built for worship. Then the Christians adopted Christmas and Easter from Mithraism, and so we need not wonder that they also brought into their literature the story about the burial of Jesus in a rock tomb. Obviously the reason for this was to make him a rock-born god like Mithra, and so associate him with the Mithraic mysteries.

Besides this, the Christians adopted from surrounding religions the idea that the disciples were amazed and perplexed because the body of the Lord was not in the tomb. Osiris was mourned for after his death, during which time his followers searched for his body, and when it was found they cried out, "We have found him ; rejoice". Tertullian (160–230) tells us that in his day it was believed that Osiris was buried and returned to life, just as this was believed about Dionysus, Attis, Adonis and others. At the festival of Easter, Mithra in effigy was laid in a rock tomb, when the people mourned for him, and then rejoiced after the body was taken out and exposed to view.

While some gods were supposed to be in their temporary tombs they were credited with descending to Hades, and so Jesus was believed to have followed this precedent and visited the underworld. Hercules, Apollo, Orpheus and Mithra descended to Hades before ascending to Heaven. By their ascent to heaven they proved themselves to be gods, as mortals remained in Hades till the resurrection day. Their ascent to heaven was known by their being seen, as etheric beings, after death, which, as in the case of Jesus, brought all the legends surrounding them into being.

The psychic stream watered all these beliefs when

in embryo and caused their germination. As it fertilised the germ which grew into the saviour-god, worshipped by Christians, so it germinated the belief which produced all the other saviour-gods. Christianity, Mithraism, and all the other beliefs we have considered, are just names for the legends, doctrines and dogmas which developed, like rank weeds, along the banks of the stream and finally hid it from sight.

Only by pushing these weeds aside can the source which brought them into being be discovered, and nature's own revelation be separated from the erroneous speculations of the theologians. When this is done we find the same psychic stream as we have with us today, which we can follow back through the years to the time of primitive man. Nature never changes. Only the opinions formed by ignorance change, just as human mentality is able to reflect to an increasing extent the rays of intellectual light shed by nature. Until the mind has developed sufficiently to catch these rays they pass by unnoticed.

From the time of primitive man these rays have been picked up to an increasing extent, and into what they will mould the human race no one can tell. Here we are considering a time when man was nearer the animal, and accepted things as they seemed to be, whereas today more people think and reason. Then the annual death and resurrection of vegetation was linked up with the death and reappearance of those who were looked back upon as god-men on earth, and as gods in heaven. So the rock tomb represented mother earth, into which life went after the death of vegetation, and from which life returned. Sorrow at the departure of life gave place to joy on its return.

Thus our ancestors symbolised in the form of legend that which was necessary to nourish them physically and mentally : food, material and immaterial, both of which are necessary, because on earth we are not only material but also etheric beings.

In the previous pages we have moved, step by step, to the culmination of this dramatic religious story, composed of the only kind of mental food our ancestors could digest. Now we have reached the pivot on which it all rests, and without which everything that has already been related of the apotheosis of Jesus would never have been conceived. Here we are at the source of the Christian Faith, the germ from which everything has developed. Now we have come to the crowning episode :

THE RESURRECTION.

The appearance of Jesus after death was considered by the early Christians to be such a supernatural event that it distinguished and raised him in their minds above the category of all human beings. They so dwelt on this subject, and it formed such a central point in their faith, that they transformed a simple natural event into an impossible and absurd legend. This legend, which is given in all four gospels, is not only irrational but also shows distinct signs of elaboration.

Each evangelist contradicts the other and, according to the *Encyclopædia Biblica*, twenty-two contradictions of a most serious character are to be found, when a comparison is made between the four accounts to be found in the New Testament. What Christians claim to be the fundamental truth of their faith rests on a basis so insecure that it does not bear serious investigation. As it stands, no thoughtful person can believe it to be true. What is false and contradictory is what has been added to the original tradition. Why this was done we shall soon discover, and what has been a mystery throughout the Christian era will be made capable of human understanding.

Christian opinion, as it finally developed to become the orthodox belief as incorporated in the creed, was that Jesus came out of the tomb in the same body as the one which was carried in and reverently laid in what was supposed to be its last resting place. If the orthodox opinion is right all the references to Jesus being seen after death are couched in terms quite different from what would be used in reference to a being in the flesh, and the question is why were such terms and expressions ever used ? There is only one answer, which is that what is natural was the first stratum of tradition and what is unnatural was the outcome of the belief that Jesus, as a god, had power to reanimate the earth body which he used as a vehicle during his temporary sojourn on earth.

We know that today apparitions are seen by some people. Those who will not go so far as to believe this will admit that the claim has been made since writing was first discovered that some have had such experiences. This claim has been made consistently down the ages and everyone of us knows at least one ghost story. Whether we believe it or not is another matter. I, personally, have never seen a ghost, but I have seen photographs of ghosts which were taken under conditions which make me think that the plates and films were not faked.

We can, therefore, say that it is more natural for one or more to have claimed that he or they had seen Jesus as an apparition after death than as a human being walking about with his own physical body. Even the most materially minded individual would say that it is more rational to believe that some of the disciples of Jesus thought that they saw him as a ghost than as a human being. Knowing that the human mind is subject to flights of fancy, it is easier to believe that one or more people were thus deluded than to think that anyone could reanimate his physical body after death and again function as a human being.

In the first case a delusion is natural, but the other is quite unnatural. Thousands have claimed to see ghosts but no one has ever claimed to see a dead man, or a dead woman, functioning in a body from which the breath of life had departed. It is a contradiction in terminology, as, if this happened, the being would not be dead. The nearest approach to this happening would come about owing to the fact that the one who was supposed to be dead was not really dead. Thus we could suppose that Jesus was taken from the cross in a comatose state and laid in the tomb. His vitality returned and he had the strength to push away the stone and appear to his disciples. This is possible but extremely unlikely.

There are several reasons why this can be ruled out, the first being that if this had occurred Jesus would never have been turned into a god. He would still have been looked upon as an ordinary human being; his recovery would have created a sensation at the time, and then been forgotten. For one to be buried in a comatose state it is necessary, presumably at

least, to die in a bed. One who is crucified could not
be buried in this state. Crucifixion does not lead to
a state of coma. Every nerve of the body is strung up
to the last and death follows from heart failure due to
extreme exhaustion. Finally, it is quite evident that
from the very earliest times it was believed that Jesus
died on the cross and was buried as a dead man, all
life having departed from his physical body. The
early Christians cursed the Jews for killing their Lord,
and if the Jews could have answered that he recovered
from his experience on the cross we would have found
it referred to in *The Talmud* or some other literature.

This, therefore, narrows the issue to the question
as to whether Jesus was seen as a spirit or in his reanimated physical body. Thus we come to the story,
as given in the gospels, and when we discover references to Jesus being "seen" and "risen" and "alive"
and "appearing" to his friends, we must conclude
that this is the earliest tradition, and that the story of
his body not being in the tomb is, along with the
legend of the burial in the rock tomb, a later elaboration. So as to make this matter clearer let me now
pick out the references in the gospels and *The Acts*
to the return of Jesus after his death, excepting in this
instance the references to his being seen by Paul.

The women who first went to the sepulchre were
told by an angel "He is not here; for he is risen"
(Matt. xxviii, 6), and then follows :

He is risen from the dead. (Matt. xxviii, 7.)
Jesus met them, saying, All hail. (Matt. xxviii, 9.)
And when they saw him, they worshipped him. (Matt.
xxviii, 17.)
He is risen; he is not here. (Mark xvi, 6.)

Now when Jesus was risen early the first day of the week, he appeared first to Mary Magdalene. (Mark xvi, 9.)

And they, when they had heard that he was alive, and had been seen of her, believed not. (Mark xvi, 11.)

After that he appeared in another form unto two of them, as they walked, and went into the country. (Mark xvi, 12.)

Afterward he appeared unto the eleven as they sat at meat, and upbraided them . . . because they believed not them which had seen him after he had risen. (Mark xvi, 14.)

After the Lord had spoken unto them, he was received up into heaven. (Mark xvi, 19.)

And it came to pass, that Jesus . . . himself drew near, and went with them. (Luke xxiv, 15.)

Yea, and certain women . . . made us astonished . . . saying, that they had also seen a vision of angels, which said that he was alive. (Luke xxiv, 22.)

Then he [Jesus] said unto them . . . Ought not Christ to have suffered these things, and to enter into his glory ? (Luke xxiv, 25.)

And their eyes were opened, and they knew him; and he vanished out of their sight. (Luke xxiv, 31.)

The Lord is risen indeed, and hath appeared to Simon. (Luke xxiv, 34.)

Jesus himself stood in the midst of them, and saith unto them, Peace be unto you. But they were terrified and affrighted, and supposed that they had seen a spirit. (Luke xxiv, 36.)

While he blessed them, he was parted from them, and carried up into heaven. (Luke xxiv, 51.)

She turned herself back, and saw Jesus standing. (John xx, 14.)

Mary Magdalene came and told the disciples that she had seen the Lord. (John xx, 18.)

When the doors were shut where the disciples were assembled . . . Jesus . . . stood in the midst, and saith unto them, Peace be unto you'. (John xx, 19.)

We have seen the Lord. (John xx, 25.)

After eight days again . . . came Jesus, the doors being shut, and stood in the midst. (John xx, 26.)

Jesus shewed himself again to the disciples at the sea of Tiberias. (John xxi, 1.)

Jesus stood on the shore. (John xxi, 4.)

This is now the third time that Jesus shewed himself to his disciples, after that he was risen from the dead. (John xxi, 14.)

Whom God hath raised up, having loosed the pains of death. (Acts ii, 24.)

This Jesus hath God raised up, whereof we all are witnesses. (Acts ii, 32.)

Ye . . . killed the Prince of Life, whom God hath raised from the dead. (Acts iii, 15.)

Jesus Christ of Nazareth . . . whom God raised from the dead. (Acts iv, 10.)

The stories told about the various appearances of Jesus after his death, as they have come down to us, are quite irrational, and devoid of meaning, if taken to mean that he went about with a physical body after his death. The foregoing references, as they stand, could be taken without difficulty to refer to Jesus being seen as a spirit. They could easily be applied to an apparition, and originally this was intended, as we find that Matthew gives the older tradition and also that which was added later. In Mark a young man spoke the following words, whereas Matthew attributes them to both a spirit and to Jesus. Originally the remark "Go into Galilee and there shall they see me", was evidently made by a spirit whom the women took to be Jesus. It is not a remark an ordinary man in the flesh would make but it is intelligible as coming from an etheric being.

When, however, intermingled with all these references to his being seen, we have the insistence on the tomb being empty, the grave clothes being laid aside, and the women being told by the angels that he had departed from the tomb, an entirely new aspect is given to the story. Here we find the evident attempt to show that Jesus had risen in his physical body, one evangelist even going to the length of saying that Jesus showed his disciples the marks on his hands and the mark made by the spear in his side.

Why this insistence on Jesus having risen in his physical body ? It is not an idea which would come naturally to anyone, and there must have been some definite reason why every evangelist should have stressed it. This we shall now soon discover. It will be noticed, however, that no such idea is conveyed in Paul's references to Jesus after his death, and nowhere throughout Paul's epistles is any attempt made to represent Jesus other than as being seen as a spirit after his death. We can definitely say that Paul knew nothing of the return of Jesus in his physical body, for the very reason that in his days this idea had not developed.

In *The Gospel of Nicodemus* we find the following reference to the reappearance: "I [Joseph of Arimathea] saw Jesus as the brightness of the sun and fell down upon the earth for fear. Then I looked upon him and said, 'Rabboni Elias'. He answered me, 'I am not Elias but Jesus of Nazareth whose body thou didst bury'." In *The Epistle to the Smyrnaeans*, by Ignatius, a second-century epistle, the writer chides those who think that when they die "they shall become mere spirits" like Jesus when he died, because he argues that Jesus rose in the flesh. This criticism of those who believed in the resurrection of the spirit, and not of the body, is an indication that some Christians, who lived when this was written, still believed as Paul did, and that pressure was being brought on them to abandon this belief for the one which was taking its place, that Jesus rose, not as a spirit, but in the flesh. The psychic stream was then slowly being covered over with the weeds of doctrine, and Christianity was becoming a religion based on legends and ceremonies.

The belief in the physical resurrection was one of later growth which came to be intertwined with the original belief that Jesus was seen as a spirit. Scholars claim to have discovered that the appearance of Jesus to his disciples as a spirit was an earlier tradition than the discovery of the empty tomb, and, though they ascribe this experience to illusion or hallucination, that is a matter for individual opinion. Professor Guignebert, in his recent work entitled *Jésus*, remarks :

Now we shall go on to show that the earliest tradition assigned the first appearances of Jesus exclusively to Galilee. Therefore the story of the discovery of the empty tomb is secondary to that which might be called the Galilean stage. This secondary character is also revealed by an examination of the episode itself. The discovery of the empty tomb has no value in itself, it is subordinate to the appearances and it has no real effect on the disciples until one or other of them has seen the risen Lord. This proves that the belief in the Resurrection was founded first on the appearances. This being so, the discovery of the empty tomb, useless as far as the disciples' faith is concerned, falls into the category of an apologetic or polemical invention and is eliminated from the realm of history.

The stories of the burial and of the discovery of the empty tomb could only have come into existence far from Jerusalem and outside the circle of the original disciples, forty years at the earliest after the death of Jesus. That is to say shortly after the destruction of Jerusalem, when it was practically impossible for anyone to undertake the smallest research on the spot. The truth is that we do not know, and in all probability the disciples knew no better, where the body of Jesus had been thrown after it had been removed from the cross, probably by the executioners. It is more likely to have been cast into the pit for the executed than laid in a new tomb.

The belief in the Resurrection, upon which Christianity has been founded, did not rest in the beginning on the assertion that Jesus, laid in the tomb on the Friday evening, came forth living on the Sunday morning, but on the statement that Jesus, after his death, was seen by several disciples.

The study of the earliest evidences for the appearances excludes therefore the discovery of the empty tomb from the primitive historical tradition, and clearly shews that belief in the resurrection of Jesus rests on these appearances. It leaves no other foundation for what is called the Easter faith than the appearances themselves.

Lagrange, another French authority, in referring to Luke's treatment of the subject, remarks "he rationalised a supernatural appearance". If Lagrange had stated that Luke had rationalised a supernormal experience it would have been more correct, as there is nothing supernatural in the universe. Professor Harnack, in his work *Neue Untersuchungen zur Apostelgeschichte*, observes, "The discovery of the empty tomb complicated and confused the tradition of the appearances and Paul knew nothing of this discovery". Alfred Loisy, in *Revue d'Histoire et de Littérature religieuse*, under the title of *La légende de Jésus*, writes in the same strain, as follows :

The accounts in the canonical and apocryphal gospels do not represent the original appearances, but the way in which the belief in the resurrection of Christ became conscious, took shape and justified itself, half a century and more after the birth of Christianity.

This last is the belief of one who has suffered for expressing his honest opinions. He became a priest in 1879 and later an abbé. He gave over many years of his life to the study of the gospels and, because of his unorthodox views, he was excommunicated from the Roman Catholic Church in France.

I shall give only one other opinion and it is that of Johannes Weiss, which is found in his magnum opus entitled *Das Urchristentum*, which was published in 1917. Here he expresses the view that Paul did not think of Jesus as having risen in his physical body, "For him Jesus's resurrection means the same thing as his glorification and exaltation", and that the stories about his return to the flesh originated for no other reason than "for the purposes of missionary apologetics". In his opinion the earliest Christology centred round Jesus as the Messiah because of his exaltation, as he had become "a being who by his very nature belonged to heaven". In his treatment of the conversion of Paul he remarks that "the vital point in it was Paul's conviction of the identity of the heavenly Messiah with the crucified Jesus".

The foregoing quotations, taken from the writings of these five authorities of international reputation, should suffice to emphasise the fact that the first tradition was to the effect that Jesus appeared after death as an etheric being, and that this psychic revelation was at a later date superimposed with the tale that he returned to earth with his old body, which in reality had shared the fate which overtakes the physical frames of all mankind.

If, moreover, we analyse critically the quotations taken from the gospels, which are tabulated a few pages further back, it becomes quite evident that they do not refer to Jesus being seen in a material body.

To convey this impression no one would say "He is risen from the dead", as the correct expression would be that he had recovered or that he, being thought dead, was not dead. Likewise it would not be said that "he appeared to Mary Magdalene". When we meet someone, we do not say that he appeared to us, or that "he appeared in another form unto two of them", or that he appeared to us as we were having breakfast.

Again, we read such remarks as "he was received up into heaven". This could not be written of one in his physical body, just as the remark attributed to Jesus, "Ought not Christ to have suffered these things and to enter into his glory", could not apply to Jesus if he were back amongst his disciples as he was before his death. When we read about their eyes being opened and that he then vanished out of their sight, we are not being told something about a person in the flesh. Further, no one would write about anyone in his earth body in words such as these : "Jesus stood in the midst of them . . . but they were terrified and supposed that they had seen a spirit". If Jesus went about after his death in his reanimated body, however did this extraordinary remark find its way into writing ? Why did the writer not say, "Jesus came in and sat down among us" ? We do not mistake people for spirits at meal-times whatever we may do at other times. Why this change of language from what was written before his death if Jesus was going amongst them as formerly ?

Why also, when Mary Magdalene told the disciples that she had seen the Lord, did they not ask why he had not come along with her, or where she had left

him, or what he was doing ? Why just the bald remark
that she had seen the Lord, which, if the orthodox
belief is correct, is quite as meaningless as is the
remark, "This is the third time that Jesus showed
himself". Such expressions as that he gave "abundant
proofs", that "some doubted", and that none cared to
ask who he was, when he appeared on the shore of the
Sea of Tiberias, are quite unnatural in reference to a
man, but can be understood with reference to a spirit.
Again, if Jesus were going about in his earth body,
presumably naked, as his grave clothes were in the
tomb, how could he appear to his disciples in a room
when the doors were shut, and then vanish from sight,
as he did on another occasion ?

One strong argument against the story of the
physical resurrection of Jesus is that neither Matthew
nor John tells us what became of him after he
had come out of the tomb. Their accounts close with
him represented as still living on earth, so they either
never heard of the story of the ascension or did not
believe it. Mark states only that "he was received
up into heaven" and Luke that "he was parted from
them and carried up into heaven". If Jesus had
actually appeared in his flesh body we would have been
given much more information than this. Matthew's
and John's silence, and Mark's and Luke's casual
reference to the parting, are sufficient in themselves
to prove that there was no accepted tradition of his
return in his old body. Two evangelists make no
attempt to account for what became of Jesus after his
resurrection, while the other two just mention his
returning to heaven in such a casual off-hand way that
one can appreciate that they do so because they

realised that their story, without some such ending, would necessitate an account of what Jesus did until he died like the rest of mankind.

To the Jewish Christians, Jesus's being translated to heaven would present no difficulties, as they believed that both Enoch and Elijah had been caught up to heaven, which are just two other examples of etheric appearances being materialised. The Gentiles had no such traditions, as their gods ascended to heaven as spirits at death. This is as it should be, as at death the etheric body is released. So we read of Krishna, as an etheric being, ascending to heaven from the pyre where he was burned. Hercules did likewise after suffering the same fate. Dionysus was seen to rise to heaven as a spirit, as was also Adonis. This is what clairvoyants see happening today when death takes place, and the experiences of the above gods are only typical of what happens to everyone. The Christian belief in the ascension of Jesus in his physical body is just as stupid and false as is the story of his physical resurrection, and I predict that before this century ends neither of these tales will be believed, except by the most ignorant of Catholics.

We are evidently not dealing here with an account about a man, and originally it was never intended to be such, as we can discover by the repeated remarks in *The Acts* about the Jews having killed Jesus. How could they have done so if he emerged from the tomb a living man, and how, if he had, could the writer of *The Acts* (xiii, 34) say that after death he had a body that would "no more return to corruption"?

Again, why are the original Greek words, which we find used, just those words which the Greeks employed when they referred to seeing an apparition ? In the sentence "he shewed himself alive . . . being seen of them" (Acts i, 3), the Greek word *optanô* is used, which is a technical term for seeing an etheric being, and when we turn to Acts xxvi, 19, and read that Paul told King Agrippa, "I was not disobedient unto the heavenly vision", we find employed in the original Greek the noun *optasia*, formed from this verb. So the same Greek expression is used when relating Paul's vision of Jesus as is used in relating the story about Jesus being seen by others after death, which is proof enough that the etheric and not the physical reappearance of Jesus was meant.

What we are now reading in the gospels is a second-century story of what had by then come to be believed, mixed up with an earlier tradition. The tradition took the line followed by Paul, and into this was entwined the story of the empty tomb and Jesus showing his pierced hands and body, together with the repeated assertions that he would rise again on the third day. This came from the belief that it was prophesied that "After two days he will revive us : in the third day he will raise us up, and we shall live in his sight" (Hosea vi, 2), which had no reference whatever to Jesus, but expressed the prevailing belief, when this passage was written, that the etheric body finally loses all connection with the physical body three days after death. This is quite in accordance with what we are told today by our friends who have passed beyond the veil, except in the case of a sudden death, when the parting takes place at once.

They tell us that it is unwise to cremate a dead body until three days have elapsed from the time of death, as in some cases it has a temporary effect on the spirit born into the new life. I remember a case which exemplifies this. At one of my séances with John C. Sloan a voice spoke, giving the name of a man whose funeral I had attended the previous day, quite unknown to the medium or anyone present. He spoke to me in evident discomfort and complained that the cremation of his earth body had rather upset him. I told him he would soon forget what had happened but he persisted by saying that he had been beside his earth body when it was burned and that its swift destruction had given him a shock. When he returned a week later he was quite normal and told me that he had now forgotten all about the incident.

We find an echo of the idea, as expressed by Hosea, in the story of the raising of Lazarus, as we read that his friends thought that there was no hope of his spirit returning as he had been dead for four days and decomposition had set in. This being so, the belief prevailed at the time we are considering that Jesus had to return to his body within three days or otherwise his spirit would finally be separated from it. Had he not done so prophecy would not have been fulfilled and this was imperative because the Psalmist had written, "Thou wilt not leave my soul in Sheol; neither wilt thou suffer thine holy one to see corruption". (Psalm xvi, 10.)

The appearance of Jesus rested on nothing tangible. The opponents of the Christian Faith naturally took this, its very pivot, to discredit all the legends which had come to surround him. They did not attempt to deny that he had lived and been crucified, because that was accepted, but they scoffed at the

Christian belief that Jesus had appeared after death, and to this what could the Christians reply ? Nothing, because by that time all the original disciples and Paul had passed away, and there was not a shred of evidence in support of the belief. Ghost stories are seldom believed except by those who have the experience, and the Jews, in the second century, were like people of the present day, scoffers at such tales. When one gets into a corner it is natural to turn to any resort to find a way out. So the answer the Christians made to the Jews crept into their literature and how this happened is not difficult to discover.

Slowly the belief in the etheric appearance of Jesus gave way to the belief that he came out of the tomb as a man in the flesh, and for this belief we can put forward several reasons. The first is that in the passion dramas of the other saviour-gods an actor came out of the stage-tomb, as representing the god's resurrection, and so it came to be believed that the god had originally returned to earth in his physical body. The second reason is that when Jesus had become a god, it was found quite easy to believe that he could reanimate his earth body. This was a much more effective and concrete way of showing that death had been conquered than the original belief in his return as a spirit, especially as the reanimation of the body on the great resurrection day for all mankind was the accepted belief of the times. This brings us to the third reason, that Jesus had first done what all mankind would do. He had led the way, had opened the proceedings, so to speak, of the general resurrection and, as this was believed to be a physical event, he must have reappeared in the flesh.

There was no evidence to guide the Christians of the second century ; tradition was vague as to how he had appeared, because there was nothing tangible handed down from generation to generation. Lastly, and probably the most potent reason of all, there was the belief that the body of the Messiah would never decay. This meant that when he left this earth he returned to heaven in the flesh and would come back in the flesh to judge the world. Then the dead would rise from their graves in the same bodies as they had when they died.

The reply the Jews made to the Christians, when they put forward the story of Jesus's body not being found in the tomb, was that the disciples had stolen the body from the grave. Matthew tries to put matters right, as throughout the burial and resurrection story the writer lays quite exceptional weight on the fact that the body of Jesus was placed in the tomb and that it was duly sealed. Under ordinary circumstances this would not have been stressed. The writer of this gospel used this argument to press home the fact that the body of Jesus was actually placed in the tomb, and that it could not have been stolen by the disciples.

To answer this accusation of the Jews, the additional information was given about Pilate putting a watch on the tomb, "lest his disciples come by night, and steal him away, and say unto the people, He is risen from the dead. . . . So they went, and made the sepulchre sure, sealing the stone, and setting a watch". (Matt. xxvii, 64.) Mark tells us that the stone was very great, but Luke and John give none of these details, and the reason Matthew dwells so much on the impossibility of the body being stolen, was because he was writing his gospel for the benefit of the Jews. This can easily be discovered by his repeated quotations from Hebrew scripture, and his constant references to the fulfilment of prophecy.

It is quite evident that when Matthew's gospel was written, Christians had to contend with the adverse criticism about the return of Jesus after his death. In those days the original belief in the etheric appearance of Jesus was growing weak as no one was alive who could establish it. As his etheric appearance could not be proved, Christians had to answer the charge that if he were seen after death then his disciples stole his body. If the Christians had replied that his body did not come into the question, as he had appeared as a spirit, the Christian Faith would have remained as Paul had left it. Instead, however, they attempted to reply to their critics by trying to prove that the disciples had never touched the body.

Why then are we told that the tomb was found to be empty ? Undoubtedly this became a settled belief in the second century, and was used as an argument in favour of the divinity of the Saviour. One who could rise from the dead in his old body could be none other than a god. This question of the empty tomb has led to endless difficulties, contradictions and irrational beliefs. In trying to believe too much the Christians produced an irrational and impossible legend. It was senseless because it created more difficulties than it solved. It changed the entire aspect of the resurrection and turned the etheric appearance of Jesus into an absurd illogical story which meant nothing.

The impression the evangelists tried to convey

was that Jesus emerged alive from the cave because he was the Christ. Consequently it was empty when the women went to dress the body with spices. This latter act was unnecessary as it had already been done when he was buried (John xix, 40), but this story had to be invented so as to refute the accusation that the disciples had stolen the body. By bringing all the evidence possible to bear on the empty tomb, which is stressed unduly, the Christians had something tangible to set off against the jeers of their opponents. *The Gospel of Peter* multiplies the details of the precautions taken to secure the body in the tomb so as to show how groundless were the charges brought against the disciples. The empty tomb was tangible proof that Jesus had conquered death by reappearing in his old body, and that was all that appealed to the mentality of the people of those days, who could only think of a resurrection of the physical body.

The Christians succumbed to the opinions prevailing in Palestine and Egypt, and, instead of holding on to the etheric reappearance of Jesus, which had turned Peter and Paul into ardent enthusiasts for the cause of Christ, they adopted the opinion that Jesus had returned in his old body. As a result the original story of his etheric return was smothered over with the legend of his return as a man. We can still trace the original story in the gospels, and it is evident that the first tradition was covered over by the later belief, which has been the accepted doctrine of the Christian Faith ever since.

So as to meet the objection that the etheric return of Jesus could not be proved, and to come into line with prevailing opinions, the Christians completely destroyed the very basis on which their faith rested. Nature, so to speak, by the return of Jesus, had forced on human minds a great psychic truth, on minds, moreover, saturated with beliefs surrounding a bodily resurrection, but, after those who had had this experience had passed on, the old idea of the resurrection of the body returned and nature's revelation was forgotten. Theology took the place of human experience because it was systematised, and had an age-long tradition behind it, whereas the other rests on the experiences of individuals whose sensitiveness to etheric conditions vary greatly and are sporadic.

So it came about that Christian doctrine became directed into the belief that Jesus anticipated the general resurrection, when all bodies would become reanimated by their spirits awaiting this event in Hades. Thus the original natural belief, on which Paul had founded the faith, was turned into one to correspond with the already established beliefs regarding the resurrection of the dead. The Christian belief in the resurrection, like everything else connected with their faith, was taken over from their neighbours.

Christianity contributed nothing new to existing religious thought, except a new name for the saviour-god. To Paul and the others in those early Christian times, Jesus had proved by his etheric appearance that he had conquered death, and that "Jesus Christ, who is . . . the first-begotten of the dead" (Rev. i, 5), had opened the door of everlasting life to the rest of mankind. The Christians of the second century materialised this and produced a story to show that he had been the first to lead the way, by his physical resurrection, for those who were daily expecting that this event would now be followed by the general resurrection of the dead.

So we have the insistence on the empty tomb as tangible proof that Jesus had risen from the grave, but it is very noticeable that he was not seen by anyone leaving the tomb, which is strange when such a point is made of it being guarded. This omission evidently struck the writer of *The Gospel of the Hebrews*, a second-century production, believed to have originated about A.D. 150, because he enlarges the story by telling us that when Jesus came out of the tomb he handed over his shroud to the servant of the High Priests, and then went off and had breakfast with his brother James.

The Gospel of Peter, another second-century work, believed to have been produced between A.D. 125 and 150, gives an even more elaborate account of how strongly guarded was the tomb and how a large crowd stood round it from Saturday morning until Jesus triumphantly walked out on Sunday morning. Then the people went to tell Pilate that Jesus was in truth the Son of God, to which Pilate retorted that it was they who had killed him and it was no longer his affair. So they all agreed to say nothing to anyone, not even to the disciples who, ignorant of the event, left Jerusalem in sorrow and tears. The inventions of the other apocryphal gospel writers need not detain us, as they are in the same strain, so we shall return to the story as found in the canonical gospels.

It must be evident to everyone that the evangelists refer to Jesus after his resurrection in quite a different way from what they do prior to his death. The story, for instance, of two disciples walking to Emmaus, is not the story relating to two men walking to a village and being joined by another man. One does not recognise a friend by his method of breaking bread, and that friend, when recognised, does not vanish from sight. The story shows distinct signs of elaboration, but this does not conceal the fact that the writer placed Jesus in quite a different category from that in which he would have placed a being in the flesh. It was a ghost story originally, and became materialised when the belief developed that Jesus had reappeared in his old body. As with their other stories so with this one, they left in part of the original tradition, which makes it absurd as it now stands.

Perhaps if I relate something which happened the other day this story will be better understood. A friend of mine, a leading citizen of Glasgow, lost his son by death, a young man of twenty-one. He told me that some weeks after his son died he was walking along Bothwell Street, one of the principal business streets of the city, when he realised that his "dead" son was walking beside him. He heard his son speak to him and he in turn answered. What particularly struck my friend was the fact that his son did not move out of the way when meeting people. He walked straight on and through those who passed by. My friend was thus accompanied for a matter of several hundred yards, when his son disappeared. In relating this story to me my informant was at a loss to understand its meaning.

I explained to him that his son had returned from the etheric world in his etheric body, a duplicate of his physical body, which enabled him to be recognised, and had taken this opportunity to pay his father a visit. This, I explained, was only possible because he, the father, was mediumistic and could give off from his body sufficient ectoplasm to enable his son to be seen, and further that he, the father, must be clairvoyant and also clairaudient to have been able to hear him speak. I suggested to him that he might read one or two books on the subject so that he could understand the matter better, but his reply to me was, "I am a Christian, and the belief that my son could return to me, and speak to me, is quite contrary to my faith. I would rather not read such books as they are all anti-Christian."

Even though such facts are anti-Christian, still they happen to be true, and I could recount many instances of a similar nature to this one. John C. Sloan, of whom I write in *On the Edge of the Etheric*, told me that when he was at sea, on duty at night, he frequently walked the deck in company with one or more etherians, and Shackleton, the explorer, tells us, in his book *South*, that on his journey in the Antarctic he experienced an etherian accompanying him. "It seemed to me," he wrote, "that often we were four, not three. I said nothing to my companions on the point but afterwards Worsley said to me 'Boss, I had a curious feeling on the march that there was another person with us'."

So, when we read the story of the two men walking to Emmaus, is it not more reasonable to believe that Jesus in his etheric body accompanied them? If he walked with them in his reanimated physical body why could they not recognise him till they sat at meat and how could he then vanish out of sight? There is no virtue in believing the impossible, and, when these old stories can be explained and understood in the light of present-day knowledge, there is nothing to be gained by accepting them as they have come down to us, just because a council of priests decreed in the fourth century that Jesus had risen in his physical body.

Besides materialising a psychic event, the narrator of this story thought he made it more interesting and arresting by adding the remark that the stranger, "beginning at Moses and all the prophets expounded unto them in all the scriptures the things concerning himself". Where are these prophesies to be found in the Old Testament? Nowhere. But to make this claim to the early Christians strengthened their faith, which was the object the writer had in view. In those days no one was critical, and many who read the gospels had never seen the Hebrew scriptures and so believed what they were told.

If we accept what we might term the spirit hypothesis, we can understand why the words "appeared" and "was seen" and "is risen" and "disappeared from sight" occur in the story about Jesus's return after death. They are quite meaningless otherwise. The story of Jesus appearing to the eleven in Jerusalem, when he showed Thomas his side, and his hands, and ate "a piece of a broiled fish", is just a story of a materialisation which many who have studied psychic phenomena have experienced. A materialised being, who returns from the other world, can, by thought, produce on his materialised body distinguishing marks which existed on his physical body. Materialised spirits have also been known in our day to eat food which, after they dematerialised, was found on the floor. As the materialised body dematerialises, the being vanishes from sight. This story of the materialisation of Jesus may have a basis of truth but, on the other hand, it may be just another instance of psychic phenomena being related to Jesus, as was evidently done in other instances.

The story of the ascension can likewise be understood as relating to a materialisation. In vanishing from sight the dematerialisation of the spirit may take place from the head downwards or from the feet upwards. If from the feet upwards one could get the impression that the being was rising off the earth, and, if a cloud of ectoplasm was also seen, the impression would be given that the being had vanished into a cloud. We are told that "a cloud received him out of their sight" (Acts i, 9), and, at a materialisation séance, after the form and features of the materialised being have vanished, a cloud of ectoplasm remains and then slowly disperses.

So we find that the stories surrounding the life of Jesus are made up of symbolic legends, or are based on psychic phenomena, but it does not follow that Jesus was actually associated with these psychic episodes. Like the prophesies, much has evidently been attributed to him which, as it has come down to us, is pure legend and quite unhistorical. The ancients, believing, as they did, that the manifestations of etheric beings on earth were related to the working of the gods, naturally surrounded those they believed to be god-men with many of the stories they knew regarding psychic manifestations. Thus we are able to trace in these ancient stories every phase known to psychic science, and nowhere are they more clearly recognised than in the legends relating to Jesus.

We have already realised that there is no historical evidence to enable us to believe that those things reported of Jesus on his return to earth as a spirit ever occurred. All that we can say is that the stories, though they have come down to us badly mutilated by the outlook of the age in which they were put in writing, have as their basis either symbolic meanings or psychic manifestations. The tearing of the veil of the Temple, for instance, is symbolic, whereas the story of the after death appearances of Jesus had a psychic basis.

The Acts tells us that "by many infallible proofs" he showed himself to them alive after his death. We can only take the author's word for it as neither he nor any of the evangelists have passed these proofs on to later generations. What would be proof to the disciples was certainly not proof to later generations, or otherwise they would never have materialised a psychic story. We are not surprised that the proofs have not come down to us ; perhaps it is surprising that all these old tales should have been preserved as they have been.

We would not expect people of the ignorance and religious fervour of the American negro to draw up a statement, signed and witnessed by leading officials, to record that one or more individuals had seen an apparition of one of their number who had died. Scientific and businesslike methods have only come into being amongst the European races, and their offshoots, within the last few hundred years. Before that, care and accuracy were not considered essential. The last thing, therefore, that any of the disciples would ever have thought of would be to prepare an accurate record, and have it properly attested, of the events which happened after the death of Jesus.

Certain authorities, including Guignebert, argue that the rather elaborate and fantastic story of Jesus being seen by the disciples on the shore of the Sea of Tiberias, has developed out of the earliest tradition of his appearance after death. The reason for this belief is that it represents the disciples back at their work again with all their hopes and anticipations behind them. They have resumed their normal occupations and Jesus has become only a memory. Here, say these authorities, we have a glimpse of reality taken from an early tradition, which has been added as an appendix to the second-century stories of the bodily resurrection of Jesus. This story is to be found in the last chapter of John's gospel and is obviously an addition, because the gospel ends naturally at the last verse of the previous chapter, with the words, "But these are written, that ye might believe that Jesus is the Christ, the Son of God ; and that, believing, ye might have life through his name".

Whence came this palpable addition to a record which originally ended with these words ? Guignebert gives his answer in the following words :

It is likely that the account is from a very early tradition, that is to say, it refers to the earliest appearance, the one, in fact, which Paul connects with Peter. Jesus appears to Peter one morning beside the lake, and perhaps to the other disciples immediately afterwards. Of all the appearances related in the gospels it is the one that is most likely to correspond to a remembered historical fact. It is not impossible that Mark related it in the original authentic ending, now lost, and which has been replaced by the apocryphal passage which has come down to us (Mark xvi, 9–20) in support of the tradition which placed the appearances in Jerusalem.

We cannot get beyond this surmise, as the fact still remains that there is no evidence whatever on which we can base an opinion as to what took place after Jesus died. All we know is that certain results followed, and the only explanation for these results is that Jesus actually appeared as a spirit to one or more of his disciples after death, possibly to Peter, who, in *The Acts*, is referred to as a trance, clairvoyant and clairaudient medium. No other cause could have brought about the results which followed the death of Jesus, and, while not taking the stories which are told about his appearance literally, and discarding entirely the attempt made at a later date to give the impression that Jesus returned to earth in his reanimated physical body, we can say that there is good circumstantial evidence that he was seen as an etheric being after death. This gave the impulse which was necessary to change deeply set ideas into a completely new line of thought, and eventually to produce the Christian Faith. The etheric appearance produced the story of the physical appearance. Without the first belief we never would have heard of the second.

There are three courses open to everyone. One is to believe that Christianity developed as the result of no specific cause. In a previous chapter we have found it impossible to accept this hypothesis. Another course is to adopt the foregoing reasoning that Jesus appeared as an etheric being, which is natural and reasonable, as we know that such things happen today. Finally we have the remaining alternative, to adopt the

Christian belief, which is irrational, illogical, and quite contrary to everything we know.

The Christian Faith is that Jesus at death descended to Hades, and then after three days reanimated his old worn-out body and trod this earth again for forty days. It also asserts that the Jews killed Jesus and that Jesus came to life again. This is the only instance in history of people being accused of killing a man who continued to live on and walk about the earth for forty days after he had been killed. Besides this the Christian Faith asserts that on the cross Jesus said to the thief, "Today thou shalt be with me in Paradise".

To make all the foregoing fit in Christians believe that Jesus died and went to Heaven, immediately to start off for Hades. He had no sooner arrived there than he returned to earth to become a man once more. Then he appeared and disappeared in a most mysterious way, frightening and mystifying his friends, and finally shot straight up to heaven in his earth body, when "a cloud received him out of their sight". And this is part of the Christian Faith "which except a man believe faithfully he cannot be saved". This, in different words, is what the great majority of Christians say they believe, and if they do not they are very dishonest in saying that they do. If they do believe that one's salvation is dependent on the acceptance of this nonsense, they can only be classed as extremely simple and foolish people.

From time to time throughout the Christian era councils of priests have met together to confirm and ratify Christian beliefs. When heresies arose, or when faith seemed to be weakening, these councils of High

Priests were called together for the purpose of issuing a report to strengthen the faithful who were assailed by doubts. Before each session began the priests comprising the council always partook of the Eucharist, as they believed that by so doing they were more likely to come to correct decisions. By partaking of this rite they believed that they were brought into closer communion with the Saviour, regarding whom they were about to deliberate.

In 1922 the two Chief Priests of the Church of England, the Archbishops of Canterbury and York, appointed a Commission to report on Christian doctrine. After sixteen years of deliberation their decisions were announced in January, 1938, and published under the name of *Doctrine in the Church of England*. In the preface we are told that, "Each morning the Chairman celebrated the Holy Communion and the daily offices were duly said. In our prayer together and in our Communions we found the direction for our common effort."

This Commission, composed chiefly of High Priests (twenty-one out of the twenty-five being priests), reasserts the othodox position, stating, for instance, that the resurrection of Jesus was "an act of God wholly unique in human history", that it was "an event as real and concrete as the crucifixion itself", and that "the majority of the Commission are agreed in holding the traditional explanation that the tomb was empty because the Lord had risen".

This can only mean that they accept the orthodox belief that he rose again in his physical body, and, as all were unanimous that the return of Jesus was as concrete and real as the crucifixion, that not one of the

members composing the Commission accepts the
return of Jesus in his etheric body as a spirit. But how
could they be otherwise than unanimous when Article 4
of the Thirty-nine Articles of Religion, as published
in the Prayer Book of the Church of England, states
that "Christ did truly rise again from death, and took
again his body, with flesh, bones . . . wherewith he
ascended into Heaven and there sitteth, until he return
to judge all men at the last day" ?

It is really difficult to get down to this mentality,
but it serves as yet another argument to support those
already put forward. If, in this more enlightened age,
minds of this order exist, how easy it is to believe that
the Christian Faith could originate nineteen hundred
years ago when the world was believed to be flat,
illness to be caused by devils, and little was known
of any science or the origin of man. In those far-off
days of limited knowledge many irrational and false
ideas combined to produce a new religion. Looking
back one wonders how it was all possible, and yet, in
our midst today, this assembly of men reiterates these
ideas of an ignorant past, which all intelligent people
have now outgrown.

In their report, in the section devoted to the
resurrection, these Christian exponents, when attempting to explain why Jesus returned from the dead, use
many curious and meaningless phrases. They give
eleven reasons to be deduced from the gospel story
of the resurrection. They are all theological in their
nature, making a mystery where there is no mystery,
and in no instance is there even a suggestion that Jesus
appeared as a spirit in his etheric body, and thus
proved that he had conquered death. "The sover-

eignty of God has been vindicated in the material creation and not outside or apart from it", and other similar fatuous phrases, which the Commission use to explain the reason for the resurrection, are just meaningless words. They sound very learned but are employed for no other reason than to make the subject mysterious and so above the level of human understanding. It would serve no useful purpose to quote the other ten reasons which it gives, as they are all equally meaningless, stupid and illogical.

If the Commission had given the subject five minutes' intelligent thought, out of the sixteen years of their deliberations, the truth would have dawned on them that the physical resurrection of Jesus was not only impossible but that it would never have produced a Paul, or the Epistles, or the Christian Faith. Does Paul not tell us that Jesus became a living spirit ? (1 Cor. xv, 45), and that he "shall change our vile [worthless] body, that it may be fashioned like unto his glorious body" ? (Phil. iii, 21.) The material cannot produce the immaterial, or the immaterial the material. They are two separate orders of existence. The etheric can only produce the etheric, the material the material, and the etheric can only manifest on the material plane as the etheric. Surely a body of men who have segregated themselves from the rest of humanity, and been relieved of the necessity of having to work like others for their daily bread, so as to enable them to give their entire thought and time to immaterial things, should have been able to think of this simple fact for themselves, even though it does not happen to come within their theological training.

No one can say that the earth body of Jesus was

the "glorious" and "glorified" body to which Paul makes reference. When, then, did Jesus obtain this shining body, if he took his earth body up to heaven with him and is presumably still functioning in it? If he is not, then when and where did he change his earth body for the glorious body in which Paul believed he appeared to him? Christians cannot possibly answer this question, and it can only be answered on the basis of the etheric appearance of Jesus, and the fact that he left his earth body on the cross when he died.

Some, who are anxious to keep within the written word of the gospels, put forward an ingenious explanation to account for the body not being in the tomb. Jesus, they say, dematerialised and rematerialised his body at will. He dematerialised it in the tomb and rematerialised it to show himself to his disciples. In support of this theory they point to instances of living people who are reported as having dematerialised in one place and rematerialised in another. Even if this be so it is no analogy, because these people were not dead. No dead body, no body, minus the etheric body and mind, has ever been known to become reanimated, and certainly no dead body can come to life and disappear from sight, to reappear alive at some other place and at some other time, and pursue this process on various occasions.

When the etheric body leaves the physical body it cannot return to it because the psychic cord between the two is severed. A baby, for instance, cannot return to its mother after the umbilical cord is severed. The psychic cord, which performs a somewhat similar function between the physical and etheric bodies, as the umbilical cord does between the mother and child, once broken can never be restored. Thus, the physical body, after the etheric structure which animates it departs, is dead and decomposition sets in.

What was there, then, first of all to dematerialise the body of Jesus and then materialise and reanimate it ? Whence came this power ? The body was as dead as a stone. Jesus was in the etheric world, functioning in his etheric body, and he could no more return to his earth body after death than anyone else. The theory is so contrary to nature that it would not be worth mentioning but for the fact that some put forward this as the explanation for the empty tomb. It is so obviously false that it is not worth pursuing further.

The entire fifteenth chapter of First Corinthians is devoted to Paul's ideas about the resurrection of Jesus and the rest of humanity. Nowhere is there a hint that Jesus rose in his earth body. Herein Paul also relates the different people by whom "he was seen". Because Jesus conquered death so shall we all, he tells us, which is logical because, if one man survives death, then so must every man, woman and child. He is likewise logical when he goes on to say that if Jesus had not survived death then no one can do so. Paul's entire eschatology thus centres round Jesus, because of his vision, which made him realise that the eschatology in which he had been brought up was false. In spite of this the old eschatology was continued by the Christians and cannot be changed, as to do so is to give up the Christian Faith, which is based on the resurrection of the physical body.

Paul also emphasises that the proof given by Jesus that he survived death is the basis of his preaching, as otherwise "our preaching is vain". Then he continues, "but some man will say, how are the dead raised up and with what body do they come?" Now, here is the essence of the subject, which he applies to Jesus, as to the rest of humanity, because he says, "The first man Adam was made a living soul, the last Adam [Jesus] was made a living spirit". Now follows his answer to his question.

"That which thou sowest, thou sowest not that body that shall be, but bare grain . . . but God giveth it a body. . . . It is sown in corruption, it is raised in incorruption; it is raised in glory . . . it is raised in power, it is sown a natural body, it is raised a spiritual [etheric] body. There is a natural body and there is a spiritual [etheric] body. As we have borne the image of the earthy [as we are flesh beings on earth] we shall also bear the image of the heavenly [we shall in the etheric world function in an etheric body]. . . . Flesh and blood cannot inherit the Kingdom of God, neither doth corruption inherit incorruption."

If we employ modern terminology we would say that flesh and blood pertain to this earth, but the incorruptible etheric body, which, while we are in the flesh, interpenetrates our physical frame, separates at death from the physical and casts it aside as of no further use. Through the etheric, our mind, which is the same after death as it is now, functions as it functioned through the body of flesh, but with greater ease. Paul, having had all this brought home to him because he had seen Jesus in his etheric body, concludes on a note of triumph when he realises all it means to humanity: "O death, where is thy sting? O grave, where is thy victory?"

The foregoing quotations from Paul's writings could have been written by anyone with psychic knowledge, and the reason why Paul wrote in this strain was because he had not only seen the risen Christ but was a medium, and knew what all such sensitive people know, that each one of us is endowed with .two bodies here on earth. What he terms the resurrection of the dead is no more than the separation of the two bodies, the one of flesh to return to earth as it is of the earth, the other to function in a new environment. Freed from the physical, it can at death respond to the vibrations of higher frequency of the etheric world, which are all about us though we cannot sense them unless we are mediumistic.

To be mediumistic means to be sufficiently sensitive to appreciate the etheric vibrations striking the etheric body. Our consciousness of the physical is due to our sensitiveness to physical vibrations. Our consciousness of etheric vibrations comes about when we are free from the physical body, but one who is a medium can be conscious of both, and at times lives in two worlds, or two states of vibration at the same time. When one is in trance, the etheric body is temporarily loosened from the physical, and thus responds more to the etheric, while the physical body responds less to the physical. It is through the etheric that our mind responds to our surroundings, so when a medium is in trance he is unconscious of his earthly surroundings and pain, and more conscious of etheric conditions. In this state his earth body can be used by etheric beings because his etheric body has become temporarily disengaged from it.

This is what we discover when we use our reason,

and allow nature to teach us what she will reveal to all who go to her with an unprejudiced and receptive mind. Mediums permit their bodies to become channels for etheric minds to work through and are amongst the most precious possessions of the human race, as through them we can learn our destiny. They open their bodies to the working of etheric laws, and, this being so, those of us who are not mediumistic must regard mediums as valuable instruments for the increase of our knowledge of the life which functions at a higher frequency of vibrations from what we experience on earth.

Those who ignore this channel nature has provided are consequently ignorant of this means of acquiring psychic knowledge, and have to rely for their religious satisfaction on rites and ceremonies, on creeds, doctrines, dogmas and holy books, which tell them those things which have been produced on earth from the imagination of the human mind. Thus they require a priesthood to guide them in the way that it thinks they should go.

Naturally the priesthood ignores and denounces nature's revelation, because nature can satisfy our deepest desires without our having recourse to any other channel than the one it provides. The only way to obtain contact between the two orders of existence is by means of a medium and, as this conflicts with the teaching of the priesthood, there has been, as we have already discovered, constant enmity from early times between the priest and the prophet. One wonders if mankind will ever become sufficiently intelligent to give the medium the place nature intends. Until this happens our civilisation is founded on an unnatural basis, and we shall be constantly disturbed by wars and social strife.

When man works against nature and ignores her laws he has to suffer, and so history is full of religious wars caused by ignorant and erroneous speculations about the other world. If he had not done so humanity today would be enjoying much more of what nature has to offer. Slowly and laboriously he has found it wise to work in partnership with nature in the material realm, and in doing so he has come to understand better nature's laws. The time is long overdue for him also to work with nature in the etheric realm, but this will only be possible when intelligence rises sufficiently to ignore the priesthood who, to the last, will oppose any knowledge of nature's psychic laws, so as to maintain the mysteries produced from Paul's speculations.

Paul, and his associates, became enthusiastic over Jesus because they received a revelation direct from the etheric world and so, during the first century of the Christian era, the belief prevailed that humanity was about to be introduced to a new heaven and a new earth, "for the first heaven and the first earth were passed away". (Rev. xxi, 1.) As this did not happen, Christians gradually materialised and symbolised the early tradition which had come down to them. Slowly, rites and ceremonies, doctrines and dogmas, took the place of gazing up into heaven for the Lord's return, and a Church organisation consequently grew up to protect these man-made ideas. Inevitably this produced the opinion that the performing of rites and ceremonies, and the holding of certain beliefs, constituted true Christianity, and so the earlier ideas, which came into being as the result of the etheric revelation, became materialised.

As apparitions are uncommon events, and only seen by certain psychically endowed people, the return of Jesus became materialised in the form in which it is now presented, in the story as it has come down to us. Just as from a fossil of a petrified fish we can deduce that once the fish was alive, so from the petrified story of the resurrection of Jesus can we discover that it once contained a live truth, one which made the medium Paul exclaim, "For I am in a strait betwixt two, having a desire to depart, and to be with Christ; which is far better: Nevertheless to abide in the flesh is more needful for you." (Phil. i, 23.)

This was turned by the priests into the belief that after death the "soul" became a disembodied entity which was purified by the fires of Purgatory, while awaiting the return to its earth body at the time of the general resurrection of the dead. This is what the Commission, to which reference was made some pages back, tells us in its report is the Christian belief, while also mentioning that after the resurrection all "souls" enter either eternal bliss in Heaven or eternal damnation in Hell. This it terms crude Christianity which ought to be rejected, but it does not say why. As it has always been Christianity, what is the authority of the Commission for going against the established and recognised creeds of its Faith?

Christianity, within three hundred years of the return of Jesus from the etheric world, had lost for ever the true meaning of the event which brought it into being, and, from then, till the present time Christians have believed that death meant for the spirit either semi-consciousness, or purification in Purgatory, till the great resurrection day, when it would return and reanimate its old physical body. In other words, Christianity carried on the Jewish and Egyptian belief concerning the dead and the final judgement. The Jews obtained this idea from Egypt where, for thousands of years, the bodies of the dead had been mummified in anticipation of the resurrection of the dead and the judgement of Osiris.

So this Commission of Christian priests, besides giving its opinion on the resurrection of Jesus, and on every phase of Christian belief, likewise gives its opinion on our life after death in these words :

But the question may be asked—and inevitably it is, in fact, asked—What is it exactly that happens when we die ? There is the discarding of the physical frame ; the soul, as we say, leaves the body. Are we to think of it as being immediately "clothed upon" with what St. Paul, in one passage, describes as its "habitation which is from Heaven"—that is to say, its new body of the resurrection ? Or, are we, in accordance with the literal and formal orthodoxy of the main Christian tradition, to think rather of a period of disembodied existence, an "intermediate state", as intervening between the death of the body and the day of "General resurrection". The problems of the relation of the temporal to the eternal order, and of the conditions of life here to the conditions of life hereafter, are involved at this point. In the light of what has been said above, the notion of a period of disembodied existence presents difficulties, and it may be that some of the questions raised cannot be answered under the conditions of earthly life. We cannot expect a coherent scheme, but must be content to employ partially irreconcilable symbolisms, and to remain otherwise agnostic.

This very profound admission of ignorance is just what happens when reason is put to one side and we do not use the gifts with which we are endowed. As a writer in *The Hibbert Journal* said in the July, 1938, issue, "No problem can be solved by mere evasion. We know that a method of sheer symbolism is no true method of faith, that a fact which is resolved into nothing but a symbol loses its spiritual significance along with its material actuality". Though the writer was dealing with quite another subject the principle is the same, and the axiom laid down applies equally to the foregoing opinion expressed by the Commission.

The agnosticism of these Christian priests is the direct result of the belief in the physical resurrection of Jesus. A god who returns after death in his physical body conveys no message to humanity of survival after death, whereas an apparition does. To the orthodox Christian the resurrection of Jesus is quite meaningless and it therefore does not cause surprise that one of our leading Bishops emphasised his doubts about survival after death in a recent broadcast.

For thousands of years mankind has supported a priesthood, and for the last seventeen hundred years Christendom has supported a Christian priesthood. This organisation has lived like a parasite on the community by claiming that it was in touch with heaven, and acted as the representative of Christ on earth, who had given into its charge the Keys of Heaven and Hell. Now the Commission, set up by the two Chief Priests of the Church of England, tells us that it knows nothing about the life after death and that we must be content to remain agnostic.

So the only revelation which has ever been given to mankind, according to the claim of the Christian Church, tells us absolutely nothing. Heaven and Hell have now both disappeared out of the Christian religion. The bribe of eternal bliss, the threat of eternal damnation, the terrible warnings and bombastic claims on which the priesthood has accumulated its vast wealth, and obtained its social position, go up in smoke ; but the wealth, the positions and the titles remain for the purpose of propagating doctrines and beliefs about a hereafter which it is now ashamed to claim to be true.

Recently, two high priests, more courageous, or perhaps more honest than the rest, have raised their voices, like Jeremiah of old, to foretell the doom of the system on which they thrive. The Moderator of the General Assembly of the Church of Scotland, The Right Reverend Dr. Thomson, as reported in the *Glasgow Herald* of the 30th October, 1934, stated publicly that, "Today the forces of Christ are in retreat practically all along the line." *The Times* of the 8th October, 1938, reported that Dr. Woodward, the Bishop of Bristol, in his presidential address to the Church Congress at Bristol, stated that, "While the very foundations of Christianity are crashing, the Church pursues its way placid and unalarmed."

So each year the churches have smaller and smaller congregations, and the priests preach about the decay of religion and the rising tide of unbelief. But why should the people worry if now there is no Hell to fear and no Heaven to anticipate ? The hope of Heaven and fear of Hell have in the past filled the churches, but, if now "we must be content to remain agnostic", why bother ?

The priests, however, are wrong in thinking that the people are less interested in their destiny than formerly. The priestly sorrow, about the decay of religion, comes from their knowledge that their services are being less and less required and that the individual, as he becomes better educated and more intelligent, is evolving a philosophy of his own as the result of studying the vast literature now available on the deeper problems of life. The people are less fearful but not less interested in their future.

Now that they understand more of the laws of nature they do not rely on priests to keep the gods in good temper, and they are finding out for themselves about their destiny, which the priests, in their own interests, have kept from them through their former stranglehold on mediumship. Education is making the priesthood unnecessary and will be the cause of its eventual extinction. Psychic knowledge, in the years to come, will take the place of religious speculations, and mediums will take the place of priests. Nature will in the end triumph over the ignorance and stupidity of mankind.

Psychic philosophy is banned by all churches and theological colleges, because it is a direct competitor with orthodox Christianity and the priesthood. The British Broadcasting Corporation, on the advice of its Religious Committee, presided over by a priest of the Church of England, refuses to open its transmitting stations to the consideration of psychic philosophy because, as the Corporation has publicly announced, it is not satisfied "that the teaching is such as can be said to be in the main stream of Christian tradition". How little those who compose its Religious Committee really know about the origin of the religion they profess ! Remove the tangled weeds of orthodoxy and the psychic stream, which brought early Christian tradition into being, is discovered, but, so long as the priests rule at Broadcasting House, the stream, which gave life to the Christian Faith, will never be exposed for the benefit of listeners who must find what comfort they can from the weeds with which it has been overgrown.

The Church cannot change its creeds, as to do so would be to admit defeat, and, for this reason, it is only a matter of time until its teachings are disbelieved by everyone, and knowledge takes the place of ignorance. If theologians only went through a course of psychic science, relying more on reason, and less on faith, ceremonials and mystical rites, they would be of more use to humanity. By expounding the comfort to be found in the Book of Nature, which, when studied and understood, gives knowledge instead of hope regarding the life hereafter, they would make more appeal to the people than they do by their theology and mysticism.

The futility of all priestly Commissions is obvious, because the members are always instructed to issue a report on the Christian Faith which is to be within the framework of that Faith. They are never commissioned to discover how the Christian Faith originated, what is true and untrue, what is symbolic or what came as the result of psychic phenomena. This last Commission was created for the purpose of producing a report which would give away as little as possible, and hold on to as much as possible. The Church of England authorities had come to realise that certain beliefs, such as eternal damnation in Hell, could not be maintained in these days. The throwing over of these had opened gaps in the structure and it was the duty of this Commission to repair the structure as best it could with the material it had at hand.

This being so, the members of the Commission were not seeking knowledge or the truth, they were not taking evidence for the purpose of comparing present-day knowledge with Christian beliefs. If they had been seekers after truth it could have been discovered in much less time than the sixteen years they took to draw up their report. If, within that time, they had paid a visit to the British Museum and read over the translations made from the inscriptions on the monuments, tombs and tablets which have been discovered, they could not, as honest men, have issued a report such as they did. If each member had also taken up a course of study in mythology and comparative religion, he would have discovered that there was nothing new in the Christian Faith, and that it was an oft-told tale.

Lastly, if they had attended séances in the rooms provided at the various psychic institutes in London, where only mediums of the best quality and highest repute are employed, they would have found that many of the Bible stories are based on the same type of phenomena as occurs today in the presence of those highly endowed people called mediums. There they could have made contact with their friends in the other world through mediumship, which would have altered their agnosticism about the after life. Then on Sunday, if they had gone to one of the numerous halls in London, at which Spiritualist services are held, they could have experienced clairvoyance and clairaudience, such as occurred for three centuries in the Apostolic Church. They would have

had no difficulty in finding ample opportunity to
obtain this evidence, as many of the large halls in
London, including the Queen's Hall, are used for
Spiritualist services every Sunday evening, and many
of the smaller ones for Sunday morning services.

If the members composing this Commission had
done all this, with the honest intention of discovering
the source and growth of the Christian Faith, they
could not have written what they did write in their
report. Fortified with their new knowledge, their
eyes would have been opened to an enlarged vista, and
they would have found the Bible a new book, containing stories of many psychic manifestations. Then
they would have understood the meaning of many of
Paul's phrases and realised how it was that their
religion commenced. Thus their difficulties over
miracles would have been solved, and they would not
have devoted so many useless words to their doctrines
and dogmas, and the physical reappearance of Jesus
after death. In a word, they would have issued a report
which could have been read with interest by all
intelligent people, and not only by the faithful.

Of course it is obvious that to expect this to
happen is to expect the impossible, because, if they had
carried through such an investigation with the intention
of arriving at the truth, they would have completely
upset the entire basis on which their Church is
founded. This would have meant that all remaining
public support would have gone and their churches
would have become empty. It is against human nature
to expect that those who live from the propagation of
a certain form of belief will do anything to show in
any way that this belief has no foundation. What

they did was what one would expect from the
priesthood ; they produced a report for the purpose
of filling up the holes and stopping the leaks which
were bringing about a waterlogged condition in the
Christian ship.

This report is a mere stopgap, and, owing to the
freedom of thought which now exists, it is doubtful
if it will have the effect intended. We cannot expect
to receive the truth about the Christian Faith from
Christian priests. They must keep the ship afloat as
long as possible, as their work and their positions
depend upon it floating. Once the ship sinks they will
have to give an explanation to the people to account
for the reason why they have accumulated such vast
wealth, and what they are doing with it. Enormous
sums have been passed over to the Church, the interest
on which is distributed amongst the priests, together
with the great revenue it draws from the recent
capitalisation of tithes.

When the ship sinks the people will expect an
account of the wealth which once belonged to them.
This day of reckoning must be staved off as long as
possible, but the admissions the Commission was
forced to make in its report have, instead of repairing
the leaking ship, opened the gaps wider than ever.
It is only a question of time till all this priestly bluffing
and misrepresentation is seen through by everyone,
and the source and growth of the Christian Faith, as
outlined in the pages of this book, are accepted as
part of our knowledge.

I have purposely broken into the consideration
of the narrative of the resurrection, as found in the
gospels, because so many people are nowadays rather

hazy as to what the Christian belief is concerning this main plank in the system. The report entitled *Doctrine in the Church of England,* which is the most up-to-date source of information available, enables me to put forward the Christian belief without fear of contradiction, while the views it expressed about our life after death gives me the opportunity of stating the orthodox Christian belief on this question, without fear of arousing objection from those who still call themselves Christians, and yet find it possible to adopt a more enlightened outlook on the subject.

So we shall now return to the days when the Christian Faith was being constructed. We have still to account for the dramatic events surrounding the last days of Jesus on earth, and explain how all these stories came to gather round him. A careful reading of the narrative relating to this period of his life must make it evident that we are not reading a connected account of a series of events. No episode is told as it would be by one who was writing a history. One has only to read an account of a trial and execution, as given in a history book, to appreciate the fact that the trial and crucifixion of Jesus were not given by eye witnesses or from reports of eye witnesses. Remarks are reported as being made about which no one could have known, but which, if dramatised, could have been put in the mouths of the actors. This will become clear as we go on. So we shall now consider

THE PASSION DRAMA

as a whole, as by this means only can it be understood. The only way to explain how this drama has come

down to us in the form in which it has, is to assume
that it developed out of a dramatic representation of the
death and resurrection of Jesus. In order to bring the
stories which were in circulation about this phase of
his life before the people, in a way that would impress
them, someone dramatised them all, on the basis of the
passion and death of the Babylonian god Bel. Doubtless this dramatist also made use of similar material relating to Osiris, as we know, from what Herodotus tells
us, that, in his day, the death and resurrection of Osiris
were likewise re-enacted in the form of a passion drama.

The production of mystery dramas, depicting
events in the life and death of the gods worshipped,
is one of the outstanding features in the religions of
Babylon, Egypt and Greece. A suffering and dying god,
his burial, followed by the search for his body, his resurrection and the rejoicing this entailed, formed the subject of many dramatic productions. It was the theme of
the age in which the gospels were produced, as it had
been for thousands of years before the Christian era. It
had a very effective appeal to people, unable to read, who
could only be influenced by what they saw and heard.

Round the gods Dionysus, Osiris, Adonis, Attis
and Mithra, to mention only some of the outstanding
saviour-gods worshipped at the opening of the
Christian era, mystery dramas were produced and performed, with the central idea, always prominently
emphasised, that they had conquered death by their
resurrection and had opened heaven to mankind.

The great mystery of redemption was thus ever
present in a form the people could understand. In
this atmosphere the Christian drama was produced,
and so the triumph of the Christian god gave to those

who witnessed these performances the same comfort as was experienced by the Pagans, who assembled to rejoice in the victory of the gods they worshipped.

Christians carried on the mystery dramas of the Pagans, the new god taking the place of the old ones, but, for two centuries, from the second to the third, there seems to have been a reaction against all stage productions, doubtless due to the influence of the Christian Jews, who were forbidden such things in the Mosaic Law. In the midst of the condemnation, with which the Apostolic Church visited the stage, its actors and votaries we find an early production known as *The Passion of Christ*, which was published in the latter part of the fourth century, to be followed by another in the fifth century, as by then it was realised that by illustrating the gospel story, by means of living pictures and sacred songs, the people were attracted to public worship.

In the writings of Proclus, Bishop of Constantinople, in the fifth century, we find him exhorting parents to come with their children to see a play entitled *The Virgin and her Child*, and alluding to the Christian mystery productions in words which enable us to realise the close similarity between the Christian and the Pagan dramatic presentations. Paul uses expressions which convey the idea that some kind of dramatic reproduction of the death of Jesus was in his mind. He was evidently thinking of him in the same light as his Pagan contemporaries thought of their Saviours, as he tells the Galatians, "before whose eyes Jesus Christ hath been evidently set forth, crucified among you." (Gal. iii, 1.) This could hardly refer to his actual crucifixion, as Jesus was not crucified amongst the Galatians.

Again, in writing to the Corinthians, he says, "For as often as ye eat this bread, and drink this cup, ye do *show* the Lord's death till he come". (1 Cor. xi, 26.) Employing the word "show" in this connection may refer to something more than the celebration of the Eucharist in church, or it may just have been his way of referring to this outward expression of the Christian Faith. His reference to being crucified with Christ (Gal. ii, 20), and his remark, "I bear in my body the marks of the Lord Jesus" (Gal. vi, 17) may again be his way of expressing the stripes (2 Cor. xi, 24) he received from the Jews, but such peculiar expressions as these may have as their genesis the suffering experienced by the actor taking the place of Jesus on the cross. In Hebrews (vi, 6), we read, "they crucify to themselves the Son of God afresh, and put him to an open shame", which points to the author having in mind a dramatic production, as does, "In the street of the great city, which spiritually is called Sodom and Egypt, where also our Lord was crucified". (Rev. xi, 8.)

Whatever all these strange expressions may mean is not important, as, with the Babylonian tablet relating to Bel in our possession, we have sufficient information to connect the gospel story with Pagan drama, the latter throwing sufficient light on how the legend came to be written in the form which has come down to us. The finding of this tablet is undoubtedly one of the most important discoveries in religious history. Here we have on a clay brick, which can be read today as easily as it was read four thousand years ago, an untampered account of the beliefs of the Babylonians concerning their Saviour. From it we find that the beliefs surrounding Jesus were not new or strange to the people of the first Christian century, and that what was believed about Jesus was believed about Bel for two thousand years before the birth of the Christian Saviour.

The record of the Babylonian Passion drama, which we read on this tablet, when placed alongside the chief events recorded in the Christian drama, is remarkably similar, and, for the purpose of comparison, I shall place the corresponding incidents opposite each other.

BABYLONIAN LEGEND	CHRISTIAN LEGEND
Bel is taken prisoner.	Jesus is taken prisoner.
Bel is tried in the Hall of Justice.	Jesus is tried in the Hall of Justice.
Bel is smitten.	Jesus is scourged.
Bel is led away to the Mount.	Jesus is led away to Golgotha (Gilgal = the hill of sacrifice).
With Bel are taken two malefactors, one of whom is released.	With Jesus two malefactors are led away ; another, Barabbas, is released.
After Bel has gone to the Mount the City breaks out into tumult.	At the death of Jesus the veil of the Temple is rent; from the graves the dead come forth, and enter the city. There is an earthquake, and darkness.
Bel's clothes are carried away.	Jesus's clothes are divided amongst the soldiers.
Bel goes down into the Mount and disappears from life.	Jesus's body is placed in a rock tomb on the side of a hill.
A weeping woman seeks him at the gate of burial.	Mary Magdalene comes weeping to the tomb to seek Jesus.
Bel is brought back to life.	Jesus comes out of the sepulchre alive.

The idea that the account given in the gospels of the last few days of Jesus on earth represents a mystery drama, relating to the arrest, trial, death and resurrection of the saviour-god Christ is not new. It has been put forward by others who formed this opinion on the knowledge we have that such dramas were performed in memory of saviour-gods who were worshipped prior to the Christian era. What is new, however, is the discovery of this Babylonian tablet, which confirms the arguments they so ably put forward. Now we have in our possession an exact account of a similar earlier passion drama, and any doubts which may have been raised as to the correctness of the former conclusions can now be dispelled.

With this tablet as our basis let us now take the gospel records and draw up the programme which the evangelists evidently copied to produce their story. We do not know where the script for the drama was produced, but as the Theological College at Alexandria had all the material at its disposal it is not unreasonable to believe that it may have emanated from that quarter.

The author had in his mind a dramatic production of the Saviour's experiences during his last days on earth, and he set out to produce a drama after the pattern of the passion play staged in Babylon. He had in his mind, when writing his play, its performance on a stage with an actor taking the place of Jesus, and other actors representing the other characters who were believed to have accompanied him when he lived on earth.

In an age which was growing tired of animal

sacrifice this dramatic reproduction of a suffering Saviour appealed to the people, as they could visualise their sins being carried by the slain Christ instead of the slain lamb, and could see the whole performance on the stage as easily as they could witness in their synagogues and temples the slaying of the lamb. At Oberammergau, in our own times, we find in the large theatre built for the purpose the same representation of the suffering Christ, and his triumph, as has been performed since early Christian days.

Bearing this in mind, let me reconstruct the passion play from which the evangelists evidently produced the gospel story of the passion and death of Jesus, remembering always that each character was an actor. The script must have run somewhat on these lines :

(1) The actor representing Jesus, seated on an ass, would ride to the theatre amid the acclamations of the population. The dramatist's source for this would be the events surrounding the Feast of Sacaea, when the victim was treated with all the respect due to a King. The story about Dionysus, already referred to, would also supply him with material for his effort. Thus the principal character, who represented the sacrificial victim, arrived at the theatre, with the crowd accompanying him. Then the people would take their seats, and he, with the other actors, would come on to the stage.

(2) The first scene opens with the victim being anointed by a woman, as this was a necessary preparation before the sacrifice.

(3) Then came the Eucharistic meal the victim had with his disciples, which was a counterpart of the

Eucharist service held in memory of Mithra, Dionysus and other saviour-gods. The playwriter either copied Paul's words, or the gospel writers did so. Another possible alternative is that Paul's account of the Last Supper was taken from the drama and inserted into his epistle to the Corinthians after his time. It is evident that each evangelist took from the drama what he thought was specially important, and made use of other material at his disposal as best suited his purpose. After the meal each episode follows in the order given in the Babylonian tablet.

(4) This scene represents the Saviour in agony and his betrayal to the authorities. He is arrested and taken off the stage under guard, to come on again in the next scene.

(5) Here we find Jesus represented as being questioned as to his sayings and doings by an actor taking the place of the High Priest, after which he is subjected to ill-treatment and then led off the stage, to appear again in the next scene.

(6) Here the victim is represented before the Roman Governor, who questions him and finds him not guilty, but the rabble on the stage demands his death, which he sanctions while dramatically washing his hands in a basin of water. Along with the victim is another prisoner, who is given the name of Barabbas, and he is released to satisfy the crowd. Now we can understand how it was possible for such a quick change to take place on the part of the people, from acclaiming the Messiah to denouncing the victim. They were different episodes, the first before the drama commenced, while the other was part of the dramatic production, which was performed by

different people from those who accompanied the victim to the theatre.

(7) In the next scene we see the mock victim being scourged, then dressed in a purple robe, a crown of thorns put on his head, a reed in his hand, and the people bowing to him in mockery. He may even be seated in the Governor's judgement seat, which episode we find mentioned in *The Gospel of Peter*. Thus, in the words of Paul, the actor will bear on his body the marks of Jesus Christ. Then he is led away off the stage.

(8) In the next scene he returns, carrying his cross, which, for dramatic effect, he is unable to bear. So it is given to another actor to carry for him. This reconciles the two accounts given in the gospels. With him come two thieves, each carrying a cross. These crosses are set up on the stage with the criminals tied on to them. During the final hours which they are supposed to live, various episodes happen, such as the members of the Sanhedrim walking past, making comments on the day's proceedings, and what the victim is supposed to have said to his followers before his arrest. Various remarks are also attributed to the thieves on either side of the Saviour, while lots are cast for his clothes. The victim representing Jesus also utters remarks suitable to the occasion. Then the time comes for him to die, and when this happens the actors show their emotions in different ways. The effect of thunder is produced behind the scenes and the "dead" rise from graves set into the stage. The body of the victim is then lifted off the cross and the scene ends.

(9) Now the audience sees the body being

prepared for burial, and then carried into a representation of a rock tomb at the far end of the stage.
After the bearers come out a stone is rolled against the
entrance.

(10) The audience wait in great expectancy
because the drama has by this time reached its height
and the greatest episode of all is about to happen.
A woman, a disciple of the victim, then approaches
the tomb to find the stone rolled away. She goes off
and brings other disciples, who enter it, only to find
that the body has disappeared. They come out in
great sorrow and look about for the body. Then the
victim dramatically comes on the stage. He has risen
from the grave and is alive once more. He then
makes appropriate remarks, after which the scene ends.

Thus ends the drama of the arrest, passion, death
and resurrection of the saviour-god Christ, which was
produced in the first century by some unknown person
or persons to be acted on the stage. When or where
this passion drama was first produced before an
audience we know not. All that can be said is that
there is every reason to believe that the evangelists
had before them, in a more or less perfect condition,
a document setting forth the words and various scenes
of this passion play and made use of it, as they thought
best, to produce the story they told about the last days
on earth of Jesus, who by then had come to be known
as the Christ. Other alternatives are that they saw
the drama for themselves, or heard an account of it
from one or more who had seen it.

We have been so accustomed to read the story
of the Passion as if it were an historical record that
our eyes have been blinded to the fact that it is a very

imperfect record, based on the outline of a drama which was produced for the purpose of a stage setting. If we take, for example, the gospel of Matthew from the twenty-sixth chapter onwards, it is not difficult to discover, if we keep this idea in mind as we read, that the one who wrote this account had beside him the script, or a report, of a passion drama relating to the death of Jesus. The narrative is a presentation of dramatic action and dialogue, with the events heaped together one after the other, irrespective of time. Nothing is said about events which must have happened, but which could not be produced on the stage, such as what took place on the journey from the Judgement Hall to Golgotha.

Let us go over the drama point by point. Jesus states that the ointment, with which he was anointed, was in preparation for his burial, a remark which could come very appropriately from one taking the part of Jesus fifty years or more after his death, but quite inappropriate as coming from one who was not even arrested. The entire record of The Last Supper is dramatic and told in order to hold an audience. Judas, as representing the Jews, is singled out as the villain of the piece, and Jesus uses words and expressions which his disciples could not have understood, but which were understood by the audience at the time the drama was produced. A hymn is then sung and the company leaves the stage, bringing the scene to an end, but before we pass on to the next scene an age-long misunderstanding must be cleared up.

The words attributed to Jesus at The Last Supper have caused endless disputes and are the mainstay of Catholic doctrine. The Protestants, though giving them lip service, refuse to believe that what Jesus is reported to have said is true, and on this assumption they have framed their doctrine. It will be remembered that the evangelists tell us that when Jesus handed the bread to his disciples he said, "Take eat, this *is my* body", and when he passed the wine round he said, "This *is my* blood of the Covenant which *is* shed for many". On these words the Catholics base their doctrine of transubstantiation, which the Protestants reject, but, so as to clear up the mystery which has exercised Christians all these years, the explanation here given, that they were copied from a passion drama, should be a decided help.

When the words were put into the mouth of the actor, Jesus had come to be looked upon as the human sacrifice accepted by Jehovah. The people associated him with the Eucharistic meal when the spirit of the animal was offered to the gods for them to eat, while the communicants consumed the body and blood in the belief that by so doing they partook of the god's immortality. With this belief prevalent it is not difficult to understand why the dramatist employed these words. He either obtained them from Paul's letter to the Corinthians, in which Paul had copied from the Pagan drama of the eucharist (if we accept the fact that Paul was the first to use them), or, if we favour the opinion of some authorities that Paul was not the originator of the Christian eucharist, from the beliefs surrounding the Pagan eucharist.

Whether Paul brought these words into the Christian Faith, or did not, is of no consequence. The idea behind them lies far back in the mists of religious beliefs, and was used by the dramatist for his scene when Jesus was depicted on the stage announcing himself to his disciples as the victim sacrificed for the sins of the world. The words, which were put into his mouth, were framed to meet the current belief of the days when the drama was produced. They cannot be taken as having been said by Jesus to his disciples, because at that time he had not reappeared, and the sacrificial ideas, which grew up as the result of this event, had not developed and would not have been understood.

Nothing is told of what was said on the way from the supper to the Mount of Olives, as that could not be portrayed on the stage, but, when the scene changes, we find Jesus and the disciples in the Garden of Gethsemane. Here we have one of the best pieces of evidence that this story comes from a dramatic reproduction of what tradition had handed down, or of what the dramatist imagined as a suitable setting for the occasion.

This account was evidently produced from a dramatic presentation of the supposed event. The disciples go to sleep and Jesus wanders off to pray. We are given the words he used in prayer. Then he returns to the disciples, and we are given the words he uses when speaking to the sleeping men. He goes off again and prays, and once more we are given his words. A second time he returns to the disciples to find them asleep. He leaves them once more and goes away a third time and prays the same words. On his return he finds them still asleep and addresses them in these words : "Sleep on now, and take your rest : behold, the hour is at hand and the son of man is betrayed into the hands of sinners."

How effective all this would be on the emotions of an audience of ardent Christians. The words put into the mouth of Jesus must have been imagined because the disciples were asleep and could not have heard them. The simplest way to explain how this incident came to be thus reported is to accept the fact that the evangelists took the words from the script of a drama of the passion of the Saviour, produced for the purpose of visibly recalling his work of redeeming mercy for mankind.

Jesus is seen standing, looking down on his disciples asleep, when Judas enters with a great multitude armed with swords and staves. This would be very effective on the stage, but it is most unlikely to have happened at the arrest of Jesus. Such a display of force was quite unnecessary for the arrest of the real Jesus, but very suitable for the stage, just as was the salutation, "Hail, Master!" which was followed by a kiss. Then all the disciples forsake Jesus and scatter, but we are not told what happened to them, as that could not have been seen on the stage.

The scene changes and we are introduced to Jesus standing before the High Priest in his palace. Peter is seen seated along with the servants, and the High Priest is upon his throne. False witnesses are brought forward and then the High Priest asks Jesus if he is the Son of God. When Jesus acquiesces the High Priest dramatically rends his clothes. Then the mob spits on the victim, buffets him and smites him with the palms of their hands. Again this is very effective on the stage but most unlikely ever to have happened at the trial of Jesus.

All this, be it remembered, is represented in the

gospels as happening about midnight, which is difficult to imagine in an Eastern city of those days when all work stopped at sunset. It is, however, quite comprehensible in a drama which had started in the afternoon and went on during the night. These dramas sometimes lasted twenty-four hours, which is the space of time, according to the gospels, that elapsed between the time of the last supper and the victim's death. This was possible on the stage, where the audience imagines the passage 'of time between the scenes, but improbable in the case of Jesus. The difference in the times of the crucifixion, as given in the gospels, may be accounted for by the different times the stage crucifixion took place, which would vary according to the time the play began.

Now we are introduced to another dramatic effect, the denial by Peter, which makes one think that the author of the play must have been a Gentile, and that it was produced for Gentile audiences, which is most probable as the Jews were all against such performances. We have already discovered that bad feeling existed between the Jewish Christians who followed Peter, and the Gentile Christians who followed Paul, and this was one way the Gentiles could show their dislike for the Jews. The conditions round Peter's denial are given in too much detail to be history,. but are just what one would expect from a dramatic production. Why all this detail about Peter when there are so many other items which are of vital importance about which nothing is said ?

The answer is to be found in what the dramatist thought would go down best with the audience. An episode like this would have much more appeal than a wordy scene depicting the chief priests and elders in council, which is passed over with the words, "And the chief priests and elders took council against Jesus to put him to death". An historian would have told us what was said at this fateful council meeting, and the reasons and arguments which influenced the decision. A dramatist, however, thinking only of effect, would pass over a discussion as quickly as possible. An historian would also have told us what happened to Jesus from the time he left the palace till he appeared before Pilate, an interval of six hours, but in a drama he goes off the stage to come on in the next scene. We are given instead, during his absence, the dramatic episode of Judas returning with the money he was paid to betray the victim, and then going off to hang himself. Even here the scriptures had to be called on to supply the details, "So they weighed for my price thirty pieces of silver." (Zec. xi, 12.)

The scene shifts again and we find Jesus before Pilate. Here also are assembled the chief priests and the elders. The meaning of this stage effect is clear. Jesus, the victim, is found innocent by Pilate, the judge, just as the sacrificed lamb was innocent of sin. The priests are the slayers of Jesus as they were of the lamb. So we have Jesus, the innocent victim, slain by the priests as a sacrificial offering.   .

The trial begins with no descriptive attempt because the audience could see everything. It consists of dramatic exclamations on behalf of Pilate, which are difficult to imagine coming from a Pagan, and he is answered equally dramatically by the people composing the mob. We can envisage Barabbas standing on the stage along with Jesus, and then Pilate shouts out, "Whom will ye that I release unto you, Barabbas or Jesus?" Now the chief priests influence the mob on the stage to shout for the release of Barabbas. This is quite possible to imagine on the stage but not in a Roman Court of Justice. Then the cry goes up, "Let him be crucified." Pilate, however, argues with the people and again they repeat the same cry. He then dramatically takes a basin, pours in water and washes his hands, disclaiming further responsibility, while the people cry, "His blood be on us and on our children", again very effective on the stage, but difficult to imagine in a Roman Court of Justice.

To the Jewish race these words drip with the blood their people have shed as the result of Christian persecution, and it is all the more tragic when we realise that they were probably never said in relation to Jesus but imagined by a Gentile dramatist as apt, and as a remark which would appeal to his audience.

Barabbas is now released and Jesus is scourged. The scourging was next in importance to the crucifixion, as in Greek tradition it was part of the sacrificial act. Its origin goes back a long way to the time when the victim, before being laid on the altar, was whipped to keep the demons away from the spirit about to be offered to the gods. In the drama of the god's death the victim had to be scourged, as it was part of the tradition surrounding the death of a victim, though there is no reason to believe that this actually happened to Jesus.

Then the soldiers and the mob gather round Jesus, stripping him, and putting on his back a scarlet robe, on his head a crown of thorns, and a reed in his right hand. Now they bow before him, and mock him, saying, "Hail, King of the Jews", after which they spit upon him, and take the reed and smite him on the head. When the mockery is over they take off the scarlet robe, put on him again his own clothes and thus lead him away to crucify him. This is all very dramatic and suitable for a stage production, but we cannot imagine that it ever occurred in the common hall of a Roman Court of Justice.

Luke does not mention the scourging, an extraordinary omission when we remember that he tells us that Jesus foretold this punishment before his arrest. Neither is it mentioned in *The Acts*, or by Paul, or in any other of the epistles. The other three evangelists, however, tell us that after the whipping, Jesus was stripped of his clothes, and the soldiers then put on him a scarlet robe. In real life one who has to suffer from this punishment has first of all his clothes taken off and is then whipped, but in these records Jesus was whipped with his clothes on. For a stage production this was necessary to hide the padding under the clothes of the actor, and thus the gospel records are in accordance with a dramatic performance, but they are not true to life, or to what happened to Jesus. It is very doubtful if he ever were whipped, and this story is much more likely to have been taken from a scene in a drama, which was inserted in the gospels, to heighten the effect and impress believers with the load of suffering borne by their Saviour.

The scene shifts again and Jesus comes on the stage with his cross. He carries a tablet, on which

are the words, "This is Jesus, the King of the Jews",
because it was the usual custom in those days to make
a condemned man carry in his own hand a tablet on
which was written the crime for which he was about
to suffer. So in the days when this play was written the
author had decided that to label Jesus as the King of
the Jews would have a dramatic appeal, and, as he had
copied other incidents from the ritual surrounding the
mock-king of Sacaea, the title was appropriate.
Perhaps this was another hit at the Jews.

The tablet, carried by Jesus, is now placed on the
stage by the cross and the victim lies down on the
cross, stretching out his arms. He is tied to the cross
and it is lifted up. The same procedure takes place
with the two thieves who are crucified on either side.
When we remember that each had a wooden support
between his legs the position, though uncomfortable,
was quite easily borne for the length of time required.

It is significant that the evangelists give no details
of the crucifixion and nothing is said about the nails
piercing the victim's hands and feet. No mention is
made of the suffering of the victim. These details
would be given by an historian recording an actual
event, but one copying his account from a drama
would not find them in his copy. On the stage such
things would not happen, and John's account of the
victim being pierced by a spear was symbolic and had
nothing to do with the drama. So Matthew remarks
laconically, "And they crucified him". In the play
the audience saw everything and the dramatist left all
these details to its imagination.

The actual time the actor victim was on the cross
would not be long, but long enough for the people

in the crowd on the stage to walk by. So we are given the actual words spoken by the chief priests and elders, and are told that they wagged their heads. While this goes on lots are cast for the victim's clothes. The dramatist obtained these ideas from the twenty-second Psalm, "All they that see me laugh me to scorn : they shoot out the lip, they shake the head, saying 'He trusted on the Lord that he would deliver him.' . . . They part my garments among them, and cast lots upon my vesture". After this is done the people on the stage sit down till the victim expires.

Now comes a dramatic touch, Jesus cries out in a loud voice. This was only possible for an actor, not for a man on the point of death. The victim then feigns death. At this point there is a great commotion, a noise like thunder and a stage earthquake being produced. From graves, set into the stage, appear the saints who were supposed to be awaiting the resurrection. They walk about the stage and mingle with the crowd, and all this so impresses the centurion in charge of the soldiers that he cries out, "Truly this was the Son of God", thus making a Gentile to be the first to recognise his divinity. So ends this dramatic scene, which represented the Saviour having suffered as a sacrifice for the sins of mankind.

The next scene opens with the body being prepared for burial. A richly dressed man offers his tomb, which is seen at the back of the stage, into which the body is carried, a stone being rolled up to its mouth. Nothing is told of what happened to the disciples after the death of their master, as they are off the stage, having disappeared on his arrest.

The scene changes. Then comes another stage

earthquake and the stone rolls away. Women come on the scene carrying spices and enter the sepulchre to find it empty, but we are supplied with the details that everything is found tidy, the grave clothes being wrapped up and put on one side, as the victim, now a god, made no hasty exit. This had all been done before he disappeared by a back exit. Consternation prevails for a time, but the reappearance of the god on the stage, greeting his disciples with, "All Hail !" is the dénouement of the drama for which the people in the audience have been waiting. He, once the victim, now the god, has conquered death. "God hath raised up . . . and made that same Jesus, whom ye have crucified, both Lord and Christ". (Acts ii, 24.)

We are not told what happens to him, and this is left to our imagination, as it was left to the imagination of the audience. When the drama ends the risen god has just finished telling his disciples to go to all the nations, baptising them in the name of the Father and of the Son and of the Holy Ghost. Ending thus on the Trinity brings us into contact with this second-century belief, but it is very far removed from the apostolic age, and the ideas of the early Christians.

These final instructions can easily be imagined as coming from the mouth of the actor, representing the risen Christ, some hundred years or more after the death of Jesus, but they are quite impossible to imagine as coming from the etheric Jesus when he reappeared as a spirit to one or more of his disciples. The oldest version of this benedictory message omits any reference to the Trinity, and instead we find the words, "in my name", which emphasises the elaboration the gospel story went through over the centuries.

With the risen Christ having finished speaking to
his disciples there was nothing further, in the opinion
of the dramatist, to be said or done. The drama had
to end on this note of triumph and, because of that, *The
Gospel of Matthew* concludes with Jesus still on earth.
The dramatist did not know what became of him after
he left the tomb, as there was no tradition about a
physical resurrection to guide him, and so he says
nothing further, confining himself strictly to this
dramatic ending.

The stories in the gospels about the various
appearances of Jesus after death came from quite
another source, and on to them was added by the
evangelists the dramatic production. They could not
be made use of by the dramatist, as a god appearing
and disappearing instantly is not a subject for the stage.
So he confined himself to depicting the victim
returning as the triumphant god and his tomb being
empty. That is what appealed to the people, his
etheric appearance having only influenced those who
witnessed it, and their contemporaries. The glimpses
the disciples had of their master as an etheric being
were all too intangible to be passed on, and that is why
they became so contaminated with the current beliefs
about the bodily resurrection of the dead.

A revelation from the etheric world is only a
revelation to the one who receives it. A psychic
revelation was the cause of every saviour-god religion,
but, owing to ignorance, the essence which leavened
the religion has always been diluted with dogma and
doctrine by succeeding generations. What the
revelation meant to the recipient could never mean
the same to those to whom he passed it on, and in its

repetition it was bound to become exaggerated. Only traces of the original belief regarding Jesus remain, but, if there had been no psychic genesis, there would never have evolved the dramatic production of his resurrection, from which came the gospel story.

Thus an apparition gave rise to this Christian passion drama, which the author compiled from other dramas of the passion and death scenes of other gods. This was worked upon by the evangelists, who set out to tell the story of the final episodes in the career of Jesus, who had become the Christ, and, as time went on, it all came to be looked upon as history. How much is history and how much is fiction no one can tell, as we have no evidence to guide us.

Mark evidently forms the groundwork for both Matthew and Luke. Matthew and Mark, the two earliest gospels, keep more closely to the script of the drama than the other two as, with the passage of time and the accumulation of doctrine and dogma, Luke and John took greater liberties than the writers of the two older gospels. There are many differences between them in detail, into which we need not enter as we are not dealing with history. This, however, does not alter the fact that everything points to all the gospels, so far as the passion drama is concerned, being originally based on a drama produced for the stage, and only from this angle can they be correctly understood.

Such is the information about the life and death of Jesus as it has come down to us. We find that it is composed of symbolic legends, myths and psychic happenings, which were put together, bit by bit, over some three hundred years for the purpose of producing a biography of the Lord and Saviour of mankind. Into these were threaded items taken from the Hebrew scriptures, which were believed to be prophetic of the Messiah, though the Jews never believed that they were related in any way to Jesus, or that the Messiah was destined to die and rise again.

The passage of nineteen centuries, since the event, has been necessary for intelligent people to discover that the Jews understood their own religion better than the Christians, whose mistaken speculations have led a third of the human race down the wrong road to end only in a mirage. Truth always triumphs in the end and, though Christians will not yet admit that their ancestors made a terrible blunder by their deification of Jesus, history in the years to come will acknowledge this to be so. Unfortunately this will never make up for all we have lost by the set-back to progress, which followed these erroneous conclusions, from which we are only now recovering.

The doctrines and dogmas, which developed out of this mistaken belief, and the Church which arose to propagate and protect it, will be the subject of the next chapter, but I trust that I have succeeded in making sense out of what is otherwise nonsense, in making clear what is dark, and intelligible that which is incomprehensible.

The acorn, in the form of a visit by an etheric visitor, slowly grew into a great theological oak tree, branching out in every direction, and drawing its nourishment from all the surrounding religious material within its reach. If this visit had been rightly interpreted, and correctly handed down, it would have removed for ever the mystery and fear of death.

There is no mystery in death as it is as natural as birth. What ignorance has made mysterious, knowledge reveals as the entrance to a fuller, freer life, and to surround it with theological speculations is to smother a great and vital truth.

We have followed through from its beginning the growth of an idea, and seen how numerous legends came into being as the result of this etheric visitation. The visitation itself was not unique as apparitions have been seen before and since. What is so striking is the way in which the dogmas, doctrines, rites and ceremonies have evolved out of this particular visitation. So much is this so that Christians can only think of it all being possible by the aid of the supernatural. Everything on earth is natural and starts from small beginnings. The Christian Faith is no exception. What we have, however, discovered is the fact that when our knowledge develops that which is termed the supernatural becomes the natural, as the supernatural is only the natural not yet understood.

Those who have raised humanity, and been its real benefactors, are the ones who, by imparting knowledge, have changed the supernatural into the natural, who have made mankind rise from off his knees, and have diverted his gaze from heaven to earth. These benefactors, who have done this down the ages, have been persecuted by the purveyors of superstition, by those who worshipped the supernatural, and derived their wealth and power from man's ignorance. The chapters which follow will tell how a mighty organisation grew up, based on the supernatural, how it strangled learning, and brought into being the time in history known as the Dark Ages.

When we think this matter over calmly, and forget all that we have been taught about the beneficence of the Christian Faith, we shall come to realise that what occurred was bound to happen under the circumstances. What the Christian Church considered was a new revelation, took the place of Greek philosophy and the knowledge of the past. It based its doctrines on much that was degrading in Judaism and Paganism, murdered or exiled all the philosophers and closed every school, college, library and university. To maintain its power, and obtain its wealth, the Church produced doctrines which still kept Hell alight in spite of all its Saviour had accomplished. So all the comfort which those who followed Paul had received was swept away by the later beliefs the theologians manufactured, and forced on the people.

The idea of offering up a victim to a god came from savagery. It was the outcome of the belief that the gods wanted the spirits of human beings to eat. Think of the millions of men, women, children and animals who have been sacrificed to the gods in this vain belief. The belief that Jesus was a victim places him amongst millions of others who have suffered to satisfy the gods. Why should he be singled out, and worshipped, and the others forgotten? The holocaust of victims, which the priests have slain, is too great in number to be comprehended, and any religion which is based on the principle of sacrifice, and a god requiring such, is a savage religion.

From the belief in a suffering and dying Saviour, Christianity evolved its doctrines, dogmas and ceremonies, all of which can be traced back to savagery, when our cannibal ancestors ate the bodies of human beings and believed that the gods relished their spirits. These dogmas and doctrines are founded on the delusion that sin is a movable quantity, and can be transferred from the people on to a human or animal victim which, when Christianity came into being, was a universal belief and practice. They postulate a cruel and revengeful deity who would not be satisfied without a blood sacrifice, and would not forgive humanity until this was carried through.

With such a god to worship, and such beliefs, there is little wonder that the history of the Christian Faith is one of cruelty, oppression and injustice, because the people are as they imagine their god to be. Through the belief in a revengeful god the Church has maintained its authority and obtained its revenue, and, through the fear it inculcated, the priests have ruled the people and kept them in subjection.

The history of how we have slowly and partially become emancipated from this tyranny is a subject in itself. At this stage of our study what interests us is to learn how this tyrannical organisation began, and this will be considered in the chapter which follows.

CHAPTER IX

CHRISTIANITY—ITS YOUTH

IT is the general impression that the gospels and epistles constitute the basis of the Christian Faith. As they have come down to us this is true, but, in studying the history of the Christian religion, we can take nothing as it appears to be, and we must always think back to the times when the religion was produced, not accepting the finished product as other than something which has been moulded into shape over the centuries.

When reading *The Acts of the Apostles* most people accept the idea that immediately after the death of Jesus a Church organisation was founded with beliefs similar to those which are accepted today. In reading the gospels, and the epistles, one also obtains the impression that the Church had only to make use of these documents to frame its beliefs. The truth is far otherwise. The New Testament documents, as we now have them, were built up, compiled and evolved along with the growing opinion as to what Christianity really was.

Gradually the theological Christ took the place of the human Jesus. Only slowly did a Church organisation come into being, and for several centuries there was no common understanding between the different Christian churches throughout the Roman Empire. Wherever Christianity was established different ideas prevailed as to the meaning to be attached to the reappearance of Jesus, and his relation to God.

Such then was the position during

THE FIRST CENTURY.

Though this was so there was, however, a common belief amongst Christian churches in the value to be attached to the exercise of those psychic gifts to which Paul refers in his letter to the Corinthians. They believed that the mediums employed by them to give clairaudience, clairvoyance and trance utterances, were acting as the connecting link between earth and heaven. The early Christians continued— what had been going on for thousands of years previously wherever priests did not rule—the use of mediums as "organs of the spirit" who were "filled with the spirit of God". The first indication of the use of mediums in Christian worship is in *The Acts*, where this is referred to on four separate occasions, the names of the mediums also being given.

The Christians also adopted the Greek terms for them and called them "vessels" and "vases", which they believed could be filled with the spirit of the Lord, and so we find Paul described as a chosen vessel of the Lord and one filled with the holy spirit. (Acts ix, 15.) The medium was also likened to a harp and the holy spirit to the plectrum, the ivory implement the player uses to pluck the strings. A medium was thus considered in the light of a human vessel, capable of containing the spirit of an etheric being, or, on the other hand, as a human instrument which could give forth sound by divine influence. A medium was also called "the oracle of God", the word oracle being derived from the Latin, meaning mouth.

Until the latter part of last century we have been confined to the works of the Church fathers for our knowledge as to what took place in those early Christian centuries, but now our range of knowledge is much greater as the result of an important discovery.

The discovery by a Greek bishop of an ancient Christian work, written in Greek, has immensely extended the range of our knowledge. This discovery was made in 1873 by Philotheus Bryennius, Metropolitan Bishop of Nicomedia. In that year he discovered the precious volume in the library of the Jerusalem Monastery of the Most Holy Sepulchre at Constantinople and published it to the world in 1883. This manuscript is known as *The Teaching of the Twelve Apostles*, though it is generally spoken of as *The Didache*. Professor Harnack, and other authorities, put its date as about 130–150, and it is not likely to be much later than that as it is quoted by Clement of Alexandria, who died in 220.

Therein we have an unblemished account of primitive Christianity. It is mostly made up of moral teachings, as the Incarnation, the Atonement, the Sacraments and other doctrines and rites are passed by unnoticed. Though we find nothing to support Christian doctrine and dogma, much is said with regard to prophetic gifts, which, during the period when this work was written, evidently continued in the early

Church, just as they did in the times of the apostles. The early Church, in the second century, consisted of a community of Christians intent on living good and pure lives in anticipation of their Lord's return. During the interval they were consoled by communications which they believed came from the etheric world, to which he had gone.

It will be remembered that in Chapter VI it was explained how the word prophet meant a medium, and, from a reading of this work, it is evident that mediums were employed in the second-century churches to give clairvoyance, clairaudience and trance addresses. They were "filled with the spirit", which meant that they were taken control of by intelligences other than their own. What is today called a medium's spirit control, was, in those days, called the holy spirit. He had other names, such as the Comforter, the Voice of God, the Spirit of the Lord, and so on, but the one in common use was the Holy Spirit.

If, after reading this work, we turn to the slanderous remarks made about mediums and mediumship by present-day Catholic and Protestant priests, we realise how far the Church has strayed from the path laid down for it by the early Christians. The writer of *The Didache* accepts quite naturally what Paul said was to be the constitution of the Church, namely "God has set some in the Church, first Apostles, secondarily Prophets, thirdly Teachers". (1 Cor. xii, 28.) So it was quite natural that, after the time of the apostles, the medium took the first place in leading Christian worship.

I have picked out from this work its references to

mediums and mediumship and these are given hereunder :

Suffer the prophets to give thanks as much as they will.

And as touching the apostles and prophets, according to the decree of the gospel so do ye.

And every prophet that speaketh in the spirit ye shall not try nor judge, for every sin shall be forgiven, but this sin shall not be forgiven.

But not every one that speaketh in the spirit is a prophet, but only if he has the manners of the Lord. By their manners then shall the false prophet and the prophet be known.

And no prophet that ordereth a table in the spirit shall eat of it, else is he a false prophet.

And every prophet that teacheth the truth, if he doeth not what he teacheth, is a false prophet.

But every approved true prophet, if he doeth aught as an outward mystery typical of the Church, but teacheth not others to do what he himself doeth, shall not be judged among you for he hath his judgement with God ; for even so did the ancient prophets also.

But whosoever shall say in the spirit, give me money, or any other thing, ye shall not hearken to him, but if he bid you give for others that are in need, let no man judge him.

Let everyone that cometh in the name of the Lord be received, and then, when ye have proved him, ye shall know for ye shall have understanding to distinguish between the right hand and the left.

But every true prophet who is minded to settle among you is worthy of his maintenance.

Thou shalt take therefore all first fruits of the produce of the wine press and threshing floor, of oxen and sheep and give them to the prophets, for they are your high priests.

In like manner when thou openest a jar of wine or oil, take the first fruits and give to the prophets.

And of money and raiment and of every chattel take the first fruits, as seemeth thee good and give according to the commandments.

From all this we discover two things of especial interest, namely that mediums were employed by Christians in their churches in the second century and also that "every prophet that speaketh in the spirit ye shall not try nor judge, for every sin shall be forgiven but this sin shall not be forgiven". So we now know that these early Christians were aware of what was the sin against the holy spirit, which, after mediumship was abolished, no Christian understood. Priests in their sermons have at one time and another made use of this undefined sin to influence their congregations in the way they wished them to think.

The words attributed to Jesus in the Revised Version of *Matthew*, that all sins will be forgiven "but the blasphemy against the Spirit shall not be forgiven" (Matt. xii, 31) has caused as much misery as the fear of Hell. Millions of Christians have lived in misery for fear of having committed this unforgivable sin, and now it turns out to be nothing worse than judging the spirit control of a medium. Everyone has the right to question and to doubt, but in those days of old, when it was considered that the spirit controlling a medium was a divine being, or a god, it was far otherwise, and all criticism was silenced by the critic being told that to criticise the holy spirit was a sin which would never be forgiven. Whether this spirit is holy or unholy matters nothing, he is judged in our more enlightened age, not by his holiness but, by what he says through his medium.

The discovery of this old work enables us to realise the reverence the early Christians had for mediums and their spirit controls, but, when these discarnate beings were forgotten, after the fourth century, and the sin was undefined, how easy it was for the simple to imagine that they had committed this unforgivable sin. Besides the terrible misery it has caused, many have become insane thinking about some evil they may have done which, on the Judgement Day, would be termed the sin against the holy spirit.

The foregoing is a summary of what this ancient work reveals to have been the state of mediumship in the Christian Church up till the middle of the second century, and we shall find, as we go on, how the bishops gradually excluded the medium from Church worship and took his or her place themselves. Then the people in the third century were taught by this new priesthood that all divine revelation was contained in the apostolic writings, and in the Old Testament, and that revelation ceased with the apostolic age.

The priests taught that the Church neither required nor could acknowledge new revelations, or even instruction, through mediums, as God had appointed the Church as his medium and the Holy Spirit as the Church's spirit control. From the fourth century onwards the Church became the only medium between God and man, and the natural medium was termed the Servant of the Devil, to be destroyed wherever discovered.

Thus the medium was abolished by the priests, who have thus continually sinned against the holy spirit, but we shall see how this all came about as we go on. Before we reach this stage we must learn how it was that doctrine accumulated round the simple early belief in the risen Christ, who was soon to return to earth to gather together all true believers.

The Youth of Christianity comprised a time of consolidation. Gradually, over the centuries, a central authority grew up, which finally, by means of excommunication, persecution and slaughter, was able to impose its will throughout Christendom. This we shall learn more about in the next chapter. We must start at the beginning and follow the development and evolution of the Christian Faith right through till it became a settled form of belief at the Council of Nicaea in 325.

Here for a moment let us turn to a psychological fact, which is that when an individual, or a body of individuals, have a fixed idea and the firm determination, and will to pursue it to the end, irrespective of persecution and opposition, they can, if the soil is favourable and the time is opportune, accomplish great things. This fact has come home to us today in a way never before because we have, within the last half-dozen years, experienced how a fixed idea, backed up by will and determination, has restored to Germany her self-respect which she lost by her defeat in the Great War. From being weak she has again become powerful, and, instead of being dictated to by the nations of Europe, she is now again mistress of her own destiny.

This is the result of one man having a fixed idea as to what he wanted. He had the strength of character and will-power, combined with fierce and persuasive oratory, to build up from small beginnings a political party which ardently believed in the political creed as laid down by their leader. To begin with, this young party originally comprised only six individuals, but it gathered more and more adherents, and the more it was opposed by the authorities in power the stronger it grew. It might have died any time after its birth had circumstances not favoured its survival. As circumstances did so the new party, with its fixed determined idea, not only overcame all opposition but finally ended as the largest and dominant party in the State. Adolf Hitler, with his fixed idea to make Germany once more a powerful nation, overcame all his opponents and became the Dictator of the German Reich.

This is a case where a fixed idea has so far achieved its purpose, and throughout history we find it repeated on many occasions, but only when the soil was suitable. Napoleon carried through his fixed idea because France needed a leader and without one was weak and disunited. Cromwell, Luther and hosts of other men achieved their purpose because of their unswerving resolution to attain their object, being determined that nothing should stand in their way.

In *Mein Kampf* Hitler stresses this fact, as therein we read that no mild expressions will ever succeed in "nationalising the masses". To get an idea over to them strength, brutality and violence are necessary. The enemy must be smashed, never bargained with. The masses simply cannot understand hand-shaking between men who are nominally opposed to one another. The fate of a Movement depends on the fanaticism, even the intolerance, which it can generate. It must attack all other Movements. After thus emphasising this brutal method he remarks that "The greatness of Christianity lay not in any effort to reconcile itself with the philosophies of the ancients, which had some likeness with its own, but in the unrelenting and bigoted expounding and defending of its own doctrines".

The method pursued by Hitler was the one adopted by the Christian Church. As its strength increased, so it brought under its sway the masses throughout the Roman Empire, and, with its doctrine of Hell for unbelievers and Heaven for believers, it gained a more complete control over the minds of men and women than did any Dictator the world has ever known. Those who supported its authority had the satisfaction of obtaining comfort from its doctrines. On the other hand, those who opposed it were treated in the same ruthless fashion as National Socialism in Germany has always treated its opponents, prison, persecution and death being the fate of all who were its enemies.

As in politics so in religion, the fixed idea can work wonders. We have already seen how Paul, with his strong will, determination and his fixed idea that Jesus was the Christ, laid the foundation of the Christian Faith. His enthusiasm was so great, his determination so strong, that he passed it on to others, so much so that in the latter half of the first century there were scattered communities throughout the Roman Empire who had become infected with the idea that Jesus was the Christ.

This was the predominant belief about Jesus, but its interpretation was another matter. Paul interpreted the Christ in one way, whereas others interpreted the meaning of his reappearance differently. Thus we find that from the time of the apostles Christian belief was in a state of flux, and this continued till the end of the fourth century. Until the Council of

Nicaea, in 325, there was no settled and ordered opinion, as everyone reserved the right to form his own ideas as to what was meant by the reappearance of Jesus. Even after this Council decided on the Nicene creed opinion was still everywhere divided, and in all probability would have remained so had the Church not obtained political power at the end of the fourth century, when it gave everyone the option of believing this creed or perishing by the sword.

When we read Church history we find that in its early centuries there existed numerous men and sects who are labelled as heretics. They were not heretics in their own time, as they only came to be looked back upon as heretics after the establishment of orthodox Christianity. After the Council of Nicaea most pre-Nicene Christians became heretics because the beliefs, as settled at Nicaea, were not the accepted opinions held prior to that Council. Prior to this Council there was no settled opinion as to what constituted heretical opinions, and those who were called heretics were only considered to be such in their own locality and not by the Church at large.

At each great centre such as Alexandria, Rome and Carthage, Christian communities came into being, over whom presided a bishop who was elected by his own people. If someone in this community came forward with a different interpretation of the meaning of the Faith from that held by the bishop, he was looked upon by him as a heretic and an outcast. The bishop in question would communicate this to all the other Christian bishops, but it did not follow that they agreed with him, and so we find that a person who was considered a heretic in one Christian centre was accepted in others as a true and worthy Christian.

The ideas common to all the early Christians were the belief in the reappearance of Jesus, the conviction that through the divine or holy spirits, who controlled the mediums, Christians were kept in touch with the etheric world, and that Jesus, as the Christ, Saviour, Mediator and Judge, would return at an early date to usher in the millennium. This latter belief was the fixed idea at which Christian enthusiasts hammered away, quite indifferent to the jeers of both the Pagans and the Jews. Whatever else they thought, Christians were unanimous on these points, and where divergencies took place these occurred on such questions as the relationship of Christ to God.

Many were the disputes which arose on such matters as to whether Christ had been a divine being from all eternity or, on the other hand, if he were just a man guided by the holy spirit during his mission on earth. Such were the two extremes of belief, and between these we find all kinds of curious ideas. Besides this there was no settled opinion as to the efficacy of baptism and on many other questions of doctrine. If one who was baptised relapsed into Paganism, and wished again to return to the Christian Faith, was a second baptism necessary ? On such issues the early history of the Christian Church is based, and it is now our business to trace its development until it reached full stature, when the Faith reached manhood.

If I had left the reader with Christianity as it was in the first century, and the conclusion that from then onwards everything was as it is preached to us today,

I would be telling only half the story. To think that the Christianity of the first century is the Christianity of today is to make a gross historical blunder. Christianity developed from a small beginning and, year by year, added to its beliefs, its doctrines and its ceremonies. Round this development grew up the Christian literature, and what we have today as the New Testament of the Christian Faith is the final outcome of three centuries of Christian imagination. So let us follow its growth step by step.

Prior to the fall of Jerusalem, as we have already learned, Paul had laid down certain doctrines which he believed were right and true. These were the leaven which was placed in the minds of the people of those days. Paul, at the end of a strenuous career, passed into the etheric order of existence where dwelt his Heavenly Christ, and left on earth the leaven he had produced to work its way into the minds of an intensely religious people. Whether they were known under the name of Jews or Pagans matters nothing. They all had spirits they wished to save. Millions then felt the weight of their sins, and it was the general opinion of the age that the world was coming to an end, when all would have to stand before the Creator and be judged.

It was an uncomfortable feeling and yet intensely real. The Pagans had their gods in whom they had been taught to trust, but faith in their saving powers was weakening. In the midst of this state of belief came the destruction of Jerusalem, which meant the end of the Temple and of the Jewish priesthood as an organised body. Many Jews found new homes throughout the Roman Empire, their faith in Jehovah shattered and their minds now receptive to new ideas. The world was at peace and prosperous. In this state the people had time and opportunity to think more than ever about their destiny.

In this peaceful world reports became more and more insistent that the Messiah the Jews were expecting had recently come to earth, as a humble individual, and paced the streets of Jerusalem unrecognised, that he had been arrested by the Jewish priests and crucified as one who was a danger to the existing Jewish religion. Soon afterwards he had come back after his death as an etheric being and appeared to some of those who were his disciples. Such was the news which spread to Rome and throughout the Empire. According to *The Acts,* within a few years from the Day of Pentecost the belief that the Messiah had come was spreading outside the bounds of Judaea, which idea was helped by the preaching and the miracles performed by the apostles. Slowly, we are told, it reached most of the countries bordering the Mediterranean Sea and finally arrived at Rome, where a Christian community became established.

Clement of Rome, who might be termed the first Church father, tells us, in a document believed to have been written by him about the beginning of the second century, that Paul himself visited "the extremity of the West" towards the end of his life, an expression which some people take to mean that he visited Spain. Paul, with his fixed idea, converted many Pagans to his outlook and, though we have no reliable record of what was done by Peter and the others, we can assume that they likewise, even if they only confined their activities to Palestine, pressed home to the Jews that the Messiah, so long awaited, had really come.

Peter, it is claimed, founded a church at Antioch, and, after presiding over it for seven years, penetrated into Parthia and other eastern countries. Though this is the orthodox opinion yet there is no evidence to support it, and it is equally doubtful if he ever visited Rome. Irenaeus, in the second century, stated that Peter never was the bishop at either Antioch or Rome but in spite of this the Church has always made these baseless claims.

Church history tells us that Bartholomew preached in India and Arabia, Andrew in Scythia, Matthew and Matthias in Ethiopia, Philip in Phrygia, that Mark founded the Church in Alexandria and Barnabas the Church in Milan. Thomas is reported to have founded the Church in Persia and to have preached in Parthia and India. All this may be true, but it is quite lacking in evidence. In its history, as in the compilation of the records of its Lord, the Church gave little thought to truth and historical honesty. We are on safer ground when we examine the writings of the Church fathers, as from them we find the progress of the Christian idea as it developed through the centuries.

The destruction of Jerusalem brought to an end the close relationship between the Christian and the Jewish Faiths. This city was the place where the first apostolic council was believed to have been held, and it was also believed to have been the scene of the Lord's death. Naturally it was regarded with veneration. The early Jewish Christians, prior to the destruction of the Temple, in embracing the new faith had not detached themselves from their earlier worship ; they had still remained Jews, and only differed from the orthodox Jew in the belief that the Messiah had actually come in the person of Jesus.

So the first Christian Church in Jerusalem (Acts ii, 46) was none other than the Temple, and there the first Christians worshipped in company with the orthodox Jews. The destruction of the Temple altered everything. What would have happened to the Christian Faith if the Temple had never been destroyed no one can say. Christianity might have become nothing more than a neo-Judaism.

If we go back in thought to the years following the death of Jesus, we can easily understand the confusion of beliefs which existed in the early Apostolic Church. This wandering healer and preacher, who had been born in humble circumstances, and had never risen above his early poverty, had preached no new doctrine and had laid down no new creed. He established no new religious belief and, so far as we know, uttered nothing new or strange. If he ever wrote anything it has not been preserved and is referred to nowhere. What was written about him did not receive his consent or approval. He established no sacraments or mysteries and inaugurated no ceremonies. He walked the valleys and hills of Galilee followed by people as humble as himself. He set up no priesthood, established no Church, and, at his death, not one single individual in the world imagined that a religion would evolve round his name.

Consequently it does not surprise us to find it

reported in *The Acts* that others had their own ideas as to the meaning of his return after death, but, in the first century, there was much greater latitude of opinion than at any other time in Christian history, if we except our own days. The only echoes we hear of discord come from those passages in the epistles of Paul and John which bear a controversial character. Besides this uncertainty as to beliefs, it seems as if the apostles had to contend with one or more who claimed to be able to perform the same wondrous works as they did. Simon of Samaria is an example, as we are told in *The Acts* (viii, 9) that he "bewitched the people of Samaria, giving out that himself was some great one". Whether he had psychic gifts or was the magician he is described to be, no one can say.

The story is interesting as Peter claimed to have genuine psychic power, which cannot, as Simon imagined, be purchased for money. Simon is represented as a mere magician and the apostles as performing their wonders through the action of the holy spirit, or, in other words, their etheric controls. The story had for its purpose the depicting of the apostles as genuine mediums, whose deeds Simon recognised could not be accomplished by magic, and this is just what magicians in our own day have also discovered. So here we have a tale of a magician converted to the belief in the genuineness of mediumship, so much so that "he continued with Philip, and wondered, beholding the miracles and signs which were done". (Acts viii, 13.)

Besides controversy as to doctrine, and the meaning of this new idea which Paul had sprung on the world, besides the apostles having to prove to the people that they were genuine mediums and not magicians, we find that the early Christians at an early date had to meet opposition not only from the Jews, but also from the Pagans. Church history, for instance, tells us that they suffered torture and persecution under the Emperor Nero, basing its information on what has come down in the writings of Tacitus, to which we have already given some consideration.

Dean Merivale, in his *History of the Romans under the Empire*, considered that this persecution .was directed against "the turbulent Jews, notorious for their appeals to the name of Christ as an expected prince or leader" ; that these "sought to implicate the true disciples, known to them and hated by them" ; and that historians, misled by the use of the name of Christ, "too readily imagined that the persecution was directed against the Christians only". This is perhaps the explanation, and when Tacitus wrote the story about fifty years later it was natural that he would associate the victims with the Christians of his time. The time of Nero, when this persecution is supposed to have happened, about the year 64, was too early for Christians to have been strong enough to make themselves sufficiently objectionable to deserve this form of treatment.

The destruction of the Temple was the final proof the Jewish Christians needed to make them realise that Jehovah was no longer with Israel, and that the Mosaic system had fulfilled its purpose and passed away. After the besieging army had accomplished its work of destruction the Christian community, which had withdrawn during the siege to beyond the Jordan, having gathered in the mountain town of Pella, returned and established itself among the ruins under one by the name of Symeon who, after the martyrdom of James, had become Bishop of Jerusalem.

The calamity which had overtaken Jerusalem had so weakened the authority of the Christians in that centre that thenceforward the Church in Jerusalem ceased to take its place as the leader of the Christian movement, and we shall find as we go on how politics, in this case as in many others, influenced the growth of this young idea. One would naturally have thought that as Jesus, now the Christ, had taken the place of the Jewish priesthood the principal seat of Christian worship would always have been Jerusalem, and that, when the city was restored sixty years later by Hadrian, the Christians would have commenced, at least in some small way, the erection of a church on the spot where once the Temple had stood. Instead of this, however, its seat became Rome, a Pagan city, and one with no connection whatever with the traditions behind the Christian Faith. How this all happened will be gradually unfolded.

The first real persecution of the Christians took place under the Emperor Domitian, and some believe that it was during this persecution that John was banished to Patmos. The persecution, however, did not last long, and Christians who were banished were soon allowed to return home. The Emperor Nerva, who followed, returned any property which had been confiscated and peace reigned once more. This brings us up to the end of the first century, and we shall now devote some thought to the growth of Christian doctrine, and to how believers fared, throughout

THE SECOND CENTURY.

Before the Christians became persecutors they were the persecuted. Whoever has a fixed idea is generally unable to appreciate the opinions of others. To begin with, the Pagans were intolerant of the Christians and hated their outspoken criticisms, and threats as to the fate of unbelievers. At the opening of the second century we find Clement of Rome writing epistles to the Church of Corinth recommending humility and the cessation of dissension. Most of his writings are considered spurious but they give one an idea of the controversies which took place at the beginning of the second century.

As the Christian Church developed, not only questions of doctrine and belief had to be considered but also matters of Church government. Though Christianity was essentially a religion of the people, and appealed to the outcast, yet, like every other religion, it could only survive as an organisation under capable leadership. So there came into being the order of deacons for the discharge of the secular administration. Then came the Presbyters or Elders, and the Bishops for the ordinary care of the congregations. At the time of the Reformation those who called themselves Presbyterians framed their Church government on the lines of the Apostolic Church, but those they called ministers were priests, both in mind and function, and were quite unlike the ministers of the early Apostolic Church.

The Episcopal form of organisation was an innovation brought into the Church in the third century by the ministers themselves, so as to obtain greater power. This intrusion was the beginning of the Christian priesthood when, entirely contrary to the basic beliefs of the religion, they captured the Church and framed its creeds, doctrines and dogmas. There has been much Christian wrangling on this subject since the Reformation, but, on every occasion, the priests have ignored the fact that the Order of the Priesthood was abolished by the coming of the Christ, and that it has no place whatever in the Christian religion, according to the ideas of the apostles, from whom both Anglican and Roman priests falsely claim their authority.

In the first two Christian centuries there were no Christian priests, and no apostle handed his authority on to any priest. In those early days the preaching of the gospel was open to everyone, and no one, except an apostle, set himself above the others in authority. The organisation of the Church was a gradual and natural evolution for the purpose of preserving ideas, rites and ceremonies, as believed by the different Christian communities scattered throughout different parts of the Roman Empire.

The first to be called a Minister of the Church was Matthias, who was chosen by the community in which he lived, but there is nothing to prove that he passed on this commission, or that he laid his hands on his successor, and thus commenced the chain of hand-laying which, it is falsely claimed, has proceeded in an unbroken line from Peter to this day. The rival claims of the Church of England and the Church of Rome on this subject are interesting, if only from the point of view of how it is possible for something to be believed, if this belief is needed as part of the structure of the system.

By the end of the second century, the organisation of the various Christian congregations was for all practical purposes identical, as they adopted as their pattern of Church organisation that of the Roman and Greek civic senates. At the head of each church was a bishop, whose function was to conduct public worship, control the church funds and keep a watch over the manners of his flock. In conducting the worship, and in ministering to the wants of the poor, he was assisted by the deacons. The presbyters were a small body whose business it was to advise the bishop. He acted as president at their meetings and he himself was a presbyter. A presbyter could act for the bishop in such matters as baptism, preaching and celebrating the Eucharist. The presbyters ranked above the deacons and the only special standing the bishop had was that he presided over the meetings of the presbyters.

The presbyters were chosen from among the deacons and the bishop was chosen from the presbyters, but in the early Church all these men continued in their ordinary occupations during the week, and gave their services mostly on Sundays. At the Sunday services only a short simple address was delivered, since the duty of "edifying", as it was called, was left to the one with charismata, meaning psychic gifts, or, as we would say today, to the one who by clairaudience, or through trance, could make contact with the etheric world,

Thus, in the early Church the medium took the principal place in the service. Mediums formed the class of persons the people wished to hear, as in Spiritualist churches today. Again, just as in Spiritualist churches today, the medium did not necessarily belong to the district or to the congregation. Mediums went about from church to church and "were held to be the organs of the spirit given by God to the whole Church". This can all be found in Tertullian's writings, all of which are accepted as authentic and genuine.

In the primitive Church the bishops and presbyters were thus ministers to the congregation, men from the local Christian community, who had obtained their ministerial positions through being elected by the congregation. They were paid for their work by receiving part or all of the collection taken at the Sunday services. The word bishop comes from the Greek, meaning an overseer, and the word presbyter is the Greek for an elder. The bishop was just the senior minister and the presbyter was his assistant.

In those days the church was not a separate building, the Christians meeting together in private rooms, and it was only towards the end of the second century that entire buildings were reserved for Christian worship and churches were built. When several churches were erected in the same district a presbyter would take charge of each, and the bishop acted as overseer of them all.

The history of the evolution of the Christian Church is well expressed in Hatch's work, *Organisation of the Early Christian Churches*. Gradually a priesthood evolved as these ministers came to consider themselves as holding the same status as the Pagan priesthood. The ministers envied the attention paid to the medium and, in consequence, a feeling of antagonism grew up between those whose business was purely secular and the one who acted as the organ of the spirit. The bishops and presbyters had, therefore, no wish to maintain apostolic usage, as this deprived them of the position to which their class had attained as the Church evolved out of the apostolic stage.

The bishops, moreover, were not slow to realise that to maintain their authority in a growing organisation an ecclesiastical order was necessary. They wished uniform thought throughout the Church, and not the maintenance of primitive Christianity. They did not want the more mystical ideas as expressed in Gnosticism, and they were determined not to have Spiritualism. When we come to consider what took place in the middle of the second century we shall discover how and why the minister became the priest, but, at the moment, we are dealing with affairs as they were when this century opens.

By now Christianity had ceased to be confounded with Judaism, and the great majority of its adherents were Gentiles. It was regarded as only an offshoot of Judaism but, just because of this, it was exposed to all the odium of a Jewish sect. So we read of many dreadful and shocking charges against the early Christians. The privacy of their séances was found cause for slander. Just what happens today doubtless happened then when a séance was in progress : the door was locked to prevent someone entering and breaking the psychic conditions.

Justin Martyr, moreover, tells us that slaves

brought reports to the authorities that their Christian masters were cannibals as they spoke openly of eating their god's body and drinking his blood. Illicit intercourse of the sexes and the practising of the black arts were imputed to them, the Jews being especially industrious in the production and propagation of such stories. Thus we find that early in the reign of Trajan an edict was issued against guilds or clubs, and this was used against the Christians.

During the reign of this Emperor, Symeon, the head of the Church in Jerusalem, suffered martyrdom for his beliefs. About this time also, Pliny the younger wrote to the Emperor those letters which have now become famous, his subject being the beliefs of the early Christians. He was undoubtedly perplexed by the novelty of the situation, as never before had a Roman pro-consul to deal with religious opinions, about which there was entire ignorance in the Roman administrative world. From what he says there were evidently no laws directed against the Christians, and so he wrote to the Emperor for instructions.

In his letter to the Emperor, he says : "I had no doubt that whatever they might confess, wilfulness and inflexible obstinacy ought to be punished". Many, as the result of this enquiry, returned to Paganism, but, of those who remained steadfast, the pro-consul was unable to discover anything to their discredit. The only crime Pliny could discover against the Christians was their habit of meeting before dawn on certain days to sing a hymn to Christ as God. Instead of discovering any truth in the slanderous stories which were told against them by their enemies, Pliny could only find that they bound themselves by an oath to abstain from theft, adultery and breach of promise, and that they partook in common of a meal in memory of their Lord.

After putting two deaconesses to torture, which cruelty failed to produce any incriminating evidence, Pliny asked the Emperor what he must now do, and whether the Christians must be punished as criminals for their beliefs or not. Trajan approved of the measures adopted by his pro-consul, and left him with large discretionary power as to what to do when the circumstances arose. The Christians, however, he told his representative, were not to be harried or sought for, but, if they were discovered to be believers, they must be punished unless they deny Christ, which would be sufficient for them to obtain release. In no case, Pliny was informed, was he to act on secret information, which prevented slaves and others informing against their masters and mistresses.

Human nature being what it is, and, knowing as we do, how fear dominates the actions of those in authority, we can well understand how the Emperor, and his officials, were afraid when they discovered how increasingly large numbers were meeting together for the purpose of worshipping a new god whom they believed was about to return to earth and displace the then existing rulers. If the Emperor, and his governors, had not themselves been imbued with the belief that the age was coming to an end, it is probable that the Christians would never have been molested. When, however, it was found that they put Christ before the Emperor, and further believed that he was the coming world King, who would judge the people and set believers and unbelievers apart, those in authority naturally considered that this sect was preaching subversive doctrines, and undermining the structure of the State.

This was not all, as one of the books used for readings at Christian worship, namely *The Revelation*, was believed by Christians to contain a prophecy of the downfall of Babylon (Rev. xviii, 2), which was interpreted as meaning Rome. This is what Justin Martyr tells us, and also that many Christians proclaimed openly the downfall of the Emperor and the Empire, which would follow the triumph of Christianity over Paganism. Besides this, the Christians showed their disloyalty by writing and speaking of the Emperor in terms of disrespect. They seemed to glory, for Christ's sake, in their disloyal attitude to those in authority, which greatly hurt the feelings of their Pagan neighbours. When asked to pray for the Emperor, in words similar to our "God save the King", they refused to do so and boasted of their disloyalty.

The Romans were not intolerant of religious beliefs, so long as these did not interfere with politics. If they had been they could easily have exterminated every professing Christian in the Roman Empire, just as the Christians in the thirteenth century entirely obliterated the Albigenses, whose only crime was the fact that their beliefs resembled Gnosticism, the form of Christian belief which was widely accepted by second-century Christians. Within twenty years the South of France, where they lived, was cleansed of this heresy by the entire population being wiped out. No more bloody affair is known in history, and the priests were in the forefront of the orthodox

Christian Army. When asked if any could be spared, the Abbot Arnold, at the taking of Beziers (July 22nd, 1209), gave the command : "Slay all. God will know his own."

It is well to remember these facts, as Church history dwells long and often on Pagan persecution, and passes lightly over the cruelties of the Christian organisation. When compared with the policy of extermination, which was pursued by the Christians after the fourth century, the Romans showed much more leniency and toleration. A study of the morals and ethics of the Stoics of those days, for instance, reveals that their ideals were every bit as high as those of the Christians.

Lecky, writing of these times in his *History of European Morals*, tells us that :

The national character . . . had early risen to a heroic level. The habits of men were unaffected, frugal, honourable and laborious. A stern discipline pervaded all ages and classes of society, the will was trained to an almost unexampled degree to repress the passions, to endure suffering and opposition. Such was the type of excellence the Roman people had attained at a time when its intellectual cultivation produced philosophical discussions, and when . . . Stoicism furnished the principles of virtue, coloured the noblest literature of the time, and guided all the developments of moral enthusiasm.

Here he is writing about the Romans, but what he says is equally applicable to the Greeks, who were a much kinder race by nature than the Romans, as is proved by their dislike of killing, and causing suffering to give onlookers pleasure. Thus there were no gladiatorial combats in Greece, and the average Greek would have looked with horror on the suffering caused to wild animals in our own times by those who hunt the fox, the otter, the stag and the hare. Anyone who has seen an otter hunt, with its cruelty and suffering, with the poor beast surrounded by a crowd of human jackals, will realise that for moral degradation there is little in our own times with which to compare it.

The early Christians were in no way superior to their neighbours but, as their beliefs took root, and eventually overgrew those of Paganism, a great deterioration in everything good and noble took place. Toleration became unknown and a violent suppression of all liberty took its place, with disastrous results to the intellectual and moral life of the then civilised world.

Gibbon, the historian, in *The Decline and Fall of the Roman Empire*, making use of the figures supplied by Eusebius, which would certainly not err on the side of an underestimate, computes that in all the persecutions of the Christians by the Pagans a number not greatly exceeding two thousand suffered death. He contrasts this with the millions who were put to death by the Christian Church as heretics, as witches, and in consequence of religious wars throughout the Christian era. This historian, for instance, refers to the fact that during the reign of Charles V over one hundred thousand victims perished in the Netherlands alone in consequence of Christian persecution, and that this is only a small fraction of the sum total of victims who fell before the ferocity of the Christian Church throughout its reign as Dictator of Christendom.

In the reign of Trajan, Ignatius, the venerable

Bishop of Antioch, suffered martyrdom in Rome about the year 115. The story runs that he was arrested and sent to Rome because an earthquake caused great damage at Antioch, which was claimed by the Christians to be a sign of their Lord's return. This angered the population and the bishop was arrested; but Eusebius (265–340), who tells the story in his *Ecclesiastical History,* seems somewhat doubtful about it, and it would be well not to take it seriously. Whatever caused the bishop's arrest does not especially interest us, but what does is the traditional belief that he was converted by John the Apostle, after which he became Bishop of Antioch about the year 70. If this claim be true, he had been responsible for this church, situated in the capital of Syria, for nearly half a century.

He was taken to Rome for his trial under the guard of ten soldiers, who treated him harshly. Nevertheless, he was allowed to meet his fellow Christians wherever he stopped on his way, and write epistles of affection and exhortation to the churches he could not visit. In the epistles he wrote to the Romans, he expressed his eager desire for the crown of martyrdom and entreated them not, through mistaken kindness, to attempt to prevent his fate. One can understand how a man of his age, believing as he did, preferred, like Paul, to depart and be with his Christ, which change to him was gain and not loss. On his arrival at Rome he was carried to the amphitheatre and there, exposed to wild beasts, he suffered death before the crowds assembled to celebrate the Feast of Saturnalia.

From his writings we get a glimpse of conditions

in the early Church. This link with the apostles tells us that "Some in the churches do most certainly have knowledge of things to come. Some have visions, some give clairaudient messages and heal the sick by the laying on of hands, and others speak in many tongues, bringing to light the secret things of man and expounding the mysteries of God". This, taken in conjunction with the writings of Paul and *The Acts*, brings the chain of psychic phenomena in the Church up to the beginning of the second century, and we shall find that it continued right on into the fourth century. Thus we have authentic evidence that mediumistic phenomena took place in the Christian Church from the time of Paul for three hundred years.

Tatian, one of the earliest Christian apologists, who lived in the first seventy years of the second century, takes up the story and tells us that "Our virgins at the distaff utter divine oracles, see visions and say the holy words that are given to them." His contemporary, Justin Martyr, tells us : "I call them prophets [mediums] who, being out of themselves and their own thoughts, do utter forth whatsoever the impelling power of the spirit wrought in them, while the divine operator served himself of them, or their organs, even as men do of a trumpet."

Irenaeus, Bishop of Lyons, who lived in the next generation, continues the chain of evidence by telling us that "We hear of many brethren in the Church possessing prophetic [mediumistic] gifts and speaking through the spirit in all kinds of tongues." After Irenaeus we come to Tertullian, who continued the same story, as we shall discover when we come to his time. He is followed by Origen in the next generation and then comes Eusebius, both of whom continue in like manner. This brings us right up to the fourth century, when the priesthood obtained control, and then we hear only about doctrines and dogma. As to psychic matters, from the fourth century onwards there is complete silence.

Under the reign of the Emperor Hadrian, who followed Trajan, the conditions of the Christians improved considerably. On the Emperor's visit to Athens, when he was initiated into the mysteries of Eleusis, he was addressed by two men in writing on the subject of the Christian religion. Here we are introduced to the first case on record of written apologies for the Christian Faith, and these are the first of a long line of similar documents which appeared throughout the next three centuries, until, in fact, Christianity needed no further apology, and the people either believed what the Church preached or were struck down by the sword.

On the plea of justice and toleration, a pro-consul of Asia, Granianus by name, when retiring from office, asked Hadrian to pass a law to stop the popular clamour against the Christians. The Emperor acceded to this request, informing the successor of Granianus, and the other provincial governors, that all persecution of Christians must cease, that they must be treated like all the other inhabitants of the Roman Empire, be brought to trial only if they had broken the law of the land, and not because of their religious beliefs.

In this reign the Jews again caused trouble by their insurrections in Egypt, Cyprus, Mesopotamia and elsewhere. These were put down with great severity and brought about fresh oppressions. Hadrian insulted the race by settling a Roman colony on the site of the Holy City. This caused a fresh revolt of the Jews in Palestine, under a leader called Barcochab, which means the son of a star, who was looked upon by his followers as the Messiah. After a long and bloody war this revolt was suppressed, many Jews were put to death, and the rest were transported from the land of their fathers.

As a further punishment, it was decreed that no Jew was ever to enter Jerusalem again except on one day in the year, the anniversary of its capture by Titus, when, in exchange for a heavy payment, they were admitted to enable them to mourn over the fallen greatness of the Holy City. The Romans built a new city on the foundations of Jerusalem and called it Ælia Capitolina. Above Mount Zion arose a new temple dedicated to Jupiter, and everything held sacred by the Jews was defiled.

During this Jewish revolt the Jews in turn persecuted the Christians in Palestine, which brought about their complete abandonment of all the Mosaic usages which, up till then, they had retained. They appointed a Gentile to be bishop of their church, and, because they thus entirely dissociated themselves from the Jews, both as regards race and religion, they were allowed by the Romans to reside in the new city. Those of their brethren, who refused to cut themselves adrift from Jewish tradition, were not allowed to live in the new city, and so they retired to Pella and other places beyond the Jordan.

Thus by revolt after revolt against the Roman

rule the Jews lost the land of their fathers, and, from that date to this, they have been wanderers on the face of the earth, with no country and no King, strangers in a strange land, always a minority and, as in the time of the Romans, incurring the enmity of those amongst whom they lived. Today we are experiencing their attempt to set up again a Jewish Kingdom in Palestine, from which they were ejected as long ago as the second century of our era.

So much for the Jews and the fate which they brought upon themselves. On the other hand the Christians, taking advantage of the respite which they enjoyed under Trajan, Hadrian and Antoninus, further improved their position by steadily gaining converts. The wider their area of influence the more certain it was that they obtained leaders from amongst the Jews and Pagans, and so we find that from now onwards one man after another came into the lime-light, because he felt convinced that he had reached the true meaning to be attached to the reappearance of Jesus.

It is to be noticed that they followed along the lines of Paul in believing that the apparition of Jesus proved that he was the Heavenly Christ. On to this they imposed one doctrine and dogma after another, and the history of the Church from now onwards is the story of one leader after another putting forward his opinion as to what these doctrines really should be. They had no lack of material from which to build up their ideas, as they had the entire Pagan and Jewish world of religious thought, right back down the centuries, from which to draw. Tatian, one of the Christian apologists, expressly states that he himself had been initiated into the Greek mysteries.

Justin (100–166), a Samarian Greek, who is better known as Justin Martyr because of the nature of his death, was one of the early outstanding exponents of the Christian Faith. Almost all we know about him is taken from his own writings.

He addressed an apology to the Emperor, the Senate and the people of Rome, about the year 140, putting forward the claims of the Christian Faith, and at Ephesus he held a discussion with a Jew named Trypho. From what he wrote of this dialogue we discover the progress of his own religious opinions, how he had tried the various forms of Greek philosophy without effect, and how eventually, when walking along the seashore in deep meditation, he was met by an old man who advised him to study the Scriptures and the gospel writings.

He goes on to tell how he did so, and also of the deep impression made on him by the strength and resolution shown by Christians at death. Becoming persuaded that the popular charges against their morals were baseless, that their Lord and Saviour was indeed the Christ, he embraced the faith and devoted his life to its defence and propagation, travelling throughout Egypt, Asia and elsewhere, dressed as a philosopher to give him the standing he believed his teaching deserved. He made his residence in Rome and there he established a school of Christian theology. So far no distinction was yet made between priest and layman, and, though not a priest, he dispensed the Eucharist.

His first apology was a bold argument against the crime of persecuting Christians for their religion in an Empire where all others were allowed to believe as they thought right.   Therein also he refuted the charges of atheism, immorality and sedition brought against the members of his faith, and also tried to prove that the psychic phenomena which developed in the presence of the apostles came from God.   He lived, however, in an age when all genuine psychic phenomena were believed to come from the same source, the Pagans attributing it to a divine agency just as did the Christians.

If Christianity was to survive as a distinct religion, it could do so only by consolidating the psychic happenings of the previous century into miraculous stories to be preached and believed as historically true.   This naturally had the effect of embalming the psychic truth for the purpose of preserving its meaning in symbolism.   Unfortunately the meaning behind the symbolism was slowly forgotten, and so the psychic stream was gradually covered over by legends, doctrines and dogmas.   So much was this the case that by the close of the second century the psychic phenomena, which had occurred in the presence of Jesus and the apostles, had been turned into miracles and acts of God, which had occurred, contrary to the normal workings of nature, so as to establish the fact that Christianity was a supernatural revelation.

Besides this, the greatest psychic happening of all, because it had given rise to the faith, was materialised into a story of the return of Jesus to earth in his physical body, which, after forty days, accompanied him on his return to heaven.   Justin was one of the early exponents of the resurrection of Jesus in his physical body, though, unfortunately, only fragments still remain of his special treatise on the subject. The Pagans, however, knew more about psychic questions than he did, and he found it impossible to persuade them that Jesus could return to earth in this unnatural way.

In his arguments for Christianity he stressed its likeness to Pagan philosophy, and argued that this philosophy was but a preparation for Christianity, which was its natural development. Christianity, in his opinion, was the fullness of light to which all the sages of the previous ages had contributed. He wrote that "those who lived according to reason were Christians" and he named many of the wise sages of the past, such as Socrates, whom he termed Christians. He would have been surprised to have been told that his religion would become so corrupt that Christians in England would hang a man because he said Socrates was in heaven, and yet that is what was done by our bigoted ancestors.

Justin composed a second apology in Rome which brought him prominently before the Pagan world because of his fierce attack on one named Crescens, who was a Cynic. Justin termed him "a very vile member of his repulsive sect" and because of this libel he was brought before the magistrate, sentenced to death, and beheaded at Rome in 166.

Under the Emperor Marcus Aurelius the condition of the Christians became worse. They had obtained respite under three Emperors but now conditions changed. The enmity against them, which had so long been noticeable amongst the people generally, spread to the Governors and Judges, so much so that they ignored the edict of

Trajan that Christians were not to be spied upon or convicted as the result of secret information. Instead of discouraging information against the Christians the authorities now began to encourage it, applying torture in order to obtain evidence, and for the purpose of forcing the victims to recant.

Marcus Aurelius was one of the most enlightened of all the Roman Emperors, if not the most enlightened, to assume the purple. He has been called "the noblest of the Pagans, the crown and flower of Stoicism", and under his rule gladiatorial contests were considerably restricted. He was celebrated for his benevolence, justice, intelligence and philosophic culture, and this antagonistic attitude towards the Christians has caused much surprise, because cruelty was not part of his nature and he was no bigot in religion. No law has been discovered as having emanated from him, in fact Tertullian says that during his reign he made no laws against the Christians, and who should know better than this Christian father who was twenty years of age when the Emperor died in 180 ? Most historians relieve the Emperor of blame and believe that the persecution was carried on by his officials unknown to him, or that he was carelessly indifferent, being engrossed with the troubles which afflicted his reign. Dr. Donaldson, in his *Critical History of Christian Literature*, acquits the Emperor of blame.

The reign of Marcus Aurelius was a period of many calamities and great public disasters. Pestilence ravaged his Empire from Ethiopia to Gaul. Famine was caused in the capital as the public granaries were destroyed by the Tiber, which rose in flood. Long and exhaustive wars were waged on the Eastern and Northern frontiers of the Empire, and one of his most distinguished generals revolted in Syria. So the Christians received from their neighbours the blame for everything that went wrong with the world in those days, just as Hitler today blames the Jews for all and every trouble which has afflicted the world throughout the twentieth century.

These troubles were used as excuses for persecuting the Christians, and it is noticeable that the fiercest persecutions always occurred immediately after the calamities of this reign. One can understand how it was possible, in an age of highly religious fervour and superstitious belief, for the Pagans to imagine that the Christians amongst them were an offence to their gods, who were sending calamities on the Empire as a punishment for their being harboured within its boundaries. This had been believed about other minorities in the preceding ages, and the Christian era is no exception. When the Christians came into power they likewise believed that every calamity was the result of the wrath of God, and the blame was always cast on heretics. Then heretic hunts would be organised, and Jews and all unbelievers were mercilessly persecuted and slaughtered.

Marcus Aurelius, like the true philosopher he was, weighed his thoughts carefully before he allowed them to become fixed ideas. His whole outlook was contrary to the Christian Faith. In his *Meditations* we find philosophical calmness, and a well-balanced judgement on all life's problems. He was a Stoic and scorned the emotionalism and want of thought connected with religion. So he criticised the

Christians because of their lack of self-control. Philosophy, however, only appeals to well-balanced minds. It is not infectious and is difficult to pass on from one to another, whereas the emotionalism of religion is catching and can spread like wildfire. Then, as now, philosophy was confined to the few, and religion attracted and comforted the masses.

We now come to one whose name has roused the emotions of Christians down the centuries. About the year 166 Polycarp suffered martyrdom for his faith. He was not noted for any new contribution made to the growing religion, but, to the historian, he is an interesting link with Jesus because Irenaeus tells us that he knew Polycarp personally, and that Polycarp "related to him his intercourse with John and the rest who had seen the Lord". His fame came from the fact that he lived to a great age and was believed to have been a disciple of John. For many years he was Bishop of Smyrna, and towards the end of his life he visited Rome for the purpose of discussing outstanding differences between the Christians of the East and those of the West. Up till then no settled date was fixed for the purpose of celebrating the Resurrection, and Polycarp came to Rome to discuss this and other questions.

Polycarp arrived at Rome and received much respect from Anicetus, then Bishop of Rome. On his return to Smyrna persecution of the Christians commenced there, on the plea that they were atheists, as none of them believed in any one of the Pagan gods. A few centuries later the same cry was raised against the Pagans by the Christians because they did not believe in Christ as God.

The charge of atheism has been a very common one, and religious history is full of the sufferings of those whose religious beliefs did not correspond with those of the majority. The god believed in by the majority in the country was always the true God, and those who thought otherwise were always branded as atheists. Even in our own time many Christians consider as atheists all who do not look on Christ as God. In the time of Polycarp, however, it was the other way round, as then Dionysus received first place amongst the majority. Polycarp, and others, in their belief that Christ was God, were in the minority and had to suffer in consequence.

So the cry arose, "Away with the atheists!" "Seek out Polycarp!" We are told that he remained calm and, unlike so many of the Christians of his time, he did not seek martyrdom. The religious hysteria of Christians in those days caused them to invite martyrdom, as they believed that so to die was pleasing unto their God. The venerable Polycarp, however, when he heard that his life was in danger, withdrew to a village, and, when his presence there was discovered, he removed to another. Here he was discovered and, when captured, is reported to have said, "God's will be done." He was then carried off to the city and, as tradition relates, replied to the pro-consul who exhorted him to renounce his faith and so save his life: "Four score and six years have I served Christ and he hath done me no wrong. How can I now blaspheme my King and Saviour?" He met his death by being burned at the stake.

The apologies of Justin Martyr did not go unanswered. In that age it was not to be expected that the Christians only had their say, and that no one rose up to reply to their claims. So we find Celsus, who was believed to be an Epicurean, launching a frontal attack on the growing faith. He charged the Christians with borrowing their beliefs from the Greeks and the Egyptians, and their ethics from Plato. He ran his caustic pen through the gospels and exposed them for what they are, symbolic legends borrowed from neighbouring religions. He argued that the Old and the New Testaments could not have come from the same god, as the doctrines of the one were quite contrary to those of the other. He ridiculed the childish beliefs of the Christians and their habit of believing anything, no matter how grotesque, if the name of Christ were attached to the story. He criticised, not only the doctrines, but the whole moral structure of the religion, claiming that it was grossly immoral that anyone should be freed from the consequences of his transgressions by belief that a god-man had suffered in his place.

Origen, about whom we shall hear later on, answered all the charges made by Celsus. The attack by Celsus seemed to stimulate the Christian leaders in the years which followed, as from now onwards increasing numbers wrote in defence of their beliefs, but not as advocates of what became orthodox Christianity in the fourth century. In fact most, if not all, of these apologists are now looked upon by the Church as heretics, and so we come to a consideration of the various "heresies" which prevailed in the second century.

We have already read in an earlier chapter how Paul was influenced in formulating his doctrines by the writings of those who were termed Gnostics, and reference was made to Philo, one of the principal exponents of this form of thought in the time of Paul. Gnosticism, as a form of belief, continued very much on the lines laid down by Philo, Christ now being introduced into the system as the Son of God, or the Logos, for whom the pre-Christian Gnostics had been waiting. What ultimately became the Holy Ghost developed out of the Gnostic belief that God communicated with the earth through angels or spirits. The chief control of a medium they called the holy spirit, to whom the early Christians also gave the name of The Comforter.

The Gnostic type of Christianity was just as likely to be true as any other, and, if it had won the fight which developed in the second century, orthodox Christianity would have been based on Gnostic principles. Here again, politics determined the course of the Christian Faith, as the opinions of the Christians at Rome ultimately overcame those of the Christians at Alexandria, the seat of Gnosticism. It was natural that this should be so, because Rome was the capital of the Empire, where gradually the opinions of the bishop of that city, and his entourage, carried weight with the other churches throughout the Empire. Here it was that Catholic Christianity was manufactured, or, in other words, the Christianity which the Bishop of Rome determined was the true faith. However, before Catholic Christianity took precedence over all the other forms, many and various were the opinions expressed by those who have come down to us under the name of the Church fathers.

In the time we are considering, all opinions were

equally orthodox. There were no heretics, and only gradually, as the power of the Church at Rome increased, did heresy develop. This was nothing more than the difference of opinion between what the so-called heretic believed and the belief as expounded by the Bishop of Rome. So what is termed Christian Gnosticism was in no way a heresy in the second century, although it became so in the fourth century, with disastrous results to its adherents. Earlier in this chapter we learnt what happened to the Albigenses in the thirteenth century because they continued this early form of the Faith. Gnosticism had a very great influence on second-century Christianity, and had several outstanding exponents, regarding whom we shall have something to say a few pages further on.

Briefly, the beliefs held by the Christian Gnostics were to the effect that there was one supreme God who had dwelt from all eternity in the fullness of light. He was the creator of successive generations of etheric beings who, the further they receded from his presence, the more imperfect they became. Matter is eternal and essentially evil. Out of this substance the world was formed, not by the supreme God, but by the Demiurge, a being who was the unconscious instrument of the divine will. Some Gnostics held that this being was antagonistic and hostile to the Supreme God. The Demiurge, or the creator of the world, was none other than Jehovah. The Gnostics who followed Marcion rejected the Jewish theology as evil, whereas others considered it to be a preparation for a higher dispensation.

Jesus, the Gnostics believed, came into the world

to deliver humanity from the wrath of the Demiurge. He was neither very God nor very man. He was an emanation from the Supreme God, from whom he had received his etheric body. Looking upon matter as evil, the Gnostics believed that it was the duty of every Christian to overcome the weakness of the flesh, and this could only be done by knowledge and not by faith. Many, therefore, sought this victory over the body by a high ascetic abstraction from the things of earth. Matter being evil, Jesus, after his victory over death, never returned to his old earth body. On this subject they were unanimous, believing, as they did, that he appeared to his disciples and Paul as an etheric being. He thus led the way for all flesh, as, by his victory over the grave, he enabled all Christian believers, provided their earth bodies had been baptised and cleansed, to enter the etheric world at death as etheric beings.

The Gnostics thus denied the Jewish and Egyptian doctrine, which so many Christians in their times were accepting, that the dead remained in Hades till some future judgement day, when they would rise again in their physical bodies, and Christ would reign on earth as the Christian king and judge. The true Christian, the Gnostics believed, thus reached heaven immediately after death and was destined to reach perfection through the course of successive incarnations.

This was essentially an oriental idea, and much of Gnosticism can be traced to the East, from which it drew much of its inspiration. They looked upon the Old Testament as the record of a savage people, and considered that the Christian revelation was contaminated by being in any way associated with the Jewish religion and its revengeful God. To the Gnostics the overcoming of evil was the aim of life, and they believed that ultimately good would triumph. All life came from God and the nearer to God it returned the purer it became. When purified, and fit for the presence of God, it returned to him who gave it, there to dwell throughout all eternity.

This, briefly, was the Christianity of a large number of professing Christians in the second century. Clement of Alexandria, the Church father and Christian saint, who was a prominent Churchman at the end of the second and the beginning of the third centuries, stated that the enlightened and perfect Christian is a Gnostic. The Gnostics adopted, as their tradition of belief, the pre-Christian Gnosticism, about which we have already read in an earlier chapter. Other sects of Christians adopted the Jewish tradition as the background of their faith. Into both these traditions the Christians worked the Christ as they imagined him, and these two sections of Christianity lived side by side during the first four Christian centuries. Those who accepted Christ and the Jewish tradition came to be known as Catholic Christians, and the others as Gnostic Christians. It so happened that the Bishops of Rome linked up Christianity with the Jewish theology and this, after the Council of Nicaea, became orthodox Christianity.

Until the Council of Nicaea these two aspects of the Christian Faith lived together as equals, and Gnosticism continued to have its adherents, even after this event, though they were excommunicated from the Catholic Church and branded as heretics.

Against Gnosticism the Catholic Church waged a bitter war, and finally exterminated all its supporters in the thirteenth century.

The Church claimed in justification for this policy of extermination that it was guided by the Holy Spirit, the god it can tell us nothing whatever about and consequently cannot define. Its priests are today quite unaware that this god evolved out of the spirit control of a medium who, in the early Christian centuries, was called the holy spirit because everything relating to mediumship in those days was considered holy. Consequently, these spirit controls were called gods, angels, and other such names, though they were none other than etheric beings who had lived on earth, had died, and returned to communicate with the people they had left behind through the instrumentality of a medium.

The Church thus took for itself what pertained to mediumship and elevated a spirit control to the rank of third person in its trinity of gods. Because a control must have a physical body as his instrument the Church claimed to be this body, this instrument and this medium, asserting that it was Christ's visible body which was controlled by the Holy Spirit.

At the service of Consecration of Bishops, as laid down in the Church of England Prayer Book, the Archbishop and Bishops present lay their hands on the head of the elected bishop, who is kneeling before them. Then the Archbishop pronounces these words : "Receive the Holy Ghost for the Office and Work of a Bishop in the Church of God, now committed unto thee by the imposition of our hands". Thus has this Church-made Holy Spirit been passed

on, so it is claimed, from the days of the apostles to
our own time. Each bishop on election is filled by
this act with this divine being, as was Jesus at his
baptism. They thus became god-men just as Jesus
did after he was filled with the Holy Spirit. Moreover, as the Holy Spirit is a part of the Godhead, the
bishops became divine beings, as, at election, each
was endowed with this part of God.

Throughout the Christian era the bishops have
claimed that this divine spirit has been passed on
from bishop to bishop by the laying on of hands.
This can only mean that each believed that, by being
so endowed, he became a god-man under the special
direction of the Holy Spirit. Thus the Church,
through its nominees the bishops, became the medium
of the Holy Spirit and took the place of the medium
produced by nature. Every decision come to by the
bishops in council was claimed to be the expression
of the will of the Holy Spirit. Their decisions were,
therefore, the will of God, which must be obeyed by
the people. These decisions were communicated to
the priests, who are termed in the Prayer Book the
Fathers in God, and they in turn instructed the people.
No change has taken place in this priestly outlook
from the time the priests captured the Church organisation in the fourth century, and what was invented
then has been retained throughout the Christian era,
and is still claimed today by both Catholic and
Protestant bishops and priests.

By spelling holy with a capital H and spirit with
a capital S the Church thus amalgamated all the spirit
controls, who act through mediums, into one in
number. This one it turned into a god and claimed

him to be its own control, specially selected by Christ to guide his Church on earth. The Church obliterated the human medium and put itself, a priestly made organisation, in his place. Instead of the medium, whom nature supplies, the Church, through its nominees the bishops, put itself forward as the only medium betwixt earth and heaven, and preached its man-made theology, instead of acting as the protector of nature's revelation through mediumship.

Since it perpetrated this gigantic fraud and crime in the fourth century it has made the most outrageous claims to inspiration and divine guidance. Before every Council meeting the bishops always prepared themselves to be controlled by the Holy Spirit by partaking of the Eucharist. This act, they claimed, brought them and Christ together through the agency of this man-made Holy Spirit. The bishops were the instruments, Christ the communicator, and the Holy Spirit the spirit control who passed on Christ's messages to earth through his mediums the bishops. Need we wonder that the bishops were always determined that no medium produced by nature was to be allowed to live ? They only were the mediums of the god specially invented for their own purposes, while nature's mediums, they asserted, were the instruments controlled by the Devil and his demons.

Thus we find, throughout the Christian era, that the bishops claim that all the decisions arrived at by them have been brought about by Christ himself, and we need go no further back than the recent Council meetings, held by the High Priests of the

Church of England, to which reference has already been made. Before each session responsible for the publication entitled *Doctrine of the Church of England*, the Eucharist was celebrated, and the priests, so they said in the introduction, carried on their deliberations in the belief that they were being guided by the Holy Spirit.

When one has the psychic key all the Christian mysteries can be unlocked. The entire edifice, called the Christian Church, built up by priestly cunning and deception, can be demolished with ease. The High Priests have always known its weakness, and that they could only gain more wealth and retain their power by suppressing all opposition. So long as they were able they persecuted, imprisoned, tortured and put to death all who stood in their way. When they were stopped perpetrating their foul deeds they then brought in legislation against blasphemy and the printing of books which told the truth and exposed their false claims. When they could not continue killing mediums they influenced governments to bring in legislation against them and this, in our own country, has never been repealed.

Any medium today can be fined or imprisoned in this Christian country for no other reason than that he or she exercises natural psychic gifts, the gifts extolled by Paul and practised in the Apostolic Church. Every attempt made to amend the Vagrants and Witchcraft Acts, under which mediums are condemned, has been opposed by the Church authorities. All the early Christian mediums, including Jesus, Paul and Peter, would be criminals under British law, if on earth today, and their chief accusers would be the Christian bishops, controlled by the Holy Spirit in his capacity as the messenger of Christ !

Such a situation would only be history repeating itself. The priests could not nowadays kill "the Prince of Life", as Peter termed Jesus in his attack on the Jewish priesthood, but one, such as Jesus seems to have been, could be fined and imprisoned. Truth is certainly stranger than fiction, and the truth about the origin, history and beliefs of the Christian Faith, and Christian Church, is certainly so strange that nineteen hundred years had to elapse before it was discovered. Those who should stand in the dock today are the Christian priests (their crime being the preaching of what is not true and making false claims about themselves and their organisation) and not the mediums whose place they have most cruelly and craftily usurped. How they did this will be explained further on in this chapter.

The fight between the priest and the medium, about which we shall now soon be reading, is all the more interesting when the foregoing facts are remembered, and now that they have been laid bare let us return to the second century. The question as to whether Christianity was to be linked with Judaism or not became the rock on which the early Christian ship split. Originally all Christians had been known as Nazarenes, but this name now became associated with those who maintained that the Mosaic Law was binding on the Christians of the Jewish race. The Ebonites went further and insisted that the Mosaic Law must be accepted by both Jewish and Gentile Christians. These two sects, after pursuing their own lines of belief, ultimately became absorbed in the orthodox Church, but the Nazarenes are known to have been a distinct sect until as late as the fifth century, and the Ebonites until the fourth century.

These two sects, the Ebonites and the Nazarenes, can be looked upon as the root out of which orthodox Christianity grew. Their adherents were opposed to Gnostic beliefs and held the opinion that Jesus was the son of Joseph and Mary, chosen to be the Messiah and Son of God because at his baptism he had received the holy spirit. They denied his virgin birth. While the Gnostics favoured Paul the Ebonites were hostile to his views, and favoured Peter, which is an echo of the old quarrel and difference of opinion between Paul and Peter.

In the first quarter of the second century we find two men of outstanding personality, Saturninus and Basilides, who founded respectively the Syrian and Alexandrian schools of Gnosticism. Saturninus, who was born in Antioch, gave forth his ideas as to the origin of the world and the beings who inhabit the etheric world. Basilides, who founded his school in Alexandria, did likewise. He denied that Jesus died for the sins of the world, and held the view that all must work out their own salvation through various incarnations. He accepted from the New Testament and the epistles only what fitted in with his speculations. He believed that at baptism Jesus became controlled by a spirit who forsook him at his crucifixion.

It would be wearisome to recount all his other ideas but enough has been said to make it evident how these early Christians differed from each other, and how far apart some of their opinions were from what eventually became orthodox Christianity. In those days there was no fixed opinion about anything, and theologians and mystics gave forth a great amount of energy and thought, just as Paul did, on the subject of the return of Jesus and his relationship to God.

To the people of the second century, theology was their all in all as it answered everything. The study of this subject revealed to them how the world was created, what were the functions of God, and the meaning to be attached to the etheric world, and the beings who lived therein. Everything, in fact, could be answered by Theology. The theologians claimed to know all that today goes under the name of science. They knew how matter was created, how the earth, the sun, the planets and the stars came into being. They knew all about God and what he had done throughout eternity, and what he intended to do throughout eternity. They knew the cause of disease, and how the devils which caused it could be driven out, in fact they knew everything, and each set forth his knowledge of these deep problems with an assurance which today can only cause amazement.

So we shall not dwell longer on the speculations of Saturninus and Basilides. Each had his own particular view as to how the earth and life came into being, which in those days was a subject about which all theologians expressed their opinions. The sun, the planets and the stars were always treated as if they were a kind of afterthought. In Genesis we are told in some detail about the creation of the earth, but the unfathomable universe is passed off with only five words, "He made the stars also", as if they were something created with what was left over after the earth was moulded into shape.

So these ancient theologians thought much and pondered long on the great problems of creation and existence, and gave forth their best, but, as their knowledge was slight and their imagination intense, they all reached different conclusions. To us today these seem very childish and foolish. Not only did they ponder over the creation of the earth but also over the creation of man. None doubted that he was a being apart from the material creation, but exactly what his composition was caused many wonderful theories. That he was a sinner was generally admitted, that his past deeds required to be pardoned by the Deity was also admitted, and that he required cleansing by baptism, through being dipped in water, none questioned. The relationship of Christ to God, and exactly what his mission was, remained a question on which unanimous agreement could not be reached. The old problems which man had pondered over for ages were accepted without controversy. It was the new one introduced by the reappearance of Jesus, over which unanimity could not be reached.

As all these questions were of intense interest to the Christians of those days, men like Saturninus and Basilides obtained considerable followings, but the one who succeeded them, Valentinus, was the most outstanding for his extraordinary speculations. He was a man of Jewish descent, a native of Egypt, having studied at Alexandria. He professed Christianity from his childhood. His views did not appeal to the Church at Rome and because of that he is now termed a heretic in Church history. He was disappointed at not being made a bishop, and later on retired to Cyprus, where he thought out and published his system of Christian Gnosticism. He died in the year 160.

His doctrine of creation, salvation, redemption and all these other theological and mystical subjects was largely influenced by his knowledge of Egyptian and Persian mysticism and the philosophy of Plato and Pythagoras. Into this he worked Jesus as the Christ, the first begotten who alone was capable of comprehending the supreme Father. His theology is so involved and mystical that sometimes it is difficult to grasp what he really means. Anyone who has studied Greek mythology will, however, at once appreciate the similarity between much of what Valentinus has written and what was written by the Greeks. The Greeks called the various etheric beings, who were responsible for the creation and management of the universe, by the name of gods, giving each a name, and Valentinus calls them etheric beings, giving them names such as Logos (=reason) and Sophia (=wisdom) and so on.

In the paragraphs which follow, I shall try to simplify his ideas and express them in words which can be followed even if they cannot be understood. Valentinus supposed a first principle from all eternity, self-existent and perfect. This, after existing in repose, resolved to manifest itself as an etheric being. From his mind were produced two spirits, the male termed "Only Begotten" and the female termed "Truth". These in turn produced two other pairs, one pair being "Reason" and "Life", the other "Man" and "the Church". These he termed first-grade beings.

From "Reason" and "Life" were produced five pairs of spirits and from "Man" and "the Church" six pairs, making up twenty-eight in all. Besides this there was an unwedded spirit named "Boundary" whose duty it was to enforce the principle of limitation and keep all existence in its proper place.

The "Only Begotten" was alone capable of comprehending the supreme Father. His knowledge was envied by the other spirits, and in proportion to their remoteness from the source so was their desire to fathom it. "Wisdom", filled with uncontrollable eagerness, issued forth from the etheric world with the intention of soaring up to the being from whence she had come, but, as she was in danger of being absorbed into the infinity of his nature, "Boundary" led her back to the sphere which she had so rashly forsaken.

The "Only Begotten" produced a new pair of spirits known as "Christ" and the "Holy Spirit". "Christ" taught the elder spirits that "Unfathomable Depth" was incomprehensible, that it could only be known through the "Only Begotten", and that the happiness of every being was to rest content with what measure of light had been allotted to him, which contentment could only come by all uniting in glorifying the Supreme Being. When this was agreed upon all the spirits combined to produce "The Saviour", the flower of the spirit world. By each spirit he was endowed with the most precious gifts possible and then allotted a host of attendant angels.

Satan and his angels now come into the picture and are known as material productions. "Wisdom" supplicates "Christ" to send to earth "The Saviour" attended by his angels, and the Demiurge sets to work on the surrounding chaos to separate the psychic from the material elements of the universe. Out of the former he builds seven heavens of which the highest is his own sphere. For every sphere he appoints a superintending angel. The Demiurge then made man, who was a creature made of psychoplasm, but "Wisdom", without the knowledge of the Demiurge, implanted in this new creature a spark of the divine. In consequence, the Demiurge and his angels stood amazed when their workmanship was completed in finding that what they had produced was something nobler than themselves.

So the Demiurge became jealous of man and placed him under the law. This man broke, and, in consequence, was thrust down from the third heaven to earth, his psychic body being enveloped with a coat of skin, or fleshly prison, thus subjecting him to the bonds of matter. In order that man might rise again to his original place in the etheric world the Demiurge inspired his prophets to promise a Messiah. He formed this Messiah by producing a psychic and immaterial body. This body was capable of performing human actions, yet was exempt from human feelings. This was the Christ who was born of the Virgin Mary, "passing through her as water passes through a tube without taking any of her substance".

For thirty years he ate and drank but derived no nourishment from his earthly food and lived as a pattern of righteousness. At his baptism the spirit of "The Saviour" descended upon him with the intention of fulfilling the prophecy which the Demiurge had not understood. Then, and only then, the Demiurge became aware of the higher etheric world and gladly yielded himself as an instrument for the advancement of the Messiah's kingdom.

Now, for the first time, was the pure truth revealed to mankind by the coming of the Christ Spirit. To the religious minded his mission was for the purpose of enlightenment, and they entered the etheric world at death because of the knowledge which united them with Christ. Those who were not religious by nature were saved by the suffering of the Messiah on the cross who, before his crucifixion, was abandoned by the Christ Spirit and his own etheric body.

The Valentinian system was acceptable to a number of Christians of those days because he used scripture as his foundation and produced his theories based on his interpretation of scriptural texts. Those who made up this sect regarded *The Gospel of John* as their authority. Initiation into its mysteries was gradual, but Irenaeus tells us that those who could pay the best had never any difficulty in learning its secrets. A remnant of the sect survived till as late as the fifth century, and this resumé of its beliefs is given as an example of the imaginative effort so prevalent amongst the early Christians.

They were for ever attempting to unravel the mysteries of creation and existence, the reason for evil, and how they thought it could be overcome. Their minds were for ever in a whirl of speculative thought, and all they imagined can only be classed under the name of mythology. When we compare their speculations with the mature and logical reasonings of the Greek philosophers we realise the childish intelligence of these men who have come down to us under the name of the Christian fathers.

Valentinus is recognised in Church history as the most important Christian theologian up till the end of the second century. He was the first man in Christendom who, for other than merely apologetic reasons, sought to fuse together mythology with the substance of the gospel. He treated Christ as the key-stone in the great structure of ideas which had been reared by Greek mystics and theologians, and he attempted to build a bridge between Greek and Christian theology.

While this imaginative system of Christian theology was making headway, a much more practical individual arose to give forth his opinions as to the meaning of things, and how everything was to be understood. This was the famous Marcion, who at least produced a scheme which could be understood, even if it has nothing more behind it than his own imagination.

He was the great anti-semitic of his day and endeavoured to dissociate the Christian religion, root and branch, from Judaism. His father was Bishop of Sinope and he himself was a presbyter in that church. By profession he was a shipmaster and traded in the Black Sea. His opinions were probably the cause of his being excommunicated from his church and, after a fruitless attempt to gain admission into the church at Rome, he started his travels to Egypt and the East for the purpose of spreading the particular opinions he had formed as to the meaning of Christ. Finally he became a Christian teacher in Rome, where, on one occasion, he tried to make friends with Polycarp, but without success, the bishop's reply to his salutation being, "I know thee for the first-born of

Satan". He died towards the end of the second century.

Marcion professed that his doctrine was contained within one of the gospels and the epistles, and he claimed that he had borrowed nothing from Greece, Egypt or Persia. He rejected the Old Testament in its entirety and built up his beliefs on the Gospel of Luke and ten of Paul's epistles. He rejected the other New Testament books because the writers were blinded by Judaism. His three principles were : the supremacy of God, who was perfect in all goodness ; the existence of the Devil, who was lord of matter, an eternal and evil being. Between these two reigned the Demiurge, a being having limited power and knowledge, whose function was to dispense justice unmixed with love or mercy. Man fell through disobedience to the laws of the Demiurge, but, through the anticipated Messiah, the son of the Demiurge, salvation could be secured. The supreme God was not satisfied with this arrangement because this Messiah was for the Jews only, and so the Supreme Being, in pity for mankind, resolved to send an even higher being to earth, namely his own son.

Jesus, the son of the Supreme Being, appeared suddenly on earth for the first time, as a materialised spirit, in the synagogue in Capernaum in the fifteenth year of the reign of Tiberius Caesar. To the Jews he pretended to be the Messiah sent by the Demiurge. The Demiurge, ignorant of the mission of Jesus, stirred up the Jews against him and, urging on the Gentiles, brought about his crucifixion. Jesus, however, was in reality a materialised being while on earth. He never had a body of flesh and went about on earth as a materialised spirit, presumably such as one sees at materialisation séances. Consequently when he was crucified he did not suffer.

This doctrine, that Jesus was crucified as a spirit, came to be known as Docetism (Greek=seem) and a distinct sect arose in the second century, the adherents of which, called Docetes, made this idea the centre of their belief. One could read this idea into some of Paul's writings, for instance, "God, sending his own son in the likeness of sinful flesh" (Romans viii, 3) and Christ "took upon him the form of a servant, and was made in the likeness of men, being found in fashion as a man". (Phil. ii, 7.)

After the crucifixion, Marcion tells us, Jesus descended to Hades and cleared the place of some of the dead Hebrews. The saints, however, would not leave as they said that they felt they were much more comfortable in Abraham's bosom. They were, however, not destined to dwell there for ever as they had the promise of the Messiah, which the Demiurge told them he would send, namely his own son, to gather them together to form a universal empire of the Jews on earth. Those saved by the death of Jesus, however, went to dwell with God as etheric beings in the etheric world.

Thus Marcion pictured a Jewish Messiah for the Jews alone, who was to come to earth as their king and, after releasing from Hades all the old Hebrew worthies, was to reign on earth as Emperor of a universal empire of the Jews. The Gentiles, on the other hand, were to find their home in Heaven in the presence of God, the supreme being of the Universe.

If this had come about it would certainly have solved once and for all the seemingly eternal Jewish question !

Marcion's bold rejection of Hebrew mythology, and his arbitrary method of putting aside what he thought favoured Judaism in the gospels and the epistles attracted many Gentile converts who, for Christ's sake, suffered persecution for their beliefs. Consequently this sect was able to boast of some martyrs. The followers of Marcion courted persecution, and seemed to thrive on hatred and tribulation. In spite of being first of all persecuted by the Pagans, and then by the orthodox Christians, the sect survived until the sixth century.

The Church, when orthodoxy became established, labelled Marcion a heretic, but in his day he was no more a heretic than anyone else. All that happened was that when the Catholic Faith evolved, under the direction of the Bishops of Rome as to what that Faith should be, the writings of Marcion were declared to be unorthodox, and not in accordance with the beliefs which had by then come to be looked upon by the church at Rome as constituting the true Catholic Faith.

Gradually the apologists obtained a wider public and, as they did so, men of position and ability amongst the Pagans took an increasing interest in what they had to say. Converts from the upper classes increased the Christian ranks and so, as time goes on, we find fewer calumnies directed against the Christians. Marcus Aurelius had passed on, leaving a profligate son by the name of Commodus, during whose reign the Church suffered no violence. The Emperor Severus, who followed him, favoured the

Christians, and it is said that he was interested in their beliefs. Still, we find that in his reign, just as in the reign of Marcus Aurelius, though the Emperor was not antagonistic, his local governors were, and so some Christians in certain districts suffered by death or banishment.

As the reign of Severus proceeded he became hostile towards both Christianity and Judaism, and issued an edict to the effect that anyone embracing either of these religions would suffer heavy penalties. It is said that he was annoyed because the Christians and Jews refused to join in his triumphant entries into Rome, the reason being that on such occasions Pagan priests took part and performed their rites and ceremonies as a token of thanksgiving to the gods. The new edict, however, did not forbid Christian worship, its purpose being merely to prevent any increase in their numbers.

In the outlying parts of the Empire, however, this edict had the effect of stimulating persecution, but many Christians obtained respite through bribing the officials. Under the three Emperors who followed Severus, the Christians did not suffer any persecution. In fact, the Emperor Elagabalus saw in Christianity such a resemblance to Paganism that he set about combining the Christian symbols with those of Paganism in a new temple he had built and dedicated to the sun. His career, however, ended before this scheme was completed.

We now find a new development in Church organisation, namely the calling together of Councils, composed of representatives of the various Christian churches throughout the Empire, for the purpose of settling differences of opinion as to doctrine and ceremony. The question as to when Easter should be held still troubled the various churches, as agreement could not be reached between the East and the West, and there were numerous other points of doctrine and usage about which no general opinion was held. This state of doubt, as to what Christianity really was, continued till finally Constantine, in the fourth century, made the priests decide exactly what the Christian religion was to be and so, once and for all, settled the matter.

We have already found that many Christians were influenced by the opinions of different men who captured public opinion by their theories, and now we come to consider the opinions put forward by another outstanding Christian, by name of Montanus, who gave his name to a new sect which was composed of his followers. Montanus, who had been a Pagan priest before his conversion to Christianity, flourished in the latter part of the second century, and from that time, and throughout the next century, Montanism spread widely amongst the Christian community. We are fortunate in having a full and unmutilated record of its beliefs, teaching and influence in the writings of Tertullian, who lived at the time its power was greatest.

The aim of the new sect was to increase the number of days given over to fasting and to make this religious rite more severe. It disapproved of second marriage, which it placed on the same level as adultery. It denounced military service and the pleasures of secular life. All knowledge outside the scriptures was considered sinful, and women were forbidden to dress otherwise than in the plainest apparel. Its adherents seem to have been the fore-runners of our Puritans.

Earlier in this chapter it was stated that up to the middle of the second century, churches employed mediums who gave trance addresses and clairaudient and clairvoyant demonstrations. With the increase in the number of churches, as only a limited number of mediums existed, their place, as the century drew to a close, was taken by the bishops and presbyters, who adopted the rôle of priests and not that of ministers to their congregations. Consequently some churches were conducting their worship without the help of mediums, and doctrine and dogma were taking the place of "the ministrations of the spirit". Montanus, in consequence, started a movement for the purpose of emphasising that those churches were mistaken in not making a greater effort to retain the form of worship hitherto carried on since apostolic times.

He accepted the Christian Faith and attacked none of its beliefs. What he claimed was, that only through mediumship could it be understood, and that those churches which did not employ mediums were departing from apostolic usage and losing contact with the etheric world. In fact, he said that they were neglecting the very foundation of their Faith. He accepted the resurrection of Jesus as a spirit, as did Paul, and claimed that only through the knowledge of clairvoyance could it be understood. In the churches which accepted his views, encourage-ment was given to trance addresses, clairvoyance and clairaudience, and some which had neglected these ministrations of the spirit returned to them when they could find suitable mediums. Montanus, who was evidently a medium, claimed to be a channel through which the holy spirit, promised to the apostles, spoke and delivered his message. He claimed that his spirit control was the Comforter promised to the disciples.

His argument was to the effect that the Comforter, or holy spirit, was none other than the etheric being who controls a medium in trance, or delivers messages to the one who is clairaudient. Anyone who was mediumistically developed was capable of enabling the Comforter to come through and deliver his messages to mankind, and, the more developed one became mediumistically, the more the revelation promised by Jesus, through the Comforter, would increase to the enlightenment of all humanity. Two women of wealth and position, Maximilla and Prisca, also described as mediums, gave their all to help forward the efforts of the new sect to re-establish mediumship in the churches which were neglecting it.

The severity of this sect's code of ethics was for the purpose of keeping pure and unspotted from the world all those who believed in its teaching, so that if any had mediumistic gifts they would be suitable channels for their controls to use to deliver the divine message. In other words, the Montanists were Christian Spiritualists, like many other Christians in the first two centuries of our era, and believed that mediums were the human instruments used by etheric beings to communicate with mankind. They claimed that these spirit communicators were none other than the Comforter promised by Jesus, which name was given to each spirit control, because of the fact that he brought the living on earth into contact with those who had passed on to the etheric world.

From what is written about the Montanists it is evident that they had studied psychic phenomena, especially what is today known as mental mediumship. They were not interested so much in what are today called physical phenomena, which resulted in what in those days were called miracles. What they developed was trance, clairvoyance and clairaudience. So, in their churches, as in the times since the apostles, the medium took first place, and trance and clairaudience formed part of their services.

Soon after the origin of this sect certain Christian bishops expressed their objection to its beliefs. Some bishops, Eusebius tells us, wished to exorcise the devils from the mediums when in trance, but this was not allowed. The Montanists claimed that they were told in the first Epistle of John (iv, 1) to try the spirits and see if they be of God. This they had done and found them to be so. Montanus was excommunicated from his church, and this caused him to organise a body of supporters to spread his belief that the Comforter, promised by Jesus (John xiv, 16), had found his way through to mankind by using the bodies of all who were mediumistically endowed.

The Bishop of Rome, Victor by name, was on the point of accepting the Montanist claims and acknowledging them as in accordance with Church usage. He was just about to admit the sect to the communion of the church at Rome, which would have meant that this church accepted the contention of Montanus that mediumship was an integral part of Christian church worship. As the church at Rome became the deciding factor as to what was to be, and what was not to be, with regard to Christian beliefs and usages, it will be realised how important Victor's decision was and how it affected the future history of the Church.

Just as Victor was replying and agreeing to the Montanist's request for admission into the church at Rome, a Christian Asiatic, Praxeas by name, arrived in Rome and visited him. Praxeas was a Priest-Confessor, who had been imprisoned for his beliefs. He persuaded Victor against the Montanists, and so influenced the bishop that he excommunicated them from the Christian Church, much to their sorrow, as they all wished to retain their membership.

Under the influence of Praxeas, who was a man of no special importance, the church at Rome now directed its policy against mediumship, and so commenced its opposition to the psychic tradition which went back to the Apostolic Church. From this event we can date the entrance of the priesthood into the Christian Church, and from now onwards it makes its influence increasingly felt. On such seeming trifles, on people and things which, at the time, are considered of little importance, great issues may hang. If Victor had not received this visit from Praxeas the Christian Church at Rome would have fallen into line with a large body of Christian opinion of those days, which would have had the effect of completely altering the direction of the Christian Faith, and the form its worship took under priestly direction.

In the second century the Faith was still unformed and much had still to be built up. In the apostolic churches there were no priests and so mediums took their proper place as the natural link between earth and heaven. This original intention continued in the first half of the second century and, to a lesser degree, thereafter up till the end of the third century. Mediums were respected and honoured in many churches, and bishops and presbyters had no established position apart from the wishes of the congregation. If a congregation wished a medium to give clairaudience no bishop could prevent it. The priests in those days were not in command and mediumship, in many churches, held the place intended by the apostles.

When Montanus was excommunicated from his church we find the first indication of the bishop usurping his position as the minister to the congregation, and going against the hitherto accepted opinion that mediums were the natural link between earth and heaven. Here we find the priest coming into command, which meant that sooner or later mediumship would be abolished from all Christian churches. This is exactly what happened, but before the priests got their way they had to wait for a century till Constantine gave them unlimited power. Until then they had to meet the wishes of the people, and so, right on until the fourth century, mediums were employed in churches, as in apostolic times, though the practice declined under priestly influence.

When the Montanists found that they could not influence Victor to alter his decision, they then accused the bishops of pursuing a policy for which there was no place in the Christian Church. Instead of being ministers, the bishops and presbyters, they said, were taking the place of the medium, which was wrong and not in accordance with apostolic tradition. All that was expected of the bishops and presbyters was to manage the secular needs of the churches under them, leaving the medium to keep the congregation in touch with the etheric world, while they presided over the services, read the passage from the scriptures, and led the praise.

This wish for the retention of the order of worship of the Apostolic Church had, however, no attraction for the Christian bishops who had much higher ambitions than merely to play second fiddle to the medium. The people were told by the bishops that they could not understand the mysteries, and that it was the divine duty of the priests to explain them and act as intermediaries between man and God. So the Christians in the fourth century took the priests at their word and, in consequence, lost their liberty.

The antagonism between Priest and Prophet has gone on down the ages, and, in the time of the Montanists, the Christian ministers shewed the same hatred towards the mediums as had their priestly predecessors for thousands of years, though they found it impossible to prevent their congregations holding the opposite opinion. Christianity, at this time, was in closer contact with the etheric world than it has ever been since. During the nineteenth century most English speaking people recovered their religious liberty, and so today we find mediumship spreading wherever priests do not rule. Nowhere is this happening in Christian churches, as the Spiritualists last century were forced to leave these and form an organisation of their own, just as were the Montanists in the second century.

At the beginning of the Christian era the medium was looked upon by Christians as the natural revealer of the other world, as one who had received his gifts from God, whereas the priesthood was a man-made institution. In consequence, mediumship was respected and encouraged, and now, as the Christian era draws to a close, it is again coming into its own and becoming understood for what it really means to mankind. Religion is entering on a new phase, with everyone freer than ever before to make contact with the unseen as his intelligence directs. This greater liberty of thought is bringing to an end vested interests working for an organisation and not for humanity. In consequence, a new vista of happiness is opening before mankind, with knowledge taking the place of faith, with teachers and mediums replacing priests, and sacred books replaced by the book of nature.

A right understanding of our place on earth, and our destiny, will some day bring about what the seers of the past have foretold would come, when "man to man the world o'er shall brothers be for a' that". This, however, will only come about when full political and religious liberty is established everywhere, and political and religious dictators are abolished.

In support of their beliefs the Montanists claimed that they were carrying out what Peter had foretold at Pentecost, when he had quoted how the prophet Joel had said, "It shall come to pass in the last days, saith God, I will pour out my spirit upon all flesh : and your sons and your daughters shall prophesy, and your young men shall see visions." (Acts ii, 17.) A large section of the Christian community, scattered as small congregations throughout the Empire, based its opinion on this text, which satisfied them that it was in accordance with God's will that the etheric world should be revealed to mankind through mediumship. Many Christians, in the time we are considering, were strenuously opposed to priestcraft being introduced into the Christian Church, and did their utmost to retain the apostolic simplicity of worship.

The dispute which went on between the bishops and the Spiritualists in the end resulted in the establishment of the episcopacy, based on the fiction that Jesus, through his apostles, had conferred on the bishops entire power over his Church on earth. This false claim, which the people in their ignorance believed from the fourth century onwards, made the priest supreme in the Christian Church, and brought to an end the participation of the medium in church services.

When Constantine made his bargain with the priests that, in exchange for a uniform Christian belief, he would raise their Church to the rank of a State organisation, the Christian religion, as represented by its priesthood, marched through the open door into the Imperial Palace, figuratively speaking, and from that time onwards worked in partnership with the Emperor. Christianity became a system of theological speculation to be imposed on everyone, whether they wished it or not. Devoid of contact with the etheric world, its one and only aim was to dominate the people by autocratic decrees issued by the Emperor on the advice of the priests.

By this bargain all the principles of the early Church, and all liberty of thought, were smothered under a mass of doctrine and dogma. A rigid creed took the place of individual belief. With this accomplished, the Christian Church then furnished itself with everything of value that could be taken from the world. That is how it ended in the fourth century, but it was not the general wish of the second and third-century Christians, who had no desire to depart from apostolic usage. Tertullian exhausted the resources of his persuasive genius to prevent the Church going the way of the priests, but otherworldliness is never a match for organisation and worldly wisdom. Thus the priests won the day in the end, though their earlier disputes with mediums in trance always made them appear foolish.

In the *Encyclopædia Britannica* we find recorded in its review of Montanism the following incident, which is probably only one of many such similar happenings :

The disputation which Bishops Zoticus of Cumana and Julian of Apamea arranged with Maximilla [the medium] and her following turned out most disastrously for its promoters. The spirit of Maximilla gained a signal victory. A certain Themison in particular having reduced the bishops to silence, Sotas, Bishop of Anchialus, attempted to refute Prisca [the name of another medium], but with no better success. He too had to retire from the field in disgrace. These proceedings were never forgotten in Asia Minor and the report of them spread far and wide. This was the commencement of the excommunication or secession, whichever it may have been, of the Montanists in Asia Minor

The same article goes on to tell of the dispute, as it developed, in these words :

The bishops gave offence to the Spiritualists on so many points that at last it could be endured no longer. The latter wished for more fasting, the prohibition of second marriages, a frank, courageous profession of Christianity in daily life and entire separation from the world. The bishops, on the other hand, sought in every way to make it as easy as possible to be a Christian, lest they should lose the greater part of their congregations. The Spiritualists would have excluded from the Church everyone who had been guilty of mortal sin. The bishops were at that time especially anxious to relax the stringency of the old disciplinary laws. And lastly, the bishops were compelled more and more to take the control of discipline into their own hands, while the Spiritualists, appealing to the old principle, that God alone can remit or retain sins, insisted that God himself, namely the spirit, was the sole judge in the congregation, and that therefore all proceedings must be conducted according to the direction of the prophets (mediums). On this point especially a conflict was inevitable. The demand that the "organ of the spirit" (the medium) should direct the whole discipline of the congregation contained implicitly a protest against the actual constitution of the Church.

Gnosticism put knowledge before faith, Montanism put mediumship before the bishops, while Catholicism stood for the Hebrew tradition and the priesthood. At one time, when the Faith was in its youth, one or other of these might equally easily have defeated the other two and been the victor. This is clearly expressed in Ritschl's work *Entstehung der Altkatholischen Kirche.*

Montanism spread throughout all Christendom, and the congregations of many churches all over the Empire went over in entirety to its beliefs. Only after it and Gnosticism were defeated did the Catholic Church arise supreme and become definitely established. Gnosticism and Montanism, the two great forces with which it had to contend, fought hard to win, but, with the church at Rome against them, the fight was in vain. So they fought and lost.

If it had not been for the Christian bishops, who had gradually established themselves as the rulers and directors of all beliefs and worship, it can be easily appreciated how Christianity could have evolved into a religion based on the same knowledge as that for which Spiritualism stands today, with no place for either doctrine or dogma. If there had been no priesthood, whose business it was to propagate doctrine, with the passage of time the Messianic beliefs surrounding the Christ would doubtless have faded away, especially as he never returned to claim his elect.

Christianity, on this assumption, might easily have evolved into an outlook on life as expressed by the seven principles of Spiritualism, of which the fatherhood of God and the brotherhood of man take first and second place. Then comes belief in communication with the other world, the conscious existence of the human spirit after death, personal responsibility, that as one sows one shall reap, and that progress hereafter is open to every human being.

By the fourth century, however, when the Church became the State Church of the Empire, and its priests had obtained control of all religious worship, Ambrose, Bishop of Milan and Christian saint, persuaded the Emperor Theodosius to issue an edict against all churches employing mediums. Thus began, from Lyons in the West to Angora in the East, the massacre of all Montanist congregations, and this slaughtering of the Spiritualists continued until the eighth century, it being particularly violent in the reign of Justinian (483–565) who, led by the priests, waged a furious war against them, with the result that most of them perished.

The Church thus obliterated mediumship from Christendom, but, whenever nature produced others having this gift, both Catholic and Protestant priests quickly exterminated them, and this went on till the eighteenth century, when the people rose up against this barbarism. If the Church had taken the opportunity it was offered and had made itself the protector, instead of the destroyer, of mediumship, how different would have been its history and the general knowledge of our destiny. That it did not do so, can be attributed to the natural ambition in man to control those under him of lesser intelligence. Those seeking power, wealth and position found intrigue, craftiness and cunning more effective than mediumship in Church affairs.

Many of the mediums in the past, as is the case today, were women, and no priest would tarnish the escutcheon of his order by allowing to take part in religious ordinances one whose sex he believed had brought all sin into the world. Some progress has, however, been made in the better understanding of the laws of nature, because we find today in Spiritualist churches that the congregations have learned to abide by natural law. There it is understood that in making contact with the other world nature is no respecter of persons, and that the only revelation from the etheric world comes through the channels fitted for it by nature, irrespective of sex, education or position. In this respect some have recovered the ground lost by the priesthood taking over the interpretation and propagation of religion.

In those early Christian centuries, when the priests were manufacturing their doctrines and creeds, they gave no thought to natural law. What was most expedient took the first place, as we shall better realise now that we are about to consider the history of Christian belief during

THE THIRD CENTURY.

At its opening there was no settled opinion as to what exactly a Christian should believe in order to secure salvation. Christian thought was not uniform, and yet its various beliefs were attracting the Pagans more and more, as they felt its claims to have a stronger appeal than their own religion, because its Saviour had died and reappeared comparatively recently. So year by year the Christian Church recorded an increased membership.

True, Christianity then was different from what became orthodox Christianity, but gradually the church at Rome came to be looked upon as the authority. Age-old beliefs were slowly crystallising round Christ and becoming accepted in Rome as the true Faith. "The Church was forced to consider how much of these older systems was true and how much was false, and, while steadfastly rejecting the falsehood, to appropriate the truth, to hallow it by a combination with the Christian principle, and so to rescue all that was precious from the wreck of a world which was passing away." So writes Canon

Robertson in his *History of the Christian Church*, and he might have added, but did not, that if Alexandria, and not Rome, had been the capital of the Roman Empire the Gnostic, and not the Hebrew tradition, would have been accepted as the basis of the Christian Faith.

The Catholic Church took from Gnosticism what it thought was true and rejected what it thought was false, basing its decisions on Hebrew tradition. Much of its literature and art came from those professing the Gnostic form of Christian belief. Christian mystics have been influenced by Gnostic thought down the centuries, and it forms the basis of Christian mysticism. Though it greatly influenced the building up of the Christian system, it was not accepted as part of its basic structure. The church at Rome had other ideas and threw its influence on the side of the Hebrew mythology. It adopted the theology produced by those Christian exponents who weaved Jesus into the Christian system as the Messiah promised to Adam. Thus had been fulfilled the promise made by Jehovah that he would deliver man from the curse of death, which had come about through Adam's desire for knowledge in the Garden of Eden.

We might well question Canon Robertson's statement that the Church appropriated the truth from the false and rescued all that was precious from the wreck of a world which was passing away. The very reverse was done. The Church ignored the psychic origin of all that became Christianity, and fostered miraculous stories, based on Pagan and Hebrew mythology. Out of this mythology it evolved its doctrines, dogmas and ceremonies, and never gave intelligent thought as to what natural laws caused the minds of men to produce all the fantastic ideas which are grouped under mysticism, mythology and theology. The Church accepted the effects and never tried to find the cause. Its own sacred and holy teaching had come from God and the mythology of the Pagans from the Devil. That was a sufficient answer and it has satisfied the faithful and the simple up till now.

The early Christian apologists gave forth everything of which they were capable, within the boundary of their knowledge, but this was limited to the discoveries of the times. They peered, so far as they were able, into the mysteries of the universe, and tried to search out and discover the infinite. In those days, when the Faith was in its youth, honesty of purpose and deep sincerity were the conspicuous features of the Christian apologists. However mistaken we now realise them to have been, they were sincere and honest of purpose, and earnestly believed that the opinions they expressed were true and in accordance with the divine will.

In our own days they have received much criticism from some who forget the limitations under which they lived. According to the Reverend Dr. Davidson, who is generally acknowledged as an authority, they accepted traditional documents uncritically, and gradually elevated them to the rank of divine documents. Dr. Davidson describes those early enthusiasts as "credulous and blundering, passionate and one-sided". In the greater light in which we now live such criticism could also be levelled at the Pagans of those days who, towards theological questions, were equally credulous, blundering, passionate and one-sided.

Contrast the limited knowledge of those days with that of the present day. We now know something of the origin of man, of the vastness of the universe and the laws of nature. We now know that man is an evolving being, having risen and not fallen, that the ancient idea of a Saviour to redeem mankind from the wrath of the gods was based on a fundamental mistaken idea of the reason for the shortcomings of the race. We now know that knowledge elevates and ignorance degrades the human species, and that the desire of the mythical Adam for greater knowledge was no sin but an attempt to reach a higher state of existence. This urge for something better, the priests, who produced the ancient story, represented as evil.

The backbone of the Christian Faith, that as in Adam all die so in Christ shall all be made alive, has been shattered by our knowledge based on research and facts, and yet we have today in our midst an army of priests, nurtured in this more enlightened age, who preach and teach the theology of an ignorant past. They make a comfortable livelihood from what they receive for spreading and inculcating ideas, which were produced by the ignorance of the first, second, third and fourth centuries of our era, when they well know that every tenet of their religion is flatly contradicted by present-day knowledge.

Through ignoring all psychic knowledge the priesthood has misinterpreted and mutilated the original Christian belief. Moreover, it has used its great influence to discourage any knowledge of the very subject on which the Christian religion is founded. While the Church had the power all with mediumistic gifts were burned. When the people put a stop to this in the eighteenth century, its priests then preached against and persecuted in every possible way these gifted people we now call mediums. Many Christians, who lived in the first four centuries of our era, would have been burned at the stake as wizards and servants of the Devil had they lived during the reign of the Christian Church, from the fifth century onwards.

The Church has thrived on doctrine and dogma, and set its face steadfastly at all times against the psychic source on which it is founded. All its energies have been concentrated on forcing the people to believe its creeds, and perform its rites and ceremonies, manufactured in an age of ignorance. It has used its might and influence to destroy the truth which it should have protected, cultivated and developed. In the third Christian century, theories and speculations, and the lust for power, led its priests off the path prepared for it by the Apostolic Church, and so everything psychic was ignored and theology took its place.

From the third century onwards we are in a different atmosphere from the first and second centuries, when considering the ideas of those Christians whose speculations produced the Christian Faith. The bishops and presbyters had by now become priests and ceased being ministers. Consequently, from now onwards, we find a general ignoring of their Lord's saying, "the works that I do shall he do also; and greater works than these shall he do" (John xiv, 12) and "he that ministereth to you the spirit, and worketh miracles among you, doeth he it by the works of the law" (Gal. iii, 5). Likewise the Church cast aside the advice given by Paul to the Thessalonians, "Quench not the spirit. Despise not prophesyings [mediumship]. Prove all things ; hold fast that which is good" (1 Thess. v, 19). Finally, it ignored the fact that in Apostolic times mediums "began to speak with other tongues, as the spirit gave them utterance" (Acts ii, 4) and "it is the spirit that beareth witness, because the spirit is truth." (1 John v, 6.)

So from now onwards we find theology replacing the belief of the Apostolic Church that the gift of mediumship, which some possess, is the road laid down by nature, or God, as the apostles termed it, over which humanity should travel in order to reach an understanding of our destiny and the great problems of existence. The apostles had found a great truth which they did not know how to handle. To them it was very real, but the theological beliefs in which they had been nurtured prevented them from understanding it in a scientific manner as we do today. So the great psychic discovery was left in the melting-pot, either to be developed in accordance with natural laws, or to be made use of to bolster up an old theology by means of legends, dogmas and doctrines. The Christian Church pursued the latter course, quite losing sight of the psychic stream which had given life to the very Faith it had been established to protect.

And yet one of the greatest champions of the Faith warned the Christians of his day of the danger the Church was running in pursuing its materialistic policy and casting aside the etheric basis out of which it had grown. Tertullian, whose opinions we are now about to consider, showed greater insight into the origin of the faith than any who succeeded him. He, and Origen, to whom I shall refer some pages further on, were the last of the Church fathers to uphold the psychic origin of the religion, and proclaim that the Christian Faith would be distorted and falsified if it did not preserve within its teaching the psychic foundation from which it arose in the first century. If those who followed Tertullian had been less materialistically minded, and less intent on worldly wealth and power, the Christian Church would have obtained its influence and strength from the psychic knowledge obtained from mediumship, instead of through the fear of Hell and the coming judgement.

Ten centuries after the time of Tertullian, Thomas Aquinas visited the Pope of his day and found him counting some money. The Pope remarked to him, "We can no longer say with St. Peter, 'silver and gold have I none'." To this Aquinas replied, "Neither can we say that, 'signs and wonders follow them that believe'." In the time of Tertullian the Church went down the wrong road and, instead of protecting and developing the psychic gifts of the people, the priests sought and achieved worldly power at the expense of natural law. The crime committed in the time of Tertullian, by the Christian priesthood, of usurping the place of the natural medium between the two worlds, is now recoiling more and more on their present-day successors, who are becoming recognised, year by year, as the preachers of false doctrines and the usurpers they really are.

Tertullian is accepted as one of the most eminent advocates of the early Christian Faith. He ranks after Augustine as the greatest of its literary exponents. Though the facts known about his life are limited, yet, from his writings, we know his views and opinions. He was a native of Carthage, born about the year 160, and his father was a centurion. He was born into a Pagan family and he tells us that until his conversion he worshipped as did his family. He took up the profession of an advocate and, in addition to his legal knowledge, he was well acquainted with natural philosophy and the Greek language.

After his conversion to Christianity he became a presbyter of the Church at Carthage and Rome. About middle life he realised that the bishops were departing from the way intended by the apostles, because of their opposition to the use of those psychic gifts, advocated by the Apostle Paul, which, he tells us, had been practised from the time of Jesus till his day. So he joined the Montanists, as their outlook was more in accordance with his own. With his remarkable power of forcible argument, his great enthusiasm and ability, the Montanists found in him a powerful advocate of their views. His writings in support of their beliefs had a great influence throughout the entire Christian community. In his work, *De Anima,* he gives us the following interesting account of the psychic gifts of a medium attached to his church :

For seeing that we acknowledge spiritual charismata, or gifts, we too have merited the attainment of the prophetic gift. We have now amongst us a sister whose lot it has been to be favoured with sundry gifts of revelation, which she experiences in the spirit by ecstatic vision amidst the sacred rites of the

Lord's Day in the church. She converses with the angels, and sometimes even with the Lord; she both sees and hears mysterious communications; some men's hearts she understands, and to them who are in need she distributes remedies. Whether it be in the reading of the Scriptures, or in the chanting of psalms, or in the preaching of sermons, or in the offering up of prayers, in all these religious services, matter and opportunity are afforded her of seeing visions.

It may possibly have happened to us, whilst this sister of ours was wrapt in the spirit, that we had discoursed in some ineffable way about the soul. After the people are dismissed at the conclusion of the sacred services, she is in the regular habit of reporting to us whatever things she may have seen in vision; for all her communications are examined with the most scrupulous care, in order that their truth may be probed. "Amongst other things," says she, "there has been shewn to me a soul in bodily shape, and a spirit has been in the habit of appearing to me; not, however, a void and empty illusion, but such as would offer itself to be even grasped by the hand, soft and transparent and of an ethereal colour, and in form resembling that of a human being in every respect." This was her vision, and for her witness there was God; and the apostle Paul most assuredly foretold that there were to be spiritual gifts in the Church.

Here we have an account of a great medium who was treated by an outstanding early Christian with the respect which was due to her, in such contrast to the way mediums have been treated since the Church organisation became controlled by the priests. This information, which has come down to us from the hand of Tertullian, proves that mediums were employed in Christian churches in the third century, as what he tells us was written in the year 211.

It is also interesting to notice how it also confirms that my argument, as set out in Chapter VI, to the effect that Paul encouraged the use of mediumship in churches, was sound and accurate, as here we find Tertullian quoting from Chapter XII of *The First Epistle to the Corinthians* in justification for mediumship in churches. It is almost unnecessary to mention that in no Christian church today is a medium permitted to exercise his or her psychic gifts before the congregation, and that in consequence the Spiritualists have had to build churches of their own, and engage public halls, so that the people can gain the comfort the early Christians received from charismata, or, as we would put it today, from psychic phenomena through mediumship.

Up to now the language used for communication and writing by all Christian churches had been Greek, and no Christian documents, not even the gospels or epistles, had appeared in Latin. Tertullian was the first to write on Christian topics in Latin, and his various treatises are the earliest specimens we have of Christian literature in this language. His masterpiece, known as *Apologeticus*, is considered the most outstanding of all Christian apologies. In another apology he emphasises the loyalty of Christians to the Emperor, but calls down vengeance on their persecutors because of the blood shed by the saints. As all Christians did in those days, he emphasises how, with the return of Christ, a new Empire would be set up on earth and the Roman Empire be overthrown.

With all the strength of his character he advocated the beliefs held by the Montanists. To marry for a second time, he considered, was nothing less than bigamy, and all who did so should be excluded from the Church. He believed in severe penance and denied the claim of the priests that they had power to remit sin. He condemned military service, doubtless because of the fact that in those days it was so intermixed with the observance of Pagan rites. He was so puritanical that he considered floral decorations sinful and contrary to nature. He writes against public amusements and those Christians who elude their persecutors, as to do so is nothing less than denying Christ. For Christ's sake, he says, Christians should provoke persecution and not try to avoid it.

Tertullian became very bitter against the Christians who did not adopt the Montanist outlook. Besides writing much against his opponents, he also continued his great work of championing the gospel of his Lord, and was for ever thrusting against Paganism and Judaism. He wrote treatises against Marcion, Valentinus, and others holding Gnostic opinions. He also wrote an attack on Praxeas, who had influenced Victor against the Montanists. This work, which he published about 213, is known as *Adversus Praxean*, from which the following is an extract :

For it was Praxeas who first, from Asia, imported this kind of perversity to Roman soil, a restless being in other respects, and puffed up besides with boasting about his martyrdom, which consisted merely in an ordinary brief, if irksome, period in prison ; whereas, even if he had surrendered his body to be burnt up, it would have profited him nothing as he had not the love of God, whose gifts [mediumship] he even violated. For, when the then Bishop of Rome was now recognising the prophesies of Montanus, Prisca and Maximilla, and, as the result of that recognition, was seeking to introduce peace to the churches of Asia and Phrygia, it was he who did, by making false statements about these very prophets and their churches, and by defending the authoritative acts of his predecessors, compel him [Victor], both to recall the letters of peace that had been already dispatched and to give up his project of welcoming their gifts [of mediumship]. So Praxeas managed two pieces of the Devil's business at Rome : he drove out prophecy and brought in heresy, and he put the Comforter to flight. Praxeas' tares have borne fruit here, having been sown above the pure teaching.

Tertullian then goes on to tell how he believes that the harm done to what he considers to be the true faith will some day be repaired. This is what he writes :

As for ourselves [the Montanists], the recognition and defence of the Comforter afterwards separated us from these carnal men (the Catholics). Those tares had, however, at that time everywhere choked the seed. For some time that fact lay hidden through hypocrisy, such was its cunning vitality, and now it has burst forth again. But it will also be again uprooted, if the Lord wills, in this present age. But, if not, at their proper season all the corrupt crops will be gathered together and, along with all other stumbling-blocks, will be burnt by unquenchable fire. But we, both always and now, more than before, as being better instructed by the Comforter, who, of course, leads us into all truth. . . .

From the foregoing it will be seen that Tertullian was a man who could express himself in strong terms. He was bitterly opposed to the Catholic priesthood superseding the medium in the Church, and, because of this, he termed them "carnal men" who had sown tares which were choking the seed of the true revelation. It will be noticed that he expressed the hope that these tares would be uprooted in his own time, but, if not, at their proper season. Little did Tertullian realise the forces he was up against, and that the "carnal men" would use the power they were then getting to batten down mediumship for sixteen hundred years. Only in our own times are the tares they sowed being uprooted and burned by "unquenchable fire", as the result of religious freedom.

Tertullian was the first to formulate the doctrine of the Trinity. He believed that the Godhead consisted of three separate persons and that the holy spirit was the god who came to earth and controlled mediums. Praxeas disagreed with him and, because of that, Tertullian wrote a book in justification of his opinions. It is of no importance to us now what those men thought about the Godhead, but what strikes one when reading these old works is the bitterness of hatred which those Christians shewed towards each other. There was no toleration of any kind and each damned the other.

Thus Church doctrine gradually developed. On the anvil of Christian opinion what became orthodox Christianity was hammered into shape over three centuries. The language of its various exponents was on many cardinal points very dissimilar. Each used contradictory terms and expressions, which were taken exception to by the others, and so the process went on while, all the time, the power of decision as to what was really true, and should be believed, and what was not, was centering more and more with the church at Rome. There, apostolic tradition was slowly being forgotten, and, gradually, Christianity crystallised and took the shape and form of the Pagan ideas with which Christians were surrounded. Slowly the new faith rose into power with ideas similar to those contained in the old religions, the name being all that was new.

Agreement, however, could not be reached as to the relation of Christ to the Godhead. His equality with God was very difficult for Christians to accept, as a very large section of the Christian community looked upon God as the Supreme Being, and Christ and the holy spirit as lower emanations from this being. Others maintained their belief in the unity of God by arguing that the Father, the Son and the Holy Ghost were three different manifestations of the Supreme Being. "From an apparition to the Supreme Being" might well be given as the title to the history of Christian beliefs from the time of Paul to the Council of Nicaea, where the matter was finally settled by Constantine himself.

The amount of unnecessary discussion which prevailed in those days in the attempt to define the Christ is amazing. Much controversy centred on the question as to whether Jesus became the Christ after baptism or at conception. Agreement could not be reached on this point any more than on the question whether he was equal or subordinate to the Supreme Being. Many were the various arguments put forward to solve this mysterious problem, which, after the Council of Nicaea, involved the Church in bloodshed, crime and persecution such as has never been laid to the charge of any other institution before or since.

From the time of Constantine onwards men, women and children suffered and died over these intangible doctrines which were evolved throughout the third century. They were not slaughtered by the Church because of any known crime, such as theft, murder or immorality, but because they could not agree with the priests on these mystical speculations for which there was not an iota of evidence. It does not matter in the slightest degree to us whether Christ is equal to or subordinate to God, or whether the Godhead is composed of one being, three beings or a dozen.   Yet, on this futile question, millions have died and suffered in the attempt made by the Church to force the people in Europe, in the countries surrounding the Mediterranean, and in America, to accept its definition of the Godhead.   There is nothing in history to parallel this record of human folly, cruelty, bigotry and intolerance.

If the Church had, at the beginning of its career, announced itself as an institution founded for the purpose of extinguishing the light of reason from the mind of man, abolishing all learning and holding up its victims to ransom on every possible occasion with the threat of Hell ; if it had announced beforehand that the sword, the stake, the rack and prison were to be its methods for the purpose of making its victims think as it wished them to think, one could say that at least it was honest in carrying out what it said it would do.   Instead of this, however, it hid its crimes under a cloak of a divine revelation, which it claimed had only come to it from God.   It made use of a simple, kind-hearted Galilean, round whom it wrapped its cruel doctrines and dogmas, and the people were given the alternative of either believing them, or perishing by the sword, or at the stake, here on earth, and in Hell for all eternity.

So when we read about all the trifling and futile arguments which went on in the third century we cannot fail to remember the unfortunate results they caused throughout the Christian era.   To the Christians of the third century, however, these questions were intensely real, so much so that men and women sacrificed everything in the attempt to get their opinions heard and believed. Nowhere were these cardinal doctrines more discussed than at Alexandria. There the controversy between philosophy and theology reached its height. There gathered many of the intellectuals of the day, as in those times philosophy was the highest pursuit of an intellectual mind. So Alexandria became the seat of a wordy war between the intellectuals of Paganism and the Christian theologians.

Though the influence of Alexandria was not such as to make the church at Rome accept the Gnostic basis for the Christian structure, still it infused into the new religion the Gnosticism and Paganism championed in its schools and colleges. There Christianity was moulded into a shape attractive to the better educated of those days. There also was situated the first Christian Church school for the teaching of proselytes who were preparing for baptism. This school ultimately developed into a seminary for the training of Christian priests, and for imparting Christian instruction to the better educated converts who had come over to the new faith.

One of the most famous principals of this Christian seminary was Clement, known as Clement of Alexandria, though it is believed that he was born in Athens. What we know of him is mainly derived from his own works. After presiding over this school for some years he had to leave it because of Pagan persecution, but he returned to Alexandria and died there about the year 220. He, and others like him, introduced into the Church a new system of thought, which had for its purpose the appreciation of Pagan philosophy. Christianity, Clement taught, was but the outcome of Pagan religious thought, the final development to which the Pagans had been striving.

He taught that Greek philosophy, as well as the Hebrew law, had laid the foundation for the Christian structure, and all that had gone before had been the gradual unfolding of the divine will, which Christianity now revealed in its final and completed form. He laid some of the stones of Christian doctrine and was the first to bring all the culture of the Greeks to bear on the exposition of Christian beliefs. The "infallible" Catholic Church made him a Saint, but, some centuries later, struck his name off the calendar as by then his opinions were not considered to be orthodox.

All knowledge, Clement argued, had divine approval and should be cultivated, as only through knowledge can one appreciate the difference between good and evil. He put forward his belief that the first information we received on earth of what he calls sacred knowledge (presumably knowledge of the here-after) came from angels communicating it to the daughters of men, who had the capacity to hear them, evidently because they were clairaudient mediums. This is a much more natural idea than the one adopted by Christianity, that all evil came into the world as the result of a woman obtaining knowledge through dis-obedience to the divine will, a priestly story which may have as its origin the fact that women have always had greater psychic power than men.

The Christians, who were influenced by the Alexandrian school, termed themselves Christian Gnostics, in order to separate their teachings from Catholic Christianity, which was unable to interpret

Christianity apart from Judaism. Clement of Alexandria was their chief exponent. They held the opinion that through the acceptance of their beliefs the highest Christian character could be attained. Those who followed the church at Rome thought otherwise and objected to the Gnostic attitude towards Hebrew scripture. The Alexandrian school, following the opinions of Philo, interpreted much in the Hebrew scriptures allegorically, whereas the Roman church looked upon it all as history.

Alexandria, as we have already seen, was the seat of intellectual Christianity (using the word intellectual in the sense it was used at that time), and Rome was the seat of the Christianity known as Catholic, of the Christianity which appealed to the masses. The name Catholic means that which is generally accepted, in other words that which is orthodox. From the intellectuals at Alexandria evolved Neo-platonism, which philosophy was for the purpose of bringing the intellectual Pagans and Christians together, and concentrating on philosophy and less on theology.

Ammonius, its founder, claimed that in this new thought all the philosophy of the ancients was concentrated, and that whereas in the past each nation had in error thought it had the whole, when in fact each had only been blessed with a part, now Neo-platonism would embrace the wisdom of all the sages who had lived on earth. The Neo-platonists accepted certain truths, considered as fundamental, which Christianity had borrowed from Paganism. These they wished to separate from the dross of Christian dogma and doctrine. In other words, they attempted to inaugurate a Pagan-Christian fellowship so as to preserve philosophy and prevent its extinction by both the Pagan and Christian priests.

Instead of Jesus being looked upon as the Saviour and Redeemer, as taught by the Christian priests, he was classed by the Neo-platonists as an outstanding sage and medium, whose object on earth was to reform religion. They claimed that the original teaching of Jesus was in conformity with their own opinions and that, if Christianity could be freed from its Egyptian idea of a Trinity of gods, in which Christ took second place in the Godhead, it could be accepted by intelligent people no matter into what religion they had been born.

The Neo-platonists aimed at uniting the wisdom of all the ages, and all the nations, into one great comprehensive scheme and system of thought. They believed in one supreme God whose trinity consisted of his mind, his spirit and his entire being. They believed in the etheric world, in which lived both good and bad beings, and they threw over polytheism because the beings, called gods, whom its votaries worshipped, were not gods, as there was only one God in the universe. Thus had the intellectuals at last arrived at a true understanding of those etheric beings who had hitherto been regarded as gods.

Neo-platonism, as expressed by its three greatest exponents, Plotinus, Amelius and Porphyry, taught that the aim of all should be to reach at-one-ment with the Divine Being. This urge was not to be confined to earth, but could be continued after death in the etheric world. Such a system of thought had strong attractions for the better balanced of those days, perplexed by the controversies of the Christians and Pagans, and disgusted with one sect of Christians hurling the words heretics and unbelievers against the other sects.

The general quarrelling and acrimonious atmosphere within the Christian ranks kept the thoughtful aloof, but in Neo-platonic philosophy they found peace and food for their minds. Philosophy, however, was no help to the masses, as they needed a god-man to worship, and its mental discipline for the attainment of the highest good was beyond their capacity. In the next chapter we shall learn how the adherents to this philosophy were exterminated by the Christians when Christianity triumphed.

Unfortunately for us all there was no room at that time for this intelligent opinion in the Christian Church, for this mode of thought, which appealed to the wise and prudent. Consequently, when it obtained power in the fourth century, it began to close all the schools, because there was nothing which was worth knowing outside the Christian scriptures. By the sixth century all the schools of philosophy, and all libraries throughout the Empire, were closed, and Simplicius, one of the last of the Neo-platonic philosophers, was driven out of Athens with his followers. With Christianity dominant everywhere around the Mediterranean he had to seek refuge at the Court of the Emperor of Persia, who stated that he considered it an honour to give refuge to a man of such learning and ability.

In philosophy the Christian Faith found the most formidable of its adversaries, because the philosophers were teaching the people to think and to use their reason and intelligence. The policy of the Church was exactly the opposite. The philosophers were few in number, and the Church was composed of the un-intelligent unthinking mob which gave it the power it desired to extinguish all learning and all discussion. As a result it became the Dictator of the western world.

Alexander Severus succeeded his cousin Elagabalus as Emperor and in this reign we again find no persecution of the Christians. Many Christians performed the duties of the Imperial household and the Emperor did nothing in any way to embarrass the Christian community. We are told that when a dispute arose over a piece of land which the victuallers of Rome claimed from the Christians, the Emperor gave his decision in favour of the Christians as he said he would rather see a Temple erected on this ground than a tavern. This tolerant Emperor planned the erection of a temple to Christ and the addition of the Christian god to the Pagan pantheon of gods. We are not told whether this actually materialised or not, but we do know that in his own private temple the image of Christ found a place alongside Isis, Osiris, Orpheus, Abraham and Apollonius of Tyana. To this Emperor, Christ was one of the gods of the past, and, through him and the others, he found his link with the divine.

Under the Emperor who followed, some persecutions broke out against the Christians, as the result of earthquakes in several provinces, but in the reigns of the next two Emperors Christians were unmolested. Origen, about whom we shall hear shortly, tells us that the outlook was so propitious that he foresaw a speedy conversion of the Empire to the Christian Faith. In his day Rome completed the thousandth anniversary of its foundation.

His optimism, however, was premature, as, in the reign of the next Emperor, Decius by name, persecution again broke out, which was welcomed by some Christians in those days because they claimed that the era of peace had degraded the morals of the Church. Origen and Cyprian, outstanding Christians of those days, tell of the pride, the luxury and the covetousness of the Christian priests, and also of the careless irreligious lives of the Christians.

During this persecution many Christians were found wanting, and, out of fear of persecution, or of the confiscation of their goods, we are told that multitudes disowned their faith. The persecution, however, did not last beyond a year as Decius was killed a year after his edict. He was succeeded by the Emperor Gallus, who reigned a short time without interfering with religious worship. Gallus was succeeded by the Emperor Valerian, who, later in his reign, tried, by persecution, to stem the increasing membership of the Christian Faith, but without success. Martyrdom again came to be looked upon as something to be welcomed, and once more the blood of the martyrs proved to be the seed of the Church.

Of the eminent men of this time notice must be taken of Origen and Cyprian. Origen (meaning son of the god Horus) was born into a Christian family at Alexandria about the year 185. Of all the theologians of the ancient Church, with the possible exception of Augustine, he was the most distinguished and influential. In an age noted for its intolerance he stands out as one of the most tolerant and courteous of men, and one always willing to consider the opinions of others. He showed great knowledge and reverence for the scripture. He studied under Clement at Alexandria, and left college with a fervent desire to preach the gospel to those he looked upon as the heathen. When persecution came his way he was eager for martyrdom but was prevented by his mother from giving himself up. Origen displayed great ability in his propaganda, and attracted many Pagans who came to hear him expounding Christian doctrine.

At the age of eighteen he took over the office of public teacher at Alexandria, and was soon afterwards appointed by his bishop to be master of the Church school. There, in his time, speculative thought was rife, and no line was drawn between orthodoxy and heresy. In order to understand the Old Testament better he studied Hebrew, but his studies were interrupted by persecution. So he visited Palestine, where he was received by Alexander, the Bishop of Jerusalem, who had been his fellow-student at Alexandria.

Because of the fact that he, a layman, preached in the churches of Palestine, his own bishop recalled him home to Alexandria and made him return to his duties in the Church school. This is the first indication we have of the change which was taking place in Church usage. The priest was now denying to the layman what had hitherto been his right, namely to preach, pray and dispense the Eucharist in the churches.

With the financial help of a rich friend Origen undertook a vast work, one, in fact, which entitles him to rank as the Father of Biblical Criticism. Much controversy was taking place as to the correct rendering of the true text of the Septuagint, the name of the Hebrew scriptures in Greek. The Septuagint was accepted by Christians, but its authority was weakened by the fact that various versions existed. In order to settle matters in dispute Origen undertook the work of writing out each verse in parallel columns.

In the first column he put the original Hebrew translation, in the second the same in Greek, in the third the version by Aquila, in the fourth the version by Symmachus, in the fifth the Septuagint, as edited from an elaborate collection of manuscripts, and in the last the version of Theodotion. This work is called the Hexapla because of its six columns. His great task lasted over twenty-eight years, and was only completed a short time before his death. Unfortunately this wonderful document perished by fire when, in the year 653, the Caesarean library was destroyed by the Arabs.

The reputation and influence of Origen increased throughout the Christian community of the Empire, and he accepted invitations to Palestine and Arabia. Then he was summoned by the mother of the Emperor to Antioch, where he discussed with her religious subjects. After this, in the year 228, he visited Greece, where he was ordained as a presbyter. Then he returned to Alexandria to discover that the Bishop of Alexandria refused to acknowledge his new status, as some of his opinions did not appeal to that authority. So he left for Caesarea and the bishop took the opportunity of depriving him of his office at the Church school at Alexandria. The bishop informed all the other churches of what he had done, and his dismissal was ratified at Rome and elsewhere, with the exception of Palestine, Phoenicia, Arabia and Achaia. This affair constitutes another example of the conflict of opinion in the early Christian Church.

After residing at Caesarea for about six years, where he taught as an independent philosophical teacher, he was compelled by persecution to take refuge in Cappadocia. When peace again reigned he returned to Caesarea, where he took a prominent part at a Church Council which was held for the purpose of deciding on the nature of the Godhead. The great question to be decided was whether the Godhead consisted of three distinct persons, and whether the Son had a distinct personality before his incarnation. The Council decided that the Godhead consisted of three distinct persons and that the Son had distinct personality before his incarnation. This decision was reached only after much wrangling and discussion, and as the result of Origen's persuasive eloquence. Shortly before his death he was imprisoned and tortured, and this hastened his end, which took place at Tyre about the year 255.

In his various works Origen writes of angels in just the same sense as the controls of mediums are spoken about today. What is today called a control he termed an angel. Some of these angels, he tells us, were responsible for the giving of clairaudience through their human mediums, and for the directing aright of the thoughts of the congregation. Origen believed correctly that some spirits are more developed than others, and he tells us that the signs and wonders of the past were still manifesting in his day.

His great aim in life was to harmonise Christianity with philosophy, by seeking to combine the truths of all systems in one Christian scheme, and thus establish the gospel in such a way as to enable the Jews and Pagans to accept the new faith. The fact that he interpreted the scriptures in a symbolic and mystical manner meant that when the Church became established he was declared a heretic, though few intelligent people would now condemn him for his deep insight. Origen was the first to examine critically what we now call the Old Testament, and his effort resulted in his arriving at the same opinion about this work as the one reached by biblical scholars of our own time. In the year 543, at a Synod held at Constantinople, he was not only branded as a heretic but was cursed by an anathema being attached to his name.

His aim was to interpret a symbolic meaning in all the stories of scriptures, which, he said, were stumbling-blocks if treated in a literal manner. He did not regard Hell as a place but as symbolical of mental suffering for wrongdoing, and he believed that those who found themselves in "outer darkness" in the hereafter were there because of their ignorance and mental indolence. To him the god of the Old Testament was unworthy of worship, which opinion offended the Catholic Church when it became constituted as a State organisation. The minds of the Catholic priests were of a mentality so like that attributed to Jehovah, and his intolerant laws so appealed to their intellects, that the more enlightened mind of this outstanding Christian was an offence to them.

It is a very remarkable fact that many of those whom the Catholic Church created saints were noted for their cruelty and bigotry ; the more bigoted the man was, the greater saint he came to be considered. So we find a man like Origen, who, in his day, was a great light in the Christian world, being passed over, while others, who took a prominent part in the persecution of Pagans, Jews and heretics, were made saints, and none had a more bloody record than Saint Dominic, the founder of the Holy Inquisition.

In concluding our short review of Origen's opinions, it is interesting to record that he believed that the etheric world is very much like this world, and that there we shall find everything more or less a duplicate of what we have here on earth. He was also in favour of mediumship and believed in communication with the departed. Like Tertullian he supported the giving of clairaudience in churches, and believed that it was part of the Church's duty to protect and cultivate this link with the other world.

He also believed that Jesus returned to earth after his death as a spirit, and he looked upon his death on the cross as representing what he termed a spiritual deliverance, not for the purpose of assuaging the wrath of an angry deity. No god, he thought, would punish mankind eternally, but only for correction. Consequently all had a chance to rise and overcome their own wickedness. Even Satan himself, he believed, could be reformed and his evil changed to good.

In Origen's day such opinions were accepted without stir, and it was only in the sixth century that the Church came to look upon him as a heretic. His piety was great, as was his knowledge of scripture, and he suffered so much for the Faith that he might well be termed a Christian martyr. By his teaching and preaching he converted a great multitude of Pagans to the Christian Faith. Though he is today looked upon by the Church as a heretic, and branded with its curse, the misfortune is that the leaders of that institution, throughout the Christian era, have not been more like him in his benevolence and width of thought.

The aim I have had before me in writing this chapter is to trace out the main Christian influences which were at work during the first three Christian centuries. Out of a great diverstiy of beliefs and opinions the Christian Church came into being in the fourth century. In the third century, as in the first and second, men arose to express their views as to what Christ meant to them. To them all he meant very much, in fact everything. Round this heavenly being their lives and thoughts were centred, and yet, when we read their opinions today, they fall very flat, because Christ today does not mean the same as he meant at the beginning of the era. Then his return to earth was awaited, not as a vague belief, but as a certainty, just as much a certainty as we today expect the sun to rise tomorrow morning.

As the centuries passed, and the anticipation did not materialise, this rampart of the Faith rotted with time and is today decaying into dust. So it is difficult for us to become enthusiastic, or indeed, interested, in the discussions relating to Christ which took place in those far-off days. If a Council of Priests were called in our own times to discuss the relationship of the different members of the Trinity to each other, how few people there would be who would be interested in the result of the discussion. The newspapers might find a corner for this news, but that would be about all. The people are not now interested in this question, as they have outgrown it, but in early Christian times it was a matter of intense interest, and many were found willing to sacrifice their lives rather than depart an iota from the opinions they had formed as to the status of Christ in Heaven.

The Christian Faith is a tradition, and those who call themselves Christians today do so because they were born into the Christian atmosphere. They accepted its tradition without giving rational or considered thought to what they were expected to believe. Absorbing a belief in this irrational way, though it gave, and still gives, them comfort, had also the effect, once they had the comfort, of making them very unwilling to study and investigate the origin of their belief. *The Psychic Stream* is not written for such people, but for those who take an intelligent interest in the deeper problems of life, and are wise enough to realise that no religion has a monopoly of truth, as many roads lead to the infinite. It is entirely a question of mental development as to the road each individual chooses to take.

The thinking person, who is interested in the history of man, is naturally interested in the causes which brought into being the various means of attaining greater at-one-ment with the divine in nature. The Christian explanation that Christians only have the true revelation, that all other religions are false, and that those who believe in them are heathen, has no weight whatever with thinking people today, and can be cast aside as worthless. During Christian times the position was far otherwise, and, in the foregoing pages of this chapter, we have had glimpses of some outstanding early Christians who were intense in their zeal to bring the people on to the road which they thought was the only one which led to God.

Cyprian (200–258) was another of these zealots. He became Bishop of Carthage, and worked hard to bring about improved discipline in the Church by means of the centralisation of authority. He was one of the first to put forward what became the strongest weapon of the Church, that there could be no forgiveness of sins or salvation outside its ranks, and that the Christian priesthood had received from Christ the keys of Heaven and Hell. He did as much as anyone to raise the Christian priesthood into the position it now occupies in the Church.

Cyprian took advantage of the progress of Montanism to produce and push forward his ecclesiastical scheme, on which the Church, both Roman and Anglican, is now built. He was the father of the episcopacy. His own church had lost many of its members by their going over to the Montanists, and this fact gave him the urge to popularise the scheme of Church organisation which he saw could fit in well with the existing conditions. He was an opportunist, and, like many a politician, struck when the opportunity was favourable. He was an absolutist and believed in the priesthood being the dictators of the entire Church. By this means only could all sectarianism come to an end. What the Church decreed, as decided by the priesthood, was to be the belief throughout the entire Christian community. So he took the opportunity, when so many were joining up with the Montanists, to advocate that those who remained, conferred on the bishops dictatorial powers as the true successors of the apostles. It is always in times of crisis that dictators make their appearance and abolish all liberty of thought.

Some historians describe the origin of the episcopacy as due to panic on the part of the bishops, who feared that the people would go over entirely to the Montanists, and continue the form of service in vogue since the time of the apostles. It was due to fear that they would lose the grip they had gradually obtained over their congregations during the past century. So the bishops saddled the Church with the present episcopal system which gave them all the power and the people none.

From this time onwards the word Priest, in Christian literature, is used to denote one previously termed a Christian minister, and the bishops are now looked upon as the High Priests of the Church. The bishops became the Church, and the Bench of Bishops elected new bishops to fill the vacancies, as they occurred, without consulting the people. Thus they got the people into their power, and, when the Church became a State institution, they sucked the very life-blood of the community by their tithes and other assessments.

This state of affairs has continued in England up to the present time. Other European countries have adjusted matters to their own satisfaction, but what interests us is what takes place in our own country. In 1936, because of the rising public indignation against this method of supporting the priesthood, an Act was passed abolishing the tithe payment. In place of tithes, fixed annuities became chargeable on land until October, 1996. These annuities are for the purpose of paying for the 3 per cent. Government Stock which has been handed over to the Church of England authorities in exchange for their waiving the right to the tithe rent charge.

The Church has thus capitalised its right to this

tenth of the produce of the land, and has now become the owner of £51,650,000 Government Stock, which makes it one of the richest close corporations in the world. This money, which it has received from the people, is the direct result of its priests preaching Hell in the days of old, and so frightening them into placing a lien on their land. To release the people from this lien the Church has now made this bargain of cash down, and the land-owners, to get out of the net in which their ancestors were caught, have now to pay, until the year 1996, for the Government Stock handed over to the Church. Such is one of the effects which was the outcome of the priests capturing the Apostolic Church in the third Christian century, and introducing Catholic Christianity, for which there was no authority whatever.

What, then, of the future? What is contained in this book is true and truth must prevail in the end. This being so it is not difficult to forecast the time when everyone will be aware of the true position of affairs. Is it to be imagined that the people will then continue to listen to parsons and priests preaching the falsehoods for which they receive their remuneration? Will the people continue to listen to and respect men who openly practise "reservations", which means saying one thing and believing another?

Will the people continue attending the celebration of the Eucharist when they realise that it is a relic of cannibalism? The present drift from Christianity is bound to continue till the churches are empty, but the priests have still their wealth on which they can live, and there will always be dishonest men who, for the sake of a sure income, will say that they believe anything. However, it is for everyone to form his own conclusions as to the future of the priesthood. Here, I am recording how it captured the Christian Church, and Cyprian, as much as anyone, helped to bring this about.

From the time of Cyprian onwards the entire constitution of the Church changed, and the bishops claimed for themselves gifts of inspiration and divine guidance which the Montanists said could only come through mediumship. Thenceforward the bishops claimed the power to rule over the Christian community, not as the chosen representatives of the people, as formerly, but, under the guidance of the Holy Spirit, as the official representatives of the apostles. On this false claim the Christian ecclesiastical organisation was formed and given legal status by Constantine. From that date to this no change has taken place in the matter of Church government, except that sections broke off, at and after the Reformation, and formed sects, some of which had as their governing principle the ministerial system in operation in the Apostolic Church.

The medium, however, was not included by these dissenters in their form of worship, in fact it would have been impossible to have done so, as mediumship, being an hereditary gift, had by then been almost extinguished. Moreover, the ministers of these sects disliked mediumship just as much as the priests of the episcopate, as, without the medium, they held a higher position towards their congregations. Though they called themselves ministers they were little, if any, better than the priests in their outlook and functions.

Twelve hundred years of priestly rule, up to the time of the Reformation, moreover, had so materialised the Christian religion that not one of the reformers knew anything about psychic gifts, or what actually took place in the early Church. Even in our own times very few Roman Catholic or Protestant priests understand their own Church history, or the meaning of Paul's references to mediumship and psychic gifts. Without the psychic key the black army go through their theological colleges unable to open the door to truth. They tramp along their dark and dingy cloisters, year after year, with their eyes shut to the light which others are enjoying outside their institutions. They live like moles and never see the light.

Cyprian was a man of wealth and devoted much of it to the poor. He suffered martyrdom for his Christian beliefs at the age of fifty-eight and his name was later added to the calendar of Christian saints. Novatain, another outstanding Christian of the time, formed a sect of his own which had its own views as to baptism and considered Church discipline to be lax.

Paul of Samosata, Bishop of Antioch, was famous for the theatrical way he conducted his services, and for his lax morality. He formed his own sect, which had its own definition of the Trinity, with which the Catholic section of Christendom could not agree. He is now labelled a heretic, because he believed that Jesus was an ordinary man who had been endowed by God at baptism with a spirit which had guided him through life.

We are told that his income in those days was

what would be equivalent to £1,600 a year, as he combined his clerical duties with those of Magistrate and City Treasurer of Antioch. This was modest, and only the beginning of the large salaries the bishops and the clergy obtained through laying claim to the tenth of the produce of the land. This claim, which they took as their right when the Church became established, was based on the Mosaic Law, but they conveniently forgot that the priesthood had been abolished by the coming of Christ! This method of obtaining revenue has continued right up to our own time, the income of the Bishop of Durham, for example, being £40,000 a year, when, in his diocese, children at the age of five were sent down the coal-mines to work ten to twelve hours a day for six days of the week, their only experience of daylight being on Sunday. Each child received one shilling a week!

Under the Emperor Gallienus the Christian religion was allowed the same status as the other religions in the State, all exiles were allowed to return home and any cemeteries which had been confiscated were restored. Christianity, for the first time in its history, was now considered lawful, though this did not mean that persecution was at an end.

About the year 270 a man by the name of Manes began to publish his opinions in Persia, and became an outstanding leader of religious thought in those parts. He wrote much and produced a system of thought which resembled some of the Gnostic systems, though it had no direct connection with them. He was influenced by neither Jewish tradition nor Greek philosophy, but rather by Zoroastrian and

Buddhist beliefs. Into his system he worked the Christian Christ and much mystical thought. His ideas, which are grouped under the name Manichaeism, became popular, and those who followed him continued as a separate sect, known as Manichaeans, into the middle ages.

We now come to the last Christian persecution, which took place in the reign of the Emperor Diocletian, who assumed the purple in the year 284. He shared his Empire with Maximian, and under these two emperors were Galerius and Constantius, the father of Constantine, who each took the title of Caesar. Diocletian took over the command of the Eastern portion of the Empire and removed his Court from Rome to Nicomedia. The ancient capital of Rome ceased to be the centre of government as Maximian, who took over the Western portion of the Empire, governed from Milan. This rearrangement of the political offices made the Pagan priests fearful that they would lose their status in the Empire. Diocletian was indifferent to religion, while Maximian was hostile to Christianity. Of the two Caesars, Galerius and Constantius, the former was hostile while the latter favoured the Christian religion.

Such, then, was the position as the third century drew to a close. Influenced by Galerius, Diocletian commenced a persecution of the Christians and burned some of their churches and sacred books. An edict was issued to the effect that all who refused to sacrifice would lose their offices, property, rank and civil privileges, and that no Christian slave could hope for liberty. All who disobeyed this were liable to torture and death. The persecution was general throughout the Empire, but in 305 Diocletian and Maximian abdicated and their positions were taken by Constantius and Galerius, who succeeded to the highest dignity of the State. Where Constantius ruled all persecution of Christians ceased, but elsewhere, under Galerius, it continued until 311, when he abandoned his effort to destroy the Christian Faith. Thus ended the last persecution of the Christians by the Pagans, and, from the beginning of the fourth century, Christians were at liberty, like the rest of Roman citizens, to worship as their conscience directed.

It is now three hundred years, or thereabouts, since the child Jesus was born somewhere in Palestine. Had his entry into the world brought about any change of thought which had effected the betterment of humanity ? If Jesus had not been born would the world, three hundred years after his birth, have been worse than it was ? Did his birth bring into vogue new elevating ideas and increase the comfort and happiness of humanity ? So far as the historian can see it did nothing to raise mankind socially, mentally or morally, or to increase his happiness. All one can find is the fact that a small proportion of the population of the Roman Empire had changed over to the worship of a new god, but, when they did so, they were no better than their Pagan neighbours, and their descendants were certainly a great deal worse.

At the end of the third century we find that the people are much the same as they were at the beginning of the first century. Socially, ethically and intellectually the Christians remained much the same as the Pagans. Because some called the saviour-god they worshipped Christ instead of Mithra, or Osiris, and the Father god Jehovah instead of Jupiter, did not make them better or kinder, or of nobler or higher character. Because of the change they received no greater comfort or happiness. They were as ignorant as formerly about the causes which brought to them happiness or misery, and they knew no more about the power that shapes the universe than did their Pagan neighbours.

If we compare this period with the three hundred years from the time of the reign of Queen Elizabeth to our own times, we shall find an extraordinary difference. Over the last three centuries the people have advanced socially, mentally and morally. There is now less pain and suffering and much greater happiness, and this can be traced to the fact that in the sixteenth century a few men began to think and explain nature's laws apart from the gods. Man began to use his reason, to think rationally, to wonder and to doubt.

When he began to commit the sin attributed to Adam and Eve he commenced to progress, and from that time onwards knowledge has taken the place of faith. This conquest by reason over faith was not lightly won, as the Christian Church used its great power to try to bring about its defeat. For three hundred years prison, torture, banishment and death were the lot of those who strayed from the orthodox path, and only slowly were the powers of darkness destroyed by the torch of knowledge.

In the first three Christian centuries there is no progress to report, only reaction, which consisted of the Christian Church slowly forcing men's minds into its own narrow groove, and thus extinguishing the light of reason. Thenceforward, till the age of science, the torch of knowledge was extinguished and mankind groped through life, existing on creeds, doctrines and dogmas. Christianity added nothing new to the world's ethical or religious thought. It added nothing new to man's knowledge of his place in the universe, and so we are not surprised, when we study the form of Christian worship at the end of the third century, to find how, in practically every feature, it corresponded with what took place in the Greek Church just prior to the opening of the Christian era, as described in Chapter IV.

The Christian Church was now an organised body under the direction of the church at Rome. Catholic Christianity was accepted by the majority of the Christian churches, but there were still various sects and considerable heresy. Upon most subjects, however, there was unanimity, but upon the greatest subject of all, the relationship of Christ to God, there was still a great difference of opinion, and in the next chapter we shall find how this was finally settled.

The Church had borrowed most of its ceremonies from Mithraism and the decorations of its buildings from Greece. Even the important ceremony of baptism had also become Paganised, and, instead of adults being baptised, this took place during infancy. Irenaeus tells us that this innovation had started in his time. The priests had by now adopted celibacy and the tonsure from Buddhism, as they did monastic life. Christmas, the birthday of Mithra, was now celebrated as the birthday of Jesus, as was Easter, the resurrection day of the saviour-gods of the past, to commemorate his reappearance. The Pagan Eucharist continued to be associated with Christ. From Paganism the Church copied its sacred vessels which, because of its wealth, were now fashioned in gold and silver.

At the Church services the congregation stood in prayer. Sunday, the Lord's Day of the Mithraists, was reserved for worship, and all business was suspended, but the Jewish taboos, relating to the Sabbath, were not now observed except by recent Jewish converts who regarded Sunday as they had done the Sabbath. With the elimination of mediumship from the Church service the sermon took the place of the clairvoyance, the clairaudience, or the trance address. Singing consisted of Old Testament psalms, and hymns based on Christian themes.

Gradually, as the years passed, pictures and images of Pagan origin were added to the churches and, as the wealth of the Christian community increased, the buildings became larger and more ornate with a degree of architectural splendour. Pictures appeared on the walls, such as a shepherd carrying a lamb. The image of a dove symbolised the Holy Ghost. A model ship represented the Church, it being the ark of salvation. A lyre and an anchor symbolised joy and hope. Christians borrowed from the Pagans pictures of Dionysus, as representing the true vine, and of the phoenix rising out of its ashes.

Likewise there were pictures of Orpheus, Apollo and Mercury, which were named "The Saviour". Images of Isis, with Horus in her arms, were labelled "The Virgin and Child", while those of the Pagan gods had their old names removed and, in their place, the name of Jesus Christ was inserted. The entire Pagan form of worship was adopted, as were the rites and ceremonies, and all the paraphernalia of the priests, including censers, incense and holy water. Even today in Saint Peter's at Rome there is an ancient statue of Jupiter, which is labelled "Saint Peter". It is the toe of the right foot of this statue that the faithful have now nearly kissed away.

Persecution brought out all that was best in the early Christian community. A persecuted minority is always clannish and shows comradeship to brothers in affliction. With the end of persecution, and as the wealth and position of the Church increased, so likewise did its uncharitableness and the worldly ambition of its priests. The love for one another, of which Christians boasted when they were weak and had many enemies, gave place to wrangling and hate. The quarrelling amongst the priests, which so angered Constantine, now made itself felt more and more, until it ended in a crescendo in his reign, and was the cause of his calling them together at Nicaea. This interesting piece of Church history we shall consider in the next chapter.

This chapter has carried the reader through the religion's youthful development. What extraordinary changes have taken place since Peter, and the other disciples, met together in the Temple at Jerusalem, as Jews, after the reappearance of Jesus, and then broke bread from house to house in memory of the master. (Acts ii, 46.) If these simple-minded Jews could have been transported forward three hundred years to find a semi-Pagan Roman Emperor sitting surrounded by three hundred Christian bishops at Nicaea, who were being forced by him to decide what they were to believe about the one the disciples had so dearly loved, could they in any way have associated this scene with their own ideas of Jesus, and what his life and death meant to them? Could Peter find anything in common with the church now called after him in Rome? Time works wonders, and the human mind produces many illogical things, but nothing more irrational, and unlike the teachings of the one it claims as its founder, has it ever produced than the Christian Faith.

We are now nearing the end of the story. We have worked back and discovered this religion's ancestors, relations and parents. We have made ourselves acquainted with its conception, birth, infancy, childhood and youth. There is only one more step to take, and that is to consider its manhood, when its beliefs became fixed and rigid, such as they have remained from the fourth century onwards. This subject we shall now take up in the chapter which follows.

CHAPTER X

CHRISTIANITY, ITS MANHOOD

CHRISTIANITY reached its manhood in the reign of Constantine, who was Roman Emperor from 313 to 337. It came of age at the Council of Nicaea. This Council might be termed its twenty-first birthday party, and Constantine honoured it with his presence. After the Council had completed its labours the Christian religion entered on its manhood. The last chapter considered the chief events relating to its growth throughout the first three centuries of the era the new religion had inaugurated. This chapter will be devoted to what took place throughout

THE FOURTH CENTURY.

It will be remembered that the father of Constantine, Constantius, was favourably disposed towards the Christians, and this policy Constantine also adopted, in fact he extended the toleration shown by his father. He, however, continued sacrificing to the gods and openly worshipped Apollo. Some historians say that this worship of Apollo continued to the end of his days.

Constantine's attitude towards all forms of religion was toleration. Whatever his other faults may have been he was no bigot, and seemed to be genuinely interested at all times in discussing theology and religion with those of similar tastes. By his various edicts the Christian religion was given the same status as the other religions of the Empire. He showed his liking for Christianity by giving large donations to different Christian communities, and also for the building of churches. He liked having Christian bishops as his companions and often they were his guests at the Imperial Palace. In the various disputes the bishops had with one another, Constantine adopted a moderate policy and tried to settle all differences amicably.

By an edict he withdrew the ban on the Church receiving legacies, which had a very important effect on its accumulation of wealth, as there could now be no dispute on the question of money which had been left to it by the faithful. Here was the beginning of the enormous possessions the Church has gathered together from that date to this. Constantine recalled all Christian exiles, and decreed that those who had been deprived of public employment, because they professed the Christian Faith, were to be reinstated. Any property left by martyrs was to be restored to their relatives, and, if the heirs could not be found, it was then to be given to the Church.

In the earlier part of his reign he had to fight rivals for the throne. These he conquered. He believed that his good fortune in war was due to his having befriended the Christians, which belief his friends the bishops were not backward in keeping constantly before him. In fact they were so successful in working on his superstitious nature that he issued an edict advising his subjects to adopt the Christian Faith. He himself did not submit to Christian baptism till on his deathbed, and throughout his life he retained the office of Pontifex Maximus, the highest in the Pagan hierarchy. The deferring of baptism until one's deathbed was very common with the early Christians, as they believed that baptism cleared them of all past sins. So the nearer death it was administered the safer they were. After infant baptism took the place of adult baptism the partaking of the Eucharist was believed to have the same effect.

Constantine took part in Pagan ceremonies, and continued to worship Apollo in the belief that Christ and Apollo stood for the same idea. On his coins he had engraved the figure of Apollo and the name of Christ. He seems to have had a special attachment to the once persecuted Faith, as he endeavoured to increase the number of converts by giving good positions and honours to all the upper-class Pagans who adopted the new religion. The poor were bribed to become Christians by liberal donations, all of which, as Eusebius says, produced an enormous amount of hypocrisy. Then he planned for sufficient churches to be built to accommodate the entire population, though, as Gibbon says, only one in twenty were Christians. He did not interfere with the Pagans worshipping as of old, but he discontinued all state-sacrificing to the gods.

Such, then, was the attitude of this semi-Christian, semi-Pagan towards the religious opinions of his subjects. In politics he was equally revolutionary, as he decided that Byzantium was in future to be the capital of the Empire. At great speed he built the new city to which he gave the name of Constantinople. Here again we find him favouring Christianity on the one hand, and Paganism on the other, by erecting numerous Christian churches, and lining the streets and squares with statues of the gods and famous men, taken from the temples and cities of Greece and Asia. Sacred Pagan relics and art adorned the Imperial Palace alongside a picture of the crucifixion of Jesus. He evidently looked upon the cross as a lucky mascot, in fact Eusebius gives as the reason for Constantine becoming a Christian that he saw a cross in the sky before a battle in which he was victorious.

No gladiatorial performances were allowed in the new city, the reason being that they did not appeal to the people of those parts. In Rome they still continued. Constantinople was the first city to have only Christian churches, as no Pagan temples were allowed. It was dedicated in 330 to the Virgin Mary and its inauguration was conducted exclusively by Christian priests. Here we find the result of the Council of Nicaea, as after it was held Christianity became the State religion of the Empire. Constantine kept his promise to the Christian priests to the effect that if they produced and agreed upon a creed he would recognise their religion. How this all came about will be told a few pages further on.

On the subject of the doctrines and beliefs of the Christian Faith he was very ignorant, and yet he seemed at times anxious to learn more, for he attended church services and listened to bishops preaching sermons. He even delivered religious discourses himself, in which he emphasised how he had been blessed through protecting the Christians, while his rivals, who had not, had been defeated by him. He seems to have been endowed with a very simple mind in religious matters and, if he had not been an emperor, he might easily have been a Pagan or a Christian priest. He caused himself to be represented on medals, coins and statues in the attitude of prayer. He kept vigils and read the scriptures.

On the other hand, he lived a grossly immoral life and was a murderer, as he killed his wife, his son and nephew. Besides this he was a sadist. The Pagans said he became a Christian after the Pagan Church denied him the Eucharist because of these murders, whereas the Christian bishops accepted him into their Church and absolved him from his crimes. Zosimus, the Greek historian of the fifth century, tells us in his history of the Roman Emperors that Constantine built the new city of Constantinople because he was so despised by the people of Rome for his wickedness. Only twice did he visit the capital, and on both occasions he received a very hostile welcome.

The seeming duality of his nature is quite in keeping with what we know of others in religious history, as one may be devoutly religious and at the same time quite immoral. Morality or ethics and religion must never be confused. Religion is the outcome of man's psychic construction, whereas morality and ethics are conditioned by how unselfish he is, how much he is prepared to put himself last and others first. The only wickedness is selfishness. The one who can live an unselfish life, without allowing the selfish to impose on his unselfishness, has the truly balanced character, and the one best fitted to produce the perfect life. Do to others as we would that they do to us has often been emphasised by the sages since the time of Confucius, and constitutes the best rule of life in the fewest possible words.

Religion can be used for selfish and unselfish purposes, according to the wisdom or zeal of the individual. The one who is constantly performing religious exercises is selfish, as they give satisfaction to the individual only. Prayer is selfish if it is centred on oneself, and unselfish if it is for others. Many of the persecutors of old believed so intensely that those who did not believe as they did, were destined for Hell, and were acting against their god, that they used every argument and fiendish instrument they could imagine to change the opinions of those they looked upon as unbelievers, so as to bring about their salvation.

"Do not I hate them, O Lord, that hate thee? I hate them with perfect hatred. I count them as mine enemies" (Psalm cxxxix, 21), say Christians on Sundays, as they drone through the Psalms, and, from what history recalls, this may be taken as the slogan of the Faith. Both Protestants and Catholics have certainly lived up to it throughout the Christian era. The Christian persecutors had ever before them the words attributed to their Saviour, "It is better for thee to enter into life halt and maimed, rather than having two hands or two feet to be cast into everlasting fire." (Matt. xviii, 8.) The missionary who changed comfort for discomfort is an outstanding example of unselfishness. By persuasion, and not by force, he tries to bring over to his opinion those who do not think as he does. So religion has nothing to do with morality, and Constantine is just one of many examples which proves that this is so.

It seems doubtful whether Helena, the mother of Constantine, was responsible for his Christian leanings, or whether he converted her to the Faith. In her later life she certainly devoted herself wholeheartedly to its propagation. In 326 she visited Palestine for the purpose of discovering those places which to Christians had become holy and sacred. The temple of Jupiter, built by Hadrian, was demolished by Constantine, and, as Eusebius naively remarks, his lavishness in supplying his mother with ample money soon enabled the people on the spot to discover the exact places where the Lord had been born, crucified and buried. Even the place from which the ascension occurred was located. On each of these a church was built. Equally astonishing is the information that the three crosses were found and also the superscription which was placed on the Saviour's cross.

Having learned something of the man who established the Christian Faith as the state religion of the Roman Empire, let us now consider the cause which made him take a decision that history proves to have been one of the most momentous ever made by man. It so happened that in the year 312 one called Arius, who was to become famous in the years which followed, aspired to become Bishop of Alexandria. A man by name of Alexander was, however, elected, and with these two men starts the story of the reason why one third of the people of the world are today known as Christians.

Arius, a presbyter of Alexandria, denied the Saviour's godhead, and argued that he could not be equal with God as he was the only begotten son. A son could not be equal to his father and could not be co-eternal with the father, as a time must have been when he was not. Otherwise the son could not have been begotten. This could mean only one thing, namely, that the son came into existence after his father. Arius took the occasion, when Alexander was discoursing on the unity of the Holy Trinity, to question him on these points. This greatly perturbed the Catholic bishop, as sides were taken for and against the unity of the Trinity, which is what generally happens on such occasions. Alexander made this the reason for calling a conference so that both sides could express their opinions. He presided and decided against Arius. From that time onwards, and for many years, this seemingly unimportant question was the burning topic of the Church.

Arius, who is described as one who lived a strict life and was of agreeable manner, found many sympathisers and, as he was a determined man, he made certain that his side was kept well to the fore. He said, in fact, that the Christian Church must now decide this question once and for all, as three hundred years was quite long enough to leave it unsettled. He was, however, forced to leave Alexandria, though he knew that he had behind him two bishops, twelve presbyters and many deacons. He took refuge in Palestine, where Eusebius, the historian, who was Bishop of Caesarea, tried to settle the quarrel by mediation. Alexander, on the other hand, sent out notices to all Christian churches warning them of Arius and his hateful opinions. As a counter move, the Bishop of Nicomedia, a friend of Arius, called together a synod of priests at Bithynia, who passed a resolution that Arius was quite orthodox in his beliefs.

Constantine was much worried by the dispute, as it threatened the very existence of the Church he had so befriended, and it rendered impossible an idea which he had formed of making Christianity the faith of the Empire. He had, moreover, to withstand the jeers of the great majority of his subjects, who were delighted at the turn of events. The Pagan priests compared the unity of belief prevailing in the ranks of their followers with the dissension and wrangling which was for ever occurring amongst the Christians. Constantine was in a quandary, as he saw that he must either stop this quarrelling amongst his friends, once and for all, or throw them over and return to the gods of his people.

His first move showed his wisdom and moderation, as he wrote a joint letter to Alexander and Arius, in which he expressed his opinion that the belief in Providence was the one essential Christian belief, and that to continue quarrelling over imaginary differences was greatly damaging the prestige of the religion. Work for peace and concord, he continued, not for strife, and settle your differences in the dignified way adopted by the Pagans.

This letter was carried by the Bishop of Cordova to Alexandria, where a synod was called. Arius, however, would not give way. Constantine was now seriously alarmed, as he and the Christians were being openly ridiculed in the theatres, and his statues were being treated with abuse and contempt. So he called together a general council of the entire Church, and fixed the meeting-place at Nicaea in Bithynia. The first meeting took place in June 325, a date that was to fix the turning-point of the history of the western world. For the first time in its history the Christian system of belief was dominated by a man who had the power to compel obedience. No Senate questioned his power, as he was the supreme autocrat of the far-flung Roman Empire.

At this stage in our study it would be wise to pause and consider what all this means. We have arrived at the stage in history when a decision was about to be taken on a subject which had exercised the thoughts of mystics and theologians for thousands of years. Every saviour-god religion had its trinity of gods, of which the Saviour was one, and the question arises as to why this was so and how the idea came into Christianity. Though Constantine, and his priests, were as ignorant of the reason as are the theologians and priests of the present day, the origin of the Trinity can easily be understood by those with psychic knowledge.

To find the origin of the belief one has to go back to the time when man discovered that he himself was a triune being with a body, spirit and mind within the one organism, three separate entities in one. When the ancients imagined the Supreme Being they pictured him in their minds as a man like themselves (Gen. i, 26), a superman more powerful than they were. He was given the same attributes as man on earth, and so they imagined him as having a body, spirit and mind.

We remember how the saviour-god idea began by one who was a sacrificial victim returning to earth to be seen as an apparition, thus proving that a new era had started in the relationship between the gods and man. From that time onwards it is easy to follow the mental steps which were taken by our ancestors in their conception of the deity. Each saviour-god religion developed the belief in one Supreme Being, who had three parts or aspects, and these three parts were intimately connected with the beliefs surrounding the saviour-god. The Supreme Being was looked upon as the Father God. He corresponded to man himself and, like man, he was able to separate his parts, as a medium can do in trance. He was able to send his spirit and mind to earth and these two emanations were treated as divine beings. Thus the deity was imagined as having the same qualities as the medium, who was considered a god-man. The medium formed the basis for man's conception of a triune god.

So we have the Father God remaining in heaven, an inscrutable being, who revealed himself to mankind by means of his mind, or Logos, which came to earth and manifested in a body of flesh. When the Logos returned to heaven, the Father God kept in touch with humanity by sending forth his spirit, who was none other than the spirit control of a medium. It was all just mystical symbolism based on theories derived from mediumship and psychic phenomena.

Such, then, were the speculations indulged in by the ancients on the subject of the relationship between the Saviour and the Father God, and the Holy Spirit and the Father God. In the course of theological evolution Jehovah became the first person in the Christian Trinity. By the Christians he was looked upon as the Father God, from whom emanated the Saviour, but when we go back to discover the origin of Jehovah we are met with a very interesting problem.

In a previous chapter reference was made to the fact that the word which has been translated "The Lord" in the Old Testament meant something quite different in the original Hebrew. In every case the word "Elohim", meaning the gods, has been translated as God, or The Lord, and the word "Yhvh", which is pronounced Jahwé, has been translated as The Lord. The name Yhvh, translated as Jehovah, occurs only four times in the Bible, whereas "The Lord" occurs 6,855 times.

Anyone who cares to read carefully what is told in the books attributed to Moses, about the relationship which existed between Moses and Jehovah, will have no difficulty in discovering that Jehovah was the spirit control of Moses. Quite possibly Jehovah was an Egyptian priest when on earth, but this is not disclosed, and all that he tells Moses is that his name his Yhvh, which can be interpreted to mean "Rain Cloud", or "What causes rain to fall". That, at least, is what is meant in the original Aramaic. In our own times many people have heard and read of "Red Cloud", the famous spirit control of Estelle Roberts, the best known medium of this generation.

Today we have the same experience of some controls giving only nature names, and this we find has been done down the ages. It seems to be an old traditional custom, which these etheric beings still maintain, and it is very interesting to find that it continues in our own time. So the Rain Cloud, or Yhvh, circle, with Moses as the medium, whose séance room became the Holy of Holies, evidently experienced just what happens today, the only difference being that Red Cloud, the control of

Estelle Roberts, is a more enlightened individual than was Rain Cloud.

This, however, does not surprise us, as mental development occurs in the etheric world just as it does here. Doubtless Rain Cloud is now a highly cultured Etherian, and would strongly dissociate himself from much in the Old Testament which both Christians and Jews attribute to him. He can always excuse himself by claiming that he suffered from the limitations he experienced during his earth life, or by pleading that his hearers did not follow out what he told them, and that they attributed to him words he never used.

Like the names of other spirit controls of the past, the name of Yhvh became so sacred that it was mentioned only by a High Priest in the Holy of Holies of the Temple, and the people, when speaking of Yhvh, referred to him as Adonai, meaning The Lord. Knowing the reverence and respect which some Spiritualists in our own times have for the controls of our leading mediums, we can understand how holy and reverent became the name Yhvh to the Hebrews.

Jesus, probably also a medium like Moses, became the Christ because of his reappearance after death. It was believed that on earth he was endowed with the Logos, or mind, of Jehovah, and also the Holy Spirit, both emanations of Jehovah. Logos is the Greek for reason. Christ was looked upon as a heavenly being, and, in time, rose to a status to enable the people to imagine him as an emanation from the Father God. This idea, which associated Christ with the Logos and the Holy Spirit, came into Christianity from Gnosticism.

After Jesus had died and reappeared, to become

the Christ, mediumship continued as it did in his time and before. The people, however, considered that those beings who had heretofore been termed holy or divine spirits, and who controlled the medium, were sent by Christ to comfort and console them during his temporary absence until he returned. As these beings were looked upon as an emanation from the Father God, they were grouped under the single name of Holy Spirit. Thus we discover that the Godhead is symbolic of man himself, having body, mind and spirit. Man imagined the Supreme Being as a trinity of gods who was one God from one aspect, and three from another aspect, a triune being in the heavens in the likeness of himself.

With the foregoing in mind the difficulty with regard to the Trinity disappears. We now know what it grew into at the time of the Council of Nicaea, but very few, if any, realised then, or realise now, that the Christian Trinity in its origin is composed of a multitude of etheric beings. We have, to begin with, Yhvh, the spirit control of Moses, then comes Christ, which is just another name for Jesus as an etheric being, and lastly we have the Holy Spirit, which is a corporate name for all the spirits who control mediums on earth.

Thus the Christian Trinity is made up of a pantheon of gods, or spirits, and it is quite a misnomer for Christians to call themselves Monotheists. The Christian Godhead contains as many gods, or spirits, as is to be found in the Pagan pantheon, whose gods were just the same as the Christian gods, namely, the spirits of those called dead. These spirits, coming back, and making their presence felt on earth, have been the cause of all theology, all mysticism and all religion. They have brought every religion into being, and Christianity is no exception.

To Jesus is attributed the remark, "No man hath seen God at any time" (John i, 18), and yet we are told of Moses talking to the Lord "face to face as a man speaketh unto his friend". (Ex. xxxiii, 11.) Here the words God and The Lord are used for two entirely different ideas. To Jesus was attributed a reference to the creator of the heavens and the earth, whereas Moses, on the occasion referred to, evidently saw and spoke to his spirit control Rain Cloud, which is not an uncommon experience for mediums to have.

Again we must remind ourselves that all the dogma which, over the previous three centuries, had come to surround Jesus was in the first instance caused by his reappearance after death. Bit by bit, from this psychic basis, the theologians raised him to be equal with the Father God, but, though they could make this claim, there was always the difficulty of getting others to believe or understand the mystery. In the other religions, which expressed the belief in a Trinity, it was accepted as a mystical expression which, though quite undefinable, represented a vital truth.

Just as the Christians transformed into historical episodes the legends which grew out of the psychic deeds attributed to Jesus, and materialised his resurrection, so they tried to materialise and define the Christian Godhead. They tried to show mathematically how one could be three and three one and, as they had nothing tangible on which to base their opinion, it was only natural that everyone would regard such a speculation from different points of view.

The Christians forgot entirely the psychic origin

of the Trinity. The idea had been handed down for thousands of years and it is quite probable that nobody knew its origin when it was being associated with Christianity. All they did know was that a Trinity of gods accompanied the belief in a saviour-god, and, as they took everything else relating to Christ from the beliefs surrounding the Pagan saviour gods, it was only natural that they would also take the belief in the Trinity, without in the least understanding its meaning. Up to the time of the Council of Nicaea, Christian theologians had been fitting Jehovah, Christ and the Holy Spirit into this old idea, but without reaching general agreement, and even then Constantine was only able to obtain a partial agreement on the subject.

The foregoing explains the reason for the quarrelling, and all the disputes which have always surrounded the belief in the Christian Trinity. They were the result of complete ignorance of the cause behind psychic phenomena, namely, that they are produced by beings who once lived on earth. Christian theologians adopted from Paganism a mystical idea based on psychic phenomena and man's physical and psychic structure. However, they knew so little about its origin that when they attempted to define it they found themselves in a sea of trouble. They tried to define something without having the necessary preliminary knowledge, and, without this basis, it was impossible to reach unanimity. To the theologians this agreement was a vital matter, as salvation depended on the Trinity being correctly and truly defined by everyone.

This, then, was the problem Constantine set

himself to solve with the aid of a multitude of priests, who were all quite ignorant of the meaning behind the dogma which the Christian Gnostics brought into Christianity. It had come down to the latter from the speculations of the pre-Christian Gnostics who became Christians by adapting their Gnostic beliefs to embrace Jesus as the Christ. So Paul, by transforming Jesus into the Christ, enabled the Gnostics to relate him to their Logos, and also to the medium's spirit control, whom they called the holy spirit.

Thus was laid the foundation of the Christian Trinity, but the trouble developed when Christians could not agree as to whether their three gods were all equal, or whether one was older and of higher status than the one to whom they allotted second place.

The whole affair seems very silly to those who think, but when people are stupid and ignorant they can only express themselves foolishly. What, however, we should remember is the reality behind all this mystical symbolism, the immaterial world of beings the ancients believed in so keenly, and yet could not quite understand or properly express. With these reflections in our minds we can now continue our history with a better understanding of the problem, and why it was that it caused so much quarrelling and bitterness.

Athanasius, made famous for a creed he never produced, tells us that there were present at Nicaea three hundred and eighteen bishops, and that these were accompanied by many of the minor clergy and some Pagan philosophers. Why the latter should have been present at a gathering which one writer of those times says "was not one which required any high intellectual qualifications" is difficult to understand, unless it was from natural curiosity.

The first Council was held before Constantine arrived, and was presided over by the Bishop of Cordova and others in turn. On this occasion Arius received the support of thirteen, seventeen and twenty-two bishops, according to three different accounts of the proceedings. No agreement could be reached and it was distinguished by the usual bitterness and bad feeling. It would have ended as it began, without agreement, but for the fact that within a fortnight of its opening Constantine arrived. The proceedings were then transferred to the Imperial Palace, and from that time onwards Constantine presided. He told the bishops that it was now or never, and that they must decide once and for all what Christianity was to stand for in the years to come.

On his arrival at Nicaea, which is situated forty-four miles from Constantinople on the other side of the Bosporus, he was welcomed by all the bishops and presbyters. Eusebius was responsible for an address of welcome which, as we might expect from one who was more a courtier than a bishop, became an extravagant panegyrical oration. Constantine then received a large deputation of bishops, who asked him to hear their individual opinions and grievances.

He commanded them to submit these in writing, and, when all were ready, he appointed a day for them to be considered. When the day arrived he took his seat on the Imperial throne and received the pleadings one by one, placing them on a table before him. After the last was received he rose and told his supplicants that "lest the contentions of the priests should become known to any one" he had decided to burn all the documents before him without reading them, and that their quarrels were nothing less than scandalous. He then announced that the Council would proceed with the business for which it was called and that a decision must be reached.

When business started Eusebius, who beforehand had been in close conference with the Emperor, sat on his right hand and continued to do so at each meeting which followed. The proceedings opened by Eusebius producing a creed which he stated contained the substance of what he had always been told was the Christian Faith. This was accepted by the followers of Arius but, just because of this, their opponents refused to do so. Then Alexander, the Bishop of Alexandria, put forward his creed, which Arius and his followers refused to accept.

A struggle then took place in which documents were torn to pieces and blows were delivered. The uproar was often so great at times that the assembly was a veritable pandemonium. In the end, by the inclusion of the Greek work *Homoousion*, which means "of the same substance", the majority adopted a creed similar to the one produced by Eusebius, but the Arians refused to accept it and protested vehemently. Constantine expressed his approval, as all he cared about was peace amongst those to whom he had given his patronage.

The Bishop of Cordova then rose and announced that the creed of Christianity had now been finally defined and accepted by a majority of the bishops of the Church. It read as follows :

We believe in one God, the Father Almighty, maker of all things, both visible and invisible; and in one Lord, Jesus Christ, the son of God, begotten of the Father, only begotten, that is to say, of the substance of the Father, God of God and Light of Light, Very God of Very God, begotten, not made, being of one substance with the Father, by whom all things were made, both things in Heaven and things on Earth; who, for us men and for our salvation, came down and was made flesh, made man, suffered and rose again on the third day, went up into the heavens, and is to come again to judge the quick and the dead; and in the Holy Ghost.

The foregoing, it will be noticed, differs from the Nicene Creed as we now know it. The creed which is now the official belief of Christianity is longer, and contains more beliefs than is contained in the one decided on at Nicaea, as given above. This question will be considered some pages further on, as some more water had to flow under the Christian bridge before an extended creed was deemed necessary.

At Nicaea the Christian belief was at long last defined and put into words. New words were employed for old theological ideas which for centuries had been used in Pagan theology. Christians now knew for what their faith stood in the opinion of the Emperor and the great majority of the bishops; Catholic Christianity was now formulated, though not definitely established. Its establishment came about at the end of the century when the Emperor Theodosius decreed the banishment or death of all who thought differently from Catholic authority.

The definition of the faith, arrived at at Nicaea, had, however, the effect of binding most of the Christian churches together into one common belief, and thus greatly strengthened the position of the

Catholic Church. As Dorner says, on the subject of the Christian theological position of that time, in his *History of the Person of Christ*, "It was clear that the Church had arrived at a point at which it could not stand still, but must choose one or other of two courses, either to take a step in advance and define the indefinite, or to go backwards into heathenism or into Judaism."

Christianity, after being in existence for three hundred years, had at last discovered who Jesus was, how he was related to the Father God, why he had come to earth, and that the Holy Ghost, undefined, was the third person in the Godhead. To make a comparison which can be better understood, let us suppose that Jesus had been crucified in 1625, the year Charles I ascended to the British Throne, and that only now, after some three hundred years have elapsed, are we made acquainted by the priests, under the compulsion of a dictator, of the theological explanation as to who he was and why he had come to earth.

Not a single priest present at the Council of Nicaea remembered to quote the words attributed to Peter, "Jesus of Nazareth, a man approved of God among you by miracles and wonders and signs, which God did by him in the midst of you as ye yourselves also know." (Acts ii, 22.) Such an omission was the result of three hundred years of theological speculation. The theologians had obliterated the human Jesus and replaced him by the theological Christ.

The introduction of the Holy Ghost at the end of the creed, as if this god had only been remembered at the last minute, enabled the Church to claim the same divine guidance as did the medium. By now Theology had replaced Spiritualism in the Church, and the priest had replaced the medium. The Church had thrown aside the instrument provided by nature for making contact with the etheric world and had calmly and coolly taken its place. It displaced nature from her own handiwork and stepped into the vacant place.

With much trumpeting and bragging, its priests told the people that God had appointed the Christian Church, and it only, to reveal his will to mankind, and had nominated the Holy Spirit to act as its guide and control. No more impudent fraud has ever been perpetrated ; nothing in history can be discovered to equal this impertinence, this throwing aside of the natural medium and substituting in his place a body of ignorant priests.

Christian theology, just as was Pagan theology, is founded on psychic phenomena. The theologians of the fourth century, making use of the speculations which had developed out of mediumship, produced an ecclesiastical organisation to take the place of the medium, and, when this was adopted, its source of origin was covered up, and on the site arose the Christian Church.

Over the grave of its victim, the medium, the Church, in fear lest its crime be discovered, erected barricades of anathemas and decrees against all who would not come inside its walls. The first to receive its holy curse were the Arians, as, before the Council of Nicaea closed, the priests performed what they considered was a very important duty, namely to anathematise Arius and all his followers, to petition the Emperor to have them banished, and to punish by death all who read their writings. To this Constantine agreed, and he then invited the bishops to a sumptuous banquet to celebrate the occasion. He again took the opportunity to advise them to live together in peace, and, before they parted, he asked for their prayers.

The peace Constantine anticipated did not come till the following century, and before this came about much bitterness continued to be expressed throughout the Church over this question of the nature of the Godhead. Eusebius was the first to break the harmony, as he was sufficiently frank to declare in a pastoral letter, which he addressed to his flock, that the creed he had signed at Nicaea was more creditable to his ingenuity than to his candour.

The Nicene Creed, however, became the weapon with which the Catholic Church destroyed two great conflicts of opinion as to the nature of the Godhead. One was known as Sabellianism, which believed God to be a Trinity, but that his three parts were inseparable and that he did not consist of three persons. The other heresy, Arianism, as we have discovered, believed the Godhead to be a Trinity, but that the Son and the Holy Ghost were subordinate, and not equal, to the Father God. Catholicism struck a balance between these two views by splitting the difference, and producing a Godhead which consisted of three separate beings who were all equal and still only one person.

A few months after the Council of Nicaea, Alexander died, and was succeeded by Athanasius, who occupied the see of Alexandria for the next forty-six years. His firm orthodoxy left its mark on the Church, so much so that when, at the end of the eighth century, some unknown person or persons produced the creed now called after him, his name was given to it so as to establish its authority amongst believers. What is today called the Athanasian Creed was quite unknown in the Church before the ninth century. Likewise the Apostles' Creed is a misnomer as it has nothing to do with the apostles. It was produced by someone unknown in the fifth century at the earliest, in fact it was not introduced into the Church until the middle of the eighth century.

Constantine, who never seems to have cared much one way or the other as to whether Arius or Alexander won over their definition of the Trinity, was persuaded by his sister a few years after the Council of Nicaea to recall Arius from exile. The Arian influence, in consequence, increased so much at Court that all Catholic bishops were dismissed from the Imperial Palace and persecuted. Here we have the first mention of Christians persecuting Christians, which is such a feature of the Faith throughout its history. Constantine ordered the readmission of Arius into the communion of the Church, but, before this could be carried through, Arius was murdered by his opponents and a year later Constantine died.

After the Council of Nicaea, Constantine decreed that the Christian religion was to be in future the religion of the Roman Empire, which edict historians think was nothing more than an astute political move. In the reign of the previous Emperor, Maximian (285–305), the Saviour-god Mithra had been raised to be the chief god and protector of the Roman Empire. This took place in 304, but, after Nicaea, Christ took his place and Mithra was deposed.

If the Emperor Julian, who became Emperor twenty-four years after the death of Constantine, had had a longer reign, Mithra would undoubtedly have returned to his former throne. Such is the power of autocrats ; they can make gods great, just as they can make them small, and they can determine the religion which is to be believed, not only in their own time, but by succeeding generations. This explains why a third of the world's population today calls itself Christian, and, what Constantine did for Christianity, King Asoka did for Buddhism in 250 B.C., when he consolidated its beliefs into fixed dogmas and doctrines at the Council of Patna.

From the religious point of view this act of Constantine was quite unnecessary, as Christians by now had the same freedom to worship as the Pagans had always enjoyed. Evidently the reason which prompted him to take this step was for the purpose of binding together his scattered Empire. Christianity had penetrated into every land of the Empire, whereas Mithraism was just one of several Pagan religions in vogue, and was not so widespread as was the Christian Faith.

One Emperor and one Faith appealed to Constantine as the right policy to pursue if all the straggling elements of his Empire were to be kept together. His reason for adopting it was more political than religious, but it had the effect of raising the Christian Faith to a status for which it was not intended. It had to be adapted to its new responsibilities which, if for the good of the State, was certainly not good for its morals. Instead of developing into a great organisation for the uplifting of humanity, Christianity became one for the harnessing of the minds of the people into a rigid code of beliefs, which all must observe as loyal citizens of the State.

The consciousness of power inspired the priests for its insignia, and they soon adorned themselves in the official robes of the Empire's officers. Soon no provincial or municipal office was without its Christian priest arrayed in gorgeous robes. No function could take place without them. Just as Christian priests today, in our own country, bless battleships before they are launched, say prayers over regimental flags and officiate at our royal and official functions, so did they in Rome.

The position which Constantine gave them they have maintained throughout our era. Political developments also increased their power, as, within a century of the death of Constantine, when Rome was abandoned by its Emperors, the Bishop of Rome became the chief citizen of the imperial city. This had the effect of bringing the religion to corruption. It produced the idea that the Christian kingdom is an earthly monarchy, to which all good Christians must contribute, and submit as loyal subjects.

The aggrandisement of the Church became the aim of the priesthood. The Church translated spiritual forces into physical equivalents. The very term spiritual, which concerns the affections, the emotions, our thoughts and ideas, in fact our entire mental being, that part of us which is the individual and passes over to the etheric world at death, is used to denote everything that belongs to the Church and the priests.

Land becomes spiritual when it passes into the

hands of the Church. Men are spiritual servants of the Church if they are priests. The bishops are Spiritual Princes and Spiritual Peers. All Church property is termed spiritual, in fact everything the Church handles ; the very garments the priests wear, are spiritual. The spiritually minded are those who are orthodox Christians, but all that pertains to a higher morality, and to a better understanding of the etheric world, has always been forgotten in the strife for wealth, worldly power, and position. Christians have brought the word Spiritual into such disrepute and contempt that for this reason it has not been used throughout this book.

The Church has not recruited its priests from men conspicuous because of their nobility of character, but often from the unscrupulous and ambitious. Such men encouraged any kind of superstitious error that tended to bring them, or the Church, increased power or wealth. In exchange for money the priests relieved the people of all their shortcomings by posing as the intermediaries between God and man. They alone could settle the difference between God and the individual, provided sufficient payment was forthcoming. The priests thus relieved the people of all need to live better lives, and of the trouble of taking serious thought of the deeper things of life. To the priests only, God had revealed the mysteries, and it was not the divine will that these should be understood by the laity.

The priests relieve their fellow Christians of all their religious worries just as a lawyer does his clients of legal worries. All that is necessary is to pay when asked, attend the Church services, employ a priest to baptise the infant, confirm the youth, perform the marriage ceremony and celebrate the Eucharist to the dying. If these ceremonies are always remembered by the individual, then he or she is a good Christian, irrespective of the life led. As every wickedness can be absolved before death there is no incentive to lead a good life, or bother about the deeper things of existence.

A Church, having such a power over the people, has always been in constant use by rulers, who fawned upon an organisation which had the power at times to make or unmake them. At times it worked with them, at others against them, according as to where its interests lay. Always it was on the side of tyranny and oppression, and against education and the elevation of the people. Its instruments in the past were persecution, war, torture and prison. All that now remains is the bribe of Heaven for those who support its claims, and the threat of Hell for those who do not, but even this weapon has become blunt and useless amongst the educated.

By employing these powerful methods it ruled wherever Christians lived and, even in our own times, we see the terrible effect it has had on our civilisation. We have made more progress within the last seventy years than in all the years right back to the fifth century, when all schools were closed and learning was abolished. The reason for this, so far as our country is concerned, is because education for everyone became compulsory under the Education Act of 1870. Only the few, before this time, were taught to read and write, and this meant that for fourteen centuries the great majority lived in a night of ignorance. Likewise, during that period, the psychic stream was forced underground and out of sight, and that which produced the faith was forgotten. When the Church abandoned the medium in favour of the priest it lost its way in the wilderness of error in which it is still wandering.

By its antagonism to mediumship it lost contact with nature's revelation, and became more and more materialistic in its outlook and beliefs. It lost touch with the meaning behind the reappearance of Jesus and so materialised a psychic event. As Principal D. S. Cairns puts it in *The Faith that Rebels*: "The miracles of the spirit gradually ceased because by compromise with the world the Church got out of touch with the pure grace of God." Though theologically expressed his meaning is clear. Eusebius, who took such a prominent part at the Council of Nicaea, also remarks that in his day psychic phenomena were declining in the Church because it had become unworthy of them.

Dr. Glover, in his book *Conflict of Religions* gives his reason for this in these words: "In the Church the ministry of the spirit and the ministry of gifts were succeeded by the ministry of office with its lower ideals of the practical and expedient." Thus the Christian Church deprived humanity of the only revelation which can come to man from the etheric world, and, if it had had its way, we would still be groping for light to lighten the darkness it brought down on humanity in the fourth century. It extinguished nature's own revelation, and put in its place its own man-made creeds, doctrines and dogmas, falsely calling them the one and only revelation given by God to man through the mediumship of his Church on earth, to which had been given all power over the minds and spirits of men.

Constantine was succeeded by his three sons. The eldest, Constantine II, who became Sovereign of Gaul, Spain and Britain, was killed in 340. He was an ardent supporter of the Nicene Creed. His third son, Constans, who was Emperor of the remainder of the Western Empire, then became Emperor of the West. He was murdered in 350, when the entire Empire devolved on Constantine's second son, Constantius II, who until then had been the Emperor of the East.

Constantius, like his father, favoured Christianity but remained unbaptised till shortly before his death. He supported the Arians and did not accept the Nicene Creed. Like his father, he was half a Pagan, and retained the chief priestship of Paganism. Moreover, on his visit to Rome in 357, he shewed his respect for the old religion. Just before his death he ordered the recall of Athanasius, who had been banished from his see at Alexandria, and also all the other banished bishops who had been exiled when the Arians gained influence with Constantine.

Constantius was followed by Julian, who reigned from 361 to 363. Lecky, in his *History of Rationalism*, describes him as "among the best men who ever sat upon a throne". He was in early life brought up as a Christian, but, after he became Emperor, he declared himself a Pagan. For that reason he is called Julian the Apostate. He was only six years old when his uncle Constantine died, and one of his earliest memories was the massacre of his father and kinsfolk in the interest of the sons of Constantine. He therefore had no cause to love the Christian Faith. Though trained to its profession, he became attracted in early life by the Faith of his ancestors. He adopted a form of Pagan philosophy which was popular in those days amongst the educated, and worshipped Mithra, whom he believed had revealed the only true God.

He was tolerant to the Jews, and gave them permission to rebuild the temple at Jerusalem. By this act he annulled the edict of Hadrian, and so the Jews had access once more to the Holy City. The Jews were enthusiastic and vigorous in making their plans for the new Temple. The foundations had been laid, and building was about to commence, when they were destroyed by an earthquake. Julian died about the time of this catastrophe, and the attempt to rebuild the Temple was abandoned because of the hostility of the Christians, who looked upon the disaster as an act of their god.

Looking back, we now see how unfortunate it was that religious prejudice thwarted the Jews in this, their last, opportunity to recover their old sacred city, and again build up a home for their nation. What a difference it would have made to them if they had had a home, and been no longer strangers in foreign lands! Christianity prevented this materialising, as Christians argued that it was contrary to the scriptures that the Temple should be rebuilt, it having been foretold that it was to remain desolate. (Matt. xxiii, 38.) Instead, they built churches in Jerusalem, and it became a place of religious pilgrimages.

In 614 Jerusalem was captured by the Persians, when the churches and holy places were destroyed, and in 637 it was captured by the Mohammedans, who built a mosque on the site of the Temple. The last chance the Jews had of recovering their native land was denied them by the Christians in the years succeeding the death of Julian, and since then Palestine has been inhabited by other races.

Throughout the Christian era Christians have constantly persecuted the unfortunate Jews. Hitler, their latest persecutor, tells us in *Mein Kampf* that in persecuting the Jews he is acting for Christ. The words he uses are these, "I believe I am acting in accordance with the will of Almighty God, because, in defending myself against the Jews, I am fighting to defend the work of Christ." Hitler is only reiterating the reason given by all former fanatics who have looked upon the Jews as the enemies of Christendom [because they "killed the Prince of Life" (Acts iii, 15)], and believed that by persecuting them they were glorifying Christ.

From the articles appearing in our religious weeklies, as I am writing this chapter, the writers take up the attitude that the Jews have had themselves to blame for their troubles because, as one writer, who is a Christian high priest, puts it, "nineteen centuries ago they spurned and crucified the Son of God". What a tragedy it is that the human race contains, and always has contained, so many political and religious zealots who have been nothing but a curse to the wise and prudent!

The Emperor Julian was no indifferent religious believer and held his opinions strongly. He announced his determination to restore the Pagan Faith to the old position it had before the time of Constantine, and, in this endeavour, produced an elaborate exposition of the false claims made by the Christians. His reign was too short to show what precise form the **Pagan** revival was to take, and how far his antagonistic attitude towards Christianity would affect the new religion, but everything he did pointed to moderation. He issued an edict of universal toleration, and then used his influence to restore the old faith and suppress the new. In no case was violence used, and he even allowed Christians to hold high offices of state. If his reign had been longer the history of Europe would undoubtedly have been different.

Julian was a brave general and ever at the front with his men. In a battle against the Persians he was killed in 363, after a short reign of two years. This was considered to be an omen in favour of Christianity, as Julian met his death in the home of Mithraism, the rival of the Christian Faith. He was a good Emperor, temperate in all things, and at all times showed self-control and zeal for the public good. He was cultured and fond of literature. One of the most remarkable features of his public life was his perfect ease and mastery in associating the cares of war and statesmanship with the assiduous cultivation of literature and philosophy. And yet he was also devoted to the old superstitions which appealed to the masses, being noted for the number of sacrifices he offered to the gods.

With the death of Julian ended any hope the Pagans might have had of their religion being restored to its old position. On the day following his death, Jovian, who was a Christian, was chosen to be Emperor, and, as the army's religious beliefs generally followed those of the Emperor, the soldiers declared themselves in favour of the Christian Faith. From that time onwards Christianity went ahead without a setback, though quarrelling still continued in its ranks between the Arians and the Catholics.

Robertson, in his *Short History of Christianity*, sums up the position at that time in these words :

At each episcopal election or expulsion, the most exalted sees of Christendom (Constantinople, Alexandria, Antioch) furnished scenes that would have disgraced a revolution. Julian has told how whole troops of those who were called heretics were massacred, notably at Cyzicus and at Samosata ; while in Paphlagonia, Bithynia, Galatia, and many other provinces, towns and villages were utterly destroyed. In one massacre at Constantinople, the second in connection with the forcible reinstalment of the semi-Arian bishop Macedonius, there perished more than three thousand people. The orthodox populace, divided in furious factions, fighting like savages in their very churches, were as brutal as their masters. Gregory of Nazianzun, whose own ferocities of utterance illustrate the character of the period, declared truly that he had never seen a synod do aught but worsen a quarrel.

Origen, in the third century, tells us that "There have been but a few now and again, easily counted, who have died for the Christian religion," and it will be remembered how Gibbon, taking the figures as supplied by Eusebius, concluded that the total number of Christians who suffered death as the result of Pagan persecution did not greatly exceed two thousand people. It is well to remember this when we find that immediately after their persecution ceased they commenced to massacre each other.

In the last chapter we read of the bitterness that existed between Tertullian, who was the first to formulate the doctrine of the Trinity, and Praxeas. From this time, until within the last few years, when a man was fined and imprisoned in Spain because he could not believe in the Trinity, this doctrine of a triune god has brought more bitterness, suffering, misery, cruelty and bloodshed than any other idea that has ever entered the mind of man, if we except human sacrifice.

There is no period during the reign of the Church when those in power have not attempted by persecution, prison and death to force upon the minority, called the unorthodox, their opinions as to how the Deity should be defined. When Calvin was in power at Geneva he was just as intolerant as were the Roman Catholics and, because Servetus could not agree with him in his definition of the Trinity, he arrested him and burned him at the stake. Servetus, who was a Spaniard and an eminent physician, was the first to discover the circulation of the blood (not Harvey), and he was the first of a long line of Protestants to be killed by Protestants in the name of Christ. The doctrine of the Holy and Blessed Trinity, to which Christians give so much devotion, can only be termed one of the most pernicious ideas which has ever entered the mind of man, and yet it is the very essence of Christianity, without which the entire Faith would crumble to pieces.

After the short renaissance which took place during the reign of Julian, conditions again deteriorated under Jovian, the Emperor who succeeded him. He was a Catholic and accepted the Nicene Creed, but, as he reigned only eight months, there was not sufficient time to exterminate all the Arians from the Church. The next Emperor, Valentinian I, was tolerant and did not interfere in Church disputes. He reigned only three years and was succeeded by Valens, who favoured the Arians. And so this ding-dong fight between these two parties in the Church went on till we come to the reign of Theodosius I, who became Emperor in 379, and with his reign the Catholic Church commenced its undisputed career.

Theodosius, who was a Spanish soldier, was an ardent advocate of the Nicene Creed and, on being made Emperor, he was admitted into the Church. Two years later, in 381, he called together a Council of Christian priests at Constantinople, at which the following creed was sanctioned and passed :

I believe in one God the Father Almighty, maker of Heaven and Earth and of all things visible and invisible, and in one Lord Jesus Christ, the only begotten Son of God, begotten of his Father before all worlds, God of God, Light of Light, Very God of Very God, Begotten, not made, Being of one substance with the Father. By whom all things were made. Who for us men and for our salvation came down from Heaven. And was incarnate by the Holy Ghost of the Virgin Mary. And was made man. And was crucified also for us under Pontius Pilate. He suffered and was buried. And the third day he rose again according to the Scriptures. And ascended into Heaven. And sitteth on the right hand of the Father. And he shall come again with glory to judge both the quick and the dead, Whose kingdom shall have no end. And I believe in the Holy Ghost, the Lord and Giver of Life, who proceedeth from the Father and the Son, who with the Father and the Son together is worshipped and glorified, Who spake by the prophets. And I believe in one Catholic and Apostolic Church. I acknowledge one baptism for the remission of sins. And I look for the resurrection of the dead and the life of the world to come.

The question may well be asked, On what authority did the Church at the end of the fourth century adopt this altered creed when, at the beginning of the century, it had produced and passed a creed which was to be the basis of the Christian Faith, and never under any circumstances to be altered? It is easier to ask the question than to answer it, as no Church historian can trace the origin of the creed as altered. It was altered and enlarged, at some unknown place, by some unknown person or persons, at some unknown date, and that is all that can be said about it. It was not composed at the Council of Constantinople in 381, as is often asserted, as it was in existence seven years before the date of that Council.

The probable explanation is that the original Nicene Creed was gradually increased in the East as the dogmatic instinct of the Church developed under the pressure of the Arian heresy. It was deemed necessary to meet the growth of heretical opinions by additional growths of authoritative Catholic opinion, and, gradually, the more comprehensive creed came to be used in the place of the one originally produced at Nicaea. Though the origin of the altered creed is unknown the fact remains that it was passed at the Council of Constantinople, and since that time it has been the official creed of the Church. It is also interesting to remember that the one hundred and fifty bishops who attended this Council were all orthodox Catholics. They all came from the Eastern churches only, and none were present from the West. Consequently, the Council of Constantinople was not a representative Council of the Christian Church.

About this time was inserted into the New Testament the verse "For there are three that bear record in heaven, The Father, the Word and the Holy Ghost, and these three are one". (1 John v, 7.)

This verse first occurred in a Latin manuscript in Spain about the year 400. It is not to be found in any of the Greek manuscripts of earlier date. The Church, however, passed this interpolation, as it corresponded to its beliefs after the time of Nicaea, and gave them scriptural authority. From that date onwards this verse became part of scripture, every word of which the priests claimed had been inspired by God.

What is today called inspirational, or automatic, writing was considered in the time of the Apostolic Church to come from God, and that is how the early Christians thought the Hebrew prophets, and the apostles, wrote the scriptures. After the canon was decided upon at the Council of Carthage, in 397, the Church announced that inspiration ceased with the apostles, and that all inspiration now rested in the Church, which was guided by the Holy Spirit to interpret the scriptures as God intended them to be understood.

From the time of the Council of Constantinople onwards the Arians had no hope of success, as, by threats and persecution, Theodosius made the Arian bishops subscribe to the creed of the Church as settled at Constantinople. All who did not accept the Catholic Faith, and the doctrine of the Holy and Blessed Trinity, "as taught by Saint Peter to the Romans", were called heretics, and severe laws were made against them. It is difficult to reconcile this with the verse quoted some pages further back, relating what Peter is reported to have believed about Jesus; in fact, from certain remarks attributed to Jesus in the gospels, he stands out as the greatest of all heretics.

It became illegal for heretics to assemble together, and all their buildings were destroyed or confiscated. Whoever refused to obey was banished, or put to death, and over a dozen Christian sects were, in consequence, almost entirely exterminated. All mediumship in the churches was forbidden, and practical effect was given to this ban by gangs of Christians, led by priests and monks, who destroyed the churches which retained the early form of worship. All mediums were put to death. The Pagan mediums received the same fate and their sanctuaries were destroyed. In 395 the sanctuary at Eleusis was entirely destroyed by a gang of Christian priests. Thus ended both Christian and Pagan contact with the etheric world, which was now shut out to mankind until the eighteenth century, when the power to kill mediums was made illegal.

In the Glasgow Exhibition of 1938 a section was reserved for the tortures inflicted on mediums throughout the Christian era. This was called "Church Discipline", and there the visitor saw the instruments of torture employed by the Protestant Church on these unfortunate people. The most up-to-date instrument exhibited was dated 1704, and this brought about the death of all those who had to suffer it. After 1712 the murdering and persecuting of mediums was made illegal, and Catholic and Protestant priests thereafter could only defame them.

From the fourth century onwards Christian priests took the place of mediums, all religious and intellectual liberty was abolished, all schools were closed, and Christendom entered the Dark Ages. Theodosius also issued edicts against Pagan worship, and from that date onwards the old religion slowly disappeared. The Mithraists were exterminated everywhere, though at that time their religion was making headway throughout the Empire. All Pagan temples were destroyed, or appropriated by the Christians, and the Pagan priests and votaries either became Christians or were banished or murdered. Many Pagans, however, found no great difficulty in making the change over to Christianity, as by now the new religion had absorbed the principal elements of the Pagan faith. Except the name of the new god there was little new for the convert to accept.

By persuasion and force the Roman Empire was Christianised, and this policy was pursued until the whole of Europe had accepted the gospel message. Thus Christ took the place of Mithra, Osiris, Dionysus, the Nordic gods, and all the other Saviours of the Pagans. Jehovah likewise took the place of Jupiter. From now onwards only two outstanding saviour-gods remained, Krishna in the East and Christ in the West. All the others were cast into oblivion, and faded from the minds of their former worshippers.

Theodosius, by his edicts, known as the Theodosian Code of 381, laid the foundation of the Inquisition, as in this code groups of priests were appointed to act as "Inquisitors of the Faith". In Article IX heresy was defined as treason against God, and all who were found guilty were treated as if they were traitors to the State. As Towner says in his *Philosophy of Civilisation* :

The office of Inquisitors of the Faith, founded by Theodosius in the fourth century, has been revived as often as Christian dissension arose. There was no period when it could be affirmed that charity, forgiveness or brotherly love existed between Christian sects. Differences of opinion, no matter how trifling, invariably led to charges of heresy, and heresy was invariably stamped out with ferocious cruelty. No pause, moderation, restraint or mercy was ever shown. . . . The persecutions of the Pagans were short, and pale when compared to the long red chapter of history which describes the persecutions of Christians by Christians.

Historians have found it difficult to estimate the number of victims who have suffered and died, as the result of Christian persecution and slaughter, during the reign of the Christian Church. However, all are agreed that very many millions of innocent people perished, through Christians destroying each other, because they differed as to doctrines or forms of worship. In Germany alone, as the result of the Thirty Years' War, fourteen million people perished for no other reason than that the opposing sides could not agree on the question of Christian doctrine. The number of mediums destroyed exceeds half a million.

The first outstanding victim of the Theodosian Code was Precillian, Bishop of Avila, a Spanish theologian who, with several of his followers, in the year 385 was tortured and then burned alive at Trèves on a charge of heresy. He was accused of the crime of communicating with the dead and holding certain Gnostic doctrines. The last victim to Protestant priests was George Aikenhead, aged nineteen, who was found guilty of a charge of heresy and hanged in Edinburgh in 1820, though Catholic priests have continued to imprison their victims up to the present century, especially in Spain. Their tyranny drove some of the people into the arms of the Communists, whose extreme acts brought about the Spanish civil war.

The Roman Catholic Church did not withdraw the terrible Theodosian Code until 1816, when a papal bull decreed that torture was to cease. In spite of its claim to being guided by the Holy Spirit, its wicked laws and practices, over fourteen hundred years, could not have been surpassed by savages. If the Christian Church had only protected mediums, instead of claiming for itself the source of their inspiration, how different our history would have been! Man's ignorance and defiance of nature's laws must often have made the gods weep!

Throughout the reign of Theodosius, Ambrose, Bishop of Milan, exerted great influence on his policy, and must therefore share with the Emperor the responsibility for the section in the Theodosian Code relating to heretics. Ambrose is the first instance we have of a Christian priest taking up the roll of a politician. Thenceforward politics, as much as religion, was the work of the Church. Under the guidance of Ambrose, Theodosius united the Christian churches throughout the Empire, and the dream of Cyprian, the father of the episcopacy, was at last realised : one Church, one Faith and one Priesthood.

Some of the greatest blackguards in history have been the most ardent believers in the Nicene Creed, and Theodosius set all who followed him an excellent example of how to be a true believer and, at the same time, an unmitigated scoundrel. In Thessalonica, in the year 390, some of the inhabitants murdered the Commander-in-Chief of the district and some of his soldiers. Theodosius promised the people pardon for

their crime and asked them to be present at a performance of games in the Circus. When they were
all assembled they were attacked by an overwhelming
force of soldiers. None was spared and every man,
woman and child was slaughtered. No distinction
was made between those who might have been guilty
of the murder and those who were innocent.

Guilty and innocent, citizen and stranger, all met
the same fate. For three hours this indiscriminate
butchery was carried on, and Gibbon tells us that
when the soldiers were tired of their ghastly work
fifteen thousand people lay dead in the Circus grounds.
Ambrose wrote a letter to Theodosius exhorting him
in the mildest terms, and with much flattery, to grieve
for what he had done, and that for the present he could
not partake of the Eucharist. He was advised that
he should do penance for his crime. Theodosius
replied that he was sorry, and eight months later he
presented himself before the bishop to receive the
Eucharist. Ambrose administered this to him,
absolved him from his crime, and assured him that he
would have a safe entry into Heaven.

The next outstanding Christian of those days was
Augustine, who is looked upon by the Christian
Church as its greatest father. No single name has
ever exercised such power over the Church, and no
mind has made such an impression upon Christian
thought. Contemporary with Augustine lived Jerome,
who translated the Hebrew scriptures into Latin.
When this great work was completed, he remarked to
Pope Damasus that it would be difficult for anyone
to recognise the original from his translation. The
Pope then commissioned him to translate the gospels

and epistles from Greek into Latin. To this request Jerome replied that it would be difficult to know where to start, as there were as many different versions of these in existence as there were copies in circulation. However, he undertook the task, trusting in God to direct him as to which were the right ones to use for his translation, and which were the ones to be rejected.

This remark made by Jerome is sufficient confirmation, if such be needed, of the truth of the remark made by Celsus, in the second century, when the gospel stories were being put together. Celsus, to whom reference was made in the previous chapter, exposed the unscrupulous methods adopted by the Christians, in manufacturing the history of their faith, in these words :

> You utter fables and you do not even possess the art of making them seem likely. . . . You have altered three, four times and oftener the texts of your own Gospels in order to deny objections made to you.

Jerome is quite candid in giving the reason why, in his opinion, mediums should not continue to be employed in churches. He writes, "We tell them that we do not so much reject prophecy as refuse to receive prophets whose utterances fail to accord with the scriptures old and new." By now the Church had, in its own interests, shut outside the Church door the holy spirits, who controlled mediums, and grouped all such visiting spirits under the name of The Holy Spirit. As we have discovered, it created a corporate name for an unlimited company of etheric beings. This vast assembly of spirits, who visit this earth, and make their presence known through mediums, the Church consolidated into one god, which it placed in the Godhead, and gave this god third rank but equal standing with Jehovah and Christ.

Jerome rejected these spirit controls because they did not accept the gospels, the epistles and the Hebrew scriptures as translated by him. These controls were well aware of the fact that these documents differed vastly from the original writings and, from the way Jerome writes, it seems as if he had been plainly told the truth by at least one visiting spirit, who had exposed the fraud the Church had perpetrated. Those who visit us today from the other world say just the same as they did then, because they tell us that the creeds, doctrines and sacred literature of the Church are false, and were produced either by fraud or ignorance of the truth.

I have been at séances, in the company of Protestant priests at various times, when those who spoke from the etheric world pointedly reminded them of the false claims and mistakes made by the Christian Church, and that they were preachers of false doctrines. Like Jerome, they did not appreciate this exposure, and said to me, when the séance ended, that those who were speaking such heresy must be devils.

We can, therefore, appreciate what Jerome felt on the subject. He put his Church's creeds, doctrines, dogmas and sacred writings before what the Christians had heretofore termed "The Conversations of the Lord", which came through "The Oracles of God", through those "filled with a holy or divine spirit". The Church extricated itself from all its difficulties by branding the Oracles of God, the mediums, as

"Servants of the Devil" and burning them. So the only revelation that has ever come, or ever can come, to mankind from the other world was extinguished by the instruments of the divine spirits being destroyed in order that the priests could rule.

Augustine, Ambrose and Jerome were the triumvirate who launched the Catholic Church on the world, with its doctrine that only those who were true Catholics could be saved, and that the Church had been given all power from God to absolve every sin and wickedness. The words the priests had put into the mouth of Jesus, that, "He that believeth and is baptised shall be saved, but he that believeth not shall be damned" (Mark xvi, 16), had brought about results even better than these interpolaters had ever imagined, and we are now witnessing, in the dogmas and doctrines these three men added to the Faith, the culmination of all that had gone before.

The malignant part played by them, in using every priestly invention to strangle all freedom of thought, will some day be appreciated, when they will come to be looked upon as unscrupulous tyrants of the worst type, and not as the saints the Christian Church describes them as being. They are paralleled today by the Nazi triumvirate in Germany, which, by similar methods, has banished all freedom of expression, and uses the same ruthless methods to achieve and maintain its stranglehold over its fellow men. Though the Christian triumvirate spent much of its time speculating on the Godhead, it had no idea of human liberty, and looked upon humanity as slaves, who had to believe as their master the Church told them, or, as Augustine said, die by the sword.

Augustine incorporated into the doctrines of the Church the worst of Paul's theology. Paul wrote that we are "by nature the children of wrath". Augustine improved on this by describing the human race as "one mass of perdition from Adam", and he then elaborated Paul's doctrines of predestination, salvation by faith, justification by grace, and the remnant of the elect, thus abolishing all the comfort that the death of Jesus had given to believers. What misery these doctrines have caused to multitudes in the Christian community, and what arrogance they have produced through many thinking that they were predestined to be saved by grace, and counted amongst the elect!

This represents what Christianity gave to the world. Let us now consider the other side and realise of what it deprived the world. It will be remembered how in Chapter IV reference was made to the fact that Alexandria, in the time of Ptolemy, was the world's intellectual centre. Though the University became a Theological College, learning did not quite die out, and, in the last chapter, we discovered how it had been revived under the influence of Neoplatonism, which was a revival of the philosophy of Greece. Philosophy and Christianity could not, however, live side by side, so we are not surprised to discover that Christians set about in a thorough manner the extermination of all rational thought.

Cyril (376–444), one of the most distinguished fathers of the Church, became Archbishop of Alexandria at a time when many were being attracted to this more philosophical outlook on life. He was a great theologian, and left many commentaries on the subject of Church doctrine, besides a treatise on the Trinity and the Incarnation. He presented to the City of Ephesus a statue of the Virgin Mary, which replaced the one to the goddess Artemis. He was one of the most bloodthirsty ruffians we have to deal with in early Church history, as, shortly after his appointment to the see of Alexandria, he displayed his zeal against the Jews, Pagans and heretics. Immediately after he became endowed with the Holy Spirit, on his election to office, he closed all non-Catholic churches in his diocese. He assailed the Jewish synagogues with an armed force, drove the Jews in thousands from the city, and exposed their houses and property to pillage. Thirty thousand Jews are said to have perished as the result of his persecution. Another of his crimes was directed against those with philosophic tendencies.

Hypatia (350–412 A.D.), described by Socrates (385–450 A.D.), the Church historian, as one of the most outstanding women of her time, fell a victim to the wrath of the Archbishop. (This historian must not be confused with his great namesake who lived in Athens nine hundred years earlier.) Hypatia was a very remarkable woman, as she was not only a philosopher but also an outstanding mathematician, being responsible for a commentary on the work of Diophantus, the inventor of Greek algebra. She was the daughter of Theon, the mathematician, astronomer and philosopher, and spent her early life studying in Athens.

She became a distinguished lecturer on philosophy in Alexandria, and came to be regarded as the recognised head of the Neoplatonic School in that city. Her lectures attracted so many of the leading people of the city that the street, in which they were held, was always crowded with chariots when a lecture was proceeding. We are told that the "fascination of her great eloquence, the charm of her rare modesty and beauty, combined with her remarkable intellectual gifts, attracted to her classroom a large number of disciples, over some of whom her influence was very great".

This outstanding woman continued to conduct her lectures during the time the Christians in Alexandria were ravaging, torturing and slaughtering the Jews, Pagans and heretics, and it does not, therefore, surprise us to read that she met a tragic end. Urged on by Cyril, the congregation from his church invaded her classroom, and dragged her out, along the streets, into their church. There the Christians stripped her naked, cut her to pieces with oyster shells, and finally burned her body piece by piece. For this crime Cyril was responsible, though it was carried out under the leadership of Peter, a lay reader in his church.

With her death died also philosophy in Alexandria, and a city which once flourished as the intellectual centre of the world became, under Christian control, a mere provincial town and of little importance. The fate which befell the intellectual life of Alexandria also overtook Athens, where the Christians likewise extinguished the light of reason and put in its place the dark night of superstition.

One of the most common delusions in the minds of Christians is that their religion brought to mankind all that was good, noble and true, and that, before this divine revelation came to humanity, the people were living in the darkness of heathenism, bowing down to gods of wood and stone. Christians believe that Christianity raised the world from savagery to a state of civilisation, and that before its time there was no such thing as lovingkindness, charity, works of healing and mercy, or any of the virtues outside of the Old Testament and the Jewish race.

This great delusion is specially propagated by Christian priests of all denominations, with the result that it is taken up and passed on by those who know no better. In consequence, this travesty of the truth continues its daily round, and will continue to do so until the average level of intelligence rises sufficiently to enable the people to find where the truth lies.

The Bishop of Rome from 402 to 417 was Innocent I. He was the first to lay claim to the status of sovereign over the entire Western Church. Though the Eastern Church rejected this claim it would still be correct to look upon him as the first Pope. From this time onwards the Bishop of Rome took the title of Pontifex Maximus, and succeeded to this Pagan office. He became the Chief Priest and the bishops were the High Priests, all of whom claimed to be controlled by the Holy Spirit.

Each Pope further claimed to be the Oracle of God, and so replaced the mediums supplied by nature, who were the oracles of their controlling spirits, the only revealers of the etheric world and its inhabitants. Besides replacing mediums, and their controlling spirits, the Pope took the titles of "Father of Princes", "The Ruler of the World" and "The Vicar of Christ". The Empire was divided into twelve provinces, over each of which reigned an Archbishop, then termed a

Patriarch, each of whom also claimed to be controlled by the Holy Spirit.

So the priesthood, which the apostles tell us was abolished by Christ, came to life again by a body of men, whose functions in the first two Christian centuries were purely ministerial, capturing the Church organisation. Once this was done the bishops assumed dictatorial powers, which they claimed to have received from Christ, through the Holy Spirit, who was their control, and they his medium. This mediumship, they claimed, was passed on from bishop to bishop, by the bishops, who were filled with this divine control, laying their hands on the head of every new bishop on his election to the position of a medium of the Church. This is what has happened in the past, happens today, and will continue to happen, so the priests claim, until the return of Christ to earth, when he will relieve his priestly mediums of the responsibility of revealing his will to mankind.

When the Christian Church was definitely established, the first wave of barbarian invasion swept over the Roman Empire. For three days, in 408, Rome was sacked and pillaged by the Visigoths. This event made a great impression everywhere, and those who had been forced to adopt the Christian Faith were not slow to express their opinions, and explain the calamity as one sent by the gods in anger against the Christians. According to Zosimus, a contemporary historian, Innocent bowed to the popular panic and gave permission for sacrifices to be made to the gods. The priests themselves were equally puzzled to account for the disaster, the more so because these barbarians were also Christians, having been converted to Christianity by missionaries sent from Constantinople. The Visigoths were amongst those who had come over to the new faith, and they were the first to break through the frontier of the Empire and usher in the age of barbarism.

This disaster led Augustine to write the greatest of all his works, *The City of God*, in which he set out his vast conception of the Catholic Church's universal ecclesiastical supremacy, and its domination over all the kingdoms of the earth. Innocent had the same idea, and it was taken up by Leo the Great, who became Pope in 440. Only the Church remained in those days to impose discipline and order in Western Europe, and this task it pursued by sheer ruthlessness until, under Charlemagne (742–814), the old empire was partially reformed under the name of the Holy Roman Empire.

Until then the Christian Church reigned supreme and its Popes lived like Emperors. At no time did its ecclesiastical supremacy reach a greater height than under Gregory the Great, who wore the papal crown from 590 till he died in 604. Gregory was more powerful than was ever a Roman Emperor. No Emperor in those days ruled in Rome, and the Pope had not only power over the bodies of men, but he, and his priests, made the people believe that they had also power over their destiny after death. He lived so sumptuously that he was the owner of a thousand slaves.

From that time onwards the Catholic Church met with one reverse after another. In the seventh century Mahomet took half of Christendom to himself. Four hundred years later what remained split in two, because those who became the Greek Church could not agree with the Catholic Church in its definition of the Trinity. The remainder was again divided in half at the Reformation, though what the Catholic Church lost by this it regained to some extent in South America. Augustine's dream of a world-wide Catholic Church, to which Kings, Emperors, Princes and all mankind must bow in subjection, was therefore never realised, and this is something humanity has been spared, and for which it can be thankful.

The priests from the fourth century onwards put themselves beyond and above the law of every land in Christendom, and became a law unto themselves. A priest could only be tried by a priest, and every parish had over it a priestly autocrat. No one was educated as there was nothing to learn outside of what the Church taught. From the time of the Emperor Justinian, by an edict in 529, all schools and libraries throughout the Empire were closed, and Europe became a vast camp of ignorant monks and nuns, who spent their time in religious observances, regarding all knowledge as sinful.

Though Gregory lived in regal state, the Church's ban on education, freedom and initiative quickly brought Christendom into the time now known as the Dark Ages, when the people lived in hovels and all their savings were used to build Cathedrals, Churches, Monasteries, Convents and Theological Colleges. We have only to compare social conditions at that time with what they were under Paganism to realise the deterioration which had taken place. Christianity and barbarism now went hand in hand, but all were true believers in the Trinity, and the divine power of the Catholic Church. Faith was supreme and knowledge neglected, with disastrous results.

From that time until our own, all progress and all reform have always found their greatest opposition from the Church authorities of all denominations. In our own country, since the Protestant Church ceased to rule, every measure for the improvement of the welfare of the people has found all, or nearly all, the bishops in the House of Lords in opposition, and, in every case, these measures have become law against their wishes.

This book, however, is not concerned with the terrible history of Catholicism and Protestantism. Historians, uninfluenced by Christian prejudice, have dealt with this subject fairly and fully. Our study has been concerned only with the source and growth of the Christian Faith. The general acceptance of the Nicene Creed, as representing Christian belief, now brings it to an end. We have found the origin of the Faith and have followed it through, from the time of its early ancestors, until it reached manhood in the fourth Christian century. Here we must leave it. Its future history is not part of the purpose of this book.

The object of *The Psychic Stream* is to correct the misrepresentations of the priests and ministers of the Christian Church, and the false assertions made by Christians. In their place it has put forward a logical and reasoned argument which, in the opinion of its author, represents the true explanation of the origin and growth of the Christian Religion in the light of our present-day knowledge. The contents of this book are certainly revolutionary, but they have at least the merit of being based on facts.

It is indeed very difficult to believe that what we have been considering in this chapter was the outcome of a few people, some three hundred years earlier, seeing one whom they took to be Jesus in his etheric body, and yet, strange and impossible as it may seem, it is a fact that there is an unbroken chain of cause and effect connecting those appearances with the beliefs incorporated in the Nicene Creed. Religious history records some extraordinary developments in belief, but none more extraordinary than this. In these pages the evolution of this idea has been traced step by step, without a break, and, strange as it may seem, the truth is that an apparition was the cause of the Christian Faith and all that this has meant to mankind.

The reason for this great transformation has been made clear throughout its development. That Jesus came to be regarded as a god was not a unique event, as, under the same circumstances, others were likewise deified, but the cause behind the Christian religion obtaining its widespread power and position has only one other parallel in Buddhism. Constantine, the autocrat of the Roman Empire, gave Christianity the position of the State Religion, and thereafter everything favoured its increase of power and influence.

Julian reigned only two years, and, but for this check, it received no other. Theodosius put the sword into its hand and retired to Constantinople, leaving the Church in command at Rome. Brute force and a fierce zeal for the establishment of a universal Church now did the rest, till all Europe, and every country surrounding the Mediterranean, was conquered and brought within the fold. Thus did Christians carry out what they believed to be their Lord's command to "go into all the world and preach the gospel to every creature." (Mark xvi, 15.)

Having now accomplished what I set out to do, my task is ended, but, to emphasise the conclusions reached, it would be well to run these over briefly in the order in which they have been set out. The remaining pages of this book will, therefore, be devoted to a review of its principal conclusions.

CHAPTER XI

EPILOGUE

WE have now arrived at the point when we can draw certain definite conclusions from the information which has passed before us. We have been enquiring into subjects having their origin in vital principles, over which in our days many thoughtful people are pondering. Many, having given up the old orthodox outlook, are keenly anxious to build up a philosophy which will be a strength and comfort to them throughout their life on earth. The study of the numerous attempts made by our ancestors, who had the same longings and aspirations as ourselves, will surely be of help to many, as today we can better realise their mistakes, though appreciating their motives.

We are now in a position to come to certain positive decisions on those theological problems, about which there has been such mystery in the past. This book, I trust, has made simple much that was difficult to understand, and I hope that it has shed a new light into many hitherto dark places. The numerous problems which have come before us, one by one, were only soluble if taken in their correct order by one armed with psychic knowledge. In order to understand the many mysteries and difficulties which confront the student of religion one had to go back to the beginning of the history of man and take one step at a time. The reason so little progress has been made in the past on this subject is because the anthropologist and mythologist have been quite ignorant of the fact that psychic occurrences do happen and that they have taken place ever since man arrived on the earth.

With this knowledge we found it possible to place our feet firmly on the first step. The next was not so difficult, and so we climbed up, step by step, out of the mist and fog below. When we reached the top, a clear panorama spread before us, we were able to see about us and know exactly where we were, in a way as never before.

Having arrived at the top, let us now go back and take each step once again so that we do not forget the lesson each has taught us. There are fifteen steps we must re-climb, and, if we remember what each and all have taught us, we are then armed with knowledge which is of vital importance to every one of us throughout our journey on earth. The first conclusion we can come to is that :

(1) A time came, as man was evolving out of the animal stage, when he dimly realised that his surroundings were more than they appeared to be. He thought differently from an animal. As his mind developed the time arrived when he discovered that he was not just a mass of moving flesh. He discovered that he had an immaterial something within his body which at first he could neither express nor understand. The germ of the idea, however, took root in his primitive mind, and from that time onwards he was a man and not an animal.

Again, he differed from an animal in having a hazy

idea that certain things were right to do and others were wrong. Thus the knowledge of good and evil took root, to grow and develop very gradually in each succeeding generation. Instinct had been supplemented by reasoned thought, though at first the latter was little better than instinct. It was, however, something different, as it developed into a knowledge of right and wrong. This gave rise to what we call Religion, which, however, must not be confused with morality and ethics.

Religion relates to the belief that man, by his acts, can please or displease the gods, or a god. One who displeased the gods was termed a sinner, and what he did to displease them was termed a sin. Ethics, on the other hand, relate to the moral code, which also has developed from small beginnings. This code is a system of principles and rules of conduct and covers the entire field of moral science. It is the result of accumulated experience as to how we should conduct ourselves so as best to secure the welfare and happiness of the human family.

(2) Man, we now know, is a trinity composed of a body of flesh, a duplicate etheric body, and a mind, which latter, through the etheric body, controls the physical body on earth, and the etheric body in the etheric world. Today it can be expressed as three different states of vibration, of which the physical body is the lowest. This body on earth houses the etheric body, at a higher rate of vibration, which in turn houses the mind, the highest state of vibration we know. This knowledge has come slowly from the evidence accumulated by those who have studied psychic phenomena.

From the evidence which has come down to us, we gather that primitive man had what we today call psychic faculties. These are the result of the etheric body responding, by sense impression, to etheric vibrations, as some individuals have been made by nature in such a fashion that the etheric body is not completely immersed in the physical. With the majority the physical body is the only one to respond by sense impression to the range of vibrations to which it is related, and so etheric vibrations pass unnoticed.

The fact, however, that we are each endowed with an etheric body is the cause of so many, to a greater or lesser degree, having an instinct that we are not only beings composed of flesh but that our personality survives the change called death. This may be described as an extra sense and is the cause of our religious emotions. But for the knowledge we have gained from those having mediumistic gifts we would be at a loss to understand and account for the religious instinct. We now know that the reason is that we are etheric beings, clothed temporarily in a covering of flesh so as to enable us to respond to physical vibrations during our time on earth.

Until now we have developed mentally, but our psychic qualities, through ignorance, prejudice and fear, have not only been neglected but suppressed. We know how feeble were the minds of our ancestors, and that only by education has intelligence developed. So likewise can our psychic faculties be developed, and it seems as if the human family is destined to progress along a path leading to increased psychic knowledge. Psychic sight and psychic hearing will enable future generations to tune in to a finer range of vibrations, and what it all will lead to some day no one can say. The gift of mediumship is certainly increasing, and it may be that this quality, when intelligently understood, will raise humanity for ever above those material activities which bring about war and human misery. These reflections are the result of known psychic developments which have taken place throughout the world over the past hundred years.

(3) Early man had these psychic faculties, and they are to be found amongst the primitive people of our own times. Through ignorance they have been mis-understood. This misinterpretation is reflected in all primitive religions, all of which are based on fear of, or affection for, the spirits of the dead, and the belief that they can harm and help humanity. The belief in spirits or gods is the foundation of all and every religion. Religion is a system of thought devoted to secure the favour of the gods, to keep them on friendly terms with mankind, and to obtain their help in time of trouble. What the ancients called gods, Christians call saints, angels and demons, which are only different words for the same beings.

Those in the tribe with psychic faculties were used as the medium between the tribe and the gods. They delivered the messages of the gods and later became known as oracles, prophets and organs of the spirit. From the experience obtained through mediumship our ancestors divided the gods into higher and lower categories, and also placed a god behind each natural phenomenon. To them was attributed all growth on earth and the movements of the heavenly bodies. Those gods who visited the earth were divided into good and bad beings, namely angels and demons, their standing being determined by their conduct when controlling their mediums. Through mediumship man discovered this order of beings surrounding him, and, on this knowledge, has grown up a theology, the science of the gods. This science, by ignoring its source of origin, in time became one of speculative thought devoid of any firm basis.

(4) Imitators of mediumship arose at an early date and those who imitated the medium were called magicians. The magician was the one who, by cunning and deception, produced effects similar to those of the medium. He rose to fame because he could duplicate his tricks at will, whereas the medium was dependent on external minds, which were not always present or willing to manifest through their instrument. Besides this, the instrument was not always able to act as the medium of the gods because the psychic faculty is so often sporadic.

The magician claimed that, by spells and incantations, he could influence and control the gods, and so order the course of nature. Out of the magician grew the priest, who claimed to be able to influence the gods by prayers, rites and ceremonies. As it was believed that the gods ate the spirits of the dead, sacrifices were offered freely to them, and it became the principal duty of the priests to feed them so as to keep them contented. The priests claimed to know whether the gods were friendly or angry with mankind, and the number and kind of spirits they wanted to eat. The priests also claimed that they were the medium of the gods in conveying their instructions to mankind.

(5) The mind of man has amongst its other qualities that of speculative imagination, of creating

new ideas out of certain known facts. The fact that
a world of etheric beings surrounds us induced early
man to imagine things for which there was no evidence,
one of which was that they were the first creation and
that man was created by them. Instead of believing
that the etheric world is populated from the earth,
he reversed the order and thought that man was the
last creation. Another mistaken idea he had was that
mankind brought upon himself all his sufferings and
death because he had transgressed against the wishes
of the gods.

So our ancestors kept on the best possible terms
with the gods by sending them human and animal
spirits to eat. On one occasion a sacrificed victim
was seen after death, and this was interpreted as
meaning that the gods had given up eating human
spirits, and that he had been .the one responsible for
thus enabling humanity to live on after death. From
this primitive idea developed the theology and legends
surrounding the saviour-gods. The tale, which was
spun ages ago, began with the disobedience of the
first man and the promise he had received from the
gods of a saviour. By the time the tale was finally
completed, thousands of years later, Jesus had been
evolved into the Saviour, after the same story had been
woven round other Christs who had achieved for
mankind what was also attributed to him.

According to the legend, Adam and all his
prototypes, under various names in the other world
religions, was punished by being placed under the
curse of "dust thou art, and unto dust shall thou
return". (Gen. iii, 19.) This curse, which was placed
on him and his descendants, meant their estrangement

from the gods while on earth, and annihilation at death. Out of this false idea, which imagined man as a fallen instead of an evolving being, all the saviour-god religions have developed.

Our early ancestors believed that the first man on earth had offended the gods by striving after knowledge, as this was a perquisite of the gods. In consequence, all mankind lay under the curse of death, which was a mystery only to be accounted for by the belief that he had angered the gods. Undoubtedly this was a priestly invention for the purpose of keeping the people ignorant, so that the priests could retain their power and live on the sacrifices offered up to feed the gods.

The theologians of those early days, however, gave man hope by prophesying that a day would come when man and the gods would again become friendly, and that a god would come to earth who would suffer and take upon himself their guilt. Thus this god would open to mankind the door of heaven which, through the wickedness of the first man, had been shut, barred and bolted against mankind. Meanwhile, lest a worse fate befell him, and so as to obtain from the gods the best from his already poor conditions on earth, he was expected to be liberal in his offerings to them in the form of sacrifices. By this means, and this only, could he be reasonably sure of good harvests, and be safe from their anger, which they expressed by sending thunder, lightning, floods and drought. So much for the legend which was the outcome of the apparition of some unknown sacrificed human victim.

(6) The sacrifice of human beings still continued,

however, in spite of the germ planted in the minds of man that the victim had broken the gods of the habit of eating human spirits. On one occasion, at some time later, after the sacrifice of a human victim, this individual was seen again as an apparition. This was taken as a sign that his sacrifice had so pleased the gods that he had broken the curse of death laid on the first man.

Consequently they had not consumed him but had allowed him to live with them. The gods were now believed to be satisfied. Because of his atoning work the victim received the titles of Saviour, Redeemer and Mediator, and the people of the tribe or nation to which he belonged, believed that he was the one the gods had sent to earth as their victim, for the purpose of breaking the curse placed on the first man, and all his descendants.

The saviour-god theology thus received further new ideas, and many and varied were the speculations these entailed. How many saviour-gods have been worshipped because of the reappearance of different sacrificed victims we know not. All we know is that mythology tells us of thirty sacrificed victims who became saviour-gods in the minds of their worshippers. One of the rites which developed out of this belief was the Eucharist, which commenced by the victim reappearing at what we would today call a séance. This was the origin of what is now known as the Real Presence.

Later, this séance developed into a ceremony which consisted of an image of the dead Saviour in dough being laid on the altar. This the people believed had been transformed by the priests into the Saviour's body, which, by eating, conferred on the communicant his immortality. In time, bread and wine took the place of the dough image, and the communicant ate the bread and drank the wine, which the priests claimed they had changed into the body and blood of the Saviour. These the worshippers consumed in the belief that they conferred on them the qualities necessary for salvation, which meant reunion or at-one-ment with the gods.

Owing to the difference in language, and a strong national sentiment, each nation had its own saviour-god, and also its own gods whom it worshipped. The fundamental ideas underlying all the beliefs, cere-monies and rites connected with each were, however, similar, because sufficient communication existed between the nations to permit of one copying from the others. Consequently, as occasion arose, after a human sacrifice, when the victim reappeared after death, he was surrounded by the same beliefs as had accumulated round all the other gods. When appari-tions were seen which were not those of slain victims, they were considered to be angels, or messengers, sent by the gods to earth to visit those specially privileged to see the heavenly beings. These visits were con-sidered to be omens of either good or evil.

(7) Generally speaking, the priests were antag-onistic to everyone endowed with psychic gifts, because they looked upon such people as competitors in their profession. Many endowed with mediumistic gifts have, right down the ages, been persecuted or destroyed by the priests, who could maintain their position only so long as the people did not realise their false claims and deception, and the fact that the

only way to get in touch with the other world was through mediumship.

(8) At the commencement of the Christian era saviour-gods were worshipped in Italy, Greece, Egypt, Persia and India. Throughout Asia religion consisted more of ancestor worship, as in that part of the world the saviour-god idea did not develop. West of Asia, however, many people found their comfort in the theological idea that a Saviour had suffered on their behalf.

Of all the nations of the western world the Jews alone had no saviour-god to worship. They alone were a peculiar people in their religious outlook. To the other nations the saviour-gods had come, and their atoning sacrifices were remembered by the worshippers partaking of the Eucharist. The Jew, on the other hand, anticipated the coming of a Messiah who would make Israel supreme by reigning in Jerusalem over all the earth.

(9) Such, then, was the position of religious opinion at the commencement of the Christian era, which era owes its origin to the fact that an apparition of a Jew, who was a priestly victim, was seen after his death. This was taken by the followers of this Jew to be a sign from heaven that he was the Messiah long promised to the Jewish race by Jehovah. Owing to Greek influence he was transformed from a Jewish Messiah into the Christ, the world Saviour.

The circumstances of this apparition are interesting as, from the different accounts we have of what took place, it is evident that at that time in Palestine there was an outburst of psychic phenomena which centred round this Jew before his death. This Jew,

Jesus by name, we can assume was a strongly developed medium, but the accounts which have come down about him are unfortunately quite unhistorical and unreliable. From these legends we are told that he chose disciples, some of whom likewise displayed psychic power. He wandered about Palestine supported by some he had healed, and spent his time healing the sick by touch and performing miracles, the exaggerated accounts of which probably had their origin in psychic happenings.

It was the method in those days to write up the deeds of mediums in this exaggerated way, and it is quite reasonable to believe that the stories surrounding Jesus came into being because of his psychic gifts. We do not know what he taught, as there is nothing reliable to tell us, but it is probable that he was, like others of his time, a reformer who was anxious to see his countrymen repent of their sins in view of the anticipated end of the age. Jesus was born a Jew, had the religious beliefs of a Jew, died a Jew and never was a Christian, as his followers have always believed.

His sayings and psychic deeds so angered the priests that they secured his arrest and death. At his arrest we are told that his disciples all dispersed and fled, and this would have been the end of everything if he had not reappeared after death to one or more of those who had been his followers.

Whatever views they and the other disciples evolved from this experience, did not alter their old form of worship, as we are told that they continued worshipping in the Temple as formerly. If no further development had taken place they might have become a Messianic sect within the Jewish religion, which sect might have developed into a Jewish saviour-god religion, just as other saviour-god religions had evolved in other lands.

(10) Paul, a Jew, likewise saw an apparition, which he took to be that of Jesus. His imaginative mind evolved out of this the belief that Jesus was the Christ who had come to earth, not for the Jews only but also for the Gentiles. Conversant as he was with the surrounding saviour-god religions, he worked up a similar system of belief round Jesus. His enthusiasm and energy were so great that he convinced some Gentiles in different parts of the Roman Empire that the Saviour awaited by the Jews had come to earth, suffered and died, not for the Jews only, but also for the Gentiles, and that the saviour-gods they worshipped were devils and not gods.

If it had not been for the fact that the old saviourgods had died so long ago, and faith in their mediatorial powers was weakening, it is doubtful if he would have made much impression. With things as they were, he was, however, successful in convincing some that the Christ had only now come in the person of Jesus, who had revealed himself to him and his disciples, after his sacrificial death, as a sign that he had by his death satisfied the Supreme Being, and removed the curse of death placed on Adam.

Paul was evidently strongly mediumistic, and it is quite possible that on many occasions Jesus made him feel aware of his etheric presence. This made Paul believe that he was the apostle of Jesus, and the one chosen by him to reveal to mankind that he was the Christ.

From this small beginning developed the beliefs which finally culminated in what is today called the Christian Faith. Its origin was due to a psychic occurrence, namely an apparition. The circumstances of the death of Jesus caused the belief that he was a priestly victim, and consequently a sin-offering to Jehovah. As he had appeared, after having been thus sacrificed, he was taken to be the Mediator, Redeemer and Saviour, just as had happened with previous priestly victims who had appeared after having been sacrificed for the sins of their people.

(11) Throughout his missionary life Paul founded various small communities, or churches, as he called them, in various parts of the Roman Empire. To them he wrote letters amplifying his beliefs regarding his Heavenly Christ, and they, like him, became equally enthusiastic and anxious to spread the gospel message. On the other hand Peter, who seems to have been mediumistic, like his master, encouraged the belief that Jesus was the Messiah for the Jews alone.

Various communities of Jews, who held this belief, met together in the various towns of Palestine. These became in time Christian sects under the name of Nazarenes and Ebonites. Only after the passage of four centuries, due to the formation of one Christian Church, under the leadership of the Bishop of Rome, were these Jewish-Christian sects welded into the common Christian belief which was determined at Nicaea in 325, when, by a majority of priests, Jesus was ranked as equal to Jehovah and the Holy Spirit.

(12) After the death of Paul, various men wrote accounts of the birth, life, death and reappearance of

Jesus, for the purpose of proving that he was the Christ. These accounts grew from small beginnings into elaborate stories. Ultimately, at the Council of Carthage, in 397, four of these writings were accepted by the Church as accurate accounts of the life and death of Jesus, because they had been added to and altered so as to keep them up to date with the development of Christian belief. These writings gradually came to be looked upon as sacred, God-inspired documents, and as containing the true Christian belief. They were used by the Christian community in their worship, and, in the sixth century, they were joined to the Hebrew scriptures to become one book under the name of the Word of God. This book differed considerably from our present Bible, which came into being as late as 1611.

The enthusiasm of Christians to spread the gospel message brought in new converts from amongst both the Pagans and the Jews, so much so that by the second century we find Christian churches scattered everywhere throughout the Roman Empire. Persecution seemed to increase the enthusiasm of the Christians, as they looked on martyrdom as a privilege because it would mean their immediate entrance into the presence of their Lord.

(13) From the time of the apostles, outstanding men came forward to testify for the Faith. They wrote apologies to prove that the Christian Christ was the one and only Christ, and that the Pagan Christs were false gods. Their zeal for the cause increased the number of Pagan converts, so much so, that by the fourth century the Christian community throughout the Roman Empire was a power which Constantine

made use of for the purpose of binding his Empire together.

(14) The Apostolic Church, the name given to the various Christian communities, which came into existence from the time of the apostles till the Church became Catholic, had, as one of its principles, the belief that spirits communicated through the mediums employed in the churches. These etheric beings, it was thought, kept intact the link between heaven and earth until the Lord's return, which was shortly expected to come about. They were termed divine and holy spirits, and were in time consolidated under the name of the Holy Spirit, who became one of the Christian gods. They were also called the Comforter, but, from what we are told of the way they expressed themselves, it is evident that they were none other than the spirit controls of those we today call mediums. By means of clairvoyance, clairaudience and trance utterances through the mediums employed, the people obtained their comfort at their church services and at private séances.

Each Apostolic church was in charge of a bishop, who, with the presbyters, accepted, as did the congregation, the form of church worship and belief which had been handed down from apostolic times. Gradually, however, the bishops formed themselves into a close corporation, or priesthood, for the purpose of regulating worship, and giving them entire authority over their congregations. This close corporation was in direct defiance of the apostolic teaching, that the priesthood had been brought to an end by the death of Jesus, who, as the Chirst, was now the one and only priest continually making intercession for his people on earth. The priests, by persecution and slaughter, stamped out all liberty of thought, and Christianity thus became an organised religion, with its beliefs unified, and sectarianism abolished. The Church, in consequence, became one united body of Christians, who believed what the bishops at the various Councils determined was to be the Christian Faith. Any remnants of the various sects who survived were absorbed or destroyed as time went on.

Christian beliefs are concerned with doctrines and dogma only. Nothing is said in any of its creeds about love and charity. They contain nothing of a moral or ethical nature. Outside the doctrines and dogmas there are no Christian principles, and neither the Christian Church, nor the Christian Faith, have ever professed any. Protestant priests in our own times talk much that is false about Christian principles, Christian charity and Christian ethics, and it is only because the people are stupid and ignorant that these falsehoods are accepted as true. Individual Christians have professed lofty principles, and lived up to them, but so have others who were not Christians. Christianity stands only for a form of theological belief which has given its adherents an outlet for their religious emotions.

On the other hand, Christianity abolished individual liberty. Individual opinion as to what Christianity was, if it differed from the findings of the bishops, was called heresy. Heretics were ex-communicated from the Church, persecuted and put to death. Mediumship was likewise abolished, as the priests decided that if mediums took part in the Church services, and acted as the connecting link between heaven and earth, they had not the necessary authority over their congregations. The medium was therefore excluded from all part in the church service, which became regulated by the ceremonies and doctrines introduced by the priests. These they copied from their Pagan neighbours, and, after Christianity had destroyed Paganism, this fact was in time forgotten.

Up to the time the Church became a State organisation Christians continued to gather round mediums, to hear and experience what took place in their presence. This was a disrupting feature and contrary to settled Church government. Consequently, mediums were termed wizards and witches, and their controls, previously called holy spirits and the Comforter, were termed devils. Mediums, instead of being considered "the oracles of God", were called "the servants of the Devil", and, in consequence, they were persecuted and exterminated by death.

The Church set itself up in the place of the medium, and called itself Christ's body, controlled by the Holy Spirit through its nominees the bishops, who endowed each other with this divine being. The bishops made the same false claims about their powers as did the priest-magicians who deluded the people into believing that they were endowed with divine power. Christianity thus reverted to the magic age and put superstition in the place of philosophy and natural law. The Church claimed to be infallible and to speak with the voice of God. In other words, its chief priests became man-made mediums, fashioned on what the Apostolic Church claimed for its mediums. It abolished nature's mediums and claimed, as it still

does today, all that in earlier days had been claimed
for the medium.

From this developed its hazy belief in what it calls
the Communion of Saints. After referring in vain to
many theological works in my attempt to discover
what exactly this phrase means, I at last discovered its
definition in *This is our Faith*, by Bernard Heywood,
Bishop of Ely, who writes as follows in the chapter
devoted to this subject :

> Let us take the phrase exactly as we have it. "Communion"
> —common union—implies fellowship. "Saints", as often in
> the New Testament, is to be understood as signifying those
> who are "called to be saints", those who belong to the "Holy"
> Church, in fact Christians. Therefore, the doctrine of the
> Communion of Saints is the doctrine that all Christian people,
> wherever they may be, on earth or in Paradise, are united to
> each other in one common fellowship because each is "a mem-
> ber of Christ". "All are one in Thee, for all are Thine".

Evidently communion does not mean communication. Consequently, Christians are quite ignorant
of everything relating to the activities and thoughts
which prevail in the etheric world. Thus they are
unaware of the fact that earth's religions mean nothing
to etheric beings. In Etheria there are no Christians,
Hindus or Buddhists, and no sects such as Catholics
and Protestants. The beliefs which make up the
various world religions fade from the mind as earth
memories are forgotten, just as we forget our nursery
stories.

The doctrines which the Church produced are in
many instances debasing, vicious and corrupt. The
entire Christian scheme of salvation is immoral, and it
is therefore not surprising that the reign of the

Christian Church has been one of the utmost wickedness. Christianity is based on a revengeful god who punished an innocent being so that the wicked could escape. Jesus became the whipping-boy for the human race. Belief, and not deeds, is the Christian passport into heaven, which was taken advantage of by the craven and degenerate. These set themselves above the unbeliever, who was often a finer and nobler character than the ignorant and stupid believer who despised him.

(15) By the end of the fourth century the Church was in control of the Roman Empire. It was everywhere the State Church and wielded a power equal to that of the Emperor. At the beginning of the fifth century, when Rome had ceased to be the capital, as Constantinople had taken its place, the Bishop of Rome became the Pope and the head of the Church, which not only controlled the religious but also the political life of the Roman Empire.

What improvement, it may be asked, did this change over from Paganism to Christianity make in the comfort the people obtained from their religious beliefs? None whatever, as they only exchanged one god for another. The religious comfort they received from their Pagan beliefs continued, but was in no way increased by their adoption of the Christian Faith. With the adoption of Christianity, however, they lost their religious liberty, education ceased and, in consequence, their social conditions greatly deteriorated. Christians owned slaves up to the nineteenth century, and the history of slavery in Christendom is a record of barbarity and wanton cruelty. So the change did not increase the happiness of mankind, as the people socially were much better off under the rule of the Roman Emperors than under the rule of the Church.

With fifteen hundred years of education lost, humanity has little to be thankful for and much to regret. Where might we not have been today, in knowledge and culture, if the Christian Church had never been brought into being? All that we can be sure of is that our knowledge and social conditions would have been no worse than they are today, and there is every reason to believe that they would have been vastly better. As to the belief in a life after death, Christianity knows only about a resurrection of the physical body at some indefinite future date, and then a judgement, when a fantastic Heaven will be the destiny of believers, whereas Hell will be the eternal abode of unbelievers. What a travesty of the truth, and wherein lies the comfort to be obtained from such a belief?

This, then, is a very brief résumé of the facts, which I have sorted out and put in their correct order throughout this book. The question now to be asked is, of what use are they to us? They are of great historical interest as they explain many things which have hitherto been mysterious and misunderstood. Besides this, they have an intimate personal bearing for everyone, and this must be emphasised because it is the fact which is of paramount importance.

Today the same psychic phenomena, which we have traced from early times, take place in our midst. Nineteen hundred years ago the psychic stream flowed strongly above ground, and, for the first two hundred years of our era, it was to be found wherever Christians gathered together. Moreover, it had swept away the priesthood from the Christian community, but, after two centuries, the black army reformed and dammed up the flood of psychic revelation. When the power of the priesthood was weakened last century, by our revival of education, which the Church had abolished in the fourth century, it lost its power to prevent the development of natural psychic gifts. So today the psychic stream has once more swollen into a flood, and mankind is again obtaining the comfort and knowledge it lost in the fourth century, when creeds and dogmas took the place of nature's own revelation.

Today we have many mediums, in whose presence the same phenomena occur as have occurred from early times. What now goes under the name of psychic phenomena is not new, because it is part of nature's laws and is as old as man himself. Supernormal phenomena have occurred from earliest times, though, in ignorance, our ancestors have misinterpreted and misunderstood their meaning. The reason why so few accept them today is because from the fourth to the eighteenth centuries mediums were destroyed by the priesthood, just as we destroy vermin. To the priesthood they were objectionable because they were living witnesses to the error in the theology by which it thrived.

The Christian priests, by their magical cunning, in making the people believe that they could influence their three gods, accumulated great wealth and power, and for this reason they have always been stronger than the medium. Nature produced only comparatively few mediums, and they have consequently always been in the minority. The result is that from early times they have been persecuted and destroyed. Since early days they have always been held up to the people by the priests as those who had given themselves over to the Devil. Mediumship is an hereditary gift, and, because of this campaign of destruction, there were never many mediums when a priesthood was in power.

At the Reformation, the power of the priesthood was weakened in those countries which became Protestant, but it was not until the eighteenth century that it was sufficiently broken to bring to an end the destruction of mediums. When this did happen, nature was again able to produce its natural link between the two worlds. From that time onwards mediumship has grown and developed, and, just as this took place, our knowledge of its various phases has likewise increased, bringing to the people greater comfort and happiness. As mediumship increases so the belief in the theology of the priests decreases.

Today we are witnessing empty Christian churches and indifference to the Christian Faith. The priests can do nothing to counteract this, as to change their creeds and doctrines would be admitting defeat. They cannot introduce Spiritualism into the services as to do so means the end of priestcraft. So they can only look on and bewail what they call the drift from religion. On the other hand, when one of our Sunday newspapers announced in October, 1938, that Estelle Roberts (to whom I have already referred as one of this country's most gifted clairvoyante and clairaudiente mediums) had agreed to give to its readers two demonstrations in London, and three in the provinces, sixty thousand applications for seats were received. All the large halls engaged were insufficient to accommodate the people anxious to be present.

On Armistice Sunday, 1938, the Royal Albert Hall, the Queen's Hall, the Wigmore Hall, and many other halls in London were occupied by people witnessing the same phenomena as occurred in the early Apostolic Church. Not only does this happen on every Armistice Sunday, but, in every city and most of our towns throughout the country, the largest halls are engaged for similar gatherings from time to time during the year. Every Sunday throughout the year in the Queen's Hall, in other large halls in London, and in all Spiritualist churches in Great Britain, to the number of approximately three thousand, there are similar clairaudient, clairvoyant and trance demonstrations as were experienced by the early Christians.

Thus it is possible today, as in the Apostolic Church, to keep in touch with the etheric world, to receive all the satisfaction and comfort this brings, and, at the same time, to discard the mistakes of the early Christians, who were influenced in their beliefs by being in contact with Pagan and Hebrew mythology, and religious doctrines which intelligent people have today outgrown.

This book is concerned with facts only, and with the history of the past in relation to our knowledge of the present day. Its purpose is to explain the source and growth of the Christian Faith in the light of modern knowledge and experience. When we find the same occurrences today as happened in the early part of the Christian era, and for thousands of years before the Christian era commenced, we must come to the conclusion that psychic phenomena are the result of natural law, which no amount of opposition will ever kill. Mankind may kill off nature's mediums, but he cannot stop nature producing others. This, nature has done from the earliest times, and only now in Protestant countries are the people becoming intelligent enough to appreciate what mediumship really means.

Mankind may misinterpret psychic phenomena and call mediums the servants of the Devil on the one hand, or their controls gods on the other. Out of psychic phenomena man may build up theologies and mythologies, imagine saviours, holy spirits and gods of all kinds. He may surround these with creeds, dogmas and doctrines. He may imagine his heavens and his hells, but the fact still remains that all these vain imaginings originate, and have originated, in the fact that man survives death, and that some, called dead, return to be seen by those with clairvoyant sight, or to communicate through mediums with their fellow men on earth.

This intimately concerns each one of us, as we likewise will survive death and be able to come back again to communicate with those we leave behind. This means that the two worlds are joined together by a uniform etheric substance, and that mediums are endowed with this link which makes the two worlds one. Nature has provided them with this, and, if we have the necessary knowledge, we can use these instruments to prove to our sightless eyes, and deaf ears, that what we call the world is something more than physical matter, and that this earth is only the core of an unseen greater world.

The foregoing pages of this book have been

devoted to a realm of life and thought which, to the great majority on earth, can be neither seen, heard nor touched. Its range of vibrations is beyond our senses, and yet how very real it has been to our ancestors and is still to us. This seems strange at first, but our individual minds are immaterial, as is this other order of life, and how real they are to everyone. They are the only reality. The unseen is the real, and the seen but a temporary experience which fades at death. All round us is a vital world of life and thought, which has impressed itself on incarnate humanity sufficiently to produce all that the foregoing pages have unfolded. The unseen has influenced the history of the past in a way few realise, and discarnate minds have often been the cause of effects on earth which produced many of the great events of history.

From what we are told by those who communicate with us from the etheric world, we learn that this greater world is composed of various states of existence, and that we on earth are in the lowest allotted to humanity. What we carry over with us at death is our mind, and its instrument which we call the etheric body. Mind, that intangible substance, by its capacity to produce images, constitutes our memory, our personality and all that makes up our character. The mind is the individual and it can never be destroyed. Our destiny is to progress from earth, through the various aspects of the etheric world, till we experience neither space nor time. Then we shall have become ; we shall have reached reality.

This knowledge has come to us because the psychic stream has forced itself once again above ground, as it did in the first three Christian centuries, and, with our greater knowledge of natural law, we are now in a position to understand correctly what it really means. We do not today turn it into mythology and weave round it legends, creeds, dogmas and doctrines. We are rising above that low state of intelligence which was responsible for the Christian Faith, above the ignorance on which its guardians have thrived, and still thrive, during their reign of office. Let us hope that the people are now intelligent enough not to allow the priests once more to divert the stream from their reach and force it underground.

Religious freedom, that priceless heritage for which our forefathers fought and died, is ours today. Let us see to it that we do not lose it once again. Let us determine that never again shall we allow the priesthood to dominate our religious beliefs and batten down all freedom of thought. If we maintain this policy, this freedom will in time clear away their false and immoral theology, which has made man a slave to a tyrant god in heaven, and salvation dependent on belief in a creed and the performance of magical rites, quite irrespective of the life lived.

Man discovered some three hundred years ago, that the reason for night and day was the movement of the earth on its own axis, and that the daily apparent movement of the sun was a delusion. This discovery did not abolish the sun or reduce its life-giving power; all it did was to alter man's perspective. Though we have discovered that what the Christian Faith stands for is likewise a delusion, this has in no way abolished the fact that we are etheric beings, and that another and a better world awaits us after death.

Here again, as with the sun, we have to alter

our perspective and adjust our outlook. The new panorama will, however, when we have outgrown our prejudices, contain a fuller and grander conception of our destiny, than did the glimpse caught by our ancestors, just as our present astronomical knowledge has opened up to us an immensely greater, and grander conception of the universe, than was within their reach.

Let us look all about us and not only in one direction. We must not, like the Materialist, concentrate our attention on the earth alone or, like the Supernaturalist, cast our eyes continually to heaven. We must be able to look to the left and to the right, unafraid that something may come upon us which will upset our preconceived ideas. The whole of nature is ours, and, whether we look downwards or upwards, we must feel that we are safe in its keeping.

We are not exiles here from any God, but each one of us is part of one great scheme which, as we develop mentally, unfolds before us. Each one of us is part of God, and God is evolving Mind which is never at rest. Each one of us has a niche in a universe, which, as we develop mentally, unfolds before us, and enables us to appreciate more and more the greatness of our heritage.

Let us, therefore, help forward the increase of knowledge, which will bring to humanity not only greater happiness but also abolish the dread of the unknown. By knowledge only will mankind understand his destiny, and only by knowledge will all the religious ignorance of the past be swept away. Knowledge, combined with wisdom, will direct the human family how to live together in peace and happiness, and bring to it all the material comforts it needs and desires. Knowledge will in time replace mystery. Knowledge will some day take the place of the Christian Faith, which is but an expression of man's yearning for something he did not understand.

Some day it will be realized that all religions were the outcome of ignorance and the product of fear. When knowledge takes the place of ignorance the dread of the unknown will cease, and we shall look upon death as our birth into a better and happier state of existence. We shall then consider death to be just as natural as is birth into this world. When this time comes, all that will remain of the Christian Faith will be the buildings, erected for its propagation, and its idle priests living on the wealth obtained from the fear their predecessors fostered.

Socrates, the Greek sage, is reported as having said just before his death, "They can kill my body but they cannot kill me." When this is properly understood, and truly believed, all that seems unjust and cruel in our world today will be appreciated in its true aspect, and not from the limited angle which the great majority regard it. Fear will then vanish from the world, and human happiness will increase just in proportion as we come to realize that we are etheric beings, and that our heritage belongs to another order of existence. The more we rely on our reason and experience, the more the Universe unfolds before us, and the greater becomes our knowledge of our relationship to it.

So will the psychic stream flow and swell into a mighty river, till it has swept from the world all ignorance as to our origin, our destiny, and what we human beings really are.

Then each and all will know that we are here on earth preparing for the great future which is our heritage, and that the change called death only means our losing contact with the physical, and experiencing in its place the etheric order of existence.

In that higher order of life our place and happiness will be determined by the character we have formed on earth, as nature's law operates there as it does here. As we sow, so shall we reap.

INDEX

ABRAHAM, 1052
"Acts of Judas Thomas," 693, 694
"Acts of Pilate," 694
"Acts of the Apostles," 386, 480, 581, 634
"Acts of the Apostles," writer of, 875
"Acts of the Apostles," writer of, inaccurate, 615
Adam, 172, 1035
Adonai, 1086
Adonis, 310, 665, 825, 880, 894, 930
worship of, 397, 708, 825
"Adversus Gentes," 784
Ælia Capitolina, 988
Æschylus, 101, 656
Æsculapius, 695, 780, 783
restored sight of two blind men, 793
temple of, 781
Agape, 110
Age of ignorance, 752
of magic, 54
of sacrifice, 542
of science, 842, 1070
of superstition, 124
Agnosticism about the after life, 926
of Christian priests, 922
Agriculture, origin of, in Egypt, 235
Ahriman, 740
Aikenhead, Geo., last victim of Protestant priests, 1114
Albigenses, 999
Alcestis, a saviour goddess, 212
Alexander, 316, 412, 431
primary cause of Christianity, 546
Bishop of Alexandria, 1080, 1092
Bishop of Jerusalem, 1054
Alexander, Severus, 1052
Alexandria, 317, 966
Theological College of, 335
the seat of all learning, 318, 319, 1049
world's intellectual centre in time of Ptolemy, 1120
decline of, 1122
Allegory in Bible, 22
All Souls' Day, 114
Altar absent in early Christian Churches, 868

Altars, no further need of, 869
discovered with speaking-tubes. 45
Ambrose, Bishop of Milan, 1030, 1115, 1119
Amelius, 1050
Amen, Egyptian god, 64
Ammonius, founder of Neo-platonism, 1049
Amos, 604
Amulets, 49
Ananias, 663, 819
heard clairaudiently, 621
Ancestor worship, 57, 105, 111, 118, 140, 146, 243
in China and Japan, 119
worship developed into Spiritualism, 118
Ancestry of Christian Eucharist, 825
Andocides, 417
Andrew, 970
Angel, another name for Etherian, 733
a messenger from God, 735
Angels, 26, 988
Angus, Dr., "The Mystery Religions and Christianity," 388
Anicetus, Bishop of Rome, 995
Animal sacrifice, 934
at an end, 530, 849
Animals, controlled by spirits, 86
cruelty to, 768
difference from savages, 37
possessing a spirit-body, 86
Animism, 83, 89
early Babylonians were believers in, 222
represented by Buddhism, 147
Ankh, 64
Annas, father-in-law of Caiaphas, 833
Annunciation, feast of the, 701
Antagonism between priest and prophet, 1025
to mediumship, 828
Anticipating the future in the Bible, 603
Antioch, headquarters of Gentile Christians, 629
Anti-Semitism, reasons for, 437
Antipater, 328
Antiquity of man, 60
Antoninus, 989

Buddha, 334, 335, 336, 420, 703, 710, 756, 765
Buddhism, 606, 1128
    founder of, 335
Buddhist beliefs, 170, 1067
Bultmann, Rudolf, 508
Burkitt, Prof., 814
    his "Jesus Christ, An Historical Outline," 482
Burning, bodies of the dead, 113
    and torturing heretics, 750

CÆSAR Augustus, 707
    Constantius, 1067
    Galerius, 1067
Cæsarian Library destroyed by Arabs by fire in year 653, 1055
Cairns, Principal, in "The Faith that Rebels", 1102
Calvary, 844
Calvin, 1108
Caodaism, 606
Carthage, 322, 323, 966
    Council of, 475, 502, 671, 675, 729, 1111, 1144
Catalepsy, 784
Catholic and Protestant priests exterminated mediums, 1031
    Christendom, 702
    Christianity, 666
    Christianity manufactured, 998
    Christians, 1001
    Church created Saints noted for their cruelty and bigotry, 1057
    Church given power to absolve every sin and wickedness, 1119
Catholicism stood for Hebrew tradition and the priesthood, 1029
Cause for every effect, 70
Celsus, 414, 467
    an Epicurean, 997
    exposed unscrupulous methods of altering the Gospels, 1117
Century, 1st, 957
    2nd, 975
    3rd, 962, 1032
    4th, 962, 965, 1019, 1074
Ceremonials in 3rd century churches, 1070
    of Christianity adopted from Osiris and Mithra, 853
Chaldean language, 137
Chaldeans, 825
Champollion, 138
Chancel, 868
Channel for messages, 652
Character development, 21
    is what really counts, 421
Charismata, 1039
    meaning psychic gifts, 977

Charismata—*continued.*
    psychic phenomena through mediumship, 1041
Charlatans imitating mediums, 42
Charlemagne, 1125
Charms and spells, 51
Childhood of Jesus, 712
Chrestos, another name for Osiris, 209, 466
Christ, 31, 209, 572, 649, 656, 879, 1011
    another name for Jesus as an Etheric Being, 1087
    as a sacrificed victim, 549
    as God, 996
    belief in the return of, from old Saviour-god ideas, 208
    instead of Mithra or Osiris, 1069
    myth, 554
    replaced the priests, 869
    Saviour-god, 938
    Saviour of the world, 586
    Spirit, 1013
    "The Bread of Life", 705
    the God, came after Jesus the man, 122
    time ripe for a new, 438
    took place of Mithra, Osiris, Dionysus, Nordic gods, etc., 1113
    took place of Jehovah, as "the living presence", 868
Christian and Pagan, words interchangeable, 450
    thought intertwined, 820
Christian barbarians, 782
    belief, 31, 478, 837, 920, 921
    belief defined at Nicæa, 1093
    belief during the 3rd century, 1032
    belief in the ascension of Jesus in his physical body, 894
    beliefs, development of, 475
    beliefs, earliest, 474
    beliefs, from whence derived, 120
    beliefs in a state of flux, 676
    beliefs, psychic origin of, 600
    Bible, 22
    Bishops, 1006
    Bishops at Nicæa, 1073
    ceremonies similar to those of Mithra, 278
    Church absorbed Paul's doctrines, 873
    Church as dictator of Christendom, 984
    Church built up by priestly cunning and deception, 1005
    Church, closing of schools by, 179

ARTHUR FINDLAY'S
TRILOGY ON SPIRITUALISM.

This important and valuable work is the outcome of the author's desire to produce, in a lucid and easily read form, all that he considered was of interest and essential for philosophic and religious belief, while, at the same time, exposing the error which surrounds these two names. His Trilogy on Spiritualism is the result of many years of thought and investigation of this subject. The reception his books have received proves that he has met a great and growing need, and succeeded in his purpose. Because of prejudice and early training some today may not appreciate his work as will future generations, because so much has to be discarded before nature's own revelation is discovered. Such a quantity of error has been taught under the cloak of a divine revelation, and it is difficult to forget what has influenced the mind in childhood. The present-day thoughtful and un-prejudiced person will, however, appreciate and find Arthur Findlay's comprehensive work very enlightening, especially now that a combined index has been compiled of these three books.

"ON THE EDGE OF THE ETHERIC."

This book, which was published in September 1931, has brought conviction of the truth of communication and survival to a larger number of enquirers than any other book ever published. From this point of view it is Spiritualism's greatest book. The explanation why this should be so is obvious on the first reading of the book. The author, not only tells his own experiences but, in simple scientific language, explains how all the supernormal occurrences he has experienced are within natural law and in accordance with reason. It is the rational, thorough and careful way the author has prepared his case that brings conviction to the reader.

The press of Great Britain, the United States, and the Dominions, without exception, gave this book a reception never before accorded a book on this subject. It was certainly the most widely reviewed book of the Winter Book Season of 1931–1932. The following extracts are a selection taken only from the British press.

The Times.—The specimens which are presented in the book as three A1 and three A2 cases of the successful exercise of Sloan's supernormal faculties are certainly very striking. This is testimony which cannot lightly be set aside.

The Morning Post.—Mr. Findlay brings a fund of sound common sense to the study of what is now often called Psychics. His book certainly places Psychics on a firmer basis than any other treatise of the kind, and should be studied by the opponents as well as the supporters of the Spiritist conceptions of life after death so-called.

Glasgow Herald.—A well-presented account of many years' experience. If some of the evidence which he produces is not genuine it would appear that mediums had almost infinite skill and knowledge to produce such phenomena. The only reasonable explanation seems to be that a considerable proportion of the evidence is genuine.

Leicester Mercury.—"On the Edge of the Etheric", by Mr. Arthur Findlay, is one of the most remarkable books written on the subject of psychic phenomena, not only because of the matter of the book, but because of the qualifications of the author and the manner of his presentation of facts.

The Glasgow Citizen.—"On the Edge of the Etheric" is welcome. The book is of more than usual interest to Glasgow in view of the fact that Mr. Findlay was for many years a prominent Stockbroker in the city before retiring to the South of England. A very interesting book.

Cambridge Daily News.—The arguments are clear and lead step by step to logical conclusions. The whole book is a lucid statement on a difficult subject.

Glasgow Daily Record & Mail.—Widespread interest has been aroused by the new book "On the Edge of the Etheric" by a Glasgow Chartered Accountant, Mr. Arthur Findlay. Mr. Findlay has written a book which bears the stamp of earnest conviction which deserves to be read with care by all. Remarkable things are recorded in this book.

Edinburgh Evening Despatch.—A member of the Glasgow Stock Exchange, and until recently a prominent member of a well-known firm of Chartered Accountants and Stockbrokers, has written a book confirming his belief in survival and communication with the other side, following a remarkable series of séances.

Evening Standard.—"On the Edge of the Etheric", written by Mr. Arthur Findlay, is remarkable for itself and for its writer. There have been many books on Psychic Phenomena, but few of them have presented their case with the lucidity of this one.

Sheffield Telegraph.—Mr. Findlay has written a valuable book that hosts have been waiting for, and it will be a valuable addition to any bookshelf.

Leicester Evening Mail.—Mr. Findlay does not try to obtain converts to his belief, but his book is written in such restrained language, and is so fascinating, that it should not be ignored by any genuine inquirer after truth.

Essex Weekly News.—His book, a mine of information, gives the result of an exhaustive investigation into Spiritualism. Mr. Findlay describes many strange experiences he has had in the last 12 years, experiences that indeed are well nigh incredible.

Aberdeen Press and Journal.—When we read this book we were compelled to review our former notions regarding Spiritualism. It is a startling treatise. The conversations recorded are amazing. We are compelled to admit that the explanation cannot be put down to fraud, telepathy, or cryptesthesia. It will confirm believers in their convictions, and must cause even sceptics to suspend judgment.

Manchester Evening News.—Mr. Arthur Findlay, who is reputed to be one of the hardest-headed commercial men in Glasgow, tells quite plainly and unemotionally experiences which he has had with Mr. John C. Sloan, the celebrated Spiritualist medium. There is no hysteria about it ; no abstruse hypotheses. It is just a straightforward statement of things Mr. Findlay has seen and heard, and will commend itself to any reader who, with an open mind, is interested in psychic research, and wants to know more of what lies beyond the veil.

Yorkshire Post.—Mr. Findlay's elucidation is easy to follow, easy to understand, and profoundly interesting.

Wolverhampton Express and Star.—"On the Edge of the Etheric", by Mr. Arthur Findlay, is a remarkable new book on psychic research. Attention has been drawn to the book recently by an attempt to "ban" it in certain church circles, in spite of the fact that the work provides evidence which should greatly strengthen the appeal of real religion. Mr. Findlay, who is a Stockbroker, a Magistrate, and a student of Physics, traces luminously the changed outlook of science with regard to the structure of matter. Mr. Findlay has written a book which is in many ways stronger than either Mr. Dennis Bradley's "Wisdom of the Gods" or the same author's "Towards the Stars", and will strengthen the evidence regarding the reliability of direct voice phenomena. Mr. Findlay is certainly right in asserting, in effect, that science and organised religion at large cannot much longer refuse to examine this important subject without forfeiting the respect of reasonable men and women.

Londoner's Diary, in the Evening Standard.—It is a truism that to have a book banned is the surest way to fly its banner before the public gaze. This enviable fate has come to Mr. Arthur Findlay's book "On the Edge of the Etheric". The "Church Times" and the Church of Scotland organ "Life and Work" will not accept an advertisement of the book. "On the Edge of the Etheric", which happened my way not long ago, is, to say the least, profoundly interesting. Mr. Findlay is no bigot, and he admits the probability that many readers will find themselves unable to accept his conclusions. This is no reason why they should not be acquainted with his conclusions. An attempt to stifle an honest expression of opinion, even on the controversial matter of psychic research, is reprehensible.

Manchester City News.—We understand that this volume is causing something of a sensation, and this is not surprising. It is a trained and precise business man's record of facts, within his own knowledge, concerning the after life. The evidence is set forth in a very convincing manner, and the deductions made therefrom have logical force. The opening chapter is a masterpiece of fine reasoning for the unprejudiced consideration of the whole case.

Bookfinder.—How this book will startle commonplace souls! It is elaborated with a wealth of interesting illustrations taken from recent discoveries in physical science and spirit-communications. This book is one of absorbing interest, and can be confidently recommended to all thoughtful readers.

Truth.—If one is suspicious of the good faith of most mediums and sceptical about the phenomena they produce, the *confessio fidei* of a man like Mr. Findlay deserves a very different reception, for his integrity is beyond question. The evidence of survival after death which Mr. Findlay brings forward is copious and interesting. Perhaps the most useful thing one can say about his book is that it is one which opponents of Spiritualism should read, and read carefully. They may remain *in statu quo* when they have done so, but they will have learned that a very sincere case can be made out for Spiritualism, and they will understand why men of powerful intellect have not considered psychic research as unworthy of their critical investigation.

Public Opinion.—Mr. Arthur Findlay has had the unique experience, for a book of this kind, of seeing it run through five editions in the course of two months. A host of reviewers have paid tribute to Mr. Findlay's investigation of psychic phenomena as worthy of consideration, in striking contrast to many books of the kind.

Birmingham Gazette.—Mr. Findlay is clearly a careful recorder, with a Scotsman's respect for facts. He is an experienced investigator.

Sheffield Independent.—Mr. Findlay adduces much interesting evidence . . . it would have been impossible for the medium, or any other person present, to have known anything about.

Weekly Scotsman.—"On the Edge of the Etheric" is a remarkable book. Mr. Findlay has approached the subject in an honest, thoroughly scientific fashion, and his conclusions, compelling thought, are at once arresting, consoling, and uplifting.

Sunday Dispatch.—The restrained and unsensational way in which it is written accounts for the demand for Mr. Arthur Findlay's remarkable book on psychic phenomena "On the Edge of the Etheric". The enormous interest taken in survival makes Mr. Findlay's contribution of undoubted importance, particularly as the sincerity of the Author is as notable as his avoidance of unduly provocative assertions.

Yorkshire Observer.—There is no disputing that this book certainly makes a distinct and valuable contribution to the many books which have preceded it on a question which is daily exciting more and more interest. It is provided with a vast wealth of evidence. A remarkable book.

Daily Herald.—"On the Edge of the Etheric" is a remarkable contribution to modern psychic literature.

Nottingham Journal.—"On the Edge of the Etheric" is a remarkable book. It claims to make the Spirit World understandable and to be revolutionizing the Scientific and Religious thought of Great Britain. This may seem a big claim, but, after reading through these pages, one puts the book down with a feeling that we have been indeed tourists in a world beyond the grave.

Aberdeen Evening Express.—This book deals with recent psychic evidences of survival after death, and deals with them in a sound common-sense manner. It has met with a remarkable response from the reading public.

Greenock Telegraph.—It is just because Mr. Findlay's reasoning fits the facts so closely that his book may lead to a profound modification in the religious convictions of thousands of his countrymen. It is a striking enquiry into survival after death, and a book which may make religious history.

Arm-Chair Science.—Read this amazing book for yourself; it is staggering.

Time and Tide.—Difficult though the acceptance of the experiences may be, the difficulty in no degree takes away from the absorbing interest of the book—rather adds to it, as the reader finds Mr. Findlay's temperate and solid recital smashing the standard objections with all the destructive finality of the Nasmyth hammer of his native city of Glasgow. Mr. Findlay is a notable witness, a leading man in a city of no small renown for hardheadedness and sound sense, a witness not to be denied.

Investor's Chronicle.—This is a very remarkable book by a Scottish Stockbroker, who retired from active business eight years ago, but is still a member of the Glasgow Stock Exchange. He was for twenty years the senior partner of the stockbroking side of one of the leading firms of Stockbrokers and Chartered Accountants in Glasgow. He certainly deals lucidly with a subject that is attracting the increasing attention of many thinking people.

Light.—Even if we pay regard only to the carefully classified cases which he grades as A1 and A2 according to the quality of the evidence, we regard it as a book of outstanding value. The facts were carefully sifted, the statements by the communicators rigidly tested, and all possibility of fraud excluded owing to the precautions taken.

"THE ROCK OF TRUTH."

The author followed a definite plan. He first of all set out to make as convincing a case as possible for survival and communication. This he did in "On the Edge of the Etheric". In "The Rock of Truth", which was published in August 1933, he commenced an examination of the claims made by the various world's religions, Christianity in particular. In the same thorough manner, as he dealt with the case of survival, he exposed the erroneous teachings of all orthodox religions, devoting particular attention to the Christian religion. After having cleared away growths, which had accumulated round man's instinctive belief in survival, he puts forward in the second half of the book, a philosophy based on facts which has proved of great assistance to all who have been unable to accept the teachings of orthodoxy. This book, when published, created a sensation as the facts and information given were so contrary to accepted opinions. It was widely and favourably reviewed, not only in Great Britain but also in the United States and British Dominions.

The Yorkshire Post.—"The Rock of Truth" is sure of a much wider circulation than scholarly treatises usually enjoy. A flame of conviction runs through the book. It is important as a sign of the times.

Psychic News.—"The Rock of Truth" is a milestone in the march towards Spiritualism. I think it is soberly the most important statement of our world in relation to the worlds surrounding it which has appeared. It is not easy for me to write with restraint about the clearest and most admirable assembly in existence of all that is known to human beings about what happens after death and about what I call "Celestial Geography". The magic of Arthur Findlay's clarity and sincerity is such that, as others will be, I am disarmed from difference. This book, together with his "On the Edge of the Etheric", will set his name permanently upon the scroll of Spiritualist fame. He is of those who have given light to this world.

Cambridge Daily News.—"The Rock of Truth" is certainly one of the best books we have seen on this subject.

Manchester City News.—Spiritualism's case is most ably championed and set forth. Searing truth in Part One is matched by almost sensational reasoning in Part Two, in which the author tells of the etheric duplicate of men's and women's physical bodies and of their existence after death. Scientifically, and with much evidence, the philosophy and certainty of Spiritualism are explained, it is all simply and palatably done. In view of the information it is hard not to believe in the possibility of communication between the two worlds. The book is likely to draw much attention, for the way in which Mr. Findlay tells of the thought and meaning of the new religion is vastly arresting.

Manchester Evening News.—"The Rock of Truth" will remain one of the most sane works on Spiritualism that has yet been published.

Leicester Mercury.—The book is very well written and forms the best statement to date of the position of the Spiritualists.

Paisley Daily Express.—It is a rich tonic of hopefulness for which we thank Mr. Findlay.

The Guardian.—There is much in "The Rock of Truth" that is well worth the most serious attention.

"THE UNFOLDING UNIVERSE."

This book completes the trilogy, and is devoted to an examination of the evolution of humanity's religious and philosophic convictions from the primitive savage up to the present day. After a study of man as a psychic being, the author gives his opinions as to the nature of the Etheric World, in which we live after death, considering the laws and conditions of life there, as he has been made to understand them from those who communicated with him from that other order of life. Here he shows the naturalness of it all, and how life continues to function after death in a world very similar to the one it has experienced on earth. He also envisages the future, considering the effect the knowledge of survival and communication will have on the religious, political and social outlook of future generations. The following is a selection of the many press reviews the book received throughout the English-speaking world.

Leicester Evening Mail.—Much is now known about life and conditions after death, and in "The Unfolding Universe" the author has succeeded to a very great extent in making the subject of Spiritualism easily understood by all. It is a volume which is almost certain to become as popular as the author's two previous works.

The Inquirer.—Mr. Findlay's book is a brave, able statement of his view. It deserves careful and impartial study.

The Spectator.—Nor can we doubt the attractiveness of the truths so discovered. Mr. Findlay's own success testifies it. I do not doubt that "The Unfolding Universe" will be equally popular.

The Scotsman.—Mr. Findlay is all for knowledge and against mysteriousness. "Ignorance and misery," he says, "are twin brothers. Spiritualism, which stands for knowledge, lifts the tragedy from life." "The Unfolding Universe" is informative and a large amount of reading and research has gone to the making of it.

Psychic News.—"The Unfolding Universe" is Arthur Findlay's greatest book. In it he gives a comprehensive picture of the Universe, as revealed by Spiritualism. His chapter on "The Age of Superstition" is a masterpiece of reasoning. The book is invigorating and is an oasis of common sense in an arid desert of theology. In his three books he has raised Spiritualism to the level of a science, has disclosed what is false in religion, while emphasising what is true. His philosophy and his psychic experiences must satisfy all human desires as to life and conduct on earth, and our destiny after death. He appeals to reason and knowledge and not to faith, never departing from the scientific method, and the conclusions of modern scientific thought.